Contents

PAGE 29

PAGE 50

PAGE 222

PAGE 238

PAGE 292

PAGE 345

PAGE 348

PAGE 438

PAGE 462

PAGE 528

PAGE 554

PUBLISHED BY

John Wiley & Sons, Inc.

111 River St., Hoboken, NJ 07030-5774

ISBN 978-0-470-89075-2

Frommer's®

Editorial by Frommer's

EDITOR
Linda Barth

PHOTO EDITOR
Cherie Cincilla

CARTOGRAPHER
Andrew Dolan

CAPTIONS
Paul Karr, Marie Morris, Laura M. Reckford, and Kathryn Williams

COVER PHOTO EDITOR
Richard Fox

COVER DESIGN
Paul Dinovo

Produced by Sideshow Media

PUBLISHER
Dan Tucker

MANAGING EDITOR
Megan McFarland

PROJECT EDITOR
Alicia Mills

PHOTO EDITOR
John Martin

PHOTO RESEARCHERS
Tessa Perliss and Julia Rydholm

DESIGN
Kevin Smith, And Smith LLC

SPOTLIGHT FEATURE DESIGN
Em Dash Design LLC

For information on our other products and services or to obtain technical support, please contact our Customer Care Department within the U.S. at 800/762-2974, outside the U.S. at 317/572-3993 or fax 317/572-4002.

Wiley also publishes its books in a variety of electronic formats. Some content that appears in print may not be available in electronic formats.

MANUFACTURED IN CHINA

5 4 3 2 1

How to Use This Guide

The Day by Day guides present a series of itineraries that take you from place to place. The itineraries are organized by time (The Best of Boston in 1 Day), by region (Southwestern Vermont), by town (Portland), and by special interest (Central & Western Massachusetts for Book Lovers). You can follow these itineraries to the letter, or customize your own based on the information we provide. Within the tours, we suggest cafes, bars, or restaurants where you can take a break. Each of these stops is marked with a coffee-cup icon ☕. In each chapter, we provide detailed hotel and restaurant reviews so you can select the places that are right for you.

The hotels, restaurants, and attractions listed in this guide have been ranked for quality, value, service, amenities, and special features using a star-rating system. Hotels, restaurants, attractions, shopping, and nightlife are rated on a scale of zero stars (recommended) to three stars (exceptional). In addition to the star-rating system, we also use a kids icon kids to point out the best bets for families.

The following **abbreviations** are used for credit cards:

AE American Express   **MC** MasterCard
DC Diners Club   **V** Visa
DISC Discover

A Note on Prices

Frommer's lists exact prices in local currency. Currency conversions fluctuate, so before departing consult a currency exchange website such as **www.oanda.com/currency/converter** to check up-to-the-minute conversion rates.

How to Contact Us

In researching this book, we discovered many wonderful places—hotels, restaurants, shops, and more. We're sure you'll find others. Please tell us about them, so we can share the information with your fellow travelers in upcoming editions. If you were disappointed with a recommendation, we'd love to know that, too. Please email us at frommersfeed back@wiley.com or write to:

Frommer's New England Day by Day, 1st Edition
Wiley Publishing, Inc.
111 River Street
Hoboken, NJ 07030-5774

Travel Resources at Frommers.com

Frommer's travel resources don't end with this guide. **Frommers.com** has travel information on more than 4,000 destinations. We update features regularly, giving you access to the most current trip-planning information and the best airfare, lodging, and car-rental bargains. You can also listen to podcasts, connect with other Frommers.com members through our active reader forums, share your travel photos, read blogs from guidebook editors and fellow travelers, and much more.

An Additional Note

Travel information can change quickly and unexpectedly, and we strongly advise you to confirm important details locally before traveling, including information on visas, health and safety, traffic and transport, accommodation, shopping and eating out. We also encourage you to stay alert while traveling and to remain aware of your surroundings. Avoid civil disturbances, and keep a close eye on cameras, purses, wallets and other valuables.

About the Authors

Kerry Acker and **Tom Gavin** are freelance editors and writers who have written and contributed to numerous books, including *Frommer's New York State*. Both spent much of their childhoods driving and vacationing around New England, and they met while attending college in Worcester, MA.

Paul Karr, a native New Englander and prize-winning journalist, has authored more than 20 travel guidebooks for *Frommer's* covering the U.S. and Canada from coast to coast, as well as various other guidebooks.

A resident of Boston's North End, **Marie Morris** grew up in New York and graduated from Harvard, where she studied history. She's a co-author of *Frommer's New England* and writes the *Frommer's Boston*, *Frommer's Boston Day by Day*, and *Boston For Dummies* guides. She has worked for Newser.com, *02138* magazine, the *Boston Herald*, *Boston* magazine, and the *New York Times*.

Laura M. Reckford is the editor of *The Barnstable Enterprise* newspaper in the town of Barnstable on Cape Cod. Formerly the managing editor of *The Falmouth Enterprise* and *Cape Cod Life* magazine, she has also been on the editorial staffs of *Good Housekeeping* and *Entertainment Weekly*. She is the author of *Frommer's Cape Cod Day by Day*, *Frommer's Cape Cod, Martha's Vineyard & Nantucket*, and a co-author of *Frommer's New England*.

About the Photographers

Ken Cedeno is a Washington, D.C.–based photojournalist who has covered politics and breaking news in Congress and the White House for more than 20 years. His clients include the Associated Press, Agence France-Presse, Reuters, UPI, and Bloomberg, as well as *Time*, *Newsweek*, the *New York Times*, the London *Sunday Times*, and other publications worldwide. He has traveled to many countries on assignment, including Costa Rica, Cuba, Croatia, Iceland, Italy, Spain, and Turkey.

Thornton Cohen is a Central America–based photographer who has spent the last 25 years in perpetual motion, observing and capturing the human experience. He has worked on several Frommer's guides as well as other international media and guidebooks. You can see more of his work at www.thorntoncohen.com.

Vincent DeWitt lives on Cape Cod with his wife and two young children. He has worked as a photographer on newspapers in Boston, Alaska, and Cape Cod and traveled to Cuba, Macedonia, Zambia, and Brazil as well as several other countries.

Caleb Kenna is based in Brandon, Vermont; his clients include *Vermont Life*, the *New York Times*, the *Boston Globe*, the *Chronicle of Higher Education*, and the Vermont Land Trust, among others. Caleb has also photographed internationally with a focus on India. More of his work can be seen www.calebkenna.com.

Mary Ellen Martel has been photographing the landscapes of Acadia National Park, Maine, and New England for nearly 40 years. As the photographer for a local fire department, she also captures images of firefighters in the line of duty.

Marianne Pernold, a freelance photographer since 1974, specializes in people and environmental photo projects. For more information, go to www.pernoldphoto.com.

Matt Teuten is a Boston–based editorial/travel assignment photographer represented by Aurora Novus. Since 2006 he has been a faculty member at the Center for Digital Imaging at Boston University.

Carl D. Walsh has been a professional photojournalist since 1984. Represented by Aurora Select, he has worked on six continents, been in contact with popes, presidents, and shamans, and has been published in some of the world's top publications.

1
The Best of New England

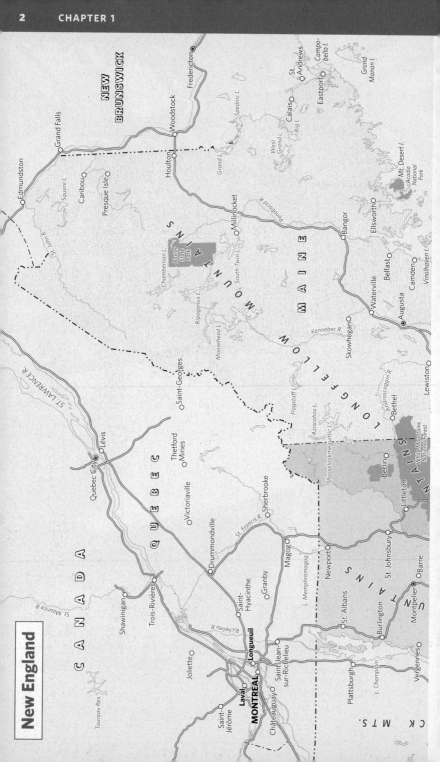

New England

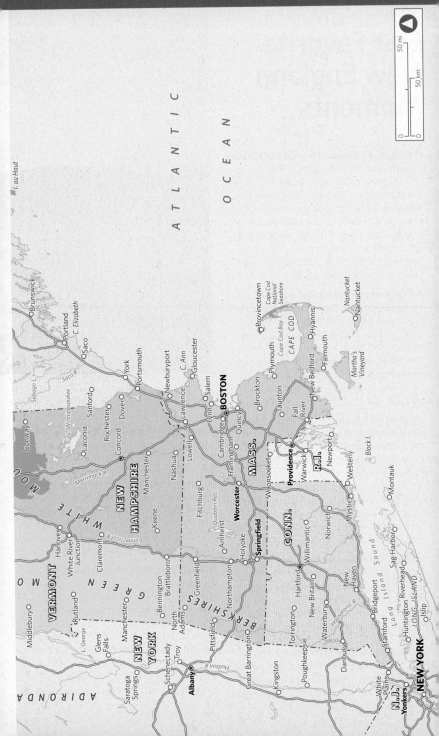

Our Favorite New England Moments

Feeling like a kid again at Fenway Park, Boston. Whether you're a lifelong fan of Boston's beloved Red Sox or you've never been to a baseball game before, the oldest park in the major leagues will likely capture your heart and linger in your memory. Cheer along with the Little Leaguer in the next seat who's armed with a glove and ready to snag a pop-up, or take a tour of the place even if you can't get tickets to a game. See p. 66, **1**.

Basking in the breeze off Boston Harbor. On a sticky summer day, enjoy the feel of the wind in your hair as the ferry to the Charlestown Navy Yard zips across the harbor. In cooler weather, chill out at a waterfront park or plaza. The prevailing east wind freshens the downtown air on all but the hottest days; grab an iced coffee and enjoy a cooling interlude. See p. 52, **9**.

Checking out the scene on Commercial Street in Provincetown, MA. Main streets don't get much more colorful than Provincetown's. You'll find intriguing shops, art galleries, and all manner of restaurants. There are also buskers, musicians, mimes, drag queens, and tourists from all over the world. A gay and lesbian mecca, the town is a northern version of Florida's Key West, colorful and cosmopolitan with a lot of heart and soul. See p. 202.

Getting the scoop in Oak Bluffs, MA. For a lively day on Martha's Vineyard, head to the harbor town of Oak Bluffs and stroll, with a Mad Martha's ice-cream cone in hand. There's plenty to do, from riding the historic Flying Horses Carousel to exploring the historic district of "gingerbread" cottages surrounding the wrought-iron tabernacle, where performances take place several evenings a week in summer. Oak Bluffs also has the Vineyard's widest selection of restaurants and the liveliest nightlife. See p. 218.

Exploring the gardens at Naumkeag, MA. The grounds of Joseph Choate's turreted shingle-style summer home in Stockbridge, Massachusetts, are dreamy. With Monument Mountain as the dramatic backdrop, we move between the distinct garden spaces—the graceful blue steps by the white birch trees, the winding gravel paths in the Rose Garden, and the tranquil shade of the Oak Lawn—and pretend we're Gilded Age grandees. See p. 253, **6**.

Waking up in Stonington Borough, CT. The best way to soak up the history-drenched atmosphere of Connecticut's ridiculously charming Stonington Borough is with an early-morning walk along Water Street. Stroll past the antiques shops, white picket fences, and old sea captains' homes up to the lighthouse, and take in the salty air. The silence of the streets is broken only by the sound of braying seagulls and distant bell buoys. See p. 284, **6**.

> *PREVIOUS PAGE Its 19th-century architecture makes Newfane a favorite southern Vermont destination.*
> *THIS PAGE Over 50 landowners make possible the multi-use Kingdom Trails system in the rolling hills of northeast Vermont.*

Sipping sunset cocktails at the Atlantic Inn, RI. The best way to end a day spent biking or swimming on Block Island, Rhode Island, is to relax in an Adirondack chair at this elegant Victorian inn high on a hill and sip mojitos while watching the sun slip into the sea. See p. 324.

Getting lost in the Northeast Kingdom, VT. The best way to experience Vermont's wild and wonderful Northeast Kingdom is to let yourself get a little bit lost. Cruise the dirt and gravel roads by car or by bike and see what you find, be it a sparkling lake, a moose, a farmstand, or a storybook village. Extra points for going in autumn, to add some color to the adventure. See p. 376.

Soaring over the scenery in New Hampshire. Buckle yourself into the open cockpit and don a headset for a breathtaking scenic ride in a biplane over the Lakes Region. The lone craft rumbles to life, heads down the runway, and hovers up into the sky as if on strings. Tune out the whir of the prop and the rush of the wind, and behold the intermingling of the mosaic of foliage with the swirls of lake not so far below. See p. 418, ❸.

Chowing down at Red's Eats, ME. When heading north up Route 1 toward midcoast Maine, traffic might briefly frustrate you in the charming village of Wiscasset. Fear not: Red's Eats stands guard at the town bridge. If you think you can find a fatter lobster roll anywhere in Maine, I challenge you to do so. See p. 517.

Viewing Portland from the water, ME. Portland the *city* is only half of the Portland *experience*. To really enjoy Maine's largest burg, you also need to get to the beach in good weather—there are plenty of sandy parks just south of town—or out on a boat. See "The Beaches of Lucky 77," p. 455.

The Best Outdoor Adventures

> Give cross country skiing a try at Vermont's Trapp Family Lodge, founded by the family *The Sound of Music* is based on.

Strolling around the Public Garden, Boston. The city's loveliest park is gorgeous year-round, with regularly changing seasonal flowers, stately trees, and a delightful assortment of statuary and fountains. The Swan Boats ply the water of the lagoon all summer; nearby, the *Make Way for Ducklings* sculptures thrill visitors of all ages. Visit in the spring if you can: There's something magical about the atmosphere when the bitter New England winter finally recedes. See p. 56, **7**.

Going back in time at Walden Pond, MA. Surrounded by trees that screen out the modern world, the pond looks much as it did when Henry David Thoreau moved to a small cabin on the shore on July 4, 1845. "I went to the woods because I wished to live deliberately," he wrote in what became his most famous book, and the lovely site remains a perfect destination for getting away from it all. The pond is the centerpiece of a state park that's popular for walking, swimming, fishing, and imagining days gone by. See p. 123, **6**.

Going for a ride, Cape Cod. The bike path everyone is talking about is the expanded (12-mile) **Shining Sea Bikeway** in Falmouth. It goes from North Falmouth to Woods Hole, passing cranberry bogs, historic farmland, and the Great Sippewissett Marsh, before getting close to Falmouth center and skirting the coastline to the bohemian fishing village of Woods Hole. This flat path is great for families, who can take on a section of it and combine it with a dip in the placid waters of Buzzards Bay. See p. 168.

Getting out on the water, Cape Cod. One of the best kayaking trips involves paddling around Barnstable Harbor and out to Sandy Neck, a primitive cottage colony with a lighthouse at the end of a 6-mile barrier beach. You can explore the Great Marsh ecosystem on the west side of the harbor, a unique marine environment with tidal creeks and islands loaded with flora, fauna, and bird life. Sandy Neck itself offers trails for hikers and isolated pristine beaches backed by low dunes. See p. 173.

> *Mountain bikers rule 57 miles of car-free carriage roads in Acadia National Park, the crown jewel of the Maine coast.*

Canoeing on the Housatonic River, CT. The pine forests and meadows of Connecticut's Litchfield Hills look even more pristine from the beautiful Housatonic. Its shallow waters are welcoming even to novices; most stretches are quiet, and the few rapids you'll encounter are mild. **Clarke Outdoors** will take you to Falls Village, where you'll begin your 10-mile trek. Pack a lunch, or disembark at the halfway point—West Cornwall's covered bridge—to eat in town. At the end of your ride, Clarke will tote you back to the shop, where you can have a hot shower. See p. 290.

Biking Block Island, RI. Even if you don't bike regularly, we strongly recommend that you rent a bicycle or bring your own. It's quite simply the best way to experience the tranquil natural beauty of the 7-mile-long island: stopping to explore the windswept bluffs, lighthouses, Rodman's Hollow, and, of course, the beaches. We especially love it in the fall, when the sun is less intense and the crowds have largely dissipated. See p. 311, ⓫.

Cross-country skiing in Stowe, VT. With the Ski Center at the beautifully sited **Trapp Family Lodge** as a starting point, you can settle into the quiet schussing of your own skis as you choose from 37 miles of groomed trails or 62 miles of backwoods terrain. Whatever path you take, make your way to the Slate and

Pasture Cabin and warm up in front of a blazing fire with a cup of hot chocolate. See p. 369.

Hiking the White Mountains, NH. We're not saying that everyone needs to tackle the mighty Presidential Range (to those who do, we offer a resounding bravo), but if you're in the vicinity of the mighty Whites, you have no excuse: Hit the trails! The crisp mountain air beckons, whether you're taking a gentle hike like the 3.25-mile Lonesome Lake trail in **Franconia Notch** or a more challenging trek, like the fairly steep 2.6-mile trip to Arethusa Falls in **Crawford Notch**. See p. 427.

Whale-watching out of Bar Harbor, ME. When in Maine, watch for wildlife; when in Bar Harbor, watch for whales. Humpbacks, minkes, finbacks—they all spend the summer fattening themselves up in the fertile waters off the coast here, and there's nothing quite like seeing them up close and personal. You're guaranteed to catch a glimpse in summer, or you get a second trip for free. See p. 463.

Mountain biking in Acadia National Park, ME. The miles and miles of handsome gravel roads and stone bridges threading through some of Acadia's best territory owe their legacy to oilman John D. Rockefeller, Jr., who envisioned horse-drawn carriages here. But to mountain bikers, it's a paradise of wide lanes, terrific views, and absolutely no cars. See p. 484.

FALL FIREWORKS
New England's Spectacular Foliage

BY KATHRYN WILLIAMS

EVERY AUTUMN, STARTING IN LATE SEPTEMBER, the forests of New England erupt in a riotous phantasmagoria of color when the leaves of the temperate region's plentiful maple, oak, birch, and beech trees turn from green to shades of red, orange, yellow, gold, russet, and purple. With the transformation comes the blessing and the bane of the locals' existence: leaf peepers. The tens of millions of enthusiasts who ply the region's back roads and byways in search of the most vibrant foliage are big business for New England's normally sleepy small towns. In 2010, fall visitors to New Hampshire alone spent more than $1 billion. While New Hampshire, Maine, and Vermont are the most-visited states, peepers also pour into Connecticut, Rhode Island, and Massachusetts. Foliage hunters looking to miss the crowds should come midweek if possible, bearing in mind that Columbus Day weekend is the busiest time. Make lodging arrangements well in advance; some B&Bs will require a 2-night minimum stay.

Jeepers Peepers: Leaf-Viewing Etiquette

Remember, while you're peeping, locals still have to get to work on time. Tips for being a good guest:

> Slow down on winding roads: There may be farming equipment, livestock, or other slow-moving peepers around the next bend.

> Don't creep along far below the speed limit.

> Pick up a parking pass in state and national parks.

> Respect deer and moose crossing signs—they are there for a reason!

> On single-lane roads, stop at a pullout or parking lot to let cars behind you pass.

> Ask for the land-owner's permission before peeping on private property.

Peak Watch

"Peak color" is the Holy Grail for peepers. The turning starts first in the cooler climates of the north and higher elevations and creeps south and into valleys. The best resource is the locals, particularly park rangers, inn keepers, and tour guides (p. 552). Each state also has a website or hotline dedicated to current foliage conditions. For up-to-date information, check these sites:

NEW HAMPSHIRE
☎ 800/258-3608; www.visitnh.gov/4-seasons/fall-harvest/foliage

VERMONT
http://www.vermontvacation.com/fall.aspx

MAINE
☎ 207/287-4900;
www.maine.gov/doc/foliage

CONNECTICUT
www.ct.gov/dep/foliage

MASSACHUSETTS
www.massvacation.com/fallfoliage

US FOREST SERVICE
☎ 800/354-4595;
www.fs.fed.us/fallcolors

Sunny Days, Cool Nights

The palette and timing of fall's color change depend on factors as variable as leaf pigments, length of night, light, temperature, and rainfall. As autumn nights grow longer and trees prepare for winter, the chlorophyll that gives leaves their green color breaks down, revealing the yellow, orange, and brown carotenoid pigments underneath. The brilliant red colors of fall come from other pigments, anthocyanins, produced in response to sugars stored in the leaf's cells. Temperate New England's typically wet springs and sunny fall days followed by crisp nights are what make the foliage in this part of the country especially stunning.

The Best Small Cities & Towns

> Main Street in Chatham, where 19th-century style meets 21st-century luxury.

Concord, MA. Centuries of history, a rich literary legacy, lovely scenery, and notable shopping are just some of the elements that make Concord irresistible. Far from being a time capsule of Revolutionary War relics and Louisa May Alcott memorabilia, it's an intriguing destination where you can have fun while learning something new. See p. 120.

Nantucket, MA. It looks as though the whalers just departed, leaving behind their grand houses, cobbled streets, and enticing shops selling luxury goods from around the world. Tourism may be rampant, but not its tackier side effects, thanks to stringent preservation measures. See p. 150.

Chatham, MA. It has to be said: Chatham is the prettiest town on Cape Cod. On a summer day, stroll Main Street past the many shops and galleries, beyond the historic houses with their white picket fences, and on down to Lighthouse Beach, where you can see across Chatham Harbor and out to the Atlantic Ocean. It's picture-perfect. See p. 194.

Newport, RI. This city by the sea possesses an astonishing array of extravagant mansions—the best representation of Gilded Age excess in the country—and a nautical heritage dating to the Colonial era. You'll also find fabulous restaurants, excellent shopping, good beaches, and hopping nightlife. See p. 326.

Brattleboro, VT. This red-brick former mill town on the Connecticut River has transformed into a thriving haven for artists and artisans, with enough galleries, idiosyncratic boutiques, and bookstores to keep you occupied. Terrific restaurants, a curious mix of urban and rural sensibilities, and access to scenic drives and outdoor fun seamlessly blend hip and hippie. See p. 386.

Portsmouth, NH. It seems all sorts of people—from the young and idealistic, to the sporty set, to retirees—find something to fancy about this old port on the Piscataqua River. Maybe it's the independent shops and surprisingly good restaurants, or perhaps it's the harbor, the neighboring islands, or all of its historic sites. Best of all, you can do all of your exploring car-free. See p. 444.

Kennebunkport, ME. It's known as the town of the Presidents Bush (George H. W. and George W.), but there are better reasons to make the trip to K-Port: good seafood, a small attractive shopping square, boats at dock, fine inns, and a looping oceanside drive. This is elegant old New England at its finest. See p. 510.

The Best Scenery

> Cadillac Mountain, the only peak in Acadia National Park accessible by car, draws crowds with its breathtaking views.

From the Skywalk Observatory, Boston. Boston's geography is confusing at best. From the 50th floor of the Prudential Center, visitors can orient themselves—and see as far away as Cape Cod and New Hampshire. The panorama is especially lovely at sunset. See p. 56, **5**.

Up-Island on Martha's Vineyard. Vineyard scenery gets spectacular up-island, in such towns as Chilmark, where you'll pass expansive meadows, family farms, and ancient stone walls. Follow State Road and the Moshup Trail to the western tip of the island, the dazzling cliffs of Aquinnah, and the quaint fishing village of Menemsha. See p. 154.

In West Cornwall, CT. We've driven through this tiny town many times, and are always surprised loses its painterly quality. A 242-foot covered bridge spans the Housatonic River—you might spot a wading fly fisherman—and a handful of 19th-century buildings make up charming Main Street. It's beautiful in the spring and lovely against winter white, but never more dazzling than in autumn. See p. 288, **5**.

On the green in Dorset, VT. With a perfect village green, anchored by the beautifully restored Dorset Inn, Dorset looks like a movie set. You might have to bite into the penny candy from the little country store to make sure it's real. With its well-manicured green and its white clapboard buildings, this spot embodies New England's special brand of small-town charm. See p. 374, **4**.

At Moss Glen Falls, VT. In the center of the state, off impossibly scenic Route 100, a short walk brings you to this staggered, shimmering cascade. It's not the biggest or baddest, but it is one of the most beautiful waterfalls in the Northeast, and the location deep in the calm of the Green Mountains can't be beat. See p. 406.

Atop Mount Washington, NH. Sure, it's the tallest peak in the Northeast, and even just a view of the old Rockpile is pretty awe inspiring. From Mount Washington on a clear day, with the White Mountains in the foreground, you can see from the Adirondacks to the Atlantic, and all the way to Canada. See p. 441.

From the summit of Cadillac Mountain, ME. Acadia National Park is chock-full of jaw-dropping views, but the best vista is the one that awaits you at the tippy-top of Cadillac Mountain: a gorgeous panorama of islands, cliffs, open sea, and little towns. And yes, you can drive to the summit. See p. 484, **7**.

The Best Museums

> The RISD Museum of Art is home to an impressive collection.

Museum of Fine Arts, Boston. Never stuffy, always enlightening, the MFA gained 53 new galleries with the opening of the Art of the Americas wing in 2010. Don't overlook the original building, which overflows with treasures from all over the world. See p. 70, ❺.

Whaling Museum, Nantucket, MA. Housed in a former candle factory, this museum is a showpiece in the region. From the 43-foot finback whale skeleton to the impressive collection of scrimshaw and nautical art, it holds plenty to interest all ages. One section re-creates the 18th-century candle factory; other rooms are devoted to kids' activities. See p. 150, ❷.

Heritage Museums and Gardens, Sandwich, MA. This site, with museum buildings on 76 landscaped acres, will impress kids and adults alike. Children might fixate on the gleaming antique cars and the old-fashioned carousel. Adults can't help but be impressed with the horticulture, including a world-renowned rhododendron collection. See p. 156, ❶.

Sterling and Francine Clark Art Institute, Williamstown, MA. The Berkshires' other major art attraction, MASS MoCA (p. 250, ❷), is one of our favorite museum-going experiences, but it is hard to top the Clark, with its far-reaching collection of Impressionist works,

excellent rotating exhibits, and the elegant Stone Hill Center—a light-filled concrete structure housing an art conservation center/gallery space, designed by self-taught Japanese architect Tadao Ando. See p. 248, ❶.

Peabody Museum of Natural History, New Haven. This world-class museum at Yale is the brainchild of legendary paleontologist O.C. Marsh, who named triceratops, stegosaurus, and brontosaurus. The dinosaur skeletons in the Great Hall set our hearts aflutter. The juvenile apatosaurus is spectacular. See p. 302, ❺.

RISD Museum of Art, Providence. For a fairly small museum, this place has quite a diverse collection. Whether you come for the Monets, Cézannes, and Renoirs, or head straight for the modernist works by artists like Cy Twombly, Roy Lichtenstein, and Andy Warhol, you're sure to be impressed. See p. 341, ❹.

Farnsworth Art Museum, Rockland, ME. This is the best of many jewel-box art museums along the coast of Maine. Expect a heavy concentration of work from the Wyeths (Andrew, N. C., and Jamie), as well as a good dose of Winslow Homer, Fairfield Porter, and William Zorach. Photography and contemporary art haven't been neglected, either. See p. 518, ❶.

The Best Historic Sites

Paul Revere House, Boston. "Listen, my children, and you shall hear" about a regular guy who was also an American hero. Revere made his living as a silversmith and his reputation as a rider who warned the local militias of the British troops advancing in April 1775. His cozy home offers a look at the comfortable life he was jeopardizing with the actions that helped start the Revolution. See p. 53, ⑩.

John F. Kennedy Hyannis Museum, Hyannis, MA. This museum has long been the most popular attraction on Cape Cod, drawing visitors to the evocative black-and-white candid photographs of the Kennedy family swimming, sailing, and playing touch football at the place they have long called home, their waterfront compound in Hyannis Port. President John F. Kennedy once called Cape Cod "the one place I can think and be alone." His allure, and that of other famous Kennedy family members, still draws people 50 years after his days in the White House. See p. 165, ⑦.

Historic Deerfield, MA. One of the most absorbing ways to experience Colonial and Early American history is by walking through this Pioneer Valley village. Heading down Main Street, everywhere you turn is another incredibly preserved or restored old house. Unlike most historic districts, Deerfield allows visitors to step in and explore many homes, appointed with period furniture, tools, and personal effects. See p. 259, ⑤.

Newport, RI. Beyond its famed summer "cottages" (grand Guilded Age mansions by another name), Newport has a fascinating and complicated history dating to the days when it rivaled New York and Boston as a major seaport (*Spotlight: Soul Liberty*, p. 336). Much of that history is still evident, thanks to well-preserved architecture. A walk around Historic Hill reveals such Colonial gems as the White Horse Tavern (1652) and Trinity Church (1725), as well as the Great Friends Meeting House (1699) and Touro Synagogue (1763), structures that attest to a rich and varied heritage. See p. 326.

> Kids whining? Introduce them to the accommodations at the Old Gaol in York, ME.

Old Gaol, York, ME. Maine's first Colonial settlement, York was founded 1624, just a few years after the Pilgrims hit Plymouth Rock. The town still possesses the highest concentration of historic buildings in the state. The Old Gaol, a 1719 barn-red building, was Maine's first jail; tour its dungeon, cells, and the jail keeper's quarters, plus a nearby tavern, a schoolhouse, and period homes, with a single all-access pass from the Old York Historic Society. See p. 502, ①.

The Best Beaches

Cahoon Hollow, Wellfleet, MA. One of the Cape's most popular beaches, this Atlantic Ocean beauty features the famous 75-foot dunes characteristic of many of the beaches that are part of the Outer Cape's National Seashore. What distinguishes Cahoon Hollow is The Beachcomber, a rocking club (and former Coast Guard station) in the parking lot. Beach lovers can go straight from daytime sun to nighttime fun. See p. 174.

Race Point, Provincetown, MA. This picturesque National Seashore beach, with a historic Coast Guard station doubling as a museum, is at the tip of the Cape Cod peninsula. The Atlantic Ocean waters here are typically on the colder side—considered refreshing to New Englanders—with ample wave action. This is a good place to watch the horizons for migrating whales. See p. 179.

Hammonassett Beach, Madison, CT. With over 2 miles of crisp, white sand, this lovely stretch is the longest shoreline park in the state. It can draw plenty of bathers on scorching days, but it often feels surprisingly private, and there always seems to be enough space that you don't feel crowded. It's the perfect place for a bundled-up amble along the ocean or boardwalk in colder weather. See p. 270.

Mansion Beach, Block Island, RI. Arrive early and drive or bike (our preference) down a long dirt road to find this beautiful, long stretch of Block Island beach. A short hike then brings you to white sand and sparkling surf, which can be quite strong, making it the ideal body-surfing spot (but not so great for young children). Set beneath rocky cliffs, it's also a great walking beach. See p. 310, **9**.

Goosewing Beach Preserve, Little Compton, RI. It's not easy to get to this serene barrier beach—you have to walk across part of another beach—which is why it's blessedly crowd free. Even if you don't swim, the mile-long slice of pebbly beach is perfect for strolling, and there's a bathtub-warm salt pond just begging to be explored. Bring your binoculars and you may be lucky enough to spot nesting piping plovers, terns, and herons. See "Getting Out of Town," p. 328.

Ogunquit Beach, ME. Ogunquit's main strand has white sand and placid ocean views, and the compact downtown is a short stroll away. It's very rare to find a beach in Maine that combines lots of sand (most of the coast is rocky), summery vistas, quiet seclusion, ample parking, and walking-distance access to shops and restaurants. See p. 507, **3**.

> As close as the Outer Cape comes to having high-rises: the 75-foot dunes at Cahoon Hollow beach.

The Best Dining Experiences

> *For a night out with your sweetheart, Nantucket's Company of the Cauldron casts a spell.*

The North End, Boston. The influence of the Italian immigrants who once dominated this old neighborhood is apparent everywhere. Wander the narrow streets, read the menus posted outside most restaurants, and pick out a place to eat. Even if you just split a pizza or settle for coffee and pastries at a cafe, you've had an experience that's possible in only a handful of American cities. See p. 97.

Nantucket, MA. This island is a foodie mecca. No other place in New England has more fine-dining restaurants within a few blocks. It's difficult to choose, but the good news is, you can't go wrong. Do you want seafood? That's easy: Straight Wharf. Innovative: American Seasons. Romantic: Company of the Cauldron. Funky eclectic: Black-Eyed Susan's. Ethnic: Corazon del Mar. The list goes on. See p. 227.

Old Inn on the Green, New Marlborough, MA. With its wide-plank floors, wrought-iron chandeliers, and wood-beamed ceilings, this 1760 former stagecoach stop gets our vote for most romantic setting in Western Massachusetts. Yet it's chef Peter Platt's vibrant, French-inflected seasonal cuisine that takes center stage. Whether you order a la carte or opt for the prix-fixe menu, your meal will be unforgettable. See p. 255.

Match, South Norwalk, CT. A central figure in the growing culinary scene in revitalized South Norwalk, Match draws praise for its daring dishes and well-curated wine list. A humming, jovial place—with a sidewalk cafe in the warmer months—Match has an informed, affable staff and a menu that features audacious choices like Peanut Butter and Grape Jelly Halibut and the trademark 8 Hour Osso Bucco. See p. 277, ②.

Claire's, Hardwick, VT. This legendary community-supported restaurant in northern Vermont is the beating heart of the state's thriving locavore scene. The kitchen uses über-local ingredients, artisanal products, and an extensive farm-to-table network to turn out consistently tantalizing meals. A gathering spot for both locals and foodie travelers, Claire's is both inspiring and delicious. See p. 379.

Portland, ME. Go highbrow or lowbrow: Fore Street and Hugo's can match New American menus with any other New England restaurant, and the waterfront diners are full of salty characters. The brewpubs are uniformly excellent, too. Curiously, you can't get a good lobster dinner in this city—head to one of Maine's fishing villages for that. See p. 501.

The Best Hotels & Resorts

> *The Chanler gives guests a chance to experience Newport's Gilded Age finery.*

Four Seasons Hotel, Boston. Often challenged, never surpassed, the Four Seasons offers its guests the finest physical appointments—from the swimming pool overlooking the Public Garden to opulent marble bathrooms to wonderful dining—and a level of service that leaves even its most luxurious competitors in the dust. See p. 111.

Cliffside Beach Club, Nantucket, MA. Situated on the beach and within walking distance to town, this is the premier lodging choice on the island. There's a sublime beachy-ness to the whole setup, from the antique wicker in the clubhouse to the colorful umbrellas set up for guests on the beach. See p. 226.

Winvian, Morris, CT. Sure, there's a two-story luxe treehouse and a suite incorporating a repurposed beaver dam, but this remarkable, ultra-exclusive resort transcends gimmickry. Composed of playful, architect-designed cottages with pebble-steam showers, waterfalls, and Bose sound systems, Winvian also has a breathtaking spa, top-of-the-line dining, and attentive staff members. See p. 291.

The Chanler, Newport, RI. This might be as close as you get to staying in a Newport mansion. Near Marble House, Rosecliffe, and the Breakers, this deluxe hotel, housed in an 1873 mansion, brings detailed character to its sumptuous decor, from the deep brown and gold of the English Tudor room to the pointed arches and rich purples in the Gothic room. See p. 334.

Equinox Resort & Spa, Manchester, VT. The Equinox has more than 200 years of colorful history, but 21st-century renovations mean that guests retire to luxurious rooms with custom-made beds. The activities—from a top-notch golf course and spa to archery school, falconry classes, and Land Rover driving lessons—make this hotel extraordinary. See p. 375.

Omni Mount Washington, Bretton Woods, NH. One of New England's grande dames, constructed in 1902, this hotel looks every bit the historic landmark it is. The setting—at the base of New Hampshire's highest peak—takes our breath away. Such recent upgrades as a 25,000-square-foot spa and an exhilarating canopy tour promise even better times ahead. See p. 443.

Inn by the Sea, Cape Elizabeth, ME. This place has it all: a sprawling lawn with Adirondack chairs, well-kept gardens, a lovely spa, high-class dining, luxurious cottages and rooms, a "green" ethos, and a boardwalk footpath leading down to one of the Portland area's prettiest beaches. See p. 500.

The Best Small Inns & B&Bs

> *Indulge your fantasies of running away to sea with a night at the Griswold Inn.*

Captain's House Inn, Chatham, MA. The 19th-century sea captain's house that anchors this exquisite property is set on two meticulously groomed acres. It feels like a private club, complete with swimming pool and tennis court. The place has a British air, from the high tea offered upon arrival to the immaculate service throughout your stay. See p. 198.

The Porches Inn at MASS MoCA, North Adams, MA. Across the street from MASS MoCA, six refurbished row houses seamlessly blend modern and rustic touches—Frette linens and rainfall showers, paint-by-numbers art and vintage Mohawk Trail collectibles—to create a one-of-a-kind lodging experience. From the rocking chairs on the porches to the brilliantly conceived color palette, we just love it here. See p. 254.

Mayflower Inn & Spa, Washington, CT. The service at this property is top-notch and the rooms are luxurious, but the spa is the jewel in the crown. In contrast to the classic New England decor of the rooms, Spa House is a serene sanctuary, overlooking a shimmering pond. Concierges shape your experience, which might incorporate a private hike or snowshoe excursion with chakra balancing. See p. 291.

The Griswold Inn, Essex, CT. We love spending the night at the Gris, a gathering spot for sailors and landlubbers alike since it opened in 1776. From the dining room hung wall-to-wall with nautical art to the taproom ceiling of horsehair and oyster shells, we can think of few other places that ooze so much character. There's even a hunt breakfast every Sunday, a tradition the British began when they occupied the Gris in the War of 1812. See p. 295.

Inn at Thorn Hill & Spa, Jackson Village, NH. Set in the foothills of the White Mountains, this handsome inn stands out for its attentive and sophisticated, though unpretentious, service. Thorn Hill is also home to one of our favorite lounges, an inviting room where you'll want to sink into a leather couch by the fire. Knowing there are 3,000 exquisite bottles of wine in the cellar doesn't hurt, either. See p. 442.

2
The Best
All–New
England
Itineraries

New England Highlights

With 2 weeks to spend in New England, you can explore urban and rural destinations, see the mountains and the ocean, and mix road trips with quality time for sightseeing, relaxing, and mingling with the locals. Resist the temptation to visit as many places as possible—longer stays in fewer destinations allow for a richer, more complete experience that's simply not possible if you're constantly on the move. On this itinerary, you'll want a car for travel beyond the Boston area, because public transit between our destinations is inconvenient and can be slow.

> PREVIOUS PAGE *Bash Bish Falls, a magnet for Berkshires hikers, is especially gorgeous during foliage season.* THIS PAGE *Traffic on the Charles River and Boston's skyline.*

START Boston is 71 miles from Newport, RI, and 110 miles from Portland, ME. TRIP LENGTH 658 miles.

1 Boston & Cambridge, MA. On Day 1, walk part of the **Freedom Trail,** beginning at **Boston Common** (p. 50, **1**), the oldest American public park. Skip through history, visiting the **Robert Gould Shaw Memorial** (p. 50, **2**), which commemorates a Civil War officer and his troops; the **Granary Burying Ground** (p. 50, **3**), final resting place of heroes of the Revolution; and **King's Chapel Burying Ground** (p. 74, **6**), with its Colonial gravestones. Pause at 19th-century **Old City Hall** (p. 51, **5**) before exploring the **Old State House Museum** (p. 51, **6**), in a 1713 building that was once the seat of the Colonial government. Stop at **Faneuil Hall** (p. 51, **7**), then enjoy the street

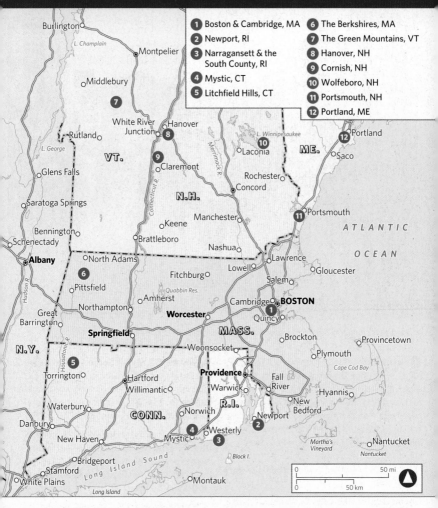

1 Boston & Cambridge, MA
2 Newport, RI
3 Narragansett & the South County, RI
4 Mystic, CT
5 Litchfield Hills, CT
6 The Berkshires, MA
7 The Green Mountains, VT
8 Hanover, NH
9 Cornish, NH
10 Wolfeboro, NH
11 Portsmouth, NH
12 Portland, ME

performers, shops, pushcarts, restaurants, and bars of **Faneuil Hall Marketplace** (p. 52, 8). Ride the **water shuttle** (p. 52, 9) across Boston Harbor to Charlestown and back, and then check out the **Paul Revere House** (p. 53, 10). Wind down on **Hanover Street** (p. 53, 11), the main drag of the **North End.** Start Day 2 at the **Museum of Fine Arts** (p. 70, 5). Later, take a **Boston Duck Tour** (p. 55, 4), and then visit the **Skywalk Observatory** (p. 56, 5). Next, do some shopping on **Newbury Street** (p. 56, 6) before a walk through the lovely **Public Garden** (p. 56, 7), where magnificent trees and seasonal flowers surround the little lagoon that's home to the **Swan Boats** (p. 65, 7). On Day 3,

take an early tour of **Fenway Park** (p. 66, 1), then cross the Back Bay Fens to the **Isabella Stewart Gardner Museum** (p. 67, 3), before a visit to Cambridge, where you'll find the **Longfellow House–Washington's Headquarters National Historic Site** (p. 88, 8) and **Harvard Yard** (p. 59, 3). ⏱ 3 days.

On the morning of Day 4, take I-93S 13 miles to Rte. 24. Go about 40 miles south, taking care in Fall River, where the highway merges with I-195. When you cross the state line, follow signs to rtes. 114 and 138 which will take you straight into Newport, where you'll spend the next 2 nights.

> *The streets along Newport Harbor abound with shops, restaurants, and summer crowds.*

2 Newport, RI. Plan to tour two of "The Cottages," including **the Breakers** (p. 331, **7**); to prevent Gilded Age overload, schedule one for Day 4 and one for Day 5. For a different perspective on the mansions, lace up your walking shoes and follow the 3½-mile **Cliff Walk** (p. 328, **4**). And be sure to set aside some time for shopping, or at least browsing, in the shops of **Lower Thames Street.** ⊙ 2 days. See p. 326.

Get an early start on Day 6, taking Rte. 138 west 7 miles to Rte. 1A south. Go 6½ miles to Narragansett, where you'll pick up Rte. 1 south.

3 Narragansett & the South County, RI. South County refers to a section of the Rhode Island coast—roughly from **Narragansett** (p. 316, **1**) to the Connecticut state line—that's well loved by locals and virtually unknown to outsiders. Work your way west on Rte. 1 south, stopping to relax at one of the area's excellent beaches. ⊙ 1 day. See p. 316.

Either spend the night in South County or head for Mystic to get a jump-start on Day 7. Rte. 1 leads to Mystic, 33 miles from Narragansett.

4 Mystic, CT. Mystic Seaport (p. 282, **3**) can easily fill Day 7, but if you prefer to branch out, spend part of the afternoon in next-door **Stonington** (p. 284, **4**) or at one of the nearby **casinos** (p. 272). ⊙ 1 day. See p. 280.

Start Day 8 early, taking I-95S 23 miles to Rte. 9 north. After about 22 miles, follow signs for I-691W, and take it to I-84W. Take exit 7 to Rte. 7 north to New Milford, where you'll pick up Rte. 202.

5 Litchfield Hills, CT. Take a little time to enjoy this detour through a particularly picturesque slice of northwestern Connecticut. ⊙ 2 hr. See p. 286.

Continue on Rte. 7 north, across the Massachusetts border.

6 The Berkshires, MA. If you haven't stopped for lunch on the road, head to **Great Barrington** (p. 236, **1**) for a good meal and a little shopping. Then visit **Stockbridge** and the **Norman Rockwell Museum** (p. 237, **2**). Spend the night in this area, or push on to **Williamstown** (p. 248, **1**) so you can get an early start on Day 9. Hit the **Sterling and Francine Clark Art Institute** (p. 248, **1**), break up your art-focused day with a drive up **Mt. Greylock** (p. 252), and then backtrack to **MASS MoCA** (p. 250, ②). ⏱ 1½ days. See p. 248.

On Day 10, take Rte. 7 north into Vermont.

⑦ **The Green Mountains, VT.** Work your way north, enjoying the vistas of the Green Mountain National Forest. Stop in **Bennington** (p. 372, ①), then detour onto Rte. 7A and take it to **Manchester** (p. 374, ③) for outlet shopping, pleasant dining, and breathtaking views. **Dorset** (p. 374, ④), which looks like a Hollywood version of a Vermont town, is a good place to pause as you continue north. Make your destination your hotel or motel; lodging options along Rte. 7 range from the ultra-luxurious **Equinox Resort & Spa** (p. 375) in Manchester to the motels that cluster around Rutland. On Day 11, take Rte. 7 north to Rutland and go east on Rte. 4. You're heading for **Woodstock** (p. 394) for excellent sightseeing, shopping, and outdoor activities; a good excursion up the road is the Simon Pearce store and restaurant in **Quechee** (p. 396, ⑤). ⏱ 2 days.

Start Day 12 by crossing into New Hampshire. From Woodstock, follow Rte. 4 east 9½ miles to I-89. Go 3 miles south to the intersection with I-91. Take I-91N 5½ miles to exit 13 and pick up Rte. 10A/Rte. 10 east for just under a mile.

⑧ **Hanover, NH.** Visit Dartmouth College (p. 432, ⑤) and its art museums. ⏱ 2 hr.

Take Rte. 10A/Rte. 10 west back to I-91 south and go 14 miles, to exit 9. Take Rte. 5/Rte. 12 south just over 4 miles and turn left at Bridge St. After crossing the river, turn left and follow Rte. 12A north for 1½ miles.

⑨ **Cornish, NH.** Take in the **Cornish-Windsor Covered Bridge** (p. 432) and visit the **Saint-Gaudens National Historic Site** (p. 432, ④), which commemorates the great sculptor. ⏱ 2 hr.

Continue on Rte. 12A north for 12 miles and follow signs to I-89S, which you'll take 6½ miles, to exit 17. Go 26 miles east on Rte. 4 to Danbury where you'll bear left onto Rte. 104 east. Go 24 miles and turn left onto Rte. 3 (Daniel Webster Hwy.). Go north for less than a mile to a right onto Rte. 25 east. After 11 miles, turn right and take Rte. 109 south 17½ miles to:

> *The neighborhood around Portsmouth's Strawbery Banke Museum dates to 1653.*

⑩ **Wolfeboro, NH.** The adorable lakeside town is a good place to take a break and explore on foot. ⏱ 1–2 hr. See p. 434, ①.

Head south on Rte. 28 for 9 miles. It merges into Rte. 11, which you'll take south for 15 miles. In Rochester, pick up Rte. 16 and continue south 20 miles. After crossing I-95, follow signs into Portsmouth, where you'll spend the night.

⑪ **Portsmouth, NH.** Begin Day 13 at the fascinating **Strawbery Banke Museum** (p. 445, ④) and leave time in the afternoon for exploring and shopping. ⏱ 1 day. See p. 444.

On Day 14, take I-95N 52 miles north to Portland, ME.

⑫ **Portland, ME.** Spend your last day in New England in this lovely port city. Visit the **Portland Museum of Art** (p. 494, ①), wander through the **Old Port** (p. 452, ①), and indulge in some of the city's justly famous cuisine (p. 501). ⏱ 1 day. See p. 494.

Southern New England Highlights

Northern New England overshadows the southern part of the region—but its higher profile often means larger crowds and steeper prices, especially at busy times. Connecticut and Rhode Island have their own appeal, with lovely coastal scenery complementing rolling green hills. A visit to the region makes a pleasant contrast to the mountains and rocky shores of the other New England states. This itinerary can enjoyably precede or follow a trip to Boston, Cape Cod, or New York; if you're starting in New York, reverse the order of the stops listed here.

> *Rose Island Lighthouse helps guide sailors in Narragansett Bay, in South County, RI.*

START Newport, RI, is 71 miles from Boston.
TRIP LENGTH 142 miles.

1 Newport, RI. For tips on making the most of your brief time in Newport, see the suggestions in "New England in 2 Weeks," earlier in this chapter. Drop the tour of the second "Cottage" or cut back on your Cliff Walk time to save a few hours. ⊕ 1 day. See p. 326.

If the weather isn't great, spend the morning of Day 2 in Newport. Otherwise, get an early start and set out along the coast. Leave Newport on Rte. 138 west and go 7 miles to Rte. 1A south. Go 6½ miles to Narragansett, where you'll pick up Rte. 1 south. Plan to spend the night in:

2 South County, RI. This is the part of the Rhode Island coast known mostly to natives—and that's a good thing. Spend some time exploring Narragansett, but be sure to schedule a bit of beach time and an appointment with some fresh seafood. ⊕ 1 day. See p. 316.

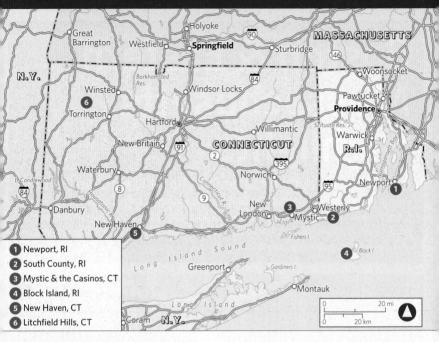

1. Newport, RI
2. South County, RI
3. Mystic & the Casinos, CT
4. Block Island, RI
5. New Haven, CT
6. Litchfield Hills, CT

On Day 3, take Rte. 1 20 miles south to Rte. 78 west. Go about 5 miles, and follow signs to I-95S, which you'll take 6 miles to exit 90. Follow signs to Mystic, CT, where you'll spend the night.

3 Mystic, CT & the Casinos.
Allow at least half a day to experience **Mystic Seaport** (p. 282, 3). It can easily fill a day. On the afternoon of Day 3, pick a casino. Ledyard, home to the **Foxwoods Resort Casino** (home to an excellent museum on Native Americans) and **MGM Grand at Foxwoods** (p. 272), is a bit closer to Mystic than **Mohegan Sun** (p. 272), in Uncasville. If casinos aren't your bag, make a side trip to **Essex** (p. 292, 2).

Start Day 4 early, taking Rte. 27 north for 1¼ miles to I-95S. Go 8 miles to exit 84. Pick up Rte. 32 south and take it about 2 miles into New London. Follow signs to the waterfront and ferry.

4 Block Island, RI.
A day trip to Block Island is a great favorite with savvy New Englanders looking to get away from it all, quickly. Leave New London early, and be sure you know the schedule for the ferry back so you don't get stranded. Spend the day on the beach, on a bike, or linger over lunch. ⏱ 1 day. See p. 320.

From New London, take I-95W 44 miles to New Haven to start Day 5.

5 New Haven, CT.
Spend the day at **Yale University** (p. 300, 1 – 3), with its fascinating museums, but plan an off-campus excursion for some world-class "apizza," the city's second-biggest draw. ⏱ 1 day. See p. 300.

On Day 6, head inland. Take Rte. 63 north about 15 miles and go right onto Rte. 8 north. After 13 miles, pick up Rte. 254 north and go about 8½ miles to a left onto Rte. 118 west. Litchfield is 1 mile up the road. To continue to Washington, take Rte. 202 west 9¾ miles to a left at Rte. 47 south and go 3 miles.

6 Litchfield Hills, CT.
In this wealthy green corner of northwestern Connecticut, you'll pass through **Litchfield** (p. 288, 4) en route to **Washington** (p. 290, 6), home of the celebrated **Mayflower Inn & Spa** (p. 291). If the pricey accommodations aren't in your budget, plan on a snack or meal in the taproom. On Day 7, hiking and boating are just two options for visitors who have time for nonmotorized sightseeing in the morning. In the afternoon, return to your arrival point or continue on your way. ⏱ 2 days. See p. 286.

Boston & Eastern Massachusetts Highlights

A week is enough time to get comfortable with the Boston area and gain a sense of what else eastern Massachusetts has to offer. You'll spend 4 days exploring the 617 area code, then branch out. Cape Ann offers breathtaking scenery and just enough attractions, while Plymouth piles on the relatable history and low-impact outdoor exploration.

> *The view from Boston's* Top of the Hub *lounge is especially memorable at sunset.*

START Boston is 41 miles from Rockport and 23 miles from Salem. **TRIP LENGTH** 160 miles.

❶ **Boston & Cambridge.** For the first 3 days, see stop ❶ in "New England Highlights" earlier in this chapter. One evening, have drinks at the **Top of the Hub** lounge (p. 116) before or after dinner; they come with a mind-blowing 52nd-floor view of the Boston area. On Day 4, either return to the **Museum of Fine Arts** (p. 70, ❺; your admission fee covers two visits within 10 days) or head back to Cambridge to visit the **Longfellow House–Washington's Headquarters National Historic Site** (p. 88, ❽) and **Mount Auburn Cemetery** (p. 88, ❿). In the afternoon, take a **whale-watching cruise** with the New England Aquarium (p. 64, ❹). ⏱ 4 days. See chapter 3.

> Mayflower II, *a replica of the original, makes its home not far from Plymouth Rock.*

On Day 5, take I-93N 11 miles until you see signs for I-95/Rte. 128 north. Go 8½ miles and merge left onto Rte. 128. Follow it 19 miles and turn left onto Rte. 127, which will take you into Gloucester and then Rockport, where you'll spend the night.

2 Rockport & Gloucester. Follow the recommendations in the Boston day trip "Cape Ann" (p. 128), which takes you from the tip of the beautiful peninsula south through two fascinating destinations. While exploring Gloucester, try to include a stop at the **Whale Center of New England** (p. 130), which will be even more interesting after your whale-watch on Day 4. ⏱ 1 day.

On Day 6, take I-93S 9 miles to the left exit onto Rte. 3 south, which you'll take 30 miles to Exit 4, Plimoth Plantation Hwy.

3 Plymouth. Start your visit with a visit to **Plimoth Plantation** (p. 134, **1**), where you can experience life as the 17th-century Pilgrims might have lived it. Continue with a visit to **Plymouth Rock** and *Mayflower II* (p. 135, **3** and **4**), a representation of the type of ship that brought the Pilgrims to the New World in 1620. ⏱ 1 day. See p. 134.

On Day 7, take I-93N 11 miles to I-95/Rte. 128 north, go 8½ miles, and merge left onto Rte. 128. Continue 2½ miles to exit 25A and follow Rte. 114 east 2 miles into downtown Salem.

1 Boston & Cambridge
2 Rockport & Gloucester
3 Plymouth
4 Salem
5 Marblehead

4 Salem. What better way to wrap up your time in New England than with a visit to the city made famous by witchcraft (or, more precisely, by accusations of witchcraft)? You'll want to visit the quirky **Salem Witch Museum** (p. 124, **1**), of course, and the excellent **Peabody Essex Museum** (p. 124, **2**). ⏱ Half-day. See p. 124.

In the afternoon on Day 7, take Rte. 114 east 4 miles to Marblehead.

5 Marblehead. On your last day, be sure to leave time to wander around seaside Marblehead's charming Old Town (p. 126, **5**). ⏱ Half-day. See p. 124.

12 Days in Boston & Farther Afield

This itinerary uses the hub-and-spoke model, with the Boston area as a base. It approximates the experience of a local resident on a "staycation": exploring Boston and Cambridge, then a series of day trips to a range of fascinating destinations, most of them less than 2 hours away. You don't need a car before Day 6. In fact, you may not need one at all—though the increased flexibility is wonderful and allows you to see and do more. Public transit is a workable option for most of this itinerary, if you allow lots of time and patience for buses and trains, money for cab fare, and energy for planning the logistics.

> Johnston Gate, erected in 1889, is the oldest gate in the wall around Harvard Yard.

START Boston is 71 miles from Newport, RI, and 110 miles from Portland, ME. **TRIP LENGTH** At least 990 miles on the road.

❶ Boston & Cambridge, MA. You'll be spending the first 3 days of your trip exploring New England's biggest city and its most charming neighbor. See chapter 3 for details. ☺ 3 days.

On Day 4, pick up a rental car and take I-93S 13 miles to Rte. 24 and continue south for about 40 miles. Be careful in Fall River, where the highway briefly merges with I-195. The route to Newport, where you'll spend the night, is clearly marked on Rtes. 114 and 138.

❷ Newport, RI. One day is just barely enough time to explore this wonderful little city. If you can add a day to your itinerary, this is the place to do it. Since you'll only have time to tour one "cottage," we suggest you make it **the Breakers** (p. 331, ❼). And definitely plan on a walk on a section of the 3½-mile **Cliff Walk** (p. 328, ❹), but not the whole thing. You'll want to leave time for shopping, dining, and wandering the narrow streets and grand boulevards. Note that the bus from Boston (make sure you know the return schedule!) is a more-than-viable option in the summer, when parking in Newport is anything but fun. Plus, having a designated driver can expand your evening options. ☺ 1 day. See p. 326.

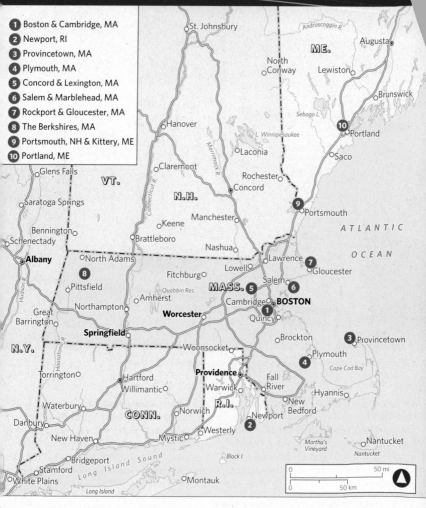

1 Boston & Cambridge, MA
2 Newport, RI
3 Provincetown, MA
4 Plymouth, MA
5 Concord & Lexington, MA
6 Salem & Marblehead, MA
7 Rockport & Gloucester, MA
8 The Berkshires, MA
9 Portsmouth, NH & Kittery, ME
10 Portland, ME

Get an early start on Day 5 as you'll be returning to Boston to pick up the fast ferry to Provincetown. It takes just 90 minutes each way but costs $83 round-trip. A cheaper option is the old-school (slow) ferry, which only operates on Saturdays, takes twice as long, and allows just 3½ hours to explore, but costs only $44. Leave your car behind—you won't need it. Plan to spend the extra three nights in or around Boston.

3 **Provincetown, MA.** P-town in the summer is one of the best places in the world for people-watching. Stroll, shop, and make time for a visit to the **Pilgrim Monument & Provincetown Museum** (p. 165, 9), which makes a good intro to tomorrow's excursion. ⏱1 day. See p. 202.

Hit the road early on Day 6, taking I-93S 9 miles. Exit left onto Rte. 3 south, which you'll take 30 miles to Exit 4, Plimoth Plantation Hwy.

4 **Plymouth, MA.** See "Boston & Eastern Massachusetts," above, for information about a day trip to Plymouth. The Pilgrims landed here in 1620 after a brief stay in **Provincetown** (see above), and the contrast raises some good questions: Were they nuts to leave such a beautiful place? Where would you rather live now? ⏱1 day. See p. 134.

> *Boats on the Piscataqua River, which separates New Hampshire from Maine.*

On Day 7, take Rte. 2 west, 10 miles, crossing I-95/Rte. 128. Pay attention when you see signs for Lincoln; where the road takes a sharp left, go straight, following signs for HISTORIC CONCORD. This is Cambridge Tpk., which leads into the center of town, about 1½ miles ahead.

5 Concord & Lexington, MA. The towns where the Revolutionary War began make a good follow-up to yesterday's Colonial focus. See the Boston day trip "Concord" for pointers. If you're using public transit, consider investing in a ticket for the **Liberty Ride** (☎ 781/862-0500, ext. 702; www.libertyride.us). The price of the tour includes transportation around and between Lexington and Concord. ⏱ 1 day. See p. 120.

Head for the North Shore on Day 8. From Boston, take I-93N 11 miles to I-95/Rte. 128 north, go 8½ miles, and merge left to stay on Rte. 128 north. Continue 2½ miles to exit 25A and follow Rte. 114 east about 2 miles into downtown Salem.

6 Salem & Marblehead, MA. Post-Revolution prosperity helped these neighboring communities grow prominent and prosperous. See the Boston day trip "Salem & Marblehead," p. 124 for an itinerary that covers both. A visit to the **Peabody Essex Museum** (p. 124, 2) in Salem makes a good introduction, as does a walk around the historic **Old Town** (p. 126, 5) section of Marblehead. ⏱ 1 day.

On Day 9, it's back to the North Shore. Take I-93N 11 miles, until you see signs for I-95/Rte. 128 north. Go 8½ miles and merge left to stay on Rte. 128. Follow it 19 miles; it ends at Rte. 127 in Gloucester. Turn left and go north 3½ miles into:

7 Rockport & Gloucester, MA. For information about visiting Rockport and Gloucester, see the Cape Ann day trip (p. 128) in chapter 3. Note that this area is an excellent 2-day destination—simply adding a **whale-watch** (p. 130) and a trip to the beach will let you fill 48 hours almost to overflowing. If you add a day here, I suggest skipping the Berkshires (see Day 10). ⏱ 1–2 days.

On Day 10, leave Boston, taking I-90 (the Mass Pike) west 123 miles to exit 2. To reach Lenox, follow Rte. 20 west for a little over 5 miles.

❽ The Berkshires, MA. This Day 10 day trip requires lots of care time but is loads of fun. Although western Massachusetts is only about 2½ hours from Boston, the area is as closely associated with getaways from New York City as it is with the Massachusetts state capital. The key to an enjoyable experience is realistic planning. Roads are narrow and traffic is relatively slow—you simply can't fit in more than two major destinations without a lot of stressful scrambling. My favorite 1-day visit starts in **Lenox** on a summer Saturday morning with a picnic breakfast during rehearsal at **Tanglewood** (p. 252, ❺). Then I'd have lunch in **Great Barrington** and hit **Stockbridge** for a visit to the **Norman Rockwell Museum** (p. 237, ❷) and some shopping. In the winter, I'd concentrate on **Williamstown**, the **Sterling and Francine Clark Art Institute** (p. 248, ❶), and **MASS MoCA** (p. 250, ❷). ⏱ 1 day. See p. 248.

Start Day 11 by taking I-93N from Boston for 11 miles to I-95N. Go 50 miles to exit 6, in Portsmouth, NH.

❾ Portsmouth, NH & Kittery, ME. The Piscataqua River, which separates New Hampshire from Maine, is your touchstone today. South of it is Portsmouth, the beautiful little city that's the jewel of New Hampshire's 18-mile coastline. Start your day here with breakfast and a visit to the **Strawbery Banke Museum** (p. 445, ❹). In the afternoon, cross the border. (Make sure Memorial Bridge is open to traffic before heading for US Rte. 1; a long-term construction project was in the late planning stages at press time.) **Kittery** (p. 504) is best known for its excellent outlet shopping, which can easily fill the rest of the day. If you

prefer to explore, consider an optional detour a bit farther up the lovely southern Maine coast. It's less than an hour on US Rte. 1 or I-95 north to artsy **Ogunquit** (p. 506) or the preppy paradise of **Kennebunkport** (p. 510). ⏱ 1 day. See p. 444.

Spend the night in Kittery, Ogunquit, or Kennebunkport. On Day 12, from Kittery, take I-95N and go 49 miles to I-295, and take that 5 miles north.

❿ Portland, ME. Spend your final day exploring Maine's loveliest port city. See "Portland" on p. 494 for a 1-day itinerary. ⏱ 1 day.

> *Norman Rockwell's Berkshires studio, as it looked in 1960.*

Travel Tip

For this itinerary, we recommend reviewing the average temperature and rainfall box on p. 563.

New England with Kids

The pleasures of a family trip to and around New England tend to be low-tech, with an element of nostalgia and the potential to shake your offspring out of their Nintendo trances—no promises, though. Families lucky enough to have 2 weeks to spend can combine two time-tested approaches: parking yourselves at or near the beach for a week, then piling into the minivan and hitting the road. This itinerary concentrates on Cape Cod and the White Mountains, with a few additional fun stops for the whole family.

> The Bourne Braves pause for the national anthem before a Cape Cod Baseball League game.

START Sandwich, on Cape Cod, is 57 miles from Boston. **TRIP LENGTH** 2 weeks and 460 miles.

1 Cape Cod, MA. One traditional way to visit the Cape—and it's an excellent tradition—is to rent a place for a week and make that your base. Allow for plenty of beach time, a trip to the **Heritage Museums and Gardens** (p. 156, **1**) in **Sandwich,** a visit to **Provincetown** (p. 202), and a **Cape Cod Baseball**

League game (p. 159). You'll start Day 8 with another trip to the beach, waiting for the worst of the turnover-day traffic to ease. ⏱ 7½ days. See chapter 4.

To leave the Cape, take Rte. 6 west to the Bourne Bridge, then follow signs to I-495N. After about 60 miles, pick up I-90 (the Massachusetts Tpk. or Mass Pike) and go west 28 miles. Exit at the Sturbridge tolls and take I-84W for about 3 miles, following signs for

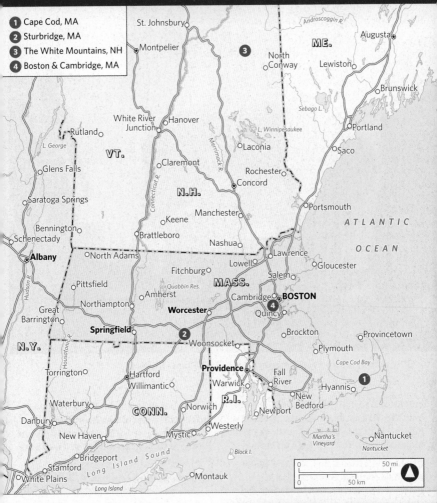

1 Cape Cod, MA
2 Sturbridge, MA
3 The White Mountains, NH
4 Boston & Cambridge, MA

Rte. 20 west. After ¾ mile, turn left onto Main St. in Sturbridge, where you'll spend the night.

2 **Sturbridge, MA.** On Day 9, be at **Old Sturbridge Village** (p. 261) when it opens, wearing sunblock and broken-in walking shoes. Spend most of the day exploring the re-creation of a 19th-century community. ⏱ 6 hr.

Take I-84E 3 miles to the Mass Pike east and go about 12 miles to the exit for I-290E. Take I-290 about 21 miles to the exit for I-495N. After 32 miles, pick up I-93N for 31 miles. At exit 23, take Rte. 104E/132N for 8½ miles, then Rte. 3 (the Daniel Webster Hwy.) north for less than a mile before turning right

> *A hand painted bellows is just one of the many period details you'll find at Old Sturbridge Village.*

> *Young visitors explore scientific principles at the Boston Children's Museum.*

ontoRte. 25 east. Go 19 miles to a left turn onto Rte. 113 east and follow it a total of 5¼ miles to a left turn at Rte. 16 north, the White Mountain Hwy. You'll spend 4 nights in:

❸ **The White Mountains, NH.** The **White Mountain National Forest** and the surrounding area abound with family activities such as hiking, fishing, birding, and kayaking. Check the weather forecast, and try to pick a sunny day to spend in and around **Jackson** and **Mount Washington** (p. 441). The 8-mile **Mount Washington Auto Road** (p. 441) is an unforgettable experience. At **Bretton Woods,** you can board the **Mount Washington Cog Railway** (p. 419, ❻). The ride is pricey and time-consuming, but irresistible to train fans. If you're visiting in the summer, be sure to spend at least part of a day at **Story Land,** 850 Rte. 16, (603-383-4186; www.storylandnh.com), a theme park custom-made for wee ones. Rides like Alice's Tea Cups are safe for infants and toddlers, while those like the Polar Coaster are for older kids. ⏱ **3 days. See chapter 9.**

Late on Day 12 or after breakfast on Day 13 (to miss the worst of rush-hour traffic), take Rte. 16 54 miles to I-95S. Continue 14 miles to Boston or Cambridge, where you'll spend the next 2 days.

❹ **Boston & Cambridge, MA.** Spend Day 13 exploring the attractions described in "Boston with Kids" (p. 62): the **Museum of Science, Faneuil Hall Marketplace,** and either the **New England Aquarium** or the **Boston Children's Museum.** If you're feeling pressed for time or just burned out on sightseeing, go directly from the marketplace to the **Public Garden** (p. 56, ❼), where you can relax under a tree and take a lazy **Swan Boat** (p.65, ❼) ride. On the morning of Day 14, if you're not racing to the airport, consider a tour of **Fenway Park** (p. 66, ❶) or a subway ride to Cambridge to visit the **Harvard Museum of Natural History** (p. 61, ❻). ⏱ **1½ days. See chapter 3.**

> Generations of New Englanders have frolicked at New Hampshire's Story Land, which opened

A Fall Foliage Tour

Some of the roads most popular with New England "leaf peepers" are unpleasant in September and October, when cars and tour buses cause unbelievable traffic for a solid 6 weeks. This itinerary steers clear of the heavily traveled White Mountains, sending you to see less visited, but equally beautiful, displays of abundant fall foliage. Beginning on Day 2, you'll need a car and, ideally, a second driver so you can trade off admiring the scenery and concentrating on the road.

> The vibrant reds and yellows of autumn in New England may draw crowds, but it is still possible to get away from it all.

START Boston is 120 miles from Brattleboro, VT, and 130 miles from Hanover, NH. **TRIP LENGTH** 258 miles from Brattleboro to Boston, 349 miles if you visit Hanover.

1 Boston & Cambridge, MA. Start your adventure with a little urban lovliness. These cities are always charming, but never more so than when the leaves are changing. Explore the winding paths at the **Public Garden** (p. 56, **7**), then walk along **Charles Street** (p. 79, **5**). Detour onto the leafy side streets of Beacon Hill or go straight to Cambridge. Spend a little time in **Harvard Yard** (p. 59, **3**), and then follow the "Harvard Square" itinerary on **Brattle**

Street (p. 88, **7**). Leave at least an hour to explore beautiful **Mount Auburn Cemetery** (p. 88, **10**). ⊕ 1 day.

Leaving Cambridge, take Rte. 2 10 miles west and bear left onto Rte. 2/2A west. Just over a mile up the road, turn left onto Rte. 126 south (Walden St.) and go about ½ mile to the Walden Pond parking lot.

2 Concord, MA. On Day 2, head straight to **Walden Pond** (p. 123, **6**), which is spectacular when the leaves are turning. Take a walk and maybe even wade a bit, if you're feeling tough (it's chilly this late in the season). ⊕ 1 hr. See p. 120.

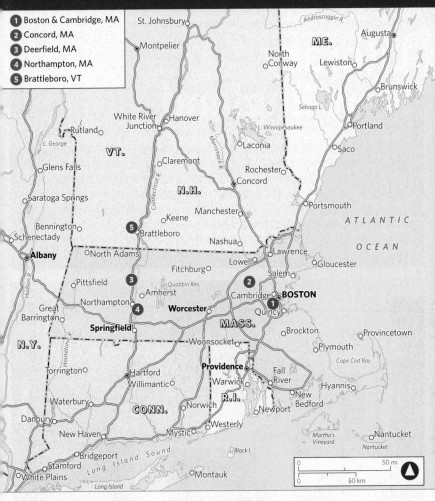

1 Boston & Cambridge, MA
2 Concord, MA
3 Deerfield, MA
4 Northampton, MA
5 Brattleboro, VT

Continue on Rte. 2 west 69 miles to Greenfield, exit onto Rte. 5/Rte. 10 south, and follow signs about 5½ miles to:

3 Deerfield, MA. Build your visit around a walking tour of **Historic Deerfield**; if you don't take one the afternoon you arrive, schedule it for the morning of Day 3 and explore on your own. ☺ 1 day (an afternoon and a morning). See p. 259, **5**.

Around midday on Day 3, take Rte. 5/Rte. 10 south for about 5½ miles and pick up I-91 south. Go to exit 20, pick up Rte. 5/Rte. 10 south, and go 1½ miles. Turn right onto Main St. in downtown Northampton. Even on the interstate, the foliage is beautiful.

4 Northampton, MA. Stop for lunch and explore this vibrant college town. ☺ 2-3 hr. See p. 257, **3**.

Return to I-91 and go 37 miles north, aiming to reach Brattleboro in time for sunset (between 5 and 6pm in the fall).

5 Brattleboro, VT. On Day 4, let your energy level be your guide. You can explore the Brattleboro area on foot, on a bike, or in a canoe—and then decide whether to continue over the border into New Hampshire. ☺ Half-day. See p. 386.

On the morning of Day 5, return to Boston by the scenic route. Take I-91S 17 miles to exit 27 and pick up Rte. 2 east. It's about 70 miles to west Cambridge.

Literary New England

Literary landmarks dot New England, which has inspired far more authors than this itinerary can accommodate. (Robert Frost, yes; Rudyard Kipling, no.) We'll go in search of big names, some expected (Nathaniel Hawthorne, Louisa May Alcott) and some perhaps not (Mark Twain). For this meandering trip, you'll need a car—ideally one equipped with GPS for navigating Vermont and New Hampshire. Stock up on audiobooks before you leave, because you're going to be on the road a fair amount, and wouldn't you rather pass the time with your favorite authors than with talk radio?

> Samuel Clemens (otherwise known as Mark Twain) and his family entertained guests in the elegant drawing room of their Hartford home.

START Hartford, CT, is 105 miles southwest of Boston. **TRIP LENGTH** 10 days and 541 miles.

❶ Hartford, CT. Mark Twain is so strongly associated with the Mississippi River that many people are surprised to learn that he was also a New Englander. Start Day 1 with a tour of the **Mark Twain House & Museum** (p. 298, ❺); afterward, stop next door at the **Harriet Beecher Stowe Center** (p. 298, ❻), the former home of the Uncle Tom's Cabin author. ⊙ 3 hr. See p. 296.

In the afternoon, leave Hartford on I-91N and go 25 miles to exit 6 in Springfield, MA. Follow signs to the Springfield Museums complex.

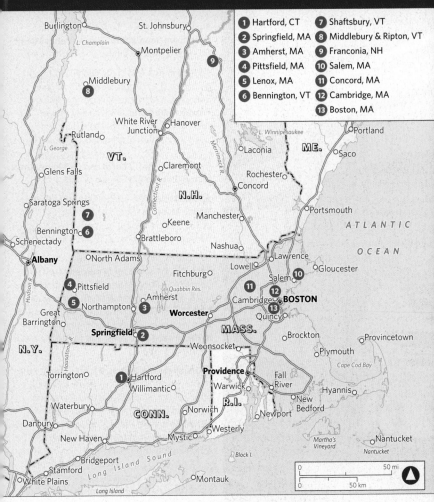

❶ Hartford, CT	❼ Shaftsbury, VT
❷ Springfield, MA	❽ Middlebury & Ripton, VT
❸ Amherst, MA	❾ Franconia, NH
❹ Pittsfield, MA	❿ Salem, MA
❺ Lenox, MA	⓫ Concord, MA
❻ Bennington, VT	⓬ Cambridge, MA
	⓭ Boston, MA

❷ **Springfield, MA.** The city is hardly a tourist magnet, but lovers of children's literature will enjoy the **Dr. Seuss National Memorial Sculpture Garden** (p. 256, ❶). Snap a few photos and get back on the road. ☺ 1 hr. See p. 256.

Take I-91N for 19 miles to exit 19, and pick up Rte. 9 east. Go 6 miles into:

❸ **Amherst, MA.** One of America's greatest poets rarely left this charming little town. A tour of the **Emily Dickinson Museum** (p. 244, ❺) allows a good look at the home of the Belle of Amherst. ☺ 2 hr. See p. 258, ❹.

Take Rte. 9 west 6 miles to I-91, and go south

13 miles to I-90 (the Massachusetts Tpk.). Go west for 35 miles to exit 2, pick up Rte. 20 west, and go 8½ miles into Pittsfield. You're in the heart of the Berkshires, where you'll spend the next 2 nights. On Day 2, explore:

❹ **Pittsfield, MA.** Tour **Arrowhead,** the house where Herman Melville was living when he wrote *Moby-Dick*. Spend the afternoon browsing the area's many excellent new and used bookstores, before heading to Lenox for the evening. ☺ 1 day. See p. 251, ❸.

Take Holmes Rd. south 1¼ miles and go left onto Rte. 20E/7S; take a right onto Rte. 7A and go south for 2 miles.

> *Edith Wharton keeps an eye on her longtime home, the Mount.*

5 Lenox, MA. In the evening on Day 2, commune with old England's brightest literary light and take in a performance at **Shakespeare & Company** in Lenox. Even if the current production is by someone other than its namesake, it's worth a visit. Begin Day 3 at **The Mount,** where *The Age of Innocence* novelist Edith Wharton lived from 1902 to 1911. Afterward, you'll have time for shopping, sightseeing, picnicking, or relaxing with (what else?) a good book. ⏱ 2 days. See p. 252, **5**.

On Day 4, take Rte. 7 north 33 miles into downtown Bennington. Turn left onto Main St. (Rte. 9) and go 1 mile.

6 Bennington, VT. In the **Old First Church** cemetery (p. 372, **1**), downhill from the Bennington Monument, you'll find **Robert Frost's tombstone.** His wife and four of their six children predeceased the great poet; they're buried here, too. ⏱ 30 min.

Backtrack to Rte. 7 north and go 3 miles, then bear right onto Rte. 7A. Go ¾ mile.

7 Shaftsbury, VT. The **Robert Frost Stone House Museum** (See "Vermont's Frost," p. 353), where the quintessential New England poet spent time in the 1920s, is a small home that's rich in history. ⏱ 2 hr.

Take Rte. 7A south for ¾ mile and turn left onto Rte. 7. Rutland lies 53 miles north. See p. 23, **7**, for suggested stops in the Green Mountains. You'll spend the night in the Rutland area or in Middlebury. Enjoy a morning in the Green Mountains, and spend the afternoon exploring:

8 Middlebury & Ripton, VT. This quaint little town—village, actually—is home to Middlebury College, where Robert Frost was once on the faculty. Writers like Eve Ensler and Vendela Vida are alums. Then go 6 miles east to the **Robert Frost Interpretive Trail** (p. 402, **5**) in Ripton. It's an easy walk, literally in the footsteps of Frost, a longtime summer resident, whose poetry is posted at various points along the path. ⏱ 4 hr. See p. 400.

In the afternoon, return to Rte. 7 north and go 8 miles to a right turn onto Rte. 17 east, which you'll follow for 25 miles to Rte. 100 north. After 5½ miles, take Rte. 100B north and go 8 miles, following signs toward I-89. Take I-89S 8 miles to exit 7 to Rte. 62 east; after 5 miles, pick up Rte. 302 east. Go 42 miles to Rte. 117, turn right and go 8 miles east. Turn right onto Rte. 116 south and go half a mile into:

9 Franconia, NH. At the quaint **Frost Place** (p. 440, **6**), you can tour the poet's home and stroll the half-mile nature trail on the property. ⏱ 1½ hr.

End your day with the long drive to the Boston area. Take I-93S 135 miles to exit 37A where you'll take I-95N 8½ miles, before bearing left onto Rte. 128 north. Go 1¾ miles to exit 25A, and pick up Rte. 114 east. It's about 3 miles to Salem, where you'll spend the night, and spend Day 6.

🔟 **Salem, MA.** Start your day with a visit to the **House of the Seven Gables** (p. 125, ❹), made famous by one of Salem's most famous former locals, 19th century novelist Nathanial Hawthorne. Next, get in touch with the town's past at the **Salem National Maritime Historic Site,** 193 Derby St. (☎ 978/740-1660; www. nps.gov/sama), and take a ranger-led tour that includes the 1819 **Custom House.** Legend has it that Hawthorne was working there when he found the embroidered letter that inspired his 1850 masterpiece *The Scarlet Letter.* In the afternoon, visit the **Peabody Essex Museum** (p. 124, ❷) and seek out the iconic portrait of Hawthorne amid the wonderful collections. ⏱ 1 day. See p. 124.

You can spend the night in Salem or press on to Concord. Take Rte. 114 west 1½ miles to Rte. 128 south, which merges with I-95S after about 3 miles. Continue 18 miles to exit 30B, then follow Rte. 2A west for 4½ miles into Concord. You'll spend the morning of Day 8 in:

🔟 **Concord, MA.** Explore the **Concord Museum** (p. 120, ❶); tour **Orchard House** (p. 121, ❷), where Louisa May Alcott wrote *Little Women;* and visit **The Wayside,** 455 Lexington Rd. (☎ 978/318-7863; www.nps. gov/mima), next door. The appealing house was Nathaniel Hawthorne's home for the last 12 years of his life. The Wayside is part of an attraction you already know about, **Minute Man National Historical Park,** and is staffed by park rangers. On Day 9, spend the morning at iconic **Walden Pond** (p. 123, ❻). See if it inspires you the way it inspired Henry David Thoreau. ⏱ 1½ days. See p. 120.

In the late morning of Day 8, take Rte. 126 less than a mile to a right turn onto Rte. 2/2A east. After 1½ miles, bear right to stay on Rte. 2 east. Go 11 miles. At the first of back-to-back traffic circles (aka "rotaries"), take the second exit; at the next one, take the first

> *A battered mailbox tells visitors they've reached the Frost Place in Franconia, NH.*

exit, onto Fresh Pond Pkwy. Go 1 mile and take a left onto Brattle St. Plan to spend the night in Boston or Cambridge.

🔟 **Harvard Square, Cambridge, MA.** Tour the **Longfellow House–Washington's Headquarters National Historic Site** (p. 88, ❽), which was once home to poet Henry Wadsworth Longfellow. Then take the 1½ mile walk down Brattle Street to **Mount Auburn Cemetery** (p. 88, 🔟). It holds the graves of Longfellow and cookbook author Fannie Farmer, among many others. ⏱ 4 hr. See p. 86.

Spend Day 9 exploring:

🔟 **Boston, MA.** There is much to see here, but be sure to visit **Beacon Hill,** one of Boston's most literary neighborhoods. It was once home to Louisa May Alcott (10 Louisburg Sq.) and Robert Frost (88 Mount Vernon St.). ⏱ 1 day. See p. 78.

All-Season Ski Country

Nonskiers can have as much winter fun as their skiing companions. In the off season, everyone can enjoy ski areas blanketed in wildflowers, lush greenery, or fall foliage rather than snow. This nonlinear itinerary concentrates on Vermont and New Hampshire, with directions from the popular destinations of Stowe and Bretton Woods. Don't let a snowy forecast deter you—the public-works departments plow constantly—but heed warnings about travel during bad storms. If you rent a vehicle, authorize at least one nonskiing driver who can drop off and pick up the skiers at the slopes, so you won't need a second car for sightseeing.

> Ferries ply Vermont's Lake Champlain year-round, through both water and ice.

START Burlington, VT, is 38 miles from Stowe, VT, and 115 miles from Bretton Woods, NH. **TRIP LENGTH** 5 days and 478 miles if you make Stowe, VT, your home base, or 829 miles if you base yourself in Bretton Woods, NH.

① **Burlington & Shelburne, VT.** Winter visitors will probably want to spend Day 1 concentrating on Burlington's adorable downtown area, which centers on a pedestrian mall, **Church Street Marketplace** (p. 380, **①**). In the summer, allow time to see the superb **Shelburne Museum** (p. 383) and to explore the Lake Champlain waterfront. To reach Shelburne from Burlington, take Rte. 7 south for 9 miles. ⊕ 1 day. See p. 380.

On Day 2, from Stowe, take Rte. 108 south for 1¼ miles and turn right onto Rte. 100 south. Follow it 9½ miles to I-89S and go 11 miles to the exit for Montpelier and St. Johnsbury. Take Rte. 2 and Memorial Dr. 2 miles and turn left onto Main St. From Bretton Woods, NH, take Rte. 302 west for 16 miles to the entrance ramp for I-93N. After 22 miles, merge onto I-91N and take it 2½ miles to the exit for Rte. 2 west. Go 34 miles, following signs for downtown Montpelier, and turn right onto Main St.

② **Montpelier, VT.** Explore the Vermont state capital on the morning of Day 2. Have lunch prepared by students from the **New England Culinary Institute** but consider skipping dessert to leave room for your next stop in Waterbury. ⊕ Half-day. See p. 404.

Take Rte. 2 west 13 miles to Rte. 100 north in Waterbury. Continue for just under 1 mile and follow the signs.

③ **Ben & Jerry's factory, Waterbury, VT.** Need we say more? ⊕ 2 hr. See p. 405, **③**.

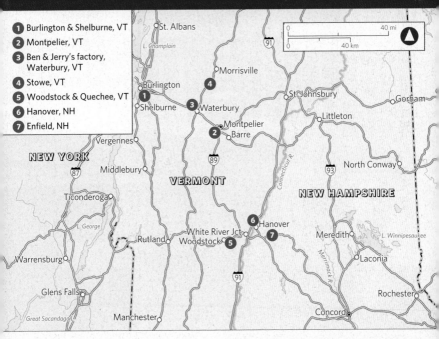

1. Burlington & Shelburne, VT
2. Montpelier, VT
3. Ben & Jerry's factory, Waterbury, VT
4. Stowe, VT
5. Woodstock & Quechee, VT
6. Hanover, NH
7. Enfield, NH

Continue on Rte. 100 for 9 miles to the turn-off for Stowe.

4 Stowe. An excellent destination for hikers of all abilities, Stowe will help you burn off some butterfat. ⏱ Half-day. See p. 408.

From Stowe, take Rte. 108 south for 1¼ miles and turn right onto Rte. 100 south. Follow it for 9½ miles to I-89S and go 61 miles to the exit for Rte. 4 west. Take it for 10 miles into downtown Woodstock, passing through Quechee about 2½ miles from the interstate. From Bretton Woods, take Rte. 302 west for 16 miles to the entrance ramp for I-93N. After 22 miles, merge onto I-91 south and go 59 miles. Take I-89N for just under 3 miles to the exit for Rte. 4 west. Follow it for 10 miles to Woodstock, passing through Quechee.

5 Woodstock & Quechee, VT. These lovely towns near the New Hampshire border combine shopping, dining, and gorgeous scenery in such abundance that you'll want to get an early start on Day 3. In the summer, allow time for a hike or a bike ride. ⏱ 1 day. See p. 394.

From Stowe, start Day 4 by taking Rte. 108 south for 1¼ miles and turning right onto Rte. 100. Follow it for 9½ miles to I-89 south and

go 63 miles. Exit at I-91 and follow it north for 5½ miles to exit 13. Follow Rte. 10A east, which becomes Rte. 10 east, for just under a mile into Hanover. From Bretton Woods, take Rte. 302 west for 16 miles and merge onto I-93N. After 22 miles, take I-91 south and go 54 miles to exit 13. Take Rte. 10A/Rte. 10 east for just under a mile.

6 Hanover, NH. In Hanover, home to **Dartmouth College** (p. 432, 5), allow time to look around the gorgeous campus and visit the **Hood Museum of Art**. ⏱ Half-day.

Take Rte. 120 south 3 miles to I-89 south, exit at Rte. 4 east, and go 2 miles. Bear right onto Rte. 4A east.

7 Enfield, NH. Less than half an hour away and well worth a detour is the **Enfield Shaker Museum** (p. 432, 5). ⏱ Half-day.

On Day 5, stick close to your home base. You're going to be traveling soon enough, so today you'll combine a visit to the nearest town or village—on foot, if that's feasible—with packing for your trip home. For tips on exploring Stowe, see p. 408. For information on Bretton Woods, see p. 429.

3
Boston &
Cambridge

Our Favorite Boston & Cambridge Moments

Every once in a while, I get a new perspective on my adopted hometown. The sun suddenly emerges from behind a cloud, making the harbor glow or illuminating the sapphire blue of the Charles River. A delighted child's laughter rings out in the Public Garden, or the wind gusts out of the east, carrying a salty Atlantic tang. An excited crowd swarms toward Fenway Park or gathers in Harvard Yard. The familiar feels new, just for a moment, and I realize yet again how endlessly fascinating Boston and Cambridge are. I'd love to help you find some serendipitous moments of your own. Let's look around.

> PREVIOUS PAGE *A full house at Fenway Park, the oldest ballpark in the majors.* THIS PAGE *Renoir's* Dance at Bougival *occupies a place of honor at the Museum of Fine Arts.*

❶ Treading in the footsteps of the Founding Fathers. Only a handful of American cities have histories as rich and varied as Boston's. Reminders of its Colonial origin dot downtown, where buildings that predate the American Revolution stand within sight of 20th- and 21st-century landmarks. A walk along the **Freedom Trail** introduces some highlights. See p. 72.

❷ Seeing old friends at the Museum of Fine Arts. Strolling through the MFA, you may find yourself bonding with the artwork. Hello, Degas dancer. How's everything, Vincent van Gogh? Are your teeth still bothering you, President Washington? Even if they're not the most valuable or significant of the museum's holdings, the most familiar ones feel like favorite neighborhood characters. See p. 70, ❺.

1. Treading in the footsteps of the Founding Fathers
2. Seeing old friends at the Museum of Fine Arts
3. Imagining yourself as an American aristocrat
4. Channeling a college student
5. Savoring a taste of Italy
6. Exploring a palace and its treasures
7. Riding on the back of a Duck (Tour)
8. Riding on the back of a Swan (Boat)
9. Watching whales
10. Cracking open a lobster
11. Taste-testing New England clam chowder
12. Wearing the numbers off your credit cards
13. Tapping your foot in time to the music
14. Breathing sea breezes on a stuffy day
15. Tracking Thanksgiving to its source

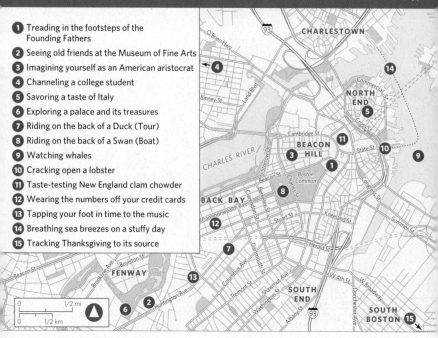

3 Imagining yourself as an American aristocrat. Picturesque **Beacon Hill** has been a blue-blood bastion for almost 400 years. Federal-style architecture makes the neighborhood a visual delight, from the red-brick facades of the graceful houses to the intricate details of a wrought-iron fence. Visitors stroll the cobblestone streets and whisper, "This is exactly what I thought Boston would look like." See p. 78.

4 Channeling a college student. Skip the piercings and ill-fitting pants and head to **Harvard Square,** the heart of a city that's also an age-old, cutting-edge college town. Beyond the brick walls and imposing gates of Harvard Yard is a festival of trendy shopping, gourmet ice cream (maybe that explains the baggy pants), and alfresco music. See p. 86.

5 Savoring a taste of Italy. What's this? A *caffè* that serves perfect espresso in the **North End?** Oh, it's Boston's version of Little Italy? But only tourists call it that? Why, yes, we really could use a break. A cappuccino would be lovely, thanks. See p. 82.

6 Exploring a palace and its treasures. Isabella Stewart Gardner commissioned the museum

that bears her name, in the style of a Venetian palazzo. The main building, Fenway Court, is effectively the largest artifact in the **Gardner Museum's** intriguing collections. See p. 67, **3**.

7 Riding on the back of a Duck (Tour). My favorite tour of Boston is amphibious and unforgettable: It trundles around the streets before slipping into the placid waters of the Charles River basin. Boston Duck Tours are wildly popular, so plan ahead—you won't be sorry. See p. 55, **4**.

8 Riding on the back of a Swan (Boat). The retro charms of the Public Garden include a teeny-tiny suspension bridge and a collection of monuments and memorials honoring nearly forgotten events and people (and George Washington). At the heart of the gorgeous park is a small body of water that's home to a fleet of pedal boats that look like giant swans. Sit back, let the iron-thighed employees do the work, and keep an eye out for the real swans who live here, too. See p. 65, **7**.

9 Watching whales. Bostonians have gone to sea since before there was a Boston, and this is the perfect reason to climb aboard the modern-day equivalent of a whaleboat.

> *Widener Library, an enduring memorial to a victim of the sinking of the* Titanic.

Armed with binoculars rather than a harpoon, you'll find the enormous mammals in their summer hangout, above the Stellwagen Bank underwater plateau off the Massachusetts coast. Cruises leave from Boston and Gloucester. See p. 130.

10 Cracking open a lobster. You don't have to visit Maine to enjoy Maine lobster, which arrives in Boston daily, year-round. No matter how much I rave about a stylish new bistro or an unusual ethnic cuisine, my out-of-town visitors almost invariably ask for a bright red crustacean. **Legal Sea Foods,** here we come. See p. 102.

11 Taste-testing New England clam chowder. The second-most-famous regional food comes in so many different versions that it actually has a cooking contest named after it. If you can't make it to Boston for **Chowderfest** during Harborfest, the city's 4th of July party, stage an ad hoc comparison. Even hard-core purists can find something unusual to like (red-skinned potatoes? not bad!). See p. 101.

12 Wearing the numbers right off your credit cards. Boston and Cambridge offer unique merchandise of all descriptions at all price points. Begin with an inspirational stroll along Newbury Street, or cross the river and walk Massachusetts Avenue (Mass Ave) from Harvard Square to Porter Square. If a big mall is more your style, you're covered—we have those too. See p. 92.

13 Tapping your foot in time to the music. From the elegance of Symphony Hall to the raucous performances of street-corner buskers, the area's live-music scene creates a unique soundtrack. Conservatory students, seasoned Broadway pros, and countless other performers put on a show just about every day. Be sure to catch a performance by the world-famous **Boston Symphony Orchestra.** See p. 117.

14 Breathing sea breezes on a stuffy day. When the summer heat grows nearly unbearable, a ride across **Boston Harbor** (for as little as $1.70) grants an interlude, however brief, of

> *Plants and flowers brighten the courtyard at the Isabella Stewart Gardner Museum.*

wind in your hair and the promise of fall. The commuter ferry is the bargain option; narrated cruises are a pricier but enjoyable alternative. See p. 52, **9**.

15 Tracking Thanksgiving to its source. Just north of the city, **Plymouth** (home of that very famous rock) celebrates the harvest holiday throughout the year—not by feeding everyone turkey and cranberry sauce, but by keeping the Pilgrims' legacy alive. I dare you to look at the *Mayflower II,* anchored on the downtown waterfront, and not be impressed by the early settlers' bravery and determination. Eating turkey afterward is optional. See p. 134.

> *The Paget family has operated the Swan Boats in the Public Garden since 1877.*

Boston in 1 Day

With just 1 day to spend in Boston, focus on the compact downtown area and explore on foot. This itinerary follows part of the Freedom Trail, which presents an opportunity to explore 3-plus centuries of history. It's an easy walk, with plenty of locals around to offer directions if you go astray. My best advice is twofold: Don't concentrate so hard on the trail that you forget to look up and around. And wear comfortable shoes.

> A costumed guide leads Freedom Trail explorers to the site of the Boston Massacre.

START Take the Red or Green Line T to Park St.

1 ★ **Boston Common.** The oldest public park in the country (bought in 1634, set aside in 1640) is a welcome splash of green in red-brick Boston. As a boy, philosopher Ralph Waldo Emerson herded his mother's cows here on the way to school. ⏱ 10 min. Bordered by Beacon, Park, Tremont, Boylston & Charles sts. Free admission. Daily 24 hr. T: Red or Green Line to Park St.

2 ★★★ **Robert Gould Shaw Memorial.** This magnificent bronze sculpture by Augustus Saint-Gaudens, unveiled in 1897, is one of the finest public memorials in the country. The plaque on the back tells the story of the men on the front, the first American army unit made up of free black soldiers. Col. Robert Gould Shaw (1837–63), who was white, led the Union Army's 54th Massachusetts Colored Regiment into battle in the Civil War. ⏱ 10 min. Beacon St. (at Park St.). Free admission. Daily 24 hr. T: Red or Green Line to Park St.

3 ★★ **Granary Burying Ground.** Established in 1660, yet far from the oldest cemetery in Boston, this one is my favorite for its variety of designs and roster of . . . occupants. The map near the entrance locates the graves of, among others, Paul Revere, Samuel Adams, and John Hancock, whose monument is almost as ostentatious as his signature. For more information, see p. 72, **5**. ⏱ 20 min. (try to visit in the morning, before tour groups flock here). Tremont St. (at Bromfield St.). Free admission. Daily 9am–5pm (until 3pm in winter). T: Red or Green Line to Park St.

4 ★ **King's Chapel Burying Ground.** The oldest graveyard in Boston dates to 1630, the same

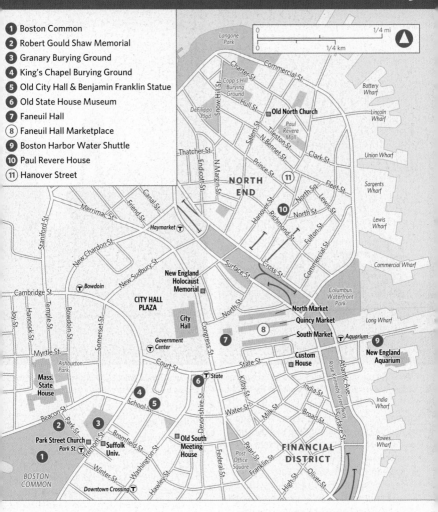

1 Boston Common
2 Robert Gould Shaw Memorial
3 Granary Burying Ground
4 King's Chapel Burying Ground
5 Old City Hall & Benjamin Franklin Statue
6 Old State House Museum
7 Faneuil Hall
8 Faneuil Hall Marketplace
9 Boston Harbor Water Shuttle
10 Paul Revere House
11 Hanover Street

year Europeans settled here. ⏱ **20 min.** (aim
for the morning, especially on summer weekends). For more information, see p. 74, ⑥.

⑤ **Old City Hall & Benjamin Franklin Statue.**
The seat of local government from 1865 to 1969,
this ornate French Second Empire building now
holds offices and a steakhouse. In front is the
city's first portrait statue, a likeness of Benjamin
Franklin, who was born a block away. ⏱ **5 min.**
School St. at City Hall Ave. (end of Province St.).
T: Blue or Orange Line to State.

⑥ ★ **Old State House Museum.** The Old State
House has stood here since 1713, when Massachusetts was a British colony and State

Street was named King Street. (In 1630s
Puritan Boston, the whipping post and stocks
awaited sinners here.) The building served
as the state capitol until the present State
House opened in 1798. Today it houses the
Bostonian Society's museum of city history, a
fascinating mix of permanent and temporary
displays. ⏱ **1 hr.** 206 Washington St. (at State
& Court sts.). ☎ 617/720-1713, ext. 21. www.
bostonhistory.org. Admission $7.50 adults, $6
seniors & students, $3 kids 6–18, free for kids 5
& under. Daily 9am–5pm (until 6pm July–Aug,
until 4pm Jan). T: Blue or Orange Line to State.

⑦ ★ kids **Faneuil Hall.** Many of the great orators
of the past 2-plus centuries inspired audiences

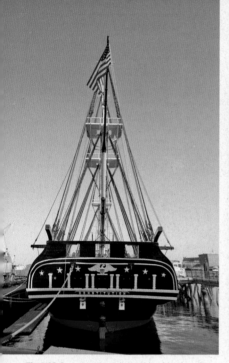

> *The USS Constitution is the world's oldest warship afloat, and is still under the command of the US Navy.*

> *Founding Father Samuel Adams (yes, the beer was named for him) keeps watch over downtown.*

to rebellion, reform, and protest here, earning the building the nickname "the cradle of liberty." One of the best-known speakers was the revolutionary firebrand Samuel Adams (yes, like the beer), whose statue stands outside, facing Congress Street. Originally erected in 1742, Faneuil Hall was a gift from prominent merchant Peter Faneuil and was expanded using a Charles Bulfinch design in 1805. National Park Service rangers tell the story in brief talks in the second-floor auditorium. Note the address—Dock Square—and the fact that there isn't a dock, or indeed any water, nearby. The seemingly random patterns etched into the plaza around the Samuel Adams statue show the shoreline at various points in the past, illustrating how landfill has transformed the city. ⏱ 5 min. (30 min. for tour). Dock Sq. (at Congress & North sts.). ☎ 617/242-5675. www.nps.gov/bost. Free admission. Daily 9am–5pm; talks every 30 min. until 4:30pm. T: Green or Blue Line to Government Center, or Orange Line to Haymarket.

⑧ 🍴 ★★ kids **Faneuil Hall Marketplace.** The five-building complex incorporates shopping, dining, drinking, live entertainment (think juggling), and people-watching. The Quincy Market building holds a huge food court. At lunch, follow the office workers—lines form at places that earn repeat business. ⏱ 30–60 min. (morning is least busy, afternoons most entertaining, especially in warm weather). Bordered by State, Congress, and North sts. and Atlantic Ave. ☎ 617/523-1300. www.faneuilhall marketplace.com. Mon–Sat 10am–9pm; Sun noon–6pm; many restaurants open earlier and close later. T: Green Line to Government Center, Orange Line to Haymarket or State, or Blue Line to Aquarium or State.

⑨ ★★★ kids **Boston Harbor Water Shuttle.** The fare for the commuter ferry that connects downtown Boston and the Charlestown Navy Yard may be the best money you spend during your visit. You can cross the Inner Harbor,

> *For Italian-style sweets, head to Hanover Street, the North End's main drag.*

turn around, and come right back, but there's plenty to look at on either end: Long Wharf adjoins the New England Aquarium, and the Charlestown pier is a 5-minute walk from USS *Constitution* (Old Ironsides) and its museum. Concentrate on the journey, not the destination—find a place on the deck and enjoy the wind in your face. In inclement weather, this is still a fun excursion—just be sure to bundle up! ⊕ 10 min. each way, but allow 1 hr. total to include wait time & a bit of exploring at either end (steer clear during the morning & evening rush hour). Long Wharf (1 block from State St. & Atlantic Ave.). ☎ 617/222-4321. www.mbta.com. One-way fare $1.70 adults, free for kids 11 & under with a paying adult. Mon–Fri 6:30am–8pm; Sat–Sun 10am–6pm. T: Blue Line to Aquarium.

🔟 ★★★ kids **Paul Revere House.** The more I learn about Paul Revere, the more I like him. On a visit to his North End home, you gain a sense of what daily life was like for a successful Colonial craftsman. Outfitted with 17th- and 18th-century furniture and fascinating artifacts (including silver pieces created by Revere), the little wood structure is open for self-guided tours, a format that allows you to set your own pace. A talented silversmith who supported a large family—he had eight children with each of his two wives—Revere played an important role in the fight for independence. He left this cozy house over and over, working to bring about what became the American Revolution—and risking his neck every time. Could I be that brave? Could you? ⊕ 45 min. (crowds fluctuate, but weekend afternoons are busiest). 19 North Sq. (btw. Richmond & Prince sts.). ☎ 617/523-2338. www.paulrevere house.org. $3.50 adults, $3 seniors & students, $1 kids 5–17, free for kids 4 & under. Apr–Dec daily 9:30am–5:15pm (until 4:15pm Apr 1–15 & Nov–Dec); Jan–Mar Tues–Sun 9:30am–4:15pm. T: Green or Orange Line to Haymarket.

⑪ 🍴 ★★ kids **Hanover Street.** This crowded street at the heart of the North End, Boston's best-known Italian-American neighborhood, is filled with restaurants, *caffès*, and out-of-towners. Explore a bit before settling down for a cappuccino, a cannoli, and some people-watching. My favorite destinations are **Mike's Pastry,** at 301 Hanover St. (☎ 617/742-3050; www.mikespastry.com; $), **Caffè Vittoria,** 296 Hanover St. (☎ 617/227-7606; www.vittoriacaffe.com; $), and **Modern Pastry,** 257 Hanover St. (☎ 617/523-3783; www.modernpastry.com).

Boston in 2 Days

If you followed the 1-day tour, you have a feel for

downtown Boston and its Colonial legacy. In the 19th century, the population moved west, into the newly created Back Bay neighborhood (built largely on landfill) and beyond to the Fenway. Compared with the tangled streets of downtown, these carefully planned neighborhoods come as a relief. This itinerary offers a good look at both. Here, too, comfortable shoes are key.

> One of the smallest suspension bridges in the world spans the Public Garden lagoon.

START Take the Orange Line T to Back Bay or the Green Line T to Copley.

① 🍽 ★ kids **Charlie's Sandwich Shoppe.** Start your day with blueberry pancakes at this longtime South End favorite. On Sundays, when Charlie's is closed, head to **Brasserie Jo** (p. 97). 429 Columbus Ave. (btw. Holyoke St. and Braddock Park). ☎ 617/536-7669. $–$$. No credit cards.

② ★★★ kids **Museum of Fine Arts.** The familiar and the undiscovered meet at the MFA, one of the best museums in the world. Plan your visit using the excellent website—you can take a tour, concentrate on a particular period, or head straight to the Art of the Americas wing, a high-tech marvel that opened in 2010. One highlight of the new space is *The Passage of the Delaware*, an 1819 painting by Thomas Sully that's a whopping 17 feet wide, but the marvels come in all sizes. You might seek out a Monet, a sculpture, a photograph, a mural, a vase, or even a piece of furniture. It's all here; use your time wisely. ⏱ 3 hr. (arrive when the doors open, visit on a weekday if possible, and, if you're traveling without kids, try to avoid school vacation weeks). See p. 70, ❺.

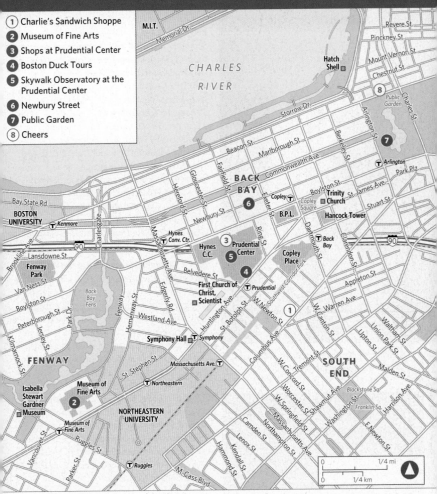

1. Charlie's Sandwich Shoppe
2. Museum of Fine Arts
3. Shops at Prudential Center
4. Boston Duck Tours
5. Skywalk Observatory at the Prudential Center
6. Newbury Street
7. Public Garden
8. Cheers

③ 🚇 kids **Shops at Prudential Center.** The Pru has a generic food court and several sit-down restaurants (including a branch of Legal Sea Foods; see p. 102). In good weather, you can picnic in the courtyard. The shops and pushcarts here are on about the same level as the dining—fine, but without much pizzazz. **800 Boylston St. (enter from Huntington Ave. near Belvidere St. or from Boylston St. btw. Fairfield and Gloucester sts.). ☎ 800/SHOP-PRU (746-7778). www.prudentialcenter. com. $–$$.**

④ ★★★ kids **Boston Duck Tours.** The best motorized tour of Boston uses revamped

World War II amphibious vehicles that sit high above the street. The con-duck-tors (ouch) are exceptionally well trained—they have to be licensed to operate the mammoth Ducks on water as well as on land, which must make memorizing some historical highlights feel like a cinch. After a relatively brief but thorough tour on land, the vehicle rolls down a ramp and cruises around the Charles River basin. Whee! A captivating combination of unusual perspectives, cooling breezes, and fascinating narration. Aim for a tour in the afternoon, when the action on the river is liveliest, but don't pass up a morning slot if that's the only option. ⏱ 80 min. for tour. Boarding behind the Prudential Center, on Huntington Ave. (near

> *The Egyptian collection is among the most popular exhibits at the Museum of Fine Arts.*

Discount Passes

A **CityPass** (☎ 888/330-5008; www.city pass.com) will save you time and money if you plan to visit the Museum of Fine Arts, Museum of Science, New England Aquarium, Skywalk Observatory at the Prudential Center, and either the Kennedy Library or the Harvard Museum of Natural History. If you visit all five, the price ($46 for adults, $29 for kids 3–11) represents at least a 47% discount for adults. You'll also cut straight to the entrance of each attraction—a tremendous relief when lines are long (especially at the aquarium). The passes, good for 9 days from first use, are on sale at participating attractions and online. The main competition for CityPass is the **Go Boston Card** (☎ 800/887-9103; www. smartdestinations.com). Prices start at $50 for 1 day, with 2-, 3-, 5-, and 7-day options available. Both passes can be great deals, but do a little math before you buy—it's only a bargain if you take full advantage of it.

Belvidere St.), or at the Museum of Science, Science Park (p. 62, ❶). Abbreviated seasonal tours ($2–$6 discount) leave from the New England Aquarium (p. 64, ❹) starting at 3pm. ☎ 800/226-7442 or 617/267-DUCK (3825). www.bostonducktours.com. Tickets $32 adults, $27 seniors & students, $22 kids 3–11, $10 kids 2 & under; $3.50/ticket online sales fee. Apr to mid-Dec daily 9am to 1 hr. before sunset (later from the aquarium). No tours mid-Dec to Mar. Timed tickets go on sale 30 days ahead online, in person & by phone; same-day in-person sales start at 8:30am (9am at the New England Aquarium). T: Green Line E to Prudential or any car to Copley for Prudential Center; Green Line to Science Park for Museum of Science; Blue Line to Aquarium for Aquarium.

❺ ★★ **Skywalk Observatory at the Prudential Center.** Having seen the Back Bay from street level, you'll get a new perspective from far above. The 50th-floor Skywalk affords views of far more than just the Back Bay—the 360-degree panorama extends as far as New Hampshire and Cape Cod when the sky is clear. Interactive audiovisual displays, including exhibits on immigration, trace Boston's history. ⊙ 1 hr. 800 Boylston St. (at Fairfield St.). ☎ 617/859-0648. www.topofthehub.net/ skywalk_home.html. Admission $13 adults, $11 seniors, $9 kids 12 & under. Daily 10am–10pm (until 8pm Nov–Mar); always call first, because the space sometimes closes for private events. T: Green Line E to Prudential, or B, C, or D to Hynes Convention Center.

❻ ★★★ **Newbury Street.** One of the best-known retail destinations in New England, Newbury Street has something for everyone. It's famous for art galleries, pricey hair salons, and pricier designer boutiques. The closer to the Public Garden, the nicer the neighborhood. Less expensive and more fun are the stores at higher-numbered addresses. Don't forget to check out the businesses above and below street level. Arlington St. to Mass Ave. ☎ 617/ 267-2224. www.newburystreetleague.org. T: Green Line to Arlington or Copley.

❼ ★★★ kids **Public Garden.** Boston's most beloved park, the nation's first public botanical garden, is a perfect place to unwind. The Public Garden's 24 acres overflow with seasonal

> *Boston Duck Tours' amphibious vehicles navigate city streets and the Charles River.*

blooms and permanent plantings; the roses, which peak in June, are particularly lovely. No matter how crowded it gets, it feels serene. The monuments and statues are delightfully miscellaneous—the oldest, the 1868 **Ether Monument,** celebrates (seriously) the first use of general anesthesia in an operation. The **Make Way for Ducklings** sculptures delight children of all ages, and the **Swan Boats,** which ply the lagoon in the summer, are a lovely reminder of the Public Garden's 19th-century roots. For more information, see p. 65, ❻ & ❼.

⑧ 🍺 kids **Cheers.** This is it, in all its touristy glory. I wouldn't even mention it, but the bar that inspired the TV series sits across the street from the Public Garden, and hardly a week goes by without an out-of-towner asking me for directions to it. 84 Beacon St. (at Brimmer St.). ☎ 617/227-9605. www.cheersboston.com. $–$$.

> *The Cheers bar (originally the Bull & Finch) inspired the seemingly immortal TV show.*

Boston & Cambridge in 3 Days

After concentrating on central Boston, this itinerary is your chance to spread out a little. The city's Dorchester neighborhood is accessible on the Red Line of the T and home to a unique attraction, John F. Kennedy's presidential library. His alma mater, Harvard, is a subway ride away in Cambridge, at the heart of an intriguing city that thrives in Boston's shadow. This itinerary includes a stop at an art museum or a natural history museum, but not both. If this is your last day before exploring beyond Boston in a rental car, you can pick it up early and use it for the trip to the Kennedy Library—but you'll probably have to pay to park in Cambridge and at your hotel.

> Dexter Gate (see p. 84) connects Harvard Yard to Massachusetts Avenue, or Mass Ave.

START Take the Red Line to JFK/UMass, then the free shuttle bus. Or drive, following the directions on the presidential library's website.

① ★★★ kids **John F. Kennedy Presidential Library & Museum.** Whether or not you remember the Kennedy era, you'll enjoy this museum. Copious collections of memorabilia, photos, and audio and video recordings illustrate the exhibits, which capture the 35th president in vibrant style. The displays begin with the 1960 presidential campaign; a 17-minute film about his early life narrated by J.F.K. himself, using cleverly edited audio clips, kicks off your visit. By the time you reach the dim room where television news reports of the assassination play in a loop, you'll want to shed a tear along with Walter Cronkite. ⊙ 2 hr. (Arrive when the doors open and you may have the place to yourself; prepare for gridlock on summer weekend afternoons). Columbia Point (off University Dr. N. near UMass-Boston). ☎ 866/JFK-1960 (535-1960) or 617/514-1600. www.jfklibrary.org. Admission $12 adults, $10 seniors & students, $9 youths 13–17, free for kids 12 & under. Surcharges may apply for special exhibitions. Daily 9am–5pm (last film at 3:55pm). T: Red Line to JFK/UMass, then take free shuttle bus.

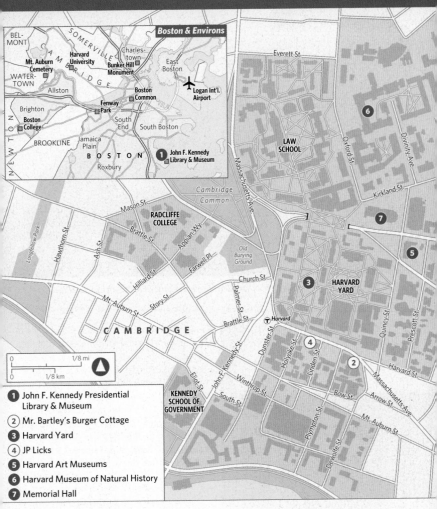

1 John F. Kennedy Presidential Library & Museum
2 Mr. Bartley's Burger Cottage
3 Harvard Yard
4 JP Licks
5 Harvard Art Museums
6 Harvard Museum of Natural History
7 Memorial Hall

Ride the shuttle bus back to the Red Line and take an Alewife-bound train to Harvard (25 min.). You'll emerge in the heart of Harvard Sq.

2 🍽 ★★★ 🧒 **Mr. Bartley's Burger Cottage.** Fantastic burgers are the thing here, but I've also had excellent veggie burgers, hummus, and cheesesteaks. The setting is also hard to beat—a charming, old-school joint that's been serving locals since the 1960s. Make sure you try the unbelievable onion rings. Closed Sunday. 1246 Mass Ave (at Plympton St.), Cambridge. ☎ 617/354-6559. $. No credit cards.

3 ★ **Harvard Yard.** Harvard, the oldest college in the country (founded in 1636), welcomes visitors and offers free guided tours when school is in session. Even without a guide, it's worth a look at the stately main campus. Two adjoining quads make up Harvard Yard, where the most popular stop is the John Harvard statue, in front of University Hall. The other most popular stop is Sever Hall, where the rounded archway around the front door forms a "whispering gallery." Stand on one side and speak softly into the molding; someone standing next to you won't be able to hear, but a listener at the other end of the archway will. Sever Hall is next to Memorial Church, which

> *Harvard's Sackler Museum is in a neighborhood the architect described as "an architectural zoo."*

> *A visit to the Kennedy Library begins with a film narrated by John F. Kennedy himself.*

is open to the public except during services. Across from the church is majestic Widener Library; climb the steps and take in the view. To begin exploring, visit the website or stop in at the Events & Information Center to take a tour or pick up a map. ⊕ 30 min.; longer if you take a tour. Events & Information Center, Holyoke Center, 1350 Mass Ave (btw. Dunster & Holyoke sts.). ☎ 617/495-1573. www.harvard.edu/visitors. Tours Mon–Sat; check website for schedule. T: Red Line to Harvard.

④ 🍦★★★ **kids** **JP Licks.** A break already? Hey, college is hard! You need gourmet ice cream, in flavors both plain and fancy. Pick out your treat, then return to the Yard and find somewhere to perch while you snack. 1312 Mass Ave (btw. Holyoke and Linden sts.). ☎ 617/492-1001. www.jplicks.com. $.

❺ ★ **Harvard Art Museums.** If you're interested in art, this is the place for you; if you prefer natural history, skip this stop and go straight to ❻, where you'll want to spend a little extra time. The university's art collections are both classic and contemporary, representing everything from Roman sculpture and Japanese woodblock prints to Impressionist masterpieces and modern photography. Happily, they're also rarely crowded, making them one of Cambridge's hidden gems. At press time, the Fogg and Busch-Reisinger museums are closed for renovation through 2013, but there's still loads to see here. Meanwhile, the long-term exhibition "Re-View" is up at the Arthur M. Sackler Museum. Incorporating objects from all three museums, spanning both time and geography, the displays focus on themes that illustrate how the disparate collections relate to one another. ⏱ 2 hr. 485 Broadway (at Quincy St.). ☎ 617/495-9400. www.harvardartmuseums.org. Admission $9 adults, $7 seniors, $6 students, free for kids 17 & under, free to MA residents before noon Sat. Tues–Sat 10am–5pm. T: Red Line to Harvard.

⑥ ★ kids Harvard Museum of Natural History. If dinosaurs aren't for you, skip this stop and spend your time looking at art. The natural history museum is one of the university's most popular attractions, thanks to its fascinating collections. They include everything from insects to dinosaurs, presented in exhibits that make discovering the wonders of the natural world seem as fun as a video game. Also here are the world-famous **Glass Flowers,** 3,000 models of hundreds of plant species that might just fool you. Yes, they look real. ⏱ 2 hr. 26 Oxford St. (near Kirkland St.). ☎ 617/495-3045. www.hmnh.harvard.edu. Admission (includes Peabody Museum of Archaeology & Ethnology) $9 adults, $7 seniors & students, $6 kids 3–18, free for kids 2 & under, free to MA residents Sun until noon year-round & Wed 3–5pm Sept–May. Daily 9am–5pm. T: Red Line to Harvard.

⑦ ★ Memorial Hall. Anything but a stereotypical red-brick Harvard building, "Mem Hall" is a Victorian-era (1874) structure in an unusual style known as Ruskin Gothic. Polychrome (multicolored) brickwork sets off quirky archways, and the floor plan mimics a Gothic cathedral, with a dining hall in place of the nave and Sanders Theatre, a lecture and concert hall, in the apse. The transept is a hall of memorials that lists the Harvard men who perished in the Civil War, but only if they fought for the Union—remember, Boston was a hotbed of the abolitionist movement. Stay away during mealtimes to avoid being trampled by hungry students. ⏱ 10 min. 45 Quincy St. (at Cambridge St.).

> Harvard's Memorial Hall abounds with stained glass and ornate architectural details.

Boston with Kids

Almost every day in the summer, I see children shuffling along the Freedom Trail like prisoners on a chain gang, looking hot, bored, and tired. Unless your kids are old enough to express interest, don't make them visit every stop. Boston offers so much else to see and do that you'll never miss the full-on Freedom Trail experience. Before you start this itinerary, note that I suggest you visit either stop 4 or stop 5 (not both), depending on how old your kids are.

> *Say hello to Mrs. Mallard and her* Make Way for Ducklings *babies in the Public Garden.*

START Take the Green Line T to Science Park.

❶ ★★★ Museum of Science. This is the best indoor family destination in the Boston area. It can be overwhelming, with some 500 exhibits—engaging hands-on activities and experiments, interactive displays, and fascinating demonstrations—but it's both educational and entertaining. I suggest that you build your visit around a few subjects you find interesting. For example, I especially like the sections that focus on the human body, dinosaurs, and medicine. Use the website before you leave home to rough out a route through the enormous museum, leaving room for inspiration to strike; the temporary exhibits are always worth a look. Also check the schedules for the Omni theater and planetarium, which can help you decide whether to budget the time and money for a longer stay—or a return visit. ⏱ 3 hr. (Buy tickets online in advance and arrive at 9am sharp to avoid the largest crowds). Science Park, off O'Brien Hwy. (Rte. 28). ☎ 617/723-2500. www.mos.org. Museum admission $21 adults, $19 seniors, $18 kids 3–11, free for kids 2 & under. Omni theater or planetarium $9 adults, $8 seniors, $7 kids ($2.50 discount after 6pm). Discounted combination tickets available. Sat–Thurs 9am–5pm (until 7pm July 5 to Labor Day), Fri 9am–9pm; theaters close later. T: Green Line to Science Park.

② 🍴 ★★ **Faneuil Hall Marketplace.** The food counters that line both sides of Quincy Market (or as the locals know it, Quin-zee Market)

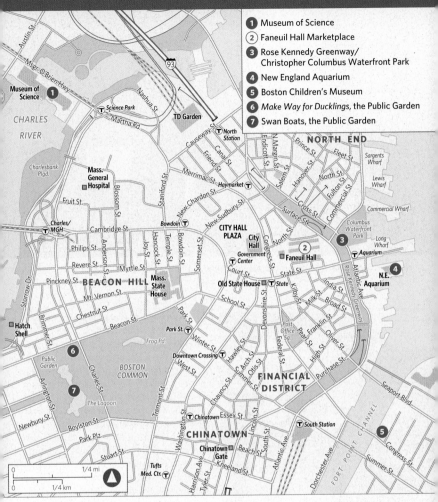

1. Museum of Science
2. Faneuil Hall Marketplace
3. Rose Kennedy Greenway/
   Christopher Columbus Waterfront Park
4. New England Aquarium
5. Boston Children's Museum
6. *Make Way for Ducklings,* the Public Garden
7. Swan Boats, the Public Garden

are a smorgasbord with something for everyone, from the hungriest omnivore to the pickiest vegetarian. Get your food to go, because you'll be picnicking across the street, away from the largest crowds. See p. 52, ⑧.

③ ★★ Rose Kennedy Greenway/Christopher Columbus Waterfront Park. Either of these green spaces is a good picnic spot. Between Faneuil Hall Marketplace and Boston Harbor is a stretch of the Rose Kennedy Greenway, the long, skinny park created when the interstate highway through downtown Boston was moved from the surface into a tunnel. This parcel holds an information center and, in season, a carousel; turn right and walk about 2 blocks to find a large fountain. Across the street from the marketplace is lovely Waterfront Park, which overlooks a marina and offers better shade than the Greenway. It has a small playground, several lawns, a rose garden, benches beneath the enormous trellis, and an excellent fountain. The fountain doesn't run all the time; press one of the four buttons around the edge to start the timed spray. ⏱ 45 min. Atlantic Ave. (at State & Richmond sts.). ☎ 617/635-4505. www.ci.boston. ma.us/parks or www.rosekennedygreenway.org. T: Blue Line to Aquarium.

> A visit to the Museum of Science can be literally electrifying.

> Near downtown Boston's skyscrapers, a carousel delights young visitors to the Rose Kennedy Greenway.

❹ ★ **New England Aquarium.** Consider skipping this stop or the next one, depending on how old your kids are and whether marine life interests them. For aficionados, the thousands of fish and aquatic mammals here make this place a big hit. The centerpiece is the Giant Ocean Tank, where the sharks are. The surrounding displays and hands-on exhibits are home to a vast variety of sea creatures. My favorites are the open-air marine mammal center, where the sea lions frolic, and the medical center, a working veterinary hospital. Other exhibits focus on sharks and rays, penguins, the Amazon, the Gulf of Maine, and tide pools. Allow an extra hour if you plan to take in a 3-D film in the adjacent theater. ⏱ 2 hr. (invest in a Boston CityPass (p. 56) to avoid the lines at the entrance). Central Wharf (½ block from State St. & Atlantic Ave.). ☎ 617/973-5200. www.newenglandaquarium.org. Admission $22 adults, $21 seniors & college students, $16 kids 3–11, free for kids 2 & under. Imax theater tickets $10–$13 adults, $8–$11 seniors & kids. Aquarium July to Labor Day Sun–Thurs 9am–6pm, Fri–Sat & holidays 9am–7pm; day after Labor Day to June Mon–Fri 9am–5pm, Sat–Sun 9am–6pm. Imax theater daily from 9:30am. T: Blue Line to Aquarium.

❺ ★★ **Boston Children's Museum.** If your kids are under 11 or so, and don't care for fish and their friends, skip the aquarium and head here. This is hands-on heaven: Kids can get comfortable with a workbench, visit Japan, learn about Boston's black community, make enormous soap bubbles, and climb around in a gigantic three-story maze. And that's just scratching the surface. Check the website before you visit to give the target audience a sense of what to expect. ⏱ 2 hr. (crowds are especially large on rainy summer weekdays). 300 Congress St. (at Sleeper St., overlooking Fort Point Channel). ☎ 617/426-6500. www. bostonchildrensmuseum.org. Admission $12 adults, $9 seniors & kids 1–15, free for kids under 1, $1 for everyone Fri after 5pm. Sat–Thurs 10am– 5pm; Fri 10am–9pm. T: Red Line to South Station, 10-min. walk.

⑥ ★★★ Make Way for Ducklings, the Public Garden. Do you know the story of Mrs. Mallard and her eight babies, Jack, Kack, Lack, Mack, Nack, Ouack, Pack, and Quack? You will soon. Robert McCloskey's 1941 book introduces young readers to Boston, where the Mallard family goes in search of a new place to live. After perilous adventures, they arrive at the Public Garden. Sculptor Nancy Schön's graceful rendering of McCloskey's charcoal drawings was unveiled in 1987, the 150th anniversary of the Public Garden. Her sculptures, created using the lost-wax process, capture the imagination of just about everyone who encounters the row of bronze waterfowl waddling in the direction of the water. ⏱ 5 min. Public Garden (near the corner of Beacon & Charles sts.).

⑦ ★★ Swan Boats, the Public Garden. End a day of interactive experiences and walking with something low-tech and sedentary: a ride on a Swan Boat. Pedaling one of these things looks like brutally hard work—for the employees at the back of each boat who actually exert themselves. Meanwhile, the passengers relax on long benches, taking in the passing scene of ducks, swans, pigeons, dogs, and humans lazing around the beautiful Public Garden. The swan-drawn boat in the opera *Lohengrin* inspired the design of the vessels, which have been the Paget family business since 1877; the current fleet consists of larger versions of the originals. If you're a fiend for planning, make sure your family is familiar with E. B. White's charming novel *The Trumpet*

> Dozens of penguins make their home at the New England Aquarium.

of the Swan before you even see a Swan Boat— you won't be sorry. ⏱ 15 min. for the ride; allow 1 hr., including a little downtime before or after. The Public Garden is bordered by Arlington, Boylston, Charles & Beacon sts.; the boats operate on the lagoon in the middle. ☎ 617/522-1966. www.swanboats.com. Tickets $2.75 adults, $2 seniors, $1.25 kids 2–15. Sat before Patriots Day to mid-June daily 10am–4pm; mid-June to Labor Day daily 10am–5pm; day after Labor Day to mid-Sept Mon–Fri noon–4pm, Sat–Sun 10am– 4pm. Closed mid-Sept to mid-Apr. T: Green Line to Arlington.

The Fenway

The Fenway neighborhood—confusingly, "the Fenway" is also the name of a street, and Fenway Park often goes by just "Fenway"—offers a unique opportunity to visit two institutions that are virtual temples in their fields: Fenway Park and the Museum of Fine Arts. Weird combination? Maybe a little. But consider this: Both places celebrate the efforts of people who do what they do better than just about anyone else. This itinerary also includes the Isabella Stewart Gardner Museum, a jewel box of an institution around the corner from the MFA. The museum bears the name of its founder, an enthusiastic Red Sox fan.

> Lansdowne Street hops before, during, and after games at Fenway Park.

START Take the Green Line T (B, C, or D train) to Kenmore and follow Brookline Ave. across the bridge over the Massachusetts Tpk.

1 ★★★ kids **Fenway Park.** The magic of Fenway Park isn't in the players or the games or the unforgettable green of the playing field or even the story of the supposed "curse" that prevailed in the 86 years between World Series titles (1918–2004). It's in the whole experience, and you can't truly understand what all the fuss is about until you see for yourself. You don't have to score scarce, expensive tickets to do so, either—tours run year-round.

Tour specifics may vary, especially in the off season, when construction is often going on. Visitors usually get to explore the stands and visit the press box and luxury seats, and they sometimes walk on the warning track and touch the left-field wall, or "Green Monster." If you do score tickets to a game, arrive early to enjoy the scene. Red Sox tickets are the most expensive in baseball, and one of the most imaginative management teams in baseball strives to make visiting Fenway worth the big bucks. Yawkey Way turns into a sort of carnival midway for ticket holders before

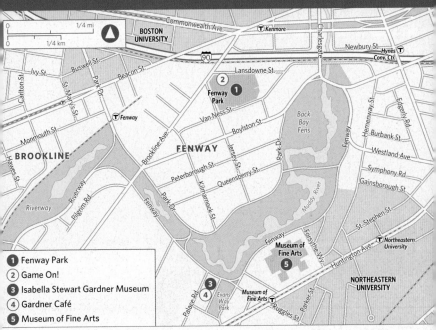

1 Fenway Park
2 Game On!
3 Isabella Stewart Gardner Museum
4 Gardner Café
5 Museum of Fine Arts

games, with concession stands, live music, and other diversions. Outside and in, the food options are numerous and varied—lobster rolls, New England clam chowder, and kosher hot dogs are just some of the alternatives to the usual ballpark fare—but the classic snack is still the Fenway Frank. New sections of seats keep cropping up in previously unused areas of the ballpark, notably including the section *above* the left-field wall, which holds the "Monster Seats." ⏱ 1½ hr. for the 50-min. tour & some exploration of the neighborhood. 4 Yawkey Way (at Brookline Ave.). ☎ 617/226-6666 for tour info; 877/733-7699 for game tickets. www.redsox.com. Tours $12 adults, $11 seniors, $10 kids 3–15, free for kids 2 & under. Daily on the hour 9am–4pm or until 3½ hr. before game time. T: Green Line B, C, or D to Kenmore.

② 🍺 kids **Game On!** The chow here is several crucial notches better than ballpark food—and you can still get an excellent dog or burger. You can also watch just about any game you're interested in on one of the 90-plus TVs. 82 Lansdowne St. (at Brookline Ave.). ☎ 617/351-7001. www.gameonboston.com. $–$$.

③ ★★ **Isabella Stewart Gardner Museum.** This engaging museum makes a perfect stop between Fenway Park and the Museum of Fine Arts; its namesake was a devoted Red Sox fan. An heiress and socialite, "Mrs. Jack" Gardner (1840–1924) was also an avid traveler and patron of the arts. The core of the museum, which opened in 1903, is her private collection of paintings, sculpture, furniture, tapestries, and decorative objects. It includes works by Botticelli, Raphael, Rembrandt, Matisse, and John Singer Sargent. Titian's *Europa,* on the third floor, is one of the most significant European paintings in an American collection; across the way in the Gothic Room is Sargent's 1888 portrait of Mrs. Gardner.

Crossing the Fens

To get from the Fenway to the Gardner Museum, you'll walk through the Back Bay Fens, a marshy section of Boston's famed Emerald Necklace of parks. The parkland here is surrounded by busy streets, and thanks to the tall grasses, drivers often can't see very far ahead; be extra cautious, and cross only at traffic lights. Allow 30 minutes for your stroll.

FENWAY PARK

Home Sweet Home of the Red Sox BY MARIE MORRIS

JOHN UPDIKE, ON ASSIGNMENT FOR *THE NEW YORKER* IN 1960, captured the magic of Fenway, describing it as a "lyric little bandbox of a ballpark." The home field of Boston 's beloved and oft-beleaguered Red Sox opened on April 20, 1912, making it the oldest venue in the Major Leagues. As Paris and the Pyramids are to world travelers, so Fenway Park is to sports fans—they have to see it at least once.

Mr. Red Sox: Ted Williams

The Red Sox have had more than their share of great players over the years, but Ted Williams (1918-2002) was the greatest of all. Mr. Red Sox, as he came to be known, played for Boston from 1939 through 1960, with time off for service as a Marine Corps pilot in World War II and the Korean conflict. Also known as the Splendid Splinter, the two-time MVP, 19-time All-Star, and first-ballot Hall of Famer was the last Major Leaguer to bat over .400 in a season (.406 in 1941). Williams smacked the longest home run ever hit in the park, which flew 502 ft. and beaned a fan sitting in Section 42, Row 37, Seat 21, on June 9, 1946. To this day, that seat is bright red in a sea of blue.

By the Numbers

Wondering what those numbers are on the front of the right-field grandstand? Like every other MLB team, the Sox retired Jackie Robinson's number 42, and, of course, there is Williams's number 9. Here is a key to the rest of the retired Boston greats:

NO. 1 infielder and coach Bobby Doerr
NO. 4 infielder and manager Joe Cronin
NO. 6 infielder and coach Johnny Pesky
NO. 8 outfielder Carl Yastrzemski
NO. 14 outfielder Jim Rice
NO. 27 catcher Carlton Fisk

The Green Monster

Wedged into its urban location, Fenway is the opposite of a prefab facility. Its eccentric contours trace the surrounding streets, which predate the park. The most notorious of the park's odd features is the left-field wall, known as the Green Monster, or simply the Wall. The 37-ft.-high structure features a hand-operated scoreboard, and the inside has enough space for an outfielder to relax there during a pitching change. The Wall officially stands a mere 310 ft. from home plate (some sources say it's closer), but hitting a ball that clears the top is tough; the "wall ball," or ground-rule double that caroms off the Green Monster, is a likelier outcome than a towering homer.

FUN FACT: The Wall wasn't painted green to match the rest of the park until 1947 (before that, it was covered in ads).

The Curse of the Bambino

By 1918, the Red Sox had won five World Series titles, but then a drought began. Hindsight and superstition linked the phenomenon to the team's sale of Babe Ruth (aka the Bambino) to the archrival New York Yankees after the 1919 season. Ruth went on to cement his reputation as one of the great baseball players of all time. Boston went on to lose the seventh and last game of the 1946, 1967, and 1975 World Series; blow a 14-game lead over the Yankees in the race for the 1978 American League title; and come within one out of winning the 1986 World Series.

In 2004, the tide turned: The Red Sox swept the St. Louis Cardinals in the World Series, breaking the "Curse of the Bambino" and inciting a celebration New Englanders are still talking about. Then, just 3 years later, the Red Sox won the World Series again in a sweep of the Colorado Rockies. And yet, the curse may still linger. In 2011, the Sox crumbled spectacularly, losing 18 out of 24 games in September, blowing a 9-game lead for the AL wild card and left fans to bemoan the team's fate once again.

> *An ornate sedan chair in the Veronese Room at the Isabella Stewart Gardner Museum.*

My favorite gallery is the Dutch Room, where the displays include a 17th-century German sculpture of an ostrich made out of silver and an actual ostrich egg. The building, which opened to the public in 1903, resembles a 15th-century Venetian palace. Three floors of galleries surround the plant- and flower-filled courtyard. Plantings change with the seasons; visitors in April can see the museum's signature blooms, orange nasturtiums, cascading from the third-level balconies. Although the terms of Mrs. Gardner's will forbid changing the permanent exhibitions, the museum is a consistently lively presence in the contemporary art world. In fact, they have a new wing, a Renzo Piano project that meticulously hews to the founder's wishes about the integrity of the original building. Opened in 2012, the building holds the main entrance, exhibition and office space, and an expanded cafe. ⏱ 2 hr. 280 The Fenway (at Museum Rd.). ☎ 617/566-1401. www.gardnermuseum.org. Admission $12 adults; $10 seniors; $5 college students with ID; free for kids 17 & under, adults named Isabella with ID & adults on their birthdays. Tues–Sun (& some Mon holidays) 11am–5pm. T: Green Line E to Museum.

④ 🍽 ★★ **Gardner Café.** The Gardner Museum has an appropriately classy cafe that's a perfect place to indulge in some sweets and a cup of tea or a glass of wine. At lunchtime, the savory food is wonderful, too. 280 The Fenway (at Museum Rd.). ☎ 617/566-1401. $-$$.

SITE GUIDE PAGE 71

⑤ ★★★ kids **Museum of Fine Arts.** The MFA is more than just art; its architecture is noteworthy, too. The British architect Sir Norman Foster of Foster + Partners designed the Art of the Americas wing. It opened in 2010 to great fanfare, and opportunities to explore, on your own or with a guide, are numerous and easy to find. Just a year later, the museum revealed a renovated wing, designed by I.M. Pei, devoted to contemporary art. The new kids on the block have somewhat eclipsed the existing galleries, so I'll spotlight something great that doesn't get as much attention as it once did but remains fascinating—the rotunda (see the Site Guide). ⏱ 3 hr. 465 Huntington Ave. (btw. Museum Rd. & Forsyth Way). ☎ 617/267-9300. www.mfa.org. Admission (good for 2 visits within 10 days) $20 adults, $18 seniors & students 18 & over, $7.50 kids 7–17 on school days before 3pm or free after 3pm & weekends, free for kids 6 & under. Voluntary contribution ($20 suggested) Wed 4–9:45pm. Tours free; multimedia guide $6 adults, $4 kids. Sat–Tues 10am–4:45pm; Wed–Fri 10am–9:45pm. Tours daily except Mon holidays; check website for schedule. T: Green Line E to Museum or Orange Line to Ruggles.

The Gardner Museum Heist

On March 18, 1990, the Isabella Stewart Gardner Museum was the victim of one of the most notorious art thefts of modern times. Thirteen pieces valued at $300 million—including Rembrandt's only seascape, *The Storm on the Sea of Galilee,* and one of just 35 known paintings by Vermeer—have been missing ever since. The theft remains one of the FBI's "Top Ten Art Crimes." The museum has not replaced the stolen works, and their empty frames still hang in the galleries, a silent tribute to the purloined treasures. Here's hoping this information is obsolete by the time of your visit.

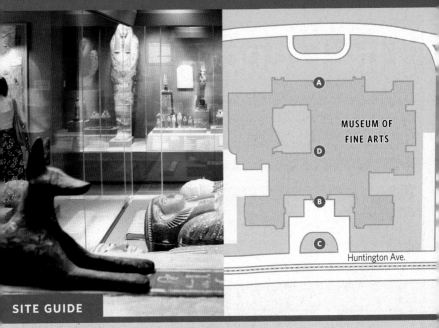

⑤ Museum of Fine Arts

The Museum of Fine Arts is famous for its incredible Egyptian collection (pictured), its Impressionist paintings, and its architecture, but the art that graces its entrances often gets overlooked. Access to the Museum of Fine Arts (1909) is through two grand entrances, the Ⓐ State Street Corporation **Fenway Entrance,** and the Bank of America Plaza on the Avenue of the Arts, which incorporates the Ⓑ **Huntington Avenue entrance.** On this itinerary, you approach the Fenway entrance, with 22 immense Ionic columns along its facade. You can't miss them, but if you do, you'll know you're in the right place when you see giant baby heads on the lawn on either side of a fountain. The bronze sculptures, by the Spanish artist Antonio López García, are formally titled **Night** and **Day**—one is asleep and one is awake. As you leave the museum, I recommend using the Huntington Avenue entrance, which is closer to the Green Line stop and gives you a look at one of Boston's most familiar pieces of public art. On this lawn is Ⓒ *Appeal to the Great Spirit,* a bronze statue of an Indian on horseback. Cast in Paris in 1909,

it's one of the finest works by American sculptor Cyrus Dallin.

Inside, a sweeping staircase leads to the rotunda, which holds one of the museum's signature elements: Ⓓ **John Singer Sargent's Rotunda Murals.** Sargent incorporated sculpture and architectural features with paintings to create the elaborate space; colorful murals depict mythological figures such as Apollo, Athena, the Muses, and Prometheus. The rotunda, which opened to the public in 1921, proved so popular that the museum wanted more. Return to the staircase, scoot out of the flow of traffic, and look up and around to take in Sargent's Colonnade Murals. Creating this space required substantial structural work; for example, the columns that allow light to pour in replaced solid walls. Apollo is here, too, as is a delightfully grisly representation of Perseus holding Medusa's severed head. This project was Sargent's final work: In 1925, the night before he was to sail from London to Boston to supervise installation of the last section, he died in his sleep.

The Freedom Trail

The Freedom Trail is a 2.5 mile walk that leads visitors to some of Boston's, and the nation's, most historic sites. A reminder: the Trail is a suggested route. Feel free to start at the end, skip a stop or two, or otherwise personalize the experience. If you'd rather go with a (costumed) guide, the Freedom Trail Foundation offers guided tours (www.thefreedomtrail.org).

> *The golden dome of the State House, capped by a statue of a cod, is the highest point on Beacon Hill.*

START Take the Red or Green Line to Park St.
TRIP LENGTH About 4 hr.

1 ★ **Boston Common.** The trail begins at the oldest American public park: 50 acres of walkways, lawns, trees, plants, ball fields, and even a cemetery. See p. 50, **1**.

2 **The Black Heritage Trail.** The 1½-mile **Black Heritage Trail** connects sites on Beacon Hill that preserve the history of 19th-century Boston. The "north slope" of the hill was the center of the free black community, and the trail links stations of the Underground Railroad, homes of famous citizens, and the first integrated public school in the city. ☉ 1½ hr. across Beacon St. from the Massachusetts State House.

SITE GUIDE PAGE 75

3 ★ **Massachusetts State House.** The state capitol is one of the signature works of the great architect Charles Bulfinch. Note the symmetry, a hallmark of Federal style, in details as large as doors and as small as moldings. Tours (guided and self-guided) explore the building. Allow time to see the statues and monuments outside; my favorite is President Kennedy. ☉ 10 min. to explore outside; 40 min. with tour. Beacon St. (at Park St.). ☎ 617/727-3676. www.mass.gov/statehouse. Free admission & tours. Mon–Fri 9am–5pm (tours 10am–3:30pm). T: Red or Green Line to Park St.

4 **Park Street Church.** The plaques across the front of this striking building describe significant events in its history. Most Bostonians know the church for its 217-foot steeple and clock tower, which plays the Westminster Quarters every 15 minutes. ☉ 20 min. 1 Park St. (at Tremont St.). ☎ 617/523-3383. www.parkstreet.org. Tours mid-June to Aug Tues–Fri 9am–4pm, Sat 9am–3pm. T: Red or Green Line to Park St.

5 ★★ **Granary Burying Ground.** Originally a section of Boston Common, this burying

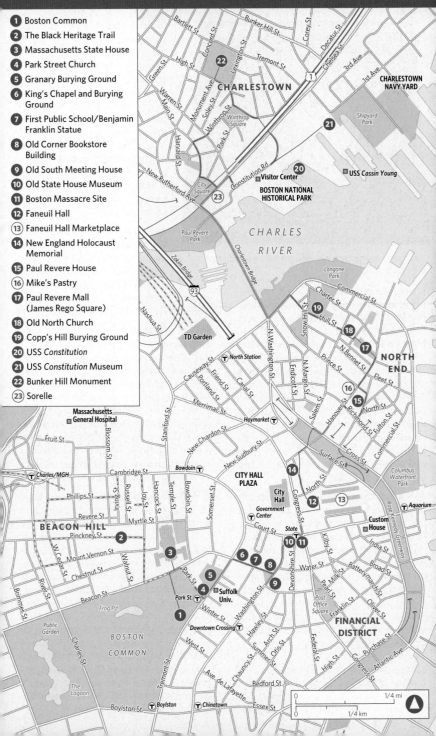

1 Boston Common
2 The Black Heritage Trail
3 Massachusetts State House
4 Park Street Church
5 Granary Burying Ground
6 King's Chapel and Burying Ground
7 First Public School/Benjamin Franklin Statue
8 Old Corner Bookstore Building
9 Old South Meeting House
10 Old State House Museum
11 Boston Massacre Site
12 Faneuil Hall
13 Faneuil Hall Marketplace
14 New England Holocaust Memorial
15 Paul Revere House
16 Mike's Pastry
17 Paul Revere Mall (James Rego Square)
18 Old North Church
19 Copp's Hill Burying Ground
20 USS Constitution
21 USS Constitution Museum
22 Bunker Hill Monument
23 Sorelle

> *Circular markers in the sidewalk point the way along the Freedom Trail.*

in Cambridge, King's Chapel was constructed by erecting the granite building around its wooden predecessor, then removing the old chapel. ⏱ 30 min. 58 Tremont St. (at School St.). ☎ 617/227-2155. www. kings-chapel.org. $2 donation suggested. Chapel year-round Sat 10am–4pm; summer Sun 1:30–4pm, Mon & Thurs-Fri 10am–4pm, Tues-Wed 10–11:15am & 1:30–4pm. Burying ground daily 8am–5:30pm (until 3pm in winter). Double-check hours on website. T: Green or Blue Line to Government Center.

7 First Public School/Benjamin Franklin Statue. A colorful sidewalk mosaic on School Street marks the site of the first American public school. The Benjamin Franklin statue sits in front of Old City Hall. School St. at City Hall Ave. (end of Province St.). See p. 51, **5**.

8 Old Corner Bookstore Building. This land once belonged to religious reformer Anne Hutchinson, who was excommunicated and banished from Massachusetts in 1638. The current structure dates to around 1712. It's best known today as the one-time home of Ticknor & Fields, publisher of such authors as Longfellow, Emerson, Thoreau, Alcott, and Stowe. Step across the street to appreciate the scale of the building, which was already old when the American Revolution was breaking out. 285 Washington St. (at School St.).

ground was laid out in 1660. It got its name from the granary, or grain-storage building, that stood on the site of Park Street Church. Solomon Willard, architect of the Bunker Hill Monument, designed the granite entrance. You'll see the graves of Paul Revere, Samuel Adams, the victims of the Boston Massacre, and Benjamin Franklin's parents. Also buried here is Isaac Vergoose's wife, Elizabeth Foster Goose, believed to be "Mother Goose." Even in death, John Hancock has style: The carving on his monument is a rebus. Look for the hand above the three birds, or cocks—"handcocks," get it? ⏱ 20 min. Tremont St. (at Bromfield St.). See p. 50, **3**.

6 ★ King's Chapel and Burying Ground. The oldest cemetery in Boston, the graveyard next to King's Chapel was established in 1630. It holds the graves of many early residents, including the first Colonial governor, John Winthrop, and Mary Chilton, the first woman to come ashore in Plymouth in 1620. The graves of William Dawes, Paul Revere's "midnight ride" counterpart, and of Elizabeth Pain, reputedly the model for Hester Prynne in *The Scarlet Letter,* are here, too. The Puritans gained an Anglican neighbor in 1686, when King's Chapel was established for British officers (it became Unitarian after the Revolution). The current chapel (1749) is the country's oldest church in continuous use. Designed by Peter Harrison, the architect of Christ Church

9 ★ kids Old South Meeting House. The Boston Tea Party, one of the pivotal political demonstrations of the pre-Revolutionary era, started here in 1773. The displays and exhibits in the former house of worship—now used for lectures, concerts, and other events—tell the story in a low-key yet compelling fashion. As you leave, look across the road at **1 Milk St.,** an office building standing roughly where Benjamin Franklin was born in 1706, at what was then 17 Milk St. The facade incorporates a bust of Benjamin Franklin and the words BIRTHPLACE OF FRANKLIN. ⏱ 40 min. 310 Washington St. (at Milk St.). ☎ 617/482-6439. www.osmh.org. Admission $6 adults, $5 seniors & students, $1 kids 6–18, free for kids 5 & under. Apr-Oct daily 9:30am–5pm; Nov-Mar daily 10am–4pm. T: Blue or Orange Line to State.

SITE GUIDE

② The Black Heritage Trail

The first stop is Ⓐ ★★ **The Robert Gould Shaw Memorial** (pictured; p. 50, ②)—Augustus Saint-Gaudens' masterpiece and one of the finest Civil War memorials anywhere. Colonel Shaw, who was white, and many of his troops perished in the Civil War battle for Fort Wagner, South Carolina, near Charleston. Continuing on the trail, you come to Ⓑ the **Charles Street Meeting House,** which opened in 1807 as the (white) Third Baptist Church and later became the First African Methodist Episcopal Church. Today the building, a stately red-brick Asher Benjamin design, holds offices and commercial space, including **Café Vanille** (p. 80, ⑥). The only buildings on the trail that are open to sightseers are the last two stops, the Ⓒ **African Meeting House** and the Ⓓ **Abiel Smith School,** which make up the **Museum of African American History** (p. 80, ⑨). In its heyday, the Meeting House (1806) was known as the "black Faneuil Hall"; the building was later a synagogue. Don't leave without venturing down **Holmes Alley,** off Smith Court—the narrow passageway is believed to have been a hiding place for fugitive slaves traveling the Underground Railroad. Free 2-hour tours of the Black Heritage Trail led

by a ranger from the National Park Service's **Boston African American National Historic Site** (☎ 617/742-5415; www.nps.gov/boaf) are available Monday through Saturday from Memorial Day weekend to Labor Day weekend, and by request at other times; call ahead for a reservation. To take a self-guided tour, pick up a brochure at the Museum of African American History or the Boston Common or State Street visitor center.

⑩ ★ kids Old State House Museum. Now dwarfed by skyscrapers, the one-time state capitol has been here since 1713. ⏱ 1 hr. See p. 51, ❻.

⑪ Boston Massacre Site. A circle of cobblestones embedded in a traffic island honors the five men killed by British troops on March 5, 1770. A waist-high marker near the curb on the Devonshire Street side of the Old State House tells the story. ⏱ 5 min. State St. (at Devonshire St.).

⑫ ★ kids Faneuil Hall. Residents of Colonial Boston came here to shop—and to take part in protests that helped lay the groundwork for the American Revolution. ⏱ 5 min.; 30 min. for tour. See p. 51, ❼.

⑬ 🍴 ★★ kids Faneuil Hall Marketplace. Yes, it's touristy, but the original "festival market" draws big crowds for a good reason. ⏱ 30–60 min. See p. 52, ❽.

⑭ ★★ kids The New England Holocaust Memorial. This memorial isn't formally on the Freedom Trail. I always include it, though—when we think about freedom, it's important to contemplate the consequences of not having it. ⏱ 10 min. Union St. (at North & Hanover sts.). ☎ 617/457-8755. www.nehm.org. T: Orange or Green Line to Haymarket.

⑮ ★★★ kids Paul Revere House. Paul Revere probably never said, "the British are coming"—but "the regulars are out" doesn't have quite the same dramatic impact, does it? ⏱ 45 min. See p. 53, ❿.

⑯ 🍴 ★ Mike's Pastry. Italian pastries are always a good idea. So are all-American treats such as brownies and chocolate chip cookies. 300 Hanover St. (at Prince St.). ☎ 617/742-3050. www.mikespastry.com. $.

⑰ ★ Paul Revere Mall (James Rego Sq.). This elegant little space connects the main drag of the North End to the neighborhood's high point, the Old North Church. ⏱ 10 min. See p. 83, ❺.

⑱ ★★ Old North Church. Brush up on the Longfellow poem "Paul Revere's Ride" before you arrive. The steeple here was the stage for "one if by land, and two if by sea." ⏱ 40 min. See p. 83, ❻.

> *Musicians and other street performers liven up Faneuil Hall Marketplace.*

19 ★ **Copp's Hill Burying Ground.** Rising property values eventually ended the practice, but in early Colonial times, residential neighborhoods often incorporated graveyards. This one opened in 1659. ⏱ 20 min. See p. 84, **7**.

20 ★★ kids **USS Constitution.** The three masts of this mighty frigate loom over the Charlestown Navy Yard, and the vessel is one of the most eye-catching sights on the harbor. On August 19, 1812, in an engagement with HMS *Guerriere* during the War of 1812, the British ship's cannonballs bounced off the *Constitution's* thick oak hull as if it were iron, and the nickname "Old Ironsides" was born. The oldest commissioned floating warship in the world (launched in 1797 and retired in 1815), Old Ironsides never lost a battle, but narrowly escaped destruction several times in its first 2 centuries. Today the 204-foot-long ship is a beloved symbol of Boston. It's an active-duty posting for the sailors who lead tours (outfitted in fancy 1812 dress uniforms), and visiting the vessel means clearing security. The tour—a fascinating overview and an opportunity to mingle with people from all over the world—is worth the slight inconvenience. ⏱ 1 hr. including security screening (arrive early to beat the tour groups). Charlestown Navy Yard. ☎ 617/242-7511. www.history.navy.mil/ussconstitution. Free admission. Apr–Oct Tues–Sun 10am–6pm, tours every 30 min. until 3:30pm; Nov–Mar Thurs–Sun 10am–4pm, tours every 30 min. until 3:30pm. T: Ferry from Long Wharf (Blue Line to Aquarium), or Green or Orange Line to North Station & 10-min. walk.

21 ★ kids **USS Constitution Museum.** The *Constitution* is, for the most part, a hands-off experience; its engaging museum is exactly the opposite. Children (and adults) push buttons, open doors, pull ropes, study artifacts, watch demonstrations of maritime crafts, and enjoy interactive exhibits. ⏱ 30 min. Building 22, off First Ave. ☎ 617/426-1812. www.ussconstitutionmuseum.org. Free admission; suggested donation $4 adults, $2 kids. Apr–Oct daily 9am–6pm; Nov–Mar daily 10am–5pm. T: Ferry from Long Wharf (Blue Line to Aquarium), or Green or Orange Line to North Station & 10-min. walk.

22 ★ **Bunker Hill Monument.** This 221-foot obelisk, designed by Solomon Willard, commemorates the Battle of Bunker Hill on June

> *The Boston skyline has included the Old North Church steeple since 1723.*

17, 1775. The British won that battle, but nearly half of their troops were killed or wounded. Partly as a consequence, royal forces abandoned Boston 9 months later (March 17, known in Boston as Evacuation Day). The exhibits in the museum across the street from the granite monument tell the story of the battle. Fair warning: The strenuous climb up 294 stairs to the top ends at a small space with frustratingly tiny windows. ⏱ 30 min. if you stay on the ground, 1 hr. if you climb the stairs. Monument Sq. (at Monument Ave.). ☎ 617/242-5641. www.nps.gov/bost. Free admission. Museum daily 9am–5pm; monument daily 9am–4:30pm (until 5:30pm July–Aug). T: Orange Line to Community College, 10-min. walk.

23 🍴 ★ **Sorelle.** Pastries, sandwiches, and salads served in a sleek contemporary space make a good transition from your Colonial excursion back to real life. 100 City Sq. (at Chelsea St.). ☎ 617/242-5980. www.sorellecafe.com. $–$$.

Beacon Hill

The views are better from the waterfront and the real estate is more expensive in the Back Bay, but the most prestigious addresses in Boston are on beautiful Beacon Hill, as they have been for most of the past 2 centuries. Post-Revolution prosperity created Boston's most prominent (in all senses of the word) neighborhood, which is a visual treat from every angle. Wear comfortable shoes.

> Governor Samuel Adams laid the cornerstone of the Massachusetts State House in 1795.

START Take the Red or Green Line to Park St. and walk up the hill.

❶ ★ **Massachusetts State House.** The construction of the state capitol, which opened in 1798, coincided with Beacon Hill's rise to fashionable status. Before the Revolution, most Bostonians lived in the area around what are now Faneuil Hall Marketplace and the North End; with peace and increasing prosperity, the population ballooned and construction boomed. The prototypical Boston building, of red brick with white marble trim, owes its iconic status to one man: Charles Bulfinch. The best-known architect of the Federal era

(1780–1820), Bulfinch designed the golden-domed central building of the State House as well as many of the graceful residences you'll see on this tour. ⏱ 10 min. to explore outside; 40 min. with tour. See p. 72, ❸.

❷ ★ **Nichols House Museum.** In contrast to the adjacent Back Bay, where many historic structures hold offices, schools, condos, and apartments, Beacon Hill retains a fair number of one-family homes (along with plenty of condos and apartments). Almost all of the private residences on the narrow streets of "the Hill" are tantalizingly close yet inaccessible to visitors. This 1804 building, which is

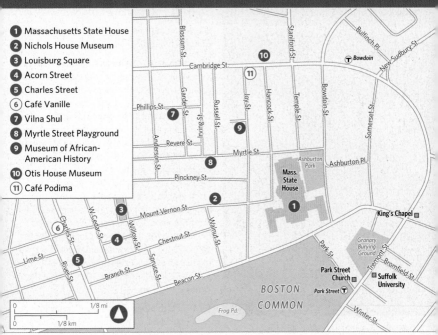

1. Massachusetts State House
2. Nichols House Museum
3. Louisburg Square
4. Acorn Street
5. Charles Street
6. Café Vanille
7. Vilna Shul
8. Myrtle Street Playground
9. Museum of African-American History
10. Otis House Museum
11. Café Podima

attributed to Charles Bulfinch, is a welcome exception. It permits a glimpse of Boston during the lifetime of the house's most famous occupant, Rose Standish Nichols (1872–1960). "Miss Rose" was a suffragist, feminist, pacifist, and pioneering landscape designer. She traveled the world, returning home with much of the art and artifacts that decorate her house, which became a museum after her death. Most of the furnishings in the four-story building are gorgeous antiques collected by several generations of the Nichols family. They moved here in 1885, not long before the novelist Henry James called Mount Vernon "the only respectable street in America." ⏱ 45 min. 55 Mount Vernon St. (at Joy & Walnut sts.). ☎ 617/227-6993. www.nicholshousemuseum.org. Admission $7. Apr-Oct Tues-Sat 11am-4pm; Nov-Mar Thurs-Sat 11am-4pm; tours every 30 min. T: Red or Green Line to Park St.

SITE GUIDE PAGE 81

③ ★★★ **Louisburg Square.** The fanciest addresses in Boston's fanciest neighborhood surround this park within a daunting iron fence. The architecture is consistent yet random, employing the same materials in a pleasing variety of styles. It's the common property of the Louisburg Square Proprietors, believed to be the oldest homeowners' association in the country. The original proprietors bought the land, which was then pasture, from the painter John Singleton Copley, and commissioned its design in 1826. The 22 houses that surround the graceful patch of grass and trees were built between 1834 and 1848; Aristides landed here in 1850. In the late 19th century, residents of Louisburg Square introduced Christmas Eve caroling and bell ringing to the United States, a tradition that continues today. ⏱ 20 min. Btw. Mount Vernon St. (at Willow St.) & Pinckney St. (at Grove St.).

④ **Acorn Street.** This adorable cobblestone thoroughfare feels like a surprise. It's something of an open secret to clued-in Bostonians—and no secret to postcard photographers. You'll see why when you get there. Btw. Willow & W. Cedar sts.

⑤ ★★ **Charles Street.** Look past the signs and merchandise to appreciate the structural details of the 19th-century buildings that line Beacon Hill's main commercial strip. One of the best streets in the city for aimless strolling, Charles Street abounds with gift and antiques shops. It's also home to

> *Café Vanille specializes in French pastry.*

such nontouristy businesses as a pharmacy, hardware store, and convenience store (the 7-Eleven at 66 Charles St., with hilariously low-key signage that follows the street's strict zoning rules). ⏱ At least 30 min. Beacon St. to Cambridge St. T: Red Line to Charles/MGH.

⑥ 🍽 ★★ **Café Vanille.** One of the best French bakeries in the city, Café Vanille is a perfect place to relax with a pastry or sandwich and a cup of strong coffee. In fine weather, try to snag a table in the outdoor seating area. 70 Charles St. ☎ 617/523-9200. www.cafevanilleboston.com. $.

⑦ **Vilna Shul.** Built in 1919 and named for Vilnius, Lithuania, this little synagogue was home to an active congregation until the mid-1980s. In the 21st century, it became the focus of a restoration project that recently allowed it to open to visitors. ⏱ 20 min. 18 Phillips St. (at Anderson & Garden sts.). ☎ 617/523-2324. www.vilnashul.org. Free admission; donations accepted. Mar 15–Thanksgiving Wed–Fri 11am–5pm, Sun 1–5pm & by appointment. T: Red or Green Line to Park St.

⑧ **Myrtle Street Playground.** Climbing all over Beacon Hill is no holiday for your legs; give them a rest at this delightful little oasis. Myrtle St. (btw. Irving & S. Russell sts.).

⑨ ★★ **Museum of African American History.** This fascinating museum offers visitors a comprehensive look at the history and contributions of blacks in Boston and Massachusetts. It occupies the **Abiel Smith School** (1834), the first American public grammar school for African-American children, and the **African Meeting House** (1806), one of the oldest black churches in the country. Changing and permanent exhibits use art, artifacts, documents, historic photographs, and other objects to explore an important era that often takes a back seat in Revolutionary War–obsessed New England. ⏱ 1 hr. 46 Joy St. (at Myrtle & Cambridge sts.). ☎ 617/725-0022. www.afroammuseum.org. Admission $5 adults, $3 seniors & youths 13–17, free for kids 12 & under. Mon–Sat 10am–4pm. T: Red or Green Line to Park St.

⑩ ★★★ **Otis House Museum.** Charles Bulfinch made his name by popularizing the Federal style in residences as well as public spaces that survive to this day (including the Massachusetts State House). This magnificent home, completed in 1796, was the first of three he designed for his friend Harrison Gray Otis. The engrossing tour touches on the history of the neighborhood, discusses historic preservation, and, most important, shows off the house and its furnishings. The architectural details share the spotlight with the story of a companionable young family bound for bigger things. Otis, a real estate developer who was later a congressman and Boston's mayor, and his wife of nearly 50 years, Sally Foster Otis, appointed their home in grand style and enjoyed a reputation for entertaining lavishly. ⏱ 45 min. 141 Cambridge St. (at Staniford St.); enter from Lynde St. ☎ 617/227-3956. www.historicnewengland.org. Tours $8. Wed–Sun 11am–4:30pm; tours every 30 min. T: Green or Blue Line to Government Center (or Blue Line to Bowdoin, on weekdays only).

⑪ 🍽 ★★ **Café Podima.** Students from nearby Suffolk University flock here, drawn by the large portions and low prices. Have a salad, sandwich, or pizza, or just grab some ice cream or frozen yogurt. 168 Cambridge St. ☎ 617/227-4959. $.

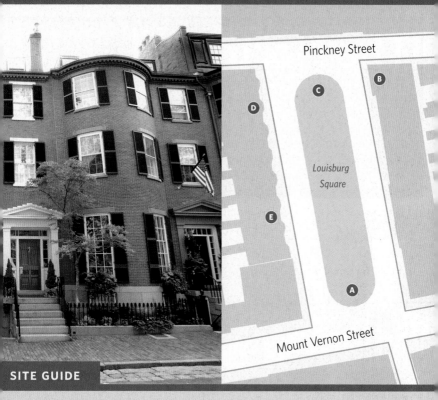

SITE GUIDE

3 Louisburg Square

An Italian marble likeness of the Athenian statesman **A Aristides the Just** anchors one end of the park. Not so long ago, lingering in front of **B 19 Louisburg Sq.** would have earned you a chat with a Secret Service agent. U.S. Senator John Kerry, the 2004 Democratic presidential candidate, lives here (and in a number of other swanky places) with his wife, Teresa Heinz Kerry. The rendering of **C Christopher Columbus** in the square, awash in greenery in the summer, is believed to be the first American statue honoring Columbus. Use him as an excuse to peer inside the fence, which was constructed to keep outsiders away after the statues on the square were vandalized. The celebrated 19th-century singer Jenny Lind—promoted as the "Swedish Nightingale" by impresario P. T. Barnum—married her accompanist in the parlor of the house at **D 20 Louisburg Sq.** in 1852. Beloved author Louisa May Alcott bought

the house at **E 10 Louisburg Sq.** in 1885, but she lived here for only about 3 years. She had contracted mercury poisoning while serving as a nurse during the Civil War, and her health was failing. In 1888, on the day after her father Bronson's funeral, Alcott died here.

The North End

Boston's best-known Italian-American neighborhood gets yuppier by the day, but it's still the area's top destination for pasta, cappuccino, pastries, and the lively street life that makes this crowded, friendly area endlessly appealing to pedestrians. As you wander around, remember to look up—among the architectural flourishes executed by the talented craftsmen who worked on many of the buildings, you may see a *nonna* (grandma) looking out the window, keeping track of the action on her street.

> Box pews like the ones in the Old North Church are traditional in old, drafty New England houses of worship.

START Take the Green or Orange Line to Haymarket and cross the Rose Kennedy Greenway.

1 ★★★ kids **Paul Revere House.** With its good water supply and easy access to the harbor, the North End was one of the first areas of Boston settled by Europeans. The Paul Revere House, the oldest surviving house downtown, was built around 1680, in the wake of a huge fire in 1676. 🕓 45 min. See p. 53, **10**.

2 **Rose Fitzgerald's birthplace.** A plaque marks the modest tenement building where President John Fitzgerald Kennedy's mother came into the world in 1890. It recalls the days when the North End was a working-class Irish and Jewish neighborhood. For much of the 20th century, the North End was Boston's best-known Italian-American area; today the neighborhood is estimated to be less than half Italian-American, having become popular with young professionals who walk to work downtown and, more recently, empty nesters fleeing the suburbs. 4 Garden Court (at Prince & Fleet sts.).

3 🍽 ★★ kids **Caffè Vittoria.** Neighborhood denizens and out-of-towners alike come here for the extensive selection of coffee drinks, the Italian baked goods, and the peerless people-watching. 296 Hanover St. (at Parmenter & Prince sts.). ☎ 617/227-7606. www.vittoria caffe.com. $.

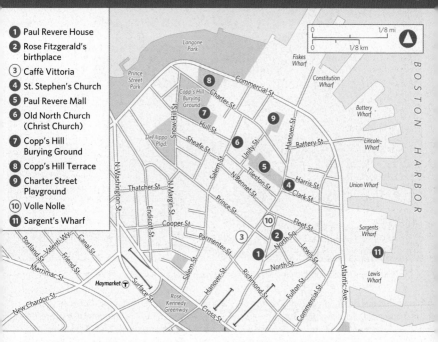

1 Paul Revere House
2 Rose Fitzgerald's birthplace
3 Caffè Vittoria
4 St. Stephen's Church
5 Paul Revere Mall
6 Old North Church (Christ Church)
7 Copp's Hill Burying Ground
8 Copp's Hill Terrace
9 Charter Street Playground
10 Volle Nolle
11 Sargent's Wharf

4 ★ **St. Stephen's Church.** St. Stephen's, one of three Roman Catholic houses of worship in the tiny North End, is the only standing church building in Boston designed by Charles Bulfinch. The design bears the hallmarks of the architect's iconic style, including the symmetry that makes Federal architecture so pleasing to the eye—step across the street to appreciate it fully. At its dedication in 1804, St. Stephen's was Unitarian; it changed with the neighborhood's population and became Catholic in 1862. A refurbishment in 1965 restored the building's original austere details, including clear (not stained) glass windows. The bell, installed in 1805, came from Paul Revere's foundry and cost $800. Rose Fitzgerald (later Rose Kennedy) was baptized here in 1890, and her funeral took place here in 1995. ⊙ 10 min. 401 Hanover St. (at Clark St.).

5 ★ **Paul Revere Mall.** Also known as James Rego Square but usually just called the Prado, this tree-shaded plaza links the commotion of Hanover Street and the serenity of the Old North Church. One of the best photo ops in the city is here: Focus on the equestrian statue of Paul Revere, then allow the church steeple to stray into the frame. The sculptor was

Cyrus Dallin, who also created the Indian on horseback in front of the Museum of Fine Arts (p. 70, 5). Wander slowly here, taking time to peruse the plaques that line the left-hand wall; they commemorate important people and places in the history of the neighborhood. ⊙ 10 min. Hanover St. (at Clark & Harris sts.).

6 ★ **Old North Church (Christ Church).** This beautifully proportioned brick edifice, designed in the style of Sir Christopher Wren, fairly overflows with historic associations. It contains the oldest American church bells (cast in Gloucester, England, and installed in 1745), the Revere family's pew, and a bust of George Washington that's believed to be the first memorial to the first president. The strongest link is with Paul Revere, who arranged for sexton Robert Newman to hang two lanterns in the steeple on the night of April 18, 1775, signaling to the rebellious colonists that British troops were leaving Boston by water ("two if by sea"), bound for Lexington and Concord. The original weather vane tops the current steeple, the church's third, which is a replica of the original. The behind-the-scenes tour takes visitors up into the spire and down to the crypt. It's definitely not for the claustrophobic, but irresistible for those who are curious

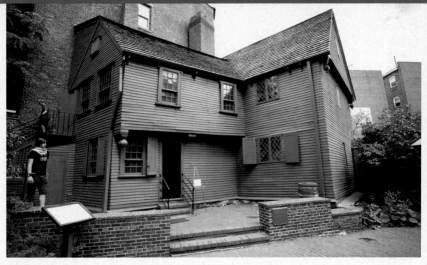

> *The Paul Revere House dates to around 1680, just 50 years after the founding of Boston.*

about Colonial times. My favorite feature of the church isn't actually in the church—it's the tranquil gardens on the north side of the building (to the left as you face the main entrance from the street). ⏱ 40 min. 193 Salem St. (at Hull St.). ☎ 617/523-6676. www.oldnorth.com. $3 donation requested. Free tours every 15 min. Behind-the-scenes tour (50 min.) $8 adults, $6 seniors & students, $5 kids 16 & under; available June weekends, daily July–Oct & Dec 25–Jan 1 & by appointment. Reservations recommended. Jan–Feb Tues–Sun 10am–4pm; March–May daily 9am–5pm; June–Oct daily 9am–6pm; Nov–Dec daily 10am–5pm. T: Orange or Green Line to Haymarket.

⑦ ★ Copp's Hill Burying Ground. Boston's second cemetery, this graveyard was established in 1659. It's at the crest of Copp's Hill, the highest point in the North End, with a panoramic view across the Inner Harbor. At the Charlestown Navy Yard, you'll see the three masts of USS *Constitution*. "Old Ironsides" was built near here, at Hartt's Shipyard (now 409 Commercial St.), and launched in 1797. The family plot of the prominent Puritan ministers Increase Mather (who was also president of Harvard) and Cotton Mather (Increase's son) is in the burying ground, as is the grave of Robert Newman, the sexton of the Old North Church in 1775 (he hung the lanterns that signified "two if by sea"). The poet Phillis

Wheatley, a freed slave, is believed to have been buried here in an unmarked grave. The graves of many slaves and free blacks are here; Boston's first black neighborhood was nearby, and an estimated 1,000 of the 10,000 or so people buried here were black. The best known is Prince Hall, who fought at Bunker Hill and later founded the first black Masonic lodge. ***Fun fact:*** The 10-foot-wide private home at 44 Hull St., across from the burying-ground entrance, is the narrowest house in Boston. ⏱ 20 min. Hull St. (at Salem & Snowhill sts.). Daily 9am–5pm (until 3pm in winter). T: Green or Orange Line to North Station.

⑧ ★★ Copp's Hill Terrace. Because the back gate of the burying ground is always locked, you'll have to walk all the way around to get to this little plaza, designed by a protégé of Frederick Law Olmsted. The seating area, on a patch of concrete that overlooks a terraced lawn, has a great view of the action on the athletic fields across the street and the harbor and Charlestown Navy Yard beyond. Commercial Street, directly below, was the location of one of the weirdest disasters ever, in this or any other city: the molasses flood of January 1919. A 2.3-million-gallon industrial storage tank blew apart, sending thousands of tons of molasses pouring through the streets, killing 21 people and injuring dozens more. Charter St. (at Snowhill & Foster sts.).

> *Wherever you go downtown, Boston Harbor is never far away.*

Detour to the Institute of Contemporary Art

From the North End, the South Boston waterfront, also known as the Seaport District, is an easy walk along the water. The crown jewel of this relatively new area is the **Institute of Contemporary Art.** Boston's first new art museum in almost a century opened in 2006 (the institution dates to 1936) and quickly became a favorite of both aficionados and sightseers. The ICA's horizon-broadening definition of art encompasses everything from painting and sculpture to film and dance. Architects Diller Scofidio + Renfro designed the building to take full advantage of its location; it juts out over the harbor, allowing breathtaking views. ⏱ 2 hr. 100 Northern Ave. (Seaport Blvd.). ☎ 617/478-3100. www.icaboston.org. Admission $15 adults, $10 seniors and students, free for kids 17 & under; free to all Thurs after 5pm. Open Tues–Sun 10am–5pm (extended hours Thurs–Fri till 9pm); also open Mon on some national holidays. T: Waterfront Silver Line bus to World Trade Center.

❾ ★ **Charter Street Playground.** Seek out this pocket park tucked between the tourist tracks of the Freedom Trail and Hanover Street, and you'll be the only out-of-towner who's here intentionally. The little patch of greenery and cobblestones is home to a sweet sculpture of a seal. Greenough Lane, off Charter St. (at Unity St.).

⓿ 🍽 ★★ **Volle Nolle.** A neighborhood favorite for sophisticated sandwiches and scrumptious baked goods, Volle Nolle isn't a typical North End sub shop—and that's a good thing. Eat in, or take a picnic to the next stop. 351 Hanover St. (at Fleet St.). ☎ 617/523-0003. $.

⓫ ★ **Sargent's Wharf.** The little park at the end of the wharf behind the parking lot is a neighborhood secret—it's not visible from the street, but it hums with activity. The free telescopes allow views of the maritime traffic on the Inner Harbor and the action at the airport, which feels close enough to touch. Off Commercial St. at Eastern Ave. (north side of 2 Atlantic Ave.).

Harvard Square

Much of the interesting architecture in and around Harvard Square is on the main Harvard University campus, and a great deal of it isn't. This tour touches on both. The school and "the Square" have been linked since they were just starting out—in the 1630s. Neither would be what it is today without the other.

> The building is just one of the funny things associated with the Harvard Lampoon.

START Take the Red Line to Harvard and follow Mass Ave to Linden St.; turn right and walk 1 block to Mount Auburn St.

❶ ★ **Harvard Lampoon Castle.** A peerless blend of form and function, the Harvard Lampoon Castle is the home of the nation's best-known undergraduate humor magazine. The triangular building is suitably madcap, with colorful trim all around and a "face" of three windows and a door on the Linden Street end. The 1909 structure is the work of Edmund Wheelwright of the Boston firm of Wheelwright & Haven, also the architect of the Longfellow Bridge and numerous cultural venues. The Lampoon is a legendary launching pad—the founders of the *National Lampoon* and dozens of writers for *Saturday Night Live,*

The Simpsons, Conan O'Brien's various efforts, and other TV hits (and misses) got their start here. 57 Mount Auburn St. & 44 Bow St. (at Linden & Plympton sts.).

❷ **Dexter Gate.** Facing the street, the engraving on this portal to Harvard Yard reads ENTER TO GROW IN WISDOM. On the other side, the inscription says DEPART TO SERVE BETTER THY COUNTRY AND THY KIND. Mass Ave (at Plympton St.).

❸ ★★ **Carpenter Center for the Visual Arts.** Completed in 1963, the Carpenter Center is the only North American building designed by the Swiss-French architect Le Corbusier. The concrete building's dynamic design encourages visitors to circulate on ramps that allow views of studio space from the public areas. The two gallery spaces are open to the public.

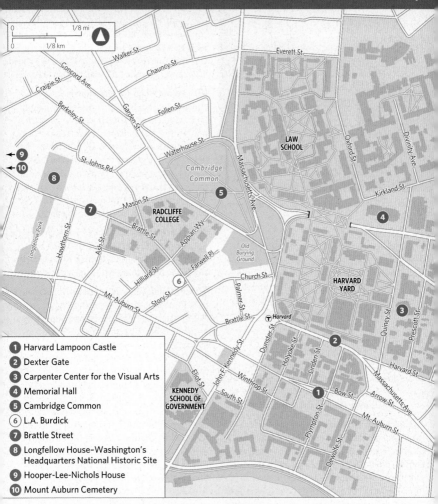

1. Harvard Lampoon Castle
2. Dexter Gate
3. Carpenter Center for the Visual Arts
4. Memorial Hall
5. Cambridge Common
6. L.A. Burdick
7. Brattle Street
8. Longfellow House–Washington's Headquarters National Historic Site
9. Hooper-Lee-Nichols House
10. Mount Auburn Cemetery

Purists deplore the way the Carpenter Center relates to its surroundings; pause across the street to contemplate the site, which does seem to cramp the building's style, even to the amateur's eye. ⏱15 min. 24 Quincy St. (at Harvard St. & Broadway). ☎617/495-3251. Free admission. Mon–Sat 10am–11pm; Sun 1–11pm.

4. ★ **Memorial Hall.** The architects of "Mem Hall," the firm of Ware & Van Brunt, won a design competition that was open only to Harvard graduates (who wonder why people think they're snobs). The cornerstone was laid in 1870 and construction completed in 1875. ⏱10 min. 45 Quincy St. (at Cambridge St.). See p. 61, 7.

SITE GUIDE PAGE 89

5. ★ **Cambridge Common.** Set aside as common land in 1631, just a year after the founding of Cambridge (then called Newtowne), the Common sometimes feels like one of the only quiet parts of Harvard Square. Legend has it that George Washington took control of the Continental Army here in July 1775, but historians have debunked the specifics. Nevertheless, a memorial surrounded by three cannons commemorates the event. A more interesting marker is on the edge of the Common. While Paul Revere was leaving Boston by boat on April 18, 1775, William Dawes slipped out of

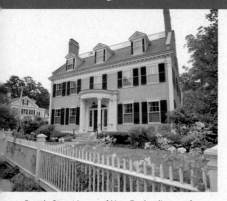

> *Brattle Street is one of New England's most famous addresses.*

town on what's now Washington Street. Both headed for Lexington and Concord, and Dawes rode through the heart of Cambridge. On Massachusetts Avenue north of Garden Street, horseshoes embedded in the sidewalk illustrate his path. ⏱ 10 min. Mass Ave & Garden St.

⑥ 🍴 ★★ **L. A. Burdick.** The cafe—one of only a few retail locations the New Hampshire–based confectioner operates—offers candy, pastries, and drinks to stay or go. **52-D Brattle St.** ☎ 617/491-4340. www.burdickchocolate.com. $-$$.

⑦ ★★★ **Brattle Street.** One of the most beautiful residential streets in the country, Brattle Street has been an exclusive address since Colonial times. It gained fame—and the nickname "Tory Row"—around the time of the Revolution because of its association with British sympathizers. The loyalists later evacuated, but some of their lovely homes survive.

⑧ ★★ **Longfellow House–Washington's Headquarters National Historic Site.** Henry Wadsworth Longfellow lived here from 1843 until his death, in 1882. The poet first made his home here as a boarder in 1837; after he married Fanny Appleton, her father made the house a wedding present. The current furnishings and books belonged to the Longfellows and their descendants. The Vassall-Craigie-Longfellow House was built in 1759 and served as George Washington's headquarters in 1775 and 1776, during the siege of Boston; note the bust of the president at the bottom of the stairs in the first-floor entry hall. ⏱ 1 hr. 105 Brattle St. (at

Longfellow Park). ☎ 617/491-1054. www.nps.gov/long. Tour $3 adults, free for kids 15 & under. June–Oct Wed–Sun 10am–4:30pm; always check ahead. T: Red Line to Harvard, 10-min. walk up Brattle St.

⑨ ★ **Hooper-Lee-Nichols House.** Originally constructed in 1685 and considerably altered and expanded since, the house has been the home of the Cambridge Historical Society since 1957. If your visit doesn't coincide with the limited open hours, learn more about the house's history on the society's website. **159 Brattle St. (at Lowell St.).** ☎ 617/547-4252. www.cambridgehistory.org. $5 adults. Mon & Wed 1–5pm. T: Red Line to Harvard, 10-min. walk up Brattle St.

Continue walking for about 15 min. on Brattle St., or return to Harvard Sq. and take the bus from the T station. Routes 71 and 73 run along Mount Auburn St. to our next stop.

⑩ ★★ **Mount Auburn Cemetery.** Consecrated in 1831, Mount Auburn was the first of the "garden cemeteries" that gained popularity as urban centers became too congested to support the expansion of downtown burying grounds. I find all cemeteries interesting; this one is a particularly fascinating combination of landscaping, statuary, sculpture, architecture, and, most important, history. You can tour on foot or in a car, using a rented tape or CD. Stop at the visitor center in Story Chapel for an overview and a look at the changing exhibits, or ask at the office or front gate for brochures and a map. The notable people buried here range from Charles Bulfinch, who died in 1844, to Bernard Malamud, who died in 1986. They include Mary Baker Eddy, Isabella Stewart Gardner, Oliver Wendell Holmes, Julia Ward Howe, Winslow Homer, Henry Wadsworth Longfellow, and abolitionist Charles Sumner, among many others—and their numbers continue to grow. Bear in mind that Mount Auburn is an active cemetery: Animals and recreational activities (including picnicking and jogging) are forbidden. ⏱ 2 hr. 580 Mount Auburn St. (at Brattle St. & Aberdeen Ave.). ☎ 617/547-7105. www.mountauburn.org. Tape or CD tour rental $7 ($15 deposit). May–Sept daily 8am–7pm; Oct–Apr daily 8am–5pm. Visitor center Apr–Oct daily 9am–4pm; closed Sun Nov–Mar & year-round during burials. T: Red Line to Harvard, then bus 71 or 73.

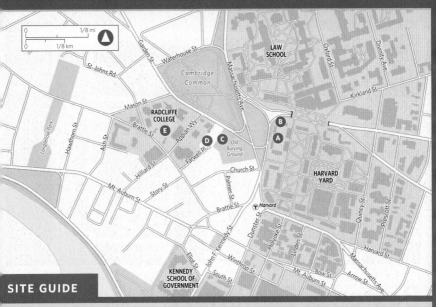

SITE GUIDE

⑤ Cambridge Common

The beaten track around Harvard Square is beaten indeed, but even this frenzied neighborhood offers some pockets of peace and (relative) quiet. One is Ⓐ **Holden Chapel,** a tiny Georgian building in Harvard Yard. Completed in 1744, it also served as a garage, a storeroom, office space, barracks for Revolutionary War troops serving under George Washington, and an anatomy lab. Nearby, in the quietest corner of the Yard, is Ⓑ **Phillips Brooks House** (1899), the name of both the building and the public-service association that makes its headquarters here. By design, the 19th-century structure matches its 18th-century neighbors. The Ⓒ **Old Burying Ground,** sometimes called the Cambridge Burying Ground, was established in 1635, a year before the university. As you explore the compact area, some 2 centuries' worth of examples can help you trace evolving fashions in gravestones. Around the corner at Zero Garden St. is Ⓓ **Christ Church,** the oldest standing church building in Cambridge. Designed by Peter Harrison, architect of King's Chapel in Boston, it opened in 1761. The building is wood, with some long-standing war wounds: British muskets made the bullet holes

in the vestibule during the Revolution. A brick wall surrounds Ⓔ **Radcliffe Yard.** Founded as the Harvard Annex in 1879 and chartered as Radcliffe College in 1894, Harvard's "sister school" existed on paper until 1999. The creation of the Radcliffe Institute for Advanced Study completed a phasing-out process that began in 1943, when Radcliffe students first gained admission to Harvard classrooms. Harvard Yard is large and dramatic, with people racing every which way; Radcliffe Yard is an enclave of serenity.

Boston & Cambridge Shopping Best Bets

Best Souvenirs
★★★ **Museum of Fine Arts Gift Shop,** Faneuil Hall Marketplace (p. 94)

Most Fun Gifts
★★★ **Joie de Vivre,** 1792 Mass Ave, Cambridge (p. 94)

Most Socially Conscious Gifts
★★★ **Ten Thousand Villages,** 694 Mass Ave, Cambridge (p. 94)

Best Offbeat Gifts
★★ **High Gear Jewelry,** 204 Hanover St. (p. 94)

Best Fancy Jewelry
★★ **John Lewis, Inc.,** 97 Newbury St. (p. 95)

Best Antiques
★★★ **Upstairs Downstairs Antiques,** 93 Charles St. (p. 92)

Best Children's Clothing
★ **The Red Wagon,** 69 Charles St. (p. 93)

Best Craft Supplies
★★ **Paper Source,** 338 Boylston St. & branches (p. 93)

Most Unexpected
★★★ **International Poster Gallery,** 205 Newbury St. (p. 92)

Best Home Decor
★ **Koo de Kir,** 65 Chestnut St. (p. 94)

Best Reason to Visit Harvard Square
★★ **Colonial Drug,** 49 Brattle St., Cambridge (p. 95)

Best Bubbles
★★★ **Lush,** 166 Newbury St. & branches (p. 95)

Best Toys for Adults
★★ **Black Ink,** 101 Charles St. & 5 Brattle St., Cambridge (p. 94)

Best Toys for Kids
★★ **Stellabella Toys,** 1967 Mass Ave & 1360 Cambridge St., Cambridge (p. 93)

Most Teen-Friendly
★**Newbury Comics,** 332 Newbury St. & branches (p. 95)

Best Salute to Texas
★**Helen's Leather Shop,** 110 Charles St. (p. 94)

> *The International Poster Gallery, a highlight of Newbury Street.*

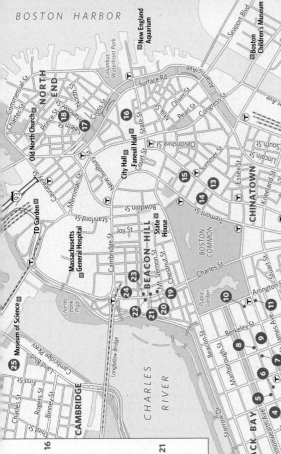

Boston Shopping

Barbara Krakow Gallery 10
Barnes & Noble 2
Barneys New York 3
Black Ink 24
CambridgeSide Galleria 25
Copley Place 3
Crush Boutique 24
DSW Shoe Warehouse 15
Eddie Bauer Outlet 13
Faneuil Hall Marketplace 16
Filene's Basement 9
Galeria Cubana 12
Helen's Leather Shop 22
High Gear Jewelry 17
International Poster Gallery 4
John Lewis, Inc. 8

Kiehl's Since 1851 7
Koo de Kir 19
Lush 6
Museum of Fine Arts Gift Shop 16
Newbury Comics 1
Paper Source 11
The Red Wagon 20
Sephora 2
The Shops at
Prudential Center 2
Society of Arts and Crafts 5
SoWa Open Market 12
Upstairs Downstairs Antiques 21
The Velvet Fly 18
Windsor Button 14

Boston & Cambridge Shopping A to Z

Antiques & Collectibles

★★★ **Upstairs Downstairs Antiques** BEACON HILL The merchandise at this subterranean shop reflects the owner's discerning eye and nose for value. 93 Charles St. (at Pinckney St.). ☎ 617/367-1950. MC, V. T: Red Line to Charles/MGH. Map p. 91.

Art

★★★ **Barbara Krakow Gallery** BACK BAY This gallery is an important destination for paintings, sculptures, drawings, and prints. 10 Newbury St. (at Arlington St.), 5th floor. ☎ 617/262-4490. www.barbarakrakowgallery.com. No credit cards. T: Green Line to Arlington. Map p. 91.

★★ **Galería Cubana** SOUTH END Cuban art direct from the island, in many styles and media, makes this destination a must. 460 Harrison Ave. (at Thayer St.). ☎ 617/292-2822. www.lagaleriacubana.com. AE, MC, V.

T: Orange Line to New England Medical Center or Silver Line to E. Berkeley St. Map p. 91.

★★★ **International Poster Gallery** BACK BAY The huge stock of vintage posters here is always worth a look. 205 Newbury St. (at Exeter & Fairfield sts.). ☎ 617/375-0076. www.international poster.com. AE, MC, V. T: Green Line to Copley. Map p. 91.

Books

★ kids **Barnes & Noble** BACK BAY A large branch of the national chain; check ahead for kids' events. There's also a location at Boston University. Shops at Prudential Center, 800 Boylston St. (at Fairfield St.). ☎ 617/247-6959. www.barnesandnoble.com. AE, DISC, MC, V. T: Green Line E to Prudential. Map p. 91. Boston University store: 660 Beacon St. (Commonwealth Ave.). ☎ 617/267-8484. www.bu. bkstore.com. T: Green Line B, C, or D to Kenmore.

> *The Harvard Coop rhymes with "hoop"—Yale calls its campus bookstore the "co-op."*

★★★ Harvard Book Store CAMBRIDGE

Great selections of new books upstairs, remainders and used books downstairs, and bookworms everywhere. Check out the high-tech machine that prints books to order. 1256 Mass Ave (at Plympton St.). ☎ 800/542-7323. www.harvard.com. AE, DISC, MC, V. T: Red Line to Harvard. Map p. 93.

Children: Fashion & Toys

★ kids The Red Wagon BEACON HILL

This welcoming space overflows with toys and gorgeous, pricey clothing and shoes for infants to preteens. 69 Charles St. (at Mount Vernon St.). ☎ 617/523-9402. www.theredwagon.com. AE, DISC, MC, V. T: Red Line to Charles/MGH. Map p. 91.

★★ Stellabella Toys CAMBRIDGE

The helpful staff can help navigate the wide selection, which includes lots of wooden toys but no guns. 1967 Mass Ave (at Allen & Beech sts.). ☎ 617/864-6290. www.stellabellatoys. com. T: Red Line to Porter. Also at 1360 Cambridge St. (Oak & Springfield sts.). ☎ 617/491-6290. T: Red Line to Central, 10-min. walk. Map p. 93.

Craft Galleries & Craft Supplies
★★ Paper Source BACK BAY

Gorgeous wrapping, writing, and craft papers complement gifts, books, stickers, stamps, and much more. 338 Boylston St. (at Arlington St.). ☎ 617/536-3444. www.paper-source.com. AE, DISC, MC, V. T: Green Line to Arlington. Map p. 91. Cambridge store: 1810 Mass Ave (Arlington St.). ☎ 617/497-1077. T: Red Line to Porter. Map p. 93.

★★ Society of Arts and Crafts BACK BAY

This nonprofit society specializes in contemporary American work. There's a gallery on the second floor. 175 Newbury St. (at Dartmouth & Exeter sts.). ☎ 617/266-1810. www.societyofcrafts.org. AE, MC, V. T: Green Line to Copley. Map p. 91.

★ Windsor Button DOWNTOWN CROSSING

Buttons, sewing notions, and everything you'd ever need for knitting and crocheting. 35 Temple Place (at Washington & Tremont sts.). ☎ 617/482-4969. www.windsorbutton.com. AE, MC, V. T: Red or Orange Line to Downtown Crossing. Map p. 91.

Cambridge Shopping

Colonial Drug 4
Harvard Book Store 5
Joie de Vivre 3
Oona's Experienced Clothing 6
Paper Source 2
Stellabella Toys 1
Ten Thousand Villages 7

> Oona's Experienced Clothing will dress you from head to toe.

Discount Shopping

★★ **Eddie Bauer Outlet** DOWNTOWN CROSSING
The sportswear specialist nicks some prices and slashes others. 500 Washington St. (at Temple Place). ☎ 617/423-4722. www.eddie bauer.com. AE, DISC, MC, V. T: Red or Orange Line to Downtown Crossing. Map p. 91.

★ **Filene's Basement** BACK BAY
This close to Newbury Street, any discount is welcome—and some of the deals here are terrific. 497 Boylston St. (at Clarendon St.). ☎ 617/424-5520. www.filenesbasement.com. AE, DISC, MC, V. T: Green Line to Copley. Map p. 91.

Fashion

★★ **Crush Boutique** BEACON HILL
Women's fashions, often by young designers, a good range of prices, and terrific service. 131 Charles St. (at Revere & Cambridge sts.). ☎ 617/720-0010. www.shopcrushboutique.com. AE, MC, V. T: Red Line to Charles/MGH. Map p. 91.

★ **Helen's Leather Shop** BEACON HILL
Western boots and shirts, leather jackets and coats, and beautiful accessories make Helen's a favorite with displaced Texans. 110 Charles St. (at Pinckney St.). ☎ 617/742-2077. www.helensleather.com. AE, DISC, MC, V. T: Red Line to Charles/MGH. Map p. 91.

★★ **Oona's Experienced Clothing** HARVARD SQUARE Oona's carries a choice stock of vintage clothing, accessories, and jewelry. 1210 Mass Ave (at Arrow St.). ☎ 617/491-2654. AE, MC, V. T: Red Line to Harvard. Map p. 93.

★ **The Velvet Fly** NORTH END
Vintage fashion, fashion with a vintage vibe, and eye-catching accessories make this boutique worth a detour from the tourist track. 28 Parmenter St. (at Hanover & Salem sts.). ☎ 617/557-4359. www.thevelvetfly.com. MC, V. T: Green or Orange Line to Haymarket. Map p. 91.

Gifts & Home Accessories

★★ kids **Black Ink** BEACON HILL
The constantly changing stock of funky gifts and household items, games, toys, and office accessories means Black Ink is never the same twice. The Harvard Square branch is equally delightful. 101 Charles St. (at Revere & Pinckney sts.). ☎ 617/723-3883. AE, DC, MC, V. T: Red Line to Charles/MGH. Map p. 91. Cambridge store: 5 Brattle St. (John F. Kennedy St.). ☎ 617/497-1221. T: Red Line to Harvard.

★★★ **Joie de Vivre** CAMBRIDGE
My favorite gift shop carries an incredible selection of sophisticated and retro toys, jewelry, notecards, puzzles, and more. 1792 Mass Ave (at Arlington St.). ☎ 617/864-8188. AE, MC, V. T: Red Line to Porter. Map p. 93.

★ **Koo de Kir** BEACON HILL
Contemporary style on Beacon Hill is unexpected but delightful—like the well-edited selection of gifts, jewelry, furniture, and home and kitchen accessories here. 65 Chestnut St. (at Charles St.). ☎ 617/723-8111. www.koodekir.com. AE, MC, V. T: Red Line to Charles/MGH. Map p. 91.

★ **Museum of Fine Arts Gift Shop** FANEUIL HALL MARKETPLACE A "greatest hits" selection of items from the museum's in-house shop. 3 S. Market Building (at Chatham Row). ☎ 617/720-1266. www.mfashop.org. AE, DISC, MC, V. T: Green or Blue Line to Government Center. Map p. 91.

★ kids **Ten Thousand Villages** CENTRAL SQUARE
The fair-trade chain specializes in handicrafts by international artisans. 694 Mass Ave (at Western Ave. & Pleasant St.). ☎ 617/876-2414. www.tenthousandvillages.com. DISC, MC, V. T: Red Line to Central. Map p. 93.

Jewelry

★★ **High Gear Jewelry** NORTH END
Classic and contemporary costume jewelry beckons from the front window of this shop on the Freedom Trail. 204 Hanover St. (at Cross

St.). ☎ 617/523-5084. MC, V. T: Green or Orange Line to Haymarket. Map p. 91.

★★★ John Lewis, Inc. BACK BAY
Unique designs crafted on the premises in platinum, gold, and silver are both lovely and imaginative. 97 Newbury St. (at Clarendon St.). ☎ 617/266-6665. www.johnlewisinc.com. MC, V. T: Green Line to Arlington. Map p. 91.

Malls & Shopping Center
★★ Copley Place BACK BAY
This enclave of boutiques and high-end mall brands, which has a branch of Neiman Marcus, adjoins the Shops at Prudential Center (see below). 100 Huntington Ave. (at Dartmouth St.). ☎ 617/369-5000. www.shopcopleyplace.com. T: Orange Line to Back Bay. Map p. 91.

★ kids Faneuil Hall Marketplace DOWNTOWN
Somewhat generic retail spread across five buildings. Check the pushcarts for more creative items. North, Congress & State sts. & Atlantic Ave. ☎ 617/338-2323. www.faneuilhallmarketplace.com. T: Green or Blue Line to Government Center, or Orange Line to Haymarket. Map p. 91.

★ kids The Shops at Prudential Center BACK BAY
The Pru, as it's known, mixes mostly unsurprising shops and boutiques with pushcarts. 800 Boylston St. (at Fairfield St.). ☎ 800/746-7778. www.prudentialcenter.com. T: Green Line E to Prudential or Green Line to Copley. Map p. 91.

Markets
★ kids SoWa Open Market SOUTH END
This funky market offers crafts, jewelry, antiques, produce, flowers, and baked goods. Open Sundays mid-May through October (10am–5pm). 460 Harrison Ave. (at Thayer St.). ☎ 800/403-8305. www.sowaopenmarket.com. Some vendors accept cash only. T: Orange Line to Back Bay, 10-min walk; or Silver Line to E. Berkeley St. Map p. 91.

Music
★ Newbury Comics BACK BAY
The novelty items, T-shirts, posters, and comics nearly outshine the new and used CDs, including imports and independent labels. 332 Newbury St. (at Hereford St. & Mass Ave). ☎ 617/236-4930. www.newburycomics.com. AE, DISC, MC, V. T: Green Line B, C, or D to Hynes Convention Center. Check website for branches. Map p. 91.

> *For memorable souvenirs, visit the Society of Arts and Crafts, on Newbury Street.*

Perfume & Cosmetics
★★ Colonial Drug CAMBRIDGE
My favorite hard-to-find fragrance is one of the 1,000 options here (along with numerous body-care products). 49 Brattle St. (at Church St. & Appian Way). ☎ 617/864-2222. www.colonialdrug.com. No credit cards. T: Red Line to Harvard. Map p. 93.

★ Kiehl's Since 1851 BACK BAY
The skin, hair, and body preparations here have a deservedly cultlike following. 112 Newbury St. (at Clarendon St.). ☎ 617/247-1777. www.kiehls.com. AE, DC, MC, V. T: Green Line to Copley. Map p. 91.

★★★ Lush BACK BAY
The U.K.-based chain is known for fresh, organic, and natural products that smell fantastic. 166 Newbury St. (at Dartmouth & Exeter sts.). ☎ 617/375-5874. www.lush.com. AE, MC, V. T: Green Line to Copley. Map p. 91. Cambridge store: 30 John F. Kennedy St. (Mount Auburn St.). ☎ 617/497-5874. T: Red Line to Harvard.

★ Sephora BACK BAY
A vast assortment of cosmetics and fragrances, with plenty of testers and helpful staff members. Shops at Prudential Center, 800 Boylston St. (at Fairfield St.). ☎ 617/262-4200. www.sephora.com. AE, DISC, MC, V. T: Green Line to Copley. Map p. 91. Cambridge store: CambridgeSide Galleria, 100 CambridgeSide Place (First St. & Land Blvd.). ☎ 617/577-1005. T: Green Line to Lechmere.

Boston & Cambridge Restaurant Best Bets

Best Seafood
★★★ **Legal Sea Foods** 255 State St. & branches (p. 102)

Best Old-Time Boston Experience
★★ **Durgin-Park** 340 Faneuil Hall Marketplace (p. 98)

Best Pizza
★★ **Pizzeria Regina** 11½ Thacher St. (p. 104)

Best for Business
★★ **Sultan's Kitchen** 116 State St. (p. 105)

Best Burgers
★★ **Mr. Bartley's Burger Cottage** 1246 Mass Ave, Cambridge (p. 102)

Best Old-School Raw Bar
★ **Ye Olde Union Oyster House** 41 Union St. (p. 105)

Best Newfangled Raw Bar
★★ **Neptune Oyster** 63 Salem St. (p. 103)

Best When Money Is No Object
★★★ **Market** 100 Stuart St., in the W Boston hotel (p. 102)

Best Down-Home Italian
★ **La Summa** 30 Fleet St. (p. 102)

Best Fancy Italian
★★★ **Mamma Maria** 3 North Sq. (p. 102)

Best Brunch
★★ **S&S Restaurant** 1334 Cambridge St., Cambridge (p. 104)

Best Mediterranean
★★ **Oleana** 134 Hampshire St., Cambridge (p. 103)

Most Romantic
★★ **UpStairs on the Square** 91 Winthrop St., Cambridge (p. 105)

Best Sushi
★ **Sakurabana** 57 Broad St. (p. 104)

Best Dim Sum
★★ **Hei La Moon** 88 Beach St. (p. 100)

Best Clam Shack
★★ **Jasper White's Summer Shack** 50 Dalton St. (p. 101)

Most Unusual Combo
★ **The Elephant Walk** 900 Beacon St. (p. 99)

Most Unusual Transatlantic Combo
★ **Taranta Cucina Meridionale** 210 Hanover St. (p. 105)

> *Red Sox fever even strikes the classy Monday Club Bar at UpStairs on the Square.*

Boston & Cambridge Restaurants A to Z

★★ kids **Artú** NORTH END *ITALIAN*
Three storefronts on the Freedom Trail make up this neighborhood favorite, which serves terrific sandwiches, pastas, and roasted meats. 6 Prince St. (at Hanover St. & North Sq.). ☎ 617/742-4336. www.artuboston.com. Entrees $6–$23. AE, MC, V. Lunch & dinner daily. T: Green or Orange Line to Haymarket. Map p. 98.

★★ **Bangkok City** BACK BAY *THAI*
The best Thai restaurant in town serves excellent takes on the usual noodle dishes, as well as a huge variety of curries. 167 Mass Ave (at Haviland St.). ☎ 617/266-8884. www.bkkcityboston.com. Entrees $8–$17. AE, DC, DISC, MC, V. Lunch & dinner Mon–Sat, dinner Sun. T: Green Line B, C, or D to Hynes Convention Center. Map p. 100.

★ **Baraka Café** CAMBRIDGE *ALGERIAN/TUNISIAN* The inauspicious location, on a dreary side street, belies the wonderfully flavorful cuisine and colorful, welcoming atmosphere. No alcohol. 80½ Pearl St. (at William St.). ☎ 617/868-3951. www.barakacafe.com. Entrees $5–$16. No credit cards. Lunch Tues–Sat, dinner Tues–Sun. T: Red Line to Central. Map p. 99.

★ kids **Barking Crab** WATERFRONT *SEAFOOD*
Grab a seat on the deck of this colorful crab shack overlooking the Fort Point Channel (which separates downtown from South Boston), sip a beer, and snack on some fresh seafood. 88 Sleeper St. (at Northern Ave.). ☎ 617/426-2722. www.barkingcrab.com. Entrees $7–$25. AE, DC, MC, V. Lunch & dinner daily. T: Blue Line to Aquarium & 10-min. walk, or Red Line to South Station & 10-min. walk. Map p. 98.

★ kids **Border Café** CAMBRIDGE *TEX-MEX*
The nonstop party, well lubricated with margaritas and beer, overshadows the tasty enchiladas, fajitas, tacos, and such at this longtime Harvard hangout. 32 Church St. (at Palmer St.). ☎ 617/864-6100. www.bordercafe.com. Entrees $7–$18. AE, MC, V. Lunch & dinner daily. T: Red Line to Harvard. Map p. 99.

★ **Brasserie Jo** BACK BAY *FRENCH*
A classic brasserie, with long hours and a wide-ranging menu, this restaurant is a delightful pit stop (and open until 1am daily). 120 Huntington Ave. (at W. Newton & Garrison sts.), in the Colonnade Hotel Boston. ☎ 617/425-3240. www.brasseriejoboston.com. Entrees $10–$32.

> *The patio at the Elephant Walk in Cambridge.*

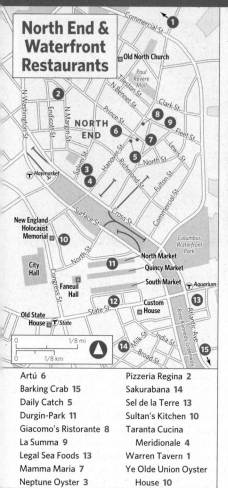

North End & Waterfront Restaurants

- Commercial St. ①
- Old North Church
- Paul Revere Mall
- Tileston St.
- N. Bennet St.
- Clark St.
- Prince St.
- Fleet St.
- Lewis St.
- North St.
- Richmond St.
- Hanover St.
- Salem St.
- Fulton St.
- Commercial St.
- Cross St.
- Surface St.
- North St.
- Columbus Waterfront Park
- North Market
- Quincy Market
- South Market
- Aquarium
- Custom House
- State St.
- Milk St.
- India St.
- Broad St.
- Rose Kennedy Greenway
- Atlantic Ave.
- N. Washington St.
- N. Margin St.
- Endicott St.
- Haymarket
- New England Holocaust Memorial ⑩
- City Hall
- Congress St.
- Faneuil Hall
- Old State House — State
- ② ⑥ ⑧ ⑨ ⑦ ⑤ ③ ④ ⑪ ⑫ ⑬ ⑭ ⑮

0 1/8 mi
0 1/8 km

Artú 6	Pizzeria Regina 2
Barking Crab 15	Sakurabana 14
Daily Catch 5	Sel de la Terre 13
Durgin-Park 11	Sultan's Kitchen 10
Giacomo's Ristorante 8	Taranta Cucina
La Summa 9	Meridionale 4
Legal Sea Foods 13	Warren Tavern 1
Mamma Maria 7	Ye Olde Union Oyster
Neptune Oyster 3	House 10

> *Giacomo's Ristorante, in the North End, is well worth the often epic wait.*

V. Dim sum, lunch & dinner daily. T: Orange Line to Chinatown. Map p. 100.

★ Daily Catch NORTH END SEAFOOD/ITALIAN

Follow the aroma of garlic to this tiny storefront, where the specialty is calamari (squid) and everything is delicious. 323 Hanover St. (at Prince St.). ☎ 617/523-8567. www.dailycatch.com. Entrees $17–$27. No credit cards. Lunch & dinner daily. T: Green or Orange Line to Haymarket. Map p. 98.

★★★ Davio's Northern Italian Steakhouse BACK BAY NORTHERN ITALIAN/STEAK

Northern Italian classics, including the best lobster risotto around, share the menu with steakhouse favorites and inventive sides. Somehow, it works beautifully. 75 Arlington St. (at Stuart St.). ☎ 617/357-4810. www.davios.com. Entrees $17–$51. AE, DC, DISC, MC, V. Lunch weekdays, dinner daily. T: Green Line to Arlington. Map p. 100.

★★ kids Durgin-Park FANEUIL HALL MARKETPLACE NEW ENGLAND

Communal tables give the dining rooms a boardinghouse feel, but they're not terribly noisy—everyone's mouth is full of delicious home-style food. 340 Faneuil Hall Marketplace (at Clinton St.). ☎ 617/227-2038. www.durgin-park.com. Entrees $10–$40, specials market

AE, DC, DISC, MC, V. Breakfast, lunch & dinner daily. T: Green Line E to Prudential. Map p. 100.

★★ The Bristol Lounge BACK BAY AMERICAN

This upscale hotel restaurant and lounge serves astoundingly good comfort food. 200 Boylston St. (at Hadassah Way), in the Four Seasons Hotel. ☎ 617/338-4400. www.fourseasons.com/boston. Entrees $18–$35. AE, DC, DISC, MC, V. Breakfast, lunch, afternoon tea & dinner daily. T: Green Line to Arlington. Map p. 100.

★★ kids China Pearl CHINATOWN CHINESE

One of the city's top dim sum destinations, China Pearl is also popular with groups and families for dinner. 9 Tyler St. (at Beach St.), 2nd floor. ☎ 617/426-4338. Entrees $7–$20. AE, MC,

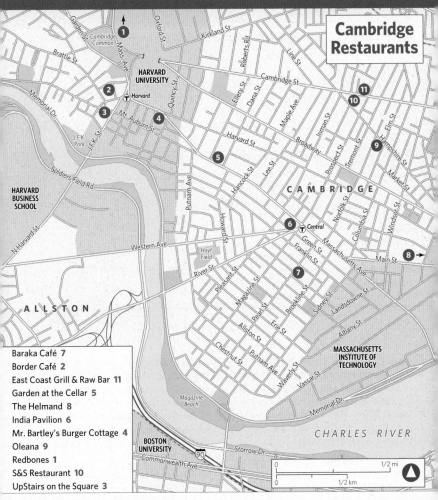

Cambridge
Restaurants

Baraka Café **7**
Border Café **2**
East Coast Grill & Raw Bar **11**
Garden at the Cellar **5**
The Helmand **8**
India Pavilion **6**
Mr. Bartley's Burger Cottage **4**
Oleana **9**
Redbones **1**
S&S Restaurant **10**
UpStairs on the Square **3**

price. AE, DC, DISC, MC, V. Lunch & dinner daily.
T: Green or Blue Line to Government Center.
Map p. 98.

★★★ kids East Coast Grill & Raw Bar CAMBRIDGE
SEAFOOD/BARBECUE
This place is a riot—of colors, flavors, and fun.
It's been one of the best seafood restaurants
in New England for more than 2 decades. 1271
Cambridge St. (at Prospect St.). ☎ 617/491-6568.
www.eastcoastgrill.net. Entrees $15–$30, fresh
seafood market price. AE, MC, V. Dinner daily,
brunch Sun. T: Red Line to Central, 10-min. walk.
Map p. 99.

★★ The Elephant Walk BACK BAY FRENCH/
CAMBODIAN French on one side, Cambodian
on the other, this is the most interesting menu
in Boston—serving some of the tastiest food.
900 Beacon St. (at Park Dr.). ☎ 617/247-1500.
www.elephantwalk.com. Entrees $8–$23. AE, DC,
DISC, MC, V. Lunch weekdays, brunch Sun, dinner
daily. T: Green Line C to St. Mary's St. Map p. 100.

★ Finale THEATER DISTRICT DESSERT/LIGHT
FARE Finale isn't a restaurant; it's a "desserte-
rie." It serves appetizer-size portions of savory
dishes—including soup, pizzas, and sandwiches—even as it answers the prayers of anyone

Back Bay & Chinatown Restaurants

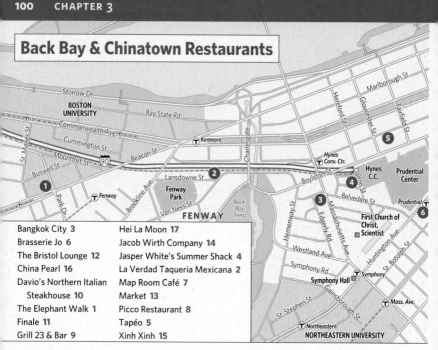

Bangkok City **3**
Brasserie Jo **6**
The Bristol Lounge **12**
China Pearl **16**
Davio's Northern Italian
   Steakhouse **10**
The Elephant Walk **1**
Finale **11**
Grill 23 & Bar **9**
Hei La Moon **17**
Jacob Wirth Company **14**
Jasper White's Summer Shack **4**
La Verdad Taqueria Mexicana **2**
Map Room Café **7**
Market **13**
Picco Restaurant **8**
Tapéo **5**
Xinh Xinh **15**

who's ever wanted to eat dessert first. 1 Columbus Ave. (at Park Plaza). ☎ 617/423-3184. www.finaledesserts.com. Entrees $6–$15. AE, MC, V. Lunch & dinner daily. T: Green Line to Arlington. Map p. 100. Also at 30 Dunster St. (Mount Auburn St.), Cambridge. ☎ 617/441-9797. Lunch & dinner daily. Map p. 100.

★★ **Garden at the Cellar** CAMBRIDGE AMERICAN Don't be fooled by the setting—a small, crowded bar. This top-notch gastropub uses the finest local ingredients in its outrageously flavorful seasonal cuisine. 991 Mass Ave (at Dana St.). ☎ 617/230-5880. www.gardenatthe cellar.com. Entrees $9–$26. MC, V. Lunch Tues-Sat, brunch Sun, dinner daily. T: Red Line to Central or Harvard, 10-min. walk. Map p. 99.

★★ **Giacomo's Ristorante** NORTH END ITALIAN/SEAFOOD The line is long, the dining room is small, and the food is worth the trouble. Be sure to check the specials board, where the kitchen promotes some of its best work. 355 Hanover St. (at Fleet St.). ☎ 617/523-9026. Entrees $14–$22. No credit cards. Dinner daily. T: Green or Orange Line to Haymarket. Map p. 98.

★ **Grill 23 & Bar** BACK BAY STEAKS
The city's top steakhouse is a magnet for the high-rolling, deal-making set. I could make a meal of the toothsome a la carte side dishes. 161 Berkeley St. (at Stuart St.). ☎ 617/542-2255. www.grill23.com. Entrees $23–$49. AE, DC, DISC, MC, V. Dinner daily. T: Green Line to Arlington. Map p. 100.

★★★ **Hei La Moon** CHINATOWN DIM SUM/CHINESE The best dim sum in the city—the variety is largest on weekends—brings huge crowds to this cavernous restaurant. It's worth the wait. 88 Beach St. (at Surface Artery). ☎ 617/338-8813. Entrees $8–$15. MC, V. Dim sum, lunch & dinner daily. T: Orange Line to New England Medical Center. Map p. 100.

★ **The Helmand** CAMBRIDGE AFGHAN
The cuisine at this elegant restaurant is reminiscent of Indian, Pakistani, and Middle Eastern food. It's flavorful, filling but not heavy, and vegetarian-friendly. 143 First St. (at Bent St.). ☎ 617/492-4646. www.helmandrestaurant cambridge.com. Entrees $13–$23. AE, MC, V. Dinner daily. T: Green Line to Lechmere. Map p. 99.

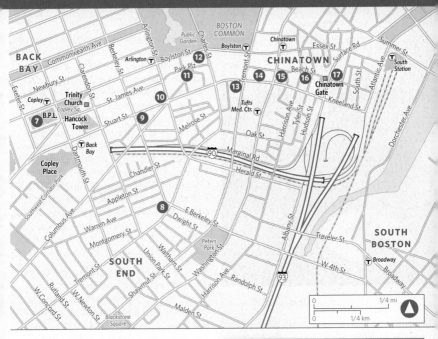

★ India Pavilion CAMBRIDGE *INDIAN*

Hit the lunch buffet to sample a wide variety of specialties, or try a house dinner for two or a *thali* (literally, "plate") selection for a good introduction. 17 Central Sq. (at Green St.). ☎ 617/547-7463. www.royalbharatinc.com. Entrees $8–$19, lunch buffet $8. AE, DC, MC, V. Lunch & dinner daily. T: Red Line to Central. Map p. 99.

★ Jacob Wirth Company THEATER DISTRICT

GERMAN/AMERICAN The long bar and wooden floor suggest a vintage saloon, and rib-sticking specialties such as wursts and Wiener schnitzel share the menu with comfort food like chicken potpie. 31–37 Stuart St. (at Tremont St.). ☎ 617/338-8586. www.jacobwirth.com. Entrees $9–$23. AE, DC, DISC, MC, V. Lunch & dinner daily. T: Green Line to Boylston. Map p. 100.

★★ kids Jasper White's Summer Shack BACK

BAY SEAFOOD The Summer Shack feels like a casual seaside place (think corn dogs, lobster rolls, and fried clams) and tastes like the brainchild of a gourmet chef (think pan-roasted lobster with chervil and chives). 50 Dalton St. (at Boylston & Scotia sts.). ☎ 617/867-9955. www.summershackrestaurant.com. Entrees

Chowderfest

Chowder, a thick soup most commonly made with clams, is a New England delicacy. More than 2,000 gallons are served up in City Hall Plaza during Chowderfest, a cornerstone of the annual Harborfest celebrations (www. bostonharborfest.com). Boston's most ambitious restaurants ladle out their "chowda" to be guzzled or shunned by voting fans. A few dollars buys you unlimited access to the hot and creamy seafood soup. (Remember that Manhattan chowder, with its tomato base, is taboo in these parts—New Englanders are fiercely picky and protective when it comes to this cream-based soup.)

> *Jacob Wirth has fed German food to hungry Bostonians since 1868.*

$8–$36. AE, DISC, MC, V. Lunch weekdays (except Nov–Mar), brunch weekends, dinner daily. T: Green Line B, C, or D to Hynes Convention Center. Map p. 100.

★ **La Summa** NORTH END *ITALIAN*
A neighborhood native owns and runs La Summa, a friendly place where many specialties are family recipes; try the handmade pasta. 30 Fleet St. (at Hanover & North sts.). ☎ 617/523-9503. www.lasumma.com. Entrees $8–$24. AE, DC, DISC, MC, V. Lunch Thurs–Sun, dinner daily. T: Green or Orange Line to Haymarket. Map p. 98.

★ **La Verdad Taqueria Mexicana** FENWAY
MEXICAN The food seems pricey, but the ingredients are top-notch. Start with the grilled corn (thank me later), and opt for tacos over a burrito. Fenway Park is across the street; before and after games, this place is a zoo. 1 Lansdowne St. (at Ipswich St.). ☎ 617/421-9595. www.laverdadtaqueria.com. Entrees $9–$19. AE, DC, DISC, MC, V. Lunch & dinner daily. T: Green Line B, C, or D to Kenmore, 10-min. walk. Map p. 100.

★★★ kids **Legal Sea Foods** WATERFRONT *SEA-FOOD* I'd love to point you to a hole in the wall and say, "There's the secret place that only the locals know about—it's the best seafood restaurant in the Boston area." I can't, though. Legal's is no secret, but it is the best. 255 State St. (at Atlantic Ave.). ☎ 617/742-5300. www.legalseafoods.com. Entrees $14–$35. AE, DC, DISC, MC, V. Lunch & dinner daily. T: Blue Line to Aquarium. Branches: Prudential Center, 800 Boylston St. (Fairfield St.), ☎ 617/266-6800, T: Green Line B, C, or D to Hynes Convention Center; Park Sq., 36 Park Plaza (Columbus Ave. & Stuart St.), ☎ 617/426-4444, T: Green Line to Arlington; Copley Place, 100 Huntington Ave. (Dartmouth St.), 2nd level, ☎ 617/266-7775, T: Orange Line to Back Bay; Charles Hotel, 20 University Rd. (Bennett St.), Cambridge, ☎ 617/491-9400, T: Red Line to Harvard; 5 Cambridge Center (Main & Ames sts.), ☎ 617/864-3400, T: Red Line to Kendall/MIT. Maps p. 98.

★★★ **Mamma Maria** NORTH END *NORTHERN ITALIAN* My favorite North End restaurant serves creative cuisine in a romantic town house. The best dish is *osso buco,* and anything with seafood is wonderful. 3 North Sq. (at Prince & Garden Court sts.). ☎ 617/523-0077. www.mammamaria.com. Entrees $26–$40. AE, DC, DISC, MC, V. Dinner daily. T: Green or Orange Line to Haymarket. Map p. 98.

★ kids **Map Room Café** BACK BAY *LIGHT FARE*
A retreat from the Back Bay's pandemonium, this self-service spot serves tasty soups, salads, sandwiches, and sweets. And you get to talk in a library. 700 Boylston St. (at Dartmouth St.), in the Boston Public Library. ☎ 617/385-5660. Entrees $5–$8. No credit cards. Breakfast & lunch Mon–Sat. T: Green Line to Copley. Map p. 100.

★★★ **Market** THEATER DISTRICT *FUSION*
Jean-Georges Vongerichten's creation has it all: amazing food, attentive service, a gorgeous setting. Considering the quality, the prices, though hardly cheap, are surprisingly reasonable. Great—more money for wine. 100 Stuart St. (at Tremont St.), in the W Boston hotel. ☎ 617/310-6790. www.marketbyjgboston.com. Entrees $21–$39. AE, DC, DISC, MC, V. Breakfast, lunch & dinner daily; brunch Sat & Sun. T: Green Line to Boylston. Map p. 100.

★★ **Mr. Bartley's Burger Cottage** CAMBRIDGE *AMERICAN* Even the throngs of tourists feel at home at this neighborhood favorite, which serves sublime burgers with all the trimmings.

1246 Mass Ave (at Plympton St.). ☎ 617/354-6559. www.bartleysburgers.com. Entrees $5–$14. No credit cards. Lunch & dinner Mon–Sat. T: Red Line to Harvard. Map p. 99.

★★ **Neptune Oyster** NORTH END *SEAFOOD*
Tiny and crammed full of hungry diners, Neptune is an open secret: Some of the best seafood dishes in the city are flying out of its busy little kitchen. Be ready to wait, especially on weekends. 63 Salem St. (at Cross St.). ☎ 617/742-3474. www.neptuneoyster.com. Entrees $14–$34, lobster market price. AE, MC, V. Lunch & dinner daily. T: Green or Orange Line to Haymarket. Map p. 98.

★★ **Oleana** CAMBRIDGE *MEDITERRANEAN*
The emphatic flavors, seasonal ingredients, and cozy atmosphere make Oleana my top choice for a shot of summer on a frosty winter night. In fine weather, try for a table on the delightful patio. 134 Hampshire St. (at Elm St.). ☎ 617/661-0505. www.oleanarestaurant.com. Entrees $22–$30. AE, MC, V. Dinner daily. T: Red Line to Central, 10-min. walk. Map p. 99.

★ kids **Picco Restaurant** SOUTH END *PIZZA*
It's all in the name, which is short for "Pizza and

Outdoor Dining

Ask for your food to go or request a table outside to take full advantage of the Boston area's all-too-brief warm season. If you don't picnic, you have some appealing options. The people-watching is especially good from the patios at Tapéo (p. 105), with its view of trendy Newbury Street, and at Picco Restaurant (below), which sees a parade of South End fashionistas and their dogs. Enjoy the view from the outdoor seating area at the Barking Crab (p. 97), a great place to relax with a drink and some messy seafood. Or get away from it all with a meal on the hideaway patio at Oleana (left), or the tranquil tables a stone's throw from the frenzy of Harvard Square at the Legal Sea Foods at the Charles Hotel (p. 102).

Ice Cream Company." The excellent pizza arrives steaming from the oven; the ice cream is a perfect chaser. 513 Tremont St. (at E. Berkeley & Clarendon sts.). ☎ 617/927-0066. www.picco restaurant.com. Pizza $11 & up. MC, V. Lunch & dinner daily. T: Orange Line to Back Bay. Map p. 100.

> Both locals and visitors pack the original Pizzeria Regina, in the North End.

> *The festive bar at Tapéo, on Newbury Street, is a popular spot for tapas.*

★★ kids **Pizzeria Regina** NORTH END *PIZZA*
That picture you have in your head of a neighborhood pizza place in an old-time Italian neighborhood? This is it. 11½ Thacher St. (at N. Margin St.). ☎ 617/227-0765. www.pizzeria regina.com. Pizza $11–$18. AE, MC, V. Lunch & dinner daily. T: Green or Orange Line to Haymarket. Map p. 98.

★ kids **Redbones** SOMERVILLE *BARBECUE*
I'm sending you off the tourist trail, but it's an easy detour, and I promise you won't be sorry: Redbones serves the best barbecue (and all the trimmings) in the Boston area. 55 Chester St. (at Elm St.). ☎ 617/628-2000. www.redbones. com. Entrees $8–$21. AE, MC, V. Lunch & dinner daily. T: Red Line to Davis. Map p. 99.

★★ kids **S&S Restaurant** CAMBRIDGE *DELI*
The best weekend-brunch restaurant in the Boston area, with lines out the door, serves classic deli food all week. 1334 Cambridge St. (at Prospect & Hampshire sts.). ☎ 617/354-0777. www.sandsrestaurant.com. Entrees $4–$18. AE, MC, V. Breakfast, lunch & dinner daily;

brunch weekends. T: Red Line to Central, 10-min. walk. Map p. 99.

★ **Sakurabana** FINANCIAL DISTRICT *SUSHI/ JAPANESE* An unassuming destination for top-notch sushi, Sakurabana is a madhouse at midday (the specials and lunch boxes are good deals) and calmer after work. 57 Broad St. (at Milk St.). ☎ 617/542-4311. www.sakurabana online.com. Entrees $11–$39, sushi $2 & up. AE, DISC, MC, V. Lunch & dinner weekdays. T: Blue Line to Aquarium. Map p. 98.

★★ **Sel de la Terre** WATERFRONT *FRENCH*
Provençal flavors raise seasonal local ingredients to a new level. I've never had a disappointing fish dish here, and carnivorous friends swear by the steak frites. 255 State St. (at Atlantic Ave.). ☎ 617/720-1300. www.seldelaterre.com. Entrees $25–$32. AE, DC, DISC, MC, V. Lunch & dinner daily, weekend brunch. T: Blue Line to Aquarium. Map p. 98. Also at 774 Boylston St. (Fairfield St.), in the Mandarin Oriental, Boston hotel. Lunch & dinner daily, weekend brunch. T: Green Line to Copley. Map p. 108.

★★ **Sultan's Kitchen** FINANCIAL DISTRICT *TURKISH* Mostly a takeout place, Sultan's Kitchen is perfect for a picnic. It also has enough tables to allow for a business lunch over delectable Middle Eastern specialties and a rainbow of salads. 116 State St. (at Broad St.). ☎ 617/728-2828. www.sultans-kitchen.com. Entrees $6–$12. AE, DC, MC, V. Lunch & dinner weekdays, lunch Sat. T: Blue Line to Aquarium. Map p. 98.

★★ **Tapéo** BACK BAY *SPANISH* A perfect place for a celebration, Tapéo specializes in tapas, flavorful appetizer-like bites that go well with sangria. 266 Newbury St. (at Fairfield & Gloucester sts.). ☎ 617/267-4799. www.tapeo.com. Entrees $24–$25, tapas $5–$16. AE, DC, MC, V. Lunch weekends, dinner daily. T: Green Line B, C, or D to Hynes Convention Center. Map p. 100.

★★ **Taranta Cucina Meridionale** NORTH END *ITALIAN/PERUVIAN* The flavors of the owner-chef's native Peru jazz up Taranta's menu, creating a peerless combination of neighborhood favorite and culinary adventure. 210 Hanover St. (at Cross St.). ☎ 617/720-0052. www.tarantarist.com. Entrees $19–$36. AE, DC, MC, V. Dinner daily. T: Green or Orange Line to Haymarket. Map p. 98.

★★ **UpStairs on the Square** CAMBRIDGE *AMERICAN* The second-floor dining room, known as the Monday Club Bar, is a cozy destination for upscale comfort food. 91 Winthrop St. (at Kennedy & Eliot sts.). ☎ 617/864-1933. www.upstairsonthesquare.com. Entrees $13–$28. AE, DC, DISC, MC, V. Lunch Mon–Sat, brunch Sun, dinner daily. T: Red Line to Harvard. Map p. 99.

★ **Warren Tavern** CHARLESTOWN *AMERICAN* Built in 1780, this historic tavern is an atmospheric spot for soups, salads, sandwiches, and classic comfort-food main courses. 2 Pleasant St. (at Main St.). ☎ 617/241-8142. www.warrentavern.com. Entrees $7–$16. DISC, MC, V. Map p. 98.

★ **Xinh Xinh** CHINATOWN *VIETNAMESE* The best Vietnamese food in town comes from this little storefront, where the friendly staff can help you navigate the mile-long menu. If you already have a favorite dish, chances are Xinh Xinh prepares a tasty version of it.

> *Ye Olde Union Oyster House has stood near Faneuil Hall since 1826.*

7 Beach St. (at Knapp St.). ☎ 617/422-0501. Entrees $6–$14. MC, V. Lunch & dinner daily. T: Orange Line to Chinatown. Map p. 100.

★ kids **Ye Olde Union Oyster House** FANEUIL HALL MARKETPLACE *SEAFOOD* The country's oldest restaurant (since 1826) is on the Freedom Trail—tourist central—but very popular with locals. 41 Union St. (at North & Hanover sts.). ☎ 617/227-2750. www.unionoysterhouse.com. Entrees $17–$29. AE, DC, DISC, MC, V. Lunch & dinner daily. T: Orange or Green Line to Haymarket. Map p. 98.

Boston & Cambridge Hotel Best Bets

Best in Boston
★★★ **Four Seasons Hotel** 200 Boylston St. (p. 111)

Best in Cambridge
★★★ **The Charles Hotel** 1 Bennett St. (p. 110)

Best City Views
★★★ **Westin Copley Place Boston** 10 Huntington Ave. (p. 113)

Best Water Views
★★ **Fairmont Battery Wharf** 3 Battery Wharf (p. 110)

Most Romantic
★★ **Eliot Hotel** 370 Commonwealth Ave. (p. 110)

Best for Families
★★ **Doubletree Guest Suites** 400 Soldiers Field Rd. (p. 110)

Best Historic Hotel
★★ **The Fairmont Copley Plaza Hotel** 138 St. James Ave. (p. 110)

Best Boutique Hotel
★★ **Fifteen Beacon** 15 Beacon St. (p. 110)

Most Hospitable to Motorists
★ **MidTown Hotel** 220 Huntington Ave. (p. 112)

Best Deal on Newbury Street
★ **Newbury Guest House** 261 Newbury St. (p. 112)

Best Access to the River
★★★ **Royal Sonesta Hotel** 40 Edwin H. Land Blvd., Cambridge (p. 113)

Best Design
★ **Bulfinch Hotel** 107 Merrimac St. (p. 107)

Best for Marathon Fanatics
★ **Charlesmark Hotel** 655 Boylston St. (p. 110)

Best for Red Sox Fanatics
★★ **Hotel Commonwealth** 500 Commonwealth Ave. (p. 111)

Best for Celtics and Bruins Fanatics
★★★ **Onyx Hotel** 155 Portland St. (p. 112)

> *Fall into the lap of luxury at the Four Seasons Hotel in Boston.*

Boston & Cambridge Hotels A to Z

Anthony's Town House OUTSKIRTS/BROOK-LINE This homey guesthouse's good-size rooms share bathrooms and have high-speed Internet. 1085 Beacon St. (at Hawes St.), Brookline. ☎ 617/566-3972. www.anthonystownhouse. com. 10 units. Doubles $78–$108. No credit cards. T: Green Line C to Hawes St.

★★ The Back Bay Hotel BACK BAY Part of an Irish chain, this luxury hotel offers plush lodgings in Boston's former police headquarters. 350 Stuart St. (at Berkeley St.). ☎ 617/266-7200. www.doylecollection.com. 225 units. Doubles $205–$505. AE, DC, DISC, MC, V. T: Orange Line to Back Bay.

★★★ Boston Harbor Hotel WATERFRONT Boston's most beautiful hotel boasts gorgeous rooms, great views, and lavish amenities. Rowes Wharf (at Atlantic Ave. & High St.). ☎ 800/752-7077. www.bhh.com. 230 units. Doubles $295–$795. AE, DC, DISC, MC, V. T: Blue Line to Aquarium.

★ kids Boston Marriott Copley Place BACK BAY A fine hotel for business or pleasure, with well-appointed, generously sized rooms. 110 Huntington Ave. (at Dartmouth St.).

☎ 800/228-9290. www.copleymarriott.com. 1,147 units. Doubles $159–$329. AE, DC, DISC, MC, V. T: Green Line to Copley.

★★ kids Boston Marriott Long Wharf WATERFRONT The great location and views complement large, sunny rooms and good business features. 296 State St. (at Atlantic Ave.). ☎ 800/228-9290. www.marriottlongwharf. com. 400 units. Doubles $249–$629. AE, DC, DISC, MC, V. T: Blue Line to Aquarium.

★ Bulfinch Hotel NORTH STATION The triangular building's smallish, custom-designed rooms are a great deal for the price. 107 Merrimac St. (at Lancaster St.). ☎ 877/267-1776. www.bulfinchhotel.com. 80 units. Doubles $169–$399. AE, DC, DISC, MC, V. T: Green or Orange Line to North Station.

★ Chandler Inn Hotel SOUTH END Small, comfortable rooms in a convenient location help the largest gay-owned property in town sell out regularly. 26 Chandler St. (at Berkeley St.). ☎ 800/842-3450. www.chandlerinn.com. 56 units. Doubles $109–$279. AE, DC, DISC, MC, V. T: Orange Line to Back Bay.

> *The austere style of the Charles Hotel's guest rooms contrasts with the plush appointments.*

Boston & Cambridge Hotels

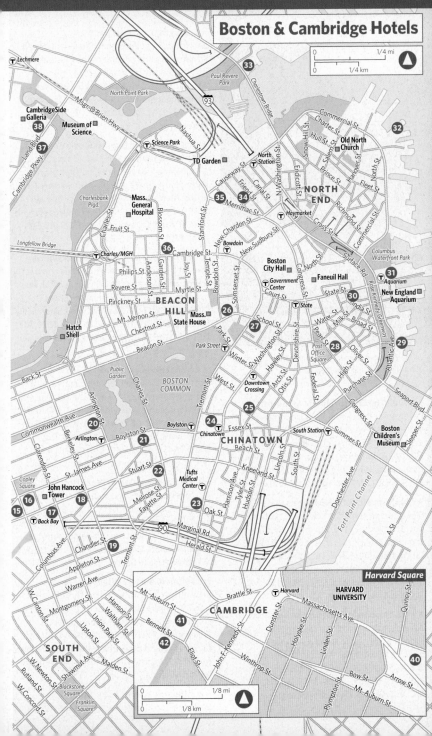

Harvard Square

> *The Fairmont Copley Plaza Hotel lobby, a riot of trompe l'oeil and ornate molding.*

★★★ kids **The Charles Hotel** CAMBRIDGE Top-notch amenities and good-size rooms packed with pampering details make the Charles Cambridge's finest hotel. 1 Bennett St. (at Eliot St.), Cambridge. ☎ 800/882-1818. www.charleshotel.com. 293 units. Doubles $299–$599. AE, DC, MC, V. T: Red Line to Harvard.

★ **Charlesmark Hotel & Lounge** BACK BAY Sleek design helps the compact, custom-outfitted rooms (many overlooking the Marathon finish line) feel large. 655 Boylston St. (at Dartmouth & Exeter sts.). ☎ 617/247-1212. www.thecharlesmark.com. 40 units. Doubles $129–$269 w/breakfast. AE, DC, DISC, MC, V. T: Green Line to Copley.

★★ kids **Colonnade Hotel Boston** BACK BAY An elegant contemporary hotel, with large rooms, great service, and a seasonal rooftop pool. 120 Huntington Ave. (at W. Newton St.). ☎ 800/962-3030. www.colonnadehotel.com. 285 units. Doubles $229–$459. AE, DC, DISC, MC, V. T: Green Line E to Prudential.

★ **Copley Square Hotel** BACK BAY Service distinguishes this hotel, with decent-size rooms done in contemporary style, from its giant corporate neighbors. 47 Huntington Ave. (at Exeter St.). ☎ 800/225-7062. www.copleysquarehotel.com. 143 units. Doubles $199–$379. AE, DC, DISC, MC, V. T: Green Line to Copley.

★★ kids **Doubletree Guest Suites** OUTSKIRTS/BROOKLINE Each sizable two-room suite has a fridge; the T isn't nearby, but this place is a good deal if you're driving. 400 Soldiers Field Rd. (at Mass. Pike Brighton/Cambridge exit). ☎ 800/222-8733. www.hiltonfamilyboston.com. 308 units. Doubles $129–$309. AE, DC, DISC, MC, V.

★★ kids **Doubletree Hotel Boston Downtown** CHINATOWN This modern hotel has compact rooms and a great location, with guest access to a huge YMCA. 821 Washington St. (at Oak & Stuart sts.). ☎ 800/222-8733. www.hiltonfamilyboston.com. 267 units. Doubles $129–$299. AE, DC, DISC, MC, V. T: Orange Line to New England Medical Center.

★★★ **Eliot Hotel** BACK BAY Most units are large, romantic suites with antique furnishings; the accommodating staff contributes to the residential feel. 370 Commonwealth Ave. (at Mass Ave.). ☎ 800/443-5468. www.eliothotel.com. 95 units. Doubles $235–$545. AE, DC, MC, V. T: Green Line B, C, or D to Hynes Convention Center.

★★ **The Fairmont Copley Plaza Hotel** BACK BAY Custom furnishings and courtly service make this luxurious hotel, built in 1912, a Boston classic. 138 St. James Ave. (at Dartmouth St. & Trinity Pl.). ☎ 800/441-1414. www.fairmont.com/copleyplaza. 383 units. Doubles from $289. AE, DC, MC, V. T: Green Line to Copley.

★★ **Fairmont Battery Wharf** NORTH END Proximity to the water makes this low-rise hotel feel like a fancy houseboat with impressive amenities. 3 Battery Wharf (at Battery & Commercial sts.). ☎ 800/441-1414. www.fairmont.com/batterywharf. 150 units. Doubles from $379. AE, DC, DISC, MC, V. T: Green Line to North Station.

★★ **Fifteen Beacon** BEACON HILL Over-the-top luxury, contemporary style, and

> *After some shopping in the Back Bay, retreat to the Mandarin Oriental.*

superb service are the hallmarks of the city's premier boutique property. 15 Beacon St. (at Somerset St.). ☎ 877/982-3226. www.xvbeacon. com. 60 units. Doubles from $295. AE, DC, DISC, MC, V. T: Red or Green Line to Park St.

★★★ **Four Seasons Hotel** BACK BAY The best hotel in New England offers its pampered guests everything they might want—for a price. 200 Boylston St. (at Hadassah Way). ☎ 800/819-5053. www.fourseasons.com/ boston. 272 units. Doubles from $425. AE, DC, DISC, MC, V. T: Green Line to Arlington.

★ kids **Hampton Inn Boston/Cambridge** CAM-BRIDGE Rooms at this business-traveler favorite offer no surprises—they're generic but comfortable. 191 Msgr. O'Brien Hwy. (at Water St.), Cambridge. ☎ 800/426-7866. www. bostoncambridge.hamptoninn.com. 114 units. Doubles $189–$359 w/breakfast. AE, DC, DISC, MC, V. T: Green Line to Lechmere.

★ **Harborside Inn** WATERFRONT This contemporary-style hotel in a renovated 19th-century warehouse near Faneuil Hall is a great value. 185 State St. (at Atlantic Ave.). ☎ 888/723-7565. www.harborsideinnboston. com. 54 units. Doubles $109–$299. AE, DC, DISC, MC, V. T: Blue Line to Aquarium.

★ **Harvard Square Hotel** CAMBRIDGE You're paying for the fantastic location, not the well-maintained but utilitarian accommodations. 110 Mount Auburn St. (at Eliot St.).

☎ 800/458-5886. www.hotelsinharvardsquare. com. 73 units. Doubles $99–$229. AE, DC, DISC, MC, V. T: Red Line to Harvard.

★★ **Hilton Boston Back Bay** BACK BAY The 26-story business hotel, with large rooms and great views from the upper floors, also suits families. 40 Dalton St. (at Scotia St.). ☎ 800/874-0663. www.hiltonfamilyboston. com. 390 units. Doubles $149–$399. AE, DC, DISC, MC, V. T: Green Line B, C, or D to Hynes Convention Center.

★ **Holiday Inn Boston at Beacon Hill** BEACON HILL Adjacent to Massachusetts General Hospital, this is a well-equipped business hotel. 5 Blossom St. (at Cambridge St.). ☎ 800/465-4329. www.hisboston.com. 303 units. Doubles $150–$400. AE, DC, DISC, MC, V. T: Red Line to Charles/MGH.

★★ **Hotel Commonwealth** BACK BAY The lavishly appointed guest rooms overlook Kenmore Square (in front) or Fenway Park (across the Mass. Pike). 500 Commonwealth Ave. (at Kenmore St.). ☎ 866/784-4000. www. hotelcommonwealth.com. 150 units. Doubles $235–$485. AE, DC, DISC, MC, V. T: Green Line B, C, or D to Kenmore.

★★ kids **Hotel Marlowe** CAMBRIDGE This posh yet funky business hotel has a family-friendly vibe and good-size rooms with elegant decor. 25 Land Blvd. (at Cambridge Pkwy.). ☎ 800/825-7040. www.hotelmarlowe.com.

236 units. Doubles $199–$449. AE, DC, DISC, MC, V. T: Green Line to Lechmere.

★ Hotel 140 BACK BAY
Small but affordable rooms (some with one twin bed) spread over three floors of a renovated former YMCA. 140 Clarendon St. (at Stuart St.). ☎ 800/714-0140. www.hotel140.com. 40 units. Doubles $119–$199 w/breakfast. AE, MC, V. T: Orange Line to Back Bay.

★★ kids Hyatt Regency Boston Financial District
DOWNTOWN CROSSING The business-oriented Hyatt, with spacious rooms and European-style appointments, slashes prices on weekends. 1 Ave. de Lafayette (at Washington St.). ☎ 800/233-1234. www.hyattregencyboston. com. 500 units. Doubles $189–$469. AE, DC, DISC, MC, V. T: Red or Orange Line to Downtown Crossing.

★★ kids The Inn at Harvard CAMBRIDGE
A retreat from busy Harvard Square, this hotel offers excellent business amenities and elegant rooms. 1201 Mass Ave (at Quincy St.). ☎ 800/458-5886. www.hotelsinharvardsquare. com. 111 units. Doubles $159–$269. AE, DC, DISC, MC, V. T: Red Line to Harvard.

★★ The Langham, Boston FINANCIAL DISTRICT
The city's top business hotel, in a prime location, does a lot of weekend leisure business. 250 Franklin St. (at Post Office Sq.). ☎ 800/791-7761. www.langhamhotels.com. 325 units. Doubles $185–$495. AE, DC, DISC, MC, V. T: Blue or Orange Line to State.

★★ The Lenox Hotel BACK BAY
The Lenox's spacious rooms make it a posh alternative to this neighborhood's business behemoths. 61 Exeter St. (at Boylston St.). ☎ 800/225-7676. www.lenoxhotel.com. 212 units. Doubles $215–$425. AE, DC, DISC, MC, V. T: Green Line to Copley.

★★ Mandarin Oriental, Boston BACK BAY
Service befitting the price keeps the international clientele coming back to this stylish property. 776 Boylston St. (at Fairfield St.). ☎ 866/526-6567. www.mandarinoriental.com/boston. 148 units. Doubles from $625. AE, DC, DISC, MC, V. T: Green Line to Copley.

★ kids The MidTown Hotel BACK BAY
This motel-like hotel—only two stories with a small lobby—has large rooms, small bathrooms, a seasonal outdoor pool, and cheap parking. 220 Huntington Ave. (at Cumberland St.). ☎ 800/343-1177. www.midtown-hotel.com. 159 units. Doubles $119–$259. AE, DC, DISC, MC, V. T: Green Line E to Symphony.

★ Newbury Guest House BACK BAY
This sophisticated inn offers comfortable accommodations at modest rates. Reserve early. 261 Newbury St. (at Fairfield & Gloucester sts.). ☎ 800/437-7668. www.newburyguesthouse. com. 32 units. Doubles $139–$279 w/breakfast. AE, DC, DISC, MC, V. T: Green Line B, C, or D to Hynes Convention Center.

★ kids Omni Parker House DOWNTOWN CROSSING
In business since 1855, the Parker House offers a range of well-kept rooms, from compact to huge. 60 School St. (at Tremont St.). ☎ 800/843-6664. www.omniparkerhouse.com. 551 units. Doubles $189–$289. AE, DC, DISC, MC, V. T: Green or Blue Line to Government Center.

★★ Onyx Hotel NORTH STATION
The contemporary boutique decor contrasts with the business amenities and gentrifying neighborhood. 155 Portland St. (at Causeway St.). ☎ 866/660-6699. www.onyxhotel.com. 112 units. Doubles $209–$349. AE, DC, DISC, MC, V. T: Green or Orange Line to North Station.

★ kids Radisson Hotel Boston THEATER DISTRICT
Large guest rooms, great views, and Sleep Number beds help make up for the location, in a transitional neighborhood. 200 Stuart St. (at Charles St. S.). ☎ 800/333-3333. www. radisson.com/bostonma. 356 units. Doubles $179–$479. AE, DC, DISC, MC, V. T: Green Line to Boylston.

★★ kids Residence Inn Boston Harbor CHARLESTOWN
This all-suite hotel on the water is a good alternative to downtown. 34–44 Charles River Ave. (at Chelsea St.). ☎ 866/296-2297. www.marriott.com/bostw. 168 units. Doubles $199–$399 w/breakfast. AE, DC, DISC, MC, V. T: Orange Line to Community College.

★★ The Ritz-Carlton, Boston Common THEATER DISTRICT
The ultramodern accommodations take up floors 9 through 12 of a high-rise tower. 10 Avery St. (at Washington St.). ☎ 800/241-3333. www.ritzcarlton.com. 193 units.

> *Many rooms at the Royal Sonesta Hotel enjoy a view of the Charles River.*

Doubles from $395. AE, DC, DISC, MC, V.
T: Green Line to Boylston.

★★ kids **Royal Sonesta Hotel** CAMBRIDGE
Luxurious and tech-savvy, the Sonesta has
spacious, modern rooms and lovely views. 40
Edwin H. Land Blvd. (at CambridgeSide Place).
☎ 800/766-3782. www.sonesta.com/boston.
400 units. Doubles $239–$319. AE, DC, DISC,
MC, V. T: Green Line to Lechmere.

★★ kids **Sheraton Boston Hotel** BACK BAY
This huge hotel has good-size contemporary
rooms and gorgeous views from higher floors.
39 Dalton St. (at Belvidere St.). ☎ 800/325-
3535. www.sheraton.com/boston. 1,215 units.
Doubles $209–$409. AE, DC, DISC, MC, V.
T: Green Line E to Prudential.

★★ **Taj Boston** BACK BAY
Known for its luxe rooms and courteous staff,
this former Ritz-Carlton got even nicer when
the Indian luxury chain took over. 15 Arlington
St. (at Newbury St.). ☎ 877/482-5267. www.
tajhotels.com. 273 units. Doubles from $249.
AE, DC, DISC, MC, V. T: Green Line to Arlington.

★★ kids **The Westin Copley Place Boston** BACK
BAY The views are so good that they over-
shadow the spacious rooms and business
amenities. 10 Huntington Ave. (at Dartmouth
St.). ☎ 800/937-8461. www.westin.com/
copleyplace. 803 units. Doubles $179–$479. AE,
DC, DISC, MC, V. T: Green Line to Copley.

B&B Booking Agencies

Bed & Breakfast Agency of Boston (☎ 800/
248-9262, 617/720-3540, or 0800/89-
5128 from the U.K.; www.boston-bn
bagency.com)

Bed and Breakfast Associates Bay Colony (☎ 888/486-6018 or 781/449-5302;
www.bnbboston.com)

Bed & Breakfast Reservations North
Shore/Greater Boston/Cape Cod (☎ 617/
964-1606 or 978/281-9505; www.bb
reserve.com)

Boston & Cambridge Nightlife & Entertainment Best Bets

Best Views
★★★ **Top of the Hub,** Prudential Center, 800 Boylston St. (p. 116)

Most Beautiful Outdoor Venue
★★ **Bank of America Pavilion,** 290 Northern Ave. (p. 119)

Best Gimmick
★★ **Bleacher Bar,** 82A Lansdowne St. (p. 116)

Best Dinner & a Show
★★ **Boston Pops,** Symphony Hall, 301 Mass Ave. (p. 116)

Best Theater Deal
★★ **Commonwealth Shakespeare Company,** Charles & Beacon sts. (p. 119)

Best Nightlife Deal
★★ **Toad,** 1912 Mass Ave, Cambridge (p. 119)

Best Sports Bar
★★ **The Fours,** 166 Canal St (p. 119)

Best Sports Venue
★★★ **Fenway Park,** 4 Yawkey Way (p. 119)

Best Family Entertainment
★ **Shear Madness,** Charles Playhouse, 74 Warrenton St. (p. 119)

Best Alfresco Pickup Joint
★ **Tia's,** 200 Atlantic Ave. (p. 116)

Best Martinis
★★ **The Bar at Taj Boston,** 15 Arlington St. (p. 116)

Best Gay Scene
★★ **Club Café,** 209 Columbus Ave. (p. 118)

Most Worth the Trip
★★★ **Johnny D's Uptown Restaurant & Music Club,** 17 Holland St., Somerville (p. 118)

Best Folk Club
★★★ **Club Passim,** 47 Palmer St., Cambridge (p. 118)

Best Rock Club
★★★ **The Middle East,** 472–480 Mass Ave, Cambridge (p. 119)

Best Comedy Club
★★ **The Comedy Studio,** 1238 Mass Ave, Cambridge (p. 117)

Best Old-School Jazz Club
★ **Wally's Cafe,** 427 Mass Ave. (p. 118)

> *Symphony Hall lightens up during the Boston Pops' season.*

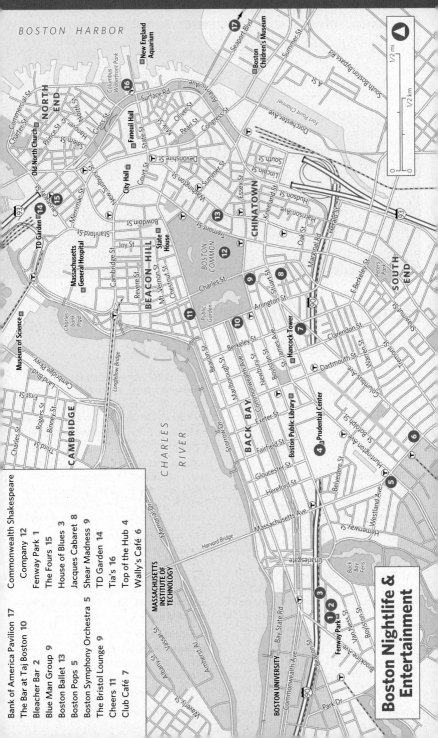

Boston Nightlife & Entertainment

Bank of America Pavilion 17
The Bar at Taj Boston 10
Bleacher Bar 2
Blue Man Group 9
Boston Ballet 13
Boston Pops 5
Boston Symphony Orchestra 5
The Bristol Lounge 9
Cheers 11
Club Café 7
Commonwealth Shakespeare Company 12
Fenway Park 1
The Fours 15
House of Blues 3
Jacques Cabaret 8
Shear Madness 9
TD Garden 14
Tia's 16
Top of the Hub 4
Wally's Café 6

Boston & Cambridge Nightlife & Entertainment A to Z

Bars & Lounges

★★ The Bar at Taj Boston BACK BAY
This aristocratic watering hole is a cozy, paneled room with a power broker clientele and killer martinis. 15 Arlington St. (at Newbury St.). ☎ 617/598-5255. T: Green Line to Arlington. Map p. 115.

★★ Bleacher Bar FENWAY
Under the Fenway Park stands, this bar has a picture window that faces the outfield. 82A Lansdowne St. (at Brookline Ave.). ☎ 617/262-2424. www.bleacherbarboston.com T: Green Line B, C, or D to Kenmore, 10-min. walk. Map p. 115.

★★★ The Bristol Lounge BACK BAY
A well-heeled older crowd comes to the Four Seasons for nightly live music and a weekend dessert buffet. 200 Boylston St. (at Charles St.). ☎ 617/338-4400. www.fourseasons.com/boston. T: Green Line to Boylston. Map p. 115.

Cheers BEACON HILL & FANEUIL HALL MARKETPLACE The bar that inspired the TV show is fun, if touristy. The Faneuil Hall location

replicates the sitcom set. 84 Beacon St. (at Brimmer St.). ☎ 617/227-9605. www.cheersboston.com. T: Green Line to Arlington. Map p. 115. Faneuil Hall: Quincy Market, South Canopy. ☎ 617/227-0150. T: Green or Blue Line to Government Center.

★ Tia's WATERFRONT
In warm weather, the patio is the busiest after-work meet market in town. 200 Atlantic Ave. (at State St.). ☎ 617/227-0828. www.tiaswaterfront.com. T: Blue Line to Aquarium. Map p. 115.

★★★ Top of the Hub BACK BAY
The 52nd-floor lounge is a gorgeous setting for romance, especially at sunset. Live jazz nightly. No jeans. Prudential Center, 800 Boylston St. (at Fairfield St.). ☎ 617/536-1775. www.topofthehub.net. T: Green Line E to Prudential. Map p. 115.

Classical Music

★★ Boston Pops BACK BAY
The playful ensemble serves refreshments at tables on the Symphony Hall floor; balcony seating has no food and drink. The season

> *The Middle East, a legendary rock club, books both bands and belly dancers.*

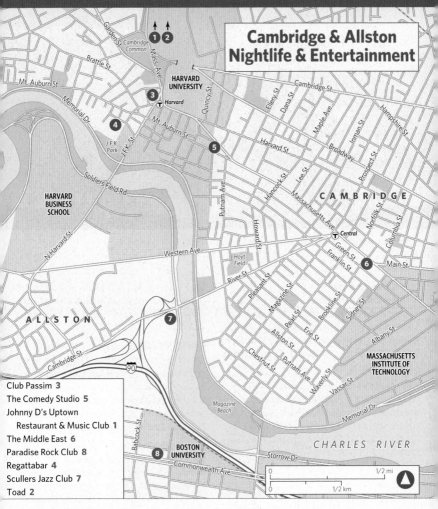

Cambridge & Allston Nightlife & Entertainment

Club Passim **3**

The Comedy Studio **5**

Johnny D's Uptown
    Restaurant & Music Club **1**

The Middle East **6**

Paradise Rock Club **8**

Regattabar **4**

Scullers Jazz Club **7**

Toad **2**

runs from May to early July (and includes their famous July 4th Fireworks Spectacular), plus December holiday programs. **301 Mass Ave (at Huntington Ave.).** ☎ **888/266-1200 or 617/266-1200 (SymphonyCharge). www.bostonpops.org.** Tickets $20–$99. **T: Green Line E to Symphony. Map p. 115.**

★★★ Boston Symphony Orchestra BACK BAY

The BSO is one of the five best American orchestras and one of the finest in the world. The season runs October through April. **301 Mass Ave (at Huntington Ave.).** ☎ **888/266-1200 or 617/266-1200 (SymphonyCharge). www.bso.org.** Tickets $29–$115; rehearsal $19. **T: Green Line E to Symphony. Map p. 115.**

Comedy

★★ The Comedy Studio CAMBRIDGE

A showcase for up-and-coming comics, who complement stand-up with sketches and improv. **1238 Mass Ave (at Bow St.).** ☎ **617/661-6507. www.thecomedystudio.com.** Cover $8–$10. **T: Red Line to Harvard. Map p. 117.**

Dance

★★ Boston Ballet THEATER DISTRICT

Best known for *The Nutcracker*, Boston Ballet is one of the country's top dance companies. Performances at the Opera House. **529 Washington St. (at Ave. de Lafayette).** ☎ **617/695-6955. www.bostonballet.org.** Tickets $25–$135. **T: Orange Line to Chinatown. Map p. 115.**

> *The Boston Pops free Fourth of July concert is a Boston tradition.*

Gay & Lesbian Clubs

★★ Club Café SOUTH END

A club, video bar, *and* restaurant, this upscale spot is a top gay nightlife destination. 209 Columbus Ave. (at Berkeley St.). ☎ 617/536-0966. www.clubcafe.com. No cover. T: Orange Line to Back Bay. Map p. 115.

★ Jacques Cabaret BAY VILLAGE

Boston's only drag club also books performance artists and, on weekends, live music. No credit cards. 79 Broadway (off Charles St. S.). ☎ 617/436-8902. www.jacquescabaret.com. Cover $6–$10. T: Green Line to Arlington. Map p. 115.

Jazz Clubs

★★★ Regattabar CAMBRIDGE

The Regattabar battles Scullers (see next listing) to book the biggest names in jazz. Everybody wins. 1 Bennett St. (at Eliot St.), Cambridge, in the Charles Hotel. ☎ 617/661-5000. www.regattabarjazz.com. Tickets $15–$35. T: Red Line to Harvard. Map p. 117.

★★★ Scullers Jazz Club ALLSTON

Scullers is harder to reach than the Regattabar (see previous listing), meaning it draws

Theater Tip

For information on touring Broadway shows, visit www.broadwayacrossamerica boston.com.

hard-core patrons. 400 Soldiers Field Rd., in the Doubletree Guest Suites hotel. ☎ 617/562-4111. www.scullersjazz.com. Tickets $18–$50. Map p. 117.

★ Wally's Café SOUTH END

This small, family-run place opened in 1947 and books mostly local talent. It attracts a serious—and seriously diverse—crowd. 427 Mass Ave (at Columbus Ave.). ☎ 617/424-1408. www.wallyscafe.com. No cover. 1-drink minimum. T: Orange Line to Mass Ave. Map p. 115.

Live-Music Clubs

★★★ Club Passim CAMBRIDGE

The place for folk music is a subterranean coffeehouse—it also serves beer, wine, and vegetarian food—founded in 1958. 47 Palmer St. (at Church St.). ☎ 617/492-7679. www.club passim.org. Cover usually $5–$20. T: Red Line to Harvard. Map p. 117.

★★ House of Blues FENWAY

The chain has a vise grip on touring artists of a certain stripe, not all of them blues musicians. 15 Lansdowne St. (at Brookline Ave.). ☎ 888/693-2583. www.houseofblues.com. Tickets $20–$45. T: Green Line B, C, or D to Kenmore. Map p. 115.

★★★ Johnny D's Uptown Restaurant & Music Club SOMERVILLE

The impressively varied schedule makes this family-run club well worth the trip. 17 Holland St. (at Davis Sq.).

☎ 617/776-2004. www.johnnyds.com. Cover usually $8–$12. T: Red Line to Davis. Map p. 117.

★★★ The Middle East CAMBRIDGE

The best (and loudest) rock club in the Boston area has four performance spaces and ultra-savvy bookers. 472–480 Mass Ave (at Brookline St.). ☎ 617/864-3278. www.mideastclub.com. Cover $8– $25. T: Red Line to Central. Map p. 117.

★ Paradise Rock Club BOSTON UNIVERSITY

Rock and alternative artists, both local and world famous, play for young crowds. 967–969 Commonwealth Ave. (at Pleasant St.). ☎ 617/562-8800 or 800/745-3000 (Ticketmaster). www.thedise.com. T: Green Line B to Pleasant St. Map p. 117.

★★ Toad CAMBRIDGE

Local rock, rockabilly, and blues artists draw a crowd that appreciates the top-notch entertainment and the price (free!). 1912 Mass Ave (at Porter Rd.). ☎ 617/497-4950. www.toadcambridge.com. No cover. T: Red Line to Porter. Map p. 117.

Popular Music
★★ Bank of America Pavilion SEAPORT DISTRICT
The huge waterfront tent is a sublime summer setting for music of all types. 290 Northern Ave. (at Congress St.). ☎ 617/728-1600 or 800/745-3000 (Ticketmaster). www.livenation.com. T: Silver Line bus to Silver Line Way. Map p. 115.

Spectator Sports
★★★ Fenway Park FENWAY
The beloved Red Sox play at the landmark park from April to October. See p. 66, ❶. 4 Yawkey Way (at Brookline Ave.). ☎ 877/733-7699 for tickets. www.redsox.com. Tickets $20–$125. T: Green Line B, C, or D to Kenmore. Map p. 115.

Discount Tickets

BosTix (☎ 617/262-8632 for info; www.bostix.org) sells full-price and discounted advance tickets and half-price same-day tickets (cash only) at booths at Faneuil Hall Marketplace (T: Green or Blue Line to Government Center) and in Copley Square (T: Green Line to Copley).

> *The House of Blues is nearly as popular as its neighbors across Lansdowne Street, the Red Sox.*

★ TD Garden NORTH STATION

The city's premier arena is home to the Celtics (NBA) and Bruins (NHL), and also hosts touring rock and pop artists. 100 Legends Way (at Causeway St.). ☎ 617/624-1000. www.tdgarden.com. T: Green or Orange Line to North Station. Map p. 115.

Sports Bar
★★ The Fours NORTH STATION
Across the street from the TD Garden, the Fours has scores of TVs and memorabilia, and good pub grub. 166 Canal St. (at Causeway St.). ☎ 617/720-4455. www.thefours.com. T: Green or Orange Line to North Station. Map p. 115.

Theater
★★ Commonwealth Shakespeare Company
BOSTON COMMON
The annual free production runs Tuesday to Sunday in July and early August. Charles & Beacon sts. ☎ 617/532-1252. www.commshakes.org. Free admission. T: Green Line to Boylston. Map p. 115.

★ Shear Madness THEATER DISTRICT

The audience helps solve a murder in this madcap show set in a hair salon; it's never the same twice. Charles Playhouse Stage II (downstairs), 74 Warrenton St. ☎ 617/426-5225. www.shearmadness.com. Tickets $42. T: Green Line to Boylston. Map p. 115.

Concord

Over the course of 3-plus centuries, Concord (locals pronouce it "conquered") has grown from a country village to a prosperous suburb. The first official battle of the Revolutionary War took place at the North Bridge on April 19, 1775. By the mid-19th century, an impressive constellation of literary stars—Ralph Waldo Emerson, Henry Wadsworth Longfellow, Henry David Thoreau, and Louisa May Alcott—called the town home. Present-day Concord preserves and honors that rich history. Let's take a look.

> Walk in Louisa May Alcott's footsteps at Orchard House, the author's longtime home.

START Follow Rte. 2 from Cambridge until you see signs for Lincoln; where the road takes a sharp left, go straight, following signs for HISTORIC CONCORD. If it's not rush hour, the trip from Boston takes 30–40 min.

❶ ★★ kids **Concord Museum.** The museum tells the story of the town in informative exhibits that incorporate intriguing artifacts, murals, films, maps, and documents. A one-time Native American settlement, Concord is perhaps best known as a Revolutionary War

battleground. In the 19th century, it was a literary and intellectual center with a thriving clock-making industry. The town was also an important player in the 20th-century historic preservation movement. Many museum displays focus on the big names: You'll see one of the lanterns immortalized by Longfellow in "Paul Revere's Ride" ("one if by land, two if by sea"), the contents of Emerson's study, and a large collection of Thoreau's belongings. The period furniture, silver, clocks, and embroidery

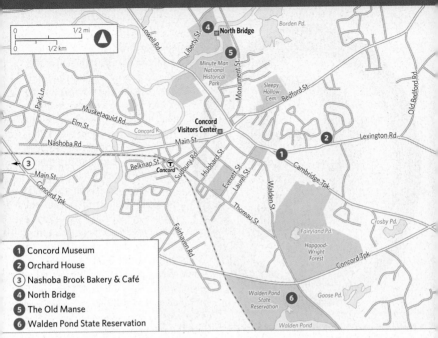

1 Concord Museum
2 Orchard House
3 Nashoba Brook Bakery & Café
4 North Bridge
5 The Old Manse
6 Walden Pond State Reservation

samplers offer an engaging look at the lives of regular people. If you're traveling with kids, be sure to pick up a Family Explorer Kit, which has some fun hands-on components. ⏱ 1–1½ hr. Cambridge Tpk. (at Lexington Rd.). ☎ 978/369-9609 (recorded info) or 978/369-9763. www.concordmuseum.org. Admission $10 adults, $8 seniors & students, $5 kids 6–17, free for kids 5 & under. June–Aug daily 9am–5pm; Apr–May & Sept–Dec Mon–Sat 9am–5pm, Sun noon–5pm; Jan–Mar Mon–Sat 11am–4pm, Sun 1–4pm.

2 ★★★ kids **Orchard House.** Louisa May Alcott lived here when she wrote her beloved novel *Little Women* (1868). Louisa and her sisters—the models for *Little Women*'s March family—are the focus of the guided tour, which is the only way to see the house, which inspired the novel's setting. Numerous heirlooms survive; I especially like Louisa's little desk and the miniature pieces of furniture that appear to be from a dollhouse (they're actually a traveling salesman's samples). Louisa's father bought this land in 1857, and the family lived here from 1858 to 1877. Check ahead for information on the extensive schedule of special events and holiday programs. ⏱ 1 hr. (on Sat in autumn, try to arrive before noon). 399 Lexington Rd. ☎ 978/369-4118. www.louisamayalcott.

org. Guided tours $9 adults, $7 seniors & students, $5 kids 6–17, free for kids 5 & under, $25 families. Apr–Oct Mon–Sat 10am–4:30pm, Sun 1–4:30pm; Nov–Mar Mon–Fri 11am–3pm, Sat 10am–4:30pm, Sun 1–4:30pm. Closed Jan 1–15.

3 🍽 **Nashoba Brook Bakery & Café.** One of the best places to assemble a picnic for your next stop, the North Bridge, is this bakery and cafe in West Concord, where the bread, pastries, soups, salads, and sandwiches are all made fresh on-site. An alternative place for provisions, in downtown Concord, is the **Cheese Shop of Concord,** 25–31 Walden St. (☎ 978/369-5778; www.concordcheeseshop.com; $), selling sandwiches, soups, and all the trimmings, including chocolates. At either place, you may want to stash away a snack for later, as Walden Pond (p. 123, 6) doesn't have a food concession. 152 Commonwealth Ave. ☎ 978/318-1999. www.slowrise.com. $.

4 ★ kids **North Bridge.** Off Monument Street outside Concord Center, a path leads to the North Bridge, a reproduction of the wooden structure that spanned the Concord River in April 1775, when the Revolutionary War

> Nineteenth-century heartthrob Nathaniel Hawthorne.

bridge. Daniel Chester French, the sculptor of the John Harvard statue in Cambridge and the seated Abraham Lincoln at the president's memorial in Washington, D.C., created the iconic image of the militia man with a musket in one hand and a plow handle in the other. A plaque on the other side of the bridge honors the British soldiers who died in the battle. Up the hill in the National Park Service visitor center, a diorama and video program illustrate the battle, and rangers are on duty in case you have questions. To get there, you can walk across the grounds or jump back in the car for the 2-minute ride. ⏱ 45 min. Minute Man National Historical Park, North Bridge Visitor Center, 174 Liberty St. (off Monument St.). ☎ 978/369-6993. www. nps.gov/mima. Free admission. Daily 9am–5pm (11am–3pm in winter).

began. Tune out the chatter of visitors and the hum of engines, and you can almost imagine the battle commemorated in Ralph Waldo Emerson's poem "Concord Hymn," the first stanza of which is engraved on the base of the *Minute Man* statue near the

⑤ ★ **The Old Manse.** A longtime family home, the Old Manse figures in an important part of the town's literary history. The Rev. William Emerson built the Old Manse in 1770, and his grandson Ralph Waldo Emerson later worked on the essay "Nature" in

Concord: Practical Matters

Driving is the most efficient way to get to and around Concord. You can also take the **MBTA commuter rail** (☎ 800/392-6100 or 617/222-3200; www.mbta.com) from Boston's North Station or Cambridge's Porter Square. Check the schedule well in advance—outbound service is limited, especially on weekends. The **Chamber of Commerce** (☎ 978/369-3120; www. concordchamberofcommerce.org) maintains a visitor center at 58 Main St., 1 block south of Monument Square. It's open daily 10am to 4pm April through October; public restrooms in the same building are open year-round. The chamber office is open year-round Monday through Friday; hours vary, so call ahead.

A Detour to Lexington

The first battle of the Revolutionary War wasn't in Concord but on Lexington's town common, now called the Battle Green. A visit will add about an hour to your excursion to Concord. Start at the **Chamber of Commerce Visitor Center,** 1875 Mass Ave (Meriam St.; ☎ 781/862-2480; www. lexingtonchamber.org). It's open daily from 9am to 5pm (Dec–Mar 10am–4pm). Step inside to see the diorama and accompanying narrative that illustrate the **Battle of Lexington.** Then head out to look around the green. The *Minuteman* statue here is of Captain John Parker, who commanded the militia. When the British confronted his troops, Parker called: "Stand your ground. Don't fire unless fired upon, but if they mean to have a war, let it begin here!"

> *Walden Pond welcomes swimmers, hikers, and leaf-peepers.*

the study. Newlywed Nathaniel Hawthorne moved here in 1842; he looks forbidding and serious in most of his portraits, but on the enlightening guided tour of the Old Manse (the only way to see the interior), you'll meet a lighthearted Hawthorne who collaborated with his new bride, Sophia Peabody, to scratch messages with her diamond ring on two windows. Henry David Thoreau planted a vegetable garden as a wedding present, and a re-creation of that project is on the grounds today. The Old Manse wasn't the permanent home of any of the town's big names. You've already seen Louisa May Alcott's house; if you're interested in visiting Emerson's or Hawthorne's, ask at the chamber of commerce office or visit the chamber website for information. ⏱ 1 hr. 269 Monument St. (at North Bridge). ☎ 978/369-3909. www.oldmanse.org. Guided tour $8 adults, $7 seniors & students, $5 kids 6–12, free for kids 5 & under, $25 families. Mid-Apr to Oct Mon–Sat 10am–5pm, Sun & holidays noon–5pm (last tour at 4:30pm). Check ahead for winter hours.

❻ ★★ kids Walden Pond State Reservation. On the way back to Boston, stop off at one of the most famous places in New England. Walden Pond was home to eccentric author Henry David Thoreau for 2 years, 2 months, and 2 days in the mid-1840s, and if not for that association, the area around the pond would likely have become valuable residential real estate many years ago. Instead, the legacy of the founder of the conservation movement is a gorgeous, surprisingly unspoiled state park property that allows hiking, swimming, fishing, and other low-impact activities but not dogs or bikes. ⏱ 1 hr. (arrive early or late in the day in the summer and fall, when the rangers close the park to newcomers after it reaches capacity 1,000). 915 Walden St./Rte. 126 (off Rte. 2). ☎ 978/369-3254. www.mass.gov/dcr/parks/walden. Free admission. Parking $5 (cash only). Daily 8am–sunset.

Salem & Marblehead

If you know Salem only because of its association with witches, you're in for a delightful surprise. Salem has been haunted by the witch trials since 1692, but it has far more to offer. Neighboring Marblehead, the self-proclaimed "Yachting Capital of America," is one of the prettiest towns in New England. It's a gorgeous place with great scenery, terrific shopping, and just enough history. Together they make a wonderful day trip.

> Abbot Hall makes a lovely backdrop for Marblehead Harbor.

START From the Boston area, take I-93N to I-95N, or take the Callahan Tunnel to Rte. 1A and follow it to Rte. 1 north. From I-95 or Rte. 1, follow the signs to Rte. 128 north. Exit at Rte. 114 east, and follow the signs to downtown Salem. From Boston, the trip takes about 45 minutes if it isn't rush hour.

1 ★★ kids **Salem Witch Museum.** Start here for an excellent overview of the 1692 witch-trial hysteria. The museum centers on a well-researched audiovisual presentation—a series of dioramas, with life-size human figures, that light up in sequence as recorded narration plays. The story gets scary—one of the "witches" was pressed to death by stones piled onto a board on his chest—but the antiprejudice message is both clear and timeless. For more on what happened in those dark days, see "The Witching Hour" on p. 532. ⏱ 1 hr. 19½ Washington Sq. (at Rte. 1A & Brown St.). ☎ 978/744-1692. www.salemwitch museum.com. Admission $8 adults, $7 seniors, $5.50 kids 6–14, free for kids 5 & under. Daily July–Aug 10am–7pm; Sept–June 10am–5pm; check ahead for extended Oct hours.

2 ★★★ **Peabody Essex Museum.** This is one of the best art museums in New England, with a growing national reputation that rests in large part on its extensive collections of Asian art and photography, American art and architecture, maritime art, and Asian, African, and Native American art. The curators

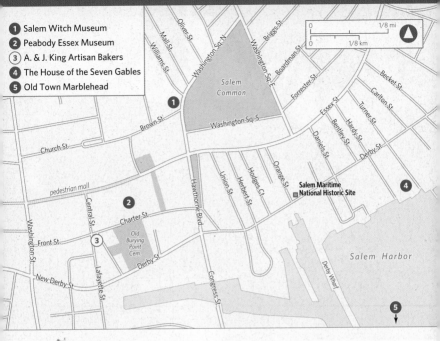

1. Salem Witch Museum
2. Peabody Essex Museum
3. A. & J. King Artisan Bakers
4. The House of the Seven Gables
5. Old Town Marblehead

strive to place objects in context, demonstrating the interplay of influences across time and cultures. On the premises is **Yin Yu Tang,** an 18th-century Qing dynasty house that was shipped to Salem from rural China. The only example of Chinese domestic architecture outside that country, the house allows an intriguing look at 2 centuries of life in China. Be sure to pick up an audio tour before exploring the house. Also be sure to peek at some of the lower-profile permanent and temporary exhibits, which are quirky, fun, and uniformly excellent. 3 hr. (build your visit around your timed ticket to Yin Yu Tang). East India Sq. (off Hawthorne Blvd. at Essex St.). ☎ 866/745-1876 or 978/745-9500. www.pem. org. Admission $15 adults, $13 seniors, $11 students, free for kids 16 & under. Yin Yu Tang admission $5 with museum admission. Tues–Sun & Mon holidays 10am–5pm.

③ 🍴 **A. & J. King Artisan Bakers.** Not far from the museum—the badge you receive for admission lets you leave and reenter—this cozy cafe serves out-of-this-world sweets and substantial sandwiches on delectable house-made bread. Closed Monday. 48 Central St. (Charter St.). ☎ 978/744-4881. www.ajkingbakery.com. $.

④ ★ kids **The House of the Seven Gables.** Nathaniel Hawthorne's scary 1851 novel inspired the name of this attraction not the other way around. Don't worry if you can't recall the story; begin your visit with the audiovisual program that recaps the book. The rambling 1668 house holds six rooms of period furniture, including pieces referred to in the novel. Guides point them out on the informative tour, which includes interesting descriptions of what life in the 1700s was like, a trip on the secret staircase, and more Q and A than many house tours permit. On the grounds are lovely period gardens that overlook the harbor. 1½ hr. 54 Turner St. (off Derby St.). ☎ 978/744-0991. www.7gables. org. Guided tour of house and grounds $13 adults, $12 seniors, $7.50 kids 5–12, free for kids 4 & under. Surcharges may apply for special exhibitions. July–Oct daily 10am–7pm (until 11pm Oct weekends); Nov–June daily 10am–5pm. Closed 1st 2 weeks of Jan.

Leave downtown Salem on Rte. 114 E. (Lafayette St.) and follow it for about 3 miles into Marblehead. At the intersection with Rte. 129, go straight onto Pleasant St. Follow it to Washington St., and look for parking.

> *The House of the Seven Gables helps bring Nathaniel Hawthorne's eerie novel to life.*

> *One of the unsettling tableaux at the Salem Witch Museum.*

⑤ ★★ Old Town Marblehead. Marblehead was founded in 1629, and it's narrow streets are filled with 17th and 18th century architecture. Wander down Washington Street toward the water, detouring if you see something interesting and taking in the architectural details and informative plaques that abound in the historic district. You'll notice the clock tower of **Abbot Hall**, Marblehead's municipal center, looming over the historic district on **Washington Sq.** at Lee St. (☎ 781/631-0528; www.marblehead. org). The highlight of this Romanesque edifice is hanging in the Selectmen's Meeting Room: Archibald M. Willard's famous painting ***The Spirit of '76.*** Even if the title doesn't ring a bell, you'll almost certainly recognize the now-iconic marching drummer boy, drummer, and fife player. The **Chamber of Commerce** (see "Practical Matters") offers an excellent walking tour on its website, but even a quick stroll on your own is rewarding. The shopping in this neighborhood is excellent. Stop at **Crosby's Marketplace,** 118 Washington St. (☎ 781/631-1741; www.crosbysmarkets.com), for picnic

> *Boats fill Marblehead Harbor all summer, and the town has a nautical feel year-round.*

provisions, then make your way down State Street to Front Street. Turn right at the entrance to the town dock, walk 1 long block to Crocker Park Lane, and, off Front St., enter **Crocker Park.** After a busy day of sightseeing, it's a great place to unwind. The park has benches, a swing, and a breathtaking view of Marblehead Harbor.

Practical Matters

Salem and Marblehead are accessible by public transit and easy to negotiate on foot. That said, if you're interested in visiting both, you'll want your own car. Yes, public transit is an option, but traveling between the downtown Salem and downtown Marblehead is devilishly complicated. If you can't drive or don't want to, you can easily find a day's worth of diversions in either place. The **MBTA** (☎ 800/392-6100 or 617/222-3200; www.mbta.com) operates commuter trains from North Station in Boston to Salem, and buses from Haymarket to Salem and Marblehead; check schedules early in the planning process, and double-check the schedule for your return trip. Tourist information is widely available. For Salem, contact **Destination Salem** (☎ 877/SALEM-MA 725-3662 or 978/744-3663; www.salem.org). In-person sources include the **National Park Service Regional Visitor Center,** 2 New Liberty St. (☎ 978/740-1650; www.nps.gov/sama), open daily from 9am to 5pm, and the **Salem Chamber of Commerce,** 265 Essex St., Suite 101 (☎ 978/744-0004; www.salem-chamber.org), open weekdays from 9am to 5pm. For Marblehead, try the **Chamber of Commerce,** 62 Pleasant St. (☎ 781/631-2868; www.marbleheadchamber. com), which is open weekdays year-round (9am–5pm) and operates a seasonal information booth (☎ 781/639-8469) on Pleasant Street near Spring Street.

Cape Ann

Jutting into the Atlantic, like Cape Cod on a much smaller scale, Cape Ann is famous for history, seafood, scenery, shopping, and summer traffic. The town of Rockport was once a center of granite excavation, and the rocky peninsula's dramatic vistas have helped sustain it as an artists' colony for centuries, drawing the likes of Winslow Homer and Childe Hassam. For hundreds of years, fishing was by far the most important trade on Cape Ann; the town of Gloucester is the nation's oldest seaport, founded in 1623, and made famous by the film *The Perfect Storm,* based on Sebastian Junger's true account of a local weather event in 1991. With the decline of the industry, tourism has become a vital part of the local economy.

START From Boston, take I-93N or Rte. 1 to Rte. 128 to Gloucester. After Exit 12, the highway crosses a bridge over the Annisquam River, then comes to a traffic circle ("rotary" to the locals). Go three-quarters of the way around and turn right onto Rte. 127 north. Follow it for about 6 miles and turn left on Gott Ave. at the sign for:

> *The* Man at the Wheel, *a timeless symbol of Gloucester.*

① ★★ kids **Halibut Point State Park, Rockport.** The views from this little park at the tip of Cape Ann are unforgettable. On a clear day, you can see Maine. Halibut Point—named for the fact that sailing ships must "haul about" here to catch the shifting winds—is a former quarry, and spring-filled quarry pools remain (swimming is forbidden). Rocky ledges lead down to the cold, rough Atlantic, where tide pools await, and a World War II observation tower holds the visitor center. Climb the 60-foot structure, or head inside to get more information. Call ahead or visit the park blog (www.halibutpoint.wordpress.com) for the schedule of tours and other events, offered on weekends from Memorial Day to Columbus Day. ⏱ 45 min. 16 Garfield Ave. (at Gott Ave.). ☎ 978/546-2997. www.mass.gov/dcr & www.the trustees.org. Free admission. Parking $2 in high season. Memorial Day weekend to Labor Day weekend daily 8am–8pm, otherwise daily dawn–dusk.

Turn left as you exit the park and follow signs on Rte. 127 south to downtown. Parking is tough, but metered spots are available.

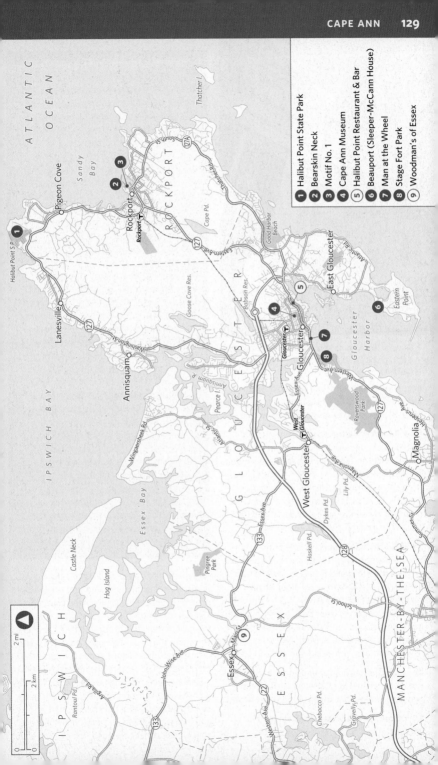

1 Halibut Point State Park
2 Bearskin Neck
3 Motif No. 1
4 Cape Ann Museum
5 Halibut Point Restaurant & Bar
6 Beauport (Sleeper-McCann House)
7 Man at the Wheel
8 Stage Fort Park
9 Woodman's of Essex

ATLANTIC OCEAN

Thatcher I.

Sandy Bay

Pigeon Cove

Halibut Point S.P.

ROCKPORT

South St.

127A

Cape Pd.

Thatcher Rd.

Rockport

Rockport

Good Harbor Beach

127

Eastern Ave.

Lanesville

127

Washington St.

Goose Cove Res.

Babson Res.

Atlantic Rd.

East Gloucester

Eastern Point

Gloucester

Gloucester Harbor

Annisquam

Annisquam R.

GLOUCESTER

Pearce I.

Essex Ave.

West Gloucester

Western Ave.

Ravenswood Park

127

Magnolia

IPSWICH BAY

Wingaersheek Rd.

Atlantic St.

Essex Ave.

Magnolia Ave.

Lily Pd.

133

Dykes Pd.

Haskell Pd.

128

School St.

MANCHESTER-BY-THE-SEA

Hesperus Ave.

Castle Neck

Hog Island

Pingree Park

ESSEX

9

Essex

Main St.

22

Western Ave.

Chebacco Pd.

Gravelly Pd.

John Wise Ave.

IPSWICH

Rantoul Pd.

Argilla Rd.

133

2 mi

2 km

> *Bearskin Neck, home to boutiques and restaurants, is Rockport's favorite destination for shopping and snacking.*

In summer, make one loop around downtown and then head to the free parking lot on Upper Main St. The shuttle bus to downtown costs $1.

② ★ **Bearskin Neck, Rockport.** Downtown Rockport abounds with shops and art galleries. Where Main and Mount Pleasant streets meet, you'll see Bearskin Neck, which extends about 3 long blocks into the Atlantic. The narrow peninsula is home to perhaps the highest concentration of gift shops you'll ever see. It ends in a plaza with a dazzling view of the water.

③ **Motif No. 1, Rockport.** This enduring symbol of Rockport is visible from several points on Bearskin Neck and from the Town Wharf, a block away. The barn-red fishing shack certainly catches the eye, but you might find yourself wondering what the big deal is. Originally constructed in 1884 and destroyed during the blizzard of 1978, Motif No. 1 was rebuilt using donations from residents and tourists.

To reach Gloucester, continue on the loop of Rte. 127 or follow Rte. 127A, which is longer and less commercial. Signs point to downtown.

④ ★ **Cape Ann Museum, Gloucester.** This lovely little museum makes an excellent

Whale-Watching in Gloucester

On Cape Ann, whale-watch cruise operators are for-profit businesses, and they're extremely competitive. Most guarantee sightings, offer a morning and an afternoon cruise plus deep-sea fishing excursions and charters, honor other firms' coupons, and offer AAA and AARP discounts. Check ahead for sailing times, prices (at least $45 for adults, less for seniors and children), and reservations, which are strongly recommended. If you're on a budget, ask whether the company imposes a fuel surcharge, and double-check the cut-off ages for kids and seniors.

In downtown Gloucester, **Cape Ann Whale Watch** (☎ 800/877-5110 or 978/283-5110; www.seethewhales.com) is the best-known operation. Also downtown are **Capt. Bill & Sons Whale Watch** (☎ 800/339-4253 or 978/283-6995; www.captbillandsons.com) and **Seven Seas Whale Watch** (☎ 888/283-1776 or 978/283-1776; www.7seas-whalewatch. com). At the Cape Ann Marina, off Route 133 south of downtown, is **Yankee Whale Watch** (☎ 800/942-5464 or 978/283-0313; www.yankeefleet.com).

If your schedule allows, plan to visit the **Whale Center of New England,** in the Gloucester Maritime Heritage Center, 24 Harbor Loop (☎ 978/271-6351; www. whalecenter.org), to see the humpback whale skeleton and explore the informative displays. It's open Monday through Saturday 9am to 5pm (call for winter hours), and admission is free.

introduction to Cape Ann's history and artists. If you're visiting on a weekend, you can take a guided tour of the highlights of the collection (Fri–Sat 11am, Sun 2pm). I could spend a day in the gallery that holds works by Fitz Henry Lane (formerly known as Fitz Hugh Lane), the Luminist painter whose light-flooded canvases show off his native Gloucester. The nation's largest collection of his paintings and drawings is here. Besides art and historic photographs, the galleries hold artifacts of the granite-quarrying and fishing industries, including real boats and ship models. Check ahead for information about

> *Motif No. 1, the famous fishing shack at the heart of Rockport Harbor.*

touring the museum's historic houses, the Capt. Elias Davis House (1804) and the White-Ellery House (1710), a rare example of First Period architecture. ⏱ 1–1½ hr. 27 Pleasant St. (1 block from Main St.). ☎ 978/283-0455. www.capeann museum.org. Admission $8 adults, $6 seniors & students, free for kids 11 & under. Mar–Jan Tues–Sat 10am–5pm, Sun 1–4pm. Closed Feb. Metered parking in lot across the street.

⑤ 🍽 **Halibut Point Restaurant & Bar, Gloucester.** This friendly tavern is known for its spicy Italian fish chowder, and it's a good place for fresh seafood, a sandwich, or a juicy burger. 289 Main St. (at Stoddards Lane). ☎ 978/281-1900. www. halibutpointrestaurant.com. $–$$.

Backtrack on Rte. 127 (Rogers St.) to East Main St. and turn right. Follow it for 1½ miles to the stone pillars that mark the entrance to Eastern Point Blvd.

⑥ ★★ **Beauport (Sleeper-McCann House), Gloucester.** Gloucester is both fishing port and exclusive summer community, and the jewel of the stylish Back Shore is this sprawling home created by interior designer and antiquarian

Henry Davis Sleeper. He made the house a showcase for his vast collection of American and European decorative art and antiques, filling its 40-plus rooms with everything from fine art to colored glass from the five-and-dime. The entertaining tour concentrates more on the gorgeous house and rooms in general than on the countless objects on display, which remain virtually as Sleeper left them when he died, in 1934. Take time to explore the grounds, which have amazing views of Gloucester Harbor. ⏱ 1 hr. 75 Eastern Point Blvd. ☎ 978/283-0800. www.historicnewengland.org. Guided tour $10 adults, $9 seniors, $5 students & kids 6–12, free (but I don't recommend it) for kids 5 & under. June–Oct 15 Tues–Sat 10am–5pm; tours on the hour (last tour 4pm).

Head south again, passing through downtown on Rte. 127. On Western Ave., cross the drawbridge and find a parking space.

⑦ ★ *Man at the Wheel*, **Gloucester.** The bronze *Memorial to the Gloucester Fisherman*, better known as the *Man at the Wheel*, is a larger-than-life symbol of the city. Leonard F. Craske's sculpture honors the more than 10,000 fishermen who lost their lives at sea

> *Swimming is forbidden in the quarries of Halibut Point State Park.*

during Gloucester's first 3 centuries. Several hundred yards west is a monument honoring the women and children who awaited their return. ⊙ 10 min. Stacey Blvd. (at Western Ave.). Daily 24 hr.

8 ★ kids **Stage Fort Park, Gloucester.** This is an optional stop; if you're starving, head to Essex. The park has lots of room to run around, a playground, beautiful scenery, and two beaches. Hough Ave. (at Western Ave.) Visitors Welcoming Center: ☎ 978/281-8865. Daily 9am–5pm summer only. Park: Daily year-round; parking Apr–Oct daily 8am–9pm.

Drive west on Rte. 133, crossing Rte. 128 and entering Essex. After about 6 miles, look for the Woodman's parking lot on the left.

9 🍴 ★★★ kids **Woodman's of Essex, Essex.** Throngs of locals and visitors descend on this rustic roadside restaurant for lobster "in the rough," chowder, steamers, corn on the cob, onion rings, and fried clams, purportedly invented here. Legend has it that Lawrence "Chubby" Woodman was the first person to fry up the mollusk, on July 3, 1916. The delicious morsels were as irresistible then as they are today, and they helped make a rousing success of the family business. In warm weather, people from all over the world flock here. In the winter, the crowd is mostly locals desperate for a taste of summer. The line is long, but it moves quickly and offers a good view of the regimented commotion in the food-prep area. Eat inside, upstairs on the deck, or out back at a picnic table. 121 Main St. ☎ 800/649-1773 or 978/768-6057. www.woodmans.com. AE, MC, V. Year-round daily lunch & dinner.

> *A feast at Woodman's of Essex, the reputed birthplace of the fried clam.*

Cape Ann: Practical Matters

Driving is the best way to see Cape Ann. If that's not an option, allow for lots of travel time. The **MBTA** commuter rail (☎ 617/222-3200; www.mbta.com) serves multiple stops on Cape Ann, including Gloucester and Rockport, from Boston's North Station. The Cape Ann Transportation Authority, or CATA (☎ 978/283-7916; www.canntran. com), runs buses from town to town on Cape Ann and operates special summer routes but has no service on Sunday. The **North of Boston Convention & Visitors Bureau** (☎ 800/742-5306 or 978/977-7760; www. northofboston.org) publishes a map and a visitor guide that includes Cape Ann. The **Cape Ann Chamber of Commerce,** 33 Commercial St., Gloucester (☎ 978/283-1601;

www.capeannvacations.com), distributes information year-round (summer Mon–Fri 9am–5pm, Sat 10am–5pm, Sun 10am–4pm; winter Mon–Fri 9am–5pm). The **Rockport Chamber of Commerce,** 170 Main St. (☎ 978/546-6575; www.rockportusa.com), operates an information booth on Upper Main Street (Rte. 127) daily from July 1 to Labor Day and on weekends from mid-May to June and early September through mid-October. In Gloucester, the **Visitors Welcoming Center** (☎ 800/649-6839 or 978/281-8865; www.gloucesterma.com) is at Stage Fort Park, off Rte. 127 at Rte. 133. It's open only during the summer (daily 9am–5pm).

Plymouth

Did you wear a construction paper hat or a feathered headdress in the Thanksgiving pageant? If you attended grade school in the United States before the heyday of political correctness, you probably did—and you probably know a little something about Plymouth. The Pilgrims. The *Mayflower*. The Rock. This town honors its history but isn't trapped in the past; it's a lively contemporary community that happens to have a lot of historic attractions.

> The 17th-century-style buildings at Plimoth Plantation give visitors a fresh perspective on the Pilgrims.

START Take I-93S and merge onto Rte. 3 south. To go directly to Plimoth Plantation, take Exit 4. Exit 6A deposits you on Rte. 44 east, which leads straight to downtown Plymouth. If it isn't rush hour, the trip from Boston takes about an hour.

❶ ★★ kids **Plimoth Plantation.** Until we perfect time travel, a visit here is the best way to experience the Pilgrims' daily life. A re-creation of a 1627 village, Plimoth Plantation approximates the conditions in the early days of the little community settled by the Puritans in 1620. Visitors wander around the farm area, visiting homes and gardens

constructed with careful attention to historic detail. The "Pilgrims" are actors who assume the personalities of members of the original community, and they take their roles seriously—kids get a kick out of their mystified reactions to questions about innovations such as TV or airplanes. You can watch them framing a house, splitting wood, shearing sheep, preserving foodstuffs, or cooking over an open hearth—all as it was done in the 1600s and using only the tools and cookware available then. Sometimes you can join the activities—perhaps planting, harvesting, witnessing a trial, or visiting a wedding party. Also open to visitors is a replica of a Wampanoag homesite

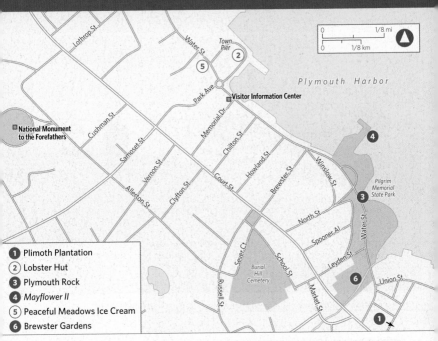

1 Plimoth Plantation
2 Lobster Hut
3 Plymouth Rock
4 Mayflower II
5 Peaceful Meadows Ice Cream
6 Brewster Gardens

that conveys a sense of how the local Indians lived. You'll be walking a lot, so wear comfortable shoes. If you plan to visit the *Mayflower II* (later in this tour), buy a discounted combination ticket. ⊕ 3 hr. (Be here when the gates open, especially in summer, when morning is the only cool part of the day). 137 Warren Ave. (at Rte. 3). ☎ 508/746-1622. www.plimoth.org. Admission (good for 2 consecutive days) $24 adults, $22 seniors, $14 kids 6–12. Plimoth Plantation & Mayflower II admission $28 adults, $26 seniors, $18 kids 6–12, free for kids 5 & under, $110 families. Late Mar to Nov daily 9am–5pm. Closed Dec to mid-Mar.

② 🍽 ★ kids **Lobster Hut.** The deck overlooking the harbor is the place to be at this self-service seafood restaurant, which is popular with out-of-towners and locals alike. Portions are reasonable, and you can order beer or wine (but only with a meal). 25 Town Wharf (off Water St.). ☎ 508/746-2270. $–$$.

③ ★★★ kids **Plymouth Rock.** At the heart of the smallest state park in Massachusetts is the legendary Plymouth Rock. Tradition tells us that the original rock was the landing

place of the *Mayflower* passengers in 1620. From a hunk 15 feet long and 3 feet wide, it diminished over the years through several relocations. In 1867, the remaining rock wound up here, perched at tide level on the peaceful shore. It's a model attraction: easy to understand, quick to visit, and unexpectedly affecting. In honor of the tricentennial of the Pilgrims' arrival, the Colonial Dames of America commissioned the enclosure, a templelike structure designed by McKim, Mead & White. ⊕ 10 min. Pilgrim Memorial State Park, Water St. (at Leyden & North sts.). ☎ 508/747-5360. www.mass.gov/dcr. Daily 24 hr.

④ ★ kids *Mayflower II.* This ship is unbelievably tiny, given its monumental role in American history. A full-scale reproduction of the type of vessel that brought the Pilgrims across the Atlantic to America in 1620, *Mayflower II* is just 106½ feet long. It's not an exact replica of the real thing, because we don't have much technical information about the original vessel, but the designer used available records to make this ship as accurate as possible. Costumed guides assume the characters of passengers to discuss the vessel and its perilous voyage, while other interpreters

> *Plymouth Harbor is home to scores of anonymous vessels and one world-famous one.*

> *Don't be surprised if visiting Plymouth Rock leaves a lump in your throat.*

John Adams & John Quincy Adams

A worthwhile detour en route to Plymouth is the **Adams National Historical Park** in Quincy, about 10 miles south of Boston. The park preserves the birthplaces of Presidents John Adams and John Quincy Adams, the house where four generations of the family lived, and other buildings associated with the political dynasty. The grounds of the 1731 Old House hold an orchard and a formal garden laid out and planted in 18th-century style. The park saw a boom in attendance after David McCullough's *John Adams* became a bestseller and then an HBO miniseries; recent crowds haven't been as large. A trolley connects the buildings, which are open for 2-hour guided tours—the only way to see the interiors—daily from 9am to 5pm in season (Apr 19–Nov 10). Admission is $5 for adults, free for children 15 and under. In the winter, call ahead for opening hours and days for the grounds and the visitor center, 1250 Hancock St. (☎ 617/770-1175; www.nps.gov/adam). The center is across the street from the Quincy Center stop on the Red Line; call or surf ahead for driving directions.

provide a contemporary perspective. It's a great place to turn children on to history as a true story—about real people. To start, ask them to imagine sharing this tiny ship with 101 other people. Just 52 of those original 102 survived their first winter in the New World and celebrated with what we now call the First Thanksgiving, in 1621. Plimoth Plantation owns and maintains the *Mayflower II* and offers discounted combination tickets. ⏱ 1 hr. State Pier. ☎ 508/746-1622. www.plimoth.org. Admission $10 adults, $9 seniors, $7 kids 6–12. Plimoth Plantation (good for 2 consecutive days) & *Mayflower II* admission $28 adults, $26 seniors, $18 kids 6–12, free for kids 5 & under, $110 families. Late Mar to Nov daily 9am–5pm. Closed Dec to mid-Mar.

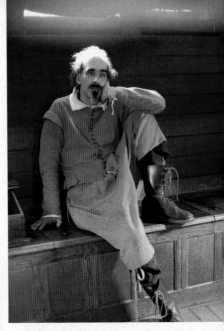

> *Costumed guides tell the story of the* Mayflower II.

Plymouth: Practical Matters

Driving to Plymouth is vastly preferable to taking public transit. Leave plenty of time if you don't drive. The **MBTA** commuter rail (☎ 800/392-6100 or 617/222-3200; www. mbta.com) from Boston's South Station serves Cordage Park, north of downtown Plymouth, and Plymouth and Brockton **buses** (☎ 508/746-4795; www.p-b.com) run to the park-and-ride lot at Exit 5 off Rte. 3. The **local bus** (☎ 508/746-0378; www.gatra.org/pal.html) takes you from the train station or bus stop to downtown Plymouth. There's a year-round visitor information center at Exit 5 that covers the whole region; for Plymouth-specific information, visit the seasonal **visitor center** at 130 Water St. (☎ 508/747-7525), across from the town pier. Information is available year-round from **Destination Plymouth,** 170 Water St. (☎ 800/ USA-1620 872-1620 or 508/747-7533; www.visit-plymouth.com). To get around without a car—or without moving the car—consider riding **America's Hometown Shuttle** (☎ 508/746-0378; www.p-b.com/ ahs.html). The narrated trolley tour covers a loop throughout the town from late June to Labor Day weekend, daily from 10am to 5pm. The fare ($15 adults, $7.50 children 6–11) includes unlimited reboarding. Check ahead for the schedule and pickup and drop-off points.

⑤ 🍽 ★ kids **Peaceful Meadows Ice Cream.** A family business that dates to 1962, Peaceful Meadows is a tasty place to refuel. Take your ice cream (fresh peach—yum) along with you to your final stop. 170 Water St. (opposite Town Wharf). ☎ 508/746-2362. www.peaceful meadowsicecream.com. $.

⑥ ★ kids **Brewster Gardens.** Backtrack along Water Street to wind down at this lovely park, on the site of the garden of an original settler, William Brewster. Two dramatic sculptures are here. The *Pilgrim Maiden*, a bronze created by Henry Hudson Kitson and erected in 1924 on a rock overlooking a small pool, honors the memory of the first female settlers. Nearby, the Plymouth Immigrant Monument is a stainless steel column decorated with figures representing people who arrived from 1700 to 2000. The monument, by Martha's Vineyard resident Barney Zeitz, was unveiled in 2001. Contemplate the art, then sit back and enjoy the greenery, or follow Town Brook up the hill to Jenney Pond, where the water wheel powers the gristmill. ⏱ 1 hr. Water & Leyden sts. ☎ 508/830-4095.

Boston & Cambridge Fast Facts

Arriving by Air

Logan International Airport (☎ 800/23-LO-GAN 235-6426; www.massport.com/logan) is the major New England airport. The best way to get across the harbor to downtown is the **MBTA bus or subway** (☎ 800/392-6100 or 617/222-3200; www.mbta.com). Kiosks in each terminal sell fare cards; see "Getting Around Boston & Cambridge," below, for information. The Silver Line bus connects each terminal to South Station, where you can exit or board the Red Line subway or commuter rail. To reach other destinations, take the free airport shuttle bus from the terminal to the Blue Line subway for the 10-minute ride downtown, then exit or transfer.

The initial **cab** fare from the airport is $10.10 ($7.50 in fees plus the initial $2.60 fare). The total fare to downtown or the Back Bay is at least $20 and can be much higher, depending on traffic. The trip to the downtown waterfront in a weather-protected **boat** takes about 7 minutes dock to dock and costs $10 one-way. The free no. 66 shuttle bus connects the airport terminals to the Logan ferry dock. **Harbor Express** (☎ 617/222-6999; www.harborexpress.com) runs scheduled ferries to Long Wharf, behind the Marriott Long Wharf hotel. Three on-call water-taxi services serve the airport and points on the harbor: **Boston Harbor Water Taxi** (☎ 617/593-9168; www.bostonharborwatertaxi.com), **City Water Taxi** (☎ 617/422-0392; www.citywatertaxi.com), and **Rowes Wharf Water Transport** (☎ 617/406-8584; www.roweswharfwatertransport.com). At the airport, ask the shuttle driver to radio ahead for water-taxi pickup; on the way back, call ahead for service. The Logan website lists numerous **shuttle van** companies that serve local hotels. One-way prices start at $14 per person, subject to fuel surcharges.

Getting Around Boston & Cambridge

ON FOOT This is the way to go if you can manage it. Even the tallest hills aren't too steep, and vehicular traffic is brutal. BY PUBLIC TRANSIT The **MBTA,** or "T" (☎ 800/392-6100 or 617/222-3200; www.mbta.com), runs subways and trolleys, buses, ferries, and the suburban commuter rail. The website has an interactive **trip planner.** The stored-value **fare system** uses paper CharlieTickets and plastic CharlieCards. CharlieTickets are easier to get (from kiosks at every station and every airport terminal), but users pay more. With a **CharlieTicket,** the subway fare is $2, the bus fare $1.50. With a **CharlieCard**—available from employees who staff most downtown subway stations and from retail locations listed on the website—subway riders pay $1.70, bus passengers $1.25. At press time, neither works on ferries or the commuter rail. Service on the Red, Green, Orange, and Blue subway lines begins at around 5:15am and ends around 12:30am. Local, express, and Silver Line buses keep shorter hours. The Boston Harbor **water shuttle** (☎ 617/227-4321) is a commuter ferry that connects Long Wharf, near the New England Aquarium, with the Charlestown Navy Yard. The one-way fare is $1.70. BY TAXI Taxis can be tough to hail on the street; your best bet is to call a dispatcher or seek out a hotel or cabstand. To call ahead, try the **Independent Taxi Operators Association,** or ITOA (☎ 617/426-8700); **Boston Cab** (☎ 617/536-5010); **Top Cab/City Cab** (☎ 617/536-5100); or **Metro Cab** (☎ 617/782-5500). In Cambridge, call **Ambassador Brattle/Yellow Cab** (☎ 617/492-1100 or 617/547-3000) or **Checker Cab** (☎ 617/497-1500). BY CAR If you plan to visit only Boston and Cambridge, there's no reason to have a car. If you arrive by car, park at the hotel and use the car for day trips. If you want to rent a car for travel beyond Boston, see p. 571 for information.

Parking

Most spaces on the street in Boston and Cambridge are metered, and many are reserved for residents. Read the signs carefully, because

Travel Tip

See p. 570 in "The Savvy Traveler" chapter for train and bus arrival information for Boston.

even an expensive garage is cheaper than a ticket. The rate is usually $1 per hour; bring plenty of quarters. On some Boston streets and in some Cambridge lots, you pay at a central machine and leave the receipt on the dashboard or the inside of the driver's-side window. Time limits range from 15 minutes to 2 hours. A full day at most garages costs no more than $30, but some downtown facilities charge as much as $45, and hourly rates can be exorbitant.

Safety

Boston and Cambridge are generally safe, especially in the areas you're likely to visit. Nevertheless, you should take the same precautions you would in any other large city. Trust your instincts—a dark, deserted street is probably deserted for a reason. Stay out of parks (including Boston Common, the Public Garden, the Esplanade, the Rose Kennedy Greenway, and Cambridge Common) at night unless you're in a crowd. Try not to walk alone late at night in the Theater District or around North Station. Public transportation in the areas you're likely to visit is busy and safe, but service stops between 12:30 and 1am. Be sure to carry cab fare and a charged phone if you're going to be out late.

Toilets

The **National Park Service visitor centers,** 15 State St. and the Charlestown Navy Yard, have public restrooms, as do most other tourist attractions, hotels, department stores, malls, and public buildings. The central branch of the **Boston Public Library** in Copley Square and most fast-food restaurants and coffee bars have reasonably clean restrooms. Some restaurants and bars, including those in tourist areas, display a sign saying that toilets are for the use of patrons only. Paying for a coffee or soft drink qualifies you as a patron. You'll find free-standing, self-cleaning pay toilets (25¢) scattered around downtown. Check carefully before using them; IV drug users have been known to take advantage of the generous time limits.

Visitor Information

The **Greater Boston Convention & Visitors Bureau** (☎ 888/733-2678 or 617/536-4100; www.bostonusa.com) offers a visitor information kit ($10 plus postage) and an iPhone app (99¢) that allows users to buy e-tickets for attractions and tours and enter by just showing the screen. The bureau also publishes a **Kids Love Boston** guide ($5) and smaller guides to specific seasons and special events. The bureau operates the **Boston Common Information Center,** 148 Tremont St. (Mon-Fri 8:30am-5pm; Sat 9am-5pm), and the **Prudential Information Center,** on the main level of the Prudential Center, 800 Boylston St. (Mon-Fri 9am-5:30pm; Sat-Sun 10am-6pm).

The **Cambridge Office for Tourism** (☎ 800/862-5678 or 617/441-2884; www.cambridge-usa.org) operates an information kiosk (Mon-Fri 9am-5pm; Sat-Sun 9am-1pm) in Harvard Square, near the T entrance at the intersection of John F. Kennedy Street and Brattle Street.

The **Massachusetts Office of Travel and Tourism** (☎ 800/227-6277 or 617/973-8500; www.massvacation.com) distributes information about the state. Its free *Getaway Guide* magazine includes attractions and lodgings listings, a map, and a calendar.

National Park Service rangers staff the **Boston National Historical Park Visitor Center** (☎ 617/242-5642; www.nps.gov/bost) and lead seasonal free tours of the Freedom Trail. At press time, the center is at 15 State St., across the street from the Old State House; it was scheduled to move to the first floor of Faneuil Hall in late 2011. The center is open daily 9am to 5pm. The ranger-staffed center at the Charlestown Navy Yard (☎ 617/242-5601) keeps the same hours.

The small outdoor information booth at Faneuil Hall Marketplace, between Quincy Market and the South Market Building, is staffed in the spring, summer, and fall (Mon-Sat 10am-6pm; Sun noon-6pm).

4
Cape Cod &
the Islands

Our Favorite Cape Cod & the Islands Moments

Sunbathing on pristine beaches, discovering inlets by kayak, and biking New England's best coastal trails are some of the peak experiences to be had on Cape Cod and the islands. Charming Main Streets lined with one-of-a-kind shops are another big draw for visitors. For visitors who like a little history in their downtime, the Cape has that too, along the fabled Old King's Highway. Here are a dozen of the region's most pleasant pastimes.

> PREVIOUS PAGE *Serenity is yours at the boardwalk at Gray's Beach in Yarmouthport.* THIS PAGE *The 12-mile Shining Sea Bikeway passes a Buzzards Bay beach, perfect for a cool dip.*

❶ Beaching it from the bays to the ocean. The options range from Old Silver Beach on Buzzards Bay to Sandy Neck on Cape Cod Bay to Craigville Beach on Nantucket Sound and Race Point on the Atlantic Ocean—all with different temperatures, wave action, and social scenes. If you're going to pick just one, make it magnificent Nauset Beach in Orleans, an Atlantic Ocean–facing beach that has more activities and amenities than any stretch of sand on the Cape. See p. 174.

❷ Biking the Shining Sea Bikeway from North Falmouth to Woods Hole. With the expanded 12-mile Shining Sea Bikeway in Falmouth, bike enthusiasts just got another scenic route to choose from, in addition to the 7-mile Cape Cod Canal trail, the 35-mile Cape Cod Rail Trail, and the 9-mile Provincelands trail through the dunes at the Cape's tip. See p. 168.

❸ Strolling Main Street. Main Streets don't get much more colorful than on Cape Cod, where unique shops offer one-of-a-kind wares

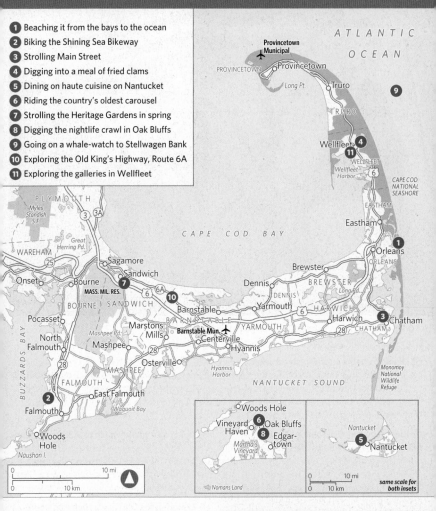

1. Beaching it from the bays to the ocean
2. Biking the Shining Sea Bikeway
3. Strolling Main Street
4. Digging into a meal of fried clams
5. Dining on haute cuisine on Nantucket
6. Riding the country's oldest carousel
7. Strolling the Heritage Gardens in spring
8. Digging the nightlife crawl in Oak Bluffs
9. Going on a whale-watch to Stellwagen Bank
10. Exploring the Old King's Highway, Route 6A
11. Exploring the galleries in Wellfleet

within strolling distance of beaches. Local favorites are Falmouth, Hyannis, Provincetown, Nantucket, and, best of all, Chatham—where you can walk to the end of the street and see the Atlantic Ocean just beyond the barrier beach. See p. 194, ❶.

❹ **Digging into a meal of fried clams.** A real Cape Codder goes belly-up at the thought of fried clams piled high with fries and onion rings. If you can only indulge once, head to Moby Dick's in Wellfleet, where they have mastered the art of fresh fish fast. For a selection of the best, see "Cape Cod for Seafood Lovers," p. 210.

> You're on vacation—go ahead and indulge with some tasty fried clams at Moby Dick's.

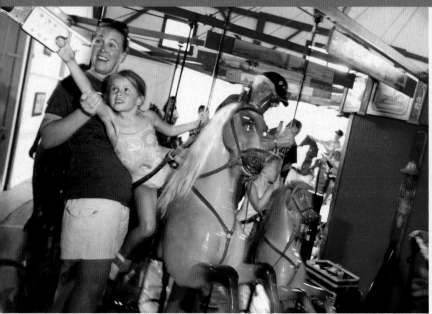

> *Grab the gold ring if you can on the Flying Horses Carousel in Oak Bluffs.*

⑤ Dining on haute cuisine on Nantucket. If up-scale dining is your thing, you'll want to head to the island of Nantucket, where chefs at two dozen upscale restaurants compete to serve the best fine dining on the island. See p. 227.

⑥ Riding the country's oldest carousel on Martha's Vineyard. It's an old-fashioned thrill, riding the Flying Horses Carousel in Oak Bluffs and reaching out to capture the brass ring. You'll see riders from 9 months to 90 years of age taking a spin on the colorful steeds. See p. 153, ②.

⑦ Strolling the Heritage Gardens in spring when the rhododendrons are in bloom. In late May and June, there's no more sensational view than the thousands of rhododendrons blooming at the Heritage Gardens in Sand-wich. The 76-acre complex displays a pre-miere collection of flowering plants in three museum buildings and along gently sloping walking trails. See p. 156, ①.

⑧ Digging the nightlife crawl in Oak Bluffs. For a fun nightlife scene, head to Oak Bluffs on Martha's Vineyard. Begin with a late dinner at one of the restaurants on the harbor. Then continue on to the Ritz Café, a classic dive bar with local bands. And no night crawl would be complete without a trip to **Back Door Donuts** (p. 221), the late-night bakery that feeds the partying crowd in an alley off Circuit Avenue. See p. 220.

⑨ Going on a whale-watch to Stellwagen Bank. It's a Cape Cod essential to take a whale-watch-ing boat to the waters off Provincetown and watch the whales cavorting in the waves. Expect flipper slaps and fluke displays. See p. 173.

⑩ Exploring the Old King's Highway, Route 6A, from Bourne to Orleans. Take a leisurely drive from one end of the Cape to the other on the Old King's Highway, with its broad range of Early American architecture and all the gift and antiques shops you could want. See p. 147, ③.

⑪ Exploring the galleries in Wellfleet and Provincetown. Gallery stroll night is Saturday, when you can stop in at half a dozen galleries and check out art while hobnobbing with the artists themselves. Your stroll will take you from Main Street to Commercial Street near the harbor, where a number of old boat shops have been converted into sophisticated galler-ies. See "An Art Lover's Paradise," p. 149.

> Flukes and flipper slaps are special greetings during a whale-watch.

Cape Cod in 3 Days

If you're lucky, you'll have a week to explore Cape Cod, which stretches 75 miles, with 15 towns all worth visiting. If you have only a few days, it's best to focus on the highlights and visit the towns of Falmouth, Barnstable, and Provincetown. You'll bike down the Shining Sea Bikeway in Falmouth and explore the science community, Woods Hole. You'll motor down the Old King's Highway and visit the Cape's unofficial capital of Hyannis, where you can pay homage to JFK's Camelot legacy. Finally, you'll take in art, culture, and the liveliest street scene this side of Manhattan at the Cape's tip in Provincetown.

> The annual Fourth of July fireworks display over Falmouth Heights Beach is the largest on the Cape & Islands.

START Falmouth is 71 miles from Boston. **TRIP LENGTH** 75 miles.

Drive to Cape Cod on Rte. 495S. Drive over the Bourne Bridge and take Rte. 28 toward Falmouth. In about 12 miles, you will arrive at a traffic light. Continue straight and take the 5th left to the Village Green.

❶ ★★★ **Falmouth.** A slice of Americana, Falmouth's charming ★★★ **Village Green** is flanked by two historic churches and surrounded by a dozen historic buildings, including the ★ **Falmouth Museums on The Green,** 55–65 Palmer Ave. (☎ 508/548-4857; www. falmouthhistoricalsociety.org). The museum tells the story of the town through exhibits in three buildings: the 1790 **Julia Wood House,**

the mid-18th-century **Conant House,** and the **Dudley Hallett Barn.** Founded in 1660 by Quakers from Sandwich, Falmouth proved to be remarkably arable territory. Today, with more than 33,000 year-round residents, it's the second-largest town on the Cape, after Barnstable. The town was the first "fashionable" Cape resort, served by trains from Boston starting in the 1870s. The area around the historic Village Green, which was used for military exercises in the pre-Revolutionary days, has several B&Bs and inns. From the Village Green, you'll want to spend some time exploring ★★ **Main Street,** where you'll find stores selling books, clothes, art, gifts, and a dozen restaurants and ice-cream shops.

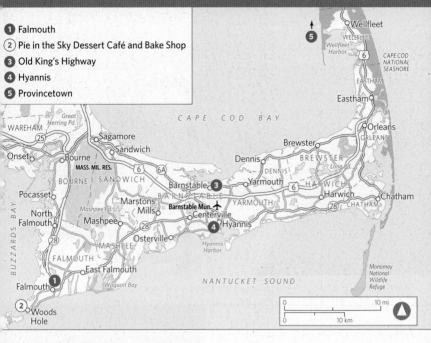

1 Falmouth
2 Pie in the Sky Dessert Café and Bake Shop
3 Old King's Highway
4 Hyannis
5 Provincetown

Wander several blocks down to **Peg Noonan Park** on the left, at the intersection of Library Lane, where in the summer free live music is performed on Friday evenings and a farmers market takes place on Thursdays. Don't miss the nearby shops in the **Queens Buyway**. Here you can buy a cup of coffee, and buy t-shirts and other souvenirs. Fit visitors can rent a bike at **Corner Cycle** in the Queens Buyway and explore the 12-mile ★★★ **Shining Sea Bikeway** (p. 168), named in honor of Falmouth native Katharine Lee Bates, who wrote the lyrics to *America the Beautiful.* The Falmouth Chamber of Commerce has maps for the entire path, complete with historical notes and points of interest. From the Village Green, it's a quick ride down Locust Street to the bike path for a 3-mile ride that skirts the coastline (on a warm day, you can stop to take a dip in Buzzards Bay) down to ★★★ **Woods Hole** (p. 182, 5), a bohemian fishing village that's also one of the top scientific communities in the world. ⏱ 1 day. Falmouth Chamber of Commerce, 20 Academy Lane, Falmouth. ☎ 508/548-8500. www.falmouthchamber.com. For detailed information on sites in Falmouth, see p. 180.

② 🍽 ★★ **Pie in the Sky Dessert Café and Bake Shop, Woods Hole.** Locals know to show up by 9am at this small bakery near the ferry terminal for the best sticky buns anywhere. Martha's Vineyard–bound passengers stop for treats before hopping on the boat. 10 Water St. ☎ 508/540-5475. $.

From Falmouth, take Rte. 28 back to the traffic rotary at the Bourne Bridge. Instead of going over the bridge, take the 1st right off the rotary and drive alongside the canal, under the Sagamore Bridge, to the town of Sandwich. The road turns into Rte. 6A, also known as the Old King's Highway. Follow for 15 miles to Barnstable Village.

3 ★★★ **Old King's Highway, Barnstable Village.** The beauty of exploring the Old King's Highway is you can make as many or as few

Travel Tip

For recommended hotels and restaurants in Falmouth, see p. 184; in Hyannis, see p. 190; in Provincetown, see p. 208.

> *A life jacket and a compass are essential gear when kayaking the waters around Cape Cod.*

stops as you like. You'll see plenty of interesting shops, from glass blowers' workshops to pottery studios, antiquarian bookstalls, antiques stores, and marvelous gift shops. People love to drive this long, winding road, a former stagecoach route, just to look at the homes, which represent a veritable history of Early American home construction, from classic Capes to Colonial, Federal, and Victorian styles of architecture. ☺ 2½ hr. For detailed information, see the tour on p. 166.

To get to Hyannis, you can take Rte. 6 to exit 6 (Rte. 132) or follow the Old King's Hwy. for about 15 miles from the Sagamore Bridge to Rte. 132. Take Rte. 132 through the airport rotary and down Barnstable Rd. to Main St.

❹ ★★★ **Hyannis.** To bask in the Kennedys' Cape Cod experience, visit the **John F. Kennedy Hyannis Museum.** A documentary on the clan is narrated by Walter Cronkite, and several rooms' worth of photos show family members at home on Cape Cod. The **Kennedy Memorial,** just above **Veterans Beach** on Ocean Avenue, is a moving tribute. Main Street, Hyannis, also has a vibrant arts district. You can walk through the **Hyannis Village Green** to the seven **art shanties in Bismore Park** on the harbor. You may catch a free musical performance in summer or even

Save Time for Beaching It

There's so much to do on Cape Cod, you might actually forget to hit the beach, but that would be a shame. In Falmouth, high points for beaching it are **Falmouth Heights Beach,** in the historic neighborhood that housed the Cape's first summer resort, and **Old Silver Beach** in North Falmouth, one of the Cape's most popular shorelines. In the town of Barnstable, there's **Sandy Neck** (pictured), a 7-mile spit of sand accessible off Route 6A. In the Outer Cape, the home of the magnificent **Cape Cod National Seashore** (essentially one big beach), there's **Nauset Beach** in Orleans; and in Provincetown, **Race Point Beach** on the Atlantic Ocean. For details on visiting all of these spots, see Cape Cod & Islands Beaches A to Z on p. 174.

Shakespeare in the park on weekend nights. Other interesting attractions within walking distance of Main Street are the **Cape Maritime Museum** on South Street, **Guyer Barn** at 230 South St. (☎ 508/790-6370; www.hyarts district.com/guyer_barn/), and **Zion Union Museum** on North Street. ⏱ ½ day. For detailed information on sites in Hyannis, see p. 186.

From Hyannis, take Rte. 6/Mid-Cape Hwy. east 19 miles. At the traffic circle, take the 2nd exit and stay on Rte. 6 E./Mid-Cape Hwy. for another 19 miles. Turn left at Rte. 6A W./Shore Rd. Continue 6 miles to Provincetown.

⑤ ★★★ **Provincetown.** This boisterous, fascinating place is a year-round destination. But during the summer season, Provincetown's streets are a celebration of individual freedom and the right to be as outrageous as imagination allows. The dozens of shops along Commercial Street are all open well into the evening, and some people come here just for the fabulous shopping. Others come for the art galleries, and still others for the dining. From Macmillan Pier in the center of town, you can take a sail on the *Bay Lady II* or a whale-watch to Stellwagen Bank. Some of the best beaches on the Cape are just down the road at **Herring Cove** and **Race Point**. P-town has a number of sidewalk cafes perfect for people-watching. Plop yourself down at a sidewalk table at ★ **Patio,** 328 Commercial St. (☎ 508/487-4003; $$), and watch the parade of colorful locals and visitors. ⏱ 1 day. Provincetown Chamber of Commerce, 307 Commercial St. (at Lopes Sq.). ☎ 508/487-3424. www.ptownchamber.com.

An Art Lover's Paradise

Bohemians began arriving on the Outer Cape more than 100 years ago, and the art colony once called the largest in the United States is still going strong. The dozens of art galleries on Commercial Street in Provincetown stay open well into the evening. Nearby Wellfleet, which bills itself as the "art gallery town," also has its share of interesting galleries specializing in crafts. Many Outer Cape galleries are open from 11am to 8pm (or later) in summer. Here are a few of my favorites.

★ **The Cove Gallery, Wellfleet.** The Cove carries the paintings and prints of well-known artists such as John Grillo, whose exuberantly colored abstract paintings are considered seminal works. 15 Commercial St. ☎ 508/349-2530. www.covegallery.com.

★ **Left Bank Gallery, Wellfleet.** Pottery, textiles, and collages share space with oil paintings at this reputable gallery, one of the oldest and largest in town. 25 Commercial St. ☎ 508/349-9451. www.leftbankgallery.com.

★ **Susan Baker Memorial Museum, North Truro.** Whimsical artist Susan Baker did not want to wait until she died to have a museum named after her, so she started one up herself. Her colorful primitive paintings of European landscapes are worth a closer look. Take the North Truro exit off Rte. 6 and follow signs toward North Truro center. 46 Rte. 6A/Shore Rd. ☎ 508/487-2557. www.susanbakerart.com.

★★ **DNA Gallery, Provincetown.** You'll likely find something politically charged at this well-respected gallery on the far East End of town. 288 Bradford St. ☎ 508/487-7700. www.dnagallery.com.

★ **Berta Walker Gallery, Provincetown.** Always worth a look, Berta Walker presents established talents with links to old Provincetown. 208 Bradford St. ☎ 508/487-6411.

★★★ **Provincetown Art Association & Museum, Provincetown.** The finest and most elegant museum on Cape Cod is worth a visit. Established in 1914 by a group of artists, the museum has a history that stretches back to the earliest days of Provincetown's art colony. There is typically an exhibit reaching back into its extraordinary collections, alongside something more contemporary. 460 Commercial St. ☎ 508/487-1750. www.paam.org. Admission $7. June-Sept Mon-Thurs 11am-8pm, Fri 11am-10pm, Sat-Sun 11am-5pm; call for off-season hours.

Nantucket in 3 Days

You could easily, and very happily, spend a week (or more) on charming little Nantucket, but if you're combining a visit to the island with a trip to the Cape, you can still see quite a bit of the island in just a few days. You'll spend most of your time in Nantucket Town, the only real hub here. The island is a bikers' dream, crisscrossed with beautifully maintained flat paths, and there is an excellent inexpensive shuttle-bus system, so take advantage.

> *You can easily explore the entire island of Nantucket by bike.*

START From the ferry, take the first left onto Easy St. and proceed 2 blocks to Main St.

❶ ★★★ **Main Street.** As soon as you step off the ferry, you'll be tempted to stroll the cobblestoned streets of Nantucket, which are lined with mostly high-end shops. Those cobblestones were originally ballast for ships that departed from these shores 150 years ago. It's fun to window-shop on Straight Wharf and South Wharf, the two piers that jut into the yacht-filled harbor. South Wharf is a mini gallery district, and its shops include nationally known artists. On Main Street and side streets, especially Centre Street, Easy Street, and Federal Street, you'll find crafters, jewelry, clothing, and gift shops. ⏲ 1–2 hr.

❷ ★★★ **Whaling Museum.** This museum is one of the top attractions in the region. It's housed in an 1846 former spermaceti-candle factory (candles made from a fluid extracted from sperm whales). The collection includes world-class crafts made by sailors, such as Nantucket baskets and scrimshaw, as well as exotic items brought back to Nantucket by whalers, including intricate sailor's valentines. A highlight is the 43-foot sperm whale skeleton, which hangs over an auditorium area where films about whaling are frequently screened. The story of Nantucket's history is all here in viewer-friendly displays, with an extensive archive of historic photos, including shots from the early days of tourism. ⏲ 2 hr. 13 Broad St. (3 blocks west of Main St.). ☎ 508/ 228-1894. www.nha.org. Admission $17 adults, $16 seniors, $8 kids; an extra $3 gets you into all the historical association sites, including the Oldest House, the Hadwen House, the Old Mill & the Quaker Meeting House. Mid-May to mid-Oct daily 10am–5pm.

Getting to the Islands

For detailed information on how to get to Nantucket, see Getting to Nantucket by Ferry, p. 229.

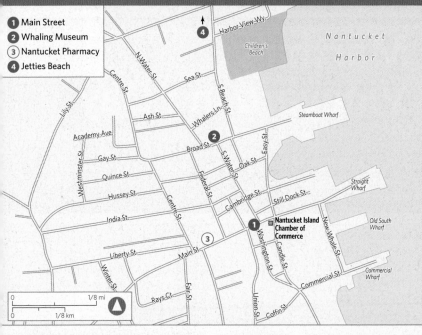

1. Main Street
2. Whaling Museum
3. Nantucket Pharmacy
4. Jetties Beach

For All the Nantucket Answers

For all its charm, Nantucket can be tough to negotiate. It can be difficult to find lodging in high season or even the shoulder seasons. Enter the **Nantucket Visitor Service and Information Bureau,** 25 Federal St., Nantucket (☎ 508/228-0925). They have up-to-the-minute vacancy information on most every accommodation on the island. They also have lists of inn and restaurant specials.

③ 🍽 ★ **Nantucket Pharmacy.** It's not easy to find a bargain on Nantucket, but this old-fashioned drugstore soda fountain qualifies. This place serves the best lunch in town, with good food at great prices. Locals love the sandwiches and the ice-cream sodas. 45 Main St. ☎ 508/228-0180. $.

From Main St., take N. Water St. 1 mile and follow signs to Jetties Beach.

④ ★★★ **Jetties Beach.** There's always a lot going on at this large family-friendly beach. It is about a 20-minute walk from town, but a shuttle-bus service runs frequently in

> The skeleton of a sperm whale that washed up on a local beach hangs from the ceiling in the Whaling Museum.

summer. It has more amenities than any other Nantucket beach, such as changing rooms, a playground with swings and a slide, public tennis courts, and a boardwalk. You can rent equipment for windsurfing, sailing, and kayaking. There are also beach-access wheelchairs. On-site is a breakfast, lunch, and dinner restaurant called The Jetties, at 4 Bathing Beach Rd. (off S. Beach St.). ⏱ 3 hr. See p. 176.

Martha's Vineyard in 1 Day

If you want to see the best of the Vineyard, you'll need good walking shoes or a sturdy bike; cars on the island are discouraged. Fortunately, an inexpensive shuttle-bus system travels to all six Vineyard towns. You get a good taste of the island, though, by just exploring the towns of Oak Bluffs and Edgartown.

> Red clay cliffs are at the heart of Aquinnah, home of the local Wampanoag tribe.

START Follow Circuit Ave. from Veira Park about ½ mile north to Bayliss Ave., then turn left at Trinity Park.

❶ ★★★ Oak Bluffs Cottage Campground. Stroll up lively Circuit Avenue and then cut through an arched walkway on the north side of the street to visit the famous "campground" of cottages, more than 300 multicolored, elaborately trimmed houses set in a 34-acre grove. The neighborhood of tightly packed cottages is a former Methodist Revival

meeting place. In the center of the circle is the **Trinity Park Tabernacle,** a magnificent open-sided chapel built in 1879. The structure is the location for community sings, concerts, and performances held all summer long, in addition to Sunday services. Once the location for 19th-century revival meetings, the cottages took the place of tents that housed worshipers during religious gatherings. Walking tours of the campground are Tuesdays and Thursdays at 10am. The Cottage Museum is decorated

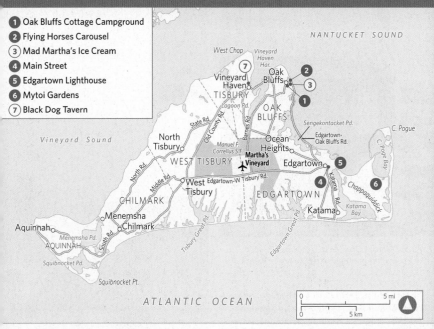

1 Oak Bluffs Cottage Campground
2 Flying Horses Carousel
3 Mad Martha's Ice Cream
4 Main Street
5 Edgartown Lighthouse
6 Mytoi Gardens
7 Black Dog Tavern

with period furnishings and displays vintage photos. ⏱ 1 hr. Cottage Museum, 1 Trinity Park Circle, Oak Bluffs. ☎ 508/693-7784. www.mvc-ma.org. Admission $2 adults, 50¢ kids 3–12. Mon-Sat 10am–4pm & Sun 1–4pm in summer only.

From Trinity Park, continue north on Circuit Ave. and turn right at Lake Ave.

2 ★★★ **Flying Horses Carousel.** You don't have to be a little kid to enjoy riding the Flying Horses Carousel in Oak Bluffs. The colorful historic steeds, with their glass eyes and manes of real horsehair, encircle America's oldest operating platform carousel. Built in 1876, the carousel is also a National Historic Landmark. Grab the brass ring for a free ride. ⏱ 10 min. Oak Bluffs Ave. (at the top of Circuit Ave.). ☎ 508/693-9481. Admission $2 per ride. Open Easter Sun–Columbus Day (mid-Oct). Summer daily 10am–10pm; reduced hours April to Memorial Day.

3 🍧 ★ **Mad Martha's Ice Cream.** No trip to Martha's Vineyard would be complete without paying homage at the famous Mad Martha's. 117 Circuit Ave. (in the center of town), Oak Bluffs. ☎ 508/693-9151. $.

> *Picture yourself in a storybook when exploring the dozens of whimsical cottages in the Martha's Vineyard Campground.*

> Mad Martha's Ice Cream is the place to get a scoop of the presidential tribute flavor, Barack My World.

You'll want to bike or drive to Edgartown. From Circuit Ave., head south on Seaview Ave. for 4 miles. Continue on to Edgartown-Oak Bluffs Rd. for 1 mile. Continue on to Upper Main St., then Main St. for ¾ mile.

④ ★★★ **Main Street.** The best shopping on the island is in Edgartown, a white-picket-fence kind of place. You might begin at the **Edgartown Visitor Center** on Main and Church streets. From there, you can check out the magnificent 1843 **Old Whaling Church,** as well as the **Dr. Daniel Fisher House,** at 99 Main St., which is an opulent 1840 Federal-style beauty. The 1672 **Vincent House,** off Main Street between Planting Field Way and Church Street, is the oldest house on the island. Walk down Main Street toward the harbor for great window-shopping, then take a left onto North Water Street. ☺ 1 hr.

Walk northeast on N. Water St. about ¼ mile toward Cottage St., then turn left.

⑤ ★★ **Edgartown Harbor Light.** For an easy romantic walk or a mini family adventure, walk down North Water Street (off Main St.) and out to the Edgartown Lighthouse to Lighthouse Beach. ☺ 30 min. See p. 214, ⑩.

Return to N. Water St., head southwest about 400 ft., then take a left onto Dagget St. Go another 350 ft., and Dagget St. turns right and becomes Dock St. Catch the ferry

> Harbor Light, beacon to mariners, doubles as a picnic spot in Edgartown.

to Chappaquiddick Island at Dock St. (see "Catching the Ferry" below for details). From the ferry, take Chappaquiddick Rd. for 2½ miles. At the sharp right curve, continue straight onto Dike Rd. (a dirt road) and follow for ¾ mile to the entrance and parking area on the left.

⑥ ★★★ **Mytoi Gardens.** If you want to feel like a Vineyard insider, take the ferry to

Seeing the Island by Bus

For a 2½-hour bus tour of the Vineyard, call **Island Transport** (☎ 508/627-8687; www.mvtour.com), or hop on one of the Island Transport buses stationed at the ferry terminals in Vineyard Haven and Oak Bluffs in the summer. The tour takes you to all six of the Vineyard's towns: Edgartown, Oak Bluffs, Vineyard Haven, West Tisbury, Chilmark, and Aquinnah. The tour stops for a half-hour at the famous red-clay cliffs of Aquinnah. Tours are $29 adults, $10 children.

> *The Vineyard's winding country roads feature ancient stone walls and colorful mailboxes.*

Chappaquiddick Island, and walk, bike, or drive the 2½ miles to Mytoi, a 14-acre secluded Japanese garden. The garden, with its numerous winding footpaths, is designed as a place of serenity and contemplation. The plantings, from a vibrant pink camellia dell to a somber stone garden, are a celebration of textures and colors. There's a small pond traversed by a footbridge. Trails from the garden connect to Poucha Pond and a salt marsh. There are picnic tables and portable toilets.

Even in the height of summer, it's uncrowded here. ⏲ 30 min. to visit the garden. Dike Rd., Chappaquiddick Island. ☎ 508/627-7689. Free admission. Year-round sunrise–sunset.

Return to Edgartown and travel back to Vineyard Haven for the ferry to the mainland. Stop for a snack at the most famous eatery on the island.

⑦ 🍽 ★ **Black Dog Tavern.** Before you hop the ferry home, stop at the Black Dog Bakery for a cup of coffee. If you want something more substantial—like a cup of chowder—walk behind the bakery to the tavern, which sits on the edge of the harbor. Yes, it is touristy (you can skip the T-shirt), but the food is good. **Beach St.** exit, Vineyard Haven Harbor. ☎ 508/683-9223. www.theblackdog.com. $–$$.

Catching the Ferry

The Edgartown–Chappaquiddick **On-Time Ferry** (☎ 508/627-9437; www.chappyferry.net) runs every 10 minutes from 7am to midnight. A round-trip is $3 per person, $10 per car plus driver, or $6 per bike plus rider.

Cape Cod with Kids

Many kids can plop down on the beach and amuse
themselves for hours on end. That's certainly one way to spend a Cape
Cod vacation, but there are so many more things to do here, both fun and
educational. The following sites, all within an easy drive of the Mid-Cape area,
will give you and your children a little break from all that sun.

> With or without sprinkles can be a tough choice at Frosty's
> on Route 6A in Dennis.

START Sandwich is 16 miles northwest of Hyannis. **TRIP LENGTH** 1 day.

❶ ★★★ Heritage Museums and Gardens. There's something for everyone on this 76-acre property, and kids will likely leave clamoring for another visit. The three museum buildings house unique collections. The round Shaker Barn is the place to find vintage automobiles, dating back to the Model T. Another building displays Native American artifacts and a collection of antique tin soldiers set up in tableaux illustrating every U.S. battle beginning with the Revolutionary War. There is a 1912 carousel with unlimited rides. The property is famous for its gardens, especially the rhododendrons, which burst forth in late spring, in colors ranging from soft pink to gaudy orange. Summer concerts are held on the lawn on Sundays at 2pm. ⏱ 2 hr. 67 Grove St., Sandwich (about ½ mile southeast of town center). ☎ 508/888-3300. www.heritagemuseumsand gardens.org. Admission $12 adults, $10 seniors 65 & over, $6 kids. April–Oct daily 10am–5pm.

Take Rte. 28 from Sandwich to the Mashpee rotary, which is west 10 miles from Hyannis or east 10 miles from Falmouth. The museum is 2 miles south of the rotary.

❷ ★★ Cape Cod Children's Museum. This place is best for little kids, with its toddler castle, puppet theater, 30-foot pirate ship, "StarLab" planetarium, and submarine. Kids can use their

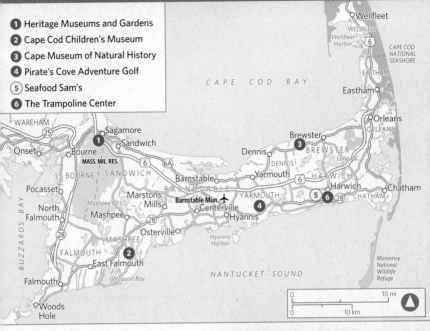

1. Heritage Museums and Gardens
2. Cape Cod Children's Museum
3. Cape Museum of Natural History
4. Pirate's Cove Adventure Golf
5. Seafood Sam's
6. The Trampoline Center

imaginations to play grown-up in a pretend diner, post office, rowboat, or train. ⏱ 1 hr. 577 Great Neck Rd. S., Mashpee. ☎ 508/539-8788. www.capecodchildrensmuseum.org. Admission $6 ages 1–59, $5 seniors. Summer Mon–Fri 10am–5pm, Sun noon–5pm; call for off-season hours. To avoid peak crowds, avoid weekends.

3 ★★★ **Cape Cod Museum of Natural History.** This interactive museum features many displays of interest to children—whale noises, a live hive of bees, and marine tanks of fish, shellfish, and reptiles. Families will have fun exploring the 85 acres of trails behind the museum, which lead to a deserted beach. 869 Main St./Rte. 6A, Brewster (about 2 miles west of Rte. 124). ☎ 508/896-3867. www.ccmnh.org. Admission $8 adults, $7 seniors, $3.50 kids. June–Sept daily 9:30am–4pm.

Take Main St./Rte. 6A east for 1½ miles to Long Pond Rd. Turn right at Rte. 124S/Harwich Rd. and continue for 5 miles. Turn right at Main St., take the 2nd left on to Forest St., go 1¼ miles, then take the 2nd right on to Sisson Rd. and bear right toward Main St./Rte. 28.

> Unlimited carousel rides come with admission to the Heritage Museum and Gardens.

> *Trampolines, go-carts, mini-golf and inflatables are among the attractions along Route 28 in Harwich.*

④ ★★ Pirate's Cove Adventure Golf. Cape Cod is a minigolf haven, but one of the most appealing courses is Pirate's Cove, which has two 18-hole courses offering caves, footbridges, and waterfalls, delivered with a bit of macabre humor. ⏱ 1 hr. 728 Main St./Rte. 28, South Yarmouth. ☎ 508/394-6200. www.

piratescove.net. May–Oct daily 10am–10pm. A round is $8.50 for ages 13 & up, $7.50 for kids 12 & under.

From Rte. 6, take exit 7 and turn left off the ramp. Take the 2nd left (about ½ mile) onto Higgins Crowell Rd. Follow Higgins Crowell to

the 2nd set of lights and take a left onto Rte. 28. Pirate's Cove is 2 miles down on the left. Look for the exploding pirate ship.

⑤ 🍽️ kids **Seafood Sam's.** This clam shack, part of a Cape chain, is the perfect family spot: it dishes out deep-fried seafood, fast, and offers a kids menu. 1006 Rte. 28, South Yarmouth. ☎ 508/394-3504. www. seafoodsams.com. $–$$. Closed late Nov–Feb. 10.

From Rte. 6, take exit 10. Take a right off the ramp toward Harwich. Follow signs to Rte. 28.

⑥ ★ **Play time in and around Harwich.** Want your kids to sleep well? There is a stretch of Route 28, in Harwich, that will surely do the trick. It's home to trampolines, go-carts, and bumper boats. Your first stop should be West Harwich's **Trampoline Center,** 296 Rte. 28, (☎ 508/432-8717) which is loads of fun, though a little bit of bouncing adds up fast. Your next stop? Harwich's **Bud's Go-Karts,** intersection of routes 28 and 139 (☎ 508/432-4964) which welcomes hot rodders as young as 8, provided they meet the height requirement (54 in.). If that's not of interest, go on to Harwichport, and try **Grand Slam Entertainment**, 322 Main St., (☎ 508/430-1155) which combines two Cape classics: boating and baseball. They offer bumper boats and batting cages. If all else fails to amuse them, there's always the **Castle in the Clouds,** 263 South St., a playground behind Harwich Elementary School—and that stop is free. 🕐 Minimum 2 hr.

Cape Cod Baseball League

The Cape league is one of the premier training grounds for Major Leaguers, and with scouts at every game, this is serious baseball. But it's also loads of fun. Kids love trying to catch a foul ball. Parents love that the games are free. There are 10 ball parks on the Cape, in Wareham, Bourne, Falmouth, Cotuit, Hyannis, Yarmouth, Harwich, Chatham, Brewster, and Orleans. The season lasts just about 6 weeks, from June through August. Game schedules are in local papers or online at www.capecod baseball.org.

Watch for Whales!

The Cape and the Islands are fabulous places to set out on a whale-watching adventure. If you're lucky, you can see finbacks, minkes, and even humpbacks on relatively quick trips. In other words, you'll get to see lots of wildlife and the kids won't have time to get bored. For more information, see p. 173.

THAR SHE BLOWS!

The Business Of Nantucket Whaling BY LAURA RECKFORD

WITH EVERY STEP ON NANTUCKET'S COBBLESTONED STREETS, visitors can sense the island's history as one of the great capitals of the whaling industry. If only those cobblestones could talk, what tales they would tell of voyages around the world. Those bricks served as ballast on whaling ships for a period, from the late 17th century to the mid–19th century, when whaling became a viable livelihood for island residents, eventually leading to the accumulation of great wealth on Nantucket. But whaling was a dangerous business for those onboard the ships who had to come practically face to face with the great leviathans in the course of harpooning them.

First Boom, Then Bust: A Whaling Timeline

LATE 1600S

Colonists begin whaling by harpooning whales close to shore.

EARLY 1700S

Whalers use single-masted sloops and, later, two-masted schooners to search for whales farther off the coast and eventually around the world. Once a whale is spotted, a harpooning crew pursues it in a much smaller, double-ended row boat or whaling boat. Sperm whales, with their superior blubber for oil and spermaceti for candles, are ideal prey.

EARLY 1800S

With the disruptions of the Revolutionary War long over, whaling begins to boom.

Voyages now include ships bearing the machinery to process whale parts. These journeys last up to 4 years at a time, with hundreds of whales killed and processed along the way. Whaling reaches its peak on Nantucket in the 1830s, bringing un-

Boom Time Treasures

In a former spermaceti candle factory near the famous whaling bar, the Brotherhood of Thieves (p. 225, ⑧), the Whaling Museum (p. 150, ②) is filled with treasures from whaling's heyday. The museum features special collections of whaling tools and artifacts, a world-renowned exhibit of whaling art such as scrimshaw and Nantucket baskets, and a 46-ft. skeleton of a sperm whale that washed up on Nantucket's beaches in 1998. For a look at the prosperity whaling brought to the island, check out two of the houses on Upper Main Street. The Hadwen House (p. 224, ③), now a museum, was built by a whaling merchant and is decorated in suitably opulent 19th-century style. Across the street, Joseph Starbuck, one of the island's most prosperous whale-oil merchants, constructed the three identical houses known as the Three Bricks (p. 224, ③) in 1836 for his three sons.

precedented wealth. Captains traveling the world bring home exotic riches. Whalers while away the long lonely hours at sea by creating scrimshaw, elaborate carvings on whalebone.

Mid-1800s
Herman Melville's classic novel, *Moby-Dick*, is published, inspired by the sperm whale that rammed and sank the Nantucket whale ship *Essex* in 1820. Nathaniel Philbrick's *In the Heart of the Sea* recounts the grisly tale of the *Essex* crew, who resorted to cannibalism to survive.

1869
With thinning whale stocks and the discovery of oil in Pennsylvania and elsewhere, the whaling industry collapses. Nantucket's final whaling ship sets sail for the last time.

1880s
Recreational boating draws visitors to the island, and by the end of the decade, tourism has become the engine of Nantucket's economy.

20th Century
A new industry, tourism, supplements the whaling industry as the island's main economic engine.

The Hunt

THE TARGET
The Right Whale, so named because it floated after being harpooned (therefore the "right" whale to hunt), shown here in Nantucket Harbor in an undated photo.

THE REWARD
Blubber could be boiled down into oil, and baleen, the filtering system that right whales use instead of teeth, could be made into tools.

Cape Cod for History Buffs

This is where the Pilgrims first landed (apologies to Plymouth) and where Europeans and Native Americans first made contact. Seventeenth- and 18th-century homes can still be found around the peninsula. In the late 19th century, tourism began on these shores, but it wasn't until a politician named John F. Kennedy made it big that things got really crazy around here. The John F. Kennedy Hyannis Museum is still one of the most popular tourist attractions on Cape Cod.

> *Iyannough of the Wampanoags—memorialized on the Hyannis Village Green—was known for his generosity to settlers.*

START Bournedale Herring Run, Buzzard's Bay, is 1 mile west of the Sagamore Bridge. **TRIP LENGTH** 1–2 days.

① ★★ **Cape Cod Canal.** The idea of New York financial wizard August Belmont, the canal was completed in 1914 at a cost of $16 million. It was widened by the Army Corps of Engineers in 1926. With a current that reverses with the tides every 6 hours, the canal is a boon for fishermen. About 30,000 boats a year use the shortcut to avoid the long trip around the treacherous shoals off the coast of the Outer Cape. There are several viewing platforms along the canal road on the Cape side. From the mainland side, you can stop at the **Bournedale Herring Run,** about 1 mile west of the Sagamore Bridge in Buzzard's Bay, to get a look. Call the Army Corps (☎ 508/759-5991) for more information. ⏰ ⅓ hr.

From Buzzard's Bay, follow signs to Bourne Bridge. Travel over the Bourne Bridge onto Cape Cod and take Trowbridge Rd., the first right at the foot of the bridge. Take a right onto Veteran's Way just after the police station, then left onto Sandwich Rd., right onto Perry Ave, and left onto Aptucxet Rd. You can park here and walk to the next two stops.

Travel Tip

For recommended restaurants and hotels in towns and villages in this tour, see pp. 190–91 and pp. 208–10.

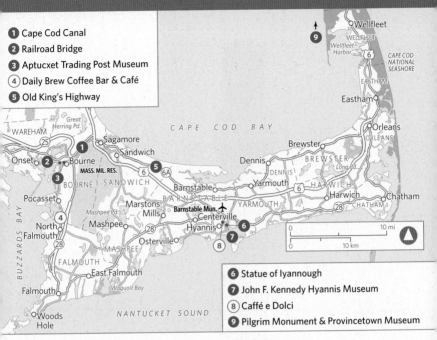

1 Cape Cod Canal
2 Railroad Bridge
3 Aptucxet Trading Post Museum
4 Daily Brew Coffee Bar & Café
5 Old King's Highway

6 Statue of Iyannough
7 John F. Kennedy Hyannis Museum
8 Caffé e Dolci
9 Pilgrim Monument & Provincetown Museum

2 ★ Railroad Bridge. This vertical-lift bridge, in Bourne, represented state-of-the-art technology when it was built over the Cape Cod Canal in 1935. Between 5 and 6pm is the best chance to catch the bridge lowering for the garbage train headed off-Cape. For the best view, try the south end of the Cape Cod Canal bike path, accessed from Aptucxet Road off Perry Avenue. ⏱ 15 min.

3 ★ Aptucxet Trading Post Museum. Long before the Cape Cod Canal was built, Native Americans were portaging goods across streams near the northern end of Buzzards Bay. The Pilgrims also recognized the area as a good trading spot with Dutch to the south, so they built a trading post here in 1627. The museum is a replica built on the spot of the old foundation. ⏱ 30 min. 24 Aptucxet Rd., Bourne Village. ☎ 508/759-9487. www.bournehistorical society.org/aptucxettradingpost.html. Admission $5 adults, $4 seniors, $2 kids. Memorial Day to Columbus Day Tues–Sat 11am–3pm.

From the Trading Post, return to Rte. 28A and continue south about 2 miles to Cataumet.

4 🍵 ★ Daily Brew Coffee Bar & Café. Stop here for great cappuccinos, baked goods, and sandwiches. 1370 Rte. 28A, Cataumet. ☎ 508/564-4755. $.

Drive northeast on Rte. 28A N/Sandwich Rd. to Bourne and the start of Rte. 28 north/Rte. 6A west, Old King's Hwy.

5 ★★★ Old King's Highway. Imagine you are Henry David Thoreau, traveling in a stagecoach on this route along the north spine of the Cape, now known as Rte. 6A. The narrow road, the curves, the old houses, even the huge shade trees that provide a dense canopy over the route are much the same as they were when he rode past in the 1860s. ⏱ 1 hr. (including stops for shopping along the route). See p. 147, 3.

Continue east on Route 6A to exit 6, Rte. 132 south. Take the exit toward Hyannis/W. Yarmouth. Merge onto Iyannough Rd./Rte. 132 east. Enter the next roundabout and take the 2nd exit onto Barnstable Rd. Turn right onto Main St.

> Get your bearings in Provincetown by spotting the Pilgrim Monument, the largest granite structure in the country.

6 ★ **Statue of Iyannough.** The Cape's Native American heritage is in evidence in the names of streets around the peninsula. The town of Mashpee is still the official home of the Wampanoag, a federally recognized tribe. Sachem Iyannough was a leader of the tribe who befriended the Pilgrims, as legend has it. ⏱ 5 min. On the Hyannis Village Green, Main St., Hyannis.

Continue on foot or by car west on Main St. to the JFK Museum.

7 ★★ **John F. Kennedy Hyannis Museum.** It has been almost 50 years since JFK was in office and his vacation home in Hyannis served as the summer White House. But this small museum of photos is still one of the most visited sites on Cape Cod. You can also visit the **Kennedy Memorial,** located above Veteran's Beach along Ocean Avenue. It is a 5-minute drive from the museum. Don't bother trying to find the **Kennedy compound;** you can't see much from the road. Instead, take a tour on a **Hy-Line Cruise** boat to see the famous houses from the water. Call ☎ 508/790-0696 for departure times and prices. ⏱ 45 min. 397 Main St., Hyannis. ☎ 508/790-3077. jfkhyannis museum.org. Admission $5 adults, $2.50 kids.

Continue west down Main St. to your next stop.

> The John F. Kennedy Museum in Hyannis has for years been among the most visited attractions on Cape Cod.

⑧ 🍴 ★ **Caffé e Dolci.** A favorite of the Kennedys—including Kennedy in-law Arnold Schwarzenegger—this cafe, run by an Italian straight from the old country, has the best espresso in town, as well as great panini and pastas. 430 Main St., Hyannis. ☎ 508/790-6900. $–$$.

After your break, take Yarmouth Rd. north out of Hyannis to Rte. 6 and go east for 49 miles to Provincetown.

9 ★ **Pilgrim Monument & Provincetown Museum.** Climb up the 116 steps of the monument to get the lay of the land, especially the intriguing curve of the Outer Cape. Then tour one of the more interesting history museums on the Cape, with artifacts and photos from Provincetown's past as a Portuguese fishing village and an arts nexus. You'll see polar bears brought back from the Arctic by Provincetown native Donald Macmillan and programs from the Provincetown Players, the troupe that launched Nobel Prize–winning playwright Eugene O'Neill. ⏱ 1 hr. High Pole Hill Rd., Provincetown. ☎ 508/487-1310. Admission $7 adults, $5 seniors & students, $3.50 kids. July to mid-Sept daily 9am–7pm.

History on the Islands

Nantucket, with its strict building regulations on preservation, is all about history. Check out the ★★★ **Whaling Museum** (p. 150, **2**), where vivid displays transport you back to the island's 19th-century glory days as one of the most prosperous ports on the east coast. There may be no better way to understand the history of Martha's Vineyard than by reading the blurbs from an oral history project on display at the ★ **Martha's Vineyard Museum,** 59 School St., at the corner of Cooke St. (☎ 508/627-4441; www.marthasvineyardhistory.org), in Edgartown. Other highlights of the museum's collection include the pre-Colonial artifacts in the Captain Francis Pease House, and the enormous Fresnel lens from the Gay Head Lighthouse that sits outside on the lawn.

Antiquing Along the Old King's Highway

The Old King's Highway, which winds through the towns of Sandwich, Barnstable, Yarmouth, Dennis, and Brewster, is the place to go for antiques store hopping. I've listed some larger multidealer shops and some small shops here. You'll find many more as you explore the route. Most antiques stores are open daily in summer 10am to 5pm or by chance or appointment.

> You never know what treasures you'll find at the antique stores along the Old King's Highway.

START Sandwich is 16 miles northwest of Hyannis. **TRIP LENGTH** 1 day.

① ★ **Sandwich Antiques Center.** This multidealer shop occupies a 6,000-square-foot building on Route 6A. Nautical items, clocks, and decoys are among the specialties. There is always a selection of antique Sandwich glass, which was once manufactured here. 131 Rte. 6A (5 min. from the Sagamore Bridge), Sandwich. ☎ 508/833-3600. www.sandwich antiquescenter.com. Daily 10am-5pm.

Head northwest on Rte. 6A toward Liberty St. for about ½ mile. Take a sharp left at Tupper Rd., then a slight left at Main St., where the museum will be on your left.

② ★ **Sandwich Glass Museum.** This fascinating museum captures the history of the town, where glassmaking flourished from 1828 to 1888. Sandwich glass is still considered some of the finest in the world. A multimillion-dollar renovation and expansion has freshened up the entire museum, and glass is displayed in light and airy rooms. Glass blowing demonstrations are featured. An excellent gift shop stocks Sandwich-glass replicas, as well as original glassworks by area artisans. 129 Main St., Sandwich. ☎ 508/888-0251. www.sandwich glassmuseum.org. Admission $5 for adults, $1.25 for children 6-14, free for children 5 and under. April-Dec daily 9:30am-5:30pm; Feb-Mar Wed-Sun 9:30am-4:30pm; closed January.

From the museum, head northwest on Main St. toward Tupper Rd. Take a slight right at Tupper Rd., then the 3rd right onto Rte. 6A going east Drive 12 miles to the next stop.

③ ★★ **Harden Studios.** An antiques shop that doubles as an art gallery, this place is highly original. The primary focus of the antiques is early Americana, with an emphasis on furniture. The building itself, the Deacon Robert

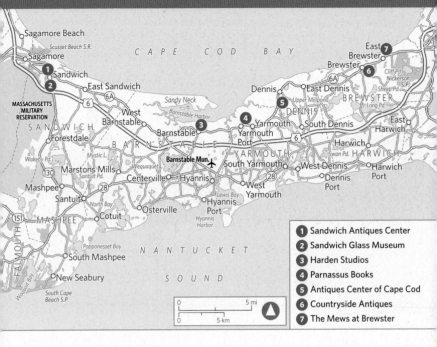

1 Sandwich Antiques Center
2 Sandwich Glass Museum
3 Harden Studios
4 Parnassus Books
5 Antiques Center of Cape Cod
6 Countryside Antiques
7 The Mews at Brewster

Davis House, was built in 1690 and is worth a visit on its own. 3264 Main St./Rte. 6A, Barnstable Village. ☎ 508/362-7711. www.harden studios.com. Open by chance or appointment.

Head southeast on Main St./Rte. 6A east toward Windsor Way. Continue to follow Rte. 6A for 2¾ miles to Yarmouth Port. Walk or drive ⅓ mile east on Main St. to:

❹ **Parnassus Books.** While you're in the neighborhood (Yarmouth Port), you might want to stop into Parnassus, where you might find a good read within the teetering stacks of books, both new and old, including specialty catalogs on a variety of subjects. 220 Main St./Rte. 6A, Yarmouth Port. ☎ 508/362-6420. www.parnassusbooks.com. Daily 10am-5pm.

From Yarmouth Port, continue down Rte. 6A for 3⅓ miles.

❺ ★★ **Antiques Center of Cape Cod.** This is the largest and busiest antiques center on Cape Cod. Among the wares offered by the more than 250 dealers are furniture, glass, art, clocks, books, jewelry, silver, pottery, and collectibles. 243 Main St./Rte. 6A, Dennis.

☎ 508/385-6400. www.antiquecenterofcape cod.com. Mon-Sat 10am-5pm; Sun 11am-5pm.

Head northeast on Main St./Rte. 6A toward Apple Lane for 7¾ miles.

❻ ★★ **Countryside Antiques.** The proprietor here roams the world in search of stylish furnishings. They're mostly old, but age and price are evidently no object. You'll find items of English, Irish, French, Swedish, and Chinese provenance. There are china, porcelain, silver, and decorative objects of all types, as well as furniture. 2052 Main St./Rte. 6A, Brewster. ☎ 508/896-1444. www.countrysideantiques inc.com. Daily 10am-5pm summer; Mon-Sat 10am-5pm, Sun 12-5pm Sun winter.

Head northeast on Main St./Rte. 6A toward Crocker Lane for 1¾ miles.

❼ ★ **The Mews at Brewster.** Representing seven dealers, this antiques store specializes in country furniture, primitives, and folk art. 2926 Main St./Rte. 6A (across from Ocean Edge Resort), Brewster. ☎ 508/896-4887. Mon-Sat 10am-5pm; Sun 11am-5pm.

> *Martha's Vineyard's sleepy roads can feel custom-made for biking.*

Outdoor Adventures A to Z

Biking

The 7-mile **Cape Cod Canal Trail** is a flat trail on both sides of the man-made waterway between the Bourne and Sagamore bridges—perfect for family outings or casual riders. To reach the trail head from the Bourne Bridge on the Cape side, take the first right off the rotary and then take a right at the T intersection for the parking area under the bridge. There are picnic facilities and toilets in season. For information, visit the Cape Cod Canal Visitor Center , 60 Ed Moffitt Dr., Sandwich (☎ 508/833-9678).

The 28-mile **Cape Cod Rail Trail** is one of New England's most popular bike paths. Once a bed of the Penn Central Railroad, the trail is relatively flat and straight. The trail head is in South Dennis off Route 134 (exit 9 off Route 6) on the east side of the street. The trail end takes you all the way to Wellfleet, just a stone's throw from the Cape Cod National Seashore. The newly expanded **Shining Sea Bikeway**, which stretches for 12 miles along the west side of town from North Falmouth to Woods Hole, is already a top regional attraction. If you bike the entire route, you'll pass cranberry bogs; a historic farm; the Great Sippewissett Marsh, which is a bird-watcher's dream; a Buzzards Bay beach along Surf Drive; and finally the atmospheric fishing village of Woods Hole. A relatively nonstrenuous ride, the trail was built on a former railroad right of way and is level nearly the entire distance.

The nice thing about biking on **Martha's Vineyard** is that you'll find not only the smooth, well-maintained paths indigenous to the Cape, but also long stretches of road with virtually no traffic. The roads, while rough in spots, traverse breathtaking country landscapes of farms and fields, divided by stone walls, and between the down-island towns of Edgartown, Vineyard Haven, and Oak Bluffs, wonderful ocean views. If you take the ferry into Vineyard Haven, it is a relatively quick ride, only a few miles, to Oak Bluffs. From Oak Bluffs to Edgartown, it is about 5 miles, but the flat paths make the ride seem easy. Besides the exercise, the best part is you don't have to find a parking spot in Edgartown.

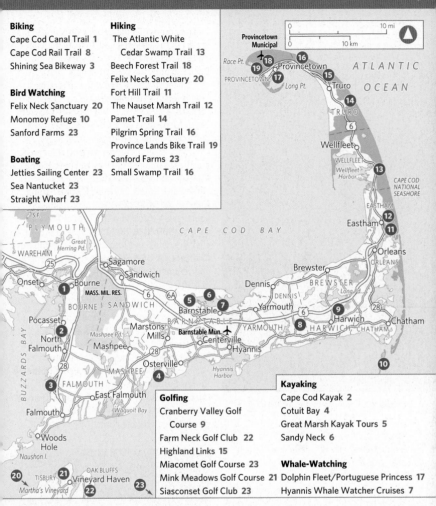

Biking
Cape Cod Canal Trail 1
Cape Cod Rail Trail 8
Shining Sea Bikeway 3

Bird Watching
Felix Neck Sanctuary 20
Monomoy Refuge 10
Sanford Farms 23

Boating
Jetties Sailing Center 23
Sea Nantucket 23
Straight Wharf 23

Hiking
The Atlantic White
   Cedar Swamp Trail 13
Beech Forest Trail 18
Felix Neck Sanctuary 20
Fort Hill Trail 11
The Nauset Marsh Trail 12
Pamet Trail 14
Pilgrim Spring Trail 16
Province Lands Bike Trail 19
Sanford Farms 23
Small Swamp Trail 16

Golfing
Cranberry Valley Golf
   Course 9
Farm Neck Golf Club 22
Highland Links 15
Miacomet Golf Course 23
Mink Meadows Golf Course 21
Siasconset Golf Club 23

Kayaking
Cape Cod Kayak 2
Cotuit Bay 4
Great Marsh Kayak Tours 5
Sandy Neck 6

Whale-Watching
Dolphin Fleet/Portuguese Princess 17
Hyannis Whale Watcher Cruises 7

Bird-watching

The Cape has a host of great bird-watching spots, including the **Monomoy Refuge** (p. 196), **Sanford Farms,** and **Felix Neck Sanctuary** (see "Hiking," below, for information on both). For details about where to go and what you might see, the Massachusetts Audubon Society (www.massaudubon.org) is an invaluable resource.

Boating

There's one-stop shopping for Nantucket's off-shore activities at **Jetties Sailing Center** (☎ 508/228-5358) at Jetties Beach, where you can rent kayaks, sailboards, and sailboats. At **Sea Nantucket**, Francis St. Beach, off Washington St. (☎ 508/228-7499), you

can rent kayaks. Deep-sea charter fishing vessels out of Straight Wharf include *The Albacore*, *The Monomoy*, and *The Absolute* (see "Fishing," below, for details). To rent a boat and motor around the harbor on your own for a half-day, a full day, or even a week, call **Nantucket Boat Rental** (☎ 508/325-1001), which is out of Slip 1 at Straight Wharf.

Fishing

Fishing is a way of life for many on Cape Cod, whether it is a hobby or a vocation, for the few who have survived regulations in the region meant to prevent overfishing. New fishing rules require a license for saltwater fishing as well as freshwater fishing. Bait and tackle

> *Surf-casting is a fun way to give fishing a try.*

The number to call to book on a vessel that is part of the **Orleans** sportfishing fleet is ☎ **508/255-9757;** The fleet heads out of Rock Harbor. A 4-hour trip costs $550.

On Martha's Vineyard, you can arrange a charter on the **Summer's Lease** out of Oak Bluffs (☎ **508/693-2880**) or **North Shore Charters** out of Menemsha (☎ **508/645-2993**; www. bassnblue.com). Half-days start at $500.

Among the charter captains on Nantucket are Ty Anderson of **Ty One On Sportfishing Charter** (☎ **508/423-5126**; www.tyoneon. com), Peter Kaizer of **Althea K Sportfishing Charter** (☎ **508/325-2167**; www.altheak sportfishing.com), Bob DeCosta of **The Albacore** (☎ **508/228-5074**; www.albacore charters.com), and Josh Eldridge of **Monomoy Charters** (☎ **508/228-6867**; www.monomoy chartersnantucket.com). Half-day trips start at $800.

Golfing

The Cape is a golfing mecca of sorts, and duffers in the know are well aware there are some very special courses here. There are several standouts for unique Cape Cod scenery.

The championship 18-hole ★★★ **Cranberry Valley Golf Course** is considered one of the top courses on the Cape. To get a tee time, call ☎ 508/430-5234, or check out www. cranberrygolfcourse.com.

stores and town halls all sell fishing licenses. Once you have a license and gear, you can surf-cast from most any beach or dock, though some are preferred. A safer bet is to take a charter fishing tour, either near shore on a so-called party boat or on a charter boat for a half-day voyage where you're likely to catch bass or blues, and sometimes flounder and scup. The fishing tackle and bait is supplied. Be aware that prices have been fluctuating of late, thanks to fluctuations in the price of fuel.

In Falmouth, you can head out on **Patriot Party Boats** for either "bottom fishing" close to shore, which costs $40 for an adult, $25 for children, or charter fishing at $70 for adults, $40 for children. Call ☎ **508/548-2626** or check out www.patriotpartyboats.com for details.

Out of Hyannis Harbor, there is Capt. Gary Brown on the **Bass Ackwards** (☎ **774/ 487-7174**).

The National Seashore

On August 7, 1961, President John F. Kennedy signed a bill designating 27,000 acres in 40 miles along the coast from Chatham to Provincetown as a new national park, the **Cape Cod National Seashore**. Along with its famous beaches, there are some great hiking and biking trails for you to explore. If you're biking, Massachusetts state law requires children 16 and younger to wear protective helmets when operating or riding as a passenger on a bicycle. For more information about the trails at Cape Cod National Seashore, call the visitor's center ☎ 508/255-3421 or vsit www.nps.gov/ caco. Beach parking is $15 per day, $3 for walkers/bikers, $45 per season. Fees are collected late June to early September; no fees the rest of the year.

> *Highland Links offers great golfing and a great view.*

The oldest golf course on Cape Cod is the 1892 Scottish-style 9-hole ★★★ **Highland Links** in North Truro (☎ 508/487-9201; www.truro-ma.gov), which shares a lofty and windblown bluff with the 1853 Highland Light. Greens fees at Highland Links, which is part of the Cape Cod National Seashore, are $33 for 9 holes, $55 for 18.

On Martha's Vineyard, there is the 18-hole ★★★ **Farm Neck Golf Club** in Oak Bluffs (☎ 508/ 693-3057) and the 9-hole **Mink Meadows Golf Course** in Vineyard Haven (☎ 508/693-0600; www.minkmeadowsgc.com).

On Nantucket, the action is at the 18-hole ★★★ **Miacomet Golf Course** (☎ 508/325-0333; www.miacometgolf.com), which costs $125 for 18 holes. A less expensive round can be found at the 9-hole **Siasconset Golf Club**, which charges $35 per round.

Hiking

There is so much great hiking on the Cape and the Islands that it's easy to while away a whole week doing nothing but strolling. Truro's ★★★ **Pilgrim Spring Trail** and ★★★ **Small Swamp Trail**, two interlocking trails at Pilgrim Heights, are high points of the Cape Cod National Seashore (see the box below). Pilgrim Spring is where the parched Pilgrims just off the Mayflower sipped their first fresh water in months. Small Swamp is named for Thomas Small, an overly-optimistic 19th-century farmer who tried to cultivate fruit trees in soil more suited to salt hay. Each trail is a .75-mile (1.2km) loop, and both trails overlook Salt Meadow, a freshwater marsh favored by hawks and osprey. Take Route 6 to Pilgrim Heights road and follow signs to the trails.

Also in Truro is the ★★★ **Pamet Trail**, which is among the more isolated parts of the Cape Cod National Seashore. You are likely not to see another person on this lovely half-mile (.8km) trail through the woods and a meadow to dunes and the beach. Start the self-guided trail at the kiosk, where maps are available.

Safety First

It goes without saying that all kayakers must know how to swim and be outfitted with safety gear. In fact, it is against the law in Massachusetts to kayak between September and June without a life jacket and flare or whistle. No matter what time of year you go, you want to be wearing gear that you will be comfortable in if you capsize and must swim to shore. A life jacket is a must, but in chilly waters in this part of the world, I also wear a half wetsuit (short pants) in July and August and a full wetsuit the rest of the year. A nautical map of whatever area you are exploring is also a critical tool, as are extra food and water, a hat, and sunscreen.

> *Most of the hikes on the Cape and the Islands are gentle enough even for small fry.*

The former Coast Guard building near the trail head on the bluff is now a youth hostel. Walk across the road, and down North Pamet Road about 500 feet (152.4m) to find the trail head. The beginning of the trail passes an abandoned cranberry bog, which is now a marsh, and an old bog building. The trail comes out of a wooded area and crosses a meadow before coming to dunes overlooking the beach. To get there, exit Rte. 6 at Pamet Roads exit and take North Pamet Road to the end.

Provincetown is home to two excellent trails. The first is the ★★★ **Beech Forest Trail**. This 1-mile (1.6km) self-guided walk gives you the lay of the land of the Province Lands (p. 203), which are dunes interspersed with beech forests. This shaded path circles a shallow freshwater pond blanketed with water lilies before heading into the woods. Among the wildlife you may see are turtles sunning themselves beside the pond. At the edge of the trail, you can see the shifting dunes gradually encroaching on the forest, and vice versa. Take Route 6 to Race Point Road and follow signs. The trail is a short drive from the Cape Cod National Seashore Province Lands Visitor Center at Race Point. You may want to stop in there before hitting the ★★★ **Province Lands Bike Trail**. Beginning at Race Point Beach (p. 179), this trail runs between 5 and 7 miles, depending on whether you take the spurs to

Herring Cove (p. 176) or Race Point beaches, and it will take you up and down dunes to give you a great sense of this terrain. You'll pass through the Beech Forest, and view several ponds. The trail can be accessed from the Province Lands Visitor Center, Beech Forest, or Race Point or Herring Cove beaches (fees may apply in beach areas).

Eastham also offers two great walks. The ★★★ **Fort Hill Trail** has one of the best scenic views over fields and marshes to the ocean. It runs 1.25 miles and connects with the Red Maple Swamp Trail. Take Route 6 to the exit at the brown Fort Hill sign on Governor Prence Road in Eastham. Another option is the ★★ **Nauset Marsh Trail**, a 1-mile hike that begins at the Salt Pond Visitor Center in Eastham (follow signs from Route 6). It winds along the edge of Salt Pond and Nauset Marsh, crosses fields, and returns to the Salt Pond Visitor Center through a recovering forest.

Wellfleet's ★★ **The Atlantic White Cedar Swamp Trail** is a great excuse to visit this charmingly weathered little town. It is located at the Marconi Station site, where Guglielmo Marconi sent the first successful transatlantic cable, to England, in 1903. This trail is just over a mile, and considered of "moderate" difficulty. It descends through a stunted oak and pine forest into a mature woodland, leads to a boardwalk that winds through the swamp, and returns via the historic "Wireless Road" (a sand road) to the starting location. Follow brown signs from Route 6 to the Marconi Site & White Cedar Swamp.

Nantucket offers lots of easy walks, but ★★ **Sanford Farms** is one of my favorite places to go for a stroll. This 300-acre conservation property is popular with runners, walkers, dog walkers, mountain bikers, and horseback riders. The Loop trail is 1.7 miles and passes Waquataquaib Pond. A 3-mile loop trail called The Barn brings you to Pasture Overlook, with views of Hummock Pond, Cisco Beach, Madaket Beach and, of course, the Atlantic Ocean. To get there, follow signs from the Whaling Museum to Madaket, and follow signs to the farm.

Martha's Vineyard's ★ **Felix Neck Sanctuary,** off Edgartown-Vineyard Haven Road (☎ 506/627-4850; www.massaudubon.org) is home to nesting pairs of osprey, a tree swallow colony, and other wildlife. This quiet,

> *Seeing the Cape from a kayak gives a whole new perspective on the place.*

lovely spot is just outside of Edgartown, about 2 miles from the center of town. Ducks and other waterfowl can be seen in the pond in the shoulder seasons. The self-guided trails from the visitor center take you through woods, meadows, and beside marshlands and Sengekontacket Pond. The orange trail leads to Waterfowl Pond, which has an observation deck with bird-sighting info. Most trails are wheelchair accessible.

Kayaking

One of the best ways to see the Cape & Islands is from the water. You can navigate through estuaries and explore uninhabited islands. Tides become important. So does weather. (Unlike in sailing, wind is bad.) There is no better place to watch an osprey swoop down for its prey. Paddling is a great way to get away from beach crowds. A few yards offshore, and suddenly you are in your own world. One of my favorite trips involves putting in off Old Shore Road in Cotuit Bay, and doing a 6-mile loop that will take you through three connected bays comprising one of the most scenic of the Cape's waterways to a barrier beach and out to Nantucket Sound. If you want to go as part of a tour, the **Massachusetts Audubon Society** (p. 568) offers a nice one, led by a naturalist.

Another of my favorites takes you along that unique 7-mile-long barrier beach called **Sandy Neck** (p. 179), where you can admire its picturesque cottage colony and lighthouse. This is a great trip for bird-watchers, because Sandy Neck and the 4,000-acre Barnstable Great Marsh nearby are such lush habitats. **Great Marsh Kayak Tours** (☎ 508/775-6447; www.greatmarshkayaktours.com) offers a range of options, including floats led by a naturalist and one timed for the sunset. Expect to pay $35 to $45 per person.

If you'd rather rent a kayak and use it whenever the mood strikes you, consider **Cape Cod Kayak** (☎ 508/563-9377; www.capecodkayak.com). Rates run from $35 for a 6-hour rental of a lightweight kayak to $345 for a week-long rental of a tandem boat.

Whale-Watching

The ★★★ **Dolphin Fleet/Portuguese Princess** (☎ 800/826-9300 or 508/240-3636; www.whalewatch.com) works with the Center for Coastal Studies so that every whale-watch voyage to Stellwagen Bank, 8 miles off the coast of Provincetown, is also a research trip for scientists. Naturalists onboard give talks as you watch the flipper-slapping, fluke-winking display. The trips leave from Macmillan Wharf in Provincetown (p. 204, ⑤). Tickets are $39 for adults, $34 for seniors, $31 for children. ★★★ **Hyannis Whale Watcher Cruises** (☎ 800/287-0374 or 508/362-6088; www.whales.net) makes the trip from Barnstable Harbor in the Mid-Cape.

Cape Cod & Islands Beaches A to Z

Parking fees are collected on Cape Cod beaches in the summer only, late June to early September. The rest of the year, the beaches are free. There is no charge for walkers and bikers at Cape Cod beaches, except the Cape Cod National Seashore beaches, which charge $3 to walkers and bikers.

> *Which beach to choose—the kittenish bay side or the lion-like ocean—is the dilemma on the Outer Cape.*

★★★ Cahoon Hollow Beach WELLFLEET

This town-run beach is big with surfers. Like all oceanside beaches on the Outer Cape, there are large sand dunes bordering the beach, which is a wide-open and beautiful expanse. What makes Cahoon Hollow distinct is that there is a restaurant/nightclub, **The Beachcomber,** next to the beach parking lot. So you can go straight from your day at the beach to an evening of listening to live music and dancing. Cahoon Hollow Rd. (off Rte. 6). Parking costs $15 per day.

★★ Chapoquoit Beach WEST FALMOUTH

One of the prettiest beaches in Falmouth and among the most serene, this is essentially a barrier beach between West Falmouth Harbor and Buzzards Bay. A beach parking sticker is needed in season (available also for renters and hotel guests). Chapoquoit Rd. (off Rte. 28A).

★★★ Coast Guard Beach EASTHAM

With the historic white Coast Guard Station perched on a bluff nearby, this popular National Seashore beach often ranks among

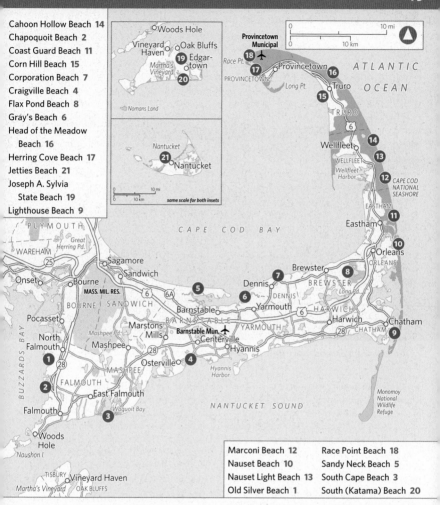

the top beaches in the country in nationwide surveys. It has lifeguards and restrooms. Bikers can access the beach from a bike path that starts at the Salt Pond Visitor Center on Rte. 6 and crosses a scenic bridge over a marsh. Big waves attract lots of boogie boarders. **Rte. 6 to Doane Rd. to Ocean View Dr.** A parking lot on Doane Rd. is accessible by shuttle bus, which runs every 10 min. Parking costs $15 a day, $45 for the season.

★★ Corn Hill Beach TRURO

This Cape Cod Bay beach, near the hill where Pilgrims found the seed corn that ensured their survival, is open to non-residents for a fee. The enormous lot assures most visitors will get a spot. Be aware of the tide schedule. At low tide, the water is too shallow for swimming unless you venture far from shore. There are portable toilets on-site. **Rte. 6 to Corn Hill Rd.** Stay right & follow to beach. Parking costs $10 per day.

★★ Corporation Beach DENNIS

This Cape Cod Bay beach was once a packet landing owned by a shipbuilding corporation. It has a number of amenities: lifeguards, snack bar, restrooms, children's play area, and wheelchair-accessible boardwalk. **Take Rte. 6A to Corporation Rd.** & follow signs to the beach. Parking costs $20 per day.

> *A big wide beach with soft sand—that's Old Silver Beach in North Falmouth in a nut—er—seashell.*

★★ Craigville Beach CENTERVILLE
Known as "Muscle Beach," this broad expanse of sand, which attracts teens and young adults, is the town of Barnstable's most popular beach. There are lifeguards and restrooms. A neighborhood on the hill above the beach is a historic Methodist camp meeting site complete with Victorian "gingerbread-style" cottages. From Rte. 28, take Old Stage Rd. and follow signs to the beach. Parking costs $15 a day.

★★ Flax Pond Beach BREWSTER
This large freshwater pond, surrounded by pines, has a bathhouse and offers watersports equipment rentals. Rte. 6A to Nickerson State Park. Follow signs in park. Parking is free.

★★ kids Gray's Beach YARMOUTHPORT
This small beach is suitable for young children, but the best part of this site is the Bass Hole boardwalk, which offers one of the area's most scenic walks. There's also a picnic area with grills. Rte. 6A to Center St. Parking is free.

★★★ Head of the Meadow Beach TRURO
This spot is known for its excellent surf. Sand dunes bordering the beach are about 100 feet tall. Half is a town beach and half is controlled by the Cape Cod National Seashore, which has lifeguard coverage. You'll likely see seals on an offshore sandbar on the south end of the beach. The parking lot is connected to the beach with a short boardwalk. The Pilgrim Heights bike path also starts here. Rte. 6 to Head of the Meadow Rd. Parking costs $15 a day.

★★★ Herring Cove Beach PROVINCETOWN
Facing west, this Cape Cod National Seashore beach on Cape Cod Bay is known for its spectacular sunsets; observers often applaud. Because it faces the bay, the waters are warmer than they are at the other Provincetown beach, Race Point. There is a bathhouse with restrooms and changing rooms, and there are lifeguards. This beach is popular with same-sex couples, particularly in the southernmost section of the beach, closer to town. Take Rte. 6 to the end and look for beach signs. Parking costs $15 a day, $45 per season.

★★★ kids Jetties Beach NANTUCKET
Located a half-mile beyond Children's Beach, Jetties is a 20-minute walk from town or an

even shorter bike ride. The parking lot fills up early on summer weekends. It's a family favorite for its mild waves, lifeguards, bathhouse, and restrooms. Facilities include the town tennis courts, volleyball nets, a skate park, and a playground; watersports equipment and chairs are also available to rent. There is also The Jetties, a full-service restaurant. The Fourth of July fireworks display is held here. Every August, Jetties hosts an intense sand-castle competition. **From town, take N. Beach St. to the beach. Beach parking is free.**

★★ kids Joseph A. Sylvia State Beach MARTHA'S VINEYARD

Stretching a mile and flanked by a paved bike path, this placid beach on the eastern shore of the island has views of Cape Cod across Nantucket Sound. Gentle and relatively warm waters make it ideal for swimming. The wooden drawbridge is a local landmark for jumping. In midsummer, this is a very busy beach. There is a shuttle-bus stop. There are no toilets. Lifeguards are posted at the Edgartown side of the beach. **Midway btw. Oak Bluffs & Edgartown on Seaview Ave. Parking is free.**

★★★ Lighthouse Beach CHATHAM

Located across the street from the Coast Guard–operated Chatham Lighthouse (p. 194, ②), this is a scenic spot. Telescopes are provided so you can look across the water to North Beach and beyond to the Atlantic Ocean. There is a huge seal colony that likes to hang out off the coast of North Beach. You can also see where the ocean has broken through the barrier beach. Because of dangerous riptides (and sharks that prey on the seals), this beach can be closed to swimming, but it's a beautiful spot nonetheless. **Main St. to Shore Rd. Take a right turn to get to the beach. Parking is free but limited to 30 min.**

★★★ Marconi Beach SOUTH WELLFLEET

This National Seashore property is lined with 50- to 100-foot (30.5m) dunes. The bluffs are so high that the beach is in shadow in the afternoon. And history buffs will want to drop by to see nearby Marconi Station (p. ###), the site of the first transatlantic wireless communication. There are restrooms, showers, and lifeguards. **Rte. 6 to Marconi Rd. Parking costs $15 per day.**

★★★ kids Nauset Beach EAST ORLEANS

Stretching southward all the way to Chatham,

this 10-mile-long barrier beach is owned by the Cape Cod National Seashore but managed by the town. It has long been one of the Cape's gonzo beach scenes: big crowds, big surf, lots of young people. There are full facilities including a snack bar serving great fried fish. A special section is reserved for surfing. There's live music at the gazebo Mondays in July and

> *Beach essentials: a hat and a bottle of sunscreen. You won't need much more than that for a lovely day at Sandy Neck.*

> Take a break from sunbathing to watch for sea life off Race Point.

August 7 to 9pm. Rte. 6A to Main St. which becomes Beach Rd. Parking costs $15 (ticket also good for Skaket Beach on Cape Cod Bay).

★★★ Nauset Light Beach EASTHAM

Next to the picturesque Nauset Lighthouse (which has a bold red stripe) is this popular Cape Cod National Seashore beach. There are lifeguards and restrooms. A nearby shady park with picnic tables is the location of the Three Sisters Lighthouses, three identical small lights. Rte. 6 to Doane Rd. to Ocean View Dr. Parking costs $15.

★★★ kids Old Silver Beach NORTH FALMOUTH

This west-facing beach (great for sunsets) is where beachgoers can enjoy the warmish waters of Buzzards Bay. Because of relatively calm waters, good sand, and a location close to the Bourne Bridge, this is a very popular spot, particularly with teenagers and young adults. Toddlers are often taken to the other side of the street where a sandbar creates a shallow area near a marsh. Amenities include a bathhouse with toilets and showers, food concessions, and lifeguards. Sailboards are available for rent. Rte. 28 to Rte. 151 to Rte. 28A to Curley Blvd. and follow signs to beach. Parking costs $20 a day.

★★★ Race Point Beach PROVINCETOWN

Of all the National Seashore beaches, this one sticks the farthest out into the Atlantic Ocean. With long stretches of pristine sand, this is a popular spot. The surf is rough, and you may spot seals or even a whale offshore. This is also the site of the Old Harbor Lifesaving Museum, open daily 2:30 to 5pm in July and August. Nearby is also the Province Lands Visitor Center (p. 203), which displays exhibits about the ecology here. Rte. 6 to Provincetown. Follow signs to the beach. Parking costs $15 a day.

★★★ kids Sandy Neck Beach SANDWICH

This 6-mile stretch of barrier beach on Cape Cod Bay is one of the Cape's prettiest and most unspoiled. With low dunes, warm bay waters, and calm surf, this is a popular spot for families with children. Off-road vehicles are allowed here when it is not the nesting season of the endangered piping plovers. It is usually closed to ORVs in June and July. At the end of Sandy Neck, there is a remote cottage colony

of summer houses off-the-grid and a lighthouse that marks the entrance to Barnstable Harbor. Rte 6A east from Sandwich, to Sandy Neck Rd. Follow signs to beach. Parking costs $15 a day.

★★★ South Cape Beach MASHPEE

This isolated and pristine Nantucket Sound beach, with both a town-run and a state-run section, is part of the 450-acre South Cape Beach State Park. There are miles of hiking trails. Rte. 28 to the Mashpee rotary. Take Great Oak Rd. for 5 miles to the end. Parking costs $7 per day.

★★★ South (Katama) Beach MARTHA'S VINEYARD

If you have time for only one trip to the beach, this popular 3-mile barrier strand boasts great wave action, sweeping dunes and relatively ample parking. It's also accessible by bike or shuttle bus. Lifeguards patrol some sections. It's one of the most popular beaches on the island, so be prepared for big crowds. Families tend to head to the left, college students to the right. From Edgartown, take Katama Rd. 4 miles (6.4km) south. Parking is free.

★★ kids Joseph A. Sylvia State Beach

MARTHA'S VINEYARD Stretching a mile and flanked by a paved bike path, this placid beach on the eastern shore of the island has views of Cape Cod across Nantucket Sound. Gentle and relatively warm waters make it ideal for swimming , and therefore very popular with families—kids will love being splashing in the shallows. The wooden drawbridge is a local landmark for jumping. In midsummer, this is a very busy beach. There is a shuttle bus stop. There are no toilets. Lifeguards are posted at the Edgartown side of the beach. Midway btw. Oak Bluffs & Edgartown on Seaview Ave. Parking is free.

Fishing on the Cape & Islands

Fishing is part of the lifeblood of the Cape and the Islands, and there are plenty of opportunities for both beginners and long-time anglers. Whether you're hoping to try surf-casting or you're aiming to spend a full day (or more) out on the high seas, this is the place to do it. For more information, see Outdoor Adventures, p. 169.

Falmouth & the Lower Cape

The second-largest town on Cape Cod and the main hub of activity on the Lower Cape, Falmouth is also one of the most scenic, with more than 68 miles of coastline. Among its eight villages is Woods Hole, a world-renowned oceanic research center. Scientists began using the fishing village as a port for research in 1871, around the same time that tourists discovered the town by the sea. One of the first resort communities laid out on the Cape was Falmouth Heights, which still retains tiny lanes and Victorian houses from the 19th century. Driving along the shore in Falmouth, past Nobska Lighthouse and Falmouth Heights Beach, is a great way to see the town. The Village Green is a good place to start your tour.

> *The Clam Shack shares space with the three-masted schooner, the* Liberte, *on Falmouth Inner Harbor.*

❶ ★★★ **Highfield Hall.** At the top of the hill, this 1878 mansion was lovingly restored over 10 years by scores of local volunteers. There are miles of walking trails in the 382 acres of **Beebe Woods** around the mansion. The hall is a cultural meeting place that hosts art exhibits and classical music concerts. The building is special-needs accessible. ⏲ 1 hr. 56 Highfield Dr. ☎ 508/495-1878. www.highfieldhall.org. Mon–Fri 10am–4pm; Sun 10am–1pm. Free admission.

❷ ★ **Peterson Farm.** At this 88-acre historic farm owned by the town, a flock of sheep graze while a llama, Scamp, watches over them. There are walking paths through fields and woods leading to Ice House Pond. ⏲ 1 hr. 109 McCallum Dr. No phone. Dawn–dusk. Free admission.

❸ ★★ **Spohr Gardens.** Tiny but dazzling, the colorful, 6-acre, privately owned Spohr Gardens flourish beside Oyster Pond. In the spring, thousands of daffodils bloom, followed by

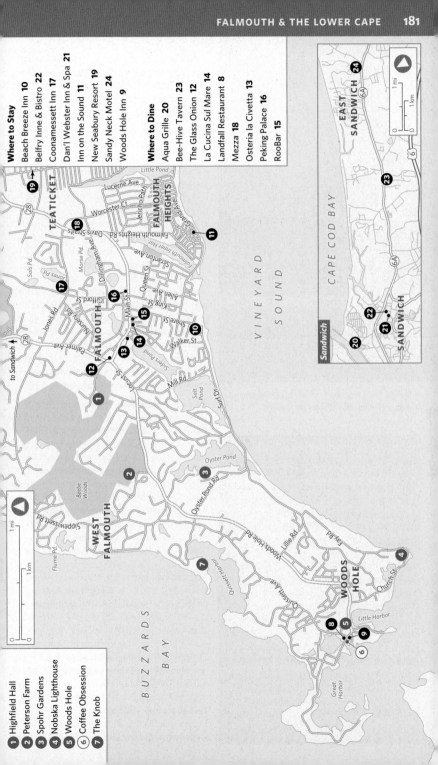

Where to Stay

Beach Breeze Inn **10**
Belfry Inne & Bistro **22**
Coonamessett Inn **17**
Dan'l Webster Inn & Spa **21**
Inn on the Sound **11**
New Seabury Resort **19**
Sandy Neck Motel **24**
Woods Hole Inn **9**

Where to Dine

Aqua Grille **20**
Bee-Hive Tavern **23**
The Glass Onion **12**
La Cucina Sul Mare **14**
Landfall Restaurant **8**
Mezza **18**
Osteria la Civetta **13**
Peking Palace **16**
RooBar **15**

1 Highfield Hall
2 Peterson Farm
3 Spohr Gardens
4 Nobska Lighthouse
5 Woods Hole
6 Coffee Obsession
7 The Knob

> Nobska Light is opened to visitors several times a year, including in December for caroling.

Going Out on the Lower Cape

Need break after a hard day on the beach? Stop by **The Captain Kidd Bar**, 77 Water St., Woods Hole (☎ 508/548-9206), which draws lobstermen and the occasional Nobel Prize winner from one of the local scientific institutions. The ★★ **Casino Wharf FX**, 286 Grand Ave, Falmouth Heights (☎ 508/540-6160; www.casinowharf.weebly.com), is a beachfront bar and restaurant with excellent views and live rock and jazz all year. Falmouth's old-school **Grumpy's Pub**, 29 Locust St. (☎ 508/540-3930), also features live music (mostly rock and blues) year-round. Also in Falmouth, **Liam Maguire's Irish Pub**, 273 Main St. (☎ 508/548-8563; www.liammaguire.com), offers Irish music by Liam himself plus other bands at a comfortable Irish pub that doubles as a sports bar. Finally, Falmouth's ★ **Quahog Republic Dive Bar**, 97 Spring Bars Rd. (☎ 508/540-4111), serves up cheap drinks nightly.

rhododendrons and day lilies. Paths wind past a collection of huge antique anchors and millstones. ⏱ 20 min. 45 Fells Rd. ☎ 508/548-0623. www.spohrgardens.org. Daily 8am–8pm. Free admission.

④ ★ Nobska Lighthouse. This 1876 lighthouse warns ships away from the bluff every 30 seconds with a flashing white light and a fog signal when the weather warrants it. The keeper's house serves as the home for the commander of Coast Guard Sector Southeastern New England. The grounds are open to the public; the lighthouse tower is open only during scheduled open houses. From the bluff across the street from the lighthouse is a great view across Vineyard Sound. On clear days, you can see the Elizabeth Islands and Martha's Vineyard. You'll see ferries making their way between Woods Hole and the island. The plaque on the lookout is dedicated to a young woman who enjoyed vacationing in Falmouth and died in one of the airplanes during the terrorist attacks on September 11, 2001. ⏱ 15 min. Off Nobska Rd. No phone. Open for tours every other Thurs & Sat morning in summer.

⑤ ★★★ Woods Hole. The main ferry departure spot for Martha's Vineyard and one of the top scientific research centers in the country, this village is always lively, with a hippie mystique and the relaxed pace of a fishing village. Walk down Water Street, the main drag, and go over the drawbridge, which raises and lowers on a schedule in summer. You'll pass the historic **Woods Hole Community Hall,** where events such as concerts, theater, festivals, and even contredansing take place year-round. Next-door is the historic firehouse, the site of craft fairs, square dances, politically charged film festivals, and farmers markets. Ahead on the left, stop by ★ **Waterfront Park** to check out the **sundial** and the **squid gate,** a clever sculpture marking the pier where a boat that researches squid is docked. At the end of Water Street, at the corner of Albatross Street, you'll see the **seal tanks** in front of the ★★ **Woods Hole Science Aquarium,** a free museum with state-of-the-art tanks full of sea creatures. You can visit the **Marine Biological Laboratory Visitors Center,** 100 Water St. (www.mbl.edu) and the ★ **Woods Hole Oceanographical Institution Exhibit Center,**

Sandwich: The Glass Town

Founded in 1637 by Puritans, Sandwich is both the Cape's oldest town and one of its quaintest. Towering oak trees, 19th-century churches, and historic houses line its winding Main Street. Sandwich's claim to fame is that it was home to the nation's first glass factories. The town still supports a number of highly skilled glass blowers. Must-see sights in Sandwich include the **kids Heritage Museums & Gardens** (pictured), Grove and Pine streets, (☎ 508/888-3300; www.heritagemuseumsand gardens.org) on 76 landscaped acres with 3 museum buildings containing an antique-car collection and a historic carousel, among other treasures.

And definitely stop in at the **Sandwich Glass Museum,** (p. 166, ②), which offers a fascinating history of the town's early industry.

> *The Falmouth farmers market on Main Street takes place Thursdays.*

⑥   🍵 **Coffee Obsession.** This hip coffee bar attracts slackers, scientists, and sailors for the best coffee in town. Coffee O., as it's known, has free Wi-Fi and a play area for children. The outdoor patio is the place to sit and watch the world go by. 38 Water St., Woods Hole. ☎ 508/540-8130. www.coffeeobsession.com. $.

❼ ★★★ **The Knob.** Named for the round tip of this peninsula that sticks out into **Quissett Harbor,** the Knob is a favorite for walkers (particularly those with dogs). Quissett Harbor, where the path starts, is a secluded and picturesque setting, filled with gleaming wooden sailboats. Walk through the woods and out along a narrow section and then up a short incline to the actual "knob," a round point that sticks out into Buzzards Bay. There are benches at the promontory, a great place to stare out to sea. 🕑 45 min.

15 School St. (☎ 508/289-2663; www.whoi. edu), where you can sit in a replica of the submersible that was used to discover the wreck of the *Titanic.* 🕑 90 min.–2 hr.

Where to Stay

> *After a day on the beach, do some more relaxing on the lawn at Falmouth's Beach Breeze Inn.*

★ Beach Breeze Inn FALMOUTH

Across the street from Surf Drive Beach, guests here beat the summertime traffic blues. There's an (unheated) pool too. 321 Shore St. ☎ 800/828-3255 or 508/548-1765. www.beachbreezeinn.com. 20 units. Doubles $179–$289. MC, V.

★★ Belfry Inne & Bistro SANDWICH

This lodging option with three historic buildings in the center of the village features antique beds and claw-foot tubs. 8 Jarves St. ☎ 800/844-4542 or 508/888-8550. www.belfryinn.com. 22 units. Doubles $149–$315 w/breakfast. AE, MC, V.

★★ Coonamessett Inn FALMOUTH

This gracious inn on 7 acres overlooking a pond has a good restaurant as well. 311 Gifford St. ☎ 508/548-2300. www.capecodrestaurants.org/coonamessett. 27 units. Doubles $170–$250 w/breakfast. AE, MC, V. .

★★ Dan'l Webster Inn & Spa SANDWICH

This large lodging and dining spot in the center of Sandwich village is a dependable bet for a comfortable stay or a hearty meal. 149 Main St. ☎ 800/444-3566 or 508/888-3622. www.danlwebsterinn.com. 46 units. Doubles $139–$249 w/breakfast. AE, DC, DISC, MC, V.

★★ Inn on the Sound FALMOUTH HEIGHTS

High on a bluff near Falmouth's premier sunning beach, this stylish B&B has a sweeping view of Vineyard Sound. 313 Grand Ave. ☎ 800/564-9668 or 508/457-9666. www.innonthesound.com. 10 units. Doubles $135–$345 w/breakfast. AE, DISC, MC, V.

★★ New Seabury Resort MASHPEE

On a private beach on Nantucket Sound, only 28 of the 1,600 condos in this resort are available for vacationers to rent. Amenities include two pools, tennis courts, and a nearby golf course. 20 Red Brook Rd. ☎ 800/999-9033 or 508/539-8322. www.newseabury.com. 28 units. Doubles $347. AE, DC, MC, V.

★ Sandy Neck Motel SANDWICH

Sitting at the entrance to Sandy Neck, the best beach in these parts, this motel has it made. 669 Rte. 6A. ☎ 800/564-3992 or 508/362-3992. www.sandyneck.com. 12 units. Doubles $129. MC, V.

★★ Woods Hole Inn WOODS HOLE

This is the place for people who want to be in the thick of it in the charming fishing village of Woods Hole. 28 Water St. ☎ 508/495-0248. www.woodsholeinn.com. 5 units. Doubles $150–$275 w/breakfast. MC, V.

Where to Dine

> *Osteria La Civetta on Main Street in Falmouth is among the top restaurants on the Cape.*

★★ **Aqua Grille** SANDWICH *NEW AMERICAN*
Overlooking Sandwich's picturesque marina, this dining spot specializes in fish, grilled or fried. 14 Gallo Rd. (next to Sandwich Marina). ☎ 508/888-8889. Entrees $10–$24 AE, DC, MC, V. Lunch & dinner daily. Closed Nov to late Apr.

★★ kids **Bee-Hive Tavern** SANDWICH *TAVERN*
This modern-day tavern offers atmosphere plus well-priced standards like burgers, sandwiches, and salads. 406 Rte. 6A. ☎ 508/833-1184. Entrees $8–$16. MC, V. Lunch & dinner daily.

★★★ **The Glass Onion** FALMOUTH *NEW AMERICAN* This upscale fine-dining establishment features locally sourced foods, like Barnstable littleneck clams, and professional service in a charming setting. 37 N. Main St. (in the Queens Buyway). ☎ 508/540-3730. Entrees $16–$33. AE, MC, V. Dinner Mon–Sat.

★★★ **La Cucina Sul Mare** FALMOUTH *SOUTHERN ITALIAN* Hearty Italian fare is featured at this family-owned restaurant on Main Street. 237 Main St. ☎ 508/548-5600. Entrees $15–$25. AE, MC, V. Lunch & dinner daily.

★★ kids **Landfall Restaurant** WOODS HOLE *SEAFOOD* A terrific harbor setting and decor of colorful salvage distinguish this landmark seafood spot. Luscombe Ave. ☎ 508/548-1758. Entrees $9–$28. AE, MC, V. Lunch & dinner daily. Closed Nov to mid-Apr.

★★ **Mezza** FALMOUTH *MEDITERRANEAN*
This place has the best thin-crust brick-oven pizza in town and delicious pasta and Middle Eastern-inspired dishes. 75 Davis Straits/Rte. 28. ☎ 508/540-6992. Entrees $15–$25. AE, MC, V. Lunch & dinner daily.

★★★ **Osteria la Civetta** FALMOUTH *NORTHERN ITALIAN* European-style dining and service are featured at this excellent restaurant where homemade pasta is the specialty. 133 Main St. ☎ 508/540-1616. Entrees $15–$26. MC, V. Lunch Wed–Sat & dinner nightly.

★★ **Peking Palace** FALMOUTH *ASIAN*
Serving Chinese, Japanese, and Thai food, this established restaurant offers many unique dishes, especially on the specials board. 452 Main St. ☎ 508/540-8204. Entrees $7–$18. AE, MC, V. Lunch & dinner daily.

★★ **RooBar** FALMOUTH *NEW AMERICAN*
Creative cuisine in an arty urban setting with brick-oven pizzas the specialty. 285 Main St. ☎ 508/548-8600. Entrees $11–$26. AE, MC, V. Dinner daily.

Hyannis & the Mid Cape

The only place on Cape Cod that resembles a city, Hyannis is actually a village in the town of Barnstable. It is the commercial and transportation hub on the Cape and the main port of departure for Nantucket. Main Street is a bustling place with several interesting museums within walking distance. In the summer, free concerts take place 3 nights a week at the harborfront park.

> Artists and crafters hawk their wares all summer at the Harbor Shanties next to Hyannis Harbor.

START Hyannis is 61 miles from Boston.

1 ★★ **John F. Kennedy Hyannis Museum.** The Cape's most popular attraction—besides the beaches—this museum contains a photographic history of the Kennedys at their summer home in Hyannis Port. The building, which used to serve as town hall, doubles as the office of the Chamber of Commerce. It is flanked by two handy buildings, the **Hyannis Public Library** and the **Hyannis Post Office.** Behind the museum and just down the road on South Street is **St. Francis Xavier Church,** where Caroline Kennedy and many other Kennedys have been married. Rose Kennedy attended Mass here every day. Also on South Street, behind the post office, is the **Hyannis Armory,** 225 South St., which is where then-President-elect John F. Kennedy gave his victory speech on November 7, 1960. ⊙ 20 min. 397 Main St., Hyannis. ☎ 508/790-3077. jfk hyannismuseum.org. Admission $6 adults, $3 seniors, $3 kids 10–16, free for kids 9 & under. Open mid-Apr to Oct Mon–Sat 9am–5pm, Sun & holidays noon–5pm; last admission 3:30pm.

2 ★ **Cape Cod Maritime Museum.** This small museum overlooking Hyannis Inner Harbor displays artifacts of ships that wrecked off the coast of Cape Cod. It also exhibits a collection of items from the U.S. Lifesaving Service, the precursor to the Coast Guard. ⊙ 30 min. 135 South St., Hyannis. ☎ 508/775-1723. www.capecod maritimemuseum.org. Admission $5 adults, $4 students & seniors, free for kids 7 & under. Mar 15–Dec 24 Tues–Sat 10am–4pm, Sun noon–4pm.

3 🍽 **Common Ground Café.** Everything is made fresh at this New Age-y sandwich shop that boasts homemade everything. Booths are set up to look like treehouses. Children will be intrigued, adults perplexed. Good grub though. 420 Main St., Hyannis. ☎ 508/778-8390. $.

4 Aselton Park. Above Hyannis Harbor on Ocean Street, this park is quite busy in the summer, hosting musical performances 3 nights a week, Shakespeare in the Park by high schoolers, and local artists in the seven artist shanties just steps away. A little farther down Ocean Street is Veterans Park, where the **John F. Kennedy Memorial** is popular with tourists. ⏱ 10 min. Free. Sunrise–sunset.

Take Gosnold St. to Scudder Ave. and follow it south to Sea St.

5 Hyannisport. Get the lay of the land in this tiny village. The unique tower above the beach is part of a private home owned by local artist Sam Barber, who paints colorful Impressionist-style paintings. Farther down is Eugenia Fortes Beach, which is named after the civil rights activist who, as a young girl in 1945, was asked by police to leave the beach because it was segregated. She refused, and went on to found the Cape chapter of the NAACP. Opposite the beach entrance is a small boulder and a rose garden dedicated to Rose Kennedy, mother of JFK and at one point the town's oldest resident. You'll gain a wonderful view of Nantucket Sound by driving up Irving Avenue to Sunset Hill past the stone church and tower of St. Andrew's-by-the-Sea to the Hyannisport Golf Course. ⏱ 20 min.

Head back into the center of Hyannis, and at the West End Rotary, take North St. for 2 blocks.

6 Zion Union Heritage Museum. This unique museum is set in a converted African-American church dedicated to preserving the African-American and Cape Verdean heritage on Cape Cod. You'll find artwork, crafts, artifacts, and exhibits that explain the impact of certain community leaders. 276 North St., Hyannis. ☎ 508/790-9466. www.zionunionheritage museum.org. Admission $5 adults, $2 students. May–Oct Tues–Sat 11am–5pm, Nov–Dec Thurs–Sat 10am–4pm, Feb–Apr Thurs–Sat 11am–5pm; Jan closed.

Treasures in Nearby Yarmouth & Dennis

House museums, an art complex, and the Edward Gorey House are among the sites worth seeking out in Dennis and Yarmouth. Head to Yarmouth Port on Route 6A, the Old King's Highway, to check out two fine historic house museums—**Winslow Crocker House,** 250 Rte. 6A (☎ 617/227-3957; www. spnea.org; admission $2.50–$4; June–Oct first and third Sat of the month 11am–5pm), and **Captain Bangs Hallett House,** 11 Strawberry Lane (☎ 508/362-3021; www.hsoy. org; admission 50¢–$3; June–Oct Thurs–Sun 1–4pm). The Winslow Crocker House is the only historic house on Cape Cod preserved by the prestigious Society for the Preservation of New England Antiquities. Not only is it a lovely example of the shingled Georgian style, but it's packed with outstanding antiques—Jacobean to Chippendale—collected in the 1930s by Mary Thacher, a descendant of the town's first land grantee. The Bangs Hallett House is an 1840 Greek Revival House named for the China trade seafarer who lived here from 1863 to 1893. It is decorated with period furnishings. Behind the house is a scenic 2-mile walking trail. Nearby is the unique **Edward Gorey House,** 8 Strawberry Lane (☎ 508/362-3909; www. edwardgoreyhouse.org; admission $2–$5; Mon–Sat 11am–4pm, Sun noon–4pm), which features exhibits about the famous illustrator in his longtime home. Farther down Route 6A in Dennis is the **Cape Museum of Art,** 60 Hope Lane (☎ 508/385-4477; www.ccma.org; admission $8; Tues–Wed and Fri–Sat 10am–5pm, Thurs 10am–8pm, Sun noon–5pm; admission free Thurs 10am–8pm), the best collection of the Cape's artistic legacy outside of Provincetown. There's also an outdoor sculpture garden. Call ahead or check the website for a schedule of special shows, lectures, concerts, and classes.

Some Beer with Your Potato Chips?

You'll find manufacturers of both in Hyannis, along with free samples. **Cape Cod Potato Chips,** at 100 Breeds Hill Rd. (at Independence Way off Rte. 132; ☎ 508/775-7253; www.capecodchips.com), are the world's best. Long a local favorite, they originate right here. Free 15-minute factory tours are offered Monday to Friday from 9am to 5pm in July and August. **Cape Cod Beer,** at 1336 Phinney's Lane (☎ 508/790-4200; www.cape codbeer.com), gives free tours of its brewery on Saturdays at 1pm and Tuesdays at 11am.

Hyannis & the Mid Cape

CAPE COD BAY

Sandwich

East Sandwich

SANDY NECK

S A N D W I C H

6A

West Barnstable

Forestdale Rd.

Quaker Meeting House Rd.

Spectacle Pd.

Great Hill Rd.

Triangle Pd.

Lawrence Pd.

B A R N S T A B L E

Cotuit Rd.

Farmersville Rd.

Peters Pd.

Race Ln.

Prospect St.

Osterville Rd.

Oak St.

Iyannough Rd.

Wakeby Pd.

Mystic L.

Old Stage Rd.

Wequaquet Lake

Phinney's Ln.

Middle Pd.

Old Falmouth Rd.

Long Pd.

Hamblin Pd.

Santuit-Newtown Rd.

Marstons Mills

Cotuit Rd.

Centerville

Falmouth Rd.

W. Main St.

Mashpee Pond

Santuit Pd.

Lovells Pd.

Falmouth Rd.

28

Long Pd.

Strawberry Hill Rd.

130

Mashpee

Main St.

8

Craigville Beach Rd.

Great Neck Rd.

Santuit

7

Main St.

North Bay

Main St.

Old Mill Rd.

S Main St.

M A S H P E E

Osterville

Centerville Harbor

Quinaquisset Ave.

Cotuit

Cotuit Bay

Grand Island

West Bay

19 20

9

1 John F. Kennedy Hyannis Museum
2 Cape Cod Maritime Museum
3 Common Ground Café
4 Aselton Park
5 Hyannis Port
6 Zion Union Heritage Museum

Where to Stay

Anchor In **18**

Ashley Manor Inn **21**

Beechwood Inn **20**

Cape Codder Resort & Spa **9**

Captain Farris House **24**

Corsair and Cross Rip Resort Motels **28**

Lamb and Lion Inn **19**

Lighthouse Inn **25**

Long Dell Inn **8**

Ocean Mist Motor Lodge **23**

Simmons Homestead Inn **10**

Where to Dine

Alberto's Ristorante **15**

Baxter's Boat House **17**

Black Cat Tavern **16**

Embargo **13**

Inaho **22**

The Naked Oyster Bistro & Raw Bar **14**

Norabella **26**

Ocean House **27**

The Paddock **11**

Regatta of Cotuit **7**

Roadhouse Café **12**

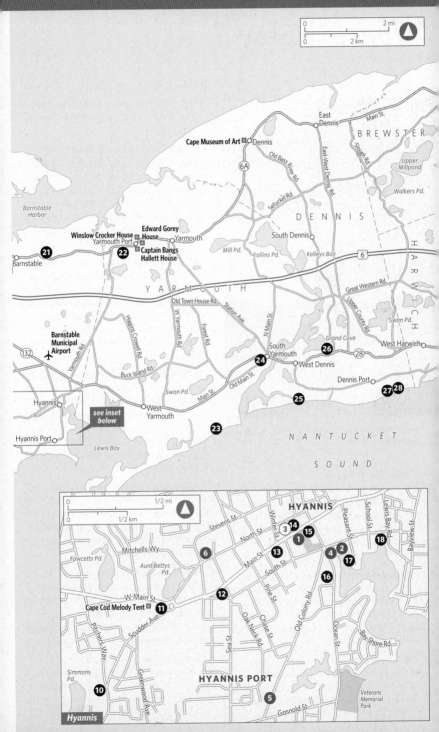

Where to Stay

> *Some antique homes along the Old King's Highway double as inns.*

★★ Anchor In HYANNIS
This motel on Hyannis Harbor is well run and with a great location. Rooms are a step above standard motel accommodations, and there is a harborfront pool. 1 South St. ☎ 508/775-0357. www.anchorin.com. 42 units. Doubles $219–$289 w/breakfast. AE, DISC, MC, V.

★★ Ashley Manor Inn BARNSTABLE VILLAGE
This pretty, historic inn is on a 2-acre property that includes a tennis court. 3660 Rte. 6A. ☎ 888/535-2246 or 508/362-8044. www. ashleymanor.net. 6 units. Doubles $175 w/ breakfast. AE, DISC, MC, V.

★★ Beechwood Inn BARNSTABLE VILLAGE
This Queen Anne Victorian is dripping with antique charm. 2839 Rte. 6A (about 1½ miles east of Rte. 132). ☎ 800/609-6618 or

508/362-6618. www.beechwoodinn.com. 6 units. Doubles $185–$210 w/breakfast. AE, DISC, MC, V.

★ Cape Codder Resort & Spa HYANNIS
The setting isn't very scenic, but this place has a lot of amenities for families, including a wave pool with two water slides and two restaurants on-site. 1225 Iyannough Rd./Rte. 132. ☎ 888/297-2200 or 508/771-3000. www.capecodderresort.com. 260 units. Doubles $159–$198. AE, MC, V.

★★ Captain Farris House BASS RIVER
This sumptuous B&B with a peaceful garden, just off bustling Rte. 28, is close to the scenic Bass River. 308 Old Main St. ☎ 800/350-9477 or 508/760-2818. www. captainfarris.com.
8 units. Doubles $185–$239 w/breakfast. AE, DISC, MC, V.

★ Corsair and Cross Rip Resort Motels DENISPORT Fresh contemporary decor puts these motels above the others along this strip of Nantucket Sound beach. 41 Chase Ave.
☎ 800/345-5140 or 508/398-2279. www. corsaircrossrip.com. 47 units. Doubles $22–$300. AE, MC, V.

★★ Lamb and Lion Inn BARNSTABLE VILLAGE
Part B&B, part motel with pool, this inn is set on a knoll in a charming section of the Old King's Highway. 2504 Rte. 6A. ☎ 800/909-6923 or 508/362-6823. 10 units. Doubles $189–$275 w/breakfast. MC, V.

★★ Lighthouse Inn WEST DENNIS
This popular resort on a private Nantucket Sound beach, with a historic lighthouse on-site, feels like old Cape Cod. 1 Lighthouse Inn Rd. ☎ 508/398-2244. www.lighthouseinn.com. 68 units. Doubles $255–$280 w/breakfast. MC, V.

★★ Long Dell Inn CENTERVILLE
This handsome 1850s sea captain's home has been welcoming guests for 80 years. These innkeepers really know hospitality, complete

with three-course breakfast. 436 S. Main St. ☎ 508/775-2750. www.longdellinn.com. 7 units. Doubles $155–$180 w/breakfast. AE, MC, V.

★ **Ocean Mist Motor Lodge** SOUTH YARMOUTH This large motel on a Nantucket Sound beach has an indoor pool. 97 S. Shore Dr. ☎ 508/398-2633. www.innseasonresorts.com. 63 units. Doubles $169–$309. MC, V.

★ **Simmons Homestead Inn** HYANNIS One of the highlights of this quirky bed-and-breakfast is the on-site museum, **Toad Hall,** a collection of 50 red sports cars. 288 Scudder Ave. (½ mile south of West End Rotary). ☎ 800/637-1649 or 508/778-4999. www.simmonshomesteadinn.com. 14 units. Doubles $180–$240 w/breakfast. AE, DISC, MC, V.

Where to Dine

★★ **Alberto's Ristorante** HYANNIS *NORTHERN ITALIAN* The hallmark at this elegant restaurant is consistency when it comes to very good food and service. 360 Main St. ☎ 508/778-1770. Entrees $11–$27. AE, DC, DISC, MC, V. Lunch & dinner daily.

★ kids **Baxter's Boat House** HYANNIS *CLAM SHACK* This Hyannis harborfront shack is the place to go for fried clams and the like. 177 Pleasant St. ☎ 508/775-7040. Entrees $9–$15. AE, MC, V. Lunch & dinner daily. Closed mid-Oct to early May.

★★ **Black Cat Tavern** HYANNIS *SEAFOOD* The top harborfront restaurant in Hyannis, this casual spot focuses on seafood, burgers, and steaks, as well as piano bar entertainment most nights in season. 165 Ocean St. ☎ 508/778-1233. Entrees $17–$31. AE, DISC, MC, V. Lunch & dinner daily.

★★ **Embargo** HYANNIS *TAPAS* Great happy hour deals can be had at this tapas bar popular with singles in the 30-to-50 age group. 453 Main St. ☎ 508/771-9700. http://embargorestaurant.com. Tapas $3–13, Entrees $8–28. AE, DISC, MC, V. Dinner Mon–Sat (4:30pm–1am).

★★ **Inaho** YARMOUTHPORT *JAPANESE* Inside this Cape Cod–style cottage is the peninsula's best sushi bar. 157 Main St. ☎ 508/362-5522. Entrees $13–$23. MC, V. Dinner Mon–Sat.

★★ **The Naked Oyster Bistro & Raw Bar** HYANNIS *SEAFOOD* The menu includes local shellfish from the owner's own aquaculture operation in Barnstable Harbor at this excellent

> *The Naked Oyster in Hyannis is the place to get a plate of oysters—naked—on the half shell.*

> *Alberto's on Main Street in Hyannis is one of many restaurants to offer outdoor seating in the summer.*

> *Hyannis is the capital of the Cape's nightlife, and many bars, including emBargo in Hyannis, feature live music.*

and very hip venue. 410 Main St. ☎ 508/778-6500. Entrees $24–$35. AE, MC, V. Lunch Tues–Fri & Sun; dinner Tues–Sun.

★★ **Norabella** WEST DENNIS *SOUTHERN ITALIAN* This chef-owned establishment is a slice of old Cape Cod, when chefs would come out to check on diners, and meals were homemade from start to finish. 702 Rte. 28. ☎ 508/398-6672. Entrees $15–$22. MC, V. Dinner nightly.

★★★ **Ocean House** DENNISPORT *NEW AMERICAN* Set on the beach overlooking Nantucket Sound, and styling itself as a New American Bistro and Bar, this fine-dining venue has always had a stellar reputation for getting local seafood preparations just right. 3 Chase Ave. (at Depot St.). ☎ 508/394-0700. Entrees $22–$34. MC, V. Dinner Tues–Sun.

An Ice-Cream Classic

At ★★ **Four Seas Ice Cream,** 360 S. Main St., Centerville (☎ 508/775-1394), exotic flavors such as cantaloupe and beach plum are a specialty.

Going Out on the Mid Cape

Hyannis is the nightlife capital of Cape Cod. You can stroll along Main Street on a summer night and find all kinds of scenes, from sports bars, to Irish pubs, to upscale venues hosting a yachting crowd. If you're looking for something a little different, try the ★★ **Barnstable Comedy Club,** 3171 Rte. 6A, Barnstable Village (☎ 508/362-6333). A local favorite since 1922, the oldest amateur theater group in the country offers a mix of old chestnuts and original farces off-season. Movie buffs should check out Dennis' ★★★ **Cape Cinema,** 35 Hope Lane (☎ 508/385-2503; www.capecinema.com), which screens art house films in a 1930s cinema with leather armchairs; an Art Deco ceiling mural by Rockwell Kent is a delight. Also in Dennis, the ★★★ **Cape Playhouse,** 820 Rte. 6A (☎ 877/385-3911; www.capeplayhouse. com), is the oldest continuously active straw-hat theater in the country (it was founded in 1927). Performances run from mid-June to early September, and children's theater performances are held on Friday mornings. In Hyannis, the ★★★ **Cape Cod Melody Tent,** 21 W. Main St. (☎ 508/775-5630; www.melody-tent.org) has hosted major performers of the past 50 years, from jazz greats to comedians.

★★ **The Paddock** HYANNIS *CONTINENTAL* With a solid reputation for good food and service, this is a sure bet for special occasions or early dinners before a night at the Melody Tent next door. 20 Scudder Ave. (at the West End Rotary). ☎ 508/775-7677. Entrees $17–$28. AE, DC, DISC, MC, V. Lunch & dinner daily. Closed Nov–Mar.

★★★ **Regatta of Cotuit** COTUIT *NEW AMERICAN* This fine-dining restaurant, set in a stately 1790 home, has long been one of the finest restaurants on the Cape. Now it also has a less expensive "Tap Room" menu. 4631 Rte. 28 (near Rte. 130). ☎ 508/428-5715. Entrees $24–$34; tap menu $10–$27. AE, MC, V. Dinner nightly.

★★ **Roadhouse Café** HYANNIS *NEW AMERICAN/ NORTHERN ITALIAN* American standards such as oysters Rockefeller and Italian pasta, heavy on the garlic, are the hallmarks here. 488 South St. ☎ 508/775-2386. Entrees $15–$26. AE, DC, DISC, MC, V. Dinner nightly.

Chatham & the Upper Cape

Said by some to be the prettiest town on the Cape and among the wealthiest, Chatham is known for its picturesque Main Street, lined with interesting shops, and manicured residential areas, where beach roses wrap around white picket fences. From Lighthouse Beach near the end of Main Street, you can look beyond a barrier beach, a favorite of seals, to the Atlantic Ocean beyond.

> Kids can watch their favorite candy being made at the Chatham Candy Manor.

START Chatham is 24 miles south of Provincetown.

1 Main Street. Chatham's tree-shaded Main Street, lined with specialty stores, offers a terrific opportunity to shop and stroll. Walking its 1-mile length from one end of Main Street to the other, you'll pass art galleries, bookstores, gift shops, candy-making shops, clothing, toys, and jewelry. The town makes it easy for wanderers. There are three large public parking lots, no parking meters, and two public restrooms. **Information booth (summer only), 533 Main St.**

2 ★★ Chatham Lighthouse. A quarter-mile south from the end of Main Street, Chatham Lighthouse is an 1876 beacon, run by the Coast Guard and visible 15 miles out to sea. It's not open for viewing, but on-site telescopes make it a great spot to take in views of the Atlantic Ocean and the "break"—the

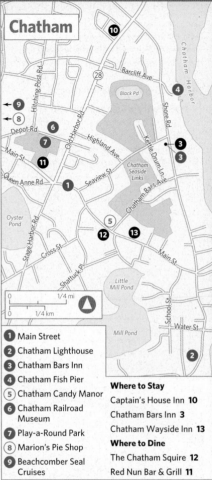

> *Chatham Light stands sentinel over Lighthouse Beach, where the undertow can be treacherous.*

Chatham

1. Main Street
2. Chatham Lighthouse
3. Chatham Bars Inn
4. Chatham Fish Pier
5. Chatham Candy Manor
6. Chatham Railroad Museum
7. Play-a-Round Park
8. Marion's Pie Shop
9. Beachcomber Seal Cruises

Where to Stay

Captain's House Inn **10**

Chatham Bars Inn **3**

Chatham Wayside Inn **13**

Where to Dine

The Chatham Squire **12**

Red Nun Bar & Grill **11**

point where the ocean broke through the barrier beach in 1987. A second break opened up a few years ago. If shopping on Main Street has tired you out, you can take a shuttle to Lighthouse Beach. Parking is restricted to 30 minutes at a time and swimming is at your own risk. The "risk" is not just the riptides. The large seal population that likes to frolic near the barrier beach has become an attraction for great white sharks. ⏱ 30 min.

3 ★★ **Chatham Bars Inn.** Begun as a private hunting lodge in 1914, this property has turned into one of the premier lodging destinations on the Cape. Stroll through the lobby, reminiscent of the grand hotels of yesteryear. Linger on the porch over coffee or a cocktail while you gaze out on the fabulous view. ⏱ 20 min. 297 Shore Rd., Chatham. ☎ 508/945-0096.

4 ★★ **Chatham Fish Pier.** Chatham has the last remaining commercial fishing fleet on the Cape. From noon on, trawlers bring in the catch of the day from fishing grounds miles offshore. You can watch the haul from an observation deck. Check out **The Provider,** a sculpture by Wood Hole artist Sig Purwin. ⏱ 30 min. Corner of Shore Rd. & Barcliff Ave., about ¼ mile north of Main St. Parking for visitors is in the upper lot.

Head back to Main St. and west a couple of blocks to the best sweet shop around.

5 ★ **Chatham Candy Manor.** Three generations of the Turner family have been hand-dipping homemade chocolates here. Why not try a chocolate-dipped strawberry? Turtles, truffles, and homemade fudge are tops. At Christmastime, there are handmade candy canes. ⏱ 15 min. 484 Main St. ☎ 508/945-0825. www.candymanor.com. $.

⑥ ★ kids **Chatham Railroad Museum.** Constructed in a whimsical "railroad Gothic style," this 1887 train station has been filled with railroading memorabilia, including models from the 1939 New York World's Fair. A 1910 caboose is out back. ⏱ 30 min. 1 block north of Main St. at the west end of town. 153 Depot St., Chatham. Donations accepted. Mid-June to mid-Sept Tues–Sat 10am–4pm.

⑦ ★ kids **Play-a-Round Park.** Opposite the Railroad Museum, this park is a must if you have kids along. Dreamed up by prominent playground designer Robert Leathers, it's a marvelous maze of tubes, rope ladders, slides, and swings. The only way you'll get going again is to promise to come back.

Monomoy, a Wildlife Reserve

The uninhabited nature reserve known as Monomoy encompasses 2,750 acres of brush-covered sand favored by some 285 species of migrating birds. Monomoy stretches south from Chatham with Nantucket Sound on one side and the Atlantic Ocean on the other; annual shoaling, when tides break up the sand, determines whether there are one or two islands. The summer and fall are the best times to watch the birds as they embark on their migration. **Monomoy Island Ferry** (☎ 508/237-0420) offers cruises to Monomoy from the Monomoy National Wildlife Refuge Headquarters on Morris Island. The price for a 90-minute cruise is $30 adults, $25 children.

Massachusetts Audubon Society's **Wellfleet Bay Wildlife Sanctuary** conducts guided natural history tours of Monomoy throughout the year (☎ 508/349-2615 for information or reservations). **Cape Cod Museum of Natural History** (p. 157, ③) also runs guided tours to Monomoy Island including overnight stays at the restored lighthouse on South Monomoy. To reach Monomoy headquarters on Morris Island, take Route 6 east to Route 137 south to Route 28. A left turn takes you through downtown Chatham (about 3 miles). Turn right at the stop sign, to the Chatham Lighthouse and Coast Guard Station. Take the first left after the lighthouse, then the first right. Follow Morris Island Road to signs for the Refuge on the left.

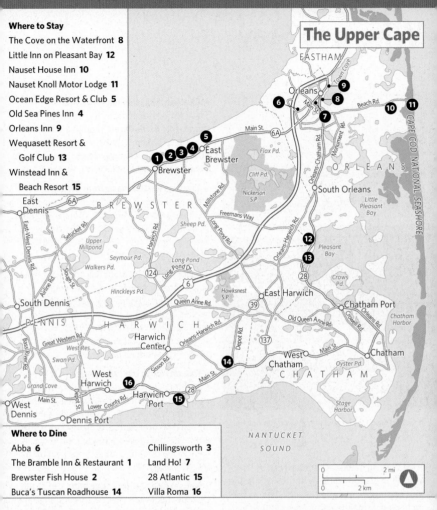

The Upper Cape

Where to Stay

The Cove on the Waterfront **8**

Little Inn on Pleasant Bay **12**

Nauset House Inn **10**

Nauset Knoll Motor Lodge **11**

Ocean Edge Resort & Club **5**

Old Sea Pines Inn **4**

Orleans Inn **9**

Wequasett Resort &
   Golf Club **13**

Winstead Inn &
   Beach Resort **15**

Where to Dine

Abba **6**	Chillingsworth **3**
The Bramble Inn & Restaurant **1**	Land Ho! **7**
Brewster Fish House **2**	28 Atlantic **15**
Buca's Tuscan Roadhouse **14**	Villa Roma **16**

Depot St. leads to Rte. 28, and from here you can drive 2 miles west to the best pie shop on Cape Cod.

⑧ 🥧 **Marion's Pie Shop.** Nearly a half-century's worth of summer visitors have come for their ration of dinner and dessert pies, from sea clam to lemon meringue. Load up on the fruit breads and sweet rolls and have a picnic on the beach. 2022 Rte. 28, about ½ mile east of Rte. 137. ☎ 508/432-9439. marionspie shopofchatham.com. $.

⑨ **Beachcomber Seal Cruises.** An enormous gray seal colony that used to hang out on Monomoy Island south of Chatham now seems to prefer being closer to shore. Some locals complain that they're ruining the fishing and fouling up the beaches, but they're awfully fun to watch. Several outfits operate seal cruises out of Chatham's harbors and from nearby Harwich. One of the best is the Beachcomber, which typically stays in the area between North Beach and the lighthouse. You park in their satellite lot on Crowell Rd., north of Rte. 28, a few miles west of the center of town. ☎ 508/945-5265. 90 min. Tours cost $27 adults, $25 seniors, $23 kids.

Where to Stay

> Get an ocean view room at the Chatham Bars Inn.

★★★ Captain's House Inn CHATHAM
You'll find great hospitality at this historic inn plus carriage house and converted barn. The meticulously maintained 2-acre grounds include a pool. 369–377 Old Harbor Rd. (about ½ mile from rotary). ☎ 800/315-0728 or 508/945-0127. www.captainshouseinn.com. 16 units. Doubles $260–$475 w/breakfast. AE, DISC, MC, V. Map p. 195.

★★★ Chatham Bars Inn CHATHAM
This grand historic resort property with inn and cottages is set on a private beach separated by a barrier beach from the Atlantic Ocean. Pool, tennis courts, 9-hole golf course, spa, and restaurants are among the amenities. 297 Shore Rd. ☎ 800/527-4884 or 508/945-0096. www.chathambarsinn.com. 205 units. Doubles $455–$725. AE, DC, MC, V. Map p. 195.

★ Chatham Wayside Inn CHATHAM
This former stagecoach stop has been thoroughly modernized, though it's a bit generic. 512 Main St. ☎ 800/242-8426 or 508/945-5550. www.waysideinn.com. 56 units. Doubles $265–$325. DISC, MC, V. Map p. 195.

★ The Cove on the Waterfront ORLEANS
Fronting the town cove, this motel complex includes a heated pool. 13 S. Orleans Rd./Rte. 28. ☎ 800/343-2233 or 508/255-1203. www.thecoveorleans.com. 47 units. Doubles $157–$196. AE, DC, DISC, MC, V. Map p. 197.

★★ Little Inn on Pleasant Bay SOUTH ORLEANS
On the coast of Pleasant Bay, between Chatham and Orleans centers, this charming inn has a peaceful aura. 654 S. Orleans Rd. ☎ 888/332-3351 or 508/255-0780. www.alittleinnonpleasantbay.com. 9 units. Doubles $245–$315 w/breakfast. AE, MC, V. Map p. 197.

★ Nauset House Inn EAST ORLEANS
A half-mile from Nauset Beach, this value-priced country inn is a cozy setting for a quiet and affordable retreat. 143 Beach Rd. (about 1 mile east of town center). ☎ 800/771-5508 or 508/255-2195. www.nausethouseinn.com. 14 units. Doubles $120–$185 w/breakfast. DISC, MC, V. Map p. 197.

★ Nauset Knoll Motor Lodge EAST ORLEANS
Overlooking Nauset Beach, this nothing-fancy motel with huge picture windows will suit minimalists to a T. It is owned by the National Park Service. 237 Beach Rd. ☎ 508/255-2364. www.capecodtravel.com/nausetknoll. 12 units. Doubles $175. MC, V. Map p. 197.

★★ Ocean Edge Resort & Club BREWSTER
This resort has a contemporary country club style with amenities such as a private Cape Cod Bay beach, a golf course, 11 tennis courts, eight pools, and four restaurants. 2907 Rte. 6A. ☎ 508/896-9000. www.oceanedge.com. 335 units. Doubles $265–$445. AE, DISC, MC, V. Map p. 197.

> *The Outer Bar & Grille at the Wequassett Inn is one of the Cape's best kept secrets.*

★ **Old Sea Pines Inn** BREWSTER

This large, reasonably priced historic inn is a great choice for families because of the casual atmosphere. 2553 Rte. 6A. ☎ 508/896-6114. www.oldseapinesinn.com. 24 units. Doubles $110–$165 w/breakfast. AE, DC, DISC, MC, V. Map p. 197.

★★ **Orleans Inn** ORLEANS

This historic mansard-roofed beauty on Town Cove includes a family-style restaurant. 3 Old Country Rd./Rte. 6A (just south of the Orleans rotary). ☎ 800/863-3039 or 508/255-2222. www.orleansinn.com. 11 units. Doubles $175–$250 w/breakfast. AE, MC, V. Map p. 197.

★★★ **Wequasett Resort & Golf Club** HARWICH

This 22-acre resort on placid and pretty Pleasant Bay has tennis, golf, swimming, sailing, and a fantastic restaurant. 2173 Rte. 28 (5 miles north of Chatham center). ☎ 800/225-7125 or 508/432-5400. www.wequassett.com. 120 units. Doubles $525–$825. AE, DC, DISC, MC, V. Map p. 197.

★★ **Winstead Inn & Beach Resort** HARWICH

This property comprises a Nantucket Sound beachfront inn and a second in-town property with a saltwater pool. 4 Braddock Lane. ☎ 800/870-4405 or 508/432-4444. www. winsteadinn.com. 21 units. Doubles $325–$525 w/breakfast. MC, V. Map p. 197.

Where to Dine

> Comfort food and a brew are on the menu at the Red Nun in Chatham.

★★★ Abba ORLEANS INTERNATIONAL
One of the best restaurants on the Lower Cape, this is where to go for fusion cuisine, a little Middle Eastern, a little European, a little New American, plus some Thai and New England thrown in. 90 Old Colony Way (at West Rd.). ☎ 508/255-8144. Entrees $18–$27. AE, MC, V. Dinner nightly. Map p. 197.

★★★ The Bramble Inn & Restaurant BREWSTER
NEW AMERICAN Often named one of the best restaurants on Cape Cod, this restaurant set in an antique home continues to impress with food that combines Mediterranean influences with exotic touches. 2019 Main St./Rte. 6A (½ mile east of Rte. 124). ☎ 508/896-7644. $20–$37. AE, DISC, MC, V. Dinner nightly. Closed Jan–Mar. Map p. 197.

★★ Brewster Fish House BREWSTER NEW
AMERICAN This intimate restaurant, in a nondescript roadhouse on Route 6A, is famous for its inspired preparation of fresh locally caught seafood. 2208 Main St./Rte. 6A (exit 12 off Rte. 6). Entrees $17–$29. MC, V. Lunch & dinner daily. Map p. 197.

★★ Buca's Tuscan Roadhouse HARWICH
NORTHERN ITALIAN With an atmosphere that's somehow romantic and festive at the same time, this place serves homemade pastas, off-the-boat fish, and tender cuts of meat, all prepared in an authentic Italian style. 4 Depot Rd. (just off Rte. 28, near Chatham border). ☎ 508/432-6900. Entrees $18–$25. AE, MC, V. Dinner nightly. Map p. 197.

★ kids Chatham Squire CHATHAM TAVERN
The unofficial center of Chatham, this is where generations of summer residents mix with year-rounders, fishermen, and landed gentry to have the best clam chowder around. 487 Main St. ☎ 508/945-0945. $11–$23. AE, DISC, MC, V. Lunch & dinner daily. Map p. 195.

★★★ Chillingsworth BREWSTER FRENCH
A longtime contender for title of fanciest restaurant on the Cape, this is where to go for a seven-course table d'hôte menu that will challenge the most shameless gourmands. A bistro offers lighter fare. 2449 Main St./Rte. 6A. From Rte. 6, take exit 10 & a right on 6A for 1½ miles. Fixed price $60–$75, bistro $17–$36. AE, DC, MC, V. Lunch & dinner daily. Map p. 197.

★ Land Ho! ORLEANS TAVERN
A longtime hit with locals, this pub offers good food, easy on the budget. Rte. 6A & Cove Rd. ☎ 508/255-5165. Entrees $9–$22. AE, DISC, MC, V. Lunch & dinner daily. Map p. 197.

★ Red Nun Bar & Grill CHATHAM PUB
This is the place for comfort food: Mama's meatloaf and cheeseburgers. 746 Main St. (next to Monomoy Theater). ☎ 508/348-0469. All under $15. MC, V. Lunch & dinner daily. Map p. 195.

Catching a Show

The Cape has a long history of local theater, and if you're interested in catching a bit of summer stock, the Upper Cape is the place to do it. Here are a few of my favorites. And if you'd rather not be indoors on a nice summer night? Consider the free Friday night band concerts in Chatham's Kate Gould Park (pictured).

★★ **Academy of Performing Arts Playhouse** ORLEANS The 162-seat arena-style stage is housed in the old town hall. Performances include musicals, drama, and poetry readings in season. Children's theater is on Friday and Saturday mornings. 120 Main St. (¾ mile from town center). ☎ 508/255-1963. www.apacape.org. Tickets $10–$22. Map p. 197.

★★ **Cape Rep Theatre** BREWSTER Performances of plays, from *Eurydice* to *Frankie and Johnny in the Clair de Lune*, take place year-round at both an indoor theater and an outdoor theater on the old Crosby estate. Summer matinees are geared for children. 3299 Rte. 6A (about 2½ miles east of Brewster center). ☎ 508/896-1888. www.caperep.org. Tickets $28. Map p. 197.

★★ **Harwich Junior Theatre** WEST HARWICH This troupe has been pleasing audiences with creative productions since 1952. Summer performances are geared to children; winter, to children and adults. 105 Division St. (take exit 9A, Rte. 134 to Rte. 28, follow 1½ miles to Division St. in Harwich, take a right to theater). ☎ 508/432-2002. www.hjtcapecod.org. Tickets $20–$25 adults, $15 kids. Map p. 197.

★★ **Monomoy Theatre** CHATHAM Every summer since 1958, the Ohio University Players have commuted to this 1930s theater to put on a play a week, from musicals to Shakespeare. In late July, they take a week off for the Monomoy Chamber Ensemble. 776 Rte. 28 (¼ mile west of the rotary). ☎ 508/945-0945. www.monomoytheatre.org. Tickets $20–$30. Map p. 195.

★★★ **28 Atlantic** HARWICH *NEW AMERICAN* This elegant and expensive restaurant at the Wequasett Inn is a place to come for special occasions. This is fine dining to the hilt, with *amuse-bouches* and all. A casual poolside Outer Bar is also on the property. 2173 Rte. 28. ☎ 508/430-3000. Entrees $21–$44. AE, DC, DISC, MC, V. Dinner nightly. Closed Dec to mid-Apr. Map p. 197.

★ **Villa Roma** HARWICH *ITALIAN* This old-style roadhouse serves nothing-fancy Italian fare. 278 Rte. 28. ☎ 508/432-6868. Entrees $10–$20. AE, MC, V. Dinner nightly. Map p. 197.

Provincetown & the Outer Cape

The town at the tip of the Cape is many things to many people: a 100-year-old art colony, a Portuguese fishing village, a dune-filled wilderness, a restaurant and shopping mecca, and a GLBT vacationland. Throughout history, the place has thrilled just about everyone who has visited, including the Pilgrims, who landed here in 1620, did the first laundry in the New World, and wrote the Mayflower Compact, in that order.

> The Lobster Pot's neon sign is a landmark in Provincetown.

START Provincetown is 116 miles from Boston.

① ★★★ Provincetown Art Association & Museum. This museum features exhibits from up-and-coming artists, established locals, and legendary figures from old Provincetown who made it nationally. Its permanent collection contains works going back to this art colony's beginnings more than 100 years ago. The sophisticated building, mixing modern architecture with old Provincetown, is also beautiful. The art association was founded in 1914 by Charles Hawthorne. In the early days, there were rivalries between the figurative painters and the Abstract Expressionists. ⏱ 40 min. 460 Commercial St. (take 1st Provincetown exit off Rte. 6, Snail Rd., and drive 1 mile). ☎ 508/487-1750. www.paam.org.

SITE GUIDE PAGE 206

② East End Galleries. Near the Art Association on Commercial Street, about a dozen galleries are worth a visit. These are a fraction of the three dozen or so galleries in town—and there are several good ones on or near Bradford Street too—but these will give you a good dose of a range of styles of artwork displayed in town. Gallery strolls take place Friday nights in summer, when all the galleries have wine-and-cheese openings and stay open 'til 10pm or so.

> *Walk to the end of Macmillan Wharf to see the giant photos that pay tribute to fisherman's wives.*

③ 🦐 ★ **Angel Foods.** This deli and specialty foods store in the far East End is the best in town. It's a great place to stock a picnic basket before going to the beach. **467 Commercial St.** ☎ 508/487-6666. $.

❹ ★★ **Provincetown Public Library.** The second floor of the library, built as a church in 1860, has a half-scale replica of the schooner *Rose Dorothea,* which won the Lipton Cup, a race from Boston to Gloucester, in 1907. The statue *Tourists,* by Chaim Gross, is out front. ⏱ 15 min. 356 Commercial St. ☎ 508/487-7094. www.ptownlib.com. Mon & Fri 10am–5pm; Tues & Thurs noon–8pm; Wed 10am–8pm; Sat 10am–2pm; Sun 1–5pm.

The Province Lands

Provincetown has two beaches within the National Seashore: **Herring Cove** (p. 176, which faces Cape Cod Bay, and **Race Point** (p. 179), which faces the Atlantic Ocean. A day pass for $15 gets you in either one or both. A season pass is $45. If you want to get into the water, Herring Cove is the place on all but the hottest days. Race Point's waters tend to be frigid, though there is great surf here for frolicking. Both have lifeguards, restrooms, and changing rooms. Nearby are miles of walking trails and a hilly bike path with sweeping dune views. The Province Lands Visitor Center has exhibits about this unique landscape and a variety of ranger-guided tours. ⏱ 30 min. (for a visit to the visitor center). Race Point Rd. ☎ 508/487-1256. www.nps.gov/caco. Free. Mid-Apr to late Nov daily 9am–5pm.

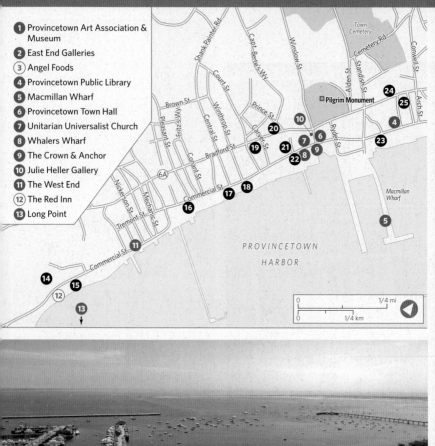

1. Provincetown Art Association & Museum
2. East End Galleries
3. Angel Foods
4. Provincetown Public Library
5. Macmillan Wharf
6. Provincetown Town Hall
7. Unitarian Universalist Church
8. Whalers Wharf
9. The Crown & Anchor
10. Julie Heller Gallery
11. The West End
12. The Red Inn
13. Long Point

> The best view in town is from the top of the Pilgrim Monument.

5 ★★★ **Macmillan Wharf.** In the 19th century, there were 52 piers jutting into Provincetown Harbor. This, the site of the town's huge municipal parking lot, is one of only a few that remain. It is the home of what remains of Provincetown's fishing fleet. Walk out to the end of the westerly pier to check out the fishing boats, the whale-watching fleet, charter boats, and pleasure boats moored in the harbor. You can also tour the pricey but entertaining **Whydah Pirate Museum** (☎ 508/487-8899; www.whydah.com; admission $10 adults, $8 seniors and children; open in summer daily 10am–7pm), at the end of the pier, which contains a small number of artifacts from the discovery of the pirate ship *Whydah*

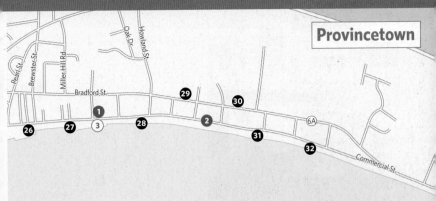

Provincetown

off Wellfleet in 1984. At the end of the pier, by looking across at Fisherman's Wharf, you can see a permanent ★★★ **art exhibit** by photographer Norma Holt and artist Ewa Nogiec, called *They Also Faced the Sea*. A tribute to Provincetown's Portuguese fishing community, the exhibit is composed of five large black-and-white portrait photos, mounted on buildings that depict Provincetown women of Portuguese descent. ⏲ 30 min.

6 ★★ **Provincetown Town Hall.** After a recent renovation, the historic Town Hall is worth a look—see it just for the 1930s murals, commissioned by the Works Progress Administration in the 1930s, that show scenes of old Provincetown when it was a fishing village. ⏲ 15 min. 260 Commercial St. ☎ 508/487-7000.

7 ★ **Unitarian Universalist Church.** Steps from the Town Hall is the "UU," where Sunday-night concerts are a summer highlight. The church, built in 1847, has a sanctuary painted in *trompe l'oeil* fashion. The lower level doubles as a theater in summer, and services are held there in the winter. ⏲ 15 min. 236 Commercial St. ☎ 508/487-9344.

8 **Whalers Wharf.** Across the street from the UU is a multistory shopping complex, which was reconstructed after being burned to the ground by a fire in February 1998. It has a theater, a fine-dining restaurant, and a number of shops and artist studios. ⏲ 20 min. 237 Commercial St.

9 **The Crown & Anchor.** Close by Whaler's Wharf is the town's biggest nightclub, actually several nightclubs, bars, a restaurant, and a cabaret in a complex that also includes an inn. You'll see performers promoting their shows in front during the day. ⏲ 1–3 hr. 247 Commercial St. ☎ 508/487-1430. www.onlyatthecrown.com.

10 ★★ **Julie Heller Gallery.** Visit this gallery set right on the beach in an old fishing shack. Artwork from old Provincetown is stacked 10 deep leaning against every wall. You'll find all the early P-town masters, Hawthorn, Avery Hofmann, Lazzell, Hensche, as well as contemporary artists. ⏲ 30 min. 2 Gosnold St. ☎ 508/487-2169.

11 ★★ **The West End.** Beginning at the Coast Guard Station, you have entered the West End of Provincetown. Here is where you will

② East End Galleries

Provincetown has long been a haven for artists, so it's no surprise that there are so many great galleries here. Many of them are clustered on or near the East End of Commercial Street, which makes doing a gallery stroll nice and easy. One of my favorites is the ④ **Berta Walker Gallery,** 208 Bradford St. (☎ 508/487-6411; www.bertawalkergallery.com). Berta is a force to be reckoned with, having nurtured many artists, and her collection includes works by Milton Avery and Robert Motherwell. The ⑤ **The Schoolhouse Gallery,** 494 Commercial St. (☎ 508/487-4800; www.schoolhouseprovincetown.com), often has provocative photography exhibits. In the same building, ⓒ **artStrand** (☎ 508/487-1153; www.artstrand.com) specializes in cutting-edge contemporary work. ⑩ **Julie Heller East,** 465 Commercial St. (☎ 508/487-2169; www.juliehellergallery.com), the new gallery from the doyenne of old Provincetown art, features contemporary artists. ⑥ **Albert Merola Gallery,** 424 Commercial St. (☎ 508/487-4424; www.albert merolagallery.com), represents some of the top names in the art world. ⑥ **Rice/Polak Gallery,** 430 Commercial St. (☎ 508/487-1052; www.ricepolakgallery.com), has maintained its top reputation over the decades for displaying intriguing works in a variety of genres and mediums. ⏱1hr.

see houses marked with plaques indicating they were floated over from Long Point across the harbor in the mid–19th century. Tourists like to take photos at Captain Jack's Wharf, a few blocks down, one of the last remaining wharves in P-town harbor and a colorful jumble of shacks that are actually individual condominiums rented out by the week. ⏱ 1 hr. At the far west end of Commercial St.

---

⑫ 🍷 ★★ **The Red Inn.** At the far end of Commercial Street is the Red Inn, a picturesque historic property with a white picket fence with climbing roses. This is a great place to have a cocktail at the end of the day. See p. 210.

⑬ ★★★ **Long Point.** To get out to Long Point, the uninhabited spit of sand that curls into Cape Cod Bay and is the very tip of Cape Cod, you can walk across the 1½-mile West End Breakwater, the giant boulders separating the harbor from the marsh, at the far west end of Commercial Street, near the Provincetown Inn. You can also get to Long Point by taking a shuttle from **Flyer's Boat Rental,** 131A Commercial St. (☎ 508/487-0898). The shuttle can pick up at Macmillan Pier or from their west-end boatyard. There are two historic **lighthouses** on Long Point. Wood End Light is the one in the approximate middle of the spit. Long Point Light, a difficult walk of 2 miles, is at the end. Shuttles run hourly in July and August and cost $15 round-trip. ⏱ 1 hr. (round-trip on the Breakwater) or 4 hr. (walking all the way to Long Point).

Historic Houses

You can discover a lot of history in P-town just by reading plaques on buildings. Blue plaques contain the dates when historic homes were constructed, and some give the names of famous people who lived there. Look for the East End garage that sits on a site where playwright Eugene O'Neill once lived. Some plaques show a house on a raft. That indicates the house was floated over from Long Point, at the tip of P-town, where there was a tiny village before creeping erosion caused the populace to give up the site. A couple dozen of the Long Point houses can be found in the west end of town.

The Outer Cape

Where to Stay

> You can't get closer to the beach than the cottages at Beach Point in North Truro.

★★ **Aerie House & Beach Club** PROVINCETOWN
With one building set on one of P-town's tallest hills on Bradford, and the other on the harbor beach, this comfortable B&B offers a wide range of rooms for guests. 184 Bradford St. ☎ 800/487-1197 or 508/487-1197. www.aeriehouse.com. 11 units. Doubles $220–$320 w/breakfast. MC, V. Map p. 205.

★★ **Anchor Inn Beach House** PROVINCETOWN
This centrally located waterfront property has very comfortable rooms, many with whirlpool tubs. 175 Commercial St. ☎ 800/858-2657 or 508/487-0432. www.anchorinnbeachhouse.com. 23 units. Doubles $275–$385 w/breakfast. AE, MC, V. Map p. 205.

★★ **Bayshore and Chandler House** PROVINCETOWN This beachfront complex in the far end of town is made up of small apartments, most with kitchenettes and picture windows facing Cape Cod Bay. 493 Commercial St. ☎ 508/487-9133. 25 units. Doubles $140–$199. MC, V. Map p. 205.

★★★ **Brass Key Guesthouse** PROVINCETOWN
This compound of six buildings around a pool is the place to stay in Provincetown, the most luxurious property and very professionally run. 67 Bradford St. ☎ 800/842-9858 or 508/487-9005. www.brasskey.com. 42 units. Doubles $400–$500 w/breakfast. AE, DISC, MC, V. Map p. 205.

★★ **Carpe Diem Guesthouse & Spa** PROVINCETOWN This top-notch guesthouse has the most deluxe spa in town, with a Finnish sauna. 12–14 Johnson St. ☎ 800/487-0132 or 508/487-4242. www.carpediemguesthouse.com. 18 units. Doubles $225–$245 w/breakfast. AE, DISC, MC, V. Map p. 205.

> *Some bubbly in your bubble bath at the Brass Key?*

★★ Crowne Pointe Historic Inn and Spa PROVINCETOWN
Perched high on Bradford Street, this deluxe lodging option includes a full-service spa. 82 Bradford St. ☎ 877/276-9631 or 508/487-6767. www.crownepointe.com. 35 units. Doubles $299–$529 w/breakfast. AE, MC, V. Map p. 205.

★★ Days Cottages TRURO
Stay in one of these famous tiny cottages lined up on a North Truro beach for an old-fashioned Cape vacation. 271 Rte. 6A. ☎ 508/487-1062. www.dayscottages.com. 23 units. Doubles $150–$180. No credit cards. Map p. 207.

★ Even'tide WELLFLEET
Set back from Route 6, this large motel is connected by a wooded path to a National Seashore ocean beach. 650 Rte. 6 (1 mile north of Eastham border). ☎ 800/368-0007 or 508/349-3410. www.eventidemotel.com. 40 units. Doubles $155–$180. AE, DISC, MC, V. Map p. 207.

★★ Kalmar Village TRURO
Spiffier than many of the motels and cottages along this spit of sand, this 1940s complex has little white cottages with black shutters surrounding a 60-foot pool. 674 Shore Rd. ☎ 508/487-0585. DISC, MC, V. Map p. 207.

★★ Land's End Inn PROVINCETOWN
With a prime 1-acre perch on Gull Hill at the far west end of town, this whimsical 1907 bungalow with million-dollar views is one of a kind. 22 Commercial St. ☎ 800/276-7088 or 508/487-0706. www.landsendinn.com. 16 units. Doubles $305–$420 w/breakfast. AE, MC, V. Map p. 205.

★ The Masthead PROVINCETOWN
This is the best-priced waterfront lodging in town. Some rooms are dowdy, others are stylish. 31–41 Commercial St. (far west end of town). ☎ 800/395-5095 or 508/487-0523. www.themasthead.com. 21 units. Doubles $225–$245. AE, DC, DISC, MC, V. Map p. 205.

★★ Surf Side Cottages WELLFLEET
Just steps from a spectacular beach with 50-foot dunes, these 1950s cottages prove that life's a beach. Ocean View Dr. (off Lecount Hollow Rd.). ☎ 508/349-3959. www.surfsidecottages.com. 18 cottages. Doubles $1,200–$2,500 weekly. MC, V. Map p. 207.

★ Surfside Hotel & Suites PROVINCETOWN
With one building overlooking the beach and another across the street, this generic motel has comfortable and updated rooms. 543 Commercial St. ☎ 508/487-1726. www.surfsideinn.cc. 88 units. Doubles $114–$169. AE, DC, DISC, MC, V. Map p. 205.

★★ Watermark Inn PROVINCETOWN
This contemporary beachfront inn on the far east end of town is on the peaceful edge of town. 603 Commercial St. ☎ 508/487-0165. www.watermark-inn.com. 10 units. Doubles $205–$470. AE, MC, V. Map p. 205.

★★ Whalewalk Inn & Spa EASTHAM
A deluxe B&B in the Outer Cape, this beauty is just off the Rail Trail and a short drive to National Seashore beaches. 220 Bridge Rd. (¼ mile west of Orleans rotary). ☎ 800/440-1281 or 508/255-0617. www.whalewalkinn.com. 16 units. Doubles $310–$365 w/breakfast. AE, DISC, MC, V. Map p. 207.

Where to Dine

> A former fishing shack, tiny Devon's features haute cuisine.

★★ **Café Edwidge** PROVINCETOWN *NEW AMERICAN* Wooden booths, rafters, and close-set tables create an intimate atmosphere here, where most specialties of the house come from the waters offshore. 333 Commercial St. ☎ 508/487-2008. Entrees $18–$29. MC, V. Breakfast & dinner daily. Map p. 205.

★★★ **Devon's** PROVINCETOWN *NEW AMERICAN* A former boat shack where Devon—your chef, waiter, host, and sometime dishwasher—does everything right, especially with the elegantly prepared food. 401½ Commercial St. ☎ 508/ 487-4773. Entrees $18–$25. DISC, MC, V. Dinner nightly. Closed Nov–Apr. Map p. 205.

★★ **Lorraine's** PROVINCETOWN *MEXICAN* Even those who shy away from Mexican restaurants should try Lorraine's for novel taste sensations, like sea scallops sautéed with tomatillos. 133 Commercial St. (far west end). ☎ 508/487-6074. Entrees $17–$26. DISC, MC, V. Dinner nightly. Map p. 205.

★★ **The Mews Restaurant & Café** PROVINCETOWN *NEW AMERICAN* You can count on fine food and suave service at this beachfront restaurant, a perennial favorite. 429 Commercial St. (east end). ☎ 508/487-1500. Entrees $18–$29. AE, DC, DISC, MC, V. Dinner nightly; Sun brunch. Map p. 205.

★★ **The Red Inn** PROVINCETOWN *NEW AMERICAN* Nothing beats the view of the restaurant seemingly at the end of the earth. Start with a glass of champagne and end with a soufflé. 15 Commercial St. (far west end). ☎ 508/487-7334. Entrees $26–$46. AE, DC, DISC, MC, V. Dinner nightly. Closed Nov–Apr. Map p. 205.

★★★ **Ross' Grill** PROVINCETOWN *NEW AMERICAN BISTRO* The place to go for an intimate dinner, this second-floor bistro has large windows overlooking the harbor and a menu with highlights like steak frites and shellfish risotto. 237 Commercial St. ☎ 508/487-8878. Entrees $22–$40. AE, MC, V. Apr–Dec lunch & dinner daily. Closed Jan–May. Map p. 205.

★★ **Wicked Oyster** WELLFLEET *SEAFOOD* A cool and casual year-round restaurant serving three square meals, from omelets to burgers to spring risotto and grilled tenderloin. 50 Main St. (just off Rte. 6). ☎ 508/349-3455. Entrees $15–$30. MC, V. Breakfast & dinner daily. Lunch off-season only. Map p. 207.

Cape Cod for Seafood Lovers

People may spend years in search of the perfect clam shack on the Cape & Islands. Eating on picnic tables using paper plates, this is low-key dining. Two of the best are in the Outer Cape. ★★ **Mac's Shack,** 91 Commercial St., Wellfleet (☎ 508/487-6333), is an attempt to run the best darn clam shack on Cape Cod. Go early or late; crowds are intense. People say ★★ kids **Moby Dick's Restaurant,** 3225 Rte. 6, Wellfleet (☎ 508/ 349-9795), wins the clam shack competition hands-down. It sure has the crowds to prove it.

Nightlife

> *You'll find the Macho Bar upstairs at the Atlantic House.*

★★ **The Atlantic House** PROVINCETOWN
This is one of the nation's most famous gay bars, featuring disco. 6 Masonic Place (off Commercial St.). ☎ 508/487-3821. Map p. 205.

★★★ **The Beachcomber** WELLFLEET
Arguably the best straight dance club on Cape Cod, the 'Comber is definitely the most scenic, set on Cahoon Hollow Beach. 1220 Old Cahoon Hollow Rd. (off Ocean View Dr. at Cahoon Hollow Beach). ☎ 508/349-6055. www.thebeachcomber.com. Cover $5–$10. Map p. 207.

★★★ **Crown & Anchor** PROVINCETOWN
Five specialty bars at this gay club include leather (the Vault), disco, comedy, drag, and cabaret. 247 Commercial St. ☎ 508/487-1430. www.onlyatthecrown.com. Cover $5 & up. Major acts $25-plus. Map p. 205.

★★ **Provincetown Theater** PROVINCETOWN
This state-of-the-art theater serves as a concert hall, dance studio, and cinema.

238 Bradford St. (east end of town). ☎ 508/487-7487. www.provincetowntheater.com. Map p. 205.

★★ **Tea Dance at the Boatslip** PROVINCETOWN
P-town's biggest outdoor gay dance party starts at 4pm daily sharp poolside at this club in the west end of town. 161 Commercial St. ☎ 508/487-1669. No cover. Map p. 205.

★★ **Vixen** PROVINCETOWN
This chic women's bar has jazz, blues, and comedy on the roster. Pool tables too. 336 Commercial St. (at the Pilgrim House). ☎ 508/487-6424. www.ptownvixen.com. Cover $20. Map p. 205.

★★★ **W.H.A.T. (Wellfleet Harbor Actors Theater)** WELLFLEET   Cape Cod's most avant garde theater can be found here. 2357 Rte. 6 (next to the post office), Wellfleet. ☎ 508/349-9428. www.what.org. Ticket prices $10–$34 for regular shows. Map p. 207.

Edgartown, Martha's Vineyard

Edgartown, with its regal sea captain's homes and white picket fences, is classic Vineyard. A good way to acclimate yourself to the pace and flavor of the island is to walk this town's picturesque streets. This walk starts at the Dr. Daniel Fisher House and meanders along for about a mile; it takes about 2 to 3 hours. For visitor information, contact the Martha's Vineyard Chamber of Commerce at Beach Road, Vineyard Haven (☎ 508/693-0085; www.mvy.com), or visit their website.

> The Whaling Church serves as a concert hall in the summer for the likes of Livingston Taylor.

START From the ferry, walk to Main St.

❶ ★ Dr. Daniel Fisher House. This historic home is a prime example of Edgartown's trademark Greek Revival opulence. A key player in the 19th-century whaling trade, Dr. Fisher amassed a fortune sufficient to found the Martha's Vineyard National Bank. Built in 1840, his proud mansion boasts such classical elements as colonnaded porticos and a delicate roof walk. The only way to view the interior (now headquarters for the Martha's Vineyard Preservation Trust) is with a guided **Vineyard Historic Walking Tour** (☎ 508/627-8619). This tour, which also takes in the neighboring Old Whaling Church, originates next door at the Vincent House Museum. Tours are offered June through September, Monday through Saturday from noon to 3pm. The cost is $7 to $10 for adults, free for children 12 and under. **99 Main St.** ☎ 508/627-8017. www.mvpreservation.org.

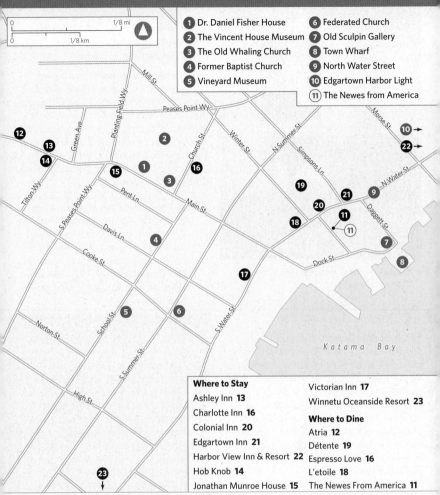

① Dr. Daniel Fisher House	⑥ Federated Church
② The Vincent House Museum	⑦ Old Sculpin Gallery
③ The Old Whaling Church	⑧ Town Wharf
④ Former Baptist Church	⑨ North Water Street
⑤ Vineyard Museum	⑩ Edgartown Harbor Light
	⑪ The Newes from America

Katama Bay

Where to Stay

Ashley Inn **13**

Charlotte Inn **16**

Colonial Inn **20**

Edgartown Inn **21**

Harbor View Inn & Resort **22**

Hob Knob **14**

Jonathan Munroe House **15**

Victorian Inn **17**

Winnetu Oceanside Resort **23**

Where to Dine

Atria **12**

Détente **19**

Espresso Love **16**

L'etoile **18**

The Newes From America **11**

② ★ **The Vincent House Museum.** This transplanted 1672 full Cape is considered the oldest surviving dwelling on the island. Off Main St. btw. Planting Field Way & Church St.

③ ★★ **The Old Whaling Church.** This magnificent 1843 Greek Revival edifice, designed by local architect Frederick Baylies, Jr., was built as a whaling boat would have been, out of massive pine beams; it boasts 27-foot windows and a 92-foot tower. Maintained by the Preservation Trust and still supporting a Methodist parish, the building is now primarily used as a performance venue. 89 Main St.

④ **Former Baptist Church.** Continuing down Main Street and turning right onto School Street,

you'll pass another Baylies monument, the 1839 Baptist Church, which, having lost its spire, was converted into a private home with a rather grand, column-fronted facade. 20 School St.

⑤ ★ **Vineyard Museum.** Two blocks farther, this fascinating museum complex was assembled by the Dukes County Historical Society. This cluster of buildings contains exhibits of Native American crafts, an entire 1765 house, an extraordinary array of maritime art, and the Gay Head Light Tower's decommissioned Fresnel lens. 59 School St. ☎ 508/627-4441. www.mvmuseum.org.

⑥ **Federated Church.** Cater-cornered across South Summer Street, you'll spot the first of

> *Antiques on display at the Martha's Vineyard Museum in Edgartown.*

Baylies' impressive endeavors, the 1828 Federated Church. S. Summer St.

7 Old Sculpin Gallery. Walk down South Summer Street to Main Street and take a right toward the water, stopping at any inviting shops along the way. Veer left on Dock Street to reach the **Old Sculpin Gallery.** The Martha's Vineyard Art Association displays its work here. The real draw is the stark old building itself, which started out as a granary and spent the better part of the 20th century as a boat-building shop. 58 Dock St. ☎ 508/627-4881. Late June to mid-September.

8 Town Wharf. Cross the street to survey the harbor from the second-floor deck at Town Wharf. You can watch the tiny On-Time ferry make its 5-minute crossing to ★★ **Chappaquiddick Island,** which is sadly probably best known as the scene of Edward Kennedy's infamous 1969 car crash, which took the life of his young staffer, Mary Jo Kopechne. ☎ 10 min. 53 Dock St.

9 North Water Street. Stroll down North Water Street to admire the many formidable captains' homes, several of which have been converted into inns. Each has a tale to tell. The 1750 **Daggett House** (no. 59), which is now a private home, started out as a 1660 tavern, and the original beehive oven is flanked by a "secret" passageway. Nathaniel Hawthorne holed up at the **Edgartown Inn** (no. 56) for nearly a year

in 1789, while writing *Twice Told Tales*—and, it is rumored, romancing a local maiden who inspired *The Scarlet Letter*. ☺ 30 min.

10 Edgartown Harbor Light. The original 1828 lighthouse was wiped out in the infamous 1938 hurricane, which caused damage throughout New England. It was replaced in 1939, and today it is one of the most photogenic spots on Martha's Vineyard. Take a stroll down to check it out, and linger on lovely Lighthouse Beach to watch the sun go down. ☺ 45 min. North Water St.

---

⑪ 🍺 **The Newes from America.** After all that walking, stop for a drink at this Colonial basement pub, which serves up specialty beers and the best French onion soup on the island. 23 Kelley St. (N. Water St.). ☎ 508/627-4397. www. kelley-house.com/dining_news_from_ america.asp. $.

Getting to the Islands by Ferry

By Ferry Most visitors take a ferry from the mainland to Martha's Vineyard or Nantucket. For the Vineyard, the main port is Woods Hole in the town of Falmouth on Cape Cod; boats also run from Falmouth Inner Harbor, Hyannis, New Bedford, Rhode Island, and Nantucket. For Nantucket, the main port is Hyannis.

The state-run **Steamship Authority** (☎ 508/477-8600 or 508/693-9130; for reservations and information, www.steam shipauthority.com; Apr 4–Sept 7 daily 7am–9pm, reduced hours the rest of the year) runs boats, including car ferries, to Martha's Vineyard and Nantucket and operates daily, year-round, weather permitting.

From Falmouth Inner Harbor You can board the *Island Queen* (☎ 508/548-4800; www.islandqueen.com) to Martha's Vineyard for a 35-minute cruise to Oak Bluffs (passengers only).

From Hyannis, Hy-Line, Ocean Street Dock (☎ 508/778-2600; www.hyline cruises.com), operates a year-round fast ferry and a conventional ferry from the Ocean Street Dock to Oak Bluffs on Martha's Vineyard and ferries year-round to Nantucket.

> North Water Street serves as Captain's House Row in Edgartown.

Where to Stay

> Watch the world go by from the front porch at the Jonathan Munroe House in Edgartown.

★ Ashley Inn
This attractive and well-priced B&B in a sea captain's home is decorated with period antiques. 129 Main St. ☎ 508/627-9655. www.ashleyinn.net. 10 units. Doubles $255–$285 w/breakfast. MC, V.

★★★ Charlotte Inn
A cluster of five historic buildings just off Main Street decorated to the nines in an English country style make up this top-notch inn, long considered the island's best. 27 S. Summer St. ☎ 508/627-4151. www.relaischateaux.com/charlotte. 25 units. Doubles $395–$695 w/breakfast. AE, MC, V.

★★ Colonial Inn
This four-story inn in the center of town has rooms decorated in a contemporary style. 38 N. Water St. ☎ 800/627-4701 or 508/627-4711. www.colonialinnmvy.com. 28 units. Doubles $245–$425 w/breakfast. AE, MC, V.

★ Edgartown Inn
This centrally located inn offers perhaps the best value on the island. 56 N. Water St. ☎ 508/627-4794. www.edgartowninn.com. 20 units. Doubles $170–$275 w/breakfast. No credit cards.

★★ Harbor View Inn & Resort
This grand 19th-century hotel has a magnificent view of Edgartown lighthouse and harbor. 131 N. Water St. ☎ 800/225-6005 or 508/627-7000. www.harbor-view.com. 124 units. Doubles $369–$625. AE, DC, MC, V.

★★ Hob Knob
This luxury boutique hotel is full of eco-friendly touches, including an organic breakfast menu. 128 Main St. ☎ 800/696-2723 or 508/627-9510. www.hobknob.com. 17 units. Doubles $420–$545 w/breakfast. AE, MC, V.

★★ Jonathan Munroe House
With its graceful wraparound and colonnaded front porch, the Jonathan Munroe House, across from the Whaling Church, stands out from the other captains' homes nearby. Rooms are immaculate and filled with antiques. 100 Main St. ☎ 877/468-6763 or 508/939-6004. www.jonathanmunroe.com. 7 units. Doubles $215–$250 w/breakfast. AE, MC, V.

★★ Victorian Inn
Just off Main Street, this inn is bigger than a B&B but with more personalized service than a large hotel. 24 S. Water St. ☎ 508/627-4784. www.thevic.com. 14 units. Doubles $245–$425 w/breakfast. MC, V.

★★★ Winnetu Oceanside Resort
One of the island's most attractive full-service resorts, this luxury hotel sits on 11 acres overlooking South Beach, which faces the Atlantic Ocean. 31 Dunes Rd., Edgartown. ☎ 866/335-1133 or 508/310-1733. www.winnetu.com. 48 units. Doubles $320–$1,200. AE, MC, V.

Where to Dine

★★★ **Atria** *NEW AMERICAN*
This fine-dining venue set in a sea captain's house is considered one of the best restaurants on island. 137 Main St. ☎ 508/627-5850. Entrees $30-$48. AE, MC, V. Dinner nightly.

★★ **Détente** *NEW AMERICAN*
The theme at this small and romantic fine-dining restaurant is seasonal specials from local farms. Off Winter St. (in Nevin Sq., behind Colonial Inn). ☎ 508/627-8810. Entrees $29-$35. AE, MC, V. Dinner nightly. Closed Feb-Mar.

★★ **Espresso Love** *AMERICAN*
Breakfast and lunch have deli standards; dinner is low-key fine dining at this casual off-the-beaten-track cafe. 17 Church St. (off Main St. behind visitor center). ☎ 508/627-9211. Entrees $12-$18. AE, MC, V. Breakfast, lunch & dinner daily.

★★★ **L'étoile** *CONTEMPORARY FRENCH* One of the Vineyard's most acclaimed chefs creates an evolving menu heightened by delicacies from around the world. 22 N. Water St. ☎ 508/627-9999. Entrees $36-$49. AE, MC, V. Dinner daily. Closed Dec-Apr.

★ kids **The Newes From America** *AMERICAN*
This historic tavern serves up good burgers and fish and chips. 23 Kelley St. (at the Kelley House). ☎ 508/627-4397. Entrees $8-$16. Lunch & dinner daily.

Going Out on Martha's Vineyard

There are now three "wet" towns on Martha's Vineyard, and three "dry" towns where alcohol is not served in restaurants, but you can bring your own. There are numerous bars in the "wet" towns of Oak Bluffs and Edgartown. Vineyard Haven, newly wet, has no bars, but you can order an alcoholic beverage in a restaurant. In Edgartown, ★★★ **Nector's,** 17 Airport Rd. (☎ 508/693-1137; www. nectarsmv.com; cover free to $17), is the island's only major nightclub. This dance hall at the airport features top musicians, comedy, theme nights, and even teen nights. In Vineyard Haven, ★★★ **Vineyard Playhouse,** 24 Church St. (☎ 508/696-6300; www. vineyardplayhouse.org; tickets $15-$30; Shakespeare tickets $15 adults, $10 children), is a 112-seat black box theater where Equity professionals put on a rich season of shows. Children's theater is performed Saturdays at 10am. Outdoor Shakespeare productions get a 3-week run beginning mid-July at Tashmoo Amphitheatre, on State Road (1 mile west of town).

Oak Bluffs, Martha's Vineyard

Oak Bluffs, the Vineyard's most bustling town, was begun as the location for revival meetings in the 19th century. Participants set up tents, which evolved over the years into cottages, decorated in the style of the time with colorful trim in the "carpenter Gothic style." With more than 300 of these "gingerbread" cottages, the town was known for years as Cottage City, until its growth necessitated a new name.

> *The whimsical gingerbread cottages are to admire, not to eat, in Oak Bluffs.*

START From the ferry terminal, go left into:

❶ Ocean Park. The heart of Oak Bluffs, this large park with bandstand is where concerts and other events, like the fireworks, are held. It is surrounded by grand homes in the Victorian style. Across from the Steamship Authority pier. ⏱ 10 min.

❷ Oak Bluffs Harbor. From here, in season, you can get a ferry to Woods Hole, Falmouth Inner Harbor, Hyannis, New Bedford, and even New York City. On the strip beside the harbor, there is a row of restaurants and bars. The best food is at **Coop de Ville,** located in the Dockside Marketplace; the best drinks (accompanied by island music) are at the **Sand Bar & Grille,** 6 Circuit Ave. Ext. The large building across the street at the head of the

harbor is the **Wesley Hotel,** a 100-year-old inn that offers relatively reasonable rates. Fishing charters take off from the southwest end of the harbor. *The Island Queen* makes a 35-minute trip to Falmouth Inner Harbor four or five times a day in summer. ⏱ 15 min.

③ 🍵 Mocha Mott's. For raspberry hot chocolate, peppermint mocha, or just the best iced coffee around, this is the place. Located below street level, down a flight of steps near the head of Circuit Avenue. 10 Circuit Ave. ☎ 508/696-1922. $.

❹ Flying Horses Carousel. Take a spin on the Flying Horses, the oldest continuously operating carousel in the country. You won't be able to resist reaching for the brass ring to try for a free ride. It's open Easter to Columbus Day, daily in the summer, and weekends in the spring and fall. ⏱ 15 min. Oak Bluffs Ave. (at the head of Circuit Ave.). $1.50 per ride. See p. 153, **❷**.

❺ Circuit Avenue. With shops, restaurants, and a little honky-tonk thrown in, this is the heart of Oak Bluffs. Come here to rock out (live music summer nights at the **Ritz Café, Offshore Ale Company,** and the **Lampost**) and then stroll through the cottage Camp Ground on a Sunday morning for a musical church service in the open-air Tabernacle. ⏱ 30 min.

❻ ★★★ Gingerbread Cottages & Tabernacle. The most famous sites in Oak Bluffs are the more than 300 cottages that make up the Camp Meeting grounds. People began coming here in 1835 for religious revival meetings.

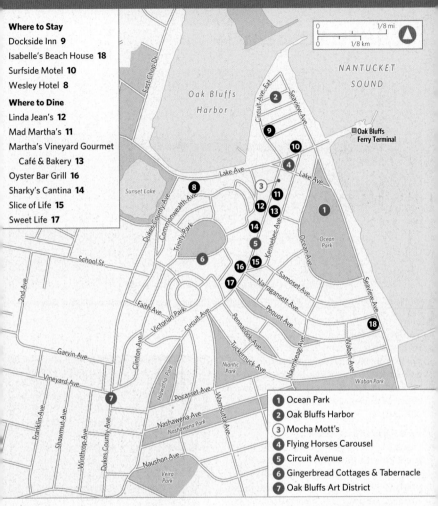

Where to Stay

Dockside Inn **9**

Isabelle's Beach House **18**

Surfside Motel **10**

Wesley Hotel **8**

Where to Dine

Linda Jean's **12**

Mad Martha's **11**

Martha's Vineyard Gourmet
   Café & Bakery **13**

Oyster Bar Grill **16**

Sharky's Cantina **14**

Slice of Life **15**

Sweet Life **17**

1 Ocean Park

2 Oak Bluffs Harbor

3 Mocha Mott's

4 Flying Horses Carousel

5 Circuit Avenue

6 Gingerbread Cottages & Tabernacle

7 Oak Bluffs Art District

Over the decades, tents were replaced by cottages. The entire campground is lit up for **Illumination Night,** held on a Wednesday in mid-August. In the center of the campground is the wrought-iron **Tabernacle,** where concerts, community sings, and other events are held all summer long. Nearby **Union Chapel,** built in 1870, is an octagonal nondenominational church at the intersection of Kennebec and Narragansett avenues. Cottages are located just north of Circuit Avenue. ⏱ 40 min. ☎ 508/693-0525. www.mvcma.org.

7 Oak Bluffs Art District. There are six hip galleries and shops here worth visiting. This relatively new arts district is anchored by the

Alison Shaw Gallery, 88 Dukes County Ave. (☎ 508/696-7429; www.alisonshaw.com), where you'll find extraordinary Vineyard photography; **Dragonfly Gallery,** 91 Dukes County Ave. (☎ 508/693-8877; www.mvdragonfly.com), a fine arts gallery representing 23 local artists; and **Pik Nik Art & Apparel,** 99 Dukes County Ave. (☎ 508/693-1366; www.piknikmv.com), with a funky selection of stuff. To get to the district, walk northwest of the Camp Ground 2 blocks along Dukes County Avenue. ⏱ 45 min. Strolls of the district when all the shops are open take place on a Sat in mid-July & mid-Aug 4–7pm. The galleries are open late May to mid-Sept daily 11am–6pm.

Where to Stay

> The surf is calm and the sand smooth at Oak Bluffs Town Beach, near the Steamship Authority ferry dock in Oak Bluffs.

★★ Dockside Inn

Set close to the harbor, this inn is perfectly located for families interested in exploring the town on foot. 9 Circuit Ave. Ext. ☎ 800/245-5979 or 508/693-2966. www.vineyardinns.com. 22 units. Doubles $220–$250 w/breakfast. AE, DISC, MC, V.

★★ Isabelle's Beach House

This grand 19th-century home, across the street from the beach, has small but pretty rooms. 83 Seaview Ave. ☎ 800/674-3129 or 508/693-3955. www.isabellesbeachhouse.com. 11 units. Doubles $275 w/breakfast. AE, DISC, MC, V.

Surfside Motel

A basic motel with a central location, this motel has particularly low prices off-season. 7 Oak Bluffs Ave. ☎ 800/537-3007 or 508/693-2500. www.mvsurfside.com. 36 units. Doubles $160–$225. MC, V.

★ Wesley Hotel

Formerly one of the grand hotels of the Vineyard, this 1879 property across the street from the harbor is now a solid entry in the "good value" category. 70 Lake Ave. ☎ 800/638-9027 or 508/693-6611. www.wesleyhotel.com. 95 units. Doubles $230–$260. AE, DC, MC, V.

Going Out in Oak Bluffs

If all that charm and fresh air haven't sapped your strength, there are plenty of ways to pass a summer night in Oak Bluffs. Young and loud are the watchwords at ★**The Lampost/Dive Bar,** 111 Circuit Ave. (☎ 508/696-9352), where DJs and occasionally bands provide music. The ★★**Offshore Ale Company**, 30 Kennebec Ave. (☎ 508/693-2626; www.offshoreale. com), is a rustic brewpub with live acoustic performers 6 nights a week. ★★**The Ritz Café**, 4 Circuit Ave. (☎ 508/693-9851; www.theritzcafe.com) is a down-and-dirty hole in the wall that features fun local bands year-round. The singles scene is hopping at the ★★**Sand Bar & Grill**, 6 Circuit Ave. Ext. (☎ 508/693-7111). For a completely different kind of scene, check out the community sings held every Wednesday in the summer at the ★★★**Trinity Park Tabernacle**, Trinity Park, on the Camp Meeting grounds (☎ 508/693-0525). This open-air wrought iron and wood church also offers summer concerts.

Where to Dine

> *The Sweet Life Cafe has one of Martha Vineyard's most extensive wine lists.*

★ Linda Jean's *DINER*

A great place to bring kids or just have a low-key meal with no pretensions, Linda Jean's has excellent breakfast and lunch selections along the lines of omelets, salads, sandwiches, and burgers. In season, dinner is served too. 25 Circuit Ave. ☎ 508/693-4093. Most items under $15. MC, V. June-Aug 8am-8pm. Call for off-season hours.

★★ Mad Martha's *ICE CREAM*

The most famous ice-cream vendor on the Cape & Islands is on Martha's Vineyard, with a second location in Edgartown (7 N. Water St.). It's pricey, but many islanders say these homemade scoops are worth it. 117 Circuit Ave. ☎ 508/693-9151. $. MC, V. May-Oct 11am-9pm.

Martha's Vineyard Gourmet Café & Bakery

BAKERY This bakery/deli is a perfect place to stop during the day for a pick-me-up. But it's late night when this place really comes alive. After a night of carousing, follow the crowds to an alley behind Circuit Avenue to the back door of this establishment (off Kennebec Ave.), known as **Back Door Donuts.** From 7:30pm-12:30am, you can pay by the back door, and they bring you just-out-of-the-oven yummies. Along with chocolate-covered donuts, favorites are apple fritters. 5 Post Office Sq. (just off Circuit Ave.). ☎ 508/693-3688. www.mvbakery.com. $10.50 per dozen donuts. MC, V. Open Mon-Sat 7am-5pm, Sun 7am-4pm.

★★ Oyster Bar Grill *STEAK/SEAFOOD*

A long oak bar and a large open kitchen frame this ample restaurant, the only island venue to specialize in steak. 57 Circuit Ave. ☎ 508/693-6600. Entrees $19-$39. AE, MC, V. Dinner nightly. Closed Dec-Apr.

★ Sharky's Cantina *MEXICAN*

A let-the-good-times-roll kind of place, this is OB's most rowdy restaurant. 31 Circuit Ave. ☎ 508/693-7501. Entrees $7-$18. MC, V. Lunch & dinner daily.

★★ Slice of Life *DELI*

This sandwich shop on the upper end of Circuit Avenue is the place to head for a low-cost but high-quality picnic lunch. The eclectic menu includes burgers and pizza. Sandwiches are made with bread baked on-site. 50 Circuit Ave. ☎ 508/693-3838. www.sliceoflife.com. Most items under $10. Daily 7am-10pm. Call for off-season hours.

★★★ Sweet Life *NEW AMERICAN*

Garden seating is preferred at this fine-dining restaurant set in a Victorian house. 63 Circuit Ave. ☎ 508/696-0200. Entrees $32-$40. AE, DISC, MC, V. Dinner nightly. Closed Nov-Apr.

Nantucket

Once the whaling capital of the world, Nantucket, with its quaint cobblestoned streets and perfectly preserved 19th-century buildings, is now a wedding and honeymoon destination. But it's also a good vacation spot for those who like to do a lot of outdoor activities. Smooth bike paths loop throughout the island. Offshore, there's boating, fishing, and kayaking, or try all three. There are several tiny villages on the island, and the largest of these is also called Nantucket. To avoid confusion, we'll be referring to it as Nantucket Town.

> Brant Point Light, a great place to watch the ferries come and go, is walking distance from town.

START From the ferry, take the 1st left, onto Easy St., to Main.

❶ Main Street. Paved with cobblestones that once served as ballast on whaling ships and lined with 19th-century buildings, Main Street is sure to charm. Strict preservation laws have meant that the town center has not changed much for the past 150 years when Nantucket was a prosperous whaling port, the third-largest city in Massachusetts and home port for 88 whaling ships. The Great Fire of 1846 destroyed much of the central business district, so most buildings date from the 1850s and after. An economic depression started by the decline of the whaling industry lasted until tourists discovered these shores in the late 19th century. The Main Street shopping area ends, appropriately, at the imposing Pacific National Bank building, and you may find use for its handy ATM. ⏱ 1–2 hr.

❷ The Hub. The primary newsstand on the island, this is a good place to get the lay of the land on Main Street. Looking across Main Street here, the water trough in the middle of the road,

An Island Festival: Nantucket Noel

The island stirs from its winter slumber for the Christmas Stroll: one last shopping/feasting spree attended by costumed carolers, Santa in a horse-drawn carriage, and a "talking" Christmas tree. This event is the pinnacle of **Nantucket Noel,** a month of festivities starting in late November. Ferries and lodging establishments book up months in advance, so plan well ahead. Call ☎ **508/228-1700** for more info.

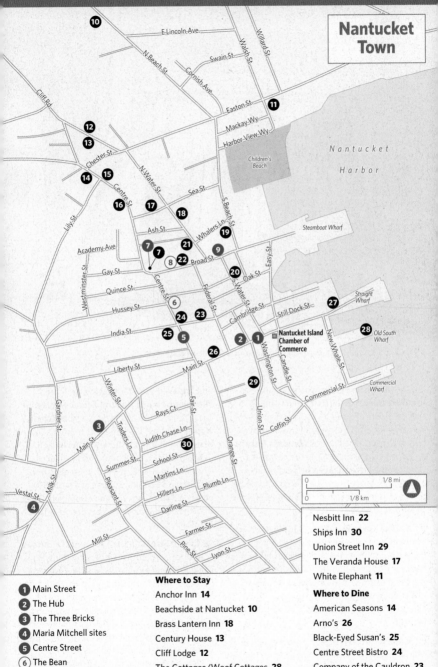

Nantucket Town

1. Main Street
2. The Hub
3. The Three Bricks
4. Maria Mitchell sites
5. Centre Street
6. The Bean
7. Jared Coffin House
8. The Brotherhood of Thieves
9. Whaling Museum

Where to Stay
Anchor Inn **14**
Beachside at Nantucket **10**
Brass Lantern Inn **18**
Century House **13**
Cliff Lodge **12**
The Cottages/Woof Cottages **28**
Jared Coffin House **7**
Martin House Inn **15**
Nantucket Whaler Guest House **21**
Nesbitt Inn **22**
Ships Inn **30**
Union Street Inn **29**
The Veranda House **17**
White Elephant **11**

Where to Dine
American Seasons **14**
Arno's **26**
Black-Eyed Susan's **25**
Centre Street Bistro **24**
Company of the Cauldron **23**
Corazon del Mar **20**
Oran Mor Bistro **19**
Straight Wharf Restaurant **27**

> *Nantucket's stately brick buildings were constructed in the whaling era.*

now filled with flowers, is where horses used to stop to quench a thirst. It wasn't until 1918 that cars were allowed on the island and that was after much of the railroad was destroyed during a storm. The famous **Compass Rose** on the side of the building on the corner of Union Street now occupied by Ralph Lauren gives the distance from Nantucket to myriad places all around the globe. ⏱ 5 min. 31 Main St. ☎ 508/325-0200.

❸ ★★ **The Three Bricks.** In 1836, Joseph Starbuck, a whale-oil merchant and ship owner, built three identical and elaborate brick houses next to each other for his three sons. Across the street is the **Hadwen House,** which is owned by the Nantucket Historical Association and is open for tours. ⏱ 5 min. 93–97 Main St.

❹ ★ **Maria Mitchell sites.** Nantucket native Maria Mitchell (1818–89) was the first female astronomer to reach acclaim, and several sites honor her achievements. On clear nights in July and August, **Loines Observatory,** at 51 Milk St. Ext., is open Monday, Wednesday,

and Friday at 9pm for viewing the stars. **Hinchman House Natural Science Museum** is at 7 Milk St. (at Vestal St.). The **Mitchell House** at 1 Vestal St., the astronomer's birthplace, offers tours. The tiny **aquarium** at 28 Washington St. is best for young children. ⏱ 30 min. ☎ 508/228-9198. www.mmo.org. Admission $6 adults, $5 kids, or a pass ($10 adults, $8 kids) gets you into all of them. Other than the observatory, the sites are open Tues–Sat 10am–4pm.

❺ **Centre Street.** In the 19th century, the several blocks of Centre Street, stretching from Main to Broad streets, used to be known as Petticoat Row for the many women who owned and operated the shops. Women traditionally ran the town of Nantucket, as their husbands traveled the seas for years at a time aboard whaling vessels. These days, Centre Street is one of the best shopping streets on the island because of the unique stores. Among them, you'll find **Dane Gallery,** which sells exquisite handblown glass at 28 Centre St. (☎ 508/228-7779);

Away Offshore

There's one-stop shopping for Nantucket's off-shore activities at **Jetties Sailing Center** (☎ 508/228-5358) at Jetties Beach, where you can rent kayaks, sailboards, and sailboats. At **Sea Nantucket,** Francis St. Beach, off Washington St. (☎ 508/228-7499), you can rent kayaks. Deep-sea charter fishing vessels out of Straight Wharf include *The Albacore* (☎ 508/228-5074), *The Monomoy* (☎ 508/228-6867), and *The Absolute* (☎ 508/325-4000). To rent a boat and motor around the harbor on your own for a half-day, a full day, or even a week, call **Nantucket Boat Rental** (☎ 508/325-1001), which is out of Slip 1 at Straight Wharf.

and **Sweet Inspirations,** with the town's best chocolates, at 26 Centre St. (☎ 508/228-5814). ⏱ 30–90 min.

⑥ 🍵 **The Bean.** The coffee here is Nantucket Coffee Roasters coffee, which is roasted on island and considered to be the best locally. With yummy baked goods too, this is the place to stop for a break. **29 Centre St.** ☎ 508/228-6215. $.

❼ ★ **Jared Coffin House.** This brick manse, the island's first three-story building, has long been a landmark in the center of town. It was built in 1845 to the specs of the social-climbing Mrs. Coffin, who abandoned Nantucket after 2 years and left the house to boarders. Now, 160-plus years later, it still serves as an inn and includes several nearby historic buildings. ⏱ 20 min. 29 Broad St. ☎ 508/228-2400. www.jaredcoffinhouse.com.

⑧ 🍵 ★★ **The Brotherhood of Thieves.** This classic whaling pub is in a 19th-century building almost completely rebuilt after a fire in recent years. To feel some of the atmospheric affects of yore, you must have a drink in the lower-level bar. But if you prefer fresh air, there is outdoor seating on a raised terrace. 23 Broad St. ☎ 508/228-2551. $$.

❾ ★★★ **Whaling Museum.** This requisite stop charts the island's whaling history. ⏱ 1 hr. See p. 150, ❷.

> The oldest house on Nantucket offers a window back to a simpler time.

Going Out on Nantucket

Nightlife isn't the big draw on Nantucket the way it is in, say, Provincetown. But there's plenty to do. ★★**The Chicken Box**, 14 Dave St. (☎ 508/228-9717, www.thechickenbox.com) is a rowdy venue popular with everyone, depending on the music act, from hip rockers to aging reggae heroes The place to go for late-night action is ★★**The Club Car**, 1 Main St. (☎ 508/228-1101) a piano bar set in a historic railway car. ★**The Muse**, 44 Surfside Rd. (☎ 508/228-1471) is a popular year-round club with live rockers in the summer.. Finally, if you'd prefer a little culture, try the ★★★**Theatre Workshop of Nantucket**, 2 Centre St. (☎ 508/228-4305, www.theatreworkshop.com). Actor John Shea, a Nantucket summer resident, is artistic director for this group that performs year-round works by Broadway-caliber writers and composers.

Where to Stay

> The world is your oyster at the hip bar at the Cliffside Beach Club..

★ Anchor Inn NANTUCKET
This historic sea captain's home next to the Old North Church has value-priced rooms. 66 Centre St. ☎ 508/228-0072. www.anchor-inn. net. 11 units. Doubles $195–$229 w/breakfast. AE, MC, V. Map p. 223.

★ Beachside at Nantucket NANTUCKET
The island's only motel is outfitted with Provençal prints and has a large heated pool. 30 N. Beach St. ☎ 800/322-4433 or 508/228-2241. www.thebeachside.com. 90 units. Doubles $355–$505 w/breakfast. AE, DC, DISC, MC, V. Map p. 223.

★★ Brass Lantern Inn NANTUCKET
This reasonably priced historic inn is a great option for people traveling with children and/ or pets. 11 N. Water St. ☎ 800/377-6609 or 508/228-4064. www.brasslanternnantucket. com. 16 units. Doubles $325–$425 w/breakfast. AE, MC, V. Map p. 223.

★★ Century House NANTUCKET
The original art on the walls at this cozy inn was created by painters the hosts invite to stay in the off-season. 10 Cliff Rd. www.century house.com/. 14 units. $155–$495 w/breakfast. AE, MC, V. Map p. 223.

★★ Cliff Lodge NANTUCKET
The rooms in the 1771 sea captain's house are cheerfully decorated with colorful quilts and splatter-painted floors. 9 Cliff Rd. ☎ 508/228-9480. www.clifflodgenantucket.com. 12 units. Doubles $195–$320 w/breakfast. AE, MC, V. Map p. 223.

★★★ Cliffside Beach Club NANTUCKET
On a beautiful beach and not far from town, this is the island's premier lodging option and on-site are a pool, a spa, and one of the island's best restaurants. 46 Jefferson Ave. ☎ 508/228-0618. www.cliffsidebeach.com. 26 units. Doubles $450–$710 w/breakfast. AE. Map p. 228.

★★★ The Cottages/Woof Cottages
NANTUCKET These well-appointed small apartments have the best location on the island, on Old South Wharf overlooking the harbor. 24 Old South Wharf. ☎ 866/838-9253 or 508/325-1499. www.harborviewcottages.com. 33 units. Doubles $490–$750. AE, MC, V. Map p. 223.

★★ Jared Coffin House NANTUCKET
This three-story brick manse is a landmark in the center of town. Two other historic buildings nearby also contain rooms. 29 Broad St. ☎ 800/248-2405 or 508/228-2400. www. jaredcoffinhouse.com. 60 units. Doubles $290–$470. AE, DC, DISC, MC, V. Map p. 223.

★ Martin House Inn NANTUCKET
One of the lower-priced B&Bs in town, this historic house is kept shipshape by the capable staff. 61 Centre St. (btw. Broad & Chester sts.). ☎ 508/228-0678. www.martinhouseinn.net. 13 units. Doubles $220–$385 w/breakfast. AE, MC, V. Map p. 223.

★★ Nantucket Whaler Guest House NANTUCKET
This 1850 sea captain's house has been converted into cute little apartments, each with its own kitchen facilities. 8 N. Water St.

☎ 508/228-6597. www.nantucketwhaler.com. 12 units. Doubles $325–$460. AE, DISC, MC, V. Map p. 223.

★ **Nesbitt Inn** NANTUCKET
This is one of the last old guesthouses with shared bathrooms on the island. 21 Broad St. ☎ 508/228-0156. 15 units. Doubles $170 w/ breakfast. MC, V. Map p. 223.

Robert B. Johnson Youth Hostel NANTUCKET
An old lifesaving station on Surfside Beach has been converted into the island's youth hostel. 31 Western Ave. ☎ 888/901-2084 or 508/228-0433. capecod.hiusa.org. 49 beds. $32–$35 members; $35–$38 nonmembers; $178 private room. MC, V. Map p. 228.

★★ **Ships Inn** NANTUCKET
This pretty, historic inn is walking distance to the town's center and contains a fine-dining dinner restaurant. 13 Fair St. ☎ 888/872-4052 or 508/228-0040. www.shipsinnnantucket. com. 12 units. Doubles $275 w/breakfast. AE, DISC, MC, V. Map p. 223.

★★ **Union Street Inn** NANTUCKET
Steps from Main Street, but in a quiet residential section, this B&B is one of the island's most stylish and best managed. 7 Union St. ☎ 888/517-0707 or 508/228-9222. www. unioninn.com. 12 units. Doubles $295–$575 w/ breakfast. AE, MC, V. Map p. 223.

★★ **The Veranda House** NANTUCKET
This stylish three-story boutique inn is in a quiet neighborhood a short walk from town. 3 Step Lane. ☎ 877/228-0695 or 508/228-0695. www. theverandahouse.com. 18 units. Doubles $309–$449 w/breakfast. AE, MC, V. Map p. 223.

★★★ **The Wauwinet** NANTUCKET
This ultradeluxe beachfront resort is Nantucket's only Relais & Châteaux property, with a fine-dining restaurant on-site. 120 Wauwinet Rd. (8 miles east of town center). ☎ 800/426-8718 or 508/228-0145. www.wauwinet.com. 35 units. Doubles $680–$1,250 w/breakfast. AE, DC, DISC, MC, V. Map p. 228.

★★★ **White Elephant** NANTUCKET
This luxury property facing the harbor is the ultimate in-town lodging. 50 Easton St. ☎ 800/445-6574 or 508/228-2500. www. whiteelephanthotel.com. 63 units. Doubles $615–$775 w/breakfast. AE, DC, DISC, MC, V. Map p. 223.

Where to Dine

★★ **American Seasons** NANTUCKET *REGIONAL AMERICAN* This romantic little restaurant offers regional food styles like New England, Pacific Coast, Wild West, or Down South, with an emphasis on sustainable and locavore-type cuisine. 80 Centre St. ☎ 508/228-8768. Entrees $34–$56. AE, DC, MC, V. Dinner nightly. Closed Nov–Apr. Map p. 223.

★ kids **Arno's** NANTUCKET *NEW AMERICAN*
This casual restaurant packs surprising style, with preparations involving steaks, fresh fish, and pasta a specialty. 41 Main St. ☎ 508/228-7001. Entrees $9–$17. AE, DC, DISC, MC, V. Breakfast, lunch & dinner daily. Closed Jan–Mar. Map p. 223.

★★★ **Black-eyed Susan's** NANTUCKET *INTERNATIONAL* This funky diner is the place to enjoy surprising food like spicy Thai fish cake and tandoori chicken with green mango chutney.

> Enjoy yummy oysters on the half shell at Corazon del Mar.

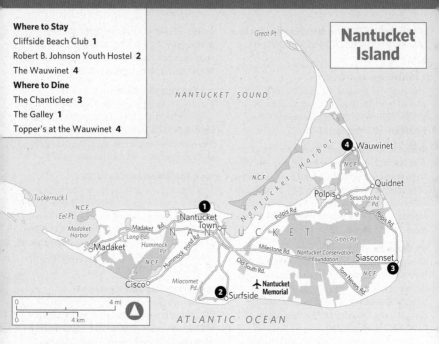

Nantucket Island

BYOB. 10 India St. (off Centre St.). ☎ 508/325-0308. Entrees $12–$25. No credit cards. Dinner nightly. Closed Nov–Mar. Map p. 223.

★ **Brotherhood of Thieves** NANTUCKET *PUB* The downstairs is what is left that is authentic at this classic whaling bar. Upstairs has been fancified. Burgers and fries a specialty. 23 Broad St. ☎ 508/228-2551. Entrees $9–$18. MC, V. Lunch & dinner daily. Closed mid-Oct to mid-May. Map p. 223.

★★ **Centre Street Bistro** NANTUCKET *NEW AMERICAN* This tiny restaurant owned by a team of top chefs is a hidden gem with reasonable prices, by Nantucket standards. The menu is creative, the food is fresh, and you can save a little by bringing your own wine or beer. 29 Centre St. ☎ 508/228-8470. Entrees $19–$25. MC, V. Dinner nightly; breakfast & lunch weekends. Map p. 223.

> ### Get the scoop
> Exceptional ice cream and other sweets can be found at ★★ **The Juice Bar,** 12 Broad St. (☎ 508/ 228-5799), Nantucket's premier place for homemade ice cream.

★★★ **The Chanticleer** NANTUCKET *FRENCH* This rose-covered cottage in 'Sconset has the atmosphere of a private club and the menu of a brasserie moderne, with dishes like *moules frites.* 9 New St., Siasconset (south side of island). ☎ 508/257-4499. Entrees $24–$43. AE, MC, V. Lunch & dinner daily. Closed mid-Oct to May. Map p. 228.

★★★ **Company of the Cauldron** NANTUCKET *CONTINENTAL* The island's most romantic restaurant—think candlelight and harp music—serves four-course fixed-price meals in two seatings. 5 India St. (btw. Centre & Federal sts.). ☎ 508/228-4016. Fixed price $60–$62. Except Mon, Lobster 4 ways for $79. MC, V. Dinner nightly. Seatings at 6:45 or 8:45pm, except Mon at 7pm. Closed mid-Oct to mid-Apr. Map p. 223.

★★★ **Corazon Del Mar** NANTUCKET *LATIN* Featuring a seafood and raw bar, as well as a tequila bar, this place offers taste sensations you can't get anywhere else on the island. 21 S. Water St. ☎ 508/228-0815. Entrees $22–$32. AE, MC, V. Dinner nightly. Closed Jan–Mar. Map p. 223.

★★★ The Galley NANTUCKET *NEW AMERICAN*
This beachfront is where you go if you want to feel like you are in a *Travel + Leisure* photo spread. 54 Jefferson Ave. (at the Cliffside Beach Club, 1 mile east of Main St.). ☎ 508/228-9641. Entrees $29–$39 AE, MC, V. Lunch & dinner daily. Closed late Sept to late May. Map p. 228.

★★★ Oran Mor Bistro NANTUCKET *NEW AMERICAN*
Climb the copper steps to the second floor of a historic building to visit this contender for best island restaurant. This sophisticated venue offers top-notch food and service. 2 S. Beach St. ☎ 508/228-8655. Entrees $26–$32. AE, MC, V. Dinner nightly. Closed mid-Dec to mid-Apr. Map p. 223.

★★★ Straight Wharf Restaurant NANTUCKET *NEW AMERICAN*
This fine-dining waterfront venue has a pair of acclaimed chefs who turn out summer favorites like watermelon gazpacho and clambake with all the fixings. There's a less expensive bar menu available. 6 Harbor Sq. (on Straight Wharf). ☎ 508/228-4499. Entrees $26–$39. AE, MC, V. Lunch/brunch Tues–Sun & dinner daily. Closed late Sept to late May. Map p. 223.

> Gathering around the piano bar at the Club Car is one of the island's great traditions.

★★★ Topper's at the Wauwinet NANTUCKET *NEW AMERICAN*
You can take a free water shuttle to this restaurant at a secluded resort, the island's fanciest. Dinner here is a major event. 22 Wauwinet Rd. (off Squam Rd.). ☎ 508/228-8768. Entrees $34–$56; 6-course fixed price $80. AE, DC, MC, V. Lunch & dinner daily. Closed Nov–Apr. Map p. 228.

Getting to Nantucket by Ferry

There are two competing high-speed ferries to Nantucket from Hyannis; both take 1 hour. The passengers-only **MV *Grey Lady,*** Hy-Line's high-speed catamaran, costs $75 round-trip, $39 one-way for adults; $51 round-trip, $29 one-way for children (☎ 800/492-8082; www.hylinecruises.com).

The Steamship Authority runs its own high-speed catamaran, the ***Iyanough,*** which costs $65 round-trip for adults and $49 round-trip for children (☎ 508/477-8600; www.steamshipauthority.com).

Both the Steamship Authority and Hy-Line also run slow ferries (2¼ hr.) to Nantucket. The Steamship Authority charges $33 round-trip, and Hy-Line charges $43 round-trip. Ferries also travel to Nantucket from Harwich Port by the **Freedom Cruise Line** (☎ 508/432-8999; www.nantucket islandferry.com), which costs $70 round-trip for adults, $51 for children.

Nantucket Goes Daffy for Daffodils

Spring's arrival is heralded on Nantucket with the region's largest spring event, ★★ **The Annual Daffodil Festival Weekend,** when masses of yellow blooms adorn everything in sight, including a parade of 100 antique cars that drive to 'Sconset for an annual Daffodil Tailgate Picnic. No fewer than three million daffodils are planted in honor of the occasion. There are a daffodil flower show, a Daffy dog parade, a children's parade, and a Daffy Hat Pageant. Book your lodging choice early for this popular late-April event. Call ☎ 508/228-1700 for more information.

Central & Western Massachusetts

Our Favorite Central & Western Mass. Moments

You're not in Beantown anymore. As you head west from the state capital, the culture changes as clearly as does the accent. Whether it's the influence of the summering elites—which has long played a part in supporting the arts in the Berkshires—or the independent-minded streak of locals who'd rather not be lumped in with the *cah pahkas* back east, you're sure to find a refreshing spirit out here. It's more earnest than cynical, deeply engaged, and setting the stage for some of our favorite times in New England.

> **PREVIOUS PAGE** *The gracious 44-room house and the perfectly manicured gardens of Naumkeag are quintessential Gilded Age Berkshires.* **THIS PAGE** *Music and moonlight enchant picnickers at Tanglewood.*

1 Picnicking at Tanglewood. Could there be a more clichéd image of the Berkshires than concertgoers sipping wine while taking in a symphony at Tanglewood? Well, it's still one of the most delightful ways to spend an afternoon or evening in this part of the state (or anywhere for that matter). We love splurging on excellent wine, cheese, charcuterie, and olives (see

Bizalion's, p. 253, **7**) and heading to Lenox. Attendees take their picnics very seriously, so remember your linens and candelabra, and flowers, of course. See p. 252, **5**.

2 Wandering the sun-drenched aisles at the Montague Book Mill. Housed in a barn-red 1842 gristmill alongside the rushing water of

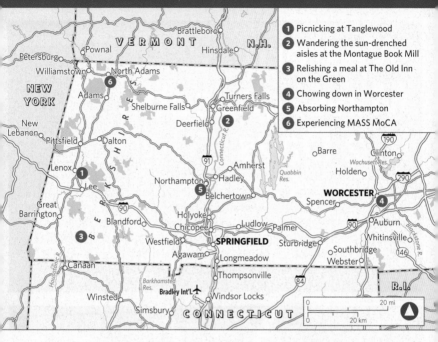

1 Picnicking at Tanglewood
2 Wandering the sun-drenched aisles at the Montague Book Mill
3 Relishing a meal at The Old Inn on the Green
4 Chowing down in Worcester
5 Absorbing Northampton
6 Experiencing MASS MoCA

the Sawmill River, this place is a book lover's paradise. You'll find rows and rows of used books for browsing and buying, and lots of atmospheric and comfy nooks for settling down and reading. Plus the rustic assemblage of buildings includes a cafe, record store, art studio, and cozy restaurant. See p. 244, **6**.

3 Relishing a meal at The Old Inn on the Green. The tiny hamlet of New Marlborough is a bit of a drive—20 minutes from Great Barrington, the closest real town—but it's worth the trip. Blazing fireplaces, candlelit chandeliers, mahogany tavern tables, and outstanding food, such as stellar local cheeses and soul-warming mains like olive oil–poached halibut with parsnip purée and black trumpet sauce. See p. 255.

4 Chowing down in Worcester. Full disclosure: We went to college in Woo-stah. In fact, we fell in love there. So, as much as we hate to admit it, we have a bit of a soft spot for the much-maligned city—most of all, its diners. And there's no diner that's purer Worcester than **Miss Woo's,** as in Miss Worcester Diner (p. 261). Housed in Worcester Lunch Car no. 812 (now on the National Registry of Historic Places), Miss Woo's does classic diner food, and does it well. Bonus: They specialize in French toast.

5 Absorbing Northampton. This happening burg has a lot going for it: good food, funky boutiques, great breweries, and a world-famous music scene. But the people are what is most special about this famously progressive college town (home to Smith): students, professors, indie rockers, foodies, and literary types, all with opinions to share. Even if you opt to not make conversation—though we encourage you to do so—you're bound to learn something simply by eavesdropping just about anywhere you go. See p. 257, **3**.

6 Experiencing MASS MoCA. This massive 19th-century mill-factory-turned-modern-art-complex would be worth a stop just to admire the architecture, but you'll be wowed by much more than the fascinating interplay of glass, brick, and steel. Thanks to its size, MASS MoCA often hosts audacious large-scale drawings and installations (such as Cai Guo Qiang's ceiling-hung cars, or Robert Wilson's *14 Stations*). We guarantee you'll end up lingering longer than you'd planned. See p. 250, **2**.

Western Massachusetts in 2 Days

Though you could easily fill a week of your time in the Berkshires, it also makes for an ideal weekend getaway, so we're focusing our 2-day itinerary exclusively on this quintessential New England destination. Tucked away in these rolling hills, a sophisticated food culture thrives, with an emphasis on local sources. The fine arts scene encompasses a range of work, from the mainstream paintings of Norman Rockwell to avant garde installations at museums such as MASS MoCA. The performing arts also have a rich heritage here.

> Its former life as a factory makes MASS MoCA an ideal setting for large-scale installations by modern and contemporary artists such as Sol LeWitt.

START Williamstown is 140 miles from Boston.
TRIP LENGTH 40 miles.

❶ **Williamstown.** Start your trip in the northwest corner of the state in this handsome little town centered on prestigious **Williams**

College. The 450-acre campus—featuring expanses of green dotted with distinctive buildings like Main Street's Gothic Thompson Memorial Chapel—sprawls through the flat center of town. Established in 1793, the college is home to the Hopkins Observatory—dating to 1838, it's the oldest in the country—and the excellent **Williams College Museum of Art.** Nearby is another stellar museum, the **Sterling and Francine Clark Art Institute,** and looming in the distance is the tallest peak in the state (3,491 ft.), **Mt. Greylock** (p. 252, "Getting Outdoors"). Drive to the top, admiring the vistas along the way, and breathe in the dramatic panoramic view of the Berkshire Hills. ⏱ 5 hr. See p. 248, ❶.

Head left onto South St. and right onto Rte. 2E; go 4½ miles to North Adams. Veer right onto W. Main St. and left at Marshall St. for 2 blocks.

❷ **MASS MoCA.** Spend some time exploring the exhibits at this spectacular contemporary art museum in nearby North Adams. ⏱ 2 hr. See p. 250, ❷.

Spend the night in North Adams or Williamstown (p. 254). On Day 2, take Rte. 2 east to Rte. 8 south and go for 18 miles to Rte. 9 west; go 3 miles north and turn left onto Rte. 7 south. Go 5 miles and turn right on Rte. 7A.

❸ **Lenox.** Catch your breath here, in the heart of the Berkshires, and explore the scenic and culturally rich little town, home to **Tanglewood.** Stop at **Haven Café and Bakery,** 8 Franklin St. (☎ 413/637-8948), for tea or a bite to eat (we love the rolled omelets). Take your time on visits to two gems: **Frelinghuysen Morris House and Studio** and **The Mount.** Also in town is **Ventfort Hall,** 104 Walker St. (☎ 413/637-3206; www.gildedage.org), a Gilded Age "cottage" built in 1893 for financier J. P. Morgan's sister Sarah. An ongoing restoration has brought the 28-room Jacobean Revival mansion back from the brink of demolition. ⏱ 4 hr. See p. 252, ❺.

Take Rte. 183 about 5 miles and turn left on Rte. 102, going 1 mile to Stockbridge.

❹ **Stockbridge.** Park on Main Street and stroll the picturesque center of this quintessential Berkshire town, captured by resident Norman

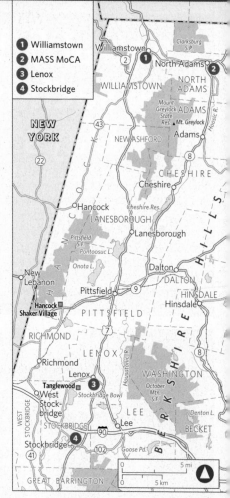

Rockwell in such paintings as *The New American LaFrance Is Here.* You'll find more of the artist's work at the **Norman Rockwell Museum.** If the weather's nice, check out the **Berkshire Botanical Garden;** then head to the Stanford White-designed mansion, **Naumkeag,** for a guided tour (don't miss the gardens). When your legs have had enough, stop for a drink at the classic **Red Lion Inn.** (After some time in the character-filled Lion's Den pub, you'll very likely want to stay for dinner, too.) ⏱ 5 hr. See p. 253, ❻.

Central & Western Massachusetts in 4 Days

In contrast to the density of Boston and Cape Cod, the western half of Massachusetts is largely rural, with small communities filling the expanses between the few cities that—though some of the largest in New England—still retain something of a small-town sensibility. In Colonial times, the west of the state was the frontier, and though the name "Pioneer Valley," referring to the central part of the state, is a tourism tag from the 1930s, it still somehow rings true: the region stands out for its often very-left-of-center politics, the intellectual influence of some of the best colleges in the country, and a homegrown, do-it-yourself sense of craft that is evident in its arts and flourishing artisanal food scenes.

> *The Homestead is now a museum dedicated to poet and former inhabitant Emily Dickinson, the "Belle of Amherst."*

START Great Barrington is 136 miles from Boston. **TRIP LENGTH** 121 miles.

1 ★ **Great Barrington.** While the gateway to the Berkshires doesn't have any sights of significance—or the Colonial atmosphere of some of its neighbors—it does have a retro-funky downtown that manages to maintain a Main Street, USA, feel despite the swarms of stylish New Yorkers who descend every weekend. Expect well-curated antiques shops and boutiques, and an eclectic selection of

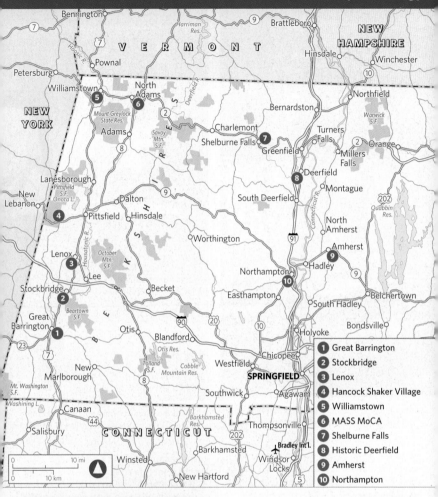

1 Great Barrington
2 Stockbridge
3 Lenox
4 Hancock Shaker Village
5 Williamstown
6 MASS MoCA
7 Shelburne Falls
8 Historic Deerfield
9 Amherst
10 Northampton

Antiquing in Sheffield

With top-end dealers and mom-and-pop operations peddling quirky flea market–style finds, the Berkshire Hills are a magnet for those who love the hunt. Many of the best shops are clustered along the Rte. 7 corridor running through Sheffield, south of Great Barrington. Some favorites are **Cupboards & Roses,** 296 S. Main St./Rte. 7 (☎ 413/229-3070), for painted Scandinavian furniture; **Hill House Antiques,** 276 Undermountain Rd. (☎ 413/229-3217), for gorgeous Arts & Crafts furnishings; and **The Splendid Peasant,** 992 Foley Rd. (☎ 413/229-8800), for American folk art.

artisanal food shops and restaurants. Wander bustling Railroad Street, and stop in at adorable **Seeds,** 34 Railroad St. (☎ 413/528-8122), for well-designed gifts. Then make for Main Street, where you'll find the superb fromagerie **Rubiner's,** 264 Main St. (☎ 413/528-0488), and, on weekends only, **Germain,** 635 Main St. (☎ 413/644-8868), which specializes in understated vintage and modern home goods. ⏲ 2 hr.

Take Rte. 7 north to Rte. 102 west, and continue onto Pine St., taking a left onto Prospect Hill Rd.

❷ ★★ **Stockbridge.** One look at this charming, classic New England town, and you'll see

> *Naumkeag is surrounded by 8 acres of landscaped gardens and 40 acres of woodland and meadow.*

> *The Norman Rockwell Museum celebrates the painter and illustrator's contribution to Americana.*

why it was so fashionable among the newly rich titans of the so-called Gilded Age. The summer "cottage" of diplomat Joseph Choate, **Naumkeag** (p. 253, ⑥) overlooks the town from its idyllic perch on Prospect Hill; the guided house tour provides an excellent look into that era. Save time for the fascinating audio tour of the elaborate grounds, conceived in stages from 1926–56 by landscape designer Fletcher Steele in collaboration with Choate's daughter Mabel.

Best known for his memorable *Saturday Evening Post* cover illustrations, iconic all-American artist Norman Rockwell spent his last 25 years in Stockbridge. With 574 paintings and drawings spanning his career, the **Norman Rockwell Museum,** 9 Glendale Rd. (☎ 413/298-4100; www.nrm.org), is the largest repository of his works, featuring many of his best-loved, nostalgic images in their full sizes. Even if you're not a fan, it's hard not to feel moved by the series *Four Freedoms,* inspired by President Franklin Roosevelt's famous speech. Check out the artist's studio too, which was moved to the museum, along with his furniture, some personal effects, and art materials. ☺ 4 hr. For more Stockbridge recommendations, see p. 253, ⑥.

The Mohawk Trail

Originally a trade route connecting native tribes from the coast all the way to what is now New York State, today the Mohawk Trail is synonymous with Rte. 2 in western Massachusetts. It traces a scenic drive from Miller's Falls to Williamstown, hooking up with a stretch of the Deerfield River, and twisting at the famous "hairpin turn" as it comes down from the hills into North Adams.

> *The simple elegance and clean, spare lines of a house at Hancock Shaker Village.*

Take Rte. 184 north to Lenox, where you'll spend the night. On the morning of Day 2, check out:

❸ ★★★ Lenox. There's plenty to see here in the epicenter of Berkshire culture. ⏱ 4 hr. See p. 252, ❺.

Take Rte. 7 north 5½ miles and continue on North St., which becomes South St. Take a right onto Rte. 20 west and go 4½ miles to:

❹ ★ Hancock Shaker Village. With a pastoral setting amid low hills, this tranquil settlement of the radical Christian sect known as the Shakers is a wonderful place to while away a few hours. A detailed audio tour gives you the lowdown on the Hancock Shakers and the 18 buildings here—including the marvel of graceful functionality that is the 1826 great round barn—while friendly and knowledgeable docents answer questions, and craftspeople demonstrate such Shaker techniques as broom and basket making. For more on the Shakers, see "The Shakers: Radical Chic" on p. 436. ⏱ 2 hr. See p. 251, ❹.

The Big Splurge

If you're in the market for an über-luxe getaway, you have some superb choices in these bucolic hills. For the ultimate all-inclusive destination spa, book a stay at **Canyon Ranch,** 165 Kemble St., Lenox (☎ 800/742-9000; www.canyonranchlenox.com; from $1,740 for 3 nights), on the tranquil grounds of the 1897 Bellefontaine Mansion, a replica of Louis XIV's Petit Trianon. You couldn't get much more luxurious than the Relais & Château **Blantyre,** 16 Blantyre Rd., Lenox (☎ 413/637-3556; www.blantyre.com; $600–$1,000 double), a Tudor-Norman mansion with sumptuous manor house decor, excellent service, and top-notch dining. (Out of your price range? Have dinner here or book a spa service.) And for sophisticated, modern rooms in a Tuscan-palazzo-style villa, visit **Wheatleigh,** Hawthorne Rd., Lenox (☎ 413/637-0610; www.wheatleigh.com; $715–$1,225 double); its exquisite restaurant is open to the public.

> *An exhibit at MASS MoCA echoes the designs of Shaker quilts.*

Take Rte. 20 east to Rte. 7 and go north for 20 miles. Spend the night in or around:

❺ ★★★ **Williamstown.** If you're visiting during the summer, try to catch one of the world-class performances during the annual theater festival. See p. 248, ❶. ⏱ 4 hr.

Take Rte. 2 east 4½ miles to North Adams, and veer right onto W. Main St. Take a left at Marshall St.

❻ ★★★ **MASS MoCA.** Each space in this astounding 19-gallery complex is bigger than the next; take your time wandering through. Even if you're not a lover of modern art, it's worth a stop to check out the very cool space. ⏱ 2 hr. See p. 250, ❷.

Take Rte. 2 (Mohawk Trail) 25 miles east and turn right on State St. Continue ¾ mile and go left on Bridge St. This is your last stop of the day—plan to spend the night in Greenfield, just east up Rte. 2 from Shelburne Falls.

Dance Fever

Every year from mid-June to August, the three stages at **Jacob's Pillow,** 358 George Carter Rd., Becket (☎ 413/243-0745; www.jacobspillow.org), welcome more than 50 dance companies. Begun in 1933 by modern dancer Ted Shawn, it's now the country's longest-running international dance festival.

❼ ★ **Shelburne Falls.** Stop off the Mohawk Trail for a stroll around this village crossing the Deerfield River. ⏱ 2 hr. See p. 260, ❻.

On Day 4, take Rte. 5/Rte. 10 about 1½ miles south from Greenfield center. Turn right on Main St. and left on Old Main St.

❽ ★★ **Historic Deerfield.** Spend a few hours traveling back in time at this complex of 11 house museums telling the story of Colonial and Early American Pioneer Valley. ⏱ 2 hr. See p. 259, ❺.

Return to US-5/MA-10 and go 5 miles south; turn left onto Rte. 116 and go south 10 miles. Take a sharp left onto Rte. 9 and follow signs for Amherst.

⑨ ★★ Amherst. Brimming with scholars and their progressive political discourse, this college town (home to Amherst College, Hampshire College, and the main campus of the University of Massachusetts) is one of the highlights of the Pioneer Valley (p. 256). Be sure to visit the fascinating **Emily Dickinson Museum.** Unpublished (except anonymously) during her lifetime, the poet was born and lived her entire life in the Federal-style house here known as *The Homestead,* and much has been made of her perceived peculiarities. Though, yes, you will see one of her infamous white dresses, the 90-minute tour takes pains to undo the caricature, dispel myths, and replace them with the facts of Dickinson's life and work. ⏱ 3 hr. See p. 244, ⑤ and p. 258, ④.

Head back up Main St., turn left at S. Pleasant, and right at Rte. 9 west for 8 miles.

⑩ ★★ Northampton. Some call it "Noho"; others, "Paradise City." No matter how you refer to this nexus of Pioneer Valley culture, a stop here makes for an excellent ending to your tour of the area. ⏱ 3 hr. See p. 257, ③.

Bread, Booze & Berkshire Blue

With a landscape defined by large swaths of green pastureland and orchards, and a food-savvy, eco-minded populace, it's not surprising that Western Massachusetts is one of the country's leaders in locavorism. You'll quickly notice that the farm-to-table ethos is taken very seriously here, and there are outstanding artisanal cheeses, breads, and other specialty foods to be found throughout the region. The **Berkshire Mountain Bakery,** 367 Park St., Housatonic (☎ 413/274-3412), is nationally recognized for its bread, especially its sourdough, while the wonderfully creamy **Berkshire Blue Cheese** (☎ 413/842-5128), made in Great Barrington by Berkshire Cheese, is available in several area specialty shops. Visit the Alpine goats at **Rawson Brook Farm,** 185 New Marlboro Rd., Monterey (☎ 413/528-2138); then buy cheese via the honor system. The guys at **Berkshire Mountain Distillers** (413/229-0219), in Sheffield, specialize in such small-batch handcrafted concoctions as Greylock Gin and Ragged Mountain Rum, found in liquor stores throughout the Berks.

> *A magnificent view from the Mohawk Trail, an old trading route and an official scenic road since 1914.*

Literary Central & Western Massachusetts

The western part of Massachusetts figured prominently in the lives of quite a few writers, as home and as inspiration for their tales: Nathaniel Hawthorne, Oliver Wendell Holmes, Emily Dickinson, Edith Wharton, and Herman Melville are just a few scribes who lived in the region. Today, there's still a wonderfully vibrant writing community—no doubt buoyed by the presence of Pioneer Valley's many excellent colleges—and some of the best independent bookstores around. Visit them (and buy books) on our 2- to 3-day itinerary.

> Settle into a cozy nook with a good book and a cuppa at the Montague Book Mill.

START Springfield is 90 miles from Boston.
TRIP LENGTH 112 miles.

1 ★ kids **Dr. Seuss National Memorial Sculpture Garden, Springfield.** Begin your tour with an imagination-firing stop at this heartwarming tribute in bronze to Theodor Seuss Geisel, native son of Springfield and beloved creator of *Green Eggs and Ham,* the Grinch, and *The Cat in the Hat.* The sculptures include such whimsical characters as Horton the elephant, Yertle the Turtle, and the Cat in the Hat himself. ⏱ ½ hr.

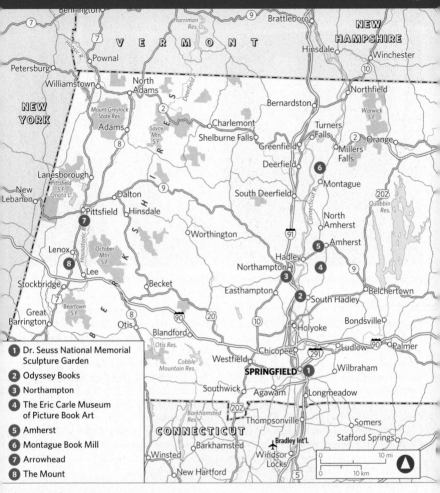

1. Dr. Seuss National Memorial Sculpture Garden
2. Odyssey Books
3. Northampton
4. The Eric Carle Museum of Picture Book Art
5. Amherst
6. Montague Book Mill
7. Arrowhead
8. The Mount

Take I-91N ½ mile out of Springfield to the left exit for I-391N, which turns into Resnick Blvd. Go ½ mile and turn right onto Rte. 202; go north 1¾ miles and exit onto Rte. 116 going north, which you'll take for 3 miles before turning left onto Rte. 47.

2 ★ **Odyssey Books.** Due in no small part to the presence of Mount Holyoke, Smith, and Amherst colleges, the Pioneer Valley is one of the most hyperliterate regions in the country, with myriad bookstores. This friendly 50-year-old, well-curated shop is the area's largest independent bookstore. New, used, and a small selection of antiquarian volumes fill the racks. ☺ ½ hr. 9 College St., South Hadley. ☎ 413/534-7307. www.odysseybks.com.

Get back on Rte. 47 and go 7 miles north, continuing onto Bay Rd; turn left at Rte. 9W and take it into Northampton.

3 ★★ **Northampton.** Home to Smith College (Sylvia Plath's alma mater), and lots of browse-worthy indie bookstores, this town is a must-see. Check out community-focused **Broadside Bookshop,** 247 Main St. (☎ 413/586-4235), for new fiction; **Raven Used Books,** 4 Old South St. (☎ 413/584-9868), for a wide-ranging selection; and **Booklink,** 150 Main St. (☎ 413/585-9955), for new travel, fiction, and nonfiction titles. ☺ 2 hr.

Take Rte. 9 1¾ mile east, and turn right on Bay Rd. Go 1¾ mile and turn left to stay on Bay Rd. for another 2½ miles.

> *Exhibits at the Emily Dickinson Museum delve deep into the life and work of the reclusive poet.*

❹ ★★ kids The Eric Carle Museum of Picture Book Art. Love children's books? Visit the country's first full-scale picture book art museum and view works by Carle, author of the classic *Very Hungry Caterpillar,* plus changing exhibits of picture book art from around the world. There are engaging attractions for wee ones, too, including an art studio where they can design their own masterpieces. ⊕ 1½ hr. 125 W Bay Rd., Amherst. ☎ 413/658-1100. www. carlemuseum.org. Admission $9 adults, $6 kids 18 and under. Open Tues–Fri 10am–4pm, Sat 10am–5pm, Sun 12–5pm (July–Aug Mon 10am–4pm as well).

Head left back out onto W. Bay Rd. and turn left on Rte. 116 going north into Amherst. Turn right at Main St.

❺ ★ Amherst. Before you hit this college town's many bookstores, visit the former home of New England's famously reclusive poet, now the **Emily Dickinson Museum,** 280 Main St. (☎ 413/542-8161; www.emily dickinsonmuseum.org). You'll see many items original to her family, but the real attraction is a tour that digs deep into the woman behind the legend—her education, controversial reputation about town, and relationship with her editor. Exhibits on unfinished poems, details on family members, and a visit to the

Evergreens—the poet's brother's home—complete the story. Then pay a visit to **Amherst Books,** 8 Main St. (☎ 800/503-5865), to stock up on poetry and literature, and to the workers' collective **Food for Thought,** 106 N. Pleasant St. (☎ 413/253-5432), for radical and progressive tomes. The **National Yiddish Book Center,** on the Hampshire College campus, 1021 West St. (☎ 413/256-4900), has a museum and bookstore specializing in Jewish culture and history. ⊕ 2 hr.

Take Pleasant St. 2½ miles north and turn left on Pine St. Go right on Montague Rd. (Rte. 63) and go 8 miles north; turn left on Rte. 47 south then right on Main St. for 1½ miles. At the fork, go left on Greenfield Rd.

❻ ★★★ Montague Book Mill. This former gristmill is the bookstore of our dreams. The multiroom Montague is all creaky floors, exposed wood ceilings, sun-dappled alcoves, and quirky corners. There are rows and rows of used books, and all sorts of inviting nooks with cozy old chairs for plopping down and burying your nose in just about any tome your heart desires. The best spots look out over the rushing Sawmill River. On warmer days, fellow bookish folk hang out on the deck outside, or at one of the tables in the alley, enjoying a beer, coffee, or treat from the **Lady Killigrew**

Café (☎ 413/367-9666). ⏱ 2 hr. 440 Green-field Rd., Montague. ☎ 413/367-9206. www.montaguebookmill.com. Daily 10am–6pm.

Return to Rte. 47 and go 4¾ miles south to Rte. 116, which you'll take north 37 miles, to the town of Savoy. There, pick up Rte. 8A and go 4½ miles south to the town of Windsor, where you'll pick up Rte. 9. Go 8½ miles west to Pittsfield, turning left at Merrill to stay on Rte. 9, and turn left at 4th St., continuing onto Elm St. Turn right at Holmes Rd. and go 2 miles.

⑦ ★ Arrowhead. Herman Melville lived here from 1850 to 1863, while he completed his masterpiece, **Moby Dick.** A 45-minute guided tour takes you through the house, now furnished with items from the Berkshire Historical Society's collection, including pieces that supposedly belonged to writers Mark Twain and Oliver Wendell Holmes, who lived down the street, and a chair owned by W. E. B. Du Bois, the Great Barrington native who co-founded the NAACP. A highlight: the view of Mt. Greylock from the upstairs study, said to have been Melville's inspiration for his whale. (The author's friend, Lenox resident Nathaniel Hawthorne, wrote in 1852: "On the hither side of Pittsfield sits Herman Melville, shaping out the gigantic conception of his 'White Whale,' while the gigantic shadow of Greylock looms upon him from his study window.") ⏱ 1½ hr. 780 Holmes Rd., Pittsfield. ☎ 413/442-1793. www.mobydick.org. Admission $12. Memorial Day to Oct 9:30am–4pm daily. Tours on the hour starting at 10am.

Turn right onto Holmes St. and again onto Rte. 7 south, which you'll take to:

> *Students of literature may find inspiration, as Herman Melville did, at Arrowhead.*

⑧ ★★ The Mount. No literary tour of the area would be complete without a visit to this gorgeous 113-acre Lenox estate, the home of groundbreaking author Edith Wharton, who wrote *House of Mirth* (1905) and the Pulitzer Prize–winning *Age of Innocence* (1920), two novels that critically examined the upper echelons of New York society. Wharton was up to the task, having been born into a wealthy, old–New York family herself. After she and her husband spent a few summers in fashionable Lenox, Wharton—also a landscape gardener and interior designer— bought this property in 1902, designing the house and formal gardens following the precepts of symmetry and balance she described in *The Decoration of Houses* (1897). Though some rooms are unfinished—the Mount's restoration is ongoing—we suggest the $2 guided tour. Look for the library, filled with some 2,600 volumes of Wharton's own collection, and save time to enjoy the gardens, where visitors can picnic. ⏱ 2 hr. Plunkett St., Lenox. ☎ 413/551-5107. www.edithwharton.org. $16 adults, $13 students with ID, free for kids 17 and under. May–Oct daily 10am–5pm.

Friday Night Fright

Did you know that Edith Wharton not only was an aficionado of supernatural tales, but also herself wrote ghost stories? Ironically—or not—her estate is reportedly haunted. If you're here on a Friday from June to October, reserve a spot on the 90-minute guided ghost tour through the haunted parts of the property, including the stables and a pet cemetery. Admission is $20 for adults and $10 for kids 8 to 16; kids 7 and under are not permitted.

BAY STATE SCRIBES
Massachusetts' Literary Lions

BY TOM GAVIN & KERRY ACKER

	Nathaniel Hawthorne 1804–64 Novelist, short-story writer	**Henry David Thoreau** 1817–62 Philosopher, poet, essayist	**Herman Melville** 1819–91 Novelist, short-story writer, poet
CLAIM TO FAME	Examined the legacy of Puritanism in New England through works striking for their psychological complexity, graceful prose, passionate allegory, and themes of good versus evil.	Dismissed in his lifetime as an acolyte of Emerson. Celebrated individualism, living close to nature, self-reliance; criticized materialism and conformity. An early proponent of civil disobedience, spent a night in jail for refusing to pay poll tax.	The tale of Captain Ahab's quest for revenge on one white whale, *Moby-Dick* is a stylistically daring, ambitious masterpiece ahead of its time, packed with symbolism, religious undertones, bawdy jokes, cultural references—and notoriously long digressions.
FUN FACT(S)	At Bowdoin College in ME, befriended Henry Wadsworth Longfellow and future president Franklin Pierce, who appointed him U.S. Consul in Liverpool, England.	He and his brother both proposed marriage to one Ellen Sewall, though neither wed her. His dying words were said to be "moose" and "Indian." Discuss.	A certain coffee franchise is named for Starbuck, Ahab's first mate on the *Pequod.* The DJ Moby (Richard Melville Hall) is a distant relative.
MUST-READ	*The Scarlet Letter*	*Walden*	*Moby-Dick,* which sold fewer than 10,000 copies when Melville was alive
STOMPING GROUND	Born in Salem, MA; studied at Bowdoin in ME; lived on Brook Farm Utopian community in West Roxbury, MA. Resided in Concord, Salem, and Lenox, MA, and then abroad, in Europe; died in Plymouth, NH.	Born in Concord, MA; graduated Concord Academy and Harvard; returned to Concord, where Emerson became his mentor and friend. Spent 2 years in a cabin by Walden Pond. Traveled frequently, but home remained Concord.	Born in New York City, moved to Albany at age 11. Many stints at sea took him as far as the South Pacific, which he wrote about in *Typee,* his first novel. Lived in Pittsfield, MA, where he befriended Hawthorne, and in New York, where he died.
QUINTESSENTIAL QUOTE	"What other dungeon is so dark as one's own heart! What jailer so inexorable as one's self!"	"If a man does not keep pace with his companions, perhaps it is because he hears a different drummer." —Walden	"To the last I grapple with thee; from hell's heart, I stab at thee; for hate's sake, I spit my last breath at thee." —Moby-Dick

FROM THE GOTHIC MELANCHOLY OF HAWTHORNE AND MELVILLE to the spare, haunting verse of Dickinson to Thoreau's poetic rhapsodies, Massachusetts writers helped define American literature with voices both groundbreaking and authentically American. The state's tradition of storytelling and its emphasis on education made it a breeding ground for greatness.

Emily Dickinson	Edith Wharton	Robert Frost
1830–86 Poet	1862–1937 Novelist, short-story writer, essayist	1874–1963 Poet
Published only seven poems in her lifetime, most of them anonymously. Used taut, economic phrases, distinct punctuation, and irregular rhythm to write poems of tremendous depth on themes of death and immortality, revealing a wholly original voice and vision.	Born into privileged Old New York society, she wrote critically yet compassionately, with wit and irony, about upper-class men and women in a world defined by convention. Her characters struggle to find happiness while adhering to rigid social mores.	America's most popular and beloved 20th-century poet. Adhered to traditional meter and verse when free verse was all the rage; seemingly simple, painstakingly crafted lines resonate for their distinctive rural New England vernacular and emotional range.
After her death, her sister discovered more than 1,700 poems in a locked box, and a poetry star was born.	Born Edith Newbold Jones, she was part of the family that inspired the phrase "keep up with the Joneses."	Never graduated from college but received more than 40 honorary degrees in his lifetime, including ones from Oxford and Cambridge, Yale, Princeton, and two from Dartmouth.
"'Hope' is the thing with feathers—"	*Age of Innocence*	"Stopping by Woods on a Snowy Evening"
Famously reclusive, Dickinson spent her whole life in Amherst save for her student years at Mount Holyoke in South Hadley and a few years undergoing medical eye treatment in Cambridge.	Born in New York City, summered in Newport, traveled throughout Europe as a child. Designed and built the Mount in Lenox, where she lived from 1902 until 1911. Then she moved to France, where she resided until her death.	Born in San Francisco; moved to Lawrence, MA; studied at Dartmouth and Harvard. Lived in Derry and Plymouth, MA; Franconia, NH; Shaftsbury and Ripton, VT; and Boston and Cambridge, MA. Died in Boston.
"Because I could not stop for Death—/ He kindly stopped for me—"—Because I Could Not Stop for Death	"The only way not to think about money is to have a great deal of it." —The House of Mirth	"Two roads diverged in a wood, and I—/ I took the one less traveled by,/ And that has made all the difference." —The Road Not Taken

The Berkshires

The thick woodlands, open pastures, and crisp mountain air are what first attracted the artists and writers who "discovered" this area in the mid–19th century. Then came the Choates, Carnegies, and other captains of industry; drawn by the bucolic splendor and the region's cultural clout, they built summer "cottages" that were in fact closer to castles, and brought with them many changes: electricity, wider roads, and a citizenry eager to support the arts. The Berks have since become a haven for artists of all stripes, and tens of thousands of visitors flock to Tanglewood, Jacob's Pillow, and the Berkshire and Williamstown Theater Festivals (below) annually—be sure to plan ahead. Expect to spend 4 to 5 days here soaking up performances while enjoying the great outdoors.

> The pedigree that afforded Edith Wharton a home like the Mount, in Lenox, above, also prepared her to write about upper class society in The Age of Innocence.

START Williamstown is 140 miles from Boston. **TRIP LENGTH** 97 miles.

❶ ★★★ Williamstown. Nestled in the mountains of the far-northwestern corner of the state, this scenic Colonial town—home to Williams College—appears sleepy, but brims with culture. Summertime, from late June to August, brings the world-class **Williamstown Theater Festival,** 1000 Main St. (☎ 413/458-3200), which has been drawing big-name talent for its innovative takes on works old and new since 1955. The **Sterling and Francine Clark Art Institute,** 225 South St. (☎ 413/458-2303; www.clarkart.edu), shows off its superb collection of Old Master paintings (della

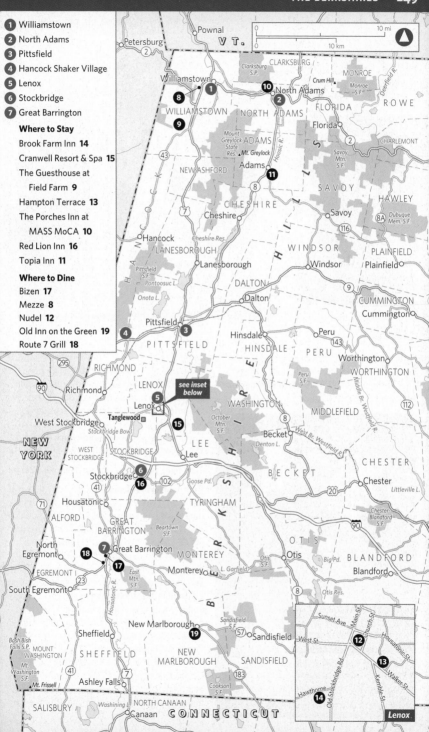

1 Williamstown
2 North Adams
3 Pittsfield
4 Hancock Shaker Village
5 Lenox
6 Stockbridge
7 Great Barrington

Where to Stay
Brook Farm Inn **14**
Cranwell Resort & Spa **15**
The Guesthouse at
    Field Farm **9**
Hampton Terrace **13**
The Porches Inn at
    MASS MoCA **10**
Red Lion Inn **16**
Topia Inn **11**

Where to Dine
Bizen **17**
Mezze **8**
Nudel **12**
Old Inn on the Green **19**
Route 7 Grill **18**

> *The impressive Impressionist collection at "the Clark" in Williamstown includes works by French masters Monet and Renoir.*

Francesca), French impressionism (Monet, Renoir), and American art (Homer, Sargent). Free to the public, **Williams College Museum of Art,** Main St./US-2 (☎ 413/597-2429; www.

Tanglewood Tip

Today's wildly popular summer festival hosts such wide-ranging acts as the Boston Symphony Orchestra, James Taylor, Mark Morris Dance Group, and *Prairie Home Companion.* Get tickets, grab picnic supplies—we love **Bizalion's** in Great Barrington (see p. 253), or **Guido's,** 1020 South St., Pittsfield (☎ 413/442-9912)— and enjoy world-class music on Tanglewood's gorgeous grounds under the stars.

wcma.org), highlights 20th-century American painting, with work by de Kooning and Rauschenberg, among others. Explore **Main Street,** with its columned homes and stately red-bricked architecture, and check out the antiques shops; we love the Early American furniture and folk art at **Saddleback Antiques,** 1396 Cold Spring Rd. (☎ 413/458-5852). ⏱ 5 hr.

Turn right onto Rte. 2 and go 4½ miles east to:

② ★★★ **North Adams.** This formerly down-at-heel mill town was transformed into an international destination in 1999, with the opening of **MASS MoCA,** at 1040 MASS MoCA Way (☎ 413/MOCA-111 [662-2111]; www.massmoca.org). The massive art and performance center, composed of 27 refurbished textile factory buildings, just might be the ideal contemporary-art viewing experience. The space—with lots of glass and brick, wooden posts, and steel beams that bear testament to its industrial past—is vast, open, and light-flooded, allowing for multiple vantage points from which to view the world-class installations (Rauschenberg), photography, and paintings (Lewitt). There are also excellent indie-leaning programs of music (Stephen

> *In addition to world-class art, visitors to MASS MoCA can enjoy a music festival featuring well-regarded performers such as Wilco and Levon Helm.*

Malkmus, Patti Smith) and theater. Want more art? Head to **Kolok Gallery** at Windsor Mill, Rte. 2 (☎ 413/346-1046), for contemporary art, and the galleries at **Eclipse Mill,** 243 Union St. (☎ 413/664-9101), for paintings, pottery, and other media. ⊙ 3 hr.

Head 18 miles south on Rte. 8 to:

❸ ★ Pittsfield. Until recently, this former wool manufacturing center was the ugly stepchild of the Berkshires—a gritty industrial town to be avoided. But feisty downtown Pittsfield has been injected with new life, thanks to such arts-focused revitalization efforts as the 2006 $22-million renovation of the century-old **Colonial Theater,** 111 South St. (☎ 413/997-4444; www.thecolonialtheatre.org), and the 2010 opening of the indy **Beacon Cinema,** 57 North St. (☎ 413/358-4780; www.thebeacon cinema.com). Stop in the **Berkshire Museum,** 39 South St. (☎ 413/443-7171; www.berksire museum.org), to see 19th-century art by Bierstadt and Innes; kids will love the hands-on excavation center in the dinosaur room and a cool interactive video art exhibit. Check out **Ferrin Gallery,** 437 North St. (☎ 413/442-1622), for contemporary sculpture and ceramics, then head to tapas joint **Mission,** 438 North St. (no phone), whose zesty *patatas bravas,* salmon BLT sliders, and Spanish wines

make for a great lunch break. Finally, lovers of *Moby Dick* won't want to miss **Arrowhead** (p. 245, ❼), where Herman Melville wrote much of his whale tale. ⊙ 2 hr.

Continue south onto South St., turn right onto Rte. 20and go 4½ miles west.

❹ ★★ kids Hancock Shaker Village. At its peak in 1830, this community was home to 300 Shakers, the intriguing sect noted for their celibacy, simplicity, and fine craftsmanship (see "The Shakers: Radical Chic" on p. 436 for more information). Now, you can explore 18 restored buildings—including the graceful 1826 stone round barn, the only circular barn ever built by the Shakers—during a self-guided tour of the tranquil grounds. A highlight: the 1830 brick dwelling, where you'll find the communal dining rooms, separated sleeping quarters of the Brethren and the Sisters, and a state-of-the-art kitchen of the period. Try to catch one of the daily activities, such as blacksmithing or sheepshearing. ⊙ 2 hr. Rte. 20 and Rte. 41, Pittsfield. ☎ 800/817-1137. www.hancockshakervillage.org. $17 adults, $8 kids 13–17. Apr–Oct daily 10am–5pm.

Take Rte. 20 east into Pittsfield, turn right onto Rte. 7 and go 5 miles south. Veer right onto Rte. 7A and go 1 mile south.

⑤ ★★★ Lenox. Both charming and sophisticated, this quiet little village is the beating cultural heart of the Berkshires. After Hawthorne, Longfellow, and actress Fanny Kemble spread the word about the beautiful mountain town in the mid-19th century, Gilded Age glitterati followed their lead. They built baronial estates like the 1893 **Ventfort Hall** (p. 235, **❸**), the 1894 Tudor-style Wyndhurst Mansion at **Cranwell** (p. 254), and the enchanting, turreted 1902 **Blantyre** (p. 239). Edith Wharton, author of the Pulitzer Prize–winning *Age of Innocence* (1920), lived and wrote on her 113-acre estate, **The Mount** (p. 245, **❽**), for 10 years. Lenox's high-culture cachet was cemented in 1936, when the Boston Symphony made **Tanglewood,** 297 West St. (☎ 413/637-1600; www.tanglewood.org), its summer home, late June through early September (p. 565). Visual artists, too, found inspiration here: Abstract artists George Morris and Suzy Frelinghuysen filled their Bauhaus-influenced 1940s house with a compelling collection of Cubist art. Now, fans of mid-century design will go gaga at the **Frelinghuysen Morris House & Studio,** 92 Hawthorne St. (☎ 413/637-0166; www.frelinghuysen.org), where the couple's prized Picassos and Legers are on view alongside their own sculpture and frescos. Downtown, check out **Charles Flint Antiques,** 52 Housatonic St. (☎ 413/637-1634), for Early American and Shaker furniture, and **Church Street Art Gallery,** 34 Church St. (☎ 413/637-9600), for compelling outsider art. ⏱ 5 hr.

Getting Outdoors

Overloaded with culture? Thankfully, there are myriad ways to experience the region's other kind of beauty—the natural kind. Seventy miles of trails traverse 3,491-foot **Mt. Greylock,** Mt. Greylock State Reservation, Lanesborough (☎ 413/499-4262; www.mass.gov/dcr/parks/mtGreylock/), including part of the Appalachian Trail. If you're feeling adventurous, consider one of the more challenging hikes in **Greylock Glen** on the steep eastern slope of the mountain. Or drive the switchback road to the summit (there's a $2 car fee). Up top, there are trails to explore, as well as **Bascom Lodge** (☎ 413/743-1591), a stone-and-wood lodge serving meals. In the southwestern corner of the state, **Bash Bish Falls State Park,** Falls Rd., Mt. Washington (☎ 413/528-0330; www.mass.gov/dcr/parks/western/bash.htm), has as its centerpiece a cascade of water plunging 80 feet to a crystalline pool. **Bartholomew's Cobble,** Rte. 7A, Ashley Falls (☎ 413/229-8600; www.thetrustees.org), offers 5 miles of trails crisscrossing 330 acres of wildflower-strewn land. Don't miss the panoramic view of the Housatonic from Hurlburt's Hill. (Call to find out more about their guided canoe tours.) The paved 11-mile **Ashuwillticook Rail Trail** (☎ 413/442-8928; www.mass.gov/dcr/parks/western/asrt.htm) runs from Adams to Lanesborough alongside scenic Cheshire Reservoir; rent bikes 300 yards from the trail at **Berkshire Outfitters,** Grove St., Adams (☎ 413/743-5900).

> *Gourmet specialty shops and restaurants line the streets of Great Barrington; on Saturdays there's a farmer's market.*

Head 5 miles south out of town on Rte. 183 (West St.), turn left onto Rte. 102 and go 1 mile.

6 ★★★ **Stockbridge.** Postcard-perfect downtown Stockbridge might be the most famous sight in the Berkshires. Anchored by the grand **Red Lion** (see "Where to Stay"), with its huge porch and old-world charm, this all-American town looks ready to be painted. Indeed it was: Not only did Norman Rockwell use his Stockbridge neighbors as his subjects, but the town itself figured often in his work. (His *Stockbridge Main Street at Christmas* is reenacted every Dec, complete with vintage cars and locals dressed in period garb.) Head to the **kids Norman Rockwell Museum** (p. 237, **2**) to see his *Saturday Evening Post* scenes of rosy-cheeked children and flag-waving small-town life, along with more socially probing works like *The Problem We All Live With.* Not surprisingly, idyllic Stockbridge was popular among Gilded Age high society. For an evocative representation of that era, take a guided tour of the 44-room 1885 Shingle-style **Naumkeag,** 5 Prospect Hill Rd. (☎ 413/298-3239; www.thetrustees.org), with a stunning hand-carved oak staircase, leather-wallpapered library, and fine art collection. You'll get a rare look at servants' quarters, while the gardens—

we love the Art Deco Blue Steps—are not to be missed. The **Berkshire Botanical Garden,** MA-183 and MA-102 (☎ 413/298-3926; www.berkshirebotanical.org), with 15 peaceful acres of flower, herb, and vegetable gardens, is a lovely spot for a stroll or a picnic. ⏱ 1 day.

Continue east on Rte. 102 for ⅓ mile, turn right onto Rte. 7 and go south for 6½ miles.

7 **Great Barrington.** While fine restaurants and a thriving locavore scene can be found throughout the region, Great Barrington is where the action is. It's as close to a hub as the Berkshires has, and it has emerged as its premier foodie destination, with artisanal cheese shops, farm-to-table eateries, and specialty food stores. In addition to the spots mentioned in "Where to Dine," check out these go-tos for gastronomes: **Bizalion's Fine Foods,** 684 Main St. (☎ 413/644-9988), for meticulously crafted French sandwiches and mouthwatering *pain au chocolat;* **Rubiner's** (p. 236, **1**), for a stellar cheese selection served up in what was once a bank; and **SoCo Creamery,** 5 Railroad St. (☎ 413/528-8560), for small-batch ice cream and gelato. For more on Great Barrington, see p. 236, **1**. ⏱ 2 hr.

Where to Stay

> *Take a load off on one of the Porches Inn's namesakes.*

★★ **Brook Farm Inn** LENOX

This sophisticated B&B is tailor-made for the Tanglewood set, with poetry readings at tea time and gorgeous breakfasts like crème brûlée French toast. We like no. 2, with French doors, a balcony, and a four-poster canopy bed. 15 Hawthorne St. ☎ 800/285-7638. www.brookfarm.com. 15 units. Doubles $149–$425 w/breakfast. AE, DISC, MC, V.

★★ kids **Cranwell Resort & Spa** LENOX

An excellent golf course, full-service spa, indoor and outdoor pools, cross-country skiing, and an ice-skating rink are some on-site perks at this historic property, whose centerpiece is a stunning Tudor mansion. With fine dining and tavern-style eats. 55 Lee Rd. ☎ 800/572-8938. www.cranwell.com. 96 units. Doubles $215–$595. AE, DISC, MC, V.

★★ **The Guesthouse at Field Farm** WILLIAMSTOWN

One of the most unusual properties we've seen, this former home of a contemporary-art collector is manna for modernists. Set amid open fields and woods, it has such touches as a Vladimir Kagan sofa, Eames chair, fine art (for example, Wolf Kahn), and outdoor sculpture. 554 Sloan Rd. ☎ 413/458-3135. www.thetrustees.org. 6 units. Doubles $150–$295 w/breakfast. AE, DISC, MC, V. May–Oct; weekends only Nov–Dec.

★★ **Hampton Terrace** LENOX

A remarkably friendly B&B with a prime location, the Hampton offers platefuls of delicious breakfasts, outstanding service, and well-appointed, spacious rooms. Public areas are inviting, too—we particularly like the 1930s red-leather bar. 91 Walker St. ☎ 800/203-0656. www.hamptonterrace.com. 14 units. Doubles $175–$345 w/breakfast. AE, DISC, MC, V.

★★ **The Porches Inn at MASS MoCA** NORTH ADAMS

A daring concept, beautifully executed. Composed of six refurbished 1890s row houses across the street from MASS MoCA, Porches weds retro-industrial chic with rustic and modern details. Mohawk Trail collectibles, paint-by-numbers art, rainfall showers, Frette linens—it's all here, and it works. 231 River St. ☎ 413/664-0400. www.porches.com. 47 units. Doubles $130–$355 w/breakfast. AE, MC, V.

★★ **Red Lion Inn** STOCKBRIDGE

A Berkshires fixture since 1773, the venerable Red Lion continues to please guests with its warm service, Victorian furnishings, and old New England charm. The chef turns out contemporary takes on classic American dishes, with a heavy emphasis on local ingredients. 30 Main St. ☎ 413/298-5130. www.redlioninn.com. 108 units. Doubles $95–$410 w/breakfast. AE, DISC, MC, V.

★★ **Topia Inn** ADAMS

The Topia makes other "green" inns look bogus. Beds are 100% organic, floors are teak or bamboo, and walls are clay-finished. Serenity reigns: Each artist-designed room (like Peacock and Aloha) is an oasis, with silk blankets and rain showers. 10 Pleasant St. ☎ 888/868-6742. www.topiainn.com. 8 units. Doubles $125–$260 w/breakfast. AE, DISC, MC, V.

Where to Dine

> *Plan ahead to be sure you get a table at tiny, tasty Nudel.*

★★ Bizen GREAT BARRINGTON *JAPANESE*
There's a huge and varied menu of Japanese fare, and the shoji-screen-and-mat atmosphere can be transporting, but crowds flock here for the top-quality, albeit expensive, sushi. 17 Railroad St. ☎ 413/528-4343. Entrees $18–$24, sushi $8–$18 per roll. AE, DISC, MC, V. Lunch & dinner daily.

★ Mezze WILLIAMSTOWN *ECLECTIC*
Popular among Williams College profs, Mezze serves seasonal contemporary fare in a sleek setting overlooking a pond. Warm beet pasta with candy-striped beets and apples is tasty and pretty; roasted Amish chicken comes with fingerlings and hen-of-the-woods mushrooms. 777 Cold Spring Rd. (Rtes. 7 & 2). ☎ 413/458-0123. www.mezzerestaurant.com. Entrees $18–$38. AE, DISC, MC, V. Dinner daily.

★★ Nudel LENOX *NEW AMERICAN*
Reservations aren't accepted at this Lilliputian place, so go for an early dinner to try some of their innovative, locally focused small plates (parsnip maple salad, anyone?) or pastas (Garganelli with chorizo, spicy roasted tomato, braised chicken). 37 Church St. ☎ 413/551-7183. www.nudelrestaurant.com. Small plates $10, large plates $18–$25. AE, DISC, MC, V. Dinner Tues–Sun.

★★★ Old Inn on the Green NEW MARLBOROUGH *AMERICAN* Candlelit, wrought-iron chandeliers and wide-plank floors make this former stagecoach stop wonderfully atmospheric, but chef-owner Peter Platt's extraordinary contemporary cuisine makes it one of the best restaurants in New England. (The $30 three-course menu is a steal.) Reserve. 134 Hartsville New Marlborough Rd. (Rte. 57, Village Green). ☎ 413/229-7924. www.oldinn.com. Entrees $26–$38. AE, MC, V. Dinner daily.

★★ kids Route 7 Grill GREAT BARRINGTON *SMOKEHOUSE* We love this place for its excellent craft beer selection; atmosphere that's welcoming to locals, weekenders, and kids; and, of course, its awesome barbecue. All meats are locally raised: The cow/pig/chicken plate lets you try them all. Don't miss the smoky beans and Guinness chocolate cake. 999 Main St. ☎ 413/528-3235. www.route7grill.com. Entrees $15–$28. AE, MC, V. Lunch Sat–Sun, dinner daily.

Local Currency

Want to support the Berkshire economy? Considering paying in **BerkShares** (www.berkshares.org), a local currency used by more than 360 businesses, and available for exchange at 13 different bank branches.

Springfield & the Pioneer Valley

The Berkshires may bask in the limelight of Tanglewood, but the Pioneer Valley is still one of our favorite parts of Massachusetts. You'll find a politically engaged, community-minded citizenry—thanks in part to the presence of a handful of top-tier colleges such as Amherst and Smith—and a thriving local culture: There's music, theater, and a great art museum in Northampton; museums and bookstores in Amherst and Hadley; and locally made crafts in Shelburne Falls. Plan on 3 to 4 days to see it all.

> *Springfield is credited as the home of modern hoops and hosts the country's Basketball Hall of Fame.*

START Springfield is 90 miles from Boston.
TRIP LENGTH 66 miles.

1 ★ **Springfield.** The largest city in western Massachusetts sits along the Connecticut River—which provided power for the mills that helped it become a manufacturing center in the 18th and 19th centuries. It's also home to the U.S. Armory as well as Smith & Wesson. The largest attraction is the 40,000-square-foot **Naismith Memorial Basketball Hall of Fame,** 1000 W. Columbus Ave. (☎ 877/4HOOPLA 446-6752; www.hoophall.com). Opened in 1968, it's named for James Naismith who is credited with inventing the game at a school in Springfield in 1891. You'll find interactive exhibits (want to be a sportscaster?), plenty of memorabilia, and a chance to test your skills on the court. The complex known as the **Springfield Museums,** 21 Edwards St. (☎ 800/625-7738; www.springfieldmuseums. org), brings together a surprisingly good yet disparate group on one compact campus around the **Dr. Seuss National Memorial Sculpture Garden.** The **Lyman and Merrie Wood Museum of Springfield History** focuses on 150 years of locally manufactured goods, including a great collection of Indian motorcycles and a Springfield-made Rolls-Royce. The **Springfield Science Museum** boasts full-size replicas of T. rex and Triceratops skeletons, and is home to the oldest American-built planetarium in the world. The **George Walter Vincent Smith Art Museum** was opened in 1896 by its millionaire namesake, who amassed impressive collections of 19th-century American paintings and Asian art. Finally, you'll find the 5 centuries' worth of European works, as well as the only permanent gallery of Currier & Ives lithographs, in the **Michele & Donald D'Amour Museum of Fine Arts.** ◷ 4 hr.

Go north on I-91N. Stay left to continue onto I-391N, which turns into Resnick Blvd. Go right onto Rte. 202 and exit onto Rte. 116 north. In 3 miles, go right at Park St. and right into campus onto Lower Lake Rd.

❷ ★★ **Mount Holyoke College Art Museum.** One of the first college art museums in the U.S. was founded in 1876 with a now rather well-known Albert Bierstadt painting—it was a year old at the time. The collection has grown to include 15,000 diverse pieces: Greek, Roman, and Egyptian arts are well represented, along with impressive Italian renaissance works, and a selection of 17th-century European paintings. ◷ 1½ hr. Lower Lake Rd., South Hadley. ☎ 413/538-2245. www.mtholyoke.edu/go/artmuseum. Free admission. Tues–Fri 11am–5pm; Sat–Sun 1–5pm.

Take Rte. 47 north for 7 miles, then continue onto Bay Rd.; go left onto Rte. 9 and go west into:

❸ ★★★ **Northampton.** There's a lot to love about this vibrant town where President Calvin Coolidge was once mayor. We hate to use the word "artsy," but it might just be appropriate, as residents include picture book author Eric Carle and half of noise-rockers Sonic Youth. The easily walkable "downtown" area includes such galleries as **R. Michelson,** 132 Main St. (☎ 413/586-3964; www.rmichelson.com); eclectic boutiques like **Pinch,** 179 Main St. (☎ 413/586-4509; www.pinchgallery.com), offering one-of-a-kind jewelry, pottery, and other handicrafts; and plenty of eats. In addition to our suggestions in "Where to

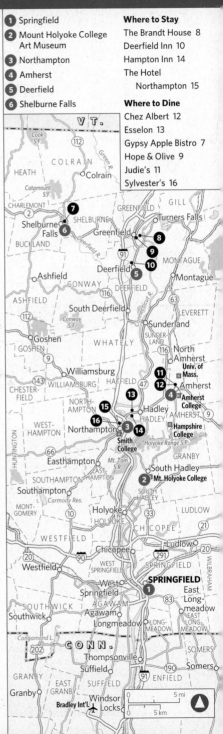

❶ Springfield
❷ Mount Holyoke College Art Museum
❸ Northampton
❹ Amherst
❺ Deerfield
❻ Shelburne Falls

Where to Stay
The Brandt House 8
Deerfield Inn 10
Hampton Inn 14
The Hotel Northampton 15

Where to Dine
Chez Albert 12
Esselon 13
Gypsy Apple Bistro 7
Hope & Olive 9
Judie's 11
Sylvester's 16

> *The Smith College Museum of Art offers a wide array of public programs.*

Country Fun

The largest fair in the northeast, **The Big E,** 1305 Memorial Ave., West Springfield (☎ 413/205-5115; www.thebige.com), is 17 days of good old-fashioned end-of-summer fun held every September. Basically, it's the state fair, for all of New England's state. There are dog shows, horse shows, antique and modern firearms shows, rides, craft shops, and a daily parade.

Dine," we recommend **Local Burger and Fries,** 16 Main St. (☎ 413/586-5857), where the grass-fed beef patties are especially popular on Friday and Saturday nights, when the place stays open until 3am. Just up Main Street is one of the largest private women's colleges in the country, **Smith College,** set on a 147-acre campus largely designed by landscaping icons Olmsted, Olmsted and Eliot in 1893. Visit the **Smith College Museum of Art,** 9 Elm St. (☎ 413/585-2760; www.smith.edu/museum), a crown jewel of the Pioneer Valley. Set in a striking contemporary space, with a 43-foot-long Tamayo mural filling its atrium, the formidable collection of 19th- and 20th-century European and American paintings—with works by Monet, Picasso, Close, and O'Keefe—is complemented by Asian, African, and Latin American art, along with rotating exhibits. Don't miss the celebrated artist-designed restrooms. ⏱ total 4 hr. Northampton Visitor Center, 99 Pleasant St. ☎ 413/584-1900. www.explorenorthampton.com. May–Oct Mon–Fri 9am–5pm, Sat–Sun noon–4pm; Nov–Apr Mon–Fri 9am–5pm.

Take Rte. 9 7 miles east to:

4 ★★ **Amherst.** Home to the University of Massachusetts, Hampshire College, and, of course, Amherst College (co-founded by dictionary publisher Noah Webster), this attractive academic axis is about as classic a New England college town as you'll find. Pleasant Street is lined with a cluster of restaurants; bars such as **Moan and Dove,** 460 West St. (☎ 413/256-1710); bookstores (p. 244, **5**); and shops like **The Clawfoot Tub,** 30 Main

Nightlife in NoHo

Perennial favorite **Iron Horse,** 20 Center St. (☎ 413/586-8686; www.iheg.com), hosts a wide variety of live music and comedy. Go to the **Calvin Theater,** 19 King St. (☎ 413/584-1444; www.iheg.com), for artists from Rufus Wainwright and Loretta Lynn to Marshall Crenshaw. Just after a good beer? Head to the 40 taps at **Dirty Truth,** 29 Main St. (☎ 413/585-5999), or sample from the wide variety of house brews at **Northampton Brewery,** 11 Brewster Court (413/584-9903).

> The Bridge of Flowers, connecting Shelburne and Buckland, was originally a trolley bridge built in 1908 by the Shelburne Falls & Colrain Street Railway.

St. (☎ 413/253-3500; www.theclawfoottub. com), with local, eco-friendly and organic furniture, kitchenware, and other home products. Set in a circa-1750 house, the **Amherst History Museum,** 67 Amity St. (☎ 413/256-0678; www.amhersthistory.org), offers guided tours telling the story of the town through the lives of the Strong and Emerson families who resided here. Be sure to pay your respects to America's great enigmatic poet at the **Emily Dickinson Museum** (p. 244, ⑤). ⏱ 3 hr.

Head right onto Main, left onto S. Pleasant St., and right onto Rte. 9W/ Rte. 116N. Go 10 miles north and turn right onto Rte. 5/Rte. 10; go 3 miles north.

⑤ kids **Deerfield.** This tiny town—home to elite prep school Deerfield Academy—earned a place in history for sustaining a raid by French and native forces in 1704; 56 villagers were killed and more than 100 more were marched as captives all the way up to Quebec. At **Historic Deerfield,** 79 Old Main St. (☎ 413/774-5581; www.historic-deerfield.org), you'll find a collection of 11 18th- and 19th-century house museums interwoven with the active 21st-century community—no docents in period garb here. Half-hour guided tours are available on the hour in most houses; others allow self-guided visits. For an overview, the **Wells-Thorn House** exemplifies how the village developed over the period from 1725 to 1850, with each room furnished in the style of a different era. The **Flynt Center** provides a deeper look into crafts of the times, exploring details of textiles and furniture construction. **Magic Wings Butterfly Conservatory,** 285 Greenfield Rd. (☎ 413/685-2805; www.magicwings. com), is a pretty enchanting place, even if you don't think of yourself as a butterfly person (really, who does?). More than 3,000 tiny fairies flit about the 8,000-square-foot greenhouse at any given time: familiar Monarchs, big black-and-white Asian swallowtails, and beautiful blue South American Morphos, to name just a few. Farther south, **Yankee Candle Village,** 25 Greenfield Rd. (☎ 413/665-8306; www.yankeecandle.com), is especially fun for kids; they'll dig the face painting, make-your-own candles, and the Bavarian Christmas Village, where it snows year-round. ⏱ 3½ hr.

> *"Flight attendants" at the Magic Wings Butterfly Conservatory will help you identify different species.*

Continue up Old Main St.; turn right onto Main St. and left onto US Rte. 5/Rte. 10 and go 2¾ miles north. Turn left onto Rte. 2A west and continue onto Rte. 2 (Mohawk Trail) going 8½ miles west. Veer left at S. Maple St. and go left at Bridge St.

6 ★ **Shelburne Falls.** The towns of Buckland and Shelburne come together at this charming crossing of the Deerfield River, connected by two short bridges—including the famous **Bridge of Flowers,** a community-supported walkway overflowing with a variety of flora. Look for the glacial potholes down by the dam, where the stone has been carved into perfect circles known as "the devil's hooves." Some small shops are clustered here: Check out the paintings and photography at the **Caroline Christie Gallery,** 9 Deerfield Ave. (☎ 413/250-8187; www.carolinechristieart.com); hand-carved, wood-fired works at **Molly Cantor Pottery,** 20 Bridge St. (☎ 413/625-2870); and blown glass at **Young and Constantin Gallery,** 10 S. Main St. (☎ 866/625-6422; www.yandcglass.com). For a light snack, **Mocha Mayas** coffeehouse, 47 Bridge St. (☎ 413/625-6292; www.mochamayas.com), is a good bet, or stop for a sandwich in **McCusker's Market,** 3 State St. (☎ 413/625-9411; www.greenfieldsmarket.coop/Pages/McCuskers.html). ⏱ 2 hr.

Getting Outdoors

Move away from the denser population center of the southern Pioneer Valley and you'll come across some great places for rafting, canoeing, and kayaking. Whatever your pleasure, we recommend contacting the nice people at **Zoar Outdoor,** 7 Main St./Rte. 2, Charlemont (☎ 800/532-7483; www.zoaroutdoor.com), located right on the Deerfield River. In addition to offering packages and outfitting for all of the above, they've pioneered ziplining in the state; their exhilarating 11- line canopy tour includes a prep course and guide. Rock-climbing courses are also available.

Worcester & Old Sturbridge

The third-largest city in New England, and home to 10 institutes of higher learning, this scruffy ex-manufacturing city always seems to get short shrift. Many travelers bypass Worcester on their way from Boston, but a few oft-overlooked gems make a stopover worthwhile. The **Higgins Armory,** 100 Barber Ave. (☎ 508/853-6015; www.higgins.org), houses the vast armor collection of local industrialist John Woodman Higgins—encompassing suits from Ancient Greece to Feudal Japan to Medieval Europe. Opened in 1898, the **Worcester Art Museum,** 55 Salisbury St. (☎ 508/799-4406; www.worcesterart.org), was the first museum in the U.S. to purchase a Monet. In addition to paintings by Gauguin, Goya, and Sargent, you'll also find ancient Roman floor mosaics from Antioch and a medieval chapel moved here in 1927. Home to Kenda—the oldest living polar bear born in captivity—the **EcoTarium,** 222 Harrington Way (☎ 508/929-2700; www.ecotarium. org), has a digital planetarium, exhibits on freshwater ecosystems and energy conservation, and a 19th-century-style naturalist's studio of taxidermy, shells, and crystals. The biggest local attraction is nearby **Old Sturbridge Village** (pictured), 1 Old Sturbridge Village Rd., Sturbridge (☎ 800/733-1830; www.osv.org). With period-dressed docents and more than 40 transplanted historic buildings on its 250 acres, it re-creates an ordinary town in early-19th-century New England. Blacksmiths, cobblers, and potters produce wares to sell at the country store; farms and gardens are seeded with period-correct heirloom varieties; and livestock are reverse-bred to approximate animals of the era. Before you leave, we insist you grab a bite at a diner in one of the original Worcester diner cars. One of the biggest diner manufacturers, the Worcester Lunch Car Company, cranked out 651 of these prefab eateries here between 1906 and 1961. Right across the street from the old factory is **Miss Worcester Diner,** 300 Southbridge St. (☎ 508/753-5600); it's changed hands several times over the years, but somehow it still feels like home. Another favorite: nearby **Corner Lunch,** 133 Lamartine St. (☎ 508/799-9866).

Where to Stay & Dine

> *Make time for a pre-dinner cocktail at the bar at Hope & Olive.*

★★ **The Brandt House** GREENFIELD
This quiet, well-appointed B&B in the valley has an outdoor Zen garden, an upstairs sunroom, and a covered deck. Breakfasts—with choices like pumpkin waffles or frittatas—are large and well executed. We like sunny room no. 6, though no. 9, with king-size bed and wood-burning fireplace, is nice as well. 29 Highland Ave. ☎ 800/235-3329. www.brandthouse.com. 9 units. Doubles $90–$245. AE, DISC, MC, V.

★★★ **Chez Albert** AMHERST *FRENCH*
This cozy yet elegant restaurant has a well-deserved reputation as the best place in town. The fine menu of locally inspired French dishes—beef bourguignon, autumn vegetable *mille-feuille,* quail with foie stuffing—is matched by a roster of artisanal wines. 27 S. Pleasant St. ☎ 413/253-3811. www.chezalbert.net. Entrees $24–$25. AE, DISC, MC, V. Lunch Tues–Fri, dinner daily.

★★ **Deerfield Inn** DEERFIELD
Right in Historic Deerfield, this 1884 country inn is a good home base for exploring the village, offering a selection of traditional yet warm and cozy rooms with Colonial charm. 81 Main St. ☎ 800/926-3865. www.deerfield

inn.com. 24 units. Doubles $155–$370 w/breakfast. AE, MC, V.

★ **Esselon** HADLEY *ECLECTIC*
It's known for its wide selection—and primary focus—of house-roasted coffees and select teas, but the food here is also quite good. On the concise menu: coconut chicken curry, burgers, and salmon teriyaki. 99 Russell St. (MA-9). ☎ 413/585-1515. Entrees $9–$16. MC, V. Breakfast & lunch Mon–Fri, dinner Tues–Sat, brunch Sat–Sun.

★★ **Gypsy Apple Bistro** SHELBURNE FALLS *BISTRO* This intimate restaurant in Shelburne Falls offers more than ample portions of exquisitely crafted, French-inspired fare. The menu changes monthly; count on artful flavor combinations and elegant preparations. Reserve. 65 Bridge St. ☎ 413/625-6345. Entrees $19–$26. MC, V. Dinner Wed–Sun.

Hampton Inn HADLEY
Centrally located in the Pioneer Valley, this well-kept and dependable chain option can be forgiven its cookie-cutter aesthetic. 24 Bay Rd. ☎ 413/586-4851. www.hamptoninn.hilton.com. 73 units. Doubles $119–$194 w/breakfast. AE, DISC, MC, V.

> *Even the decor is creative at Judie's.*

> *Adirondack chairs grace the lawn of the Deerfield Inn.*

★★ **Hope & Olive** GREENFIELD *NEW AMERICAN*
We were so happy to discover this place. With
a convivial bar serving fantastic cocktails and an
ever-shifting array of microbrews, the kitchen
turns out such well-executed, seasonal standouts as lobster and corn fritters with avocado-
lime aioli, fried bread and tomato napoleon, and
pumpkin lasagna. 44 Hope St. ☎ 413/774-3150.
www.hopeandolive.com. Entrees $11–$23. AE,
DISC, MC, V. Lunch & dinner Tues–Sun.

★★ kids **The Hotel Northampton** NORTHAMP-
TON This big Colonial revival hotel—with comfy rooms decorated in classic New England inn
fashion—is right in the heart of Northampton.
You couldn't ask for a better location, and
it also includes the historic Wiggins Tavern
(est. 1786), moved here from New Hampshire
in 1930. 36 King St. ☎ 413/584-3100. www.
hotelnorthampton.com. 106 units. Doubles
$155–$287. AE, DISC, MC, V.

★ kids **Judie's** AMHERST *NEW AMERICAN*
Enormous popovers—preferably with apple
butter—are the hook, but the ambitious menu
lists a variety of inventive dishes. We had an
amazing appetizer of puff pastry, tomato, goat
cheese, scallops, and balsamic over spinach,
followed by an equally toothsome lamb shank.
51 N. Pleasant St. ☎ 413/253-3491. www.judies
restaurant.com. Entrees $10–$17. AE, DISC, MC,
V. Lunch & dinner daily.

★★ **Sylvester's** NORTHAMPTON *BREAKFAST/*
DINER This lively local fave has fantastic
French toast—with cinnamon bun and banana
bread variations—and other organic/local
breakfast staples. You won't go wrong with
the sandwiches either. On your way out,
stop at the attached bakery for treats to take
home. 111 Pleasant St. ☎ 413/586-5343. www.
sylvestersrestaurant.com. Entrees $5–$11. AE,
DISC, MC, V. Breakfast & lunch daily.

6 Connecticut

Our Favorite Connecticut Moments

With no mountains to rival those of New Hampshire and Vermont, or cities to compare to Boston or Newport, Connecticut might be easy to overlook compared to its neighbors to the north and east. Indeed, its charms are subtler, and many a traveler has simply driven through the state en route to other points in New England. That's a shame, because the sophisticated restaurants and boutiques of the Gold Coast, the antiques shops and pristine countryside of the Litchfield Hills, New Haven's thriving intellectual and arts scene, and the maritime heritage of the Mystic Coast rank as some of the best in the region.

> *PREVIOUS PAGE A covered bridge in West Cornwall, in the Litchfield Hills. THIS PAGE SoNo, Norwalk's once seedy 19th-century waterfront, is now the place to be.*

❶ Getting immersed in the painted panels at the Florence Griswold. The dining room at the house that is now the Florence Griswold Museum—center of the American Impressionist **Lyme Art Colony** (p. 292, ❶)—holds one of Connecticut's most remarkable treasures. During the colony's heyday in the early 1900s, artists such as Willard Metcalf and Henry Ward Ranger took to painting directly on some of the home's interiors. The dining room features 38 painted panels—seascapes, country scenes, still lifes—by 30 different artists. It's an astonishing chronicle of Impressionism in America. See p. 271, ❺.

❷ Taking a break at Dottie's Diner. This bright, aqua-toned Woodbury diner has welcomed many a weary antiquer and yet still feels like a gathering place for locals. But atmosphere is just a part of this joint's appeal. The real draw is the donuts—especially the chocolate-covered ones—which are positively addictive. The chicken-only pot pies, which are just as satisfying in their own savory way, are an added bonus. See p. 289.

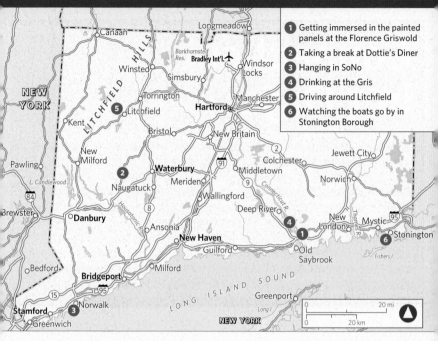

1 Getting immersed in the painted panels at the Florence Griswold
2 Taking a break at Dottie's Diner
3 Hanging in SoNo
4 Drinking at the Gris
5 Driving around Litchfield
6 Watching the boats go by in Stonington Borough

3 **Hanging in SoNo.** It's easy to dismiss the SoNo moniker as a Manhattan-inspired marketing gimmick, but the historic South Norwalk waterfront—with its narrow streets and red-bricked 19th-century factory buildings—has more than a little charm. Browse the idiosyncratic boutiques, drink a pint at the **Ginger Man**, follow up with dinner at **Match**, and save room for chocolate at the marvelous **Chocopologie**. See p. 277, 2.

4 **Drinking at the Gris.** A beautiful mahogany bar, a roaring fireplace, entertaining temperance posters, and wall-to-wall marine art: The Griswold Inn thrums with character. The taproom itself was originally a schoolhouse, moved here by oxen in 1801, and sports a ceiling made of oyster shells and horsehair. The clientele is a convivial mix of locals, yachtie types, and tourists. There's no better place in Connecticut to get your drink on—especially during one of their sea shanty nights , when the crowd enthusiastically sings along. See p. 295.

5 **Driving around Litchfield.** Pockets of this part of the state are nothing less than enchanting. We love driving Rte. 7 from Bull's Bridge, through the charming town of **Kent** (p. 286, 1) and past nearby 250-foot Kent Falls, up through Cornwall Bridge, and on to postcard-worthy **West Cornwall** (p. 288, 3), with its idyllic red covered bridge. Another gem: the bucolic Shore Road loop around tranquil **Lake Waramaug** (p. 290, 5), culminating with a sunset drink at the Hopkins Inn, overlooking the sparkling water. See p. 286.

6 **Watching the boats go by in Stonington Borough.** The old fishing and whaling village of Stonington was settled in 1649, and is now home to the state's last remaining commercial fishing fleet. There's a lot to love here: the stone lighthouse, the narrow tree-lined streets, the stately homes of sea captains of ages past, and water just about everywhere you turn. This is a spot for lingering and leisurely exploring. For us, the place is never more romantic than in the early morning, when you might catch the fishing boats heading out to sea in the break-of-dawn mist. See p. 284, 4.

Connecticut in 3 Days

Adopting its name from the Algonquian "Quinnehtukqut"—approximately meaning "beside the long tidal river"—Connecticut has largely been defined by its relationship with bodies of water. Water was a lifeline, whether for the fishing and trade of Long Island Sound, or for the communities that grew up alongside the Connecticut River, which cuts right up from Old Lyme to Canada. Our 3-day itinerary covers just a sliver of the state, but throws this connection into relief, taking you from the culturally rich port city of New Haven up the coast to where the traffic thins, and you'll encounter a vibrant Colonial past and a decidedly nautical character. You'll visit some of the state's best museums, a world-famous university, landmark eateries, and Connecticut's showpieces—Mystic Seaport and the Native American casinos.

> The seaport of Mystic was drawing visitors (and sailors) long before Julia Roberts made it famous in the 1988 film Mystic Pizza.

START New Haven is 40 miles from Hartford.
TRIP LENGTH 93 miles.

❶ ★★ New Haven. On the northern edge of Long Island Sound, and famously the site of Yale University, New Haven was once home to the Quinnipiac tribe. Threatened by their Pequot neighbors, the tribe sold their land to well-off Puritan settlers from Massachusetts in 1638 in exchange for protection. By the 1700s, the port had grown into an educational center and manufacturing city, but it struggled with economic decline in the 20th century. Despite its scruffy rep, crime rates

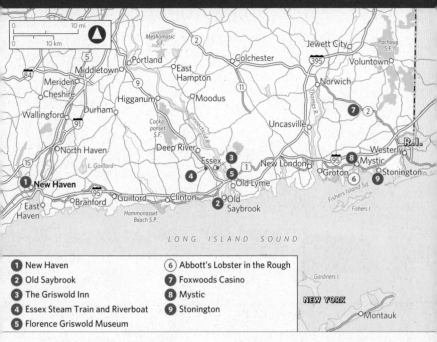

1. New Haven
2. Old Saybrook
3. The Griswold Inn
4. Essex Steam Train and Riverboat
5. Florence Griswold Museum
6. Abbott's Lobster in the Rough
7. Foxwoods Casino
8. Mystic
9. Stonington

are down, and there is plenty to love about the home of the Colt revolver and the Winchester rifle. Much of what is notable can be traced to venerable Yale, which provides excellent museums and arts options, and a surrounding neighborhood with an abundance of dining choices. Start at the Louis Kahn–designed **Yale Center for British Art** (p. 300, ②), and view the most significant British art collection outside the U.K., with works ranging from Joshua Reynolds to Damien Hirst. Next, stroll through the leafy and largely Gothic **Yale Campus** (p. 301, ③), and check out the variety of other architectural styles the school has assembled since is founding in 1701. Take a break at legendary **Frank Pepe** (p. 392), home of New Haven–style pizza, to dig into a lightly charred slice of cheesy bliss. Finally, visit the **Peabody Museum of Natural History** (p. 302, ⑤), where a sizable collection of dinosaur fossils is complemented by exhibits on evolution, Egyptian artifacts, and wildlife dioramas illustrating local ecology. ⏱ Half-day. See p. 300.

Take I-95N 29 miles to exit 67. Follow Rte. 154 south into:

② **Old Saybrook.** The coast east of New Haven is dotted with charming little historic towns. One is picturesque Old Saybrook, the first Colonial settlement (1635) on New England's southern shore. It is famous both for being the home of actress Katharine Hepburn and for its lovely views of Long Island Sound, thanks to its setting at the mouth of the Connecticut River. For a pretty drive, take Rte. 154 through the center of Old Saybrook, then continue out of town to Saybrook Point, where the road starts to follow the coastline, providing gorgeous vistas. Stop at **Saybrook Point Park** for a stroll along the water. ⏱ 1 hr.

Head 4 miles north on Rte. 154. Go right on to West Ave., and make a slight right onto Main St.

③ ★★ **The Griswold Inn.** Whether you stop in for a drink or stay for dinner, the wonderful Gris is an essential stop on your tour. With brick sidewalks, white-clapboard buildings, and not a McDonald's around, the unspoiled Connecticut River town of **Essex** (p. 292, ②) dates back to 1776, and the Griswold Inn claims to be the oldest continuously operated tavern in the country. It's got buckets of atmosphere—an

> *Now a state park, Gillette Castle, in East Haddam near Essex, was once the home of Sherlock Holmes actor William Gillette.*

Hit the Beach

At ★ kids **Hammonassett Beach State Park,** on Boston Post Road in Madison (☎ 203/245-2785), there are 2 miles of sandy beach, trails, a boardwalk, and a nature center. Though parking fees can be steep in season ($13–$22), they're discounted after 4pm. If you can, stop by for an afternoon shoreline walk or hike.

unmatched collection of nautical art, a huge potbellied stove, a taproom ceiling of shells and horsehairs, and, usually, live music. If you're the sing-along type, you may have just found paradise. ⏲ 2 hr. See p. 295.

On Day 2, take Rte. 154 north for ¼ mile, and turn left onto Railroad Ave.

❹ ★★ kids **Essex Steam Train and Riverboat.** Climb aboard a 1920s steam locomotive in Essex for a relaxing 1-hour ride through meadow and marsh before boarding the paddle-wheeler *Becky Thatcher.* Amid the quiet beauty of the landscape, you'll get a good look at elegant **Goodspeed Opera House** (p. 294) and striking **Gillette Castle** (p. 293, ❸). (***Bonus:*** If it's fall, you're in for a dazzling display of foliage.) You'll need to make reservations for this trip in advance—be sure to book the 11am departure so you'll have time for the rest of today's adventures. ⏲ 2½ hr. See p. 292, ❷ .

Get on Rte. 154 south and take a quick right onto 621, following the ramp onto Rte. 9 south. From there, take I-95N to exit 70, where you'll pick up Rte. 156 west and then Rte. 1 north for ¾ mile.

❺ ★★★ Florence Griswold Museum. Spend an hour or so in Old Lyme, exploring the art in Miss Florence's grand Georgian home, the beating heart of American Impressionism in the early 1900s. Don't miss the pièce de résistance: the painted panels in the dining room. ⏱ 1½ hr. See p. 292, **❶**.

Get back on I-95N. to exit 85, and then take Rte. 1 2 miles north. Turn right onto Groton Long Pond Rd., then left onto S. Elm St., right at Mosher St., right onto Ward Ave., left onto Main St., and right onto Pearl St.

⑥ 🍽 ★★ Abbott's Lobster in the Rough, Groton. This riverside seafood shack in Noank is worth the detour—and the ensuing wait. The hot lobster roll might be the best we've had. See p. 285.

Retrace your route to S. Elm St. and turn right. Continue 10 miles west on Rte. 215, turning left at W. Mystic Ave. Continue on

A Must-See

Long before there were shipbuilding towns or cute Colonial villages, Connecticut was home to about 16 Algonquin tribes. While the state was the site of such notable events as the bloody 1637 **Pequot War** (see "State of the Pequot" on p. 274 for more information), there are precious few museums in New England that explore the Native American experience with much substance. But there's a notable exception. The $193-million **Mashantucket Pequot Museum** (p. 294, **❹**), opened in 1998 using funds from the breathtakingly successful Foxwoods Casino, is an excellent place to learn about Native American history. Connecticut's indigenous culture comes to life through films, dioramas, and even a re-creation of a Pequot village, complete with life-size figures fishing and cooking, along with computer-generated sounds and smells. It's well worth a stop, so do your best to squeeze in a visit while you're at Foxwoods (see right).

> *The 1920s Essex Steam Train will spirit you along the Connecticut River Valley to Deep River Landing.*

State Hwy. 614, and turn right onto Rte. 184 going east. Go left onto Shewville Rd. and go 4 miles, and right onto Rte. 214 east and go 2 miles. Turn left and take Trolley Line Blvd. 1 mile to Foxwoods, where you'll spend the night (see "Going Gambling" on p. 272).

❼ ★ Foxwoods Casino. For the past 15 years or so, southeastern Connecticut has meant one thing to many people—gambling. Foxwoods is one of two thriving casinos operating on Native American property here (Mohegan Sun is the other), and it provides a veritable microeconomy where you can drink, dine, sleep, shop, and, if you're lucky, make some money. See p. 272.

Going Gambling : Connecticut's Native American Casinos

It doesn't quite have the cachet of Las Vegas, but Connecticut is home to two Native American casino resorts—Foxwoods and Mohegan Sun—that are among the country's best places to court Lady Luck. Navigating the ins and outs of both mammoth properties will give you an aerobic workout and they are often inundated with East Coast day-trippers, but they are nonetheless fun places to gamble. They're also great places to stay and dine, though you'll generally pay a hefty price for the privilege. With nearly 340,000 square feet of gaming space, **Foxwoods Resort Casino,** 340 Trolley Line Blvd., Mashantucket (☎ 800/369-9663; www.foxwoods.com), is the largest casino complex in the U.S. There are table games galore, almost 7,400 slot machines, a poker room, and even bingo. For sheer variety it can't be beat, but we find it a bit unwieldy to navigate and a little too generic. That said, if you're also looking for a casino with accommodations, Foxwoods is your best bet, with four hotel options. At the top of the list is the resort's **MGM Grand,** whose sleek rooms offer high-thread-count linens on pillow-top beds, and large rainfall showers. Ask for one of the higher rooms with expansive views of the surrounding forest. Your next best bet is the slightly older but centrally located, 24-story **Grand Pequot Tower.** The **Great Cedar Hotel** has smaller rooms, and the simpler **Two Trees Inn** is a shuttle bus ride away. On the dining front, its 38 restaurants range from fast food to gourmet fare created by such celebrity chefs as Tom Colicchio and David Burke. The full-service **G. Spa & Salon** and a host of entertainment and nightlife options—including a theater that attracts major headliners—are on the premises in case you need a break from the roulette wheel.

Five miles away, **Mohegan Sun,** 1 Mohegan Sun Blvd., Uncasville (☎ 888/226-7711; www.mohegansun.com), is the nation's second-largest casino, with nearly 300,000 square feet of gaming space (7,000 slots, all the required table games, and a first-rate poker room). Its warmer, Native American theme makes it a bit less intimidating than Foxwoods, and free nightly entertainment, at the Wolf Den on the casino floor, may help take the sting out of a losing night.

The fully equipped rooms at Mohegan Sun are large and comfy, though the walls are a little thin; rooms with river views are the most desirable. The resort's 30-plus restaurants range from the ubiquitous Starbucks to fine dining by the likes of such culinary notables as Bobby Flay and Todd English. Entertainment, nightlife, and spa offerings are similarly diverse.

> If Beluga whales and African penguins don't interest you, the 20-ft. tall, sea nettle-shaped jellyfish exhibit at the Mystic Aquarium should get your attention. 310A

On Day 3, follow your route back down Shewville Rd. and continue onto Rte. 27 south into:

8 ★★★ Mystic. From a grisly early conflict with the Pequot tribe (p. 274) to success as a major port and shipbuilding center, a big story is behind this tiny seaside village of 4,000 residents. Get a taste of this past at **Mystic Seaport** (p. 282, **3**). You won't have enough time to fully explore this living museum, but that's okay—hitting the highlights will do. In our opinion, that means paying a visit to the shipyard, where experts are restoring the last surviving wooden whaling ship; stopping in some of the living history shops in the Seafaring Village; and exploring the Exhibit Galleries. If you still have time, head to the **Mystic Aquarium & Institute for Exploration** (p. 282, **3**); don't miss the beluga whales and African penguins. ☺ Half-day.

Take Rte. 1 2 miles north out of Mystic and turn right onto Rte. 1Alt (N. Water St.) then left to stay on Rte. 1Alt (now Trumbull Ave.). Turn right onto Alpha Ave. and left onto Water St.

9 ★★★ Stonington Borough. End your tour with a walk—or drive—through the narrow (and we mean really, really narrow) streets of this charming fishing village, one of our favorite towns in New England. Stop for a sunset drink at the ★ **Dog Watch Café,** Dodson Boatyard, 194 Water St. (☎ 860/415-4510), before grabbing dinner at **Noah's** (p. 285). ☺ 2 hr. See p. 284, **4**.

Spending the Night

There are plenty of quaint places to stay in Essex, Old Lyme, and Ivoryton—see our suggestions on p. 295.

STATE OF THE PEQUOT

The Fall & Resurrection of Connecticut's Lost Tribe

BY KERRY ACKER & TOM GAVIN

ONE OF THE MOST DOMINANT TRIBES IN THE NORTHEAST before the arrival of Europeans, the Pequot nation numbered some 6,000 at the turn of the 17th century but declined swiftly over the following decades. Weakened by the smallpox epidemic of 1633, they also split from the Mohegans, who—along with Pequot rivals the Narragansett—allied with the English in a war that would all but decimate the once powerful Pequot and set the tone for native–settler relations. Barely surviving into the 20th century, the tribe organized anew and focused on rebuilding. With their savvy pursuit of the gambling market, culminating in the masterstroke of the Foxwoods Casino, they have attained dominance once again as the wealthiest tribe in the United States.

Who They Were

Whether or not their name actually means "destroyers" in Narragansett, as one interpretation goes, there's little doubt that the Pequot were considered aggressive by many of their neighbors. At its peak, the nation controlled some 250 sq. miles of land along the southeastern coast of Connecticut from modern day Mystic to Niantic and inland up the Connecticut River. Their strength was based not in numbers but in a strong central authority, resulting in a highly organized military and tenacious trade practices. Today the Mashantucket Pequot, formed by one line of descendants from the original tribe, maintain a reservation of just over 2 sq. miles in Ledyard. The Pequot language—a dialect of Eastern Algonquian—was forbidden after the war and disappeared, but recently the tribe has organized an effort to revive the lost tongue.

The Comeback

Subjugated by the Mohegans and later removed to small reservations, the few Pequot who survived the war were forbidden to use the tribe's name, but their lineage carried on. Toward the end of the 18th century, more than half moved to Oneida territory in New York. Down to one reservation in Mashantucket, few Pequot were left by the mid–20th century. But in the 1970s, the tribe rebounded, approving a constitution, electing the first tribal chairman, suing to reclaim land in Ledyard that was sold by the state in the 1850s, and petitioning for federal recognition. With tribal members returning to Mashantucket, 1986 saw the opening of high stakes bingo. In 1992, the Foxwoods Casino (p. 272) opened, followed by the Pequot Museum (p.294, **4**) in 1998.

The Pequot War

The first substantial conflict of its kind in New England, the Pequot War had profound repercussions, shifting the balance of power and making way for colonial expansion. As the Massachusetts Bay and Plymouth colonies grew, tensions over trade and territory led to conflict with the Pequot. When trader John Oldham was murdered in 1636, the Puritans responded with decisive force to quash the "heathens." The loss of hundreds of Pequot women and children in the Mystic Massacre of 1637 diminished the beleaguered tribe. With the Treaty of Hartford in 1638, the Pequot Nation was officially dissolved.

Connecticut in 1 Week

Quietly Tucked between the massive sprawl of New York City and the Yankee charm of Boston, little Connecticut is often overlooked, written off by many as a flat expanse of faceless bedroom communities. That is a shame. While it is in fact flat—the highest point is a mere 2,380 feet—the third-smallest state in the union is actually a land of great contrasts: swanky towns and down-at-heel industrial centers, genteel communities and salty fishing villages, quaint farms and huge casino complexes. Our weeklong itinerary gives you ample opportunity to see it all.

> "It is a home—& the word never had so much meaning before," said Samuel Clemens of the residence that is now the Mark Twain House & Museum.

START New Haven is 40 miles from Hartford. **TRIP LENGTH** 259 miles.

❶ ★ Greenwich & the Gold Coast. Both geographically and culturally, this is the closest Yankee Connecticut gets to Manhattan chic. Fairfield County gets its nickname from the (mostly) wealthy communities that line the southwestern coast; stylish restaurants, galleries, and boutiques cater to this crowd of mover and shakers. Spend a day exploring two sides of the area's personality. First stop: **Greenwich,** home to the hedge funds that helped put the gold on the coast. You'll find mansions, yacht clubs, and top-tier shopping. Head to Greenwich Avenue—the town's answer to Rodeo Drive—and check out **Michael Kors,** 279 Greenwich Ave. (☎ 203/618-1200), for luxe ready-to-wear; **Design Within Reach,** 86 Greenwich Ave. (☎ 203/422-2013), for

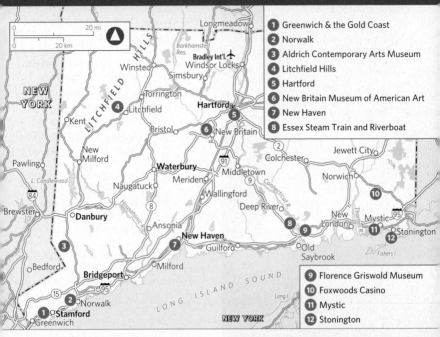

1. Greenwich & the Gold Coast
2. Norwalk
3. Aldrich Contemporary Arts Museum
4. Litchfield Hills
5. Hartford
6. New Britain Museum of American Art
7. New Haven
8. Essex Steam Train and Riverboat

9. Florence Griswold Museum
10. Foxwoods Casino
11. Mystic
12. Stonington

contemporary furniture; and **WishList,** 350 Greenwich Ave. (☎ 203/629-4600), for up-to-the-minute separates. ⊙ Half-day.

Norwalk is 15 miles northeast of Greenwich on I-95N.

2 Norwalk. When you've had your fill of Greenwich, continue on to **Norwalk,** for less glitz and more grit. This once-struggling mill town has experienced something of a renaissance over the past decade, boasting a mini arts and culinary scene in SoNo, its restored 19th-century waterfront. Galerie **SoNo,** 135 Washington St. (☎ 203/831-8332), features works by such artists as Wolf Kahn and Joan Miro. Stop in for a pint at **The Ginger Man,** serving 52 draft beers at 99 Washington St. (☎ 203/354-0163), and exquisite chocolates at **Chocopologie,** 12 S. Main St. (☎ 203/854-4754). For dinner, we love the consistently creative New American cuisine at **Match,** 98 Washington St. (☎ 203/852-1088). If you have the time, consider a trip out to visit Sheffield Island, at the entrance to Norwalk's harbor (☎ 800/838-3006; www.seaport.org). You'll be given a tour of the island's 1868 lighthouse and have time to wander the beaches and trails of the Stuart B. McKinney Wildlife Refuge. ⊙ Half-day.

> *Sheffield Island Lighthouse, visible from Norwalk, can be visited by ferry.*

> *See how the other half lives on Connecticut's Gold Coast.*

On the morning of Day 2, take I-95N from Stamford or I-95S from Southport to exit 15 where you'll pick up Rte. 7. Go north 3¾ miles, then turn left to stay on Rte. 7 for another 2 miles. Turn left at Rte. 33 and go north 8¾ miles.

❸ ★★ **Aldrich Contemporary Arts Museum.** A welcome drive away from the coast brings you to this gem in Ridgefield exhibiting a regularly changing selection of works by the likes of pioneering video artist Beryl Korot and screen printer Gary Lichtenstein. Don't miss the camera obscura room. ⏱ 2 hr. 258 Main St., Ridgefield. ☎ 203/438-4519. www.aldrichart. org. Admission $7 adults, $4 students 18–22. Tues–Sun noon–5pm.

Follow signs for I-84E and take it 3½ miles to the left exit for Rte. 7 going north. When you reach New Milford, either continue on to Kent, or pick up Rte. 202 east to Litchfield, where you'll spend the next 2 nights.

❹ ★★★ **The Litchfield Hills.** There's not much in the way of excitement in this lush northwestern corner of the state, and for many, that's precisely the point. A-list actors (Meryl Streep), celebrity chefs (Danny Meyer), and art stars (Jasper Johns) all have homes here, embracing the bucolic—and blueblood—charms of these rolling hills. Fertile fields, bubbling streams, and flower-strewn valleys are the main attractions. There's also a wealth of history: The town of **Litchfield,** the site of the first law school in the country (1773), was a safe haven for Continental forces during the Revolutionary War, and claims abound that George Washington spent the night at one place or another. Vestiges of the region's Colonial past are still evident, most distinctly in its graceful town greens. But the scenic landscape and tiny jewel-like villages—such as **West Cornwall, Warren,** and **New Preston**—are best experienced as part of a meandering, leisurely drive.

Spend Days 2 and 3 wandering, stopping in antiques shops (p. 289), posh boutiques, and great restaurants (p. 291). Save time for an outdoor adventure—be it a hike at **White Memorial** (p. 289, ❹), a paddle on the **Housatonic River** (p. 290) or fly-fishing (p. 290). And don't miss **Lake Waramaug** (p. 290, ❺). Finally, you have excellent lodging choices, including **Winvian** (p. 291), one of the most unique resorts in the east, and the **Mayflower Inn & Spa** (p. 291), the *ne plus ultra* of spas. ⏱ 2½ days.

On Day 4, get up early and head east on Rte. 118 out of Litchfield and turn right onto Rte. 254 south. Go 7¼ miles and turn left onto Rte. 6 east for 16 miles. Merge onto I-84, go 7¾ miles, and take exit 50 into Hartford, where you'll spend the night.

❺ ★ **Hartford.** By the late 19th century, Connecticut's largest city, founded in 1636 by Puritan preacher Thomas Hooker, was the wealthiest in the country. It flourished first as a port, then as a center of the insurance trade, set up to protect shipping merchants from pirates, fires, and other risks. The next 100 years were

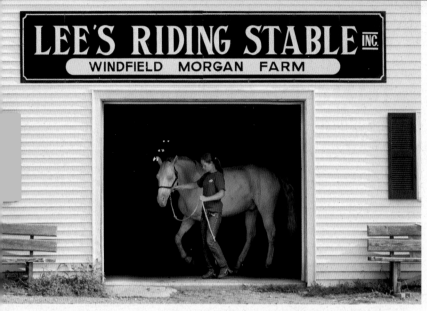

> *A riding stable in Litchfield speaks to the rural idyll characteristic of the northwest corner of the state.*

less kind to the capital, and by the mid-1900s, the middle class had fled. Nowadays, the city faces challenges—many of the companies that earned it the title "Insurance Capital of the World" have since left—but if you look past the gray appearance, you'll be surprised by its riches. We suggest you spend the day exploring the **Old State House** (p. 296, ②), the state-of-the-art **Connecticut Science Center** (p. 297, ③), and the **Mark Twain House & Museum** (p. 298, ⑤). ⏱ 1 day. See p. 296.

On Day 5, plan an early stop in New Britain en route to New Haven. Take I-84W for 13 miles. Get off at exit 35, onto Rte. 72 and go east 1 mile to exit 7. Make a sharp left onto Rte. 372 west, and take the first right onto W. Main St. After ¾ mile, turn right onto Lexington St.

⑥ ★★ **New Britain Museum of American Art.** The first museum in the U.S. dedicated entirely to American Art, with a collection covering Colonial and Federal portraits (Gilbert Stuart), the Hudson River School (Thomas Cole), American Impressionism (Childe Hassam), Modernism (Milton Avery), and the work of hometown hero Sol LeWitt. ⏱ 2 hr. 56 Lexington St., New Britain. ☎ 860/229-0257. www.nbmaa.org. $10 adults, $8 students 12–18.

Head back up Lexington St. and go right onto W. Main St. for ½ mile. Make a right at Main St., a quick left onto Arch St., and the first left onto Elm St. Stay right to merge onto Rte. 9 south, go 6 miles to exit 20S onto I-91S, and go 27 miles. Take exit 2; turn right onto Hamilton St. and right onto Chapel St.

⑦ ★★ **New Haven.** Spend the rest of Day 5 exploring this college town, following our suggestions on p. 268, ①, and then head to **the Griswold Inn** (p. 295). See p. 300.

⑧–⑬ Follow stops ④ to ⑨ on our "Connecticut in 3 Days" Tour (p. 268).

Spending the Night on the Gold Coast

There are plenty of great choices in this area, but the two we recommend are the understated-yet-luxe **Delamar Southport,** 275 Old Post Rd., Southport (☎ 203/259-2800; www.thedelamar.com), and the stylish **Hotel Zero Degrees,** 909 Washington Blvd., Stamford (☎ 203/363-7900; www.hotelzerodegrees.com).

Mystic & the Southeast Coast

Just beyond I-95, along the Connecticut coast east of New Haven, is a clutch of small, centuries-old settlements, some of which have colorful seafaring histories—pretty Stonington Borough was a whaling and sealing village, while Mystic was a shipbuilding center. Our tour takes you through these and other quietly appealing towns, includes the family-friendly attractions of Mystic Seaport and Mystic Aquarium—along with a submarine museum—and offers ideas for getting onto or into the water. Find a cozy inn to use as a base and plan to spend 3 or 4 days touring.

> It's hard to escape all things nautical in Mystic. But then why would you want to?

START Guilford is 38 miles from Hartford.
TRIP LENGTH 53 miles.

❶ Guilford. This pleasant Colonial burg claims not only the largest town green in New England—crisscrossed with paths, it's tranquil and welcoming—but also some fine historic houses, including the ★★ 🧒 **Henry Whitfield State Museum,** 248 Old Whitfield St. (☎ 203/453-2457; www.cultureandtourism.org). Built in 1639, it's New England's oldest stone house, once home to Henry Whitfield, one of the Puritan founders of the Guilford colony. Inside, you'll find a re-creation of how it may have looked in the 17th century, with space-saving innovations from the era such as a desk that turns into a chair, and a predecessor to the Murphy bed. The regional visitors' center is on the museum's premises. ⏱ **45 min.**

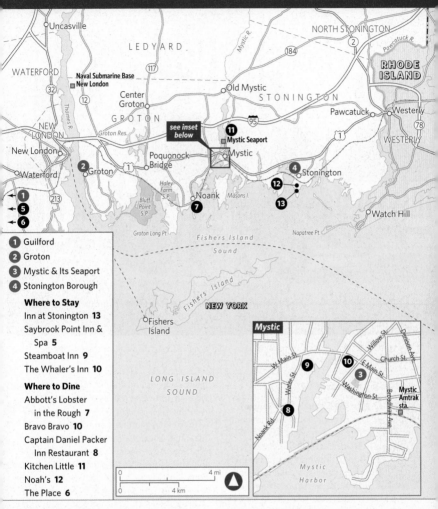

1 Guilford
2 Groton
3 Mystic & Its Seaport
4 Stonington Borough

Where to Stay
Inn at Stonington **13**
Saybrook Point Inn & Spa **5**
Steamboat Inn **9**
The Whaler's Inn **10**

Where to Dine
Abbott's Lobster in the Rough **7**
Bravo Bravo **10**
Captain Daniel Packer Inn Restaurant **8**
Kitchen Little **11**
Noah's **12**
The Place **6**

Head north on Whitfield St. and turn right at Boston St. (Rte. 146 east). After 1 mile, go left at Goose Ln. and take a quick right onto I-95N. Take left exit 86 to Rte. 12 1½ miles north into:

2 **Groton.** This industrial port town may not look like much, but it lays claim to the free ★★ kids **Submarine Force Museum,** 1 Crystal Lake Rd. (☎ 800/343-0079; www.ussnautilus. org). Popular among families and war buffs alike, this waterside museum is a worthwhile visit, offering a combo of submarine history—for example, a replica of David Bushnell's Colonial-era "Turtle," created in nearby Old Saybrook—and cool-for-kids gadgetry, such as periscopes they can use to scan the Thames

for danger. The audio tour aboard the *Nautilus,* the first nuclear sub, is not to be missed, unless of course you suffer from claustrophobia. Groton is also a good place to set out on a **fishing trip.** We suggest a cod-fishing excursion aboard the **Hel-Cat II,** 181 Thames St. (☎ 860/535-2066; www.helcat.com)—half-day trips last 6 hours and cost about $55. Finally, visit **Fort Griswold Battlefield State Park,** 57 Fort St. (☎ 860/449-6877), where in 1781 the traitorous Benedict Arnold led a British force against the Americans and ordered the massacre of 88 prisoners after they'd surrendered. ⏱ 3 hr. (more if you're going fishing). www.town.groton.ct.us.

> *The artillery in Stonington's Cannon Square was used by defenders of the small town to hold off the British navy in the War of 1812.*

Take I-95N 5 miles to exit 90.

SITE GUIDE PAGE 283

❸ ★★ kids **Mystic & Its Seaport.** One of our favorite New England shoreline getaways, Mystic boasts a charming Main Street—with a historic drawbridge and a lineup of boutiques and galleries—and two major attractions. First up is the ★★ **Mystic Aquarium & Institute for Exploration,** 55 Coogan Blvd. (☎ 860/572-5955; www.mysticaquarium.org). We're suckers for aquariums in general, but this one—with its attractive indoor/outdoor layout—is especially appealing. We love watching the enchanting beluga whales and staring at the mesmerizing jellyfish, but we're most excited about the Nautilus Live Theater, where you can interact with ocean researchers around the globe in real time. The aquarium gets crowded, so go on a weekday—and try to catch a feeding of the African penguins. As much as we love the aquarium, Mystic's marquee attraction is the ★★★ kids **Mystic Seaport,** 75 Greenmanville Ave. (☎ 888/973-2767; www.mysticseaport. org). After all that touring, wind down with a stroll on Main Street. **Whyevernot,** 17 W. Main St. (☎ 860/536-6209), is a gallery-cum–gift shop stocking one-of-a-kind crafts and knickknacks, while **Clad In,** 24 W. Main St. (☎ 860/572-8442), traffics in rare, high-quality women's wear from international designers. Of course, you'll need an ice cream from **Mystic Drawbridge Ice Cream,** 2 W. Main St. (☎ 860/572-7978). ⏱ **2 days.**

Take Rte. 1 north 2½ miles, and go right onto Rte. 1Alt (N. Water St.). Stay on Rte. 1Alt, take a right onto Alpha Ave. Turn left onto Water St.

The Thimble Islands

Off the coast of Branford, this little-known pink-granite archipelago has a colorful history that includes tales of Captain Kidd. Learn about them aboard **The Sea Mist,** Stony Creek Dock (☎ 203/488-8905; www.thimbleislandcruise.com). Admission is $10 for adults and $5 kids 12 and under.

SITE GUIDE

3 Mystic Seaport

This 19-acre complex goes far to connect visitors to our maritime past: you'll find 60 historic buildings, a working preservation shipyard, four historic vessels, and nautical exhibits. Buy tickets and pick up a daily guide (activities may include a talk about a day in the life of a sailor to scrimshaw lessons) at the **A** **Visitor Center.** At the **B** ★★ **Henry B. duPont Preservation Shipyard,** climb aboard the *Charles W. Morgan* (1841)—the world's only extant wooden whale ship, and the crown jewel of the Seaport—to watch it being painstakingly restored. Hop on the steamboat **C** ★ **Sabino** (1908), for a 30-minute daily cruise ($5.50 adults, $4.50 kids 6–17) or a 90-minute nightly cruise ($14 adults, $12 kids 6–17). For $5, you can also take a half-hour sail on the 20-foot catboat **D** *Breck Marshall.* The 50-foot-long **E** ★ **Mystic River Scale Model,** a replica of the region in its shipbuilding heyday (1850–70),

is worth a look-see, as is the square-rigged training ship **F** *Joseph Conrad* (1882). In ★★ **Seafaring Village,** make sure to stop in the **G** **Shipsmith Shop** (1885), where harpoons, cutting irons, and other ironworks for whaling ships were once manufactured. Lucky for you, you can still see an expert blacksmith hammering out iron and working with molten metal. Also visit the **H** **Hoop Shop, I** **Shipcarver's Shop,** and **J** **Mystic Print Shop,** where more talented craftsmen in period garb demonstrate their skills. Grab a snack at **K** **Schaefer's Spouter Tavern;** if you're lucky, you'll hear shanties emanating from the **L** **Chapel.** Learn about celestial navigation at the very cool **M** ★★ **Treworgy Planetarium,** and don't miss the **N** **Children's Museum** if you've got wee ones in tow. Last, stop in at the **O** **Museum Store** to browse the excellent nautical prints and ship models on offer.

④ ★★ **Stonington Borough.** You'll find Colonial, Georgian, and Federal-style homes in this peaceful, well-preserved town, where salty air blows through tree-lined streets that evoke its rich seafaring history. There are no major sights to speak of, but this former Yankee whaling stronghold is one of our favorite places in the state. Park in the lot at tiny **DuBois Beach** (arrive early to get a spot), then walk the length of ★★ **Water Street,** pausing to admire the flower gardens and historic homes once owned by sea captains, and stopping in antiques shops like **Devon House,** 72 Water St (☎ 860/535-4452), and **Roberto Freitas,** 156 Water St. (☎ 860/535-1797). But first, visit the 1823 lighthouse, a handsome stone structure housing the **Museum of the Stonington Historical Society,** 7 Water St. (☎ 860/535-1440; www.stoningtonhistory.org), for a taste of old Stonington. See such curios as an old shoe found in the wall of a local house (to ward off evil spirits) and a 19th-century doctor's house call cane, with medicines stashed down the length of the hollow tube. Ascend the narrow staircase to survey the vista that this old lighthouse used to guard. ⏱ 2 hr.

Where to Stay

> Stay right on the water at Mystic's Steamboat Inn.

★★★ Inn at Stonington STONINGTON
This welcoming waterfront inn combines quiet elegance with modern comfort. Halls hung with photos from the town's maritime heyday lead to cozy rooms with plush beds, gas fireplaces, and oversize bathrooms. Get a waterview room with balcony, from which you can watch boats pass by in the early-morning mist. 60 Water St. ☎ 860/535-2000. www.innatstonington.com. 18 units. Doubles $150–$445 w/breakfast. MC, V.

★★ kids Saybrook Point Inn & Spa OLD SAYBROOK
Sparkling, large, and well-appointed rooms—along with friendly service, two pools, and a fabulous spa—make for an excellent overnight here. Splurge on a seaview room, and have a drink at the Marina Bar. 2 Bridge St.

☎ 800/243-0212. www.saybrook.com. 81 units. Doubles $199–$529. AE, DISC, MC, V.

★★ Steamboat Inn MYSTIC
You couldn't ask for a better setting: It's right on the Mystic River. Score an upstairs room, and get great river views and a fireplace. Service here is excellent, and accommodations are very well maintained. 73 Steamboat Wharf. ☎ 860/536-8300. www.steamboatinnmystic.com. 11 units. Doubles $150–$300 w/breakfast. AE, DISC, MC, V.

★★ The Whaler's Inn MYSTIC
Sprawling over five buildings, the Whaler's has a stellar location in downtown Mystic, within walking distance of a variety of restaurants. Rooms are spacious and comfy; we suggest the Hoxie House, with whirlpool tubs, gas fireplaces, and four-poster beds. Best of all, from some rooms you can see boats cruising beneath the open drawbridge. 20 E. Main St. ☎ 800/243-2588. www.whalersinnmystic.com. 49 units. Doubles $109–$259 w/breakfast. AE, DISC, MC, V.

Beach Break
You may need a day at the beach after all this museum-going. We like the mellow shallow waters and fine white sand at ★★ kids **Rocky Neck State Park** on West Main Street in East Lyme (☎ 860/739-5471), wherwhere you can hike the trails and watch for osprey in the summer, cranes and herons in the fall.

Where to Dine

> *From the sea to the bun at Abbott's Lobster in the Rough.*

★★ kids **Abbott's Lobster in the Rough** NOANK
SEAFOOD A stone's throw from the water,
Abbott's is the place to be for casual alfresco
seafood dining. BYOB, come early, and order
up clams, corn, and the best buttery-hot lobster roll around. 117 Pearl St. ☎ 860/536-7719.
Entrees $5–$35. Cash only. Memorial Day to
Labor Day lunch & dinner daily; early May &
after Labor Day Fri–Sun.

★★ **Bravo Bravo** MYSTIC MEDITERRANEAN
A sleek, candlelit setting, top-notch martinis, and an Italian-inflected seafood-heavy
menu—the champagne-and-lobster risotto is
a standout—make this a local hot spot. Be sure
to reserve. 20 E. Main St. ☎ 860/536-3228. Entrees $19–$35. AE, DISC, MC, V. Lunch Tues–Sat,
dinner Tues–Sun.

★★ **Captain Daniel Packer Inn Restaurant**
MYSTIC NEW ENGLAND We love eating ha-
zelnut chicken and crab cakes with the locals
downstairs in this convivial historic pub, where
the low-beam ceilings and dark wood seem to
whisper tales from the building's salty past,
especially after you've had a few. 32 Water St.
☎ 860/536-3555. Entrees $22–$29. AE, MC, V.
Lunch & dinner daily.

★★ **Kitchen Little** MYSTIC BREAKFAST
About as perfect a little breakfast joint as we
could hope for, with outdoor seating right off
the river. Be sure to order one of the dishes
featuring *chourico*, the fiery Portuguese sausage. 135 Greenmanville Rd. ☎ 860/536-2122.
Entrees $4–$15. Cash only. Breakfast daily, lunch
Mon–Fri.

★★ **Noah's** STONINGTON BOROUGH AMERICAN
Well-prepared fresh fish (our native flounder
was sublime), rich house-made desserts,
and warm, efficient service are the norm at
this much-loved chef-owned mainstay. 113
Water St. ☎ 860/535-3925. Entrees $10–$25.
AE, DISC, MC, V. Breakfast, lunch & dinner
Tues–Sun.

★★ **The Place** GUILFORD SEAFOOD Grab a tree-
stump seat, pull up to a bright red cable-spool
table, and feast on wood-roasted lobster,
littlenecks, and bluefish at this cheery open-
air spot. BYOB and sides. 901 Boston Post Rd.
☎ 203/453-9276. Entrees $9–$17. Cash only.
Late Apr to Sept dinner daily, lunch Sat–Sun; Oct
lunch & dinner Fri, Sat & Sun.

The Litchfield Hills

With their pine-clad rises, open fields, clear lakes, and streams, the unspoiled Litchfield Hills are renowned for their beauty. Settled in the mid–18th century, the region has some history: The tony town of Litchfield itself was home to the first law school in the United States. Idyllic village greens, white steepled churches, and stately Colonial houses still dot the landscape. You could spend weeks doing nothing in these bucolic hills, but our 2- to 3-day tour takes you through some of the more picturesque towns and vistas, and includes a drive around a gorgeous, fish-filled lake, a stop in an antiques mecca, and opportunities to hike one of the many trails that crisscross the area.

> *The Kent area offers a variety of hiking options, including at Kent Falls State Park and Bull's Bridge.*

START Kent is 52 miles northwest of Hartford. **TRIP LENGTH** 50 miles.

1 ★★ **Kent.** Kent brims with shops, bookstores, and galleries—and weekending tourists. Visit on a weekday, when the small-town charm is most salient, or embrace the crowds and arrive on a weekend, when more attractions are open. Stop in at the ★ **Sloane-Stanley Museum,** 31 Kent-Cornwall Rd.

(☎ 860/927-3849), to see artist Eric Sloane's cool collection of Early American implements like the dog treadmill/butter churner. Don't leave without sampling the Belgian hot chocolate or unforgettable ice cream at ★★ **Belgique Patisserie,** 1 Bridge St. (☎ 860/927-3681). If you're not in the mood to shop, get outdoors —Kent Falls State Park and Bull's Bridge offer lovely and beginner-friendly trails. ⏱ **2 hr.**

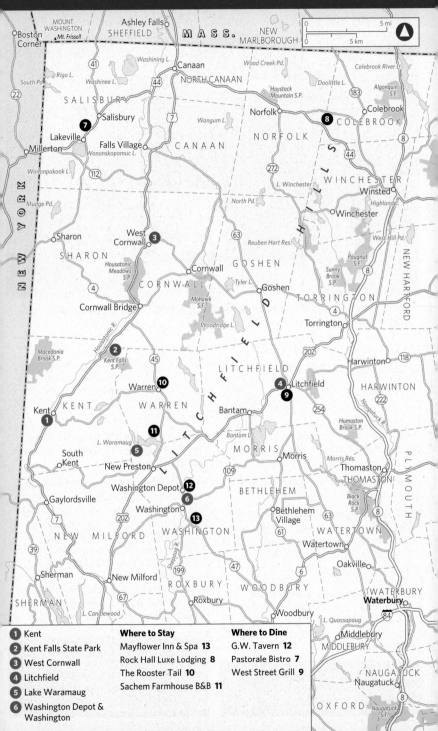

> *The covered bridge in West Cornwall (not to be confused with the town of Cornwall Bridge, nearby) is one of only two in the state still passable by cars.*

Head 4½ miles north out of town on Rte. 7.

2 [kids] **Kent Falls State Park.** If it's a weekday, hike up the steep quarter-mile trail to the top of the 250-foot falls. If you're here on the weekend and don't want to fork over the parking fee, admire the cascade from the road. ⏱ 45 min. 462 Kent-Cornwall Rd., Kent. ☎ 860/927-3238. $15 parking on weekends May–Oct. Daily 8am–sunset.

Continue 9 miles north on Rte. 7 and turn right onto Rte. 128 east, to:

3 ★★ **West Cornwall.** An 1864 red covered bridge, fly fishermen casting in the Housatonic below—the tiny town is almost impossibly picturesque, especially when the foliage is blazing. To explore it, get out of the car and walk. Rare book fans will salivate over the collection at **Barbara Farnsworth Bookseller,** 407 Rte. 128 (☎ 860/672-6571; www.farnsworthbooks.com), while anyone will appreciate the handmade crafts at the **Cornwall**

Bridge Pottery Store, 415 Sharon Goshen Tpk. (☎ 800/501-6545; www.cbpots.com), and the pure lines of the reproduction Shaker furniture at **Ian Ingersoll's** showroom, 422 Sharon Goshen Tpk. (☎ 800/237-4926; www.ianingersoll.com). ⏱ 2 hr.

Continue east onto Rte. 128 and continue onto CT-4E. Go right onto Rte. 63 south, and continue for 6 miles, into:

4 ★★ **Litchfield.** A stagecoach stop on the road between Hartford and New York, Litchfield was thriving by the Revolutionary War. But its golden age came soon after, when local merchants grew rich from the China trade, and lawyer Tapping Reeve founded Litchfield Law School (1784), the first law school in the U.S., attended by such notables as Noah Webster and Aaron Burr. The hands-on museum at **Tapping Reeve House & Law School,** 82 South St. (☎ 860/567-4501;

Hello? Hello?

Cellphone coverage in this area is pretty spotty, so plan accordingly.

Information, Please

Each of these towns has much to recommend it—too much to go into this book, sadly. Check out the indispensable www.litchfieldhills.com for more information.

Antiquing in Woodbury

In the southern fringes of the Litchfield Hills, Woodbury has a well-established reputation as one of the best destinations for top-quality antiques in New England. Though some of the museum-caliber shops are way out of our price range, we love to browse anyway. The town is an easy drive south on Rte. 47, about 20 minutes from Washington. Note that Woodbury isn't walkable, so you'll be driving from shop to shop; call ahead as some stores are open by appointment only. Before you start your hunt, head to **Dottie's Diner,** 740 Main St. (☎ 203/263-2516), purveyors of the state's best donuts. The chocolate-covered cinnamon donuts are heavenly, but the plain cinnamon variety—moist and pillowy in the middle, crispy on the outside—is equally addictive.

Begin at **Black Pearl,** 161 Main St. S. (☎ 203/266-0299), more museum than gallery, with fine art (paintings and sculptures), Asian antiquities, and rare furniture. At **Country Loft,** 557 Main St. S. (☎ 203/266-4500; www.countryloftantiques.com), you'll find oodles of 18th- and 19th-century French furniture, fun kitchen implements, and other objets d'art, as well as an impressive collection of vintage wine accouterments. Friendly **George Champion,** 442 Main St. S. (☎ 203/263-8442; www.georgechampioncompany.com/modernshop), housed in a little white chapel-like building, showcases bold mid-century furniture and decorative objects—a welcome departure from the usual Woodbury antique fare. The **Elemental Garden,** 259 Main St. S. (☎ 203/263-6500; www.theelementalgarden.com) has birdbaths, statuary, sundials, and other enchanting fine garden antiques, mostly from England and France. Sprawling throughout the red barn at **Monique Shay,** 920 Main St. S. (☎ 203/263-3186), is a huge stash of charming French Canadian painted pine and maple cupboards and tables.

> *Tapping Reeve founded Litchfield Law School, the first in America, in 1784.*

www.litchfieldhistoricalsociety.org; $5 adults, $3 kids 14–17), examines what life was like for a student during the school's heyday. Genteel Litchfield has a classic town green, lined with a handful of upscale boutiques, along with some antiques shops. Pop into **Les Plaisirs de la Maison,** 33 West St. (☎ 860/567-2555) for French-country wares. Before leaving town, spend some time at 4,000-acre ★★ kids **White Memorial Conservation Center,** 80 Whitehall Rd. (☎ 860/567-0857; www.whitememorial cc.org; $6 adults, $3 kids 6–12). Visit the nature museum, where you can see a fluorescent rock cave, explore the intriguing art of taxidermy, and feel different animal furs—then take a gentle hike on one of the 35 miles of trails. ⊙ 3 hr.

On the Fly

The Housatonic is one of the best rivers in the country for trout fly-fishing. **Housatonic River Outfitters,** 24 Kent Rd. (☎ 860/672-1010; www.dryflies.com), offers guided wading and boating trips ($150–$350 per person). Just remember, you'll need a fishing license—go to www.ct.gov/dep for information on how to get one.

Return to Rte. 202 and go west 9 miles. Turn right onto Rte. 45 north and then go left onto W. Shore Rd.

5 ★★ **Lake Waramaug.** Sparkling Waramaug—which means "good fishing place"—is great for swimming and boating too. Its tranquillity and surrounding pastoral scenery make for a lovely loop drive, especially in the fall when the golds and reds reflect on the water. From the crossroads hamlet of **New Preston,** follow 45 north (East Shore Rd.), then turn left onto West Shore Road at the lake. Stay on the Shore Roads, which continue to hug the lake. Stop in for a tasting at **Hopkins Vineyard,** 25 Hopkins Rd., Warren (☎ 860/868-7954; www.hopkinsvineyard.com), or a sunset drink on the patio overlooking the lake at the **Hopkins Inn,** 22 Hopkins Rd., New Preston (☎ 860/868-7295; www.thehopkinsinn.com); then continue on to the hamlet of New Preston. ⊙ 2 hr. www.lakewaramaug.com.

Continue on N. Shore Rd. and turn right onto Rte. 45 south. Go left onto Rte. 202 east, and right onto Rte. 47 south.

6 ★ **Washington Depot & Washington.** Tiny Washington Depot has a few shops of interest, among them **the Hickory Stick Bookshop,** 2 Greenhill Rd. (☎ 860/868-0525; www.hickorystickbookshop.com), which has a terrific children's section. A bit farther on, you'll come across one of Connecticut's best-preserved towns. Washington (settled 1734) has a graceful village green surrounded by beautiful white historic buildings, like the 1802 Congregational Meeting House. Visit the kids **Institute for American Indian Studies,** 38 Curtis Rd. (☎ 860/868-0518; www.birdstone.org; admission $5 adults, $3 kids), a small well-curated museum that includes a collection of Native American artifacts and crafts up through the 20th century, and a simulated Algonquian village. ⊙ 2 hr.

Get Out on the Water

Rent a canoe or kayak and paddle down a 10-mile stretch of the Housatonic. ★ **Clarke Outdoors,** 163 Rte. 7, West Cornwall (☎ 860/672-6365; www.clarkeoutdoors.com; 2-person canoe $50–$55, 1-person kayak $30–$30 with life vest) has got you covered.

Where to Stay & Dine

★ [kids] **G.W. Tavern** WASHINGTON DEPOT *AMERICAN* With a cathedral ceiling and a patio overlooking the Shepaug River, the G.W. is an atmospheric stalwart for tasty pub food—fish and chips, pot pie—and a lively (albeit loud) nightlife scene. 20 Bee Brook Rd. ☎ 860/868-6633. www.gwtavern.com. Entrees $11–$32. AE, DISC, MC, V. Lunch & dinner daily.

★★★ **Mayflower Inn & Spa** WASHINGTON This genteel Relais & Château property has gorgeously manicured grounds, a polished Colonial-manor-house decor, and an acclaimed dining room with a top-drawer wine list. But the spa—20,000 square feet of white, stream-lined serenity—is one of the most beautiful in the country. 118 Woodbury Rd. (Rte. 47). ☎ 860/868-9466. www.mayflowerinn.com. 30 units. Doubles $545–$830; suites $875–$1,600 w/ breakfast. AE, MC, V.

★★ **Pastorale Bistro** LAKEVILLE *FRENCH* A convivial, locally loved, converted 1760s Colonial that turns out freshened-up bistro classics and New American specialties in a warm and cozy setting. 223 Main St. ☎ 860/435-1011. www.pastoralebistro.com. Entrees $12–$26. MC, V. Brunch Sun, dinner Tues–Sun.

★★ **Rock Hall Luxe Lodging** COLEBROOK Highly personalized service is one reason this circa-1912 Addison Mizner–designed inn is so special. Others: lavish breakfast with house-cured gravlax; romantic fire pit and outdoor hot tub; and Chamber 2, with fireplace, hand-carved furniture, and original marble enclosed spray shower. 19 Rock Hall Rd. ☎ 860/379-2230. www.19rockhallroad.com. 5 units. Doubles $275–$550 w/breakfast. AE, DISC, MC, V.

★★ **The Rooster Tail** WARREN All six suites at this friendly inn have king-size beds, rainfall showers, heated floors, and flatscreen TVs—for the area, it's unexpectedly luxe. The restaurant serves a fantastic brunch and dinner. 11 Cornwall Rd. ☎ 860/868-3100. www.roostertailinn.com. 6 units. Doubles $295–$550 w/breakfast. AE, MC, V.

★ **Sachem Farmhouse B&B** WARREN This sunny 1870 B&B overlooking Lake Waramaug has four nicely appointed rooms: two with private bathroom, two with shared. All are equipped with antiques and four-poster beds, and come with a farmhouse breakfast using organic eggs from their own hens. 15 Hopkins Rd. ☎ 860/868-0359. www.thesachemfarmhouse.com. 4 units. Doubles $195–$295 w/breakfast. AE, MC, V.

★★ **West Street Grill** LITCHFIELD *CONTEMPORARY* It's more than 20 years old, but this restaurant retains the same Tribeca-in-the-country cachet that has attracted the likes of George Clooney and Mick Jagger. The kitchen excels at such well-prepared creations as chicken faux gras brûlée (with black truffle butter and apricot ginger chutney)—and caramelized scallops. 43 West St. ☎ 860/567-3885. www.weststreetgrill.com. Entrees $14–$38. AE, DISC, MC, V. Lunch & dinner daily.

The Big Splurge

Book a stay at one of the 18 themed cottages at ★★★ **Winvian,** 155 Alain White Rd., Morris (☎ 860/567-9600; www.winvian.com; 19 units; doubles $650–$1,250 a la carte w/ breakfast; $1,250–$1,950 all-inclusive; AE, MC, V). Choose the enchanting two-story treehouse, retrofitted helicopter, or playful Beaver Lodge (our fave, incorporating a reconstructed beaver dam into the ceiling). You'll get posh details such as fireplaces, waterfall tubs, and pebble steam showers, along with superb service and dining.

The Connecticut River Valley

The largest river in New England—dividing the region
from Long Island Sound right up to Canada—the Connecticut was central to travel, trade, and community long before the arrival of the Dutch and English in the 17th century. While the earliest European settlements were mainly agricultural, the region grew to become a preindustrial center for ship making and ivory products, a destination for artists, and even the target of a British occupation in 1814. Today, you'll find a strong sense of this history in the communities that line the southernmost stretch of the river. Plan to spend about 3 days here.

> *Leaf peepers from all over the world stream into the picturesque Connecticut River Valley for fall foliage season.*

START Old Lyme is 42 miles southeast of Hartford. **TRIP LENGTH** 53 miles.

➊ Old Lyme. Dotted with Colonial and federal-era homes, this small town at the mouth of the river is the home of American Impressionism, as celebrated at the ★★★ **Florence Griswold Museum,** 96 Lyme St. (☎ 860/434-5542; www.flogris. org). The pastoral landscape was already attracting artists when Ms. Griswold began taking boarders in the late 1890s, and her house soon became the unofficial home to the Lyme Art Colony. The house is presented much as it was 100 years ago—the highlight is the kitchen, where panels and cupboards are painted with scenes by Henry Ward Ranger, Childe Hassam, and others. The Krieble Gallery shows a large collection of related works. ⏲ 2 hr.

Take I-95S to exit 69 and pick up Rte. 9 north. Take exit 3 to Rte. 154 north, turn left onto Saybrook Rd. and right onto West Rd.

➋ ★★ Essex. Attacked by the British in the War of 1812, and a center for both ship building and the ivory trade, this charming, walkable village is steeped in Colonial and Early American history. Stop by the ★ **kids** **Connecticut River Museum,** 67 Main St. (☎ 860/767-8269; www.ctrivermuseum. org), where you'll see a replica of the first military submarine, affectionately named

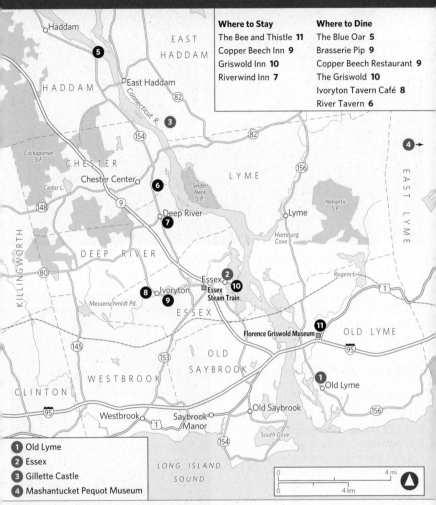

Where to Stay

The Bee and Thistle 11
Copper Beech Inn 9
Griswold Inn 10
Riverwind Inn 7

Where to Dine

The Blue Oar 5
Brasserie Pip 9
Copper Beech Restaurant 9
The Griswold 10
Ivoryton Tavern Café 8
River Tavern 6

1 Old Lyme
2 Essex
3 Gillette Castle
4 Mashantucket Pequot Museum

the "Turtle," and a display of wares—ivory, witch hazel—illuminating the trade that thrived here through the era of the steamboat. Don't miss a drink or dinner at the famous **Griswold Inn** (p. 295). To see more of the surrounding valley, hop on the ★★ **Kids Essex Steam Train and Riverboat,** 1 Railroad Ave. (☎ 860/767-0103; www.essexsteamtrain. com), for a 12-mile chug through farmlands and wetlands. Embarking on the triple-decker, Mississippi River–style paddle boat in Deep River, you'll loop up to East Haddam, as your guide talks about the life of the river and landmarks like **Gillette Castle** (3). ⏱ 4½ hr.

Get back onto Rte. 154, go north for 8¼ miles, and turn right onto Rte. 82 east. Cross the swing bridge and pass the Goodspeed Opera House. After ¾ mile, turn right to stay on Rte. 82. Go right at River Rd.

3 ★ **Gillette Castle, East Haddam.** What is that crumbling edifice on the hillside? William Gillette—the stage actor best known for his definitive portrayal of Sherlock Holmes—allegedly designed this 24-room mansion himself. Based (loosely) on French medieval castles, it contains many questionable inventions, including a system of hidden mirrors for surveillance and a liquor cabinet that confounded all who

> *Sit back and enjoy dinner, murder mystery theater, or simply the view as the crew feeds the boiler on the Essex Steam Train.*

attempted to open it—much to Gillette's delight. ⏱ 1 hr. 67 River Rd. ☎ 860/526-2336. $10 adults, $4 kids 6–12. Castle tours daily 10am–5pm Memorial Day to Columbus Day.

Turn right onto River Rd. (continue to Geer Hill Rd.) and left at Rte. 148 east. Continue onto Rte. 82 and go east for 19 miles. In Norwich, go right onto Water St. and right onto Rte. 2; go 7½ miles east to:

❹ ★★ kids **Mashantucket Pequot Museum, Mashantucket.** From the Native American creation stories to the re-created 16th-century Pequot Village, everything here is detailed and engaging. Highlights include displays of regional wildlife over the millenniums, films on tool creation and culture clash, and a 185-foot observation tower with a panoramic view of the reservation. ⏱ 2½ hr. 110 Pequot Trail. ☎ 800/411-9671. www.pequotmuseum.org. $15 adults, $10 kids 6–15. Wed–Sat 10am–4pm.

Goodspeed Opera House

If you're interested in theater, history, or both, try to catch a show where the original productions of *Annie, Man of La Mancha,* and other classic musicals were performed. Constructed in 1876 by shipping magnate and theater fan William Goodspeed, the Opera House (☎ 860/873-8664; www.goodspeed. org) has never staged an actual opera—but that doesn't make it any less of a blast.

Yes, *That* Lyme

Record of the illness dates back to 1883, but the tick-borne ailment known as **Lyme disease** was named and categorized after a large outbreak among teenagers in the towns of Lyme and Old Lyme in the 1970s. Of course, it's not just a local phenomenon—Lyme disease is the most common vector-borne illness in the U.S.

Where to Stay & Dine

★★ **The Bee and Thistle Inn & Spa** OLD LYME
The grounds are lovely, the rooms—most with four-poster beds, some with fireplaces—well-appointed and romantic, but the on-site restaurant is the star here. 100 Lyme St. ☎ 860/434-1667. www.beeandthistleinn.com. 9 units. Doubles $135–$250 w/breakfast. AE, DISC, MC, V.

kids **The Blue Oar** HADDAM *SEAFOOD*
This is what a meal by the water is all about: Order your lobster roll at the counter, grab one of the picnic benches, and let the river roll by. BYOB. 16 Snyder Rd. ☎ 860/345-2994. Lunch entrees $6–$16; dinner entrees $22–26. Cash only. May–Oct lunch & dinner daily.

★★ **Brasserie Pip** IVORYTON *FRENCH/AMERICAN* The more casual side of Copper Beech—you can get a cheeseburger over here—but every bit as good, thanks to the award-winning chef shared by the two venues. 46 Main St. ☎ 860/767-0330. Entrees $16–$27. AE, DISC, MC, V. Dinner daily.

★★ **Copper Beech Inn** IVORYTON
This inn defines country elegance. We're partial to room no. 105, with its sumptuous red and white color scheme and antique pedestal soak tub. 46 Main St. ☎ 860/767-0330. www.copperbeechinn.com. 22 units. Doubles $175–$375 w/breakfast. AE, DISC, MC, V.

★★★ **Copper Beech Restaurant** IVORYTON
FRENCH/AMERICAN With more than 500 wines on the list and a fantastic locally sourced seasonal menu, the Copper Beech is worth dressing up for—the house-made baguettes have a reputation of their own. 46 Main St. ☎ 860/767-0330. Prix fixe $54. AE, DISC, MC, V. Dinner daily.

★ kids **The Griswold Inn** ESSEX
A historic inn (in operation since 1776) that exudes warmth, the Gris is the centerpiece of Essex. The main building offers classic New England inn rooms, while suites in the annex building provide more space. 36 Main St. ☎ 860/767-1776. www.griswoldinn.com. 30 units. Doubles $100–$370 w/breakfast. AE, DISC, MC, V.

★★ **The Griswold** ESSEX *NEW AMERICAN*
Dining in a converted covered bridge, surrounded by a wall-to-wall collection of

> *The Riverwind Inn was built in 1854 and has been operating as a B&B since 1985.*

maritime art? We're sold already, but The Gris delivers satisfying upscale tavern fare, too. 36 Main St. ☎ 860/767-1776. Entrees $17–$30. AE, MC, V. Lunch & dinner daily.

★ **Ivoryton Tavern Café** IVORYTON *PUB*
The Little Burger might be the largest patty you've ever seen, while the Tavern Burger is enough to emasculate even the toughest carnivore. 8 Summitt St. ☎ 860/767-1449. www.ivorytoninn.com. Entrees $9–$20. AE, DISC, MC, V. Lunch & dinner daily.

★ **Riverwind Inn** DEEP RIVER
With a rustic and homey atmosphere, individually styled rooms, and a full country breakfast served every morning, the Riverwind straddles the line between inn and B&B. Our favorite room is "Willow," on the first floor, with its white-iron and brass bed and private porch. 209 Main St. ☎ 860/526-2014. www.riverwindinn.com. 8 units. Doubles $128–$240 w/breakfast. AE, DISC, MC, V.

★★ **River Tavern** CHESTER *NEW AMERICAN*
Make the drive to adorable Chester for the warm and jovial atmosphere here—and for the daily menu of creative dishes such as Kungpao Stonington Monkfish. 23 Main St. ☎ 860/526-9417. www.rivertavernchester.net. Entrees $26–$32. AE, DISC, MC, V. Lunch & dinner daily.

Hartford

We'll be honest: Hartford isn't the most exciting city,
and a surprisingly high crime rate doesn't raise its appeal (downtown is one of the safer areas, but be aware). It is, however, one of the country's oldest cities, and full of history. It's home to the first public art museum and the first park paid for with public funds. The *Hartford Courant* (1764), the country's oldest continuously published newspaper, actually predates the U.S. itself. Perhaps most significantly, the Fundamental Orders document, inspired by a sermon given by colony founder Thomas Hooker and ratified in 1639, is seen by many as the forerunner to the U.S. Constitution, earning the state its nickname. You'll be impressed by the culture the city has to offer. You can hit all the sites on this tour in 2 days.

> A painting of George Washington by presidential portraitist Gilbert Stuart hangs in the Old State House's Senate chamber.

START **Wethersfield** is 7 miles west of Hartford. TRIP LENGTH 7 miles.

❶ ★ **Webb-Deane-Stevens Museum, Wethersfield.** It's tough to stand out as a historic home in a town where more than 300 of them line the streets. But each of the three National Historic Landmarks that make up this museum has an intriguing story: one was George Washington's temporary headquarters, the second was home of our country's first diplomat, and the third was a middle-class house of the early 19th century. ⏱ 1½ hr. 211 Main St. ☎ 860/529-0612. www. webb-deane-stevens.org. $8 adults, $4 kids 5-18. May–Oct Mon and Wed–Sat 10am–4pm, Sun 1–4pm; April & Nov weekends only; Dec Mon–Sat 10am–4pm, Sun 1–4pm.

Head north on Main St. (past the church) and turn right onto Hart St., follow it to the right, and go left at Great Meadow Rd. Pick up I-91N and take exit 32B onto Trumbull St. Turn left onto Morgan St. and right onto Main St.

❷ kids **Old State House.** One of the oldest state houses in the country, this restored 1796 Federal-style building was the site of the first hearings for the *Amistad* trial (see box on p. 298). Today, you can tour the legislative chambers and peek into the peculiar Museum of Natural and Other Curiosities (two-headed calf anybody?), a re-creation of one that was here 200 years ago. Down in the basement is an extensive, kid-friendly exhibit on the history of Hartford. ⏱ 1 hr. 800 Main St.

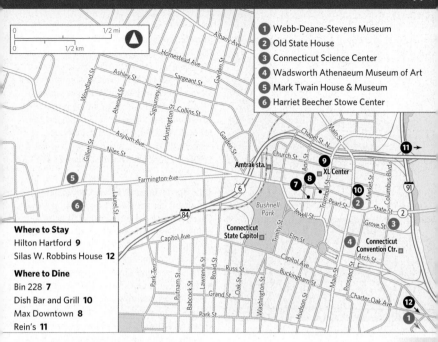

1 Webb-Deane-Stevens Museum
2 Old State House
3 Connecticut Science Center
4 Wadsworth Athenaeum Museum of Art
5 Mark Twain House & Museum
6 Harriet Beecher Stowe Center

Where to Stay

Hilton Hartford **9**
Silas W. Robbins House **12**

Where to Dine

Bin 228 **7**
Dish Bar and Grill **10**
Max Downtown **8**
Rein's **11**

☎ 860/522-6766. www.ctosh.org. $6 adults, $3 kids 6-17. July 4 to Columbus Day Tues–Sat 10am–5pm; Columbus Day to July 4 Mon–Fri 10am–5pm.

3 ★★ kids **Connecticut Science Center.** Opened in 2009, this excellent recent addition to downtown Hartford—in a dazzling, modern (and green) building—is reason enough to visit the city. Featuring 150 highly interactive

> The Webb-Deane-Stevens Museum took painstaking care with restoration of the three houses.

For Better or For Worse

While this historic city contributed significantly to America's founding with its proto constitution, it also played a large role in the secessionist movement of 1814. The New England Federalists objected strenuously to the policies of Presidents Jefferson and Madison, coming to a head with the War of 1812. A convention of New England delegates was called to Hartford, eventually compromising to bring proposed constitutional amendments to Washington. Many Americans saw their threat of secession as tantamount to treason, striking a blow to the popularity of the Federalist Party, which soon dissolved.

> *Twain purchased the oak mantel in his library from Ayton Castle in Scotland.*

exhibits, covering topics from forensics to sports to space travel, the museum is great fun: We love the multisensory Sight and Sound Experience, where you can dance in a light chamber to create sound, and Hurricane Force, which simulates 78 mph category 1 winds. The 3-D film theater is state-of-the-art. ⏱ 2 hr. 250 Columbus Blvd. ☎ 860/SCIENCE (724-3623). www.ctsciencecenter.org. $17 adults, $14 kids 3–17; movies extra. Tues–Sun & select Mon 10am–5pm.

4 ★★ **Wadsworth Athenaeum Museum of Art.** The oldest public art museum in the United States—with impressive holdings of Hudson River School paintings originally belonging to Daniel Wadsworth (he was a wealthy patron of Thomas Cole)—this was also the first American museum to acquire surrealist art. The collection features Picasso, Monet, Warhol, Klimt, Giacometti, Avery, and LeWitt. ⏱ 2 hr. 600 Main St. ☎ 860/838-4161. www.wadsworthatheneum.org. $5 adults, free for kids 13 & under. Wed–Fri 11am–5pm; Sat–Sun 10am–5pm.

5 ★ **Mark Twain House & Museum.** From 1874 to 1891, Samuel Clemens made his home—and wrote his most significant works—in this 25-room Gothic house, one of the state's most famous attractions. Walk past the Tiffany silver stenciling on the wainscoting in the entrance hall, note the books in the library where he told stories to his children and read new works to friends, and visit the billiard room, where the writing happened. ⏱ 1 hr. 351 Farmington Ave. ☎ 860/247-0998. www.marktwainhouse.org. Admission $15 adults, $9 kids 6–16. Mon–Sat 9:30am–5:30pm; Sun noon–5:30pm. Closed Tues Jan–Mar.

6 ★ **Harriet Beecher Stowe Center.** Best known for her antislavery book, *Uncle Tom's Cabin,* Stowe lived in this house from 1872 until her death in 1896. Much of what you see belonged to her or her family, including her own oil and watercolor works, and a large collection of materials from both the abolitionist-activist Beecher family and the Stowe family, collected by Stowe's grandniece and center founder Katherine Seymour Day. ⏱ 1 hr. 77 Forest St. ☎ 860/522-9258. www.harrietbeecherstowecenter.org. $9 adults, $6 kids 5–16. June–Oct Tues–Sat 9:30am–4:30pm, Sun noon–4:30pm; Nov–May Wed–Sat 9:30am–4:30pm, Sun noon–4:30pm.

The *Amistad*

In June of 1839, the Spanish schooner *Amistad* left Havana, Cuba, with a cargo of some 50 kidnapped and enslaved Africans. Three days into the journey, a revolt led by Senge Pieh left both the captain and the cook dead, and 2 months later the troubled ship ended up at Montauk Point, New York. Jailed in New Haven for piracy and murder, the Africans were assisted by local abolitionists during hearings in Hartford. The U.S. District Court determined they were fraudulently bought and sold as native Cuban slaves, but President Martin Van Buren, facing heat from pro-slavery constituents—and from Spain, who requested extradition—appealed the decision. Former president John Quincy Adams, who hadn't argued a case in more than 30 years, defended the Africans in front of the U.S. Supreme Court, which upheld the ruling, returning them to Sierra Leone in late 1841.

Where to Stay & Dine

★★ **Bin 228** HARTFORD *WINE BAR*
This low-lit, sophisticated wine bar, featuring an all-Italian wine list, panini such as sopressatta and fontina, and small plates like Gorgonzola-stuffed dates, makes for a great date night. 228 Pearl St. ☎ 860/244-9463. www.thebin228.com. Entrees $8–$12. AE, DISC, MC, V. Lunch & dinner Mon–Sat.

★ **Dish Bar & Grill** HARTFORD *NEW AMERICAN*
With a sleek atmosphere attracting an after-work crowd, Dish turns out modern twists on comfort food like trio of tuna, Maine lobster pot pie, and Cuban braised pork shank. 900 Main St. ☎ 860/249-3474. www.dishbarandgrill.com. Entrees $17–$38. AE, DISC, MC, V. Lunch Mon–Fri, dinner daily.

kids **Hilton Hartford** HARTFORD
A well-kept, dependable choice for staying downtown—theaters and many restaurants are an easy walk down Trumbull Street. Parking in the lot is pricey, but par for the course in Hartford. 315 Trumbull St. ☎ 860/728-5151. www.hilton.com. 404 units. Doubles $119–$269. AE, DISC, MC, V.

★★★ **Max Downtown** HARTFORD *CHOPHOUSE*
If you're dressing up for a special meal, dine here. While you can order the Arborio-crusted ahi tuna, steaks are the main event here—from classic strips to the rosemary-Parmesan-crusted veal porterhouse. 185 Asylum St. ☎ 860/522-2530. Entrees $23–$37. AE, DISC, MC, V. Lunch Mon–Fri, dinner daily.

Tragedy at the Circus

In 1944, the Ringling Brothers, Barnum & Bailey Circus was in Hartford entertaining a crowd of thousands when the canvas tent—waterproofed with paraffin and gasoline—caught fire, raining flames on trapped spectators as the poles collapsed. The death toll of 168, with countless others injured, is one of the most deadly fires in U.S. history. Circus officials went to prison for negligence, but nobody was ever charged with starting the fire.

> *The well-appointed parlor of the Silas W. Robbins House.*

★ **Rein's** VERNON *DELI*
This semilegendary stop off the I-84 draws travelers and locals alike with it's "way-off-Broadway" Reubens and buckets of pickles. Be prepared to wait, or order ahead—it's always busy, but the ever-friendly staff keeps the traffic moving. 435 Hartford Tpk., Vernon. ☎ 860/875-1344. www.reinsdeli.com. Entrees $5–$13 AE, DISC, MC, V. Breakfast, lunch & dinner daily.

★★★ **Silas W. Robbins House** WETHERSFIELD
Sitting on 2 beautiful acres in the largest historic district in Connecticut, this 1873 Second Empire–style stunner opened in 2008 after 6 years of painstaking restoration following a 1996 fire. Guest rooms and public spaces—parlor, den, tearoom, and dining room—are exquisitely decorated in Victorian fashion; guest rooms have flatscreen TVs. 185 Broad St., Wethersfield. ☎ 860/571-8733. www.silaswrobbins.com. 5 units. Doubles $195–$325 w/ breakfast. AE, DISC, MC, V.

New Haven

The second-largest city in Connecticut means two things to most people: Yale and pizza. Not necessarily in that order. But the Elm City—nicknamed for its 19th-century public tree-planting program—has some intriguing history. Settled in 1637 by an English Puritan community, the colony grew into a port for trade with Asia and the West Indies. Later, Yale grad Eli Whitney built a factory here to manufacture his groundbreaking cotton gin (patented 1794). In the post–Civil War era, the city also pumped out locks, clocks, and Winchester rifles. By the 1950s, however, the city fell on hard times—like Hartford, Bridgeport, and others facing mass exodus to the suburbs. Today, it still struggles, though the neighborhoods around Yale are enjoying a resurgence—with edgy shops, farm-to-table eateries, and stylish cafes—thanks to ongoing revitalization efforts. Plan to spend 1 day here.

> If someone says he went to school in New Haven, you know he means Yale.

START New Haven is 40 miles from Hartford.

1 ★★ **Yale University Art Gallery.** Housed in the first building commissioned to architect Louis Kahn, this three-story museum contains more than 187,000 pieces. The collection ranges from ancient Greek and Roman artifacts and African masks to a European collection with works by Fra Angelico and Rubens, and modern gems such as Van Gogh's *The Night Café*, as well as work by Basquiat, Rothko, Mondrian, and Richter. ⏱ 2 hr. 1111 Chapel St. ☎ 203/432-9658. artgallery.yale.edu. Free admission. Tues–Sat 10am–5pm (Thurs until 8pm Sep–June), Sun 1–6pm.

2 ★★ **Yale Center for British Art.** Founded by noted philanthropist Paul Mellon—who also donated countless works to the National Gallery in Washington, D.C.—this extraordinary museum holds the most important collection of British art outside the U.K. Turner, Constable, and Gainsborough landscapes are well represented, as are portraits by William Hogarth and Joshua Reynolds. The glass and matte-steel structure—the first museum building to include retail shops by design—is the last completed work by Louis Kahn. ⏱ 1½ hr. 1080 Chapel St. ☎ 203/432-2800. ycba.yale.edu. Free admission. Tues–Sat 10am–5pm; Sun noon–5pm.

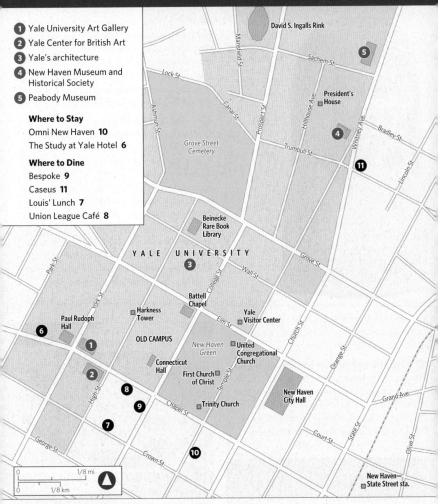

David S. Ingalls Rink

President's House

Grove Street Cemetery

Beinecke Rare Book Library

YALE UNIVERSITY

3

Battell Chapel

Harkness Tower

Yale Visitor Center

Paul Rudoph Hall

6

OLD CAMPUS

New Haven Green

United Congregational Church

Connecticut Hall

First Church of Christ

Trinity Church

New Haven City Hall

New Haven— State Street sta.

0   1/8 mi
0   1/8 km

3 Yale's architecture. Founded in 1701, the third-oldest university in the U.S. spreads across 310 acres on the central campus alone, with more than 250 buildings spanning an array of architectural styles. You've already been to two of them—head next to **Connecticut Hall.** This 1757 Georgian building is the second structure built for the school, and the oldest still standing. Gothic styles dominate much of the campus; at 216 feet (1 ft. for every year of the school's existence at the time it was built), the Collegiate Gothic **Harkness Tower** from 1921 is an easy one to find. **Battel Chapel,** dating to 1876, was erected as a Civil War memorial; its High Victorian

Gothic features include Tiffany windows and a largely solid oak interior. Built in 1963, Gordon Bunshaft's six-floor **Beinecke Rare Book Library**—one of the largest buildings in the world dedicated to rare books—has big square panels of translucent marble in place of windows, allowing only indirect, filtered sunlight inside. The 1963 **Paul Rudolph Hall** (originally the Yale Art and Architecture Building) is an early and excellent example of the Brutalism School (from the French *beton brut,* referring to the raw concrete often used in this style), and incorporates 37 levels in its nine stories. Finally, the **David S. Ingalls Rink**—nicknamed "the Yale whale" for its distinctive swooping

> *The Yale Peabody Museum's extensive and eclectic collection includes some fascinating Egyptian artifacts.*

of artist and inventor Samuel F. B. Morse. The small room upstairs chronicles the story of the *Amistad* (p. 298)—the triangle trade, the mutiny, the trials, and the resulting social implications. ⏱ 45 min. 114 Whitney Ave. ☎ 203/562-4183. www.newhavenmuseum.org. $4 adults, $2 kids 12–18. Tues–Fri 10am–5pm; Sat noon–5pm.

⑤ ★★ kids Peabody Museum. Established in 1866 with a gift from proto-philanthropist George Peabody, Yale's mineral collection soon gave way to a focus on the interests of Peabody's nephew—founder, director, and paleontologist O. C. Marsh. Dinosaurs still figure prominently, from the mounted apatosaurus skeleton in the great hall to the new torosaurus sculpture outside. Don't miss the bird collection, as well as the famous North American habitat dioramas. ⏱ 2½ hr. 170 Whitney Ave. ☎ 203/432-3775. www.peabody.yale.edu. $7 adults, $5 kids 3–18. Mon–Sat 10am–5pm; Sun noon–5pm.

shape—was completed in 1958 by architect Eero Saarinen, designer of the Gateway Arch in St. Louis. ⏱ 1 hr.

④ ★ New Haven Museum and Historical Society. Stop here for a concise history of the city, from its origins as a Puritan utopia, through industrialization, and into the 20th century. Displays include a cotton gin manufactured in 1803 by Eli Whitney, and assorted creations

Puritan Utopia

In 1638, English clergyman John Davenport and wealthy merchant Theophilus Eaton led a group of Puritans from Massachusetts to the bay of New Haven, where they set out not only to establish "a new Utopia," governed by the Bible, but also to build a prosperous port. The citizens agreed to strictly follow Scriptures and not English law, going so far as to abolish juries. They also laid out a grid of eight streets and nine squares, with the town common in the center—thus creating the country's first planned city. Though the colony expanded over the next few years, they were soon overshadowed by Boston and New York, and in 1664 the experiment in independence ended when the colony merged with the Connecticut colony.

A-beets, with Mutz (trans. Pizza, with Mozzarella)

Frank Pepe, 157 Wooster St. (☎ 203/865-5762), who opened his pizzeria in 1925, is regarded as the inventor of New Haven-style pizza: crispy thin crust with tomato sauce, garlic, oregano, and grated Romano—no mozzarella. His white clam pie later became a signature. Local contenders have their fans, too: **Sally's Apizza,** 237 Wooster St. (☎ 203/624-5271), is the Red Sox to Pepe's Yankees; **Modern Apizza,** 874 State St. (☎ 203/776-5306), is another favorite; and **The Spot,** 163 Wooster St. (☎ 203/865-7602), is an annex of Pepe's. Whichever pie you choose, be sure to wash it down with a local Foxon Park soda.

Where to Stay & Dine

★★ Bespoke ECLECTIC

One of New Haven's most happening restaurants, Bespoke turns out inspired farm-to-table cuisine in a stylish stone-and-brick setting. Start with the grilled merguez sausage, and move on to the northern steamed clams with chorizo in lobster ginger broth or coffee-cured hanger steak with roasted peppers and cocoa nibs. 266 College St. ☎ 203/562-4644. www.bespoke newhaven.com. Entrees $24–$27. AE, MC, V. Lunch Fri–Sat, dinner Mon–Sat, brunch Sun.

★ Caseus FROMAGERIE/BISTRO

This cozy bistro and wine bar—all brick walls and stone tiles—is indeed cheese heaven, with an over-the-top mac 'n' cheese and even a standout *poutine*. (Now it operates a food truck specializing in gourmet grilled cheese; follow them on www.thecheesetruck.com.) A nice wine selection and two taps of rotating microbrews balance the palate. 93 Whitney Ave. ☎ 203/624-3373. www.casseusnewhaven. com. Entrees $11–$24. DISC, MC, V. Lunch Mon–Sat, dinner Wed–Sat.

★ kids Louis' Lunch BURGERS

Some would have you believe that this local fave, established in 1895, invented the hamburger (sandwich). Have a seat for lunch, enjoy the trad pub atmosphere, and leave the details to the historians. 263 Crown St. ☎ 203/562-5507. www.louislunch.com. Burgers $5. Cash only. Lunch Tues & Wed; lunch & dinner Thurs-Sat; closed in August.

★ kids Omni New Haven

The perennial choice of visiting families and academics, with classic color schemes warming up the business modern decor. Ask for a room that overlooks the university campus. 155 Temple St. ☎ 203/772-6664. www.omni hotels.com. 305 units. Doubles $159–$309. AE, DISC, MC, V.

★★ The Study at Yale Hotel

We like the King Study rooms at this sleek and stylish boutique hotel for the extra space (a den), on top of touches like Bose stereos, Frette linens, and blackout shades. The 24-hour cafe doesn't hurt, either. 1157 Chapel St.

> *The Union League Café's Beaux Arts-style dining room is as impressive as the terrific French cuisine.*

☎ 203/503-3900. www.studyhotels.com. 124 units. Doubles $159–$459. AE, DISC, MC, V.

★★★ Union League Café FRENCH

This upscale brasserie, consistently ranked among the state's best, is the place to go for the city's most exquisite food and wine, highly professional service, and relaxed, yet unstuffy ambience. If time is tight, consider having your *canard aux navets* at the bar. 1032 Chapel St. ☎ 203/562-4299. www.unionleaguecafe.com. Entrees $22–$32. AE, MC, V. Lunch Mon–Fri, dinner Mon–Sat.

Our Favorite Rhode Island Moments

Little Rhody traces its independent streak to 1636, when founder and preacher Roger Williams insisted on the separation of church and state in his new settlement, Providence, now the capital. The first colony to renounce allegiance to Great Britain, it was the last to ratify the U.S. Constitution, holding out for the inclusion of the Bill of Rights. Though it's the tiniest in the union, the Ocean State has a seemingly endless supply of beautiful coastline. Rhode Island may not draw crowds the way Cape Cod does, but that's all the better for those who decide to pay a visit.

> PREVIOUS PAGE *The opulent ballroom of William Vanderbilt's Marble House, Newport.*
> THIS PAGE *The carousel at Watch Hill.*

1 Hiking on Block Island. Lovely Block Island has an abundance of nature trails thanks to the fact that nearly half of its land is protected. You can cross meadows laced with milkweed, wander through wood- and shrub land, and circle sparkling ponds enlivened by butterflies and buzzing dragonflies. The beautiful glacier-dug depression that is **Rodman's Hollow** (p. 320, **1**) is delicious in the spring when the shadbush blooms. In the fall, migrating songbirds abound on the wind-whipped **Clayhead Trail** (p. 323, **6**). See p. 320.

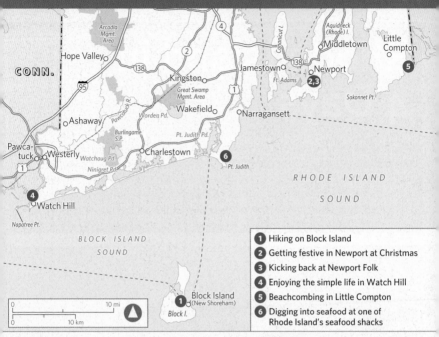

1 Hiking on Block Island
2 Getting festive in Newport at Christmas
3 Kicking back at Newport Folk
4 Enjoying the simple life in Watch Hill
5 Beachcombing in Little Compton
6 Digging into seafood at one of Rhode Island's seafood shacks

2 Getting festive in Newport at Christmas. For the entire month of December, elegant Newport becomes a holiday wonderland. The harbor and streets are strung with white lights setting the whole town aglow, and the festive spirit is infectious. Best of all, eternally glamorous coastal mansions such as **The Breakers** (p. 331, **7**), **Marble House** (p. 331, **9**), and **The Elms** (p. 330, **6**) are festooned with poinsettias, wreaths, and gold ornaments galore, creating dazzling Yuletide displays. See p. 326.

3 Kicking back at Newport Folk. While we've long since traded the pure exhilaration of outdoor music festivals for the more intimate pleasures of club performances, we make an exception for the legendary Newport Folk Festival. More than 50 years after its debut, the festival is still surprising, thanks in large part to its very broad definition of folk music (recent performers include the Low Anthem and Sharon Jones and the Dap Kings). The backdrop for these performances is a stunning view of Newport Harbor. See p. 333.

4 Enjoying the simple life in Watch Hill. Secluded Watch Hill may be home to elegant Victorian mansions, but the vibe in the little sea-sprayed hamlet on the Atlantic is decidedly mellow. The teeny main street has just a few boutiques and a restaurant or two, and there is very little to explore besides a lighthouse, beaches, and a carousel that dates back to 1876. But, really, what else do you need? Be sure to visit the splendid **Ocean House** (p. 319) for a sunset cocktail on the porch. See p. 318, **4**.

5 Beachcombing in Little Compton. The drive to and through laid-back Little Compton—with its hayfields, stone walls, and white picket fences—is memorable in and of itself. While it's only 45 minutes from Newport, this bucolic coastal town feels worlds away from the rest of Rhode Island, with beaches less discovered and trod upon. **Pebbly Goosewing Beach Preserve,** one of the most serene and pristine stretches of beach in Rhode Island, is a wonderful place to walk, regardless of the season. See p. 328.

6 Digging into seafood at one of Rhode Island's seafood shacks. Little Rhody is a top contender for some of the best old-school seafood in the nation. By old-school, we basically mean fried, and we especially recommend clam cakes cooked this way—from Newport's **Flo's Clam Shack** (p. 335) or Narragansett's **Aunt Carrie's** (p. 319). Both these legendary eateries are essential stops on any Rhode Island tour.

Rhode Island in 4 Days

If you have 4 days to explore the Ocean State, we recommend focusing on the two areas that draw the most interest: Newport and Block Island, both seaside cities, yet completely distinct from one another. Newport, with its mansions, Colonial and maritime history, beaches, and boats, is all about abundance. Block Island, on the other hand, is for getting away from it all and relaxing—even if your idea of taking it easy involves a lot of walking or cycling.

> *Rough Point, the Gothic-Tudor estate of generous but troubled tobacco heiress Doris Duke, was opened to the public in 2000.*

START Newport is 30 miles from Providence.
TRIP LENGTH 40 miles.

1 ★★★ **Newport Mansions.** There is no better way to begin your time in Rhode Island than in Newport, and no better way to begin your time in Newport than with a drive down Bellevue Avenue to explore these massive monuments to the spoils of the Gilded Age. Start at the appropriately imposing **The Elms** (p. 330, **6**), from 1901, and then head to the

distinctive **Chateau-sur-Mer** (p. ###) built some 50 years earlier, to contrast construction from the beginning and end of this era. Next, make your way to Doris Duke's magnificent **Rough Point** (p. 331, **8**), and conclude with William Vanderbilt's unrestrained grandiosity at **Marble House** (p. 331, **9**). ⏱ 6 hr.

2 ★ **Cliff Walk, Newport.** Finish your afternoon with a stroll high up along the bluffs on the southeast of the city, with the majesty

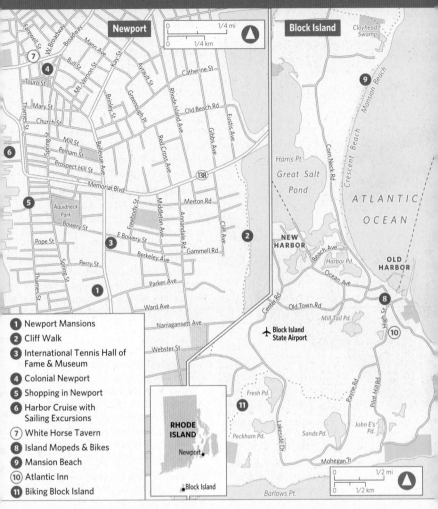

Newport

Block Island

0   1/4 mi
0   1/4 km

Clayhead Swamp

Farewell St.
W. Broadway
Broadway
Mann Ave.
Kay St.
Catherine St.
7
4
Mt. Vernon St.
Bull St.
Ayrault St.
Touro St.
Binney St.
Greenough Pl.
Rhode Island Ave.
Old Beach Rd.
Eustis Ave.
Mary St.
Church St.
Gibbs Ave.
Thames St.
Mill St.
Spring St.
Pelham St.
Bellevue Ave.
6
Red Cross Ave.
138
Prospect Hill St.
Memorial Blvd.
Merton Rd.
5
Aquidneck Park
Freebody St.
Middleton Ave.
Annandale Rd.
Cliff Ave.
Bowery St.
E. Bowery St.
3
Gammell Rd.
2
Pope St.
Berkeley Ave.
Perry St.
Spring St.
Thames St.
Parker Ave.
1
Ward Ave.
Narragansett Ave.
Webster St.

9

Harris Pt.
Great Salt Pond

Corn Neck Rd.
Crescent Beach
Mansion Beach

ATLANTIC OCEAN

NEW HARBOR
Beach Ave.
Harbor Pd.
Ocean Ave.

OLD HARBOR

Center Rd.
Old Town Rd.
Mill Tail Pd.
8
High St.
10

✈ **Block Island State Airport**

Fresh Pd.
11
Peckham Pd.
Lakeside Dr.
Sands Pd.
Payne Rd.
Pilot Hill Rd.
John E's Pd.
Mohegan Tr.

0   1/2 mi
0   1/2 km

Barlows Pt.

RHODE ISLAND
Newport ●
Block Island ●

1. Newport Mansions
2. Cliff Walk
3. International Tennis Hall of Fame & Museum
4. Colonial Newport
5. Shopping in Newport
6. Harbor Cruise with Sailing Excursions
7. White Horse Tavern
8. Island Mopeds & Bikes
9. Mansion Beach
10. Atlantic Inn
11. Biking Block Island

of the mansions to the west and the waves crashing below. The entire stretch is some 3½ miles, but you'll be forgiven if you don't walk a complete 7-mile round-trip. While you can access the walk from several points, parking is scarce unless you start up by Memorial Avenue, where you can find a spot by Easton's Beach. ⏱ 1 hr. See p. 328, **4**.

Spend the night in Newport, and start Day 2 with a visit to:

3 **International Tennis Hall of Fame and Museum, Newport.** Start your day with a visit to this tribute to the history of the game. It's housed in the former Newport Casino, a grand, storied

Victorian-era social club designed by prominent American architects McKim, Mead & White. The museum is so beautiful—with its dark wooden shingles, elegant clock tower, arcaded galleries, and gorgeous latticework—that even non–tennis fans will enjoy it here. ⏱ 1½ hr. See p. 332, **11**.

4 ★ **Colonial Newport.** You can soak up a lot of atmosphere just by strolling these well-preserved streets, but the Newport Historical Society's **Discover Colonial Newport Inside & Out** guided tour will provide deeper insight into the area's fascinating history. Hear the stories about the communities that shared this neighborhood—from the Puritan exiles

> *The relatively quiet Mansion Beach on Block Island.*

who settled here in 1638 to the Jews, Quakers, and others who soon followed—struggling with religious differences, zealously defying English rule, and coming together to keep the burgeoning port town vital. ⏱ 2 hr. Brick Market Museum, 127 Thames St. ☎ 401/841-8770. www.newporthistorytours.org. Admission $12 adults, $5 kids 12 & under. Jun–Oct Mon–Sat 10:30am, Sun 11:30am; Apr–May & Nov Sat 10:30am only.

⑤ **Shopping in Newport.** Lower Thames Street (below Memorial Ave.) brims with charming storefronts and small boutiques. We love the **Newport Restoration Foundation Store,** 415

Thames St. (☎ 401/324-6111), for its well-edited selection of jewelry and gifts; and cute **Cabbage Rose,** 493 Thames St. (☎ 401/846-7006), stands out for its up-to-the-minute women's clothing retailers, such as Juicy Couture. Browse the masterly handblown glass vases at **Thames Glass,** 688 Thames St. (☎ 401/846-0576), and check out **Island Outfitters,** 473 Thames St. (☎ 410/848-9215), if you're looking for clothing and accessories by Lily Pulitzer and other classic New England resort-wear designers. ⏱ 2 hr.

⑥ ★ **Harbor Cruise with Sailing Excursions, Newport.** There are many ways to get out on the water in Newport, but we suggest you set sail aboard the *Adirondack II,* an 80-foot wooden-hulled, turn-of-the-century-style schooner. The cruise will give you a view of the city's port from afar, where you'll see bayside mansions, lighthouses, and Fort Adams—a 19th-century military post that is now home to the Newport Folk and Jazz Festivals. ⏱ 1½ hr. See p. 333, ⑫.

⑦ 🍽 ★★ **White Horse Tavern, Newport.** Newport abounds with excellent dining options (p. 335), but a stop at this historic spot should be mandatory. Dating back to 1652, the White Horse maintains its Colonial-era atmosphere with wide-plank floors, low-beamed ceilings, and blazing fireplace. 26 Marlborough St. ☎ 401/849-3600. $$$. See p. 355.

Start early on Day 3 to catch the 9:15am ferry to Block Island (p. 320). Once you arrive, head up Water St. to:

⑧ **Island Mopeds & Bikes, Block Island.** Bikes are by far the best way to get around the island, so head here to gear up for your stay. 41 Water St. ☎ 401/741-2329; www.biomopeds.com.

Drop your bags at your hotel, where you'll be spending the next 2 nights, and head for:

⑨ ★★ **Mansion Beach, Block Island.** After Newport's relatively bustling itinerary, you'll probably want some time to relax, and this is a great place to do it. Sure, there are plenty of sandy expanses to choose from on Block Island, but we prefer the pleasantly secluded Mansion: It's got towering granite cliffs above, soft white sand, and waves just right for body surfing.

> *Two wheels are the best way to get around on compact (7 miles long and 3 miles wide) Block Island.*

Take a left on Corn Neck Rd. and head into town. There, turn left onto Dodge St. and continue on to Water St. before turning right onto High St.

---

⑩ 🍸 ★★ **Atlantic Inn, Block Island.** Wrap up your day at this perennial favorite for a late-afternoon-into-sunset cocktail. Be sure to grab a chair out on the lawn. See p. 324.

On Day 4, climb aboard your bike and head west on West Side Rd. for a morning drive.

⑪ ★★ **Biking Block Island.** Ready to get rolling? The best way—frankly, the only way—to see much of this beautiful island is on two wheels, and we don't mean scooters. Bicycles afford you access to dirt roads and other paths

that are off-limits to cars, and you'll move along at a slower pace that allows you to appreciate your surroundings all the more. The loop around the island consists of 8½ gentle miles, easy enough even for novice bikers. Starting at **Payne's Killer Donuts** (see "Sweet Spot," p. 323), near Payne's Harbor View Inn, grab a fresh donut and head west on West Side Road, continuing onto Cooneymus Road. Stop at **Rodman's Hollow** (p. 320, ❶) for a short hike, and head on to **Mohegan Bluffs** (p. 322, ❷), 150 feet up from the crashing surf. Finish up the loop by continuing onto Spring Street and back into town. The trip will take most of your morning, but your afternoon is free, so take your time—bask on a beach, linger in town, or simply coast along at your own pace. ⏱ 3–4 hr. to bike the loop.

Rhode Island in 1 Week

With a week in Rhode Island, you can comfortably explore two cities, Block Island, and a bit of South County. A cultural melting pot, the state capital of Providence—Rhode Island's original Colonial settlement—grew into a big city during the Industrial Revolution. The state's other Colonial harbor, Newport, stayed close to its maritime roots, becoming a summer resort that defined the extravagance of the Gilded Age. To help you wind down before returning home, low-key South County and delightful Block Island deliver on the promise of the Ocean State, with plenty of beachfront.

> The art museum at the Rhode Island School of Design (RISD, pronounced riz-dee).

START Providence is 50 miles from Boston, MA. **TRIP LENGTH** 132 miles.

1 Providence. Your first stop in this historic capital city should be the ★★ **John Brown House** (p. 340, **2**). Pronounced by sixth U.S. president John Quincy Adams "the most magnificent and elegant private mansion that I have seen on this continent," this Georgian house was built in 1788 for prominent businessman John Brown. It hosted no fewer than four of America's first six presidents; by the early 20th century, then-owner and transportation titan Marsden Perry had added modern innovations such as the side jet shower and Otis elevator. The guides present the history and development of Providence through the lives of those who occupied this historic mansion. When you're finished, stroll north on Benefit Street to take in the Colonial-era homes along the ★ **Mile of History** before heading for the ★★ **RISD Museum of Art** (p. 341, **4**). Step into the French blue Grand Gallery and take in the salonlike exhibition of European paintings from the Renaissance through the 19th century. However

Where to Stay & Dine

For hotels and restaurants in Providence, see p. 344; in Newport, see p. 334; on Block Island, see p. 324; in South County, see p. 319.

Webster
L. Chaubunagungamaug
(Webster L.)
395
Slatersville
Woonsocket
Pascoag
Buck Hill
Mgmt. Area
102
Pascoag Res.
Chepachet
44
Greenville
295
North Scituate
Johnston
Scituate Res.
6
Danielson
Foster
Cranston
Moosup
West
Warwick
Coventry
Warwick
East
Greenwich
4
Arcadia
Mgmt.
Area
102
Voluntown
Exeter
Wickford
95
Hope Valley
138
Kingston
2
Ashaway
Great Swamp
Mgmt. Area
1
Wakefield
Pawca-
tuck
Westerly
Charlestown
4
1
Watchaug Pd.
Burlingame
S.P.
Ninigret Pd.
Pt. Judith Pd.
5
Watch Hill
Napatree Pt.

Foxborough
Mansfield
1
Easton
95
Diamond Hill
Res.
Cumberland Hill
Norton Res.
Manville
Norton
495
Valley
Falls
Attleboro
Lonsdale
Central Falls
Taunton
146
Pawtucket
44
Centredale
MASSACHUSETTS
1 PROVIDENCE
East Providence
138
10
Seekonk
Somerset
195
Barrington
T.F. Green
Warren
Watuppa Pd.
NARRAGANSETT BAY
114
Mt.-Hope
Bay
Bristol
Fall River
24
Prudence I.
Tiverton
Portsmouth
Sakonnet R.
Conanicut I.
Aquidneck
(Rhode) I.
Little
Compton
Middletown
Jamestown
138
2 Newport
Ft. Adams
Sakonnet Pt.
Narragansett
Pt. Judith

RHODE ISLAND
SOUND

BLOCK ISLAND
SOUND

Block Island
3 (New Shoreham)
Block I.

0   10 mi
0   10 km

1 Providence
2 Newport
3 Block Island
4 Aunt Carrie's
5 Watch Hill

> *Rent a bike and take to the low, undulating hills of the interior of Block Island.*

impressive, it's a mere glimpse of the considerable holdings here, ranging from Egyptian artifacts to Latin American art to works by Picasso and Warhol. If you're not in the mood for a museum, or if you're traveling with kids, consider stopping in at the ★★★ **Roger Williams Zoo,** 1000 Elmwood Ave. (☎ 401/785-3510; www.rwpzoo.org). Opened in 1872, it's probably the best zoo in all of New England. The indoor/outdoor complex is home to more than 160 species from different habitats around the world—see elephants, giraffes,

Play Ball!

Looking for a good old-fashioned ballgame? The **Pawtucket Red Sox** (or PawSox, as they're known here) are the much-loved Triple-A farm team for the Boston Red Sox. You can catch a game at McCoy Stadium in Pawtucket, just outside of Providence. The PawSox hold the distinction of playing in the longest game in pro baseball history, against the Rochester Red Wings on April 18,1981. Play was suspended at 4am, after 32 innings, and resumed on June 23, when the Sox—with future stars Cal Ripken Jr. and Wade Boggs—finally won 3-2. For information on schedules and tickets, call ☎ 401/724-7300 or visit www.pawsox.ccom.

snow leopards, and plenty more as you walk the mile-long path that winds through the 40-acre property. ⏱ Half-day. See p. 338.

Spend the night in Providence, and get an early start on Day 2. Take I-95S 9 miles and take a slight left onto Rte. 4 south. After 10 miles, continue on to Rte. 1 south, to Rte. 138 east, over the bridge and into Newport, where you'll spend the next 2 nights.

② ★ **Newport.** Follow stops ① to ⑦ on our "Rhode Island in 4 Days" tour, p. 308. ⏱ 2 days.

On the morning of Day 4, take the ferry to Block Island, where you'll spend the next 3 nights. To get to the ferry, return across the bridge on Rte. 138 west, and pick up Rte. 1 south. Go 7 miles to Rte. 108 and take it 4 miles south. Turn right onto Galilee Escape Rd. and at the end go left on Great Island Rd.—the ferry is across the street. On the island, head straight out of the lot to Water St. to rent a bike (p. 310).

③ ★★★ **Block Island.** For the first 2 days, follow stops ⑧ to ⑪ on our "Rhode Island in 4 Days" tour. On day 3 of your stay, spend some time on Scotch Beach. When you've had your fill of sand and sun, explore **Old Harbor** with a light and leisurely walk around the only town on the island. Grab a cone at the **Ice Cream Place,** 232 Water St. (☎ 401/466-2145),

The Gaspee Affair

Even before the famous Boston Tea Party, this clash in the waters of Rhode Island presaged the coming Revolution. It was June of 1772 when William Dudingston—the local British Lieutenant responsible for enforcing customs laws, who had a reputation for harassing vessels and confiscating cargo—attempted to detain a local boat, but ran his HMS *Gaspee* aground north of Warwick. Led by local merchant John Brown, 55 men gathered and set out from Providence, capturing and abandoning the *Gaspee* crew onshore while looting and setting fire to the schooner. There was no dressing up as "Mohawks" here, as in Boston, but the furious English were still unable to apprehend the offenders, so arrests were never made.

> *The current Ocean House is the reincarnation of a Victorian resort where the well-heeled came for croquet and crumpets.*

check out the jewelry and glassware at the nearby gallery **234 Water** (p. 322, ④), pick through antiques and vintage home items at **Lazy Fish** (p. 322, ④), and browse the other shops hugging the main drag. ⏱ 3 days.

On the morning of Day 7, catch the early ferry back to Point Judith. Head left out of the lot onto Great Island Rd. and right onto Galilee Escape Rd. Turn right onto Rte. 108 south to Narragansett.

④ 🦞 **Aunt Carrie's.** Back on the mainland, a short ride up from the ferry terminal will bring you to this little crab-shack crossroads. Yes, it's still morning, but that doesn't mean you can't enjoy some amazing clam cakes, chowder, or lobster sandwich on homemade bread (or all three). Just make sure to leave room for a slice of the homemade rhubarb pie. 1240 Ocean Rd., Narragansett. ☎ 401/783-7930. $.

Continue 4½ miles south on Rte. 108 and go left onto Rte. 1 south. Go 16 miles and turn left onto Rte. 1 Scenic/Rte. 1A and take it 5 miles to:

❺ ★★ **Watch Hill.** Roll into this graceful seaside village tucked away in a corner of Westerly. Walk the strip of Bay Street, stop by the **Flying Horse Carousel** (p. 318, ④), and take a

trek out over the dunes to **Napatree Point** (p. 318, ④). As the day comes to a close, head up to the **Ocean House** (p. 319) for a drink, dinner, or—depending on how big of a splurge you have in mind—your last night in Rhode Island. ⏱ Half-day. See p. 318, ④.

Get Rolling: Segway Tours

For a thrilling view of the harbor and nearby Jamestown, along a 10-mile stretch of Ocean Drive on the southwest coast of Newport, hop on a two-wheeled, self-balancing electric people mover from **Segway Tours,** 438 Thames St. (☎ 401/619-4010; www.segwayofnewport.com). Training is included in the price of their $75 "Scenic Ocean Tour," provided you're 16 and have a valid driver's license. Reservations are recommended.

South County Shore

"South County" is actually the local term for Washington County, including Block Island, which is also the town of New Shoreham. Despite the confusing nomenclature, a sense of calm and simplicity radiates throughout these sleepy little towns—most of which grew out of agricultural and fishing communities—distinguishing the area from Providence and Newport. While most people come to this part of the state to swim and sunbathe on New England's best stretches of glorious beach, there's much more here for nature lovers. Plan to spend 3 days here, with time set aside for an excursion on the water.

> *The Towers, survivors of a fire that destroyed the rest of a Gilded Age casino, as well as several hurricanes, are a Narragansett good luck symbol.*

START Narragansett is 31 miles from Providence. **TRIP LENGTH** 36 miles.

① ★ **Narragansett.** This long, narrow town hugging the bay is all about the beach, making it a fitting gateway to laid-back South County. Look for the 1880 **Narragansett Towers,** 35 Ocean Rd., distinctive shingled structures built by McKim, Mead & White, and the last remaining evidence of the spectacular Narragansett Pier Casino, which burned down in 1900. Make time for a scoop or two at **Nana's Ice Cream & Gelato Café,** 28A Pier Market Place (☎ 401/782-2705). **Narragansett Town Beach,** 39 Boston Neck Rd. (☎ 401/789-1044), is where locals go for volleyball, swimming, and some of the best surfing in the east. The milder surf at **Scarborough State Beach,** 870 Ocean Rd. (☎ 401/789-2324), draws families and students from far and wide. ⏱ 1 hr.

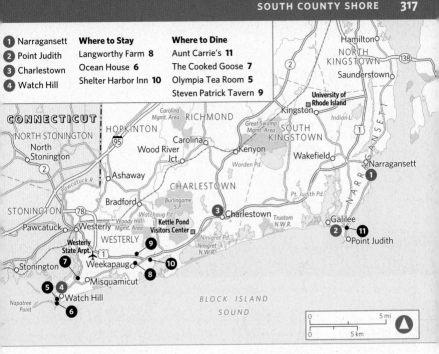

1 Narragansett
2 Point Judith
3 Charlestown
4 Watch Hill

Where to Stay
Langworthy Farm 8
Ocean House 6
Shelter Harbor Inn 10

Where to Dine
Aunt Carrie's 11
The Cooked Goose 7
Olympia Tea Room 5
Steven Patrick Tavern 9

Take Ocean Rd. 5 miles south and continue onto Rte. 108 south, which ends at:

2 ★ **Point Judith.** A commercial fishing center for the past 100 years, the scruffy port of Galilee in Point Judith is a great base for fishing, whale-watching, and other excursions (see below)—and for watching the trawlers come and go. At the breachway you'll find the Block Island Ferry, souvenir shops, and seafood restaurants. Nearby **Salty Brine State Beach,** 254 Great Island Rd. (☎ 401/789-8374), is a short stretch of sand that is good for boat-watching, while family-oriented **Roger Wheeler State Park Beach,** 100 Sand Hill Cove (☎ 401/789-8374), has swing sets and picnic tables; both have calm waters, making them great for family swims. The 1857 **Point Judith Lighthouse,** 1460 Ocean Rd., lies at the end of a mile-long peninsula where many ships have met their demise. The octagonal tower now used for Coast Guard navigation is off-limits to visitors, but you can walk the grounds, or sit up by the seawall and stare at the surf. ⏱ 1½ hr.

Take Rte. 108 north 5 miles to the 2nd exit at the traffic circle onto Rte. 1 and continue south for 12 miles.

3 **Charlestown.** Dominated by the 2,500-acre Narragansett Tribal Lands, mellow Charlestown is home to the state's largest salt pond, 1,700-acre Ninigret Pond. **Ninigret National Wildlife Refuge,** 50 Bend Rd. (☎ 401/364-912; www.fws.gov/ninigret), set on the pond, is an 868-acre expanse of varied habitats where more than 250 species of birds visit annually. On rainy days, don't miss the **Kettle Pond Visitors Center** for kid-friendly ecology exhibits. For a nice walk—and bird-watching—check out East Beach, a 2½-mile secluded swath of barrier beach, part of the **Ninigret Wildlife Conservation Area,** East Beach Rd. (☎ 401/322-0450; www.riparks.com). Come early, before the 100-car lot fills up. Also worth a stop: the hippie-founded **Fantastic Umbrella Factory,** 4820 Old Post Rd. (☎ 401/364-6616), where quirky shops clustered around gardens sell local crafts, vintage eyeglasses, musical instruments—and swords. Bonus: There's a petting zoo with an emu. ⏱ 2 hr.

Take Rte. 1 south for 6 miles. Go left to follow Rte. 1 Scenic/Rte. 1A for 5 miles, and turn left at Watch Hill Rd., continuing onto Wauwinnet Ave. and Bay St.

> *You can't go inside the octagonal brick lighthouse at Point Judith, but it makes for an excellent photo op.*

4 ★★ **Watch Hill.** Finish your visit at this charming Victorian beachfront resort at the southwestern tip of the state. Long a subdued summer retreat for the upper crust, Watch Hill has a distinct old-fashioned vibe permeating its boutique-lined main street (Bay Street), while beautiful gingerbread mansions—and the majestic Ocean House hotel—preside over it all. Try for 2-hour parking on Bay, but be prepared to pay $20 for a spot in the main lot. Grab a house-made ice-cream cone, or a lobster roll, at family-run **St. Clair Annex,** on Bay St. (☎ 401/348-8407), and stop to check out the chain-hung hand-carved wooden horses at the 1876 **Flying Horse Carousel,** also on Bay (☎ 401/348-6007; $1 kids 12 and under). Walk over the dunes to the far end of **Napatree Point Conservation Area** (☎ 800/732-7636). You'll see great views in all directions, including the **Watch Hill Lighthouse,** 14 Lighthouse Rd. (☎ 401/596-7761), itself worth a visit if you have the time. ⏱ 1½ hr.

Getting Out on the Water

South County is famous for its coastline, so take advantage. **Frances Fleet** in Point Judith (☎ 401/783-4988; www.francesfleet.com) runs whale-watching excursions. The 4½-hour trip will cost you $40 ($30 kids 11 and under), but you'll likely see gorgeous finbacks or humpbacks. They also do fluke fishing trips in summer ($70 full day, $40 half). In Wakefield, **Snappa** (☎ 401/782-4040; www.snappacharters.com) offers sport fishing ($425 for 4 hr. with 6 people; full day $825 and up) and even shark-cage diving (yes, really—call for details and pricing). Finally, **Rhode Island Bay Cruises** in North Kingstown (☎ 401/295-4040; www.rhodeislandbaycruises.com) runs a popular lighthouse tour.

A Beach Alternative

South County's most popular beach of all is **Misquamicut State Beach** in Westerly (☎ 401/596-9097). The atmosphere at this always-crowded spot is decidedly downscale compared to the elegant stretches of sand you'll find in, say, Watch Hill, but there are more facilities here, and water slides and surf shops line the street. But if you like a honky-tonk vibe to go along with your sunbathing, this is the spot for you. Bear in mind that all of the beaches run by the Rhode Island State Parks department charge a $12- to $14-per-car beach entrance fee. For more information on the area's beaches, go to www.riparks.com.

Where to Stay & Dine

★★ **Aunt Carrie's** NARRAGANSETT *SEAFOOD/ DESSERT* It's the take-out seafood and delicious pies that built the reputation of this clam shack, but we can't resist a cone of their chocolate peanut-butter-chip ice cream either. 1240 Ocean Rd. ☎ 401/783-6219. www.auntcarriesri. com. Entrees $12–$25. AE, MC, V. Lunch & dinner daily Memorial Day–Labor Day; Apr–May Fri–Sun; Sep Sat–Sun.

★ **The Cooked Goose** WESTERLY *BREAKFAST* Neither fancy nor greasy, this cheerful local gathering spot serves delicious morning fare. We're picky about pancakes, and these are some fluffy flapjacks. 92 Watch Hill Rd. ☎ 401/ 348-9888. www.thecookedgoose.com. Entrees $4–$13. MC, V. Breakfast & lunch daily.

★ **Iggy's Doughboys & Chowder House** NARRAGANSETT *SEAFOOD* Brave the famously long lines at this local legend, right across the way from Aunt Carrie's, and be rewarded with doughboys (fried balls of pizza dough, dusted with sugar or cinnamon—a Rhode Island specialty), clam cakes, other and deep-fried goodness. 10 Wagner St. ☎ 401/322-8883. www.iggys doughboys.com. 24 units. Doubles $106–$258 w/breakfast. AE, MC, V.

★ **Langworthy Farm** WESTERLY Part winery, part bed-and-breakfast, this Victorian farmhouse is a good choice for romantic getaways (read: no kids). Choose a suite for the extra space—the Gov. Ward room has a gas fireplace. 308 Shore Rd. (Rte. 1A). ☎ 401/322-7791. www.langworthyfarm.com. 8 units. Doubles $120–$180 w/breakfast. DISC, MC, V.

★★★ **Ocean House** WATCH HILL Sitting high on wind-swept Watch Hill overlooking the sea, this glorious property opened in 2010 to much fanfare as a respectful re-creation of the grande dame that once occupied the same spot. The rooms are splendid and the spa is par excellence. The spacious wraparound porch (perfect for afternoon cocktails), croquet in the yard, and private beach make it clear why this place was a stomping ground for high society during the Victorian era. 1 Bluff Ave. ☎ 401/584-7000.

> *Dining at the Ocean House includes a Sunday jazz brunch.*

www.oceanhouseri.com. 49 units. Doubles $260–$1,180. AE, DISC, MC, V.

★★ **Olympia Tea Room** WATCH HILL *NEW AMERICAN* Elegant and atmospheric, this Watch Hill institution has a top-tier wine list, with more than 70 wines available by the glass. Sidewalk tables overlook the harbor, and the kitchen turns out some inspired seafood dishes and great desserts. 74 Bay St. ☎ 401/348-8211. www.olympiatearoom.com. Entrees $20–$32. AE, DISC, MC, V. May–Nov lunch & dinner daily.

★★ **Shelter Harbor Inn** WESTERLY This warm country inn, converted from an early-19th-century farmhouse, spreads across three buildings. Rooms are cozy—ask for one out back with a private deck. The large rooftop deck, hot tub, and grill are open to all guests. 10 Wagner St. ☎ 401/322-8883. www.shelter harborinn.com. 24 units. Doubles $106–$258 w/ breakfast. AE, MC, V.

South County Farm Stands

For summery-sweet corn, tomatoes, and baked goodies, don't miss **Sunset Farms,** 505 Point Judith Rd., in Narragansett (☎ 401/789-4070), or **Carpenter's,** 522 Matunuck Rd., in Wakefield (☎ 401/783-7550). **Manfredi Farms,** 77 Dunn's Corner Rd., Westerly (☎ 401/322-0027), is a nice choice for pick-your-own berries and flowers—and they run a petting zoo.

Block Island

With its wind-swept cliffs and rolling green hills studded with stone walls, it's no wonder this tiny island evokes so many comparisons to Ireland. It's a world apart from the mainland—with no traffic lights, no chains, and protected land encompassing almost half the island. It likely looks much as it did when English settlers first arrived in 1661, and during the 19th-century tourism boom, when grand hotels with long porches and mansard roofs sprang up. Nowadays, the population swells from 1,000 to 20,000 in the summer, and Old Harbor (the only town) can feel clogged. We prefer September, when the water is still warm, and the roads are less crowded and perfect for cycling— the best way to see the island. Most stops on our 2-day bicycle tour are open summer through early fall.

> Block Island's North Lighthouse, the fourth at this location, was built to warn mariners of perilous Sandy Point.

START The Block Island Ferry Terminal in Galilee is 37 miles from Providence.

1 ★★ **Rodman's Hollow.** This beautiful, glacier-carved ravine, which drops below sea level, was the first piece of property set aside for conservation on Block Island. Bike down Black Rock Road for ¼ mile until you see a gate marking the trail entrance. Lock up your bike, then set out on the winding paths through blackberry bushes and wildflowers, to clay cliffs and Black Rock beach, popular with surfers and nude bathers. Don't forget to wear tick repellant, and watch for marsh hawks. ⏲ 2 hr. Nature Conservancy. High St. ☎ 401/466-2129.

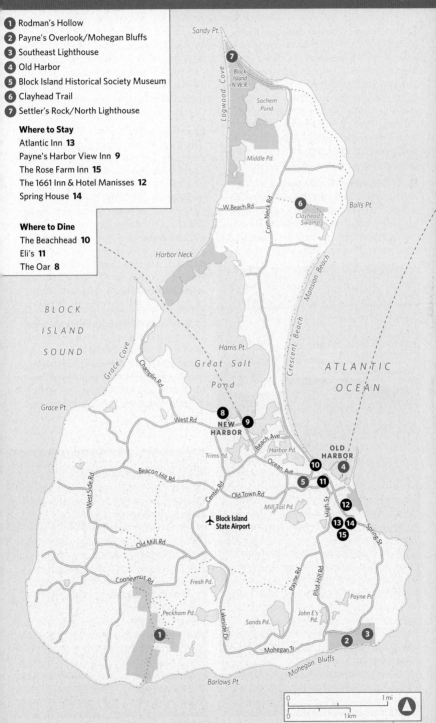

1 Rodman's Hollow
2 Payne's Overlook/Mohegan Bluffs
3 Southeast Lighthouse
4 Old Harbor
5 Block Island Historical Society Museum
6 Clayhead Trail
7 Settler's Rock/North Lighthouse

Where to Stay
Atlantic Inn 13
Payne's Harbor View Inn 9
The Rose Farm Inn 15
The 1661 Inn & Hotel Manisses 12
Spring House 14

Where to Dine
The Beachhead 10
Eli's 11
The Oar 8

② ★★★ **Payne's Overlook/Mohegan Bluffs.** Block Island's most dramatic scenery can be found here. The reasonably fit should take the long, wooden staircase 250 steps down, pausing to admire the stunning 150-foot cliffs above, the rocky shore below, and the gorgeous view of the Southeast Lighthouse to the east. There's a little beach at the bottom, though swimming can be dangerous. ⏱ 2 hr. Block Island Chamber of Commerce, at Old Harbor ferry landing. ☎ 800/383-2474.

③ ★★ 🄺🄸🄳🅂 **Southeast Lighthouse.** In the early 1990s, when erosion left this red-brick 1875 sentinel 50 feet from the cliff's edge, islanders banded together, raised $2 million, and moved the lighthouse 250 feet back. Now, restorations are ongoing, and there are even plans in the works for overnight accommodations. The little exhibit inside is free, but you'll have to pay for a tour of the tower. ⏱ 30 min. ☎ 401/466-5009. Tower tours $10 adults, $5 kids. Weekends Memorial Day to late June & Labor Day to Columbus Day; daily late June to Labor Day 10am–4pm. Grounds sunrise–sunset.

④ ★★ **Old Harbor.** The only village on the island, this is where most of the restaurants, boutiques, and inns are located, and where most ferries dock year-round. Spend some time wandering around the shops: We love **Lazy Fish,** at 235 Dodge St. (☎ 401/466-2990), which sells a hodgepodge of vintage and new home wares, furniture, and artwork; and **234 Water** (☎ 401/441-1463), specializing in one-of-a-kind items like jewelry and glassware. Head to co-op-run **Spring Street Gallery,** Spring St. (☎ 401/466-5374), and **Jessie Edwards Studio,** Post Office Bldg. (☎ 401/466-5314), for local art. ⏱ 2 hr.

⑤ **Block Island Historical Society Museum.** Make a quick stop in this mansard-roofed building with a collection of vintage island photos, quilts, furniture, and Native American artifacts. ⏱ 30 min. 18 Old Town Rd. ☎ 401/466-2481. Admission $5 adults, $3 students 16 and over. Mid-June to early Sept 11am–4pm.

Getting There & Getting Around

The best way to reach Block Island is by ferry. If you're coming from points south and west, you'll likely depart from New London, Connecticut, on the **Block Island Express** (☎ 860/444-4624; www.goblockisland.com). The high-speed service, which costs adults $24 for a one-way trip, will have you there in 1¼ hours. If you're coming from Newport, you'll take a ferry run by **Interstate Navigation** (☎ 866/783-7996; www.blockislandferry.com). The trip will take 2 hours and cost adults about $11 one way. If you insist on bringing your car (our advice: don't), you'll depart from Point Judith. Plan to spend $100 round-trip and book early. (If you're visiting in July or Aug, reserve as early as late Jan.) Otherwise, leave your car at the docks at any of the three departure points. Parking will run you anywhere from $3 to $20 a day. Bringing a bike? Expect to shell out about $3 each way.

Best Beaches on the Block

Here are some our favorites, all of which are part of Crescent Beach, the long stretch of sand on the island's east coast, from Old Harbor to Clay Head.

Fred Benson (aka Town) Beach. A stone's throw from town, this is a good family beach: The water is very shallow, plus there are lifeguards, concessions, and plenty of parking spots for those who have a car. If you're looking for peace, head elsewhere.

Scotch Beach. Summering students and families gather at this beach with white sand, few rocks, and a small parking lot.

Mansion Beach. Come by bike—car parking is limited. Surf can be rough; it's excellent for bodysurfing, but sometimes not so great for young kids. Head north for a walk beneath the cliffs and starfish spotting.

> *Settler's Rock is on Cow Cove, so named for the bovine passengers of the colonists' ship that landed here in 1661.*

6 ★★ kids **Clayhead Trail.** To find the trail head, look for a granite post across the way from a yellow Victorian house. Follow the road for 4/10 mile to a parking lot with a bike rack; lock up your wheels, then walk. The path will first head east to gorgeous 150-foot-high cliffs, then north all the way to Settlers' Rock. Other inter-connected trails along the way, known as "the Maze," will bring you to lovely views of farm-land and the coast. ⊙ 2 hr. Block Island Conser-vancy. ☎ 401/466-3111. www.biconservancy.org. Free admission.

7 ★★★ kids **Settler's Rock/North Lighthouse.** This northernmost part of the Block is one of the island's prettiest areas, especially during sunset. A granite plaque marks the spot—known as Settler's Rock—where English colonists from Massachusetts landed in 1661 (though the island was named by Dutchman Adrian Block, who named it for himself after sailing here in 1614). Tranquil **Sachem Pond,** a freshwater pond and a feeding area for swans and water birds, is right across the road. Walk the ¾ mile along the beach to the 1867 granite

North Lighthouse, hauled here by oxen, where a small first-floor museum explores the history of the lighthouse, some island shipwrecks, and area ecology. ⊙ 2 hr. ☎ 401/466-3200. Free admission. July to Labor Day 10am–4pm.

Beyond the Sand & Sea

We could spend weeks here swimming, eating, drinking, and generally lazing about, but there are other fun adventures to be had on the Block. For an exhilarating ride in the air, go parasailing with **Block Island Parasail,** Old Harbor Dock (☎ 401/864-2474; www.blockislandparasail.com). For $75 and up, you can fly solo or tandem. Reservations are accepted only on the day you want to parasail. **Rustic Rides Farm,** West Side Rd. (☎ 401/466-5060), offers trail and beach excursions on horseback. A 1-hour slow-paced ride will cost you $40 ($55 on the beach), while a 1-hour fast-paced ride will set you back $45. With all that water, wildlife, and scenery, BI is an excellent place for a paddle. Take a guided kayak tour with the knowledgeable folks at **Pond & Beyond** (☎ 401/466-5105; www.blockisland.com/kayakbi). A 2½-hour tour costs $50 per person. Looking for a good fish tale? **Block Island Fishworks,** Ocean Ave. (☎ 401/466-5392), will hook you up. Four hours of blue and bass fishing on a six-person charter will cost $450 to $500.

Sweet Spot

Our favorite island ritual is biking to **Payne's Killer Donuts,** Payne's Dock (☎ 401/466-5572) in New Harbor for early-morning donuts. The earlier you arrive, the warmer and more delicious your plain, sugar, or cinnamon confection will be. Eat one while checking out the morning marina activity.

Where to Stay

> Hotel Manisses has seventeen rooms named after local shipwrecks.

★★ Atlantic Inn

Set on a hilltop, with expansive vistas over the sea, the Atlantic offers a gorgeous veranda and spic-and-span rooms with period furnishings. The kitchen has an excellent reputation, and the wine list is the best on BI. Come here for sunset cocktails at least once during your stay. High St. ☎ 800/224-7422. www.atlanticinn. com. 21 units. Doubles $165–$290 w/breakfast. DISC, MC, V.

★ Payne's Harbor View Inn

This inn has some of the island's most spacious and modern rooms. Most have whirlpool tubs, some have private decks—as well as a lovely porch and water views. In summer, donuts from the adjacent **Payne's Killer Donuts** are a legendary local treat (open Memorial Day to Columbus Day daily 7am–7pm). Old Town Rd. ☎ 401/466-5758. www.paynesharbor viewinn.com. 10 units. Doubles $150–$395 w/ breakfast. MC, V.

★ The Rose Farm Inn

Surrounded by meadows and flower gardens, Rose Farm stands out for its tranquil setting, within walking distance of town. The most luxurious rooms—with whirlpool bathtubs, decks, and some with canopy beds—are in the Captain Rose House. Roslyn Rd. ☎ 401/466-2034. www.rosefarminn.com. 17 units. Doubles $139–$309 w/breakfast. AE, DISC, MC, V.

★★ The 1661 Inn & Hotel Manisses

Stained glass, floral wallpaper, wicker, and antiques are the order of the day at the dainty Manisses, with one of the best dining rooms on the island. Also on offer: after-dinner flaming coffees (alcohol-infused coffee set aflame) in the parlor, and a meadow full of emus, kangaroos, and a camel. The 1661 Inn, up the hill, is where guests of both properties partake in the huge champagne breakfast. Spring St. ☎ 401/466-2421. www.blockislandresorts.com. 26 units. Doubles $75–$460 (room w/deck & spa tub) w/breakfast. MC, V.

★ Spring House

With its distinct red mansard roof and great lawn overlooking the sea, this venerable hotel is one of BI's most beloved, popular for weddings. Town is steps away, and rooms are big by island standards; nab a corner room facing the ocean. Thursday-night martini nights are very popular. 902 Spring St. ☎ 800/234-9263. www.springhousehotel.com. 50 units. Doubles $125–$400 w/breakfast. AE, MC, V.

Reality Check

While you'll get buckets of charm at BI's old Victorian inns, you'll also likely get thin walls, small rooms, and no A/C. Not your cup of tea? Consider renting a house instead. Ranging from tiny $1,450-a-week seaside cottages to huge $8,000-a-week compounds, these places tend to fill up early; book in January. The reputable **Sullivan** (☎ 401/466-5521; www.blockislandhouses.com) or **Attwood Real Estate** (☎ 401/466-5582; www.attwoodrealestate.com) can help you find the perfect vacation spot to call home.

Where to Dine

> *Family dining on the porch of the Beachhead.*

★ **The Beachhead** *AMERICAN*
With a wide variety of apps, burgers, and beer, and a prime location across from the beach, the family-friendly Beachhead is a great bet for a casual lunch. But dinner here—bouillabaisse, lobster mac 'n' cheese—is surprisingly good, too. Corn Neck Rd. ☎ 401/466-2249. Entrees $9–$29. MC, V. Lunch & dinner daily.

★★ **Eli's** *AMERICAN*
Tiny, friendly, and always packed, Eli's serves up some of the island's most thoughtfully prepared meals. Reservations aren't accepted, so get there very early, and dig into apps like watermelon, feta, and fennel salad or tuna nachos, and flavorsome mains like cioppino. 456 Chapel St. ☎ 401/466-5230. www.elisblockisland.com. Entrees $19–$29. DISC, MC, V. Mid-March to mid-Nov dinner daily.

★★ **The Oar** *AMERICAN*
With hundreds of painted oars adorning the walls and ceilings, lots of locals and boaters, and a festive ambience no matter what time of day, the Oar is a fun New Harbor spot for breakfast, lunch, dinner—or one of their famous mudslides. 221 Jobs Hill Rd. ☎ 401/466-8820. Entrees $5–$29. AE, MC, V. May–Oct breakfast, lunch & dinner daily.

Hitting the Town

If your idea of island fun includes an après-beach scene, you've come to the right place. Across the street from the ferry, the porch bar at the **National,** Water St. (☎ 800/225-2449), has greeted and bade farewell to BI travelers for ages. Hard-partying **Captain Nick's,** 69 Ocean Ave. (☎ 401/ 466-5670), and **McGovern's Yellow Kittens,** Corn Neck Rd. (☎ 401/466-5855), host live music in season. **McNamara's,** Beach Ave. (☎ 401/466-2930), is a newish Irish-themed pub. If you want to flee the tourist yahoo scene, head to **Club Soda,** 35 Connecticut Ave. (☎ 401/466-5397), where there's foosball, pool tables, pub grub, and lots of locals.
★★ **Mahogany Shoals,** Payne's Dock (☎ 401/466-5572), is our favorite spot for a beer on the Block. With slanted wooden floors and loads of salty sailor attitude, the bar is best when Walter McDonough holds court, singing Irish tunes and giving good *craic.*

Newport

On the southern tip of Aquidneck Island, Newport is one of New England's premier seaside destinations. A longtime host to The America's Cup, the most prestigious race in the sailing world, Newport is also famous for its legendary folk and jazz summer festivals. Founded in 1639 as an enclave of religious tolerance—Baptists, Quakers, and Jews all lived and thrived here—by the mid-1700s, Newport had grown into a cosmopolitan city rivaling New York and Boston. The turn of the 19th century saw the arrival of prosperous titans of industry, who built their extravagant summer "cottages" on Bellevue Avenue. Nowadays, you'll find an active modern waterfront full of shops, restaurants, and boat cruises—and plenty of opportunities to explore this dynamic city's vibrant past. You can see quite a bit in a day, but if you'd really like to explore, plan to spend 4 days here.

> Rosecliff, completed in 1902 to the tune of $2.5 million, hosted many famous guests, including magician Harry Houdini and composer Cole Porter.

START Newport is 30 miles from Providence.

❶ ★ Newport Historical Society Museum. The former Brick Market building, built in 1762, this museum makes a nice starting point for your tour, providing a decent overview to Newport's colorful history. Included in the collection are exhibits on Goddard and Townshend craftsmen, candle making, rum distilling, and a printing press belonging to James Franklin—Ben's brother. ⏱ 1 hr. 127 Thames St. ☎ 401/841-8770. www.newporthistorical. org. Suggested donation $4 adults, $2 kids 5-12. Daily 10am-5pm.

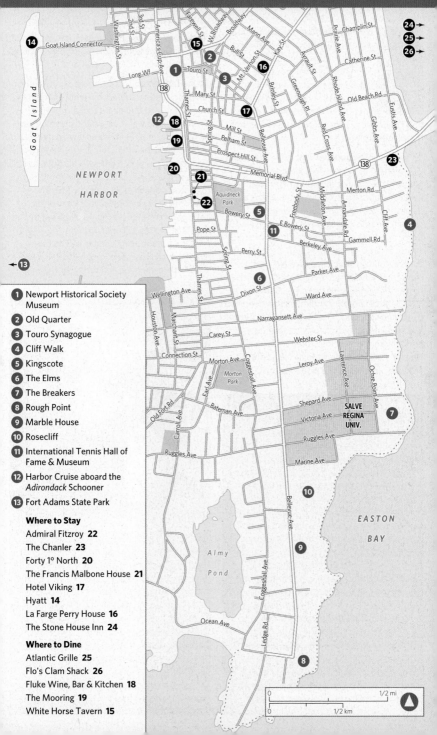

1 Newport Historical Society Museum
2 Old Quarter
3 Touro Synagogue
4 Cliff Walk
5 Kingscote
6 The Elms
7 The Breakers
8 Rough Point
9 Marble House
10 Rosecliff
11 International Tennis Hall of Fame & Museum
12 Harbor Cruise aboard the *Adirondack* Schooner
13 Fort Adams State Park

Where to Stay
Admiral Fitzroy **22**
The Chanler **23**
Forty 1° North **20**
The Francis Malbone House **21**
Hotel Viking **17**
Hyatt **14**
La Farge Perry House **16**
The Stone House Inn **24**

Where to Dine
Atlantic Grille **25**
Flo's Clam Shack **26**
Fluke Wine, Bar & Kitchen **18**
The Mooring **19**
White Horse Tavern **15**

② ★★★ **Old Quarter.** This section of town is home to astonishingly well-preserved architectural gems from the Colonial era, some of which were restored thanks to the largess of heiress Doris Duke, founder of the Newport Restoration Foundation. Take a few hours to admire the architecture. ⏱ **3 hr.**

SITE GUIDE PAGE 329

③ ★★ **Touro Synagogue.** Built in 1763, graceful Georgian-style Touro is the oldest active synagogue in the U.S. Designed by Peter Harrison, it was the house of worship for Newport's flourishing Jewish community, who had a presence since Sephardic Jews arrived in 1658, drawn by the colony's promise of tolerance. (George Washington sent a letter to the congregation in which he vowed to give "to bigotry no sanction, to persecution no assistance.") Docents are excellent, and there's a 500-year-old Torah, handwritten on deerskin. By guided tour only. The **Loeb Visitors Center** features interactive exhibits celebrating Newport's history of religious freedom (see "Soul Liberty" on p. 336 for more on Newport's incredible openness). ⏱ **2 hr. 85 Touro St.**

☎ 401/847-4794. www.loeb-tourovisitorscenter.org. Admission $12 adults, free for kids 12 & under. See website for tour schedule & visitors center hours.

④ ★★ **Cliff Walk.** This stunning 3½-mile path hugs the eastern shore of Newport, stretching from Memorial Boulevard to Bailey's Beach. With dramatic water views and crashing surf on one side, and the massive lawns of the mansions on the other, this is a must-see. You can access the walk from several spots, but if you're game to tackle the whole thing, get to Easton's Beach early, park for $10, and set off. For the first half-mile, your view of the cottages will be blocked by hedges, but by the 40 Steps, things will open up, and you'll soon pass the breathtaking estates of The Breakers, Marble House, and Rough Point. Parts of the path are unpaved and rocky, so wear good

The Cottages

There is a lot to see and do in Newport, but the biggest draw of all is "the cottages," as the grand mansions designed by the likes of Richard Upjohn and Richard Morris Hunt are known. These opulent summer-only estates were built by coal barons and other giants of industry—the Vanderbilts, the Astors—who amassed huge post-Civil War, pre-income-tax fortunes. They speak volumes about the greed and extravagance that defined the Gilded Age. You can explore only one or two, or see them all. Either way, discounts are available if you buy a package deal through www.newportmansions.org. You can explore **The Elms** (p. 330, ⑥), **The Breakers** (p. 331, ⑦), and **Marble House** (p. 331, ⑨) through excellent, multilayered, and colorful self-guided audio tours, some of which include the recollections of people who worked or lived in the cottages. All other mansions mentioned can be seen by guided tour only. You don't need to buy tickets in advance.

Getting Out of Town

We recommend skipping a few cottages and spending part of a day savoring the bucolic charms of the region on a pleasant drive to **Sakonnet Point.** Stop for an ice cream at **Gray's,** 16 East Rd. (☎ 401/624-4500), in historic Tiverton Four Corners. Then continue on to **Little Compton,** a town of farm stands, open fields, and stone walls. Take a walk on pristine **Goosewing Beach Preserve,** at the end of South Shore Rd. (☎ 401/635-4400), before dropping in for a tasting at **Sakonnet Vineyards,** 162 W. Main Rd. (☎ 800/919-4637).

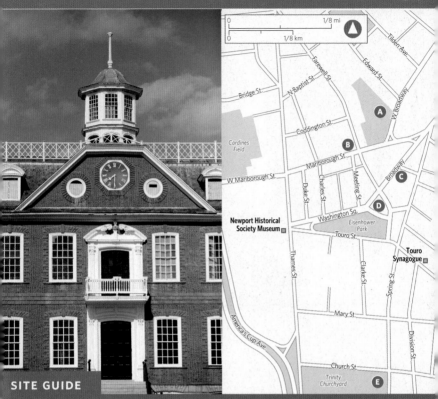

SITE GUIDE

2 Old Quarter

One of the religious sects that found safe harbor in colonial Newport were the Society of Friends (also known as Quakers), who built the A ★ **Great Friends Meeting House** (☎ 401/846-0813 for guided tours) in 1699. Now the oldest religious structure in Newport, the austere post-and-beam building served as home base for the Friends, which for the better part of the pre-Revolutionary years. Next, stop in at the still-thriving B ★★ **White Horse Tavern** (p. 335). Built in 1673, it was once the watering hole of choice for the state's General Assembly and other Colonial-era VIPs. The bright red C **Wanton-Lyman-Hazard House** (☎ 401/846-0813 for guided tours), built around 1697, is the oldest surviving home in Newport. After Parliament enacted the Stamp Act in 1765, which required colonists to pay a direct tax on just about all printed materials, an

angry mob stormed the place, then occupied by staunch Loyalist Martin Howard (notice his name is not among those attached to the house), who was whisked safely out of Newport by the British. Your stroll through history will next take you to the 1736 D **Colony House** (☎ 401/846-0813 for guided tours), where in 1766 Newport's citizenry celebrated the repeal of said Stamp Act. Make your way down Spring Street, admiring some of the Colonial homes restored by the **Newport Restoration Foundation** (look for the NRF sign; www.newportrestoration.org); and end your tour at E ★ **Trinity Church** (☎ 401/846-0660; www.trinitynewport.org) which was completed in 1725 and, whose wooden spire dominates the skyline. George Washington worshiped here, as did many other historic figures.

> *Alva Vanderbilt, a preeminent Newport hostess, envisioned Marble House, now a National Historic Landmark, as her "temple to the arts."*

shoes, and don't forget sunblock. ⏱1 hr. www.cliffwalk.com.

⑤ ★ Kingscote. Start your mansion tour here, at one of Newport's first cottages built expressly for summer use, and one of our personal favorites. Masterminded by Richard Upjohn, this 1841 Gothic-Revival-style home with lots of towers and arches was commissioned by a Southerner, who failed to return when the Civil War began. In 1880, the new owner hired Stanford White to design the show-stopping dining room: With cork ceilings, Tiffany colored glass, and a screen with elaborate spindle work, it's widely recognized as one of the most beautiful rooms of the period. Guided tours run every half-hour. ⏱1 hr. 253 Bellevue Ave. ☎ 401/847-1000. www.newportmansions.org.

Admission $14 adults, $5 kids 6–17. Early May to early Oct 10am–5pm.

⑥ ★★★ The Elms. Coal titan Edward Berwind's $1.4-million 1901 home took as inspiration the mid-18th-century Parisian Chateau d'Asnieres, but it came equipped with some of the most advanced technologies of the time—it was one of the first fully electrified cottages. Highlights of this house include formal French sunken gardens, and a unique behind-the-scenes tour ($15 adults, $5 kids 6–17), guiding guests through the boiler room, kitchen, servants quarters, rooftop, and an underground tunnel system used for transporting coal to the basement. By self-guided audio tour. ⏱2 hr. 367 Bellevue Ave. ☎ 401/847-1000. www.newportmansions.org. Admission $14 adults, $5

> *A private tour of Rough Point includes the entire first floor, the master bedroom, and special exhibits on topics such as Duke's sporting life.*

kids 6-17. Early Jan to early Apr weekends 10am–4pm; early Apr–Dec daily 10am–5pm.

7 ★★★ **The Breakers.** Just when you thought things couldn't get any more decadent, you'll see the 1895 Richard Morris Hunt–designed Renaissance-style palazzo of Cornelius Vanderbilt, the most opulent mansion of all. The music room was created and decorated in pure gold in a French workshop, then reassembled in Newport. The jaw-dropping dining room is hung with 12-foot Baccarat crystal chandeliers and anchored by 12 huge rose alabaster columns, while the two-story great hall sports a towering grand staircase and slabs of pink African marble and green Italian marble. By self-guided audio tour. ⏱ 2 hr. 44 Ochre Point Ave. ☎ 401/847-1000. www.newportmansions.org. Admission $19 adults, $5 kids 6–17. Early Jan to early Apr daily 10am–4pm; early Apr–Dec daily 9am–5pm.

8 ★★ **Rough Point.** This fascinating home—filled with the spectacular art (Renoir, Van Dyck), furnishings (French furniture and Turkish rugs), and antiques (Chinese porcelains) collected by Doris Duke—looks exactly the way it did when the eccentric and generous heiress-philanthropist lived here. Tours are intimate, and guides are very knowledgeable about Duke's life and work. Look for the tables belonging to Catherine the Great. By guided tour only. ⏱ 1 hr. 680 Bellevue Ave. ☎ 401/847-8344. www.newportrestoration.org. Admission $25 adults, free for kids 11 & under. Early Apr to early May Thurs–Sat 10am–2pm; early May to early Nov Tues–Sat 9:45am–3:45pm.

9 ★★ **Marble House.** Richard Morris Hunt designed this colossus, the cottage that ushered in an era of palatial one-upmanship in Newport. Inspired by the Petit Trianon at Versailles, it cost $11 million in 1892, and includes such extravagances as a ballroom covered entirely in 22-karat gold leaf. William Vanderbilt presented it as a gift to wife Alva, the socialite and later women's suffrage leader, on her 39th birthday. They divorced 3 years later, but Alva returned after her second husband died in 1908, and built the Chinese Tea Room out by the cliffs. ⏱ 1 hr. 596 Bellevue Ave. ☎ 401/847-1000. www.newportmansions.org. Admission $14 adults, $5

> *Stone lions guard an entrance to Rosecliff, which was privately owned until 1971.*

kids 6–17. Early Jan to early Apr weekends 10am–4pm; early Apr to Dec daily 10am–5pm.

⑩ ★ Rosecliff. This 1902 terra-cotta Stanford White–designed cottage, constructed for silver heiress Tessie Oelrichs and modeled after the Grand Trianon at Versailles, has Newport's largest ballroom, stupendous ocean views, and a gorgeous lawn with a fountain that was once filled with swans, part of the famous Bal Blanc (white ball) held here in 1904. Frequent guest Cole Porter wrote many songs here. It's all very Gatsbyesque, which is probably why parts of the film *The Great Gatsby* were shot here in 1973. By guided tour. ⏱ 1 hr. 548 Bellevue Ave. ☎ 401/847-1000. www.newport

---

More Mansions, Please!

Not enough mansions for you? Check out the Italian woodwork and Victorian Gothic architecture at the grand **Chateau-sur-Mer,** the Asian-inspired dining room and striking Shingle-style design of the **Isaac Bell House,** and the 1748 **Hunter House,** the only Newport mansion that was lived in year-round. www.newportmansions.org.

---

mansions.org. Admission $14 adults, $5 kids 6–17. Apr to mid-Nov 10am–5pm (last tour).

⑪ ★ International Tennis Hall of Fame & Museum. Sixteen fascinating galleries explore the history of tennis, through such items as Venus Williams' racy black lace dress and Bobby Riggs' warm-up gear from the Battle of the Sexes Match. Even visitors with little interest in tennis will appreciate the beauty of the grounds. The McKim, Mead & White–designed Shingle-style buildings were formerly home to the Casino, created as a playground for Newport's Gilded Age gentry. (After James Gordon Bennett was kicked out of the gentlemen-only Newport Reading Room—he had dared a friend to ride his horse up onto

Nightlife in Newport

Is it any surprise that this sailing town has a vibrant drinking scene? On the wharf, **Clarke Cooke House,** 1 Bannister's Wharf (☎ 401/846-4500), is a four-story building that is home to the swanky **Skybar** and the **Boom Boom Room** dance club. **Perro Salado,** 19 Charles St. (☎ 401/619-4777), has great margaritas, while the funky **Salvation Café,** 140 Broadway (☎ 401/847-2620), is known for their jars of sangria and tiki bar. Head to **Newport Blues Café,** 286 Thames (☎ 401/841-5510), for live music, and **POP,** 162 Broadway (☎ 401/846-8456), for martinis.

the club's front porch—he built the Casino as revenge.) The grass courts here are the oldest competitive grass courts open to the public, and you can still rent them out. ⏱ 1½ hr. 194 Bellevue Ave. ☎ 401/849-3990. www.tennis fame.com. Admission $11 adults, free for kids 16 & under. Daily 9:30am–5pm.

12 ★★ kids **Harbor Cruise aboard the *Adirondack Schooner*.** There's no place in the U.S. with a richer nautical history than Newport: city-by-the-sea, world-class sailing center. Don't you think you need to get out on the water? The classic Schooner *Adirondack II* does it in style, showing you such sights as Fort Adams, Hammersmith Farms (Jackie Kennedy's childhood home), and the historic lighthouse, while offering $1 drinks. ⏱ 1½ hr. Bowen's Wharf. ☎ 401/847-0000. www.sail-newport.com. Rates vary depending on cruise length.

13 ★ **Fort Adams State Park.** This 105-acre park with gorgeous views of Narragansett Bay is perhaps most famous for hosting Newport Jazz and Folk, but it's also a lovely place for swimming, sailing, and fishing. And, of course, there's history. Take a tour to explore the tunnels and living quarters of the soldiers who lived here from 1824 to1950. Guided tour only, on the hour. ⏱ 1½ hr. 90 Fort Adams Dr. ☎ 401/841-0707. www.fortadams.org. Admission $10 adults, $5 kids 6–18. Memorial Day to Columbus Day 10am–4pm.

Festival Time

Newport likes to party, and we strongly suggest you join right in. Here are three of our favorite city celebrations.

Newport Folk Festival (www.newportfolk fest.net). It's not just your father's folk music anymore, though you'll still catch the likes of Doc Watson and Pete Seeger alongside Iron and Wine and Fleet Foxes at this 2-day summer tradition at Fort Adams.

Newport Jazz (www.newportjazzfest. net). This 3-day summer festival has been going strong since 1954; recent years have seen Chick Corea, Tony Bennett, and Etta James grace one of the two stages at Fort Adams and the Tennis Hall of Fame.

Christmas in Newport (www.christmas innewport.org). Newport celebrates the holidays throughout the month of December, with such events as lantern tours, a tree lighting, and performances of *The Nutcracker*. The Breakers, Marble House, and The Elms are all open, and decked out in wreaths, flowers, and sumptuous holiday finery.

Where to Stay

> *Sumptuous digs at the Chanler.*

★ Admiral Fitzroy

In the market for a clean, well-run, welcoming B&B with a prime location? Look for the bright red door smack in the middle of the action on Thames. 398 Thames St. ☎ 866/848-8780. www. admiralfitzroy.com. 18 units. Doubles $105–$325 w/breakfast. AE, MC, V.

★★★ The Chanler

For a taste of what life was like for Newport's Gilded Age aristocracy, come to this "cottage"-turned-elegant-hotel. Staff is courteous, a private car is on hand for excursions within Newport, and the hotel is perched at the start of the Cliff Walk. Each room is unique—our favorites feature ocean views, private Jacuzzis, and gas fireplaces. 117 Memorial Blvd. ☎ 401/847-1300. www.thechanler.com. 20 units. Doubles $259–$1,499 w/breakfast. AE, DISC, MC, V.

★★★ Forty 1° North

This newcomer to Newport's high-end hotel scene has a lot going for it, including its location, on a marina in the heart of downtown. It's both eco-friendly (think sustainable building materials) and high-tech (we loved the in-room iPad). The rooms are chic but comfortable, and the views of Newport Harbor are amazing. 351 Thames St. ☎ 401/846-8018. www.41north.com. 24 units. Doubles $239–$650. AE, MC, V.

★★ The Francis Malbone House

Courteous hosts, lavish breakfasts and teas, and tastefully appointed guest rooms (high thread-count linens, working fireplaces in some), are a few reasons we recommend this well-located 1760 inn. 392 Thames St. ☎ 800/846-0392. www. malbone.com. 20 units. Doubles $150–$495 w/breakfast. AE, MC, V.

★ Hotel Viking

Around since 1926, this venerable hotel was once the crème de la crème of the Newport scene. Amenities include an indoor pool, a spa, and a rooftop bar with the best view in town. One Bellevue Ave. ☎ 800/556-7126. www.hotelviking.com. 209 units. Doubles $99–$1,599. AE, DISC, MC, V.

★★ [kids] Hyatt

An outdoor saltwater pool, loads of activities, and s'mores at the fire pit make this a good option for kids, but grownups will cotton to the top-tier spa and the prime setting on Goat Island. 1 Goat Island. ☎ 401/851-1234. www. newport.hyatt.com. 264 units. Doubles $109–$1,500 (for Premier Suite). AE, DISC, MC, V.

★★ La Farge Perry House

This B&B stands out not only for its warm hospitality and sumptuous rooms but also for its outstanding breakfasts, including scrumptious baked goods like blueberry scuffins (a scone muffin). 24 Kay St. ☎ 401/847-2223. www. lafargeperry.com. 5 units. Doubles $99–$499 w/breakfast. AE, MC, V.

★★ The Stone House Inn

For a secluded sanctuary by the sea, come to this 1854 Italianate villa and barn, with understated modern decor and eco-conscious touches like cork floors and reclaimed wood. Splurge on the huge Osprey Suite and get serene ocean views, a deep soaking tub, a spacious steam shower, and an ultraplush king bed. With a fab spa, a cozy tavern, and an excellent restaurant. 122 Sakonnet Point Rd., Little Compton. ☎ 401/635-2222. www.stonehouse1854.com. 13 units. Doubles $155–$625 w/breakfast. AE, DISC, MC, V.

Where to Dine

> Clamcakes are the house specialty at Flo's Clam Shack, a local staple for more than 75 years.

★ **Atlantic Grille** MIDDLETOWN BREAKFAST
Have breakfast at this cheery Middletown eatery on a weekend, when bennies (variations on benedict) are served. We love the Atlantic Bennie—with bacon on a grilled corn muffin—the *chourico* hash, and specials like pumpkin-pie pancakes. 91 Aquidneck Ave., Middletown. ☎ 401/849-4440. www.atlanticgrille.com. Entrees $2.25–$13. AE, DISC, MC, V. Breakfast & lunch daily.

★ **Flo's Clam Shack** MIDDLETOWN SEAFOOD SHACK Fun and funky—hung with nets, buoys, and American flags—Flo's is a quintessential clam shack with a local following right by Easton's Beach. There's a raw bar upstairs with great ocean views. 4 Wave Ave., Middletown. ☎ 401/847-8141. www.flosclamshack. net. Entrees $2–$20. Cash only. Memorial Day to Labor Day lunch & dinner daily; Mar to Memorial Day & Labor Day to Jan 1 lunch & dinner Thurs–Sun.

★★★ **Fluke Wine, Bar & Kitchen** NEW AMERICAN Our favorite restaurant in Newport has a knowledgeable and friendly staff, farm-to-table plates (for example, lamb meatballs and bacon-wrapped almond-filled dates), a great wine list, and finely crafted drinks. Reserve a table upstairs to watch the sun set over the harbor—and save room for s'mores. 41 Bowen's Wharf. ☎ 401/849-7778. www.flukewinebar. com. Small plates $8–$12, large plates $14–$38. AE, MC, V. Mid-Nov to Apr dinner Wed–Sat; May to mid-Nov dinner daily.

★★ **The Mooring** SEAFOOD
This large, casual-sophisticated eatery right on the wharf has a stellar reputation for fresh seafood. Be sure to get a "bag of doughnuts" (lobster, crab, and shrimp fritters with chipotle maple aioli). Sayer's Wharf. ☎ 401/846-2260. www.mooringrestaurant.com. Entrees $19–$44. AE, DISC, MC, V. Dinner daily.

★★ **White Horse Tavern** TRADITIONAL
You can't get much more atmospheric than this 1673 dimly tavern with wide-plank floors, low ceilings, and cane chairs—it claims to be the oldest in America. Expect dishes like Beef Wellington and butter-poached lobster. 6 Marlborough St. ☎ 401/849-3600. www.white horsetavern.us. Entrees $12–$40. AE, DISC, MC, V. Lunch & dinner Mon–Sat, brunch Sun.

SOUL LIBERTY

Roger Williams's Legacy in Rhode Island

BY KERRY ACKER & TOM GAVIN

BEFORE THOMAS JEFFERSON WROTE ABOUT SEPARATION OF CHURCH AND STATE, Roger Williams brought his unique vision of religious freedom to the New World. The bright, outspoken preacher from London believed in "soul liberty"—the radical proposition that only an individual's conscience, rather than an institution or the influence of others, can lead one to God. After clashing with church officials in Boston and Salem, he spent 2 years in Plymouth, where was tried for heresy; fled south to avoid deportation; and lived among the Narragansett Indians before founding Providence Plantation—a controversial haven where dissenters, separatists, and the persecuted could all live together in peace.

Native Relations

Williams insisted on fair dealings with indigenous peoples—a rare stance in his day. He challenged the Massachusetts Bay Colony's charter, which had not considered the local tribes' use of the territory. In 1636, he purchased from the Narragansett people the land that became Providence Plantation. He studied native tongues, publishing *A Key into the Language of America*. He also advocated for the Narragansett, securing them an alliance with the English in the Pequot War and facilitating the sale of Narragansett land that became Newport and Portsmouth.

Separation of Church & State

Whereas the Puritans in Boston wanted to "purify" the Anglican Church, Williams wanted to separate from it entirely. A devout believer, he founded Providence on the belief that the wall between the "garden of the church and the wilderness of the world" was essential for both the church and the citizenry to shield religious authorities from the corruptions of civil power, and to ensure the individual's right to worship according to conscience, without membership in a sanctioned group. In 1644, he cited Biblical support for this separation of church and state in his best-known work, *The Bloudy Tenent of Persecution for Cause of Conscience*.

Jews & Gentiles

Most of the colonists were Protestant, but Newport supported a thriving Jewish community, starting with the arrival of Spanish and Portuguese families coming from Barbados in 1658. Founding the Congregation Jeshuat Israel, they purchased land in 1677 for the first Jewish burial ground in America. Over the next century, more families arrived from Curaçao and directly from Portugal. The Touro Synagogue—America's first, dating to 1763—served as a meeting place in 1781 for George Washington's visit; his 1790 letter to "the Hebrew Congregation in Newport" confirmed the budding nation's commitment to religious freedom, stating the U.S. would give "to bigotry no sanction, to persecution no assistance."

Safe Haven for Heretical Christians

Cofounder of the first Baptist church in America in 1638, Williams had already left the faith by the time John Clarke, the most important early Baptist

in America, started a church in Newport. Despite Williams's dissatisfaction with all organized religions, he and Clarke continued to work together, securing a charter for the colony of Rhode Island in 1663. There the Quakers—persecuted, imprisoned, and hanged elsewhere—found refuge in the 1650s, establishing a vital community decades before William Penn's settlement farther south. The Quaker Society of Friends emphasized equality for all—including women and slaves. While the slave trade thrived in Rhode Island for another century, the Quakers became instrumental in pushing for emancipation.

The Legacy Today

Today Brown University, founded in 1764 in Providence, would do Roger Williams proud. A thriving sector of the Rhode Island capital's culture and economy, Brown was the first Ivy League school to admit all religions, and famously emphasizes diversity in both student body and curriculum as a vital component to learning, understanding, and serving the community.

Providence

A staunch advocate of religious freedom, Protestant preacher Roger Williams founded Providence in 1636, after purchasing the land from Narragansett chiefs. His settlement was the country's first to implement a separation of church and state, and—far from the anarchy his critics predicted—a community grew where religious dissenters from elsewhere could all be accepted. In the 19th century, the city became a manufacturing powerhouse, with a thriving textile, jewelry, and silver industry that attracted multitudes of immigrants from Italy, Portugal, and elsewhere. Although the Depression brought a major drop in population accompanied by a rise in organized crime, today's Providence is a multiethnic enclave with a flourishing downtown ("downcity"), a burgeoning arts and dining scene, and a proud populace that embraces it all—even politicians who have spent time in jail. Two days should be enough time to explore downcity; Federal Hill; and College Hill–dominated East Side, with Brown and RISD campuses, eclectic shopping, and historic Benefit Street homes.

> Firelight illuminates the arched bridges of Providence's three rivers for the unique annual WaterFire art installation.

START Providence is 50 miles from Boston, MA.

❶ ★ State House. This white marble American Renaissance–style building, designed by iconic late-19th-century architects McKim, Mead & White, has one of the largest self-supporting marble-covered domes in the world; only those at St. Peter's Basilica, the Taj Mahal, and—curiously—the Minnesota State capital building are larger. Take the self-guided tour for a look at the chambers, and admire the gilded ceiling and marble pilasters of the State Reception Room and the ornate ceiling of the State House Library. ⏱ 1 hr. 82 Smith St. ☎ 401/222-2357. www.rilin.state.ri.us/statehousetour. Free admission. Mon–Fri 8:30am–4:30pm.

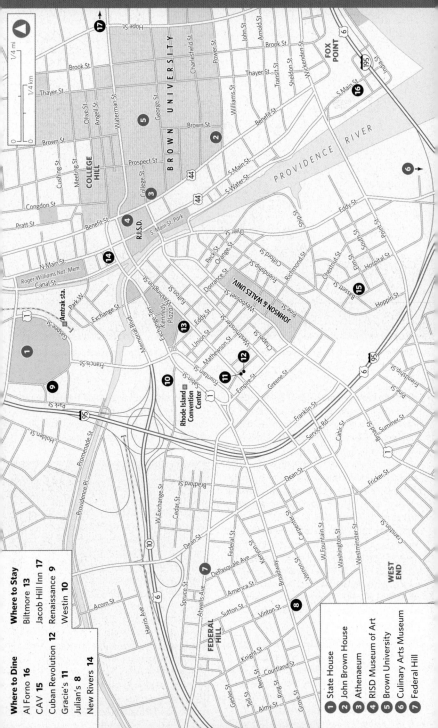

> The dome of the State House, topped by a gilded statue of "Independent Man," commands Providence's city center.

2 ★ **John Brown House.** This 1788 Georgian home was quite a mansion for its time, as Brown—not to be confused with the famous abolitionist—was a prominent slave trader and merchant in the China trade. The house was later occupied by the well-to-do Gammell family, and finally by transportation magnate Marsden Perry, when he wasn't in his Newport mansion or elsewhere. The interior represents all these eras—with its full-length Carolina pine floors, 1908 Otis Elevator, Gilbert Stuart Portraits—and the docents go deep into the stories of each owner, making for an engrossing tour. ⏱ 1½ hr. 52 Power St. ☎ 401/273-7507. www.rihs.org/museums.html. Admission $8 adults, $4 kids 7–17. Tours Fri–Sat 10:30am, noon, 1:30pm & 3pm; Apr–Nov also Tues–Fri 1:30 & 3pm.

3 **Athenaeum.** A major part of the early city's social and intellectual life, this membership library—designed by William Strickland, one of the leading Greek Revival architects of the day—opened in 1838, as an outgrowth of the earlier Providence Library Company. As a nonmember, you can still leaf through books among the glorious two-story stacks where Poe and Lovecraft once browsed. ⏱ 1 hr. 251 Benefit St. ☎ 401/421-6970. www.providence

WaterFire

This community event starring fire and water—started in 1994 by sculptor Barnaby Evans and re-created every year since 1996—has been a key component of the city's renaissance. Crowds gather along the banks of the Woonasquatucket, Moshassuck, and Providence rivers to gawk at 100 flickering bonfires on the water; a changing roster of amplified music chosen by Evans is an integral part of the show. To keep the tradition alive, donate $5 (look for the blue balloons to locate "ambassador stations"). For a more intimate experience, contact La Gondola (☎ 401/421-8877; www.gondolari.com) to boat down the river among the braziers. Check www.waterfire.org for the schedule.

> *The breadth of the Museum of Art at the Rhode Island School of Design extends from an Egyptian coffin to contemporary works.*

athenaeum.org. Free admission. Mon–Thurs 9am–7pm; Fri–Sat 9am–5pm; Sun 1–5pm.

❹ ★★ RISD Museum of Art. As one of the finest art schools in the country, the Rhode Island School of Design has a reputation to uphold here. But far from restricting its scope to, say, modern and contemporary works, the collection encompasses a wide range of fine and decorative arts: Egyptian mummy, Japanese prints, a huge 12th-century Buddha, Goddard and Townsend furniture, Renaissance and Baroque works, 18th- and 19th-century American paintings, and paintings by French Impressionists, Picasso, and Warhol, to name a few. ⏱ 2 hr. 224 Benefit St. ☎ 401/454-6500. www.risdmuseum.org. Admission $10 adults, $3 kids 5–18. Tues–Sun 10am–5pm. Closed Aug.

❺ Brown University. Founded in 1764—and the first Ivy Leaguer to accept students of all religions—Brown moved to its current location in 1770. Comprising 143 acres and 235 buildings, the main campus largely consists of Georgian buildings such as University Hall (1770), which originally housed the entire college, while numerous, smaller Victorian

> *Soak in the knowledge at the Providence Athenaeum.*

> *Brown University is known for its diversity.*

houses—like the Corliss-Bracket House (1887), where the admissions offices are—came into the fold as the university expanded. A self-guided tour map is available at the Steven Roberts Campus Center, 75 Waterman St. ⊙ 1 hr.

6 ★ **Culinary Arts Museum.** *Attention foodies:* You'll find White House china, kitchen gadgets, rare cookbooks dating back to the 16th century, and thousands of menus from around the world at this tribute to all things

Hitting the Shops

In the mood to spend a little? This artsy town has great choices. Downcity, head to indie bookstore **Symposium,** 240 Westminster (☎ 401/273-7900); **Homestyle,** 229 Westminster (☎ 401/227-1159), for cool home goods; and **Elsa Arms,** 231 Westminster (☎ 401/383-5558), for über-stylish women's wear. On the East Side, Thayer Street is lined with vintage clothing and commercial shops, but don't miss the one-of-a-kind art and wares at **RISD Works,** 20 N. Main St. (☎ 401/277-4949). South Main and Wickenden streets are also fun to browse.

Buddy Cianci, Mayor of Scandal

Love him or hate him, nobody can deny that Vincent A. "Buddy" Cianci, Jr., has left an indelible mark on Providence. As the capital's longest-serving (21 years over two stints), first Italian, and first Republican mayor since the Great Depression, the charismatic and media-savvy politician helped turn the city around in the late 1970s. He was then forced to resign after pleading guilty to assaulting a man he believed was having an affair with his wife—wielding a lit cigarette, an ashtray, and a fireplace log, no less. Miraculously, he won the office again in '91 and really hit his stride, pushing the arts and revitalizing downtown with Waterplace Park and the Providence Place Mall. So popular that he ran unopposed in '98, he was brought down again in 2002. This time he was convicted of racketeering as part of a local FBI corruption investigation called "Operation Plunder Dome." The mayor, who originally ran for office on an anticorruption platform, got 5 years in the slammer. When he got out in 2007, he promptly ditched his trademark toupee and hit the airwaves as a popular radio talk show host. Look out—he'll be eligible to run again in 2014.

> *Sweets at Sciallo Brothers Bakery.*

culinary at Johnson and Wales University. The Diner Museum is a big hit, with a collection of items donated by the likes of Julia Child. ⏲1 hr. 315 Harborside Blvd. ☎ 401/598-2805. www.culinary.org. Admission $7 adults, $2 kids 5–18. Tues–Sun 10am–5pm.

7 ★ Federal Hill. Providence's multiethnic heritage makes the city a food lover's dream. While great eats can be found throughout the city, don't miss Little Italy. Concentrated around Atwell's Avenue, the area overflows with Italian eats, from red-sauce standards to creative modern variations. More than a restaurant, the market at **Constantino's Ristorante,** 265 Atwells Ave. (☎ 401/528-1100), draws a crowd for cheeses, cured meats, and other Italian goodies. Enjoy traditional Tuscan dishes in close quarters at **Siena,** 128 Atwells Ave. (☎ 401/521-3311), or eclectic choices at the sidewalk cafe of **Mediterraneo Caffe,** 134 Atwells Ave. (☎ 401/331-7760). **Sciallo Brothers Bakery,** 275 Atwells Ave. (☎ 401/421-0986), is an old standby for cakes and other baked goods; go to **Pastiche,** 92 Spruce St. (☎ 401/861-5190), for unforgettable pastries. ⏲ 2 hr.

Providence Nightlife

There are plenty of places to get a drink in this town, but for entertainment, the non-profit **AS 220,** 115 Empire St. (☎ 401/831-9327; www.as220.org), presents new and vital works in all modes—poetry slams, traditional Irish music, punk rock, and free jazz. Larger acts, from Wilco to Wu-Tang Clan, appear at **Lupos Heartbreak Hotel,** 79 Washington St. (☎ 401/331-LUPO 5876; www.lupos.com). The **Providence Performing Arts Center,** 220 Weybosset St. (☎ 401/421-2787; www.ppacri.org)—started in 1928 as Loew's Movie Palace—hosts such shows as *Mamma Mia, the Lion King,* Blue Man Group, and the Alvin Ailey dance troupe. The 1938 art deco **Avon Cinema,** 260 Thayer St. (☎ 401/421-AVON 2866; www.avoncinema.com), screens an excellent selection of foreign, independent, and lost classics.

Where to Stay

> The glass elevator in the grand lobby of the Providence Biltmore.

★★★ Biltmore PROVIDENCE

Step into the grand entrance of this downtown 1922 hotel, where the stairway, crystal chandelier, bronze ceiling, and distinctive glass elevator demand your attention. Rooms, all with king beds, retain much of their old-world charm without feeling even the slightest bit fusty, while the spa is a nice up-to-date touch. 11 Dorrance St. ☎ 401/421-0700. www. providencebiltmore.com. 292 units. Doubles $139–$599. AE, MC, V.

★★ Jacob Hill Inn SEEKONK

The owners greet you like family upon your arrival at this sumptuous former hunt club in the nearby town of Seekonk, just over the Massachusetts border. Expect stellar hospitality, spic-and-span rooms with fireplaces and Jacuzzis, a delicious breakfast, and a gorgeous billiards room. 120 Jacob St. ☎ 401/527-3629. www.inn-providence-ri.com. 12 units. Doubles $179–$459 w/breakfast. AE, DISC, MC, V.

★★ Renaissance PROVIDENCE

High on a hill overlooking downtown, this former Masonic temple—left unfinished in 1928—has been transformed into a sleek hotel with spacious rooms and bold colors adding a modern flair to the Doric columns and marble floors. 5 Ave. of the Arts. ☎ 401/919-5000. www.marriott.com. 272 units. Doubles $169–$299. AE, DISC, MC, V.

★★★ Westin PROVIDENCE

Connected to the Providence Place mall and convention center, this Starwood property is the destination of choice for many business travelers, but that doesn't mean it's bland. Rooms are stylish and very comfortable, with patented Heavenly mattresses and pillows. 1 W. Exchange St. ☎ 800/937-8461. www. starwoodhotels.com/westin. 364 units. Doubles $229–$314. AE, DISC, MC, V.

Where to Dine

★★ Al Forno PROVIDENCE *ITALIAN*
At this standout, you'll find traditional red-sauce favorites along with more creative choices like zucchini Swiss chard and ricotta ravioli with basil pesto, or shells baked with pumpkin cream pancetta and five cheeses. 577 S. Main St. ☎ 401/273-9670. www.alforno.com. Entrees $20–$33. AE, DISC, MC, V. Dinner Tues–Sat.

★★ CAV PROVIDENCE *ECLECTIC*
The unique decor of African and Asian art and antiques suits the imaginative dishes at this atmospheric place. It excels in continental fare with touches from Southeast Asia and the Middle East. 14 Imperial Place. ☎ 401/751-9164. www.cavrestaurant.com. Entrees $15–$32. AE, DISC, MC, V. Lunch & dinner daily.

★ Cuban Revolution PROVIDENCE *CUBAN*
Follow the music to this funky and spirited mini-chain for pressed sandwiches, stuffed pepper dews, steak chimichurris, or picadillos. 50 Aborn St. ☎ 401/331-8829. www.thecuban revolution.com. Entrees $10–$18. AE, DISC, MC, V. Lunch & dinner daily.

★★ Gracie's PROVIDENCE *NEW AMERICAN*
Knowledgeable wait staff serve locally focused, seasonal dishes like oven-roasted rabbit and wild striped bass. Save room for such sweets as rhubarb mascarpone cheesecake. 194 Washington St. ☎ 401/272-7811. www. graciesprovidence.com. Entrees $10–$38. AE, MC, V. Dinner Tues–Sat.

★★ Julian's PROVIDENCE *AMERICAN*
Dinner is great at this gritty, decidedly hip, exposed-brick, TV-in-the-john destination, but it's the brunch menu that reels us in: ricotta-stuffed French toast, peach cobbler pancakes, and a

> Eastern flavors and exotic decor mingle at CAV.

great selection of savory benedicts. Be prepared for a long wait. 318 Broadway. ☎ 401/861-1770. www.juliansprovidence.com. Entrees $4–$15. AE, DISC, MC, V. Breakfast, lunch & dinner daily.

★★ New Rivers PROVIDENCE *NEW AMERICAN*
The very seasonal menu at this cute and cozy farm-to-table spot is full of bright and clean flavors, with delectable items such as duck fat fingerlings, horseradish-rubbed T-bone, and ricotta tortellini with kale-charred pine nuts. 7 Steeple St. ☎ 401/751-0350. www.newrivers restaurant.com. Entrees $16–$27. AE, MC, V. Dinner Mon–Sat.

The Best Burger in Town

Dating back to 1893, the Haven Brothers' legendary diner on wheels serves burgers and other classic cheap eats for lunch on Spruce Street, before rolling to City Hall, where they serve from late afternoon into the wee hours. Catch it if you can! For exact hours and locations, call ☎ 401/861-7777.

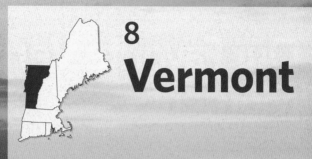

Our Favorite Vermont Moments

Pressed to name our favorite things about Vermont, we plead the Fifth. Heck, we couldn't even name our favorite season in the Green Mountain State. Let's just say that between the vast, untrammeled spaces; the lush valleys and rolling emerald hills of the Green Mountains; the hip and crunchy cities; the profusion of eco-minded farms and restaurants; disarmingly adorable villages; and fiercely independent, free-thinking citizenry, Vermont's attractions are broad and numerous. Here are some of our choice moments.

> PREVIOUS PAGE *A sunset kayaking excursion on Lake Champlain.* THIS PAGE *Shredding the powder at one of Vermont's premier ski resorts.*

❶ **Gawking at the massive puppets at the Bread and Puppet Museum.** This quirky museum that houses larger-than-life papier-mâché puppets used by a radical political theater group—found in a dilapidated barn along the back roads of the Northeast Kingdom—represents some of the best parts of Vermont culture: artsy, independent, progressive, and just a little bit weird. See p. 378, ❸.

❷ **Dining at one of Vermont's great locavore restaurants.** While others may dabble in the farm-to-table thing, using locally sourced ingredients from nearby farms and small businesses is a way of life for Vermont's restaurateurs and chefs. So put down your greasy donut and do the right thing—for your palate, the community, and the environment: Enjoy a fabulous meal at **Claire's** (p. 379) or the **Inn at Weathersfield** (p. 391).

❸ **Soaking up Brattleboro.** If this is what happens when artsy meets hippie meets outdoorsy, we're all for it. Drop by the boutiques, bookstores, and cafes, and talk to the local folks in this vibrant, indie-spirited, and community-minded city. See p. 386.

❹ **Getting lost in the Northeast Kingdom during fall foliage season.** Lose the GPS; choose a dirt road; and pass fields, rolling meadows, and other scenes of unspoiled beauty. Turn here, come across shimmering **Lake Willoughby** (p. 378, ❹). Drive

> *You don't have to be a local to enjoy the locavore menu at Claire's restaurant in Hardwick, a partner of the Center for an Agricultural Economy.*

on, through thick red- and gold-blazed forest, until left is as good as right, and—wait, are you in Canada? No, but turn again and stumble across the **Parker Pie Company** (p. 379). Life is good. See p. 376.

5 **Traveling back in time at Plymouth Notch.** The pristine setting and well-preserved buildings of the **President Calvin Coolidge State Historic Site** (p. 390, **1**) make it easy to imagine what life was like when the 30th president was growing up here. The general store, the dance hall that served as a temporary White House in 1924, the one-room schoolhouse—by the time you're done looking around you'll want to quit your job, ditch your iPad, slow down, and simplify.

6 **Visiting a cheese maker.** Cheese being one of our favorite things, we love to meet those responsible for this divine delectable. **Shelburne Farms** (p. 383) and **Grafton** (p. 391, **2**) are great places to see the process, but we also recommend driving out to **Consider Bardwell Farm,** 1333 Vermont 153, West Pawlet (☎ 802/645-9928), or **Vermont Shepherd Farm,** 281 Patch Farm Rd., Putney (☎ 802/387-4473), to see the animals and talk to the farmers.

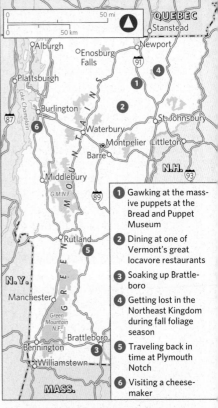

1 Gawking at the massive puppets at the Bread and Puppet Museum

2 Dining at one of Vermont's great locavore restaurants

3 Soaking up Brattleboro

4 Getting lost in the Northeast Kingdom during fall foliage season

5 Traveling back in time at Plymouth Notch

6 Visiting a cheesemaker

7 **Hitting the slopes.** The beauty, and the surprising silence, of Vermont's snow covered mountains make for the East's best skiing. Whether you're going downhill or cross country, be sure to hit the trails. Our favorite? **Stowe,** of course. See p. 408.

Travel Alert: Hurricane & Hundred-Year Flooding

On August 28, 2011, Vermont was hit by the remnants of Hurricane Irene, and, thanks to a whopping 7 inches of rain, suffered its worst flooding in nearly a century. The resulting damage ranged from water-soaked homes and businesses to washed out bridges and roads. Vermonters are a hardy bunch, and repairs were soon underway, but given the enormous extent of the damage, it would be wise to call ahead when making plans.

Vermont in 4 Days

Four days? It's a short time to spend in such a vast, beautiful state, but our tour gives you a glimpse—from your car and on foot—of what makes Vermont so distinct. This itinerary focuses on the southern part of the state, from Bennington—where a motley group of patriots fended off British troops and turned the tide of the Revolutionary War—to arty, progressive Brattleboro. The Green Mountain state has more than its share of archetypal white-clapboard towns, complete with spired churches and charming greens, but it still manages to feel crowded with weekending tourists, especially during fall foliage and ski season. Plan accordingly. And while there are properties catering to those in search of that idealized Vermont experience, with maple syrup and quaintness galore, you'll also find authentic hardworking towns, along with waterfalls and farms, general stores and antiques, pottery makers and cheese makers.

> The best view of the Quechee (pronounced kwee-chee) Gorge is from the bottom, accessible by a gravel path from the parking lot.

START Bennington is 122 miles from Burlington. **TRIP LENGTH** 166 miles.

1 ★★ **Bennington.** Start your tour in this pleasant, historic, working-class town in the southwest corner. ☺ 3 hr. See p. 372, **1**.

2 **Molly Stark Trail.** Cross the south of the state on this scenic byway, otherwise known as VT-9. ☺ 1–2 hr. See p. 360, **1**.

3 ★★★ **Brattleboro.** Explore this folksy arts-centric former mill town tucked into the Connecticut River Valley. Stop in at the **Brattleboro Museum & Art Center** to catch contemporary artwork, then stroll Main Street, checking out indie boutiques, bookstores, and galleries. Even if you're not traveling with kids, pay a visit to **Retreat Farm & Trails** (p. 387, **2**) for some quality time with the cute animals at the petting

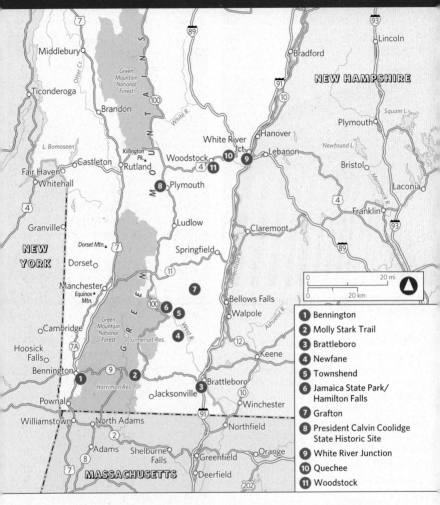

1. Bennington
2. Molly Stark Trail
3. Brattleboro
4. Newfane
5. Townshend
6. Jamaica State Park/ Hamilton Falls
7. Grafton
8. President Calvin Coolidge State Historic Site
9. White River Junction
10. Quechee
11. Woodstock

zoo, to explore some of the 9 miles of the trail network (good for mountain biking, snow-shoeing, and hiking), and to watch the cheese making at the on-site **Grafton Cheese Factory.** If you plan your visit to coincide with **Gallery Walk** (p. 387), taking place on the first Friday of every month, you'll experience Brattleboro at its best. ⏲ 4 hr. See p. 386, ❶.

Spend the night in or near Brattleboro. On Day 2, head north on Main St. and go left to stay on Rte. 30 north for 11 miles.

❹ ★★ kids **Newfane.** First, skip breakfast at your hotel and stop at the **Newfane Café and Creamery,** 550 Route 30 (☎ 802/365-4442).

This excellent order-from-the-counter spot serves up an ever-changing menu of creatively prepared dishes, with a keen focus on fresh-ness and flavor. They have a great selection of just-baked croissants and quiches, and they care about details: For example, iced coffee comes with coffee ice cubes.

Continue on into the achingly beautiful

Travel Tip

This is a tour designed for the summer or early-autumn months—many sites and shops close or have truncated hours in the off-season.

> *White picket fences and a slower pace of life contribute to the charm of Newfane.*

white-clapboard village of Newfane to admire the historic buildings, including the graceful 19th-century columned Greek Revival courthouse. Visit the **Historical Society of Windham County** to get context and check out local artifacts, and drop in at the charming **Newfane Country Store,** 598 VT-30 (☎ 802/365-7916), to browse through rows of candy, hand-painted pottery, quilts, and other Vermont delectables. ⏱ 1 hr. See p. 388, **5**.

Continue 5 miles north on Rte. 30.

5 ★★ **Townshend.** Another white-clapboard town on a green, but Townshend also has the three-span 277-foot 1870 **Scott Covered Bridge;** one of its spans is the state's longest at 166 feet. Cars aren't allowed, but you can still walk through and admire the latticework. Just west of the village, a bright yellow farmhouse is home to **Twitchell House Antiques,** Rte. 30 (☎ 802/365-9224), where you'll find vintage lamps, clocks, kitchenware, and all sorts of goodies. ⏱ 2 hr. See p. 388, **6**.

Take Rte. 30 north for 4½ miles. Turn right and take Windham Hill Rd. for 4⅓ miles, take a left at Burbee Pond Rd., and go left at W. Windham Rd., which you'll follow for 2¾ miles.

The Green Mountain Boys

After the French and Indian War (1754–63), the territory between the Connecticut and Hudson rivers was in hot dispute. By the time the British king deemed the region to be the property of New York in 1764, settlers from New Hampshire had already established farms. So when the Yorkers (or landholders from New York) began to stake their claim, trouble ensued.

When a New York sheriff and 300 Yorkers sought to take over some of those farms in 1771, a ragtag group of militiamen from Bennington, led by Ethan Allen, blocked them. These Green Mountain Boys, as the armed band came to be called, expanded and led an all-out campaign against the Yorkers, burning their buildings, beating them, and generally terrorizing them. Their efforts effectively worked: By 1777, Vermont was an independent republic, with its own constitution, the first in the nation to guarantee voting rights to all free men and ban slavery. (It officially joined the Union in 1791.)

But the Boys—now a source of tremendous pride among Vermonters—didn't end their work there: They joined the Revolution. In 1775, just under 100 of them, led by both Ethan Allen and Benedict Arnold, captured Fort Ticonderoga. Though Allen was captured and remained a prisoner of the British until 1778, the Green Mountain Boys went on to play a crucial role in the Battle of Bennington (1777), when they fought off British General Johnny Burgoyne and his troops as the Tories attempted to seize desperately needed supplies from the Continental army's storehouse in Bennington (now the site of the Bennington Battle Monument; p. 372, **1**). Considerably weakened, the British army surrendered after their defeat in Saratoga, 2 months after Bennington.

6 kids ★★ **Jamaica State Park/Hamilton Falls.** The West River flows through this popular park, so it sees plenty of canoeing and kayaking activity. But Jamaica also features the dazzling Hamilton Falls, which drop 125 feet, creating three large pools along the way. Don't be tempted to jump in: Swimming is prohibited. ⏱ 1 hr. ☎ 802/874-4600. www.vtstateparks.com. Early May to Columbus Day daily 10am-9pm.

Take Rte. 30 4½ miles south and turn left onto Rte. 35, which you'll take 3½ miles north. Veer left at Townshend Rd. and continue onto Grafton Rd. for 5½ miles. Turn right onto Rte. 121 east and take it into:

7 ★★ **Grafton.** Idyllic little Grafton completes Day 2's trifecta of storybook Vermont towns. After walking around the village, hiking at the **Grafton Ponds Outdoor Center,** and sampling cheese at the **Grafton Village Cheese Shop,** enjoy dinner at the **Old Tavern** (p. 391). ⏱ 3 hr. See p. 391, **2**.

Spend the night in Grafton. On Day 3, get back on Rte. 35, going north 7 miles. In Chester, turn right on S. Main St. and left on Maple St., which becomes Rte. 103 north. Go 12 miles to Rte. 100, and take a right to go north for 11 miles to the junction of Rte. 100A, which you'll take north for 1 mile.

8 kids ★★★ **President Calvin Coolidge State Historic Site.** Our nation's 30th president, Calvin Coolidge—famous for his Yankee reticence, he was nicknamed "Silent Cal"—was born and raised in Vermont, right here in Plymouth Notch. Spend a few hours stepping back in time, checking out the exhibits—don't miss the cheese factory!—and savoring the setting. ⏱ 2 hr. See p. 390, **1**.

Vermont's Frost

Though he was born in San Francisco, died in Boston, wintered in Florida, attended colleges in Massachusetts and New Hampshire, and even lived for a stretch in England, Vermont claims Robert Frost as one of its own. Frost created much of his poetry—using regional vernacular to evoke the scenery, moods, and people of rural northern New England—while he lived in Vermont. The state's official poet laureate wrote many of the poems contained in his Pulitzer Prize-winning collection *New Hampshire*—including "Stopping by Woods on a Snowy Evening"—during his time in Shaftsbury (1920-38), just north of Bennington.

You can visit his former home there, the **Robert Frost Stone House Museum,** 7A, Shaftsbury (☎ 802/447-6200; www.frostfriends.org). The cabin (pictured) he purchased in Ripton in 1939—near **Middlebury College's Bread Loaf campus** (p. 402), which he co-founded—served as his summer home until his passing in 1963. He is buried in **Bennington** (p. 372, **1**).

> *Conductors on the Green Mountain Flyer railroad.*

> *An artisan crafts handblown stemware at the workshop at Simon Pearce at the Mill.*

Continue north on Rte. 100A for 6 miles to Rte. 4, which you'll take west 22 miles. Turn left onto Rte. 5 north and continue onto Main St.

9 **White River Junction.** Wander around town, then hop on the 2:30pm **Green Mountain Railroad.** Enjoy the scenery along the **Connecticut River,** and the 45-minute stop at the **Montshire Museum of Science,** included in the ticket. ⊙ 2 hr. See p. 397, **8**.

Head back out Rte. 5 north, and turn right onto Rte. 4, going 7 miles east.

10 ★★ **Quechee.** Explore the trails skirting **Quechee Gorge** (p. 397, **7**)—if it's midweek, you might avoid the crowds. Then end Day 3 at **Simon Pearce at the Mill** (p. 396, **5**), a historic woolen-mill-turned-retail store/workshop/restaurant. The Irish-born Pearce and his team of skilled craftsmen create exquisite handblown vases, stemware, and other sparkling glassware and pottery on-site. You can watch the artisans at work—then savor a superb meal and an amazing view overlooking the Ottauquechee River. ⊙ 3 hr.

Travel Tip

In Newfane on a Sunday? You're in luck. At the **Newfane Flea Market** (☎ 802/365-4000), just north of the town center on Rte. 30, open every Sunday May to October, around 200 dealers hawk antiques, crafts, and cheap clothes; of course, there's food.

Plan Ahead

On Day 3, you'll want to call the **Marsh-Billings-Rockefeller National Historic Park** (☎ 802/457-3368) to make reservations for Day 4's morning tour.

> A horse-drawn sleigh tour of Billings Farm, the legacy of native Vermonter and president of the North Pacific Railroad, Frederick Billings.

Head another 7 miles west on Rte. 4 and spend the night in or around:

⓫ ★★ **Woodstock.** On your final day, make straight for the Carriage Barn Visitor Center at **Marsh-Billings-Rockefeller National Historical Park** (p. 395, ❷) to meet the ranger who will lead you on your hour-long tour of the mansion, home to three pioneering conservationists at different times: George Marsh, Frederick Billings, and Laurance Rockefeller. The guides do a bang-up job of explaining the history of conservation, the house, and the people who lived in it. Afterward, walk some of the lovely trails on the property. Then head across the street to **Billings Farm & Museum** (p. 396, ❸) to spend a few hours; aim to catch the daily 3:15pm milking. Wrap up your tour of the Green Mountain State by browsing the shops of sophisticated Woodstock (p. 394, ❶). ☺ 1 day.

Green State Politics

One of only four states that were once independent republics—along with Texas, California, and Hawaii—Vermont has a reputation for liberalness. It was the first state to ratify civil unions (in 2000). It is also one of only four in which billboards are banned, to preserve Vermont's "scenic resources". Yet despite the left-leaning stereotype, Vermont went Democratic on a presidential ticket only once before the '90s—in 1964—and Senator Patrick Leahy, incumbent since 1975, is the only elected Democratic senator in the state's history. Of course, his fellow senator, Bernie Sanders, is a socialist who caucuses with the Democrats but was elected as an independent. Likewise in the House of Representatives, only two Democrats have ever occupied Vermont's single seat.

Vermont in 1 Week

Originally claimed by the French—who settled around Lake Champlain in 1666—the Green Mountain State (Les Monts Verts?) was the first place to hold Roman Catholic services in the overwhelmingly Protestant colonies. Even after the Treaty of Paris gave England control in 1763, Vermont proved a feisty territory, remaining independent after the Revolutionary War and abolishing slavery in 1777. You'll start off with a taste of this history in Bennington, before heading deeper into the Green Mountains for the natural beauty that is the state's calling card. With ample pit stops for cheese and maple goods, you'll end up in the big city (pop. 38,889) of Burlington.

> Moss Glen Falls, arguably the most photogenic in a state full of waterfalls, is easily accessible from Route 100.

START Bennington is 122 miles from Burlington. **TRIP LENGTH** 330 miles.

1 ★★ Bennington. Begin your visit in this historic working-class town in southwestern Vermont. ◷ 3 hr. See p. 372, **1**.

Head north on Rte. 7 and turn left onto Rte. 7A, taking it 20 miles to Manchester, where you'll spend the night.

2 ★★ Manchester. While many come here for the designer shopping (nearby outlets include such brands as Ann Taylor, Brooks Brothers, and Kate Spade), Manchester—composed of genteel, historic Manchester Village and the more commercial Manchester Center—is worth some time exploring. Grab a cup at the **Spiral Press Café,** 15 Bonnet St. (☎ 802/362-9944), and browse the fabulous **Northshire Bookstore** in Manchester Center, then drive back down Rte. 7A to the common for a walk around the old part of town. Get your art fix at the **Southern Vermont Arts Center,** and don't miss **Hildene,** the grand Georgian Revival mansion where President Lincoln's son Robert Todd Lincoln spent his summers. ◷ 4 hr. See p. 374, **3**.

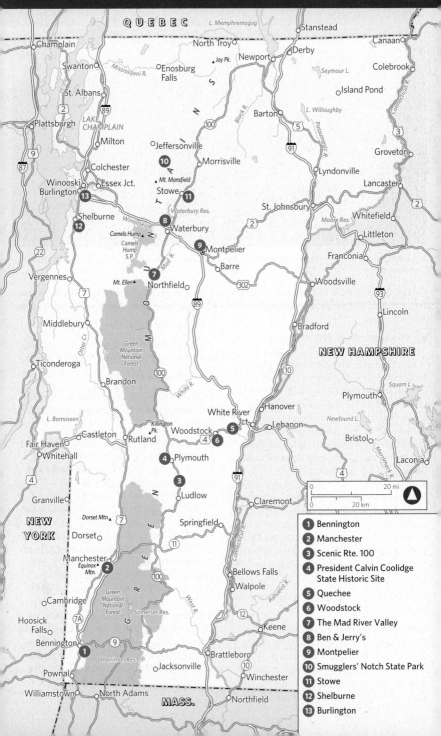

QUEBEC

L. Memphremagog

Champlain

North Troy

Stanstead

Swanton

Enosburg Falls

Jay Pk.

Newport

Derby

Canaan

Colebrook

St. Albans

Mississquoi R.

89

Island Pond

Plattsburgh

LAKE CHAMPLAIN

Milton

Jeffersonville

Barton

L. Willoughby

Seymour L.

5

91

Groton

9

Colchester

10

Morrisville

Lyndonville

Lancaster

87

Winooski

Burlington

Essex Jct.

13

Mt. Mansfield

Stowe

11

St. Johnsbury

Whitefield

Shelburne

12

Waterbury Res.

8

Waterbury

Winooski R.

2

Moore Res.

Littleton

Franconia

Camels Hump

Camels Hump S.P.

9

Montpelier

302

Woodsville

93

Lincoln

22

Mt. Ellen

7

Northfield

Barre

Vergennes

7

Middlebury

Otter Cr.

89

Bradford

NEW HAMPSHIRE

Ticonderoga

Green Mountain National Forest

100

White R.

10

Plymouth

Brandon

Squam L.

Newfound L.

L. Bomoseen

Castleton

Killington Pk.

Woodstock

White River Jct.

Hanover

Lebanon

Bristol

Laconia

Fair Haven

Whitehall

Rutland

4

6

5

91

4

4

Plymouth

Claremont

20 mi

20 km

Granville

3

Ludlow

Springfield

NEW YORK

Dorset Mtn.

7

Dorset

11

Bennington

Manchester

2

Equinox Mtn.

100

Bellows Falls

Walpole

Cambridge

Green Mountain National Forest

Somerset Res.

West R.

12

Keene

Hoosick Falls

7A

Bennington

9

Harriman Res.

Jacksonville

Brattleboro

10

Winchester

Pownal

Williamstown

North Adams

MASS.

Northfield

1. Bennington
2. Manchester
3. Scenic Rte. 100
4. President Calvin Coolidge State Historic Site
5. Quechee
6. Woodstock
7. The Mad River Valley
8. Ben & Jerry's
9. Montpelier
10. Smugglers' Notch State Park
11. Stowe
12. Shelburne
13. Burlington

> *A panoramic view of the magnificent Green Mountains, which gave Vermont its name, from the French monts verts.*

On Day 2, take Rte. 11 15 miles east and turn left onto Rte. 100 north to begin your drive on:

3 ★★★ **Scenic Route 100.** Winding its way up the middle of Vermont, Rte. 100 (aka VT-100) is the loveliest way to traverse the Green Mountains by car. Must-stops along the way include **Taylor Farm,** 825 Route 11, Londonderry (☎ 802/824-5690; www.taylorfarmvermont. com)—Vermont's only producer of Gouda cheese—where you can pick up a snack and check out their small herd of cows and goats; and the wonderfully old-time **Vermont Country Store,** 657 Main St., Weston (☎ 802/824-3184), where you can stretch your legs browsing their two wood-planked floors of Vermont-made food (cheese, maple syrup, penny candy, and so on), clothing, and other more hard-to-find local goods. Farther north you'll pass **Okemo Ski Area** (p. 371) in Ludlow before you make your way along the beautiful stretch of Lake Rescue, Echo Lake, and Amherst Lake. ☉ 2 hr.

After 26 miles, turn right onto Rte. 100A and go north 1 mile.

4 ★★★ kids **President Calvin Coolidge State Historic Site.** Stroll around the idyllic village where the 30th president was born and raised—and where he was sworn in while vacationing in 1923, upon hearing news of Warren G. Harding's untimely passing. ☉ 2 hr. See p. 390, **1**.

Return to Rte. 100N and go north 5½ miles. Turn right onto Rte. 4 and go 21 miles east to:

5 ★ **Quechee.** ☉ 2 hr. See p. 354, **10**.

Backtrack 7 miles west on Rte. 4 to Woodstock, where you'll spend the next 2 nights.

6 ★★ **Woodstock.** ☉ 1 day. See p. 355, **11**.

On Day 4, take Rte. 12 15 miles north to Rte. 107 west, and continue 8 miles to Rte. 100 north.

7 ★★ **Mad River Valley.** Get back on VT-100 for more of the glorious Green Mountains. Stop off in Rochester at **Sandy's Books and Bakery,** 30 N. Main St. (☎ 802/767-4258), for a snack, and pull off to the left above Granville to walk up to the resplendent **Moss Glen Falls** (p. 406). About 7½ miles north, take a right at Main Street into the village of **Warren** (p. 404, **1**), and stop to see the handcrafted gifts at **Creator's Shop,** 384 Main St. (☎ 802/496-2604), or grab a bite at the rustic-meets-sophisticated **Warren Store** (p. 404, **1**). Turn right at Brook Road and follow it onto East Warren Road to continue the detour at a higher elevation, with stunning views on both sides. Coming back down into the little town of **Waitsfield** (p. 405, **2**), cross the **Great Eddy Covered Bridge** (p. 405, **2**). ☉ 3½ hr.

From Waitsfield, take Rte. 100 north 14 miles to:

⑧ ★ kids Ben & Jerry's. Tour the home base of these ice-cream icons, and be prepared for some corny humor mixed in with the story of how hippie dreamers Ben Cohen and Jerry Greenfield became Ben & Jerry's unlikely corporate kingpins (with souls!). Also come hungry enough to enjoy the free samples. ⏱ 1 hr. See p. 405, ❸.

Take Rte. 11 south 1¼ miles and turn left onto Rte. 2 going east 12 miles to:

⑨ ★ Montpelier. Brush up on Vermont history and explore the shops of the smallest state capital in the country. ⏱ 3 hr. See p. 406, ❹.

Spend the night in or near Montpelier. On Day 5, it's back on Rte. 100 north to Stowe. There, pick up Rte. 108 and take it 10 miles north to:

⑩ Smugglers' Notch State Park. Resist the temptation to stop in Stowe just yet, and head a few miles north of town to this park for a hike. The drive through the towering cliffs of "the notch" itself is pretty cool, too. ⏱ 1½ hr. See p. 410, ❺.

Return 6 miles south on Rte. 108 to:

⑪ ★★ Stowe. This small resort town is the very definition of "ski village," situated at the base of Vermont's tallest peak, **Mount Mansfield** (p. 408, ❶). Catch a gondola ride to the top, drink in the view, and have a snack at the **Cliff House** (p. 409), a farm-to-table restaurant. Stroll down Main Street, visit the **Vermont Ski Museum** (p. 409, ❷), and build up an appetite on the **Stowe Recreation Path** (p. 410, ❹), which starts from the lot right behind the historic **Stowe Community Church** (p. 409, ❸). ⏱ 6 hr. See p. 408.

On Day 6, take Rte. 100S 10 miles to Waterbury and get on I-89 N. Go 24 miles to I-189W, taking it 1½ miles, and then turn onto US-7S for 5 miles.

⑫ ★★★ Shelburne. Bordering Burlington to the south, this smallish town has some of the biggest attractions in the state. ⏱ 1 day. See p. 383.

Spend the night in or around Burlington.

⑬ ★★★ Burlington. Do we have to give you an excuse to tour the **Lake Champlain Chocolates** (p. 382, ❻) factory before noon? Well, you

won't be alone. Besides the informative peek behind the curtain of the magical substance, there will be "educational" samples along the way, and more waiting in the gift shop. Next, get to know Lake Champlain from the bottom up, starting at the **ECHO Lake Aquarium** (p. 381, ❸). ECHO is all about interactive learning—for all ages. The local ecology is the springboard for discovery, from tide pools and shipwrecks to the mysterious Loch Ness–like monster known as **Champ(y)** (p. 382). Afterward, hook up with **Lake Champlain Cruises** to get out on the water yourself. Spend the rest of the afternoon strolling around one of Northern New England's most happening cities. At **Church Street Marketplace** (p. 380, ❶), a pedestrian mall 4 blocks long at the center of Burlington's active downtown area, you'll find loads of food, drink, shopping, live music venues, street performers, and more. Don't miss **Firehouse Center for the Visual Arts** right in the thick of it, for rotating contemporary art exhibits. ⏱ 1 day. See p. 380.

> You can explore Lake Champlain by all means of watercraft.

Vermont's Most Scenic Drives

With the rolling, velvety texture of the Green Mountains spread over much of the state—and large swaths of land untrammeled by industry or sprawl—you have a wide range of options for scenic driving. Those we recommend cover the state from top to bottom, through some of the best-loved roads (we're looking at you, Rte. 100) and some more hidden paths. While these journeys are certainly gorgeous during fall foliage, Vermont's landscape can be downright magical in the colder months, when the snowy woods get winter quiet, ice ponds glisten, and villages turn into scenes from Currier & Ives. That said, summer offers rewarding vistas, too—though it can be buggy—and there's plenty of outdoor fun to be had in the warm weather. Keep in mind that the estimated times below don't include stops, which could lengthen your outing considerably.

> A scenic drive along Route 5A offers views of Lake Willoughby, a glacial lake over 300 feet deep.

START Vermont Rte. 9.

1 ★ Molly Stark Trail. Running across the southern margin of the state, the Molly Stark Trail, a Vermont Scenic Byway, is a nice and easy ride on Vermont Rte. 9 from Bennington (p. 372, **1**) to Brattleboro (p. 386). Along the way are seven obelisks with information about the trail, such as who on earth Molly Stark is.

For the record, she's the wife of John Stark, a Continental army general under whose leadership the troops prevailed in the Battle of Bennington (p. 352). He famously invoked her name in a rallying cry at that battle and Molly has since been heralded as a symbolic character, though she never actually lived in Vermont.

QUEBEC

L. Memphremagog

Champlain

Swanton

St. Albans

Plattsburgh

LAKE CHAMPLAIN

Milton

Colchester

Winooski
Burlington

Essex Jct.

Shelburne

Vergennes

Middlebury

Ticonderoga

Brandon

Fair Haven

Whitehall

Granville

NEW YORK

Dorset

Manchester

Cambridge

Hoosick
Falls

Bennington

Pownal

Williamstown

North Adams

MASS.

North Troy

Enosburg
Falls

Jay Pk.

Newport

Derby

Stanstead

Canaan

Colebrook

Island Pond

Jeffersonville

Morrisville

Barton

Lyndonville

Groveton

Lancaster

Mt. Mansfield

Stowe

St. Johnsbury

Whitefield

Littleton

Waterbury Res.

Waterbury

Montpelier

Barre

Franconia

Woodsville

Lincoln

Camels Hump

Camels
Hump
S.P.

Mt. Ellen

Northfield

Bradford

NEW HAMPSHIRE

Green
Mountain
National
Forest

White R.

Plymouth

Middlebury

Killington
Pk.

Woodstock

White River
Jct.

Hanover

Lebanon

Bristol

Laconia

Rutland

Castleton

Plymouth

Ludlow

Claremont

Franklin

Dorset Mtn.

Manchester

Equinox
Mtn.

Springfield

Concord

Suncook

Green
Mountain
National
Forest

Bellows Falls

Walpole

Hillsborough

Somerset Res.

Keene

Harriman Res.

Jacksonville

Brattleboro

Winchester

Northfield

20 mi

20 km

1 The Molly Stark Trail

2 Route 14 and Lake Willoughby

3 Manchester to Grafton

4 Route 100

5 Montgomery to Smugglers' Notch

> Stop to enjoy the scenery at Smugglers' Notch, a narrow gap in the ridges north of Stowe, so-called for its history as an illicit trade route.

You can access the trail from the cities at either end, where you'll also happen to find some of the biggest traffic bottlenecks in the state. Routes 8 and 100 meet up with Molly at different points in the middle—if you're going to catch only part of this trail, the eastern half is the more scenic. Stop in the quaint village of **Wilmington** (p. 388, ❹) to check out the goods at **Tallulah's Antiques,** 179 Rte. 9 (☎ 802/464-8417), and chow on berry pancakes or pie at cozy **Dot's Diner,** 3 W. Main St. (☎ 802/464-7284); then be sure to take a break at the **Hogback Mountain Scenic Overlook** (p. 388, ❸) for the 100-mile view. ⏱ 1¼ hr. 40 miles.

❷ ★★ **Route 14 and Lake Willoughby.** This two-parter combines some of our favorite spots in the Northeast Kingdom, the wonderfully wild northeast corner of Vermont characterized by vast stretches of farmland and meadow, pine forests, and tiny villages scattered here and there (p. 376). As a whole, this drive takes a great couple of hours, but you could also break it up based on your day. Start in little **Lyndonville,** the town of covered bridges just a few miles north of regional hub **St. Johnsbury** (p. 376, ❶). Heading north on Main Street (Rte. 5 north), stay straight to continue onto Rte. 114 north, and in half a mile turn left onto Darling Hill Rd. This takes you up on a rise where farmland on either side yields to great views; you'll also pass the **Wildflower Inn** (p. 379), **The Inn at Mountain View Farm** (p. 379), and **Burke Mountain Ski Academy** (p. 370)—shortly after

the last two, turn left onto West Darling Hill Rd., left onto Bugbee Cross Rd., and right to head north on Rte. 5. Pass through the little town of West Burke and veer right onto Rte. 5A north, then make your way to the stunning **Lake Willoughby** (p. 378, ❹). At the top of the lake, stay left to continue on Rte. 16 and turn right onto Rte. 5. At Rte. 58, turn left heading west, and in tiny Irasburg, go left again to head south on Rte. 14.

The second half is a much simpler route—stay on Rte. 14 south and enjoy the ride. After 11 miles, take a detour through **Craftsbury** (p. 377, ❷) by turning left onto North Craftsbury Rd. Pass through this idyllic village (if it's a Saturday in the summer, stop at the Craftsbury Common **Farmer's Market;** www.townofcraftsbury.com), and make your way back onto Rte. 14 south. From here, you'll ride alongside **Lakes Eligo and Hardwick** before rolling into the town of **Hardwick** (see below). Have dinner at the legendary **Claire's** (p. 379), the first

> ### Travel Tip
>
> Looking to leaf-peep? The **fall foliage** usually starts mid-September and runs into late October, but the first 2 weekends in October are Vermont's busiest time. Go to www.vermontvacation.com to get a foliage forecast and book as early as possible. For more on the state's awe-inspiring autumn show, see "Fall Fireworks" on p. 8.

community-supported restaurant in the country. ⏱ 2¼ hr. 71 miles.

❸ Manchester to Grafton. This shorter drive cuts across the state and brings you from great shopping to great cheese—or the reverse. Head out of Manchester going north on Rte. 7A, and turn right onto Rte. 11 east. In the tiny hamlet of Peru, you'll pass **Bromley Mountain** (p. 370), which has tons of outdoor fun, such as climbing walls, alpine slides, and ziplines; farther on is **Londonderry,** home to **Taylor Farm** (p. 358, ❸)—stop for some cheese or ice cream. Continue on Rte. 11 for another 4 miles, then turn right onto Rte. 121. From here, you go deep into wilderness— passing nary a town—until you come upon **Grafton** (p. 391, ❷). Take a break here, and get a drink at the **Old Tavern** (p. 391). ⏱ 45 min. 30 miles.

❹ ★★★ Route 100. Ah, the venerable Route 100. Might as well call it Green Mountain Highway. Running right up the range (and the state) like a twisted spine, this road will lead you to almost every ski area worth visiting along the way, and, if you time it right, offers a spectacular show of fall foliage.. Though the entire 200 miles of it is beautiful, it takes 5 hours to drive, so we're recommending a shorter version.. Start in the village of **Weston**—pick up a snack for the ride at the **Vermont Country Store** (p. 358, ❸)—and head north. You'll pass Rescue, Echo, and Amherst lakes; take a left at Rte. 100A if you want to break it up, and check out the **Calvin Coolidge State Historic Site** (p. 390, ❶). Pass nearby **Killington Ski Area** (p. 371), and just north of **Warren** (p. 404, ❶), stop off on the left for a short walk to the magnificent **Moss Glen Falls** (p. 406). In **Waterbury** (p. 405, ❸), both the **Cold Hollow Cider Mill** and **Ben and Jerry's** (p. 405, ❸) factory may tempt. Otherwise, the final stretch leads right into the picturesque village of **Stowe** (p. 408). ⏱ 2½ hr. 100 miles.

❺ ★★ Montgomery to Smugglers' Notch. While all roads don't, in fact, lead to Stowe, here's yet another great route that ends up in that quintessential Vermont ski village. Start in the little town of **Montgomery** (p. 378), and see how many covered bridges you can count. Head south on Rte. 118 through Montgomery Center, and drive on. Turn right when you reach the intersection with Rte. 109, passing through the impossibly small Belvidere Center, and continue on through Waterville, turning right onto Rte. 108. Take a break here in Jeffersonville and grab a bite at **158 Main Restaurant & Bakery,** 158 Main St. (☎ 802/644-8100)—we love the Southern Benedict, with biscuits and gravy— or the **Mix Café,** 55 Church St. (☎ 802/644-6371), whose kitchen turns out seasonally inspired goodness like gingerbread waffles with maple whipped cream. Follow Rte. 108 south out of town and soon you're heading into **Smugglers' Notch** (p. 410, ❺). This narrow mountain pass, named for the locals who trafficked illegal goods across the Canadian border 200 years ago, cuts through 1,000-foot ridges and winds its way down a narrow path, leading you right into **Stowe** (p. 408). ⏱ 1¼ hr. 42 miles.

Finer Diners

Both the **Blue Benn** (p. 373, ❶) in Bennington and the **Chelsea Royal Diner** (p. 389) in West Brattleboro—mainstays among locals in their respective areas, and great places to shoot the breeze with them—are on the Molly Stark Trail. They are also ideally located for travelers entering the state from the south. So, after your long drive to Vermont, you can reward yourself with some of the finest diner food and ambience you're likely to find in New England. Chances are, you'll return on your way out.

Food for Thought

The Northeast Kingdom—actually, the whole of Vermont—is replete with folks who are passionate about sustainability, their food, their farms, and their communities. But the story of how the former granite town of **Hardwick** has reinvented itself as a model for locavorism—and revitalized the rural economy—is worth highlighting. For an in-depth, honest look at how an inspired group of like-minded people came together to develop a local food system—from seed producers to composters to vegetable growers to restaurants like **Claire's**—read Ben Hewitt's *The Town That Food Saved: How One Community Found Vitality in Local Food.*

Vermont with Kids

The thought of the Green Mountains can hardly exist without the accompanying thought of skiing, but there is actually plenty to do up here in the summertime, especially for kids. From the thrill of rock climbing to science museums to good old-fashioned farm visits, most of these places are ready to entertain you for the better part of a day, so plan on 3 or 4 days in total for this itinerary.

> The ECHO Lake Aquarium and Science Center in Burlington introduces kids to the Ecology, Culture, History, and Opportunity of the area.

START Waterbury is 46 miles from Burlington. **TRIP LENGTH** 177 miles.

1 ★ **Ben & Jerry's Factory.** This fun tour will start your day off with a sugar rush. ⏱ 1 hr. See p. 405, **3**.

Take I-89 north 25 miles to exit 14 and follow signs into:

2 ★★ **Burlington.** At the **ECHO Lake Aquarium** (p. 381, **3**), hands-on exhibits like the Animal Care Room and the Champlain Sea Tide Pool engage kids while providing some educational heft, and everyone loves filming a weather broadcast against the green screen. Afterward, enjoy a boat ride with **Lake Champlain Cruises** (p. 381, **4**). ⏱ 3 hr.

Take Rte. 7 south for 7 miles to:

3 ★★★ **Shelburne.** The **Shelburne Museum** (p. 383) is both a gargantuan, and unique. Translation: there's more than enough here to keep both wee ones and teens occupied. Older kids will find the blacksmith, printing, and weaving shops engrossing, while stops like the steamboat *Ticonderoga* and lighthouse please all ages. At **Shelburne Farms** (p. 383), take the wagon ride from the visitors' center (every 30 min.) out to the farmyard, and be sure to time your arrival to catch the cow milking at 11am or 2pm. ⏱ 5 hr.

Take Rte. 7 south 14 miles; turn right onto Rte. 22A south. After 1¾ miles, turn right

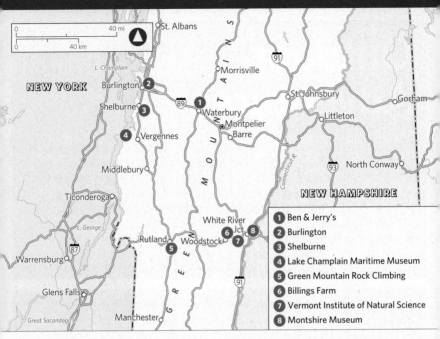

1 Ben & Jerry's
2 Burlington
3 Shelburne
4 Lake Champlain Maritime Museum
5 Green Mountain Rock Climbing
6 Billings Farm
7 Vermont Institute of Natural Science
8 Montshire Museum

onto Panton Rd., go 1½ miles, and turn right onto Basin Harbor Rd.

4 ★ Lake Champlain Maritime Museum. Exhibits on shipwrecks, Colonial maritime history, and underwater discoveries give a fascinating look into the Champlain Valley from the perspective of boating, with a collection of crafts used over hundreds of years. See boats in the process of being restored and built, and watch the conservation lab carefully investigate artifacts. ⊕ 2 hr. 4472 Basin Harbor Rd., Vergennes. ☎ 802/475-2022. www.lcmm. org. $10 adults, $6 kids 5-17. Daily 10am-5pm.

Return to Rte. 7 and take it south 45 miles to Rutland, where you'll pick up Rte. 4 east and go 1 mile to:

5 ★ Green Mountain Rock Climbing. Time to burn off some energy! The colorfully painted indoor climbing wall at Green Mountain is 25 feet tall and covers 8,000 square feet, with 30 top rope stations—plenty of room for plenty of climbers. Gear and instruction are provided. ⊕ 2 hr. 223 Woodstock Ave., Rutland. ☎ 802/ 773-3343. www.vermontclimbing.com. $15

adults, $12 kids 6-12. Mon-Thurs 2-8pm; Fri 2-10pm; Sat 10am-6pm; Sun 12-5pm.

Continue on Rte. 4 east 29 miles into Woodstock, and turn left onto Elm St. Just over the bridge, veer right onto River Rd.

6 ★★ Billings Farm. If the kids want to get right to the animals, they won't be let down here: See chickens, horses, oxen, and young calves in the nursery, and watch the cows being milked. ⊕ 2 hr. See p. 396, **3**.

Head back down River Rd. Go left onto Pleasant St. and stay on Rte. 4/Rte. 12 east for about 6½ miles.

7 ★ Vermont Institute of Natural Science. The live raptor shows are fun for all ages. ⊕ 2 hr. See p. 396, **6**.

Take Rte. 4 east 3 miles to I-89 south to I-91N to exit 13. Off the ramp, turn right at Rte. 10A east and a very quick right onto Montshire Rd.

8 ★★ Montshire Museum. This science museum has lots of hands-on activities indoors and out, including trails. ⊕ 2 hr. See p. 397, **8**.

Outdoor Adventures

For all four seasons, and throughout the state, Vermont offers a dizzying amount of outdoor fun. Looking for an outfitter or tour guide? The Vermont Outdoor Guide Association is a helpful resource; go to www. voga.org for a statewide list of guide services and tours. The well-established Vermont Adventure Tours is another company to keep in mind for tours and guides for such activities as hiking, rock and ice climbing, mountaineering, snowshoeing, biking, and paddling. And in addition to what's listed below, consider horseback riding, dog sledding, hot-air ballooning—even scuba diving amid shipwrecks in Lake Champlain.

> *Experience Vermont's awesome fall foliage along the Stowe Recreation Path.*

Biking

Mountain bikers, road warriors, and casual cyclists alike can all find terrain in the Green Mountain State to suit their pleasure. Excellent riding options for road cyclists are pretty much around every corner; two paths particularly worth mentioning are the **Stowe Recreation Path** (p. 410, ④) and the **Burlington Bike Path** (p. 381, ②). Looking to do a multiday group tour? The well-established **Vermont Bicycle Touring** (☎ 800/245-3868; www.vbt.com) is a great resource.

Voted "Best Trail Network in North America" by *Bike* magazine, **Kingdom Trails,** 478 Rte. 114, East Burke (☎ 802/626-0737; www. kingdomtrails.com), in the Northeast Kingdom has 150 miles of single-track and old farm roads, so mountain bikers of all levels will find suitable paths. Go to **East Burke Sports,** 439 Rte. 114 (☎ 802/626-3215; www.eastburkesports.com), for maps and equipment rentals. (Bike rental will cost $30–$90.) Near Barre, the **Millstone Hill Touring Center,** 34 Church Hill Rd., Websterville (☎ 802/479-1000;

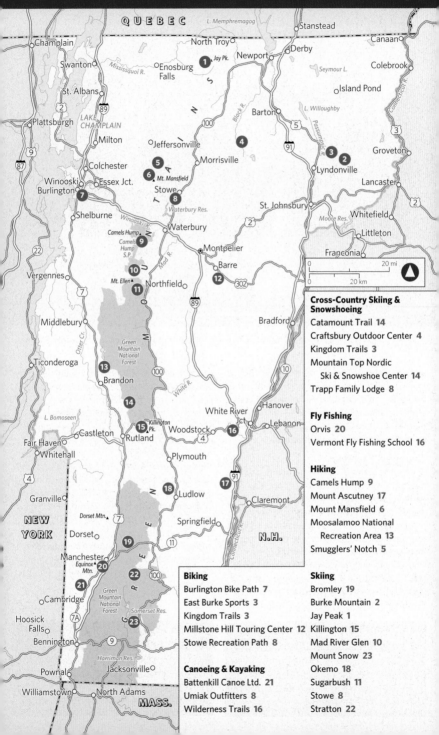

Cross-Country Skiing & Snowshoeing
Catamount Trail **14**
Craftsbury Outdoor Center **4**
Kingdom Trails **3**
Mountain Top Nordic
  Ski & Snowshoe Center **14**
Trapp Family Lodge **8**

Fly Fishing
Orvis **20**
Vermont Fly Fishing School **16**

Hiking
Camels Hump **9**
Mount Ascutney **17**
Mount Mansfield **6**
Moosalamoo National
  Recreation Area **13**
Smugglers' Notch **5**

Biking
Burlington Bike Path **7**
East Burke Sports **3**
Kingdom Trails **3**
Millstone Hill Touring Center **12**
Stowe Recreation Path **8**

Canoeing & Kayaking
Battenkill Canoe Ltd. **21**
Umiak Outfitters **8**
Wilderness Trails **16**

Skiing
Bromley **19**
Burke Mountain **2**
Jay Peak **1**
Killington **15**
Mad River Glen **10**
Mount Snow **23**
Okemo **18**
Sugarbush **11**
Stowe **8**
Stratton **22**

> *All campsites in the relatively wild Green River Reservoir State Park can be reached only by paddling to them.*

www.millstonehill.com), has more than 50 miles of single-track for experienced mountain bikers, and miles of old quarry roads and rail beds for families to enjoy. There's also summer lift service at such ski slopes as **Sugarbush, Mount Snow,** and **Killington.**

Canoeing & Kayaking

With more than 700 lakes and ponds, and rivers and streams aplenty, Vermont is a paddling paradise. The Battenkill River, which wanders through some of Southern Vermont's most gorgeous countryside—passing beneath four covered bridges on its way to the Hudson River in New York—is a great place to start. Consistently well-reviewed **Battenkill Canoe Ltd,** 6328 Historic Rte. 7A, Arlington (☎ 877/228-8365; www.battenkill.com), specializes in multiple-day trips, including inn-to-inn

tours (5-day trip around $1,575) and walking-and-paddling combos. They also rent boats (tandem canoe $60–$65, single kayak $35–$40). In Stowe, **Umiak Outfitters,** 849 S. Main St. (☎ 802/253-2317; www.umiak.com), rents canoes and kayaks (single $30 for 4 hr., $20 for 2 hr.), offers self-guided river trips on the Winooski and Lamoille rivers, and runs specialty tours such as a 3-hour combo paddle and wine tasting ($49). Quechee's **Wilderness Trails** (at the Vermont Fly Fishing School), Main St. (☎ 802/295-7620; www.scenesofvermont.com), will customize an outing for you, from leisurely family paddles on Dewey's Mill Pond to a more adventurous Connecticut River journey combined with fly-fishing sessions.

For Bike Beginners

New to mountain biking? No worries! The friendly folks at **IdeRide** (☎ 802/745-7112; www.ideride.com) will customize your tour and guide you through East Burke's very cool Kingdom Trails.

Après-Snowshoe?

Snowshoers and schussers who make the 3-mile trek from Trapp's ski center to their wonderful **Slayton Pasture Cabin** are well rewarded for their effort: A wood-burning fire, hot chocolate, and homemade soups await.

Cross-Country Skiing & Snowshoeing

There's nothing quite like gliding through a gentle winter snowfall, with nothing but the whoosh of your skis to break up the snowy silence. Vermont has some 30 cross-country touring centers throughout the state, which offer great snowshoe terrain as well. Stowe's **Trapp Family Lodge** (p. 411) skiing center, the first cross-country center in the country, has 37 miles of groomed trails and 62 miles of wild backcountry terrain. A day pass is $22 adults, $14 kids 12 to 18, and $5 kids 6 to 11; ski, boot, and pole rentals are $25 for adults and $15 for kids; snowshoe daily rentals are $20.

Near **Killington,** we suggest the family-friendly **Mountain Top Nordic Ski & Snowshoe Center,** 195 Mountain Top Rd., Chittenden (☎ 802/483-2311; www.mountaintopinn.com), with 37 miles of scenic trails. A day pass is $20 adults, $16 kids 7 to 18; snowshoe/ski rentals are $20 adults, $16 kids 7 to 18. From Mountain Top, there's easy access to the 300-mile **Catamount Trail,** which runs the length of the state, following old logging roads, snowmobile paths, and groomed trails. Go to www.catamounttrail.org for details on various sections of the trail.

In the unspoiled North Country, **Kingdom Trails** (see above) has stunning views and 47 miles of trails suitable for snowshoe/cross-country, while the **Craftsbury Outdoor Center,** 535 Lost Nation Rd., Craftsbury Common (☎ 802/586-7767; www.craftsbury.com), offers well-groomed paths through some of the most pristine countryside in New England. A bonus: the cool programs like animal tracking and orienteering. A day pass is $10 adults, $5 students, free for kids 6 and under; ski, boot, and pole rental is $15 adults, $10 students; snowshoe rentals are $5.

Fly-Fishing

The clear, spring-fed Battenkill River is a haven for trout fishing. Never tied a fly before? Learn now with the best: The renowned instructors at **Orvis,** 4145 Main St., Manchester (☎ 802/362-4604; www.orvis.com), will teach you how to read currents, choose gear, tie flies, and perfect your casting technique. (It's $235 for the 1-day school.) In Quechee, consider the **Vermont Fly Fishing School,** Main St. (☎ 802/295-7620; www.scenesofvermont.com), for half-day trout-fishing classes for $175.

Hiking

The glorious 270-mile **Long Trail** (www.greenmountainclub.org), the granddaddy of long-distance footpaths in the U.S., runs the length of the Green Mountains, meandering through woodland, valley, and rolling pasture. It starts at the Massachusetts border, joins up with the Appalachian Trail for about 100 miles, and continues to the Canadian border. Day hikers have plenty of access to the trail, along with 175 miles of side trails—pick up the authoritative **Long Trail Guide,** published by the Green Mountain Club, for detailed information. (Come foliage season, forget

> *The Long Trail was built by the Green Mountain Club between 1910 and 1930.*

Travel Tip

If you're fishing, don't forget your Vermont **license:** 1-, 3-, and 7-day temporary licenses are available on the spot from $20 to $30 at a variety of agents; see www.vtfishandwildlife.com for details.

> *The medium-difficulty Blue Heaven slope on Killington Peak, the popular resort's tallest.*

about the car: This is the way to see the blaze.) Those tackling the length of the trail, or doing any multiday hike, can take advantage of the 70 very basic overnight shelters found trailside.

Most of the state's best sites for hiking—including **Mount Mansfield, Mount Ascutney, Smugglers' Notch,** and **Camel's Hump,** among many others—are found within the state parks system. Their website, www.vt stateparks.com, is an excellent resource.

The pristine 16,000-acre **Moosalamoo National Recreation Area** (☎ 802/747-7900; www.moosalamoo.org) in the Green Mountain National Forest offers not only wonderfully quiet hiking opportunities on 70 miles of trails but also cross-country skiing, mountain biking, and snowmobiling.

Skiing

Vermont has the best skiing in the east. There, we said it. The 10 areas listed here all have their own particular standout qualities, whether it's size, location, or family-friendly amenities. Most ski-area openings and closings depend on the weather conditions in a given year—expect things to start up in late November and stay open into April, with some

of the best skiing in March (days are longer and sunnier, and it's also the snowiest month). Rates below indicate a range, which varies across weekdays, weekends, and holidays.

★ **Bromley.** The only south-facing ski area in New England, Bromley offers a distinctly more balmy experience than most. It has a reputation for great family programs, and its 45 trails cater equally well to skiers and riders. 3984 VT-11, Peru. ☎ 802/824-5522. www.bromley. com. $44–$69 adults, $44–$59 kids 13–17, $39–$45 kids 6–12, free for kids 5 & under.

★★ **Burke Mountain.** Home to the prestigious Burke Mountain Ski Academy—which has placed 45 students in the Olympics—Burke is refreshingly off the beaten path, in a beautiful part of the Northeast Kingdom. Of course, with a 2,011-foot vertical drop, it also has plenty of great skiing, with far less slope traffic than most major areas in the state. 223 Sherburne Lodge Rd., East Burke. ☎ 802/626-3322. www.skiburke. com. $64–$66 adults, $47–$49 youth 12–17, $41–$43 kids 6–11, free for kids 5 & under.

★★★ **Jay Peak.** The great white north. With an average snowfall several feet greater than most other mountains in Vermont (29.6 ft.),

Jay is far enough north that it is rarely as crowded as resorts farther south, and offers excellent terrain for serious skiers. 4850 VT-242, Jay. ☎ 802/988-9601. www.jaypeakresort.com. $69 adults, $49 kids 6–18, $10 kids 5 & under.

★★★ **Killington.** If you want the biggest, here it is: 141 trails over six mountains, with a vertical drop of over 3,000 feet (the state's highest), and plenty of variety of trails. Not surprisingly, it also has some of the biggest crowds. 4763 Killington Rd., Killington. ☎ 802/422-3261. www.killington.com. $49–$86 adults, $42–$73 kids 13–18, $34–$60 kids 6–12, free for kids 5 & under.

★★★ **Mad River Glen.** Their slogan is "Ski it if you can," and they mean it—more than half the 45 trails at this rough-and-tumble peak are double diamonds. With a substantial 2,037-foot vertical drop, this cooperative-owned area is also one of only three ski resorts in the country that have banned snowboarding—get outta the way, punk! 62 Mad River Resort Rd., Waitsfield. ☎ 802/496-3551. www.madriverglen.com. $39–$69 adults, $39–$56 kids 6–17, free for kids 5 & under.

★ **Mount Snow.** Location, location, location. For day-trippers or weekenders, Mount Snow is an easier trip than most, and draws crowds accordingly. 39 Mount Snow Rd., West Dover. ☎ 802/464-3333. www.mountsnow.com. $72–$79 adults, $56–$62 seniors & kids 6–18, free for kids 5 & under.

★★ **Okemo.** With 119 trails over 632 acres of terrain, Okemo's sizable spread runs the gamut of difficulty, and offers a nice selection of family-oriented programs. 77 Okemo Ridge Rd., Ludlow. ☎ 802/228-4041. www.okemo.com. $74–$81 adults, $65–$71 kids 13–18, $50–$55 kids 7–12, free for kids 6 & under.

★★ **Sugarbush.** The second-tallest ski area in the state—with the second-highest vertical drop (2,600 ft.)—Sugarbush has 53 miles of trails, and not quite the crush of skiers as King Killington. 1840 Sugarbush Access Rd., Warren. ☎ 800/53-SUGAR (537-8427). www.sugarbush.com. $79–$84 adults, $60–$66 kids 7–18, free for kids 6 & under.

Beat the Winter Blahs

Yes, Vermont is the ski capital of the East, but we confess we might love the après-ski scene even more. Two of our favorites are **The Alchemist** (p. 407) in Waterbury and **The Shed,** 1859 Mountain Rd., Stowe (☎ 802/253-4364), where excellent hand-crafted brews meet post-alpine conviviality perfectly. Two more perennial crowd pleasers: the **Rusty Nail** (p. 410, ❹), also in Stowe, and the classic **Wobbly Barn,** 2229 Killington Rd., Killington (☎ 802/422-6171).

★★★ **Stowe.** Stowe's Mount Mansfield is the tallest summit in Vermont (4,395 ft.), and if that's not enough, the ski area also includes Spruce Peak. The town itself is a popular destination year-round, but the 116 trails spread over these two mountains ensure that winter is still big news up here. 5781 Mountain Rd., Stowe. ☎ 800/253-3000. www.stowe.com. $59–$84 adults, $48–$66 kids 6–12, free for kids 5 & under.

★★ **Stratton.** A popular resort that's not too far for out-of-staters, Stratton Mountain is the de facto home of snowboarding; Jake Burton created his first boards while living nearby. As another matter of interest, both the Long Trail and the Appalachian Trail were conceived on (and pass over) this mountain, too. 5 Village Lodge Rd., S. Londonderry. ☎ 800/STRATTON (787-2886). www.stratton.com. $72–$84 adults, $63–$70 kids 13–17, $56–$60 kids 7–12, free for kids 6 & under.

Southwestern Vermont

Cross the border from Massachusetts or New York, and you can immediately feel the difference: Maybe it's the verdant hills and pastures, or the white-clapboard houses, but you just know you're in Vermont. These towns hum with much of what's distinct about the state—antiques shops, country stores, covered bridges, and pretty town commons. There's history too: The pivotal 1777 Battle of Bennington was actually fought in New York, but it was Bennington's stockpile of supplies the British were after. Even with the outlet traffic, you can get around the area in 3 days.

> Mount Equinox, one of the highest peaks in southern Vermont, offers spectacular views from its Sky Line Drive.

START Bennington is 122 miles from Burlington. **TRIP LENGTH** 36 miles.

1 ★★ **Bennington.** Home to prestigious Bennington College, renowned for its writing program, this hardworking little city is famous for the Revolutionary War battle of the same name (p. 352), which led to the surrender of British General Burgoyne at Saratoga. Visit Vermont's tallest structure (306 ft.), the 1891 **Bennington Battle Monument,** 15 Monument Circle (☎ 802/447-0550; www.historicvermont.org/bennington); ride up the elevator for a view of three states. Down the street is the 1806 **First Congregational Church of Bennington,** Rte. 9 (☎ 802/447-1223; www.oldfirstchurchbenn.org); in the cemetery, pay your respects at poet Robert Frost's grave.

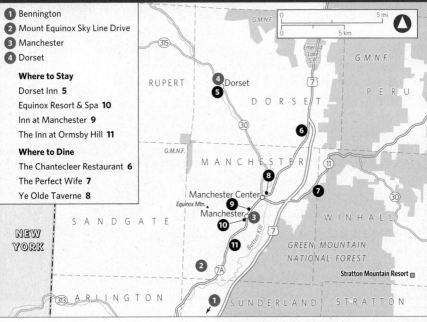

1 Bennington
2 Mount Equinox Sky Line Drive
3 Manchester
4 Dorset

Where to Stay
Dorset Inn 5
Equinox Resort & Spa 10
Inn at Manchester 9
The Inn at Ormsby Hill 11

Where to Dine
The Chantecleer Restaurant 6
The Perfect Wife 7
Ye Olde Taverne 8

(Follow the signs—it sure ain't the road less traveled!) The **Bennington Museum,** 75 Main St. (☎ 802/447-1571; www.bennington museum.org), houses an eclectic collection of early American portraits, regional artifacts, and contemporary art, plus the world's largest exhibit of Grandma Moses paintings. Take a self-guided tour at **Bennington Potters,** 324 Country St. (☎ 800/205-8033; www. benningtonpotters.com), to learn about the meticulously crafted pottery, then head to the adjacent shop to purchase the much-sought-after wares. Don't miss the legendary **Blue Benn Diner,** 318 North St. (☎ 802/442-5140). The massive, ever-changing menu includes such delectables as turkey croquettes, corn bread French toast, and crunch berry pancakes. ⏱ 4 hr. www.bennington.com.

Take Rte. 7 north to Rte. 7A, which you'll take north 17 miles to:

2 ★ **Mount Equinox Sky Line Drive.** Drive up 5¼ miles to the 3,848-foot summit of Mount Equinox for a panoramic view of the Green Mountains, Adirondacks, Taconic Range, Berkshires, and White Mountains. Stay for a picnic, or hike the easy ⅓ mile out to Lookout Rock. ⏱ 1½ hr. Rte 7A btw. Manchester & Arlington. ☎ 800/362-1114. www.equinoxmountain.com.

> The Bennington Battle Monument was built on the site of a key weapons cache during the Revolutionary War.

> *President Abraham Lincoln's famous top hat now resides at Hildene, a far cry from the log cabin in which the former owner's father was born.*

$12 per car, plus $2 per passenger. May–June Mon–Wed 9am–5pm, Thurs–Sun 9am–sunset; July–Oct daily 9am–sunset.

Return down Mount Equinox Sky Line Drive and make a left onto Rte. 7A, going north 4 miles to:

❸ ★★ **Manchester.** Anchored by the elegant Equinox Resort, genteel and tidy Manchester Village has been a stamping ground for the rich since the post–Civil War era. One of its most famous citizens was Robert Todd Lincoln (son of Abe), whose former summer home, 412-acre **Hildene,** 1005 Hildene Rd. (☎ 800/578-1788; www.hildene.org), should be your first stop in town. Stroll the gorgeous grounds, and tour the 24-room Georgian Revival mansion, whose fascinating artifacts include President Lincoln's top hat. The regionally focused **Southern Vermont Arts Center,** West Rd. (☎ 802/362-1405; www.svac.org), houses a permanent collection, rotating exhibits, and the well-regarded **Café Mamie** (www.cafemamie.com). In commercial Manchester Center, north of the village, the **American Museum of Fly Fishing,** 4104 Main St. (☎ 802/362-3300; www.amff.com), shows a stellar trove of antique rods—including those of Daniel Webster and Ernest Hemingway—as part of the world's largest repository of all things angling-related. Save time for the excellent, indie **Northshire Bookstore,** 4869 Main St. (☎ 802/362-2200), and, of course, hit the **designer outlets** at 97 Depot St. (www.manchesterdesigneroutlets.com): Michael Kors, Betsy Johnson, Coach, and Kate Spade all await. ⏱ 1 day.

From Manchester Center, take Rte. 30 north for about 6 miles.

❹ ★★ **Dorset.** Drop in to the irresistible **Redux Fine Art & Antiques Gallery,** 3266 Rte. 30 (☎ 802/867-4211), before parking by the village green in this artsy, beautifully preserved white-clapboard town. Surrounded by marble quarries—if it's hot, head to the **Dorset Quarry,** now a pretty swimming hole—Dorset supplied the marble for such landmarks as the New York Public Library, as well as its own sidewalks and all-marble church on the green. Check out the penny candy and cheeses in the **Dorset Union Store** on the green (☎ 802/867-4400), and stop for Asian-inflected tapas at the **Inn at West View Farm,** 2928 Rte. 30 (☎ 800/769-4903). ⏱ 2 hr. www.dorsetvt.com.

Where to Stay & Dine

★★ The Chantecleer Restaurant EAST DORSET
CONTINENTAL Some of the finest haute cuisine in this part of Vermont, served in a converted barn. French- and Swiss-inspired dishes include frog's legs, Dover sole, and roasted Long Island duckling. VT-7A. ☎ 802/362-1616. www.chantecleerrestaurant.com. Entrees $28–$48. AE, MC, V. Dinner Wed–Sun.

★★ Dorset Inn DORSET
The oldest continually operated inn in Vermont, right on the green in pretty Dorset. Many of the rooms have been beautifully renovated—we like the Myrick room—and come with heated floors, whirlpools, and flatscreen TVs. 8 Church St. ☎ 802/867-5500. www.dorsetinn.com. 25 units. Doubles $185–$425 w/ breakfast. AE, DISC, MC, V.

★★★ Equinox Resort & Spa MANCHESTER VILLAGE A grand old inn on the outside, the *ne plus ultra* of resort luxury on the inside, thanks to a $20-million renovation that transformed guest rooms into stylish chocolate, beige, and blue havens. Golf, visit the spa, attend archery classes, and even learn how to handle Harris hawks at the British School of Falconry. 3567 Main St. ☎ 800/362-4747. www.equinoxresort.com. 195 units. Doubles $179–$799. AE, DISC, MC, V.

★★ Inn at Manchester MANCHESTER VILLAGE
This warm and friendly country inn offers well-appointed bright and cheery rooms—we like Forget-Me-Not and Sage Suite—plus a splendid breakfast. It's the perfect place to relax, whether on the inviting porch, by the pool, or in the hammock. 3967 Main St. ☎ 800/273-1793. www.innatmanchester.com. 18 units. Doubles $155–$295 w/breakfast. AE, DISC, MC, V.

★★ The Inn at Ormsby Hill MANCHESTER CENTER This polished and sophisticated inn, dating to 1764, seems tailor-made for weary urbanites looking for a romantic getaway: Rooms have fireplaces and large Jacuzzis, and breakfasts are spectacular. 1842 Main St. ☎ 800/670-2841. www.ormsbyhill.com. 10 units. Doubles $205–$535 w/breakfast. AE, MC, V.

> Haute cuisine amidst rustic elegance at the Chantecleer.

★★ The Perfect Wife MANCHESTER *NEW AMERICAN* A hit in the area, serving one of the best filets we have had in Vermont. The tavern upstairs has its own menu, a great draught selection, and live music. 2594 Depot St. ☎ 802/362-2817. www.perfectwife.com. Entrees $20–$30. AE, MC, V. June–Nov dinner Mon–Sat, Dec–May dinner Tues–Sat.

★ Ye Olde Taverne MANCHESTER CENTER *AMERICAN* Delicious takes on Yankee-style fine dining in a charming, atmospheric Colonial setting: cranberry fritters, chicken pot pies, pumpkin bisque, traditional pot roast . . . you get the picture. 5183 Main St. ☎ 802/362-0611. Entrees $17–$30. AE, DISC MC, V. Dinner daily.

The Northeast Kingdom

The Northeast Kingdom really does feel undiscovered and a bit otherworldly—full of dense forests, rolling meadows, and sparkling lakes, dotted with picture-perfect farms—and it just might be our favorite region of the state. Though sparsely populated it is home to visionary artists, farmers, and hippies, and some of the most earnest and independent Vermonters you'll meet. Here in the land of the collapsing barn, your visit is all about the driving; get lost on dirt roads, forget GPS (and your cellphone—service is spotty at best), and get set to wander. Given the distances, plan on 3 or 4 days.

> The clear, cold waters of Lake Willoughby have been said to resemble Scandinavian fjords.

START St. Johnsbury is 59 miles from Burlington. **TRIP LENGTH** 134 miles.

① ★ **St. Johnsbury.** The gateway to the Kingdom has a population of around 7,500, as big as a town gets up here. The **St. Johnsbury Athenaeum Art Gallery and Free Public Library,** 1171 Main St. (☎ 802/748-8291; www.stjathenaeum.org)—a National Historic Landmark—is notable enough for its beautiful architecture, but is also home to the Horace Fairbanks collection of 19th-century European and American paintings. The Victorian-style **Fairbanks Museum & Planetarium,** 1302 Main St. (☎ 802/748-2372; www.fairbanks museum.org), houses a collection of numerous taxidermied birds and mammals, a wide variety of international curios, and some real oddities, such as the patriotic bug art of John Hampson. And we love the **Stephen Huneck Gallery and Dog Chapel,** 143 Parks Rd. (☎ 800/449-2580; www.dogmt.com), the masterwork of Vermont illustrator and artist

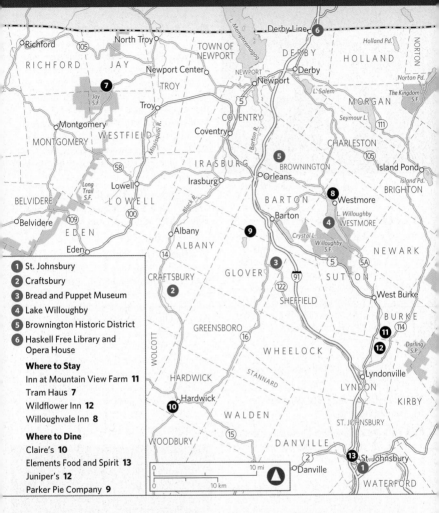

1 St. Johnsbury
2 Craftsbury
3 Bread and Puppet Museum
4 Lake Willoughby
5 Brownington Historic District
6 Haskell Free Library and Opera House

Where to Stay
Inn at Mountain View Farm 11
Tram Haus 7
Wildflower Inn 12
Willoughvale Inn 8

Where to Dine
Claire's 10
Elements Food and Spirit 13
Juniper's 12
Parker Pie Company 9

Stephen Huneck, who passed away in 2010. It's a chapel for dogs—they are allowed inside—and an essential stop for canine lovers, but the site is so poignant, even nonanimal types will tear up. ◷ 3 hr.

Go west on Rte. 2 for 11 miles. Turn right onto Rte. 15 and go 13 miles west. In Hardwick, turn right onto Rte. 14 north; go 7 miles to:

2 ★ **Craftsbury.** This quintessential Vermont hamlet—all white clapboard, rolling hills, and expanses of green—is simply a picture-perfect pass-through town. ◷ 30 min.

In Craftsbury, turn right onto Creek Rd., go 1 mile, and turn right onto Ketchum Hill Rd. and again onto E. Craftsbury Rd. Turn left on Shadow Lake Rd. (Mud Island Rd.) and go 8½ miles to Rte. 16 north; continue 1¾ miles, and turn right onto Rte. 122 south. Go ¾ mile to:

Sugar Stop

Red Sky Trading, 2894 Glover St. (☎ 802/525-4736), a little-red-barn shop in Glover, is a great place to drop in. Even if you're not in the market for adorable vintage housewares and local jams, the cream puffs and cider donuts are sure to make you happy.

> *The Bread and Puppet Museum houses "cheap art" of the political theater troupe.*

❸ ★★★ Bread and Puppet Museum. This seemingly abandoned, dilapidated dairy barn houses the complete collection of papier-mâché puppets—gigantic, sometimes creepy, and wildly intriguing—from the radical lefty political theater group Bread and Puppet, started in the '60s in New York City by Peter Schumann and moved here in 1975. An overgrown, painted school bus outside is an honor system store for "disposable" art. ⏱ 45 min. 753 Heights Rd., Glover. ☎ 802/525-3031. www. breadandpuppet.org. Donation encouraged. June–Oct daily 10am–5pm.

Return to Rte. 16 and go 12 miles north (through Barton) to:

❹ ★★★ Lake Willoughby. Coming up over the hills, this stunning glacial lake appears almost out of nowhere, and just keeps unfolding as you head down along VT-16. It's a nearly nonstop, gorgeous view, with plenty of spots along the way to stop and take it all in. ⏱ 45 min. Rte. 5A & Rte. 16, Westmore.

Take Rte. 5A north, turning left onto Rte. 58 west. Go 2½ miles and turn right onto Hunt Hill Rd., then left onto Schoolhouse Rd., continuing onto Old Stone House Rd.

Covered-Bridge Madness

In the far-northwest reaches of the Kingdom, you'll find no fewer than seven covered bridges in the little town of **Montgomery.** Leave the map at home and make it a scavenger hunt, as they are all accessible from main roads, though some are more easily visible than others.

❺ ★★ Brownington Historic District. You'll think, "This can't be right," as you find yourself in downtown Brownington among a 55-acre complex of six early-19th-century buildings. It includes **Athenian Hall** (the Old Stone House Museum), which was constructed by Rev. Alexander Twilight—believed to be the first African-American college grad *and* legislator. ⏱ 1 hr. 109 Old Stone House Rd., Brownington. ☎ 802/754-2022. www.oldstonehousemuseum. org. $6 adults, $3 students. May 15–Oct 15 Wed–Sun 11am–5pm.

Turn right onto Hinman Settler Rd. and go 8 miles to Rte. 5 north; go 4 miles and take a slight right at Caswell Ave. Watch out for Canada on your left.

❻ ★ Haskell Free Library and Opera House. This 1904 Queen Anne Revival building is right on the Canadian border, literally—a line of tape on the floor indicates the divide. Dance back and forth across it, but don't head out the wrong door without your passport. They house a permanent collection of some 20,000 volumes in English, with a smaller, rotating selection of books in French. A tour walks you through the opera house, as well. ⏱ 1 hr. 93 Caswell Ave., Derby Line. ☎ 802/ 873-3022. www.haskellopera.org. $5 adults for tour. Library: Tues–Wed & Fri–Sat 10am– 5pm; tours hourly.

Local Heroes

We love the landscape of the Kingdom—all wild woodsiness and rich, green pasturelands—but, for us, it's the idealistic farmers, award-winning cheese makers, and other passionate locavore leaders that make it such a neat place to visit. Be sure to include stops at pick-your-own berry, apple, and pumpkin farms; sample produce from the roadside farm stands; and dig in to some of the region's grass-fed beef and free-range poultry available at local eateries. See "Vermont Cheese" on p. 392 to read about the exciting cheese making that's happening up here, or see p. 363 to find out more about **Hardwick**'s visionary local-food-system model. Try your darnedest to stop in both **Claire's** and **Parker Pie Company** (see right).

Where to Stay & Dine

★★★ **Claire's** HARDWICK *NEW AMERICAN*
The menu created daily at this thoroughly locavore (or "localvore," as Vermonters prefer) mecca is always inspired, and always delicious. Meat lovers and vegetarians alike will find much to chew on. Their partner in philosophy, the Center for an Agricultural Economy, is right next door. 41 S. Main St. ☎ 802/472-7053. Entrees $12–$26. DISC, MC, V. Dinner Thurs–Tues, brunch Sun.

★ **Elements Food and Spirit** ST. JOHNSBURY *NEW AMERICAN* Thoughtfully prepared meals with an emphasis on—you guessed it!—local ingredients reign here, in dishes like Sriracha deviled eggs and root beer ribs; there's a nice selection of vegetarian options, too. Get a table on the deck. 98 Mill St. ☎ 802/748-8400. Entrees $12–$22. AE, DISC, MC, V. Dinner Tues–Sat.

★ **Inn at Mountain View Farm** EAST BURKE
This 440-acre historic farm boasts a fabulous hilltop view; hike on miles of trails right from the property. The rooms exude simple country elegance, with touches like poster, wrought iron, or sleigh beds. Darling Hill Rd. ☎ 802/626-9224. www.innmtnview.com. 14 units. Doubles $175–$275 w/breakfast. DISC, MC, V. Closed Nov to mid-May.

★ **Juniper's** LYNDONVILLE *AMERICAN*
This eatery at the Wildflower Inn (see below) is known for its farm-to-table goodness in entrees like baked stuffed chicken and grilled filet mignon—locally sourced, of course. 2059 Darling Hill Rd. ☎ 800/627-8310. Entrees $15–$27. AE, DISC, MC, V. Dinner Mon–Sat, lunch daily mid-June to Labor Day.

★★ **Parker Pie Company** WEST GLOVER *PIZZA*
We'll come clean: We have a crush on this place, located in the back of a general store in tiny, rural West Glover. The local-ingredient, artisanal pizzas and sandwiches are lip-smacking good, there's a fabulous draft selection, and it attracts a wonderful mix of Vermonters and in-the-know out-of-towners. 161 County Rd. ☎ 802/525-3366. Entrees $9–$23. AE, DISC, MC, V. Lunch & dinner daily, brunch Sun.

> From farm to table at Claire's in Hardwick.

★★ **Tram Haus** JAY
Opened in December 2009, the Tram Haus melds modern luxury—huge rooms and tubs, flatscreen TVs, slate-and-wood decor—with rustic touches like tree-stump tables and locally made wool blankets. We love the friendly, down-to-earth service; most of the staff are avid skiers and riders. 4050 VT-242. ☎ 800/451-4449. www.jaypeakresort.com. 57 units. Doubles $189–$799. AE, DISC, MC, V.

★★ **Wildflower Inn** LYNDONVILLE
High on a hill, this family-friendly spot—with a children's barn and indoor playground—is great for hiking and other activities. The fresh morning air is more renewing than any spa, and don't skip the wholesome, cooked-to-order breakfast. 2059 Darling Hill Rd. ☎ 802/626-8310. www.wildflowerinn.com. 24 units. Doubles $130–$474 w/breakfast. AE, DISC, MC, V.

★ **Willoughvale Inn** WESTMORE
Given its location, you don't come here if you're not after a great view of beautiful Lake Willoughby—make sure your room has one. 793 Vermont 5A S. ☎ 802/525-4123. www.willoughvale.com. 18 units. Doubles $155–$319 w/breakfast. AE, MC, V.

Burlington

It is far and away the densest population center in Vermont, so it's no surprise that Burlington offers a variety of cultural, culinary, and nightlife options all but unheard of in much of the Green Mountain State. And while exploring this college town—it's home to the University of Vermont (UVM)—you won't have quite the experience of natural beauty that the more rural regions promise, but the location on Lake Champlain, with the Adirondacks looming in the west, makes a pretty good consolation prize. Plus, the people are some of the most well-educated, green-minded, and outdoorsy you'll meet. Our 3-day itinerary takes you through Burlington's highlights, and includes nearby Shelburne, which offers some of its own don't-miss attractions.

> *If you're craving more activity than a cruise offers, consider renting a kayak from one of the many outfitters on Lake Champlain.*

START Burlington is 216 miles from Boston, MA.

❶ ★★ Church Street Marketplace. This 4-block brick pedestrian mall is Burlington's center for art, food, and shopping. (This is Vermont, so expect a focus on the local, sustainable, and independent.) The **Firehouse Center for the Visual Arts,** 135 Church St. (☎ 802/865-7166), exhibits contemporary works, and store/gallery hybrid **Frog Hollow,** 85 Church St. (☎ 802/863-6458), showcases the fine art and crafts of Vermont artisans. **Burlington Records,** 170 Bank St. (☎ 802/881-0303), sells vinyl LPs and vintage instruments, while bibliophiles gather at indie mainstay **Crow Bookshop,** 14 Church St. (☎ 802/862-0848). Style-conscious ladies make tracks to **Stella Shoes,** 96 Church St. (☎ 802/864-2800), for fab footwear like Gentle Souls, and **Sweet Lady Jane,** 40 Church St. (☎ 802/862-5051), stocked with such brands as Free People and Triple Five Soul. ⏱ 3 hr.

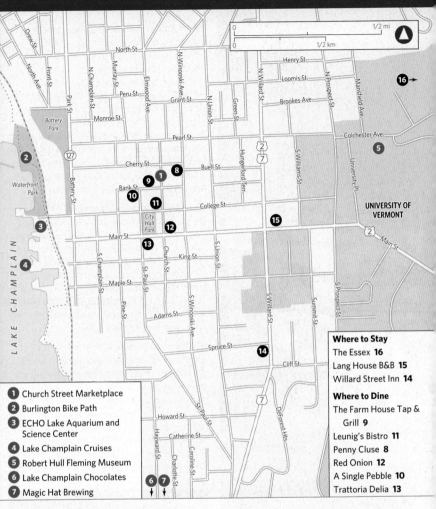

- **1** Church Street Marketplace
- **2** Burlington Bike Path
- **3** ECHO Lake Aquarium and Science Center
- **4** Lake Champlain Cruises
- **5** Robert Hull Fleming Museum
- **6** Lake Champlain Chocolates
- **7** Magic Hat Brewing

Where to Stay

The Essex **16**

Lang House B&B **15**

Willard Street Inn **14**

Where to Dine

The Farm House Tap & Grill **9**

Leunig's Bistro **11**

Penny Cluse **8**

Red Onion **12**

A Single Pebble **10**

Trattoria Delia **13**

2 ★★ **Burlington Bike Path.** Take a ride on this gentle 7.5-mile paved trail hugging the shore of Lake Champlain, offering terrific views of the Adirondacks. The path, used by walkers and inline skaters too, links several waterfront parks, so there are ample places to relax. Rent bikes ($23 for 4 hr.) at the **Local Motion Trailside Center** (☎ 802/652-2453; www.local motion.org), right next to Union Station, the best place to start your trek. ⏱ 2 hr. ☎ 802/864-0123. www.enjoyburlington.com.

3 ★★ kids **ECHO Lake Aquarium and Science Center.** This highly interactive science center focusing on the ecology of the Lake Champlain basin makes an excellent outing for kids, but

adults, too, can't help but have a blast here. You can get on camera and report the weather, study a replica of a shipwreck, discover juicy Champy (see "Vermont's Very Own Loch Ness Monster!" p. 382) stories, and explore an Atlantic tide-pool tank filled with anemones and sea stars. ⏱ 2 hr. 1 College St. ☎ 877/324-6386. www.echovermont.org. $9.50 adults ($11 summer), $7.50 kids 3-17 ($8.50 summer). Daily 10am-5pm.

4 ★ **Lake Champlain Cruises.** At 110 miles long and 12 miles at its widest, Champlain is the largest lake in New England. Lake Champlain Cruises offers a leisurely hourlong ride on its 115-foot Northern Lights, a replica of a late

❺ ★★ Robert Hull Fleming Museum. On the University of Vermont campus, the Fleming offers a tidy art collection encompassing permanent and changing exhibits. You'll find ancient Egyptian artifacts; Asian and African sculpture; European pieces by Durer, Goya, and Rodin; and American works from Bierstadt, Homer, and Warhol. ⏱1½ hr. 61 Colchester Ave. ☎ 802/656-0750. www.uvm.edu/~fleming. $5 adults, free for kids 6 & under. May to Labor Day Tues–Fri noon–4pm, Sat–Sun 1–5pm; Labor Day to Apr Tues & Thurs–Fri 9am–4pm, Wed 9am–8pm, Sat–Sun 1–5pm.

❻ ★ Lake Champlain Chocolates. We're suckers for the dark and dreamy sweet stuff, and the tour here presents a great opportunity to indulge. In 30 minutes, you'll learn about the process of bringing cacao from tree to table; all the while, factory production is visible behind the glass, and "educational" samples are on the table. ⏱1 hr. 705 Pine St. ☎ 802/864-1808. www.lakechamplainchocolates.com. Free admission. Mon–Fri 9am–2pm.

❼ Magic Hat Brewing. The tour here walks you through the nether regions of this cavernous building while investigating the history of brewing in America, as well as Magic Hat's own chapter of the story. At the end, sample any of the many brews on tap at the bar in the psychedelic gift shop. ⏱1 hr. 5 Bartlett Bay Rd., S. Burlington. ☎ 802/658-2739. www.magichat.net. Free admission. Mon–Thurs 10am–6pm; Fri–Sat 10am–7pm; Sun noon–5pm; tour hours vary wildly.

> All-natural confections at Lake Champlain Chocolates are made with local butter and cream.

19th century steamboat. You'll learn about the lake's fascinating history, including ship-building and shipwrecks, and maybe even catch a glimpse of Champy. Check out the old maps and menus on display in the boat's lounge. ⏱1½ hr. 1 King St. ☎ 802/864-9669. www.lakechamplaincruises.com. See website for rates & schedules. Mid-June to mid-Oct.

Vermont's Very Own Loch Ness Monster!

Some call it **Champ,** others **Champy**—whatever its name, this horned aquatic creature is said to have been spotted hundreds of times since Samuel de Champlain allegedly reported seeing it in 1609. Both the Abenakis and the Iroquois have legends about a mysterious serpentine lake dweller, and P. T. Barnum once offered $50,000 for its capture. Some theorize that Champy is a primitive whale, others that it's a long-necked reptile cousin of a plesiosaur. Whatever it is, both New York and Vermont legislators have taken its existence seriously enough to have added Champ to endangered species lists.

Shelburne

Four miles south of Burlington, the pastoral town of ★★★ **Shelburne** claims two of the state's best attractions, making for a great overnight visit. **Shelburne Farms,** 1611 Harbor Rd. (☎ 802/985-8498; www.shelburne farms.org), a 1,400-acre establishment devoted to conservationism and education, is the legacy of William Seward Webb and Lila Vanderbilt, who founded the farm as a model agricultural estate. The Olmsted-designed grounds are reason enough to visit (admission $8 adults, $5 kids 3-17; tours extra), but with cheese making (p. 392) and kids' activities like cow milking and egg collecting—plus a well-preserved mansion and stunning views of Lake Champlain—you could get lost here for days. Consider a stay at the **Inn at Shelburne Farms** (doubles $165-$465), the former country home of the Webbs, which boasts much of the house's original furniture.

The **Shelburne Museum,** 6000 Shelburne Rd. (☎ 802/985-3346; www.shelburne museum.org), is unlike any museum we've seen. It's sprawling and eclectic—150,000 works are on display in 39 different settings, 25 of which are relocated historic structures. Here sits a steamship on dry land, there a lighthouse, and yonder a round barn. Exhibits include French impressionist and Hudson River School paintings, along with folk-art, tool, and toy collections. It's frankly overwhelming; fortunately, your $20 ticket ($10 for kids 5-17) allows admission on a second day. **Shelburne Vineyard,** 6308 Shelburne Rd. (☎ 802/985-8222; www. shelburnevineyard.com), has been turning out award-winning wines since their first vintage was released in 2001. Their commitment to sustainability is underscored by their LEED-certified winery and tasting room (tastings $4).

Where to Stay & Dine

> Leunig's claims the "panache of Paris, and the value of Vermont."

★★★ The Essex ESSEX JUNCTION

You'll find friendly, efficient service and spic-and-span rooms throughout the three buildings here; we prefer the cheery Easter-egg tones of the rooms in the main inn. There's a beautiful indoor lap pool, an outdoor pool and hot tub, a spa, a top-tier fitness room and tennis courts, a golf course, a climbing wall and zipline (!), and, last but not least, a renowned culinary school. 70 Essex Way. ☎ 800/727-4295. www.vtculinaryresort.com. 120 units. Doubles $220–$279. AE, DISC, MC, V.

★ The Farmhouse Tap & Grill BURLINGTON

BREWPUB The boisterous taproom bar here has a great selection of artisanal drafts, and—bonus—stays open late. The menu skews to upscale comfort food that celebrates the local bounty—farmhouse meatloaf, corncakes with greens, and chicken and biscuits. Reservations are a good idea. 160 Bank St. ☎ 802/859-0888. www.farmhousetg.com. Entrees $11–$17. AE, MC, V. Lunch & dinner daily.

★★ Lang House B&B BURLINGTON

With an excellent location within walking distance of downtown, this 1881 service-focused B&B features gorgeous woodwork and stained-glass windows, as well as rooms that are handsomely appointed with antique armoires and other period touches. Delicious breakfasts rely on local ingredients. 360 Main St. ☎ 877/919-9799. www.langhouse.com. 11 units. Doubles $165–$245 w/breakfast. AE, DISC, MC, V.

★★ Leunig's Bistro & Café BURLINGTON CONTINENTAL

A festive spot right at Church Street Marketplace, Leunig's specializes in such creative fare as maple and cardamom pork loin and pomegranate-elderflower-glazed scallops. Veg choices, too, are inspired—like pumpkin falafel and quinoa chili. 115 Church St. ☎ 802/863-3759. www.leungsbistro.com. Lunch entrees $11–$15, dinner entrees $18–$31. AE, DISC, MC, V. Lunch Mon–Fri, brunch Sat–Sun, dinner daily.

★★ **Penny Cluse Cafe** BURLINGTON *ECLECTIC*
Arrive early and be prepared to wait: This breakfast joint is always jumpin'. You'll find friendly service along with your pile of cheesy, oniony home fries; gingerbread pancakes; or zydeco breakfast. Lunch too. 169 Cherry St. ☎ 802/651-8834. www.pennycluse.com. Entrees $7–$10. AE, MC, V. Breakfast & lunch daily.

★ **Red Onion** BURLINGTON *DELI*
This hole-in-the-wall is a Burlington staple—wholesome and hearty sandwiches on house-baked bread with thinly sliced meats followed by huge snickerdoodles and other yummy treats. 140½ Church St. ☎ 802/865-2563. www.redonioncafe.webs.com. Sandwiches $6 and up. V, MC, D. Breakfast & lunch daily.

★★ **A Single Pebble** BURLINGTON *CHINESE*
What do you get when you cross a Vermont commitment to freshness with authentic Szechuan, banquet-style cooking? One of the finest dining experiences in the state. Standout dishes include their signature red-oil chicken, dry-fried green beans with pork bits, and lemon-sesame crispy shrimp in lemon-ginger glaze. 133 Bank St. ☎ 802/865-5200. www.asinglepebble.com. Entrees $10–$20. DISC, MC, V. Lunch & dinner daily.

★★ **Trattoria Delia** BURLINGTON *ITALIAN*
Impeccably prepared Italian food, friendly servers, and a transporting atmosphere—a large stone fireplace, exposed beams—make this one of the best dining experiences you'll have in Burlington. Get reservations. 152 St. Paul's St. ☎ 802/864-5253. www.trattoriadelia.com. Entrees $14–$30. MC, V. Dinner daily.

★★ **Willard Street Inn** BURLINGTON
Open this Inn's brass-handled double doors to find a stunning cherry-paneled foyer and grand staircase. Some guest rooms are cozier than others, but all retain a similar spirit with either canopy beds, four posters, leather headboards, or other touches. Breakfast is served in the black-and-white-marble-floored solarium. 349 S. Willard St. ☎ 802/651-8710. www.willardstreetinn.com. 14 units. Doubles $160–$255 w/breakfast. AE, DISC, MC, V.

Burlington After Dark

A dance floor, bar, and lounge draw the young and artsy to **Red Square,** 136 Church St. (☎ 802/859-8909). For live music (Ben Kweller, Wu-Tang Clan), head to **Higher Ground,** 1214 Williston Rd., South Burlington (☎ 802/652-0777); or **Nectar's,** 188 Main St. (☎ 802/658-4771), where Phish got its start. Beer lovers have choices: **Vermont Pub & Brewery,** 144 College St. (☎ 802/865-0500), is the state's oldest craft brewery; divey **Three Needs,** 207 College St. (☎ 02/658-0889), has fine house and local brews; and **American Flatbread,** 115 St. Paul St. (☎ 802/861-2999), offers a kick-ass draft selection.

Brattleboro & the Southeast

Even in a state known for its independent streak, there's nowhere quite like New-Age-y yet hip, earnest yet stylish, community-minded and colorful Brattleboro. It's worth taking a day or so to get to know this artsy, gritty mill town on the Connecticut River. But while the focus of this itinerary would appear to be here—most of the get-out-and-do components are in Brattleboro—it's actually all about the driving. Or, better said, the wandering. The surrounding hills and villages aren't packed with attractions, per se; rather, they are pastoral and peaceful—wonderful places to relax and soak up the scenery, or just admire from your car. We'd suggest a day or two doing just that.

> Hogback Mountain has a popular scenic overlook, as well as a 600-acre conservation area and a natural history museum.

START Brattleboro is 151 miles from Burlington. TRIP LENGTH 45 miles.

❶ ★★★ **Brattleboro.** Start your tour with a walk around the cool shops, cafes, and galleries of this surprisingly happenin' town set in a pretty river valley. Check out the new and vintage furniture at **Distinctive Décor,** 85 Main St. (☎ 802/246-1219); eclectic garden and housewares at **Verde,** 133 Main St. (☎ 802/258-3908); **Gallery in the Woods** craft store and gallery, 145 Main St. (☎ 802/257-4777); cute **Dragonfly Dry Goods,** 136 Main St. (☎ 866/866/927-0099); and **Mystery on Main Street Books,** 119 Main St. (☎ 802/258-2211). Stop in the **Brattleboro Museum & Art Center,** 10 Vernon St. (☎ 802/257-0124; www.brattleboro museum.org), where there's always something compelling to see—be it photography, installations, a lecture, or a musical program. ⏱ 3 hr. Brattleboro Chamber of Commerce, 180 Main St. ☎ 877/254-4565. www.brattleborochamber.org.

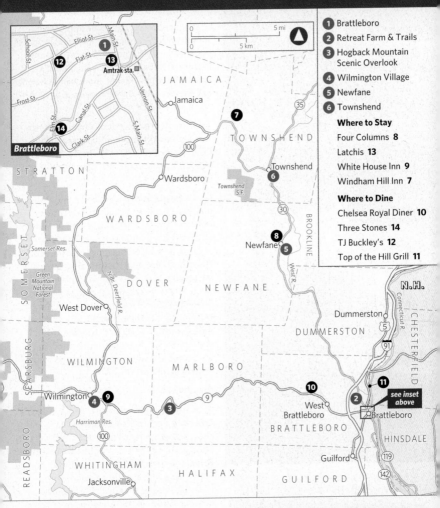

Map legend:

1. Brattleboro
2. Retreat Farm & Trails
3. Hogback Mountain Scenic Overlook
4. Wilmington Village
5. Newfane
6. Townshend

Where to Stay

Four Columns **8**
Latchis **13**
White House Inn **9**
Windham Hill Inn **7**

Where to Dine

Chelsea Royal Diner **10**
Three Stones **14**
TJ Buckley's **12**
Top of the Hill Grill **11**

2 ★★ **Retreat Farm & Trails.** This wonderful little place, just outside downtown Brattleboro, consists of a 9-mile network of trails, a petting zoo (piglets! emus!), and even a cheese shop. The Windham Foundation, which runs the farm, owns **Grafton Village Cheese Shop,** 400 Linden St. (☎ 800/472-3866; www.graftonvillagecheese.com); visitors can watch cheese making through a viewing area, then choose from an excellent selection of local cheeses. ⏱ 2–3 hr. Zoo: 350 Linden St. (Rte. 30). ☎ 802/257-2240. www.theretreatfarm.com. $6 kids 12 & over, $5 kids 2–11.

Take Rte. 9 west out of Brattleboro and go 12 miles.

Brattleboro Events

On the first Friday of every month, downtown comes alive during **Gallery Walk** (www.gallerywalk.org), when galleries, restaurants, and bars exhibit a broad swath of art, musicians play on the street, and the town bustles. The city also hosts the very-Vermont **Strolling of the Heifers** (www.strollingoftheheifers.com), an annual summer celebration of Vermont's farms featuring a parade of heifers—and goats, poultry, floats, and clowns. Watch them march, then enjoy food and dancing at the **Dairy Festival.**

> *Life is still Rockwellian in Newfane, nestled within the picturesque West River Valley.*

③ ★★ Hogback Mountain Scenic Overlook. You won't be alone, but we still recommend a stop at this unbeatable 100-mile, three-state view. It's beautiful any time of year, but is especially lovely in the fall. ⏱ 30 min. www.hogback.org.

Continue 5 miles to:

④ ★ Wilmington Village. At the intersection between routes 9 and 100, Wilmington is a crossroads town that sees a lot of action during Vermont's peak seasons. (Avoid it during foliage weekends, when crowds overwhelm it.) It's a pleasant village to explore, with some boutiques, antiques shops, and restaurants. It also has a long history as a summer destination, and so has some impressive 18th- and 19th-century architecture, including the Shingle-style Stanford White–designed **Memorial Hall,** 14 W. Main St., and adjacent **Crafts Inn.** ⏱ 1 hr. Mount Snow Valley Chamber of Commerce, Rte. 9, Wilmington. ☎ 877/887-6884. www.visitvermont.com.

Take Rte. 100 north out of Wilmington; go 4 miles, and turn right onto Dover Hill Rd. Continue onto E. Dover Rd. and onto Grimes Hill Rd. Turn left onto Rte. 30 north and go 2 miles.

⑤ ★★ Newfane. We hate to use this phrase, but there's no way around it: Newfane is postcard perfect, the quintessential Vermont village. Pretty white-clapboard buildings abound, and the 60 buildings that make up **Newfane's National Historic District,** including the graceful Greek Revival courthouse on the pretty town green, can be viewed on a self-guided tour. Pick up a free walking-tour brochure at the **Historical Society of Windham County,** Rte. 30 (☎ 802/365-4148; www.historicalsocietyofwindhamcounty.org), also home to a worthwhile collection of local artifacts. ⏱ 1½ hr.

Continue north on Rte. 30 for 5 miles.

⑥ ★ Townshend. Yet another idyllic little village, with a charming gazebo, fountain, and church. Make sure to have a look at the oft-photographed 1870 166-foot **Scott Covered Bridge,** Vermont's longest single-span bridge. Follow up a with an easy but refreshing hike (3.5 miles round-trip) up Bald Mountain, passing waterfalls and great views, in **Townshend State Park,** 2755 State Forest Rd. (☎ 802/365-7500; www.vtstateparks.com). ⏱ Half-day. www.townshendvt.net.

Following Kipling

A stay at **Naulakha,** 707 Kipling Rd., Dummerston (☎ 802/254-6868), a unique four-bedroom Shingle-style house, could be the highlight of your visit. Rudyard Kipling wrote the *Jungle Book* stories while living here, but even nonliterary types will love the breathtaking views—and skiing in the meadow where the sport was introduced in Vermont. It's $275 to $425 a night (sleeps eight).

Where to Stay & Dine

★ **Chelsea Royal Diner** WEST BRATTLEBORO
DINER The diner of our dreams. It's set in an
authentic, sun-drenched Worcester dining car,
and there's delicious breakfasts—with eggs
from their backyard chickens!—great Reubens,
grilled meatloaf sandwiches, and milkshakes.
487 Marlboro Rd. ☎ 802/254-8399. www.
chelsearoyaldiner.com. Entrees $4–$13. Cash
only. Breakfast, lunch & dinner daily.

★★ **Four Columns** NEWFANE
A Greek Revival mansion with some of the
most beautiful rooms we've seen in Vermont,
and top-tier dining. We love no. 6 (with a
through-room fireplace and huge bathroom
with soaking bathtub) and no. 4 (with green
and purple accents, cathedral ceilings, and
a two-person spa tub overlooking the village
green). 21 West St. ☎ 800/787-6633. www.
fourcolumnsinn.com. 15 units. Doubles $175–
$400 w/breakfast. AE, DISC, MC, V.

★ **Latchis** BRATTLEBORO
Smack in the middle of Brattleboro, this historic Art Deco–style hotel is a great bet if
you want to stay within walking distance of
downtown's restaurants and shops. Rooms
are basic, but sunny and clean. 50 Main St.
☎ 800/798-6301. www.latchis.com. 30 units.
Doubles $80–$200. AE, MC, V.

★★ **Three Stones** BRATTLEBORO *MEXICAN*
What a charming little gem. There's a limited
menu, but the Mayan food here is exquisitely
prepared and authentic. Our *panucho* tortilla
was spot-on, but the spicy-chocolate *boca
negra* dessert was the showstopper. 105 Canal
St. ☎ 802/246-1035. www.3stonesrestaurant.
com. Entrees $6–$14. MC, V. Dinner Wed-Sat.

★★ **TJ Buckley's** BRATTLEBORO *NEW AMERI-
CAN* For the best meal in Brattleboro, splurge
and head to this teeny menu-less (you'll
choose from five nightly selections) eatery in
a restored caboose, where the chef is so close
you can see your succulent meat and seafood
dishes being prepared. You'll need reservations, so be sure to plan ahead. 132 Elliot St.
☎ 802/257-4922. Entrees with salad $40. Cash
only. Dinner Wed–Sun.

> *"Uptown dining" in a restored 20-seat train car at
TJ Buckley's.*

★ **Top of the Hill Grill** BRATTLEBORO *BARBECUE*
Order up pulled pork, jambalaya, or hickory-
smoked ribs at this cool little seasonal place
with picnic tables overlooking a pond. Don't
forget the corn bread, and BYOB. Putney Rd.
☎ 802/258-9178. www.topofthehillgrill.com.
Entrees $2–$25. Cash only. Apr–Oct lunch &
dinner daily.

★ **White House Inn** EAST WILMINGTON
This relaxed and characterful 1915 Colonial
Revival mansion on Rte. 9 is a good choice for
an overnight, especially in winter, when guests
can go tubing on-site. 178 Rte 9. ☎ 802/464-
2135. www.whitehouseinn.com. 16 units. Doubles $150–$325 w/breakfast. AE, DISC, MC, V.

★★★ **Windham Hill Inn** WEST TOWNSHEND
A drive down a quiet dirt road brings you to the
most luxurious and comfortable inn in the area.
The refined yet unpretentious Relais & Château property has excellent service along with
stunning views, miles of trails, and rooms like
Meadowlook, a loft suite with a handcrafted
canopy bed, soak tub, and hearth fireplace. 311
Lawrence Dr. ☎ 800/944-4080. www.windham
hillinn.com. 21 units. Doubles $215–$505 w/
breakfast. AE, DISC, MC, V.

Grafton & Plymouth Notch

It's worth lingering at these two magical places. The boy-hood home of lawyer, Massachusetts governor, and 30th U.S. president Calvin Coolidge, set in almost impossibly scenic Plymouth Notch, is truly a state treasure, while the storybook village of Grafton is home to the equally precious cheddar of the same name. This works as a day trip, but we suggest overnighting at one of the recommended inns.

> *Nearly all of the teeny village of Plymouth Notch is part of the President Calvin Coolidge State Historic Site.*

START Plymouth Notch is 104 miles from Burlington. **TRIP LENGTH** 41 miles.

1 ★★ **President Calvin Coolidge State Historic Site.** Born on July 4, 1872, conservative, sober, and famously laconic "Silent Cal" stated in 1933, "I feel I no longer fit in with these times"—and it's hard not to get nostalgic for a simpler, less technological era as you tour this idyllic spot, his birthplace and boyhood home. The historic district, composed of a dozen restored buildings—among them a one-room schoolhouse, a general store, and the church he attended—looks very much as it did during the president's youth, and the setting is simply beautiful. One must-see is the Coolidge homestead, the modest clapboard house where then–vice president Coolidge received word of President Harding's death in 1923. Coolidge's father, a notary public, administered the presidential oath himself. ⏱ 2 hr. 3780 Rte. 100A,

Plymouth Notch. ☎ 802/672-3773. www.historic
vermont.org/coolidge. $7.50 adults, $2 kids
6–14. Late May to mid-Oct daily 9:30am–5pm.

Take Rte. 100 south to Londonderry, where
you'll pick up Rte. 11 east. Go 4 miles and turn
right onto Rte. 121 east. Go 10 miles; we're
taking on a slightly longer than necessary
route because it's a beautiful ride.

2 ★★ **Grafton.** The postcard-perfect village of
Grafton wasn't always so. By the Depression
era, the town—a thriving stagecoach stop in
the 19th century—was in disrepair. In 1963,
the Windham Foundation, formed by two
brothers, began slowly purchasing and restoring the center of town. Now, holdings include
some 55 properties, including the **Old Tavern**
(see below) and the **Grafton Village Cheese
Company** (p. 392); even jaded travelers can't
deny the appeal of the graceful, bucolic little
village. Take a stroll, stopping in **Grafton
Forge Blacksmith,** 72 School St. (☎ 802/843-
1029); **Gallery North Star,** 151 Townshend
Rd. (☎ 802/843-2465); and **Hunter Gallery,**
74 Main St. (☎ 802/843-1440). Then pick up
some cloth-bound cheddar from the **Grafton
Village Cheese Shop,** 533 Townshend Rd.
(☎ 800/472-3866); their production facility
is a half mile down the street, where on select
days visitors can watch cheese making. ⏱ 3 hr.

1 Calvin Coolidge National Historic Site
2 Grafton

Where to Stay & Dine
The Inn at Wethersfield **3**
The Old Tavern at Grafton **4**

Where to Stay & Dine

★★★ **The Inn at Weathersfield** PERKINSVILLE
We can't wait to get back here. Set back from
the road amid a pine grove, this Georgian-
style inn feels like a well-kept secret. Rooms
are cozy and country-elegant; some have
working fireplaces, four-poster beds, spa
showers, or claw-foot tubs. The locally focused restaurant—one of Vermont's finest—is
a destination itself. Acclaimed chef Jason
Tostrup turns out such mains as veal cassoulet
with carrot confit, lamb sausage, and white
beans; the more casual tavern might offer
chicken under a brick. 1342 Rte. 106. ☎ 802/
263-9217. www.weathersfieldinn.com. 12 units.
Doubles $139–$299. DISC, MC, V.

★★ **The Old Tavern at Grafton** GRAFTON
The centerpiece of Grafton Village, and a
delightful place to spend a night or two. The
inviting porch is filled with rockers for reading; rooms and cottages are well maintained
and graciously appointed with antique wing
chairs and canopy beds. Enjoy tennis, a swim
pond, and free access to hiking, canoeing, and
mountain biking at nearby **Grafton Ponds
Outdoor Center.** The restaurant serves a
delicious seasonally inspired menu, while the
tavern—housed in a two-story barn—offers a
fine selection of beer. 92 Main St. ☎ 800/843-
1801. www.oldtavern.com. 45 units. Doubles
$140–$325 w/breakfast. AE, DISC, MC, V.

VERMONT CHEESE

White Gold from the Green Mountains BY KERRY ACKER & TOM GAVIN

VERMONT—HOME TO MORE CHEESE MAKERS per capita than any other state—is ground zero for the burgeoning American artisanal cheese scene. A host of small farms has built a reputation for a surprisingly diverse range of top-tier handcrafted cheese, beyond the excellent traditional cheddars for which the state is best known.

Look Sharp

Named for Cheddar village in Somerset County, England, this ever-popular cheese has been made in Vermont for more than 200 years. Cheddaring, which refers to the cutting, stacking, and repeated turning of the matted curds to drain moisture, is thought to create cheddar's distinct texture. To witness the process and sample some award-winning results, visit **Shelburne Farms** (www.shelburnefarms.org), which uses the raw milk of their own brown Swiss cows; **Grafton** (www.graftonvillagecheese.com), where local farmers' Jersey cow milk is transformed into their fabulous cheddar; and **Cabot** (www.cabotcheese.coop), a co-op of 1,260 farmers producing some 30 cheeses, including the marvelous Clothbound Cheddar, cave-aged at Jasper Hill Farm.

Visiting Cheese Farms

Vermont farmers make a sincere effort to connect people to their food at its source. The following cheese makers offer guests a glimpse at the creameries—and efforts—behind the cheeses. These are small, hard-working farms, so call ahead and be prepared to get dirty.

BLUE LEDGE Painter-farmers run this family farm in a red barn surrounded by pastures and Champlain Valley wetlands. Visitors get to meet Nubian, Alpine, and Lamancha goats and buy cheese straight from the cave. (www.blueledgefarm.com)

▲ **CONSIDER BARDWELL** With a pond, 100 goats, and 300 scenic acres, this farmstead allows guests to hike, mingle with the animals, and picnic. There's an on-site self-serve shop and a cafe on weekends. (www.considerbardwellfarm.com)

▲ **FAT TOAD** This sweet farmstead allows you to take a self-guided tour to meet the friendly resident goats. At the self-service store, you can taste and buy the farm's goat milk caramels. Their cheese is made down the road at Turkey Hill Farm, where you can buy raw milk, eggs, and meat, too. (www.fattoadfarm.com)

TAYLOR Holstein and Jersey cows produce Vermont's only Goudas, including the signature Aged Gouda. For guests, the farm runs cheese making workshops, horse-drawn wagon rides, a shop selling Vermont food products, and milking and cheese making demonstrations. (www.taylorfarmvermont.com)

VERMONT SHEPHERD The country's oldest (1993) maker of sheep milk cheese. Walk the trail across postcard-perfect fields where 250 sheep graze; view cheese making through a window; see milkings; visit the cave; and buy cheese at the honor-system shop. (www.vermontshepherd.com)

Best Bites

BAYLEY HAZEN BLUE
Jasper Hill Farm
Dry and crumbly blue made with raw milk from the farm's Ayrshire cows and aged 4 to 6 months. (www.jasperhillfarm.com)

DOUBLE-CREAM CREMONT
Vermont Butter & Cheese
Sublime blend of tangy crème fraiche, cow, and goat milk with a creamy texture and nutty notes. (www.vermontcreamery.com)

TOMME
Twig Farm
Aged 80 days, this mild, semi-hard raw goat milk cheese is one of the best, with a smooth texture and sweet, herbal flavor. (www.twigfarm.com)

Woodstock, Quechee & White River Junction

Naysayers will grumble about the glut of tourists who come to Woodstock on weekends. Our sage advice to them: Avoid the weekends! There are good reasons why this refined, historic town—lined with Greek Revival and Federal-style buildings, wrought-iron lampposts, and antiques stores, all framed around a graceful village green—is so popular. There are chic boutiques and upscale eateries, but Woodstock still retains its Norman Rockwell charm (a chalkboard in town announces local events), and the bucolic landscape surrounding it looks much as it did when it was settled in 1760. This 2- or 3-day tour, which takes you around Woodstock and neighboring areas, is best done in the summer or early fall. (Many attractions have limited hours, or close entirely, otherwise.)

> Idyllic Woodstock, originally settled in 1765, soon began attracting wealthy families from the big city.

START Woodstock is 98 miles from Burlington. **TRIP LENGTH** 24 miles.

❶ ★★★ **Woodstock.** Begin at the **Woodstock Historical Society,** 26 Elm St. (☎ 802/457-1822; www.woodstockhistorical.org), housed in the former home (1807) of village merchant Charles Dana, where you'll find photographs, period furniture, fine art, and some Early American toys. Then, hit the shops! **F. H. Gillingham & Sons,** 16 Elm St. (☎ 802/457-2100), is one of the oldest general stores in the state, with all the fixin's, and then some. Co-operatively run **Collective,** 47 Central St. (☎ 802/457-1298), has finely crafted jewelry, pottery, and metalwork. Go to quirky-cool **Noushka,** 49 Central St. (☎ 802/457-4844), for playful gifts and kids' stuff, and the **Yankee Bookshop,** 12 Central St. (☎ 802/457-2411), to get your literary fix. Cooks: Head to **Aubergine,** 1 Elm St. (☎ 802/457-1340), to stock up on kitchenware. ⏱ 2 hr.

Go north on Elm St., cross the bridge and head right onto River Rd., and veer right to stay on it.

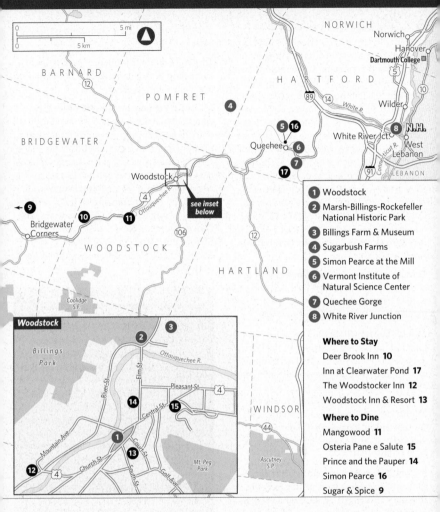

1 Woodstock
2 Marsh-Billings-Rockefeller National Historic Park
3 Billings Farm & Museum
4 Sugarbush Farms
5 Simon Pearce at the Mill
6 Vermont Institute of Natural Science Center
7 Quechee Gorge
8 White River Junction

Where to Stay
Deer Brook Inn **10**
Inn at Clearwater Pond **17**
The Woodstocker Inn **12**
Woodstock Inn & Resort **13**

Where to Dine
Mangowood **11**
Osteria Pane e Salute **15**
Prince and the Pauper **14**
Simon Pearce **16**
Sugar & Spice **9**

2 ★★★ **Marsh-Billings-Rockefeller National Historical Park.** George Perkins Marsh, Frederick Billings, and Laurance Rockefeller were all dedicated conservationists; all three made their home at one point in this mansion. (Built in 1805 in the Federal style, it was Marsh's boyhood home; Billings renovated it in the Stick style in 1869, and remodeled it again in 1885 in the Queen Anne style; Rockefeller and his wife, Mary French, a granddaughter of Billings, came into the estate in 1954.) Reserve a spot for an hour-long guided tour to learn about their legacies, and see an extensive collection of American landscape paintings.

Then, take a hike to visit the Pogue, a pond near the summit of Mount Tom, with a nice view of Woodstock. ⏱ 3 hr. 5302 River Rd. (VT-12), Woodstock. ☎ 802/457-3368. www.nps. gov/mabi. Guided tour: $8 adults, free for kids 15 & under. Late May to Oct daily 10am–5pm. Trails open year-round dawn–dusk.

Travel Tip

Hitting both Billings Farm and the Marsh-Billings-Rockefeller National Historical Park? We hope so. Buy a **combination ticket** ($17 adults, $15 kids 16–17; valid for 2 days), and save a few bucks.

❸ ★★ kids **Billings Farm & Museum.** Founded by railroad magnate Frederick Billings in 1871, this extraordinary farm offers visitors a look into Vermont's agricultural history, along with access to the goings-on of a working farm. Start with the half-hour film, providing an excellent overview of the farm and its sustainability efforts. Then stop in to see the sheep, calf nursery, and horses; time your visit with afternoon milking at the dairy barn. Also on offer: smart interactive exhibits, fun programs such as butter churning and wagon rides, and a restored 1890 farmhouse, complete with cistern and creamery. ⏱ 2 hr. 5302 River Rd. (Rte. 12), Woodstock. ☎ 802/457-2355. www.billingsfarm.org. $12 adults, $6 kids 5-15, $3 kids 3-4. May-Oct daily 10am-5pm; Nov-Feb Sat-Sun 10am-3:30pm.

Continue up River Rd. for 1½ miles. Veer left onto High Pastures Rd., go 1¾ miles, and make a slight left to stay on it. Turn right at the fork onto Sugarbush Farm Rd. and go ½ mile.

❹ ★ kids **Sugarbush Farms.** This homey family farm is a fun place to mingle with chickens, goats, and rabbits; learn about syrup making on the maple trail; and, best of all, taste sample after sample of cheese, syrup, and jam. ⏱ 1 hr. 591 Sugarbush Farm Rd., Woodstock. ☎ 800/281-1757. www.sugarbushfarm.com. Free admission. Mon-Fri 8am-5pm; Sat-Sun 9am-5pm. (Call to confirm hours in winter & early spring.)

Return to High Pastures Rd., go left at the fork onto Spaulding Ln. and stay left onto Hillside Rd. Turn left onto Quechee's Main St. and go about 2 miles.

❺ ★ **Simon Pearce at the Mill.** Yes, it's crowded, but weekends are the best time to visit. Not only can you shop for the internationally renowned glass master Pearce's beautifully crafted glassware and pottery and enjoy a fantastic meal (see below) overlooking the falls, but you can watch the artisans at work. Be sure to check out the hydroelectric turbine, which harnesses the power of the roaring Ottauquechee River, and generates enough electricity for the entire facility. ⏱ 1 hr. 1760 Main St., Quechee. ☎ 802/295-2771. www.simonpearce.com. Store daily 10am-9pm; glass blowing daily 10am-9pm; pottery making Sat-Sun 10am-4pm.

Turn right out of the lot onto Main St. and again onto Waterman Hill Rd. Take a left onto Rte. 4 east and go ⅓ mile.

❻ ★★ kids **Vermont Institute of Natural Science Center.** Pretty please: Visit this delightful outdoor museum and research center, a sanctuary for some 40 beautiful birds of prey, including eagles, falcons, and owls, all of which have sustained injuries and can't be released back into the wild. The live raptor shows are a highlight, and you can hike on trails by the Quechee Gorge. ⏱ 2 hr. 6565 Woodstock Rd. (Rte. 4), Quechee. ☎ 802/359-5000. www.vinsweb.org. $11 adults, $8.50 kids 4-17. Mid-Apr to Oct daily 9am-5:30pm; Nov to mid-Apr daily 10am-4pm.

A Tale of Three Conservationists

Improbably, three environmental luminaries occupied the same house here in Woodstock at different times. Born here, **George Perkins Marsh** was widely regarded as the progenitor of conservationism in the modern era. His insight that humankind's actions can have lasting, damaging effects on their surrounding ecosystems may seem obvious today, but were groundbreaking when he first published *Man and Nature* in 1864. The book had a profound effect on **Frederick Billings,** who bought the Marsh estate in 1861. Having opened the first law practice in San Francisco at the height of the gold rush—and making a fortune as president of the Northern Pacific Railroad—Billings brought a progressive-minded industrialist's approach to conservation, helping to introduce reforestation efforts (the state had lost 75% of its trees by the late 19th c.) in what is now the oldest actively managed forest in the country. His granddaughter, Mary French Rockefeller, moved into the house with husband **Laurance Spelman Rockefeller** in 1954. The venture-capital pioneer was already a keen advocate of conservation himself, opening several environmentally conscious resorts and helping to create and expand national parks throughout the country.

> *Sample some of Vermont's finest, tapped onsite, after you learn how it's made at Sugarbush Farms.*

Continue east on Rte. 4 east for ½ mile.

7 ★★ kids **Quechee Gorge.** This mile-long, 165-foot-deep glacier-sculpted chasm is a popular stop for the tour-bus crowd, most of whom seem to view it from the overlooks on the Rte. 4 bridge; hike down a short trail to the bottom of the gorge to avoid the throngs and take in the mighty chasm from an interesting vantage point. The Vermont Institute of Natural Science Center (see above) has trails that run along the gorge on its property. ⊙ 45 min. Quechee Gorge Visitor Center. Rte. 4, Quechee. ☎ 802/295-6852. Mid-May to Oct daily 9am–5pm.

Continue 6 miles east on Rte. 4 and turn left onto Rte. 5 north to:

8 ★ kids **White River Junction.** Within spitting distance of Hanover, New Hampshire—home to Dartmouth College and its fine museums—this former railroad center has reinvented itself as a minihaven for artists and their ilk.

The Tip Top Building, once an industrial bakery, now houses just under 40 artist's studios, along with the **Tip Top Café,** 85 N. Main St. (☎ 802/295-3312; www.tiptopcafevermont. com), a bistro serving up New American dishes like pumpkin falafel and ginger and pork meatloaf. Stop in the hip and friendly **Revolution,** 26 N. Main St. (☎ 802/295-6487), to scope out the vintage and locally designed clothing and merch, and see what's going on at **Northern Stage,** 12 W. Main St. (☎ 802/296-7000), one of the state's best theater companies. Hop aboard the White River Flyer (pulled by a vintage diesel locomotive) run by **Green Mountain Railroad,** 102 Railroad Row (☎ 800/707-3530), for a scenic round-trip ride along the Connecticut River; the ticket includes a 45-minute stop at the very cool, hands-on **Montshire Museum of Science,** 1 Montshire Rd., Norwich (☎ 802/649-2200; www.montshire.org). ⊙ 3 hr.

Out & About

Looking for some paddling or fly-fishing fun? **Wilderness Trails** (p. 368) in Quechee will customize an outing for you. **Kedron Valley Stables,** South Woodstock (☎ 802/457-1480), leads guided horseback trail rides (1-hr. ride for group of three to six: $40 per person) and horse-drawn sleigh rides in winter (45-min. ride for one to three people: $100 per ride).

Up, Up & Away

The only thing more fun than spotting a hot-air balloon in the air is being in one. Float along in blissful silence with **Balloons Over New England,** Main St., Quechee (☎ 800/788-5562; www.balloonsovernew england.com), which launches from the village green in Quechee. Call for pricing; dress warmly.

Where to Stay & Dine

> *The Inn at Clearwater Pond's lovely landscape.*

★★ **Deer Brook Inn** WOODSTOCK
Though this B&B is just a wee bit out of town, no matter: Rooms sparkle, beds are cozy, and innkeepers George and David serve up tantalizing three-course breakfasts and warm, down-to-earth hospitality. It's also affordable. 535 Woodstock Rd. ☎ 802/672-3713. www. deerbrookinn.com. 5 units. Doubles $120–$195 w/breakfast. AE, MC, V.

★ **Inn at Clearwater Pond** QUECHEE
We like this inn for its serene, pastoral setting just a mile from Quechee; its inviting sitting areas indoors and out; and, most of all, for the charming cottage, with exposed beams, a wood stove, a four-poster bed, and a claw-foot tub. 984 Quechee-Hartland Rd. ☎ 888/918-4466. www.innatclearwaterpond.com. 5 units. Doubles $165–$295 w/breakfast. Cash & checks only.

★★ **Mangowood** WOODSTOCK ASIAN FUSION
Apps and mains at this chef-owned restaurant at the Lincoln Inn are packed with Asian-inflected flavors: Think maple tamarind duck or peanut-pesto coconut risotto. Don't miss the "To Die For Sticky Pudding"; it's, well, to die for. 530 Woodstock Rd. ☎ 802/457-3312. Entrees $21. AE, MC, V. Dinner Tues-Sat; call ahead in spring.

★★ **Osteria Pane e Salute** WOODSTOCK TRATTORIA
Book now: You're in for a rare treat at this tiny, rustic-modern wine bar and eatery. The menu is small—there's always exquisite thin-crust pizzas—but count on meticulously prepared authentic regional Italian dishes with a razor-sharp focus on fresh, local ingredients. Much of the produce comes from the proprietors' own garden. 61 Central St. ☎ 802/457-4882. Entrees $15–$21. AE, DISC, MC, V. Dinner Thurs-Sun. Closed Apr & Nov.

★ **Prince and the Pauper** WOODSTOCK AMERICAN
Tucked away down an alley, this is a Woodstock go-to spot for fine dining. With exposed beams and candlelight, it's a nice night out for

> *Elegant dining on Simon Pearce tableware at the eponymous restaurant.*

couples, but relaxed enough for families. Dine prix-fixe style—lamb in puff pastry is a signature—but we also recommend the affordable bistro menu. 24 Elm St. ☎ 802/457-1818. Prix fixe $49; entrees $14–$24. AE, DISC, MC, V. Dinner daily.

★★★ **Simon Pearce** QUECHEE *CONTEMPORARY*
Consistently top-tier, local farm-focused cuisine served on Simon Pearce dinnerware, with stunning views overlooking rushing falls and a covered bridge—you're just about guaranteed a great dining experience. 1760 Quechee Main St. ☎ 802/295-1470. Lunch entrees $13–$17; dinner entrees $22–$32. AE, DISC, MC, V. Lunch & dinner daily.

★ **Sugar & Spice** MENDON *BREAKFAST*
Get yer hearty country breakfast at this red-roofed barn/sugar house. Eat outside on the deck, and be sure to taste their maple candy. The pumpkin pancakes are a forkful of autumn. Rte. 4. ☎ 802/773-7832. Entrees $6–$10. DISC, MC, V. Breakfast & lunch daily.

★★ **The Woodstocker Inn** WOODSTOCK
As soon as you spot this canary yellow, superfriendly British-run B&B, you know you're in for a different type of Woodstock stay. The sensibility here is eco-minded and whimsical and design-y and comfortable—with some of the most striking, quirky-luxe bathrooms you'll see in New England. Extra points for stellar service. 61 River St., Woodstock. ☎ 866/662-1439. www.woodstockervt.com. 9 units. Doubles $130–$395 w/breakfast. MC, V.

★★★ **Woodstock Inn & Resort** WOODSTOCK
The standard-bearer for resort-style luxury in Central Vermont, the Woodstock is the town centerpiece, set right on the village green. Rooms come gussied up with high-thread-count linens, flatscreen TVs, oversize shower heads, and hand-dyed wool blankets, while a 2010-opened spa completes the long list of top-notch amenities. Your meal in the **main dining room** will be one of the most memorable in the state. Also on-site: the **Red Rooster,** whose bright, sleek interiors are a refreshing departure from the standard cozy-country theme so prevalent in Vermont. The kitchen excels at inspired, local-centric fare; spot-on burgers make it a good lunch option too. 14 The Green. ☎ 800/448-7900. www.woodstock inn.com. 142 units. Doubles $149–$660. AE, MC, V.

Middlebury

We envy the students at Middlebury College: Not only are they surrounded by a wealth of international art and culture, but it all happens against the backdrop of an attractive town on the banks of Otter Creek, tucked between the Green Mountains and Lake Champlain. So they get small-town New England charm, along with big-city sophistication—plus access to beautiful scenery and outdoor adventures. This 1- to 2-day itinerary will help you discover for yourself some of the pleasures—simple and otherwise—of Middlebury, as well as a few riches in the surrounding hills and villages of the fertile Lower Champlain Valley.

> *The Morgan horse is one of the earliest breeds developed in the United States; UVM Morgans are prized for both recreational use and breeding.*

START Vergennes is 30 miles from Burlington. **TRIP LENGTH** 32 miles.

1 kids ★★ **Lake Champlain Maritime Museum.** This multiple-structure museum examines the history of Lake Champlain; we particularly like the nautical archaeology center, where you'll learn the juicy details of Champlain's famous shipwrecks. Also look for the exhibit on the horse-powered ferry. ⏱ 2 hr. See p. 365, **4**.

Go east on Basin Harbor Rd. for 4¾ miles and turn left at Panton Rd. After 1½ miles, turn left at Rte. 22A north for ¾ mile, and right at Monkton Rd. Go right onto Rte. 7 south for 7¼ miles. Turn right onto Campground Rd. for 1 mile and left at Pearson Rd. for 1 mile. Continue over the bridge onto Morgan Horse Farm Rd., and in 2 miles turn left at Battell Dr.

2 kids **UVM Morgan Horse Farm.** Stop by the tranquil grounds of this National Historic Site to

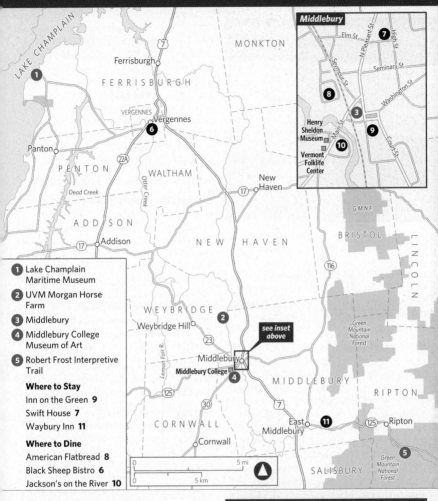

1 Lake Champlain Maritime Museum
2 UVM Morgan Horse Farm
3 Middlebury
4 Middlebury College Museum of Art
5 Robert Frost Interpretive Trail

Where to Stay
Inn on the Green **9**
Swift House **7**
Waybury Inn **11**

Where to Dine
American Flatbread **8**
Black Sheep Bistro **6**
Jackson's on the River **10**

take a half-hour guided tour of the stables, and see some examples of the legendary Morgan breed in action. Even nonhorsey types can't help but admire the beauty of the fine riding beasts—and the farm. ⏲ 45 min. 74 Battell Dr., Weybridge. ☎ 802/388-2011. www.uvm.edu/morgan. $5 adults. May–Oct daily 9am–4pm.

Pulp Mill Bridge

Erected between 1808 and 1820 over Otter Creek, this 195-foot structure at Seymour Street and Covered Bridge Road is the oldest covered bridge in Vermont, and the only two-laned version in the state that still sees daily use.

New England Pewter

First put to use in the Bronze Age, this tin-based alloy was made into flatware and tableware for English nobility in the Middle Ages. It was already one of England's biggest exports when it finally reached North America. Still a luxury for most (though much less expensive than silver), New World pewter ware began as the work of artisans trained in the English tradition. The combination of high demand and restrictions on English tin exports meant Colonial pewterers had to melt down old or worn pieces to create new work, which contributes to the relative rarity of Early American pewter.

> *Robert Frost drew inspiration from the natural beauty of this part of the state—and it's easy to see why.*

Go left onto Battell Dr. and turn left onto Morgan Horse Farm Rd. Turn left onto Pulp Mill Bridge Rd. and continue on Seymour Rd. Continue onto Elm St. and turn right onto Rte. 7 south.

❸ ★★ **Middlebury.** Chartered in 1761, this small college town is chock-full of buildings on the National Register of Historic Places. At the center of town, the **Vermont Folklife Center,** 88 Main St. (☎ 802/388-4964; www.vermont folklifecenter.org), has changing exhibits celebrating the state's cultural traditions; stop by the shop for quilts, decoys, and other crafts. Visit the **Henry Sheldon Museum,** 1 Park St. (☎ 802/388-2117; www.henrysheldonmuseum. org), for its portraits and period furniture, and head to **Edgewater Gallery,** 1 Mill St. (☎ 802/ 458-0098), for work by Vermont-based artists. Walk down Frog Hollow Alley, admire the rushing falls, and ogle the sparkly vintage wares at **Bejewelled,** 1 Frog Hollow Alley

(☎ 802/388-2799), before grabbing a cinnamon twist at **Otter Creek Bakery,** 14 College St. (☎ 802/388-3371). At **Danforth Pewter,** 52 Seymour St. (☎ 802/388-0098; www. danforthpewter.com), watch talented artisans spin, detail, and fill molds of pewter through a viewing window; of course, exquisite jewelry and ornaments are available in the shop. ⏱ Half-day. Addison County Chamber of Commerce, 93 Court St. ☎ 802/388-7951. www. addisoncounty.com.

Take Rte. 30 3 miles south out of town to:

❹ Middlebury College Museum of Art. Housed in the attractive Mahaney Center for the Arts, the small and eclectic collection runs the gamut from urns of antiquity to 20th-century pieces by Alexander Calder, Robert Rauschenberg, and Andy Warhol. Photography holdings here are particularly strong, including the work of Berenice Abbot and time-lapse-photography pioneer Eadweard Muybridge. ⏱ 1 hr. Mahaney Center for the Arts, Middlebury College, 72 Porter Field Rd. ☎ 802/443-5007. museum.middlebury.edu. Free admission.

Take Rte. 7 south for 3¾ miles. Turn left onto Rte. 125 east and go 6¼ miles.

❺ ★ **Robert Frost Interpretive Trail.** Though New England is peppered with sites associated with its most prominent poet, this short nature trail is still worthwhile. You'll encounter plaques containing his poetry, and both the scenery and his words seem to spring to life. Down the road, past the **Green Mountain National Forest Wayside,** a dirt road on the left leads to a small lot by the cabin where Frost worked and spent summers and falls from 1939 until his death in 1963. ⏱ 1-2 hr. Rte. 125, Ripton. ☎ 802/747-6700. www.fs.fed.us. Daily sunrise–sunset.

Llama Time

Stop by kids **Moonlit Alpacas,** 2170 Rte. 125, Cornwall (☎ 802/462-3519; www.moon litalpacas.com), a friendly, beautifully sited farm, to get up close and personal with more than 100 adorable alpacas and cria, their young. Look for Comet, the most affectionate alpaca you'll ever meet. With a small shop. Free admission Wednesday to Sunday 10am to 4pm.

The Bread Loaf

A short drive beyond the Robert Frost area, **Middlebury College's Bread Loaf campus,** Rte. 125, Ripton, is a cluster of mustard yellow buildings situated in a beautiful spot on a hill, with fields on both sides giving way to forest and mountains. Worth the drive through since you're already in the area.

Where to Stay & Dine

> *American Flatbread serves pies from its wood-fire pizza oven.*

★ **American Flatbread** MIDDLEBURY *PIZZA*
Beloved by families, foodies, and pizza hounds alike, this bustling local- and organically driven artisanal pie place (part of a minichain) in a cavernous space in the Marble Works building also has awesome microbrews. 137 Maple St. ☎ 802/388-3300. www.americanflatbread.com. Flatbreads $14–$24. AE, MC, V. Dinner Tues–Sat.

★★ **Black Sheep Bistro** VERGENNES *BISTRO*
There's good service; a low-key yet sophisticated, intimate atmosphere; and well-executed entrees (like cumin-rubbed pork chop with peach chipotle salsa) to be had here. All mains are $19, and all come with a cone of pommes frites. 253 Main St. ☎ 802/877-9991. Entrees $19. MC, V. Dinner daily.

★★ **Inn on the Green** MIDDLEBURY
A beautiful 1803 Federal-style, antiques-filled inn, with friendly, efficient service and an excellent location on the town common. One perk: Breakfast is brought to your room. Stay in the sun-drenched Addison suite. 71 S. Pleasant St. ☎ 888/244-7512. www.innonthegreen.com. 11 units. Doubles $129–$299 w/breakfast. AE, DISC, MC, V.

Jackson's on the River MIDDLEBURY *AMERICAN*
Sunflower yellow walls and a pleasant porch over Otter Creek make this a nice spot for a casual bite. A decent draft selection accompanies twists on comfort food staples, like four-cheese macaroni with chorizo and bacon or pulled-pork quesadillas. 7 Bakery Lane. ☎ 802/388-4182. www.jacksonsonthe river.com. Entrees $9–$19. AE, MC, V. Lunch & dinner daily, closed Wed.

★★ **Swift House** MIDDLEBURY
This whitewashed Federal-style former governor's mansion has warm and inviting rooms beautifully appointed in classic New England inn style—poster beds, a mix of antique and contemporary pieces—but the spacious suites in the carriage house, most with working fireplaces, are the most plush. Breakfasts are both excellent and huge. 25 Stewart Lane. ☎ 866/388-9925. www.swifthouseinn.com. 21 units. Doubles $129–$289 w/breakfast. AE, DISC, MC, V.

★★ **Waybury Inn** EAST MIDDLEBURY
Some people stay at the Waybury because it appeared on *The Bob Newhart Show;* we like it because it's cozy and welcoming, and the public areas have a warm Adirondack lodge feel. Rooms are smallish, but are kitted out with such details as sleigh beds and claw-foot tubs. There is also an excellent on-site restaurant and pub. 457 E. Main St. ☎ 800/348-1810. www.wayburyinn.com. 13 units. Doubles $105–$285 w/breakfast. AE, MC, V.

Montpelier & the Mad River Valley

The smallest state capital in America, Montpelier can hardly even be called a city. At under 8,000 residents, it looks and feels like a small town, with a few colorful blocks of shops, restaurants, and municipal buildings. To the south, the Mad River Valley hides most of its riches off the main drag of Rte. 100—take the time to get lost and you'll be rewarded. Settled in the late 18th century, many of the farms and fields of the early communities are intact. In contrast, nearby Barre quickly blossomed in the 19th century, attracting waves of skilled labor immigrants to its booming granite industry; it's still the "Granite Capital of the World." Plan on 3 days to cover the combined area.

> In warmer weather, you can take your gourmet sandwich from the Warren Store deli onto the deck overlooking a brook.

START Warren is 46 miles from Burlington.
TRIP LENGTH 40 miles.

1 ★★ **Warren.** A clutch of clapboard houses heralds the center of this so-classic-Vermont-it's-almost-not-real hamlet. Pick up a nice bottle of wine and browse crafts from around the world at the **Warren Store,** Main St. (☎ 802/496-3864), then have a look-see at the regional art at the **Parade Gallery,** 270 Main St. (☎ 802/496-5445). ⏱ 1 hr. Mad River Valley Chamber of Commerce, General Wait House, Rte. 100. ☎ 800/828-4748. www.madrivervalley.com.

Turn right onto Brook Rd. After 2½ miles, turn left to continue onto E. Warren Rd. and enjoy a scenic 5½ miles. Continue onto Bridge Rd. and turn right on Rte. 100 north.

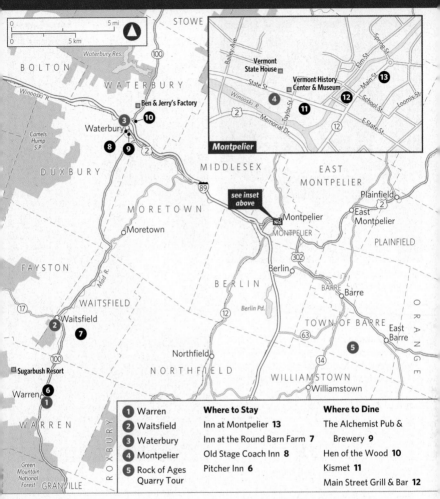

① Warren	**Where to Stay**	**Where to Dine**
② Waitsfield	Inn at Montpelier **13**	The Alchemist Pub &
③ Waterbury	Inn at the Round Barn Farm **7**	Brewery **9**
④ Montpelier	Old Stage Coach Inn **8**	Hen of the Wood **10**
⑤ Rock of Ages	Pitcher Inn **6**	Kismet **11**
Quarry Tour		Main Street Grill & Bar **12**

② ★★ **Waitsfield.** Coming into this artsy whistle stop, you'll cross the 137-foot **Great Eddy Covered Bridge**—dating to 1833, it's the oldest continuously operating covered bridge in the state. The handful of galleries and craft shops here make for good browsing; don't miss **The Store,** 5275 Main St. (☎ 800/639-0831), for kitchenware and antique furniture, and the co-op-run **Artisans' Gallery,** 20 Bridge St. (☎ 802/496-6256). ⏱ 1 hr.

Continue north on Rte. 100 for 17 miles.

③ ★ 🧒 **Waterbury.** The tiny town is a vibrant crossroads of food and drink, starting with craft brewery **The Alchemist** (see p. 407) at the town center and fanning outward along the main routes. Follow your nose (and the tour buses) to the **Cold Hollow Cider Mill,** 3600 Waterbury-Stowe Rd. (☎ 800/3-AP PLES [327-7537]; www.coldhollow.com), for all things apple; the cider donuts are delicious. Nearby, the flagship factory of ice cream king-pins **Ben & Jerry's,** 1281 Waterbury-Stowe Rd. (☎ 802/882-1240; www.benjerry.com) offers a pun-filled tour ($3 adults) that is actually pretty entertaining. Starting with a biopic moo-vie(!), you'll get the story of Ben and Jerry, along with a look at how their production methods have evolved. You'll also see the sweet stuff being processed and then—free samples! ⏱ 2 hr.

> *Free samples are only one of the draws at the Ben & Jerry's flagship.*

Take Rte. 100 1 1/2 miles south; turn left onto Rte. 2 east and go 12 miles.

❹ ★★ **Montpelier.** First settled in 1787—when Vermont was still an independent republic—this town became the state capital in 1805, allegedly due to its central location, reincorporating as a city along the way. Visit the **State House,** 115 State St. (☎ 802/828-2228; www.vtstatehouse. org), the only one in the U.S. with a gold dome, and the second on this foundation—original columns bear scars from an 1850s fire. The guided tour (every 30 min. July–Oct) walks you through the chambers while dishing out anecdotes and historic factoids.

One of the best history museums in New England, the **Vermont History Center & Museum,** 109 State St. (☎ 802/828-2291; www. vermonthistory.org), presents a timeline of Vermont's story with vivid exhibits that simulate a particular spot from a given era—the Green Mountain Boys (p. 352) at the Catamount Tavern, for example. A film re-creates three debates pivotal in the nation's history: the abolition of slavery, woman's suffrage, and civil unions. Admission is $5 adults, $3 kids 6 to 17.

Among the shops along Main and State streets you'll find indie bookstores aplenty: Check out eclectic **Rivendell Books,** 100 Main St. (☎ 802/223-3928), for new and used titles; and **Bear Pond,** 77 Main St. (☎ 802/229-0774), for new works. ⏱ 4 hr.

Moss Glen Falls

Located just off the west side of Rte. 100 between Warren and Granville, this is by no means the largest waterfall you'll see, but **Moss Glen Falls'** staggered cascade gets top honors for sheer beauty.

Take Rte. 2 for 1½ miles east. At the traffic circle, take the first exit to Rte. 302 east and go 4¾ miles. Turn right onto N. Main St.; after 1¾ mile, turn left onto Middle Rd. After 1½ miles, turn left onto Graniteville Rd.

❺ ★ kids **Rock of Ages Quarry Tour.** From the visitor's center, a narrated bus tour takes you up to the largest-dimension granite quarry in the world. Some 600 feet down, you'll see where and how the huge blocks of stone are excavated, and discover how this process has changed with new technologies. If it sounds dull then we're not doing it justice—it's actually quite fascinating. ⏱ 1 hr. 558 Graniteville Rd., Barre. ☎ 802/476-3119. www.rockofages. com. $5 adults, $2.50 kids 6–12. Tours: Late May to mid-Sept Mon–Sat 9:15am–3:35pm; mid-Sept to Oct daily 9:15am–3:35pm.

Where to Stay & Dine

★★ **The Alchemist Pub and Brewery** WATER-BURY *BREWPUB* Locals, tourists, and infants alike congregate at this always-hopping seven-barrel brewpub that turns out top-quality ales like Donovan's Red and Heady Topper. Tasty, locally sourced mains include porter-braised chicken leg, or bratwurst, kielbasa, and pierogi in a tangle of sauerkraut. 23 S. Main St. ☎ 802/244-4120. www.alchemistbeer.com. Entrees $7–$17. MC, V. Dinner daily.

★★★ **Hen of the Wood** WATERBURY *AMERICAN* Reserve *far* in advance. Simply put, you'll have one of the best meals in Vermont here. Dishes are locally focused and perfectly pitched—grass-fed rib-eye with tarragon aioli, seared Maine scallop with roasted fennel and green-olive brown butter—while the wine list has a North American artisanal focus. With a whooshing waterfall right outside and candle-light, it's just about perfect. 92 Stowe St. ☎ 802/244-7300. www.henofthewood.com. Entrees $16–$31. AE, DISC, MC, V. Dinner Tues–Sat.

★★ **Inn at Montpelier** MONTPELIER With an excellent location a short walk from downtown, this Federal-style inn has a gorgeous wraparound porch, ideal for afternoon reading. Rooms are well kept; service is warm and gracious. 147 Main St. ☎ 802/223-2727. www.innatmontpelier.com. 19 units. Doubles $132–$229 w/breakfast. AE, MC, V.

★★ **Inn at the Round Barn Farm** WAITSFIELD Set on a hill amid a meadow, mountain, and pond, this renovated farmhouse has as its centerpiece a massive round barn—at turns an art gallery, event space, and more. With Tempur-Pedic beds, gorgeous views, and lavish breakfasts, it's as inviting a getaway destination as you're likely to find. Ask about the dog-led snowshoeing excursions. 1661 E. Warren Rd. ☎ 802/496-2276. www.theroundbarn.com. 12 units. Doubles $165–$315 w/breakfast. AE, MC, V.

★★ **Kismet** MONTPELIER *NEW AMERICAN* A 2010 move brought this foodie fave—and their loyal following—to a more heavily trafficked spot on Main Street, so now the eggs *en cocotte;* baked polenta with roasted tomato, ricotta, and

> *Pitch-perfect seasonal fare at Hen of the Wood.*

basil; and other farm-fresh brunch dishes can be savored by even more happy customers. 52 State St. ☎ 802/262-3500. www.kismetkitchens.com. Entrees $10–$20. Cash or check only. Breakfast & lunch daily, dinner Thurs–Sat.

★★ **Main Street Grill & Bar** MONTPELIER *AMERICAN* This is the testing ground for the New England Culinary Institute, and includes a great Sunday brunch, a tapas menu, and imaginative farm-to-table dishes that often hit the bull's-eye. Their sister eatery, **La Brioche,** is down the block at 89 Main St. 118 Main St. ☎ 802/223-3188. Entrees $16–$22. AE, DISC, MC, V. Lunch Tues–Sun, dinner Tues–Sat.

★ **Old Stage Coach Inn** WATERBURY Waterbury center is steps away from this antiques-filled 19th-century house. Room nos. 7 and 8 are spacious and charming, with cathedral ceilings and exposed beams, but everybody gets the huge, cooked-to-order breakfast. (Some rooms have a shared bathroom.) 18 N. Main St. ☎ 800/262-2206. www.oldstagecoach.com. 11 units. Doubles $80–$190 w/breakfast. AE, DISC, MC, V.

★★★ **Pitcher Inn** WARREN The classic New England–inn exterior of this Relais & Châteaux property only hints at the level of luxury inside. Each room was designed by a different architect, and each is an exquisitely realized embodiment of a Vermont-inspired theme, from the rustic post-and-beam style of "Ski" to the chalkboards in "School Room"; whimsical objets d'art and one-of-a-kind pieces abound. 175 Main St. ☎ 802/496-6350. www.pitcherinn.com. 11 units. Doubles $425–$650 w/breakfast. AE, DISC, MC, V.

Stowe

Mount Mansfield presides over the idyllic church-steeple-

and-covered-bridge village of Stowe, a lovely place to visit any time of year. And indeed, there's no shortage of visitors: There's an international presence here, chockablock options for the upscale traveler, and, of course, the Stowe Mountain ski resort has a loyal following. But, despite the condo developments and occasional tourist-oriented shop, the town retains its historic charm and appeal. The main street is walkable—our 2- or 3-day tour has time built in to stroll around the shops—and views are gorgeous from pretty much anywhere you look. The itinerary here is for summer or early fall—we're pretty sure you'll figure out how to keep busy in winter months.

> *The mostly flat and level Stowe Recreation Path is ideal for outdoor enthusiasts of all ages and abilities.*

START Stowe is 46 miles from Burlington.

1 kids ★★★ **Mount Mansfield & Stowe Mountain Lodge.** At 4,395 feet, Mount Mansfield is the highest peak in Vermont, and home to the popular Stowe Mountain Lodge (p. 411). In the summer, travel up the zigzagging route to the summit ridge along the auto **Toll Road** ($26 per car; July to mid-Oct daily 9am–4pm), or ride up the **Gondola Skyride** to take in the incredible views. At the top, take a short hike up the rocks and planks to the Frenchman's Pile for gorgeous panoramic vistas of Lake Champlain, the White Mountains, the Adirondacks, and of course the Green Mountains. Then we suggest a ride on the 2,300-foot **Alpine Slide**—it's awesome. In the winter, hit Stowe's slopes—they're some of New England's finest. ⏱ Minimum 3 hr. 5781 Mountain Rd. ☎ 802/253-3000. www.stowe.com. Gondola: $24 adults, $16 kids 6–17, free for kids 5 & under. Mid-June to mid-Oct

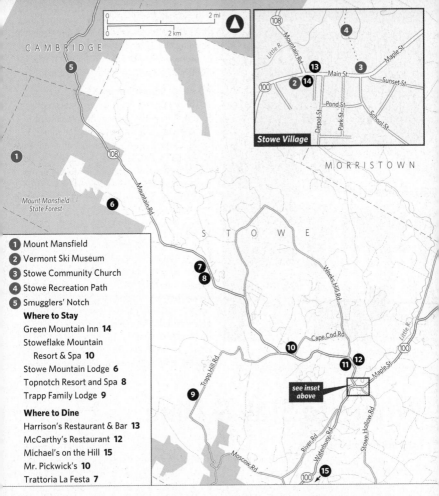

1 Mount Mansfield

2 Vermont Ski Museum

3 Stowe Community Church

4 Stowe Recreation Path

5 Smugglers' Notch

Where to Stay

Green Mountain Inn **14**

Stoweflake Mountain
    Resort & Spa **10**

Stowe Mountain Lodge **6**

Topnotch Resort and Spa **8**

Trapp Family Lodge **9**

Where to Dine

Harrison's Restaurant & Bar **13**

McCarthy's Restaurant **12**

Michael's on the Hill **15**

Mr. Pickwick's **10**

Trattoria La Festa **7**

daily 10am–4:30pm. Slide: $21 adults, $19 kids. Mid-June to mid-Sept daily; mid-Sept to mid-Oct weekends only.

2 ★ **Vermont Ski Museum.** Smack in the center of the village of Stowe, this little shrine to all things that go *shoosh* is a fun stop even in the off season. The walls are lined with gear from the 1920s to the present, accompanied by heroic stories and informative blurbs on all facets of the history of skiing—from recreation to competition to the 10th Mountain Division of the U.S. Army. ⏱ 30 min. 1 S. Main St. ☎ 802/253-9911. www.vermontskimuseum.org. $3 suggested donation. Wed–Sun noon–5pm.

3 **Stowe Community Church.** With its steeple visible from a distance as you come down into the valley of Stowe, this building marks more than the geographic center of the village. Since its construction in 1863, it had served as a house of worship for Methodist, Universalist,

A Bite at the Top

Isolated at the top of the mountain, you might expect to be disappointed by your only option, but the **Cliff House** is no flabby fry and greasy burger joint. You get farm-to-table dishes, along with breathtaking views. 5781 Mountain Rd. ☎ 802/253-3000. www.stowe.com. $$.

> *Stowe Community Church draws members and guests from all backgrounds and denominations.*

Congregationalist, and Baptist communities, but in 1920 they united under a single minister, forming one of the first interdenominational churches in the country. ⏱ 15 min. 137 Main St. ☎ 802/253-7257. www.stowechurch.org.

④ ★★ kids **Stowe Recreation Path.** Starting at the Stowe Community Church, this motorless route winds in and around Mountain Road throughout the town and village for some 5½ miles. Distinct from the heavily trafficked roads, it's perfect for walking, running, biking, or blading—and even snowshoeing in the winter. There are bike racks along the way to start and stop at your leisure—say, for a drink at **The Rusty Nail**, 190 Mountain Rd. (☎ 802/253-6245; www.rustynailbar.com). ⏱ 2 hr. 137 Main St.

⑤ ★★ **Smugglers' Notch.** "The Notch" is a narrow, winding stretch of Route 108 just north of Stowe, where the cliffs tower on either side of you up to 1,000 feet. The ride through is gorgeous, but we suggest you hike, have a picnic, or just stop to enjoy the scenery at **Smugglers' Notch State Park** (p. 370 for hiking information), located on the south side of the pass, just north of town. ⏱ 1–2 hr. 6443 Mountain Rd. ☎ 802/253-4014. www.vtstateparks.com. Road closes in winter.

Where to Stay & Dine

★ **Green Mountain Inn** STOWE
This attractive historic inn in downtown Stowe has grown considerably over the last 25 years—adding luxurious suites and even town houses to the original 1833 property—but still retains a classic ambience. 18 Main St. ☎ 802/253-7301. www.greenmountaininn.com. 105 units. Doubles $139–$439. AE, DISC, MC, V.

★★ **Harrison's Restaurant & Bar** STOWE AMERICAN A bit of a hidden gem—though it's right in the center of the village—this cozy downstairs room is a choice spot for locals and those in the know, with mouthwatering dishes like maple-glazed Scottish salmon and ancho-rubbed pork tenderloin. 25 Main St. ☎ 802/253-7773. www.harrisonsstowe.com. Entrees $13–$28. AE, DISC, MC, V. Dinner daily.

★ **McCarthy's Restaurant** STOWE BREAKFAST
The most popular place in town in the morning. That's no fluke: down-home service, a satisfying diner-style breakfast, and—in pricey Stowe—quite affordable. 454 Mountain Rd. ☎ 802/253-8626. Entrees $6–$10. Cash only. Breakfast & lunch daily.

★★ **Michael's on the Hill** WATERBURY CONTINENTAL Just south of town, this is an excellent option for that special meal, offering seasonally inspired dishes like Maine lobster with puréed corn and leek fondue, or spice-rubbed

Travel Tip

The 420-seat **Spruce Peak Arts Center,** 7320 Mountain Rd. (☎ 802/760-4634; www.sprucepeakarts.org), opened its doors in December 2010, hosting musical acts such as James Taylor, Shawn Colvin, the Wailers, and Little Feat. Dance, film, theater, and comedy round out the calendar.

venison with rösti, along with an award-winning wine list. 4182 Waterbury-Stowe Rd. ☎ 802/244-7476. www.michaelsonthehill.com. Entrees $25–$43. DISC, MC, V. Dinner Wed–Mon.

★ **Mr. Pickwick's Gastropub** STOWE *GASTROPUB* This convivial British-themed pub/restaurant, with more than 150 beers and dark wood booths, serves up not only tasty English classics like bangers and mash, but also well-crafted entrees like duck two ways and Japanese Kobe sirloin. 433 Mountain Rd. ☎ 802/253-7558. www.mrpickwicks.com. Entrees $21–$74. AE, DISC, MC, V. Breakfast, lunch & dinner daily.

★ **Stoweflake Mountain Resort & Spa** STOWE On-site golf, indoor and outdoor pools, spacious rooms, kids' programs . . . but the real reason to come here is the excellent, world-class spa, which offers more than 120 treatments, massaging waterfalls, and soaking pools. 1746 Mountain Rd. ☎ 802/253-7355. www.stoweflake.com. 120 units. Doubles $179–$499. AE, DISC, MC, V.

★★★ **Stowe Mountain Lodge** STOWE Spectacularly sited at the base of Mount Mansfield, this huge resort—a new model for luxury, sustainability, and service in Stowe—opened in 2008. The timber-and-shingle exteriors, stone-and-wood interiors, light-flooded corner guest rooms, and wraparound porches are particularly dreamy. The spa, outdoor pool, and golf course are all top of the line. 7412 Mountain Rd. ☎ 888/4-STOWE-VT (478-6938). www.stowemountainlodge.com. 139 units. Doubles $199–$1,049. AE, DISC, MC, V.

★★ **Topnotch Resort and Spa** STOWE Topnotch has gorgeous grounds, a top-tier tennis program, horseback riding, and a beautiful spa and outdoor hot tub, among other perks. Rooms, done up in a charming French-country rustic style, are comfy and spacious. 4000 Mountain Rd. ☎ 800/451-8686. www.topnotchresort.com. 108 units. Doubles $145–$575. AE, DISC, MC, V.

★★★ **Trapp Family Lodge** STOWE Set a mile or two up into the hills, this European-style complex has some of the best views in the area, with rooms to match; our fave is no. 562, with a balcony and wood-burning

> *The Green Mountain Inn offers two restaurants, a heated pool, and afternoon tea.*

fireplace. Amenities include a cross-country ski center, biking and hiking trails, maple sugaring, and even a brewery. 700 Trapp Hill Rd. ☎ 802/253-8511. www.trappfamily.com. 96 units. Doubles $199–$559. AE, DISC, MC, V.

★ **Trattoria La Festa** STOWE *ITALIAN* A dependable choice for Italian, the interior of this restored barn has been transformed by the triple play of red walls, red tablecloths, and red sauce. 480 Mountain Rd. ☎ 802/253-8480. www.trattoriastowe.com. Entrees $16–$25. AE, MC, V. Apr–May & Oct–Nov lunch & dinner Thurs–Sat, June–Sept & Dec–Mar lunch & dinner daily.

Emily's Bridge

Otherwise known as **Gold Brook Bridge,** this structure just a few miles south of the town center—at Covered Bridge Road and Gold Brook Road—is allegedly haunted by one unhappy lady named Emily. Perhaps a 19th-century Juliet who hanged herself when her lover didn't meet to elope . . . or did she crash her carriage off into the ravine? The story varies, though legends have circulated of white apparition sightings, or cars and horses being mysteriously slashed on the bridge. While Emily's existence remains unproven, this hasn't stopped the curious or spook-obsessed from looking for clues or evidence—do *you* dare cross this 1844 structure at night?

9
New
Hampshire

Our Favorite New Hampshire Moments

While we can't deny that many of New Hampshire's glories can be found amid the towering snowcapped peaks of the White Mountains, there are also riches to be discovered in the shimmering waters of the Lakes Region, cobblestone streets of Portsmouth, bucolic backcountry roads of the Monadnock and Upper Valley, and local flavor of small towns throughout the state.

❶ Creeping up Mount Washington. This isn't any old train: Climbing straight up the side of the mountain, the cog railway looks like a cockeyed cartoon locomotive—even the boiler on the engine is tilted. As you slowly ascend at a bold angle, the brakeman hollers out the history of the train. Arriving at the crisp (summer highs in the mid 50s), spectacular summit of the tallest peak in the Northeast, you'll have time to explore and take in the panoramic view. See p. 419, ❻.

❷ Flying low over Lake Winnipesaukee with Lakes Biplane. When we reserved a flight on this scenic biplane, our pilot good-naturedly assured us it would be the highlight of our trip—he was right. The ride, in an open-cockpit upgraded version of the classic WACO plane of the 1930s, was exhilarating and wondrous—a truly special experience. Equipped with your own headset and mic, you'll get a taste of how incredible it was to fly in the early 20th century. See p. 418, ❸.

❸ Soaking at the top of the Mountain View Grand Resort. If you enjoy a good spa soak—and if you don't, well, come on—imagine a setting

> PREVIOUS PAGE *New Hampshire's winter landscapes can be both bleak and beautiful.* THIS PAGE *The top of the world from Mount Washington.*

that's not a windowless room buried somewhere in a building, but rather a private chamber with a panoramic, 360-degree view of the outdoors. Now put it on top of a sprawling, five-story inn at the top of a cleared hill in the mountains. See p. 443.

❹ Indulging at the Black Trumpet Bistro. While New Hampshire isn't known as a culinary destination, the little city of Portsmouth has some gems, and the Black Trumpet is at the top of the list. Across from the harbor, this candlelit sanctuary with copper tabletops and brick walls perfectly complements the exquisitely conceived and prepared creative American cuisine. See p. 447.

❺ Spotting a moose. You've seen them in museums and on mantles, but it's still quite a surprise to come across a live moose in the wild. These enormous herbivores (they can weigh up to 1,500 lb.) make for an imposing presence, even if they're just moseying across the road in peace. Go out prowling around dusk, or hook up with **Gorham Moose Tours'** excellent tour and see if you get lucky. Just be sure to keep a safe distance—these guys may look placid, but they can deliver a swift kick if they feel threatened. See p. 424, ❸.

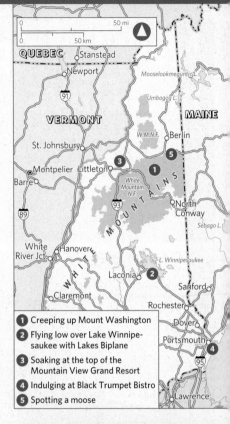

❶ Creeping up Mount Washington
❷ Flying low over Lake Winnipesaukee with Lakes Biplane
❸ Soaking at the top of the Mountain View Grand Resort
❹ Indulging at Black Trumpet Bistro
❺ Spotting a moose

> *The wine bar at the Black Trumpet Bistro was a ship's chandlery in the 19th century.*

New Hampshire in 3 Days

Given 3 days to explore, it's tempting to settle for just one locale and take your time—but this wouldn't be fair to the grand and diverse Granite State. If we have to chisel it down, there are three must-see areas: Portsmouth, Winnipesaukee, and Mount Washington. This neatly breaks into three digestible chunks: 1 day in a great little port city chock-full of history, 1 day driving—and flying—around the lovely Lakes region, and 1 day of getting out and up into the rugged White Mountains.

> A wooden walkway leads to the breathtaking Flume, a natural 800-foot gorge in Franconia Notch State Park.

START Portsmouth is 58 miles from Boston.
TRIP LENGTH 188 miles.

1 Portsmouth. With maritime trade, ship-building, and ale making all figuring prominently in its past, this town is an enchanting place to explore. The most comprehensive look into its past can be found at the open-air, living-history museum ★★★ **Strawbery Banke**

(p. 445, **4**). Guided tours of the original homes and buildings from different eras of Portsmouth's past—spanning 400 years—illustrate how this neighborhood developed (or didn't) over time, and how the port city's life changed as the nation grew. Afterward, get out on the water with **Portsmouth Harbor Cruises** (p. 444, **2**). And don't miss out on

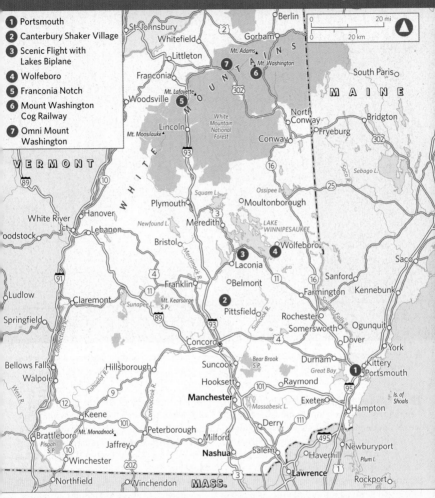

1. Portsmouth
2. Canterbury Shaker Village
3. Scenic Flight with Lakes Biplane
4. Wolfeboro
5. Franconia Notch
6. Mount Washington Cog Railway
7. Omni Mount Washington

just soaking up the atmosphere of this place; fun and crafty boutiques, food shops, cafes, and galleries line the tangle of streets that compose downtown Portsmouth, most concentrated around Market Street. You could easily spend a day poking around stores, checking out the waterfront surrounded by the flower gardens of **Prescott Park** (Marcy St. and Court St.), and wandering charming alleyways. ⏱1 day. See p. 444.

On Day 2, take the Rte. 1 Bypass north out of Portsmouth. At the traffic circle, take the first exit onto Rte. 16 and go north 21 miles to exit 15, onto Rte. 11 west. After 15 miles, turn left onto Rte. 28 south, then a quick right to

stay on Rte. 11 for another 17 miles. Turn right onto Lilypond Rd. and right onto Aviation Dr.

2 ★★ Canterbury Shaker Village. Get here early and enjoy this excellent museum located on the site of a former Shaker settlement. ⏱3 hr. See p. 436, **5**.

Old Man of the Mountain

Named by Nathaniel Hawthorne in 1850, this shoulder of granite ledges in Franconia—which appeared as a 40-foot-tall man's face in profile, and was visible from I-93—has been on the state emblem since 1945. Sadly, the ledge crumbled in 2003.

> *Though the focus is on the architecture at the living history museum of Strawbery Banke, costumed reenactors will show you around.*

❸ ★★★ Scenic Flight with Lakes Biplane.
You're in the Lakes region for only a day, so we recommend you splurge and sign up for a 20-minute ride in this open-cockpit biplane. It's a singular experience, and what a fantastic location for it—the tapestry of lakes and islands forms a breathtaking scene that rolls below you as far as the eye can see. The plane feels as if it's moving in slow motion, hanging a mere 1,000 feet above the landscape, and your pilot Phil is happy to share details of the route from his cockpit behind you. (There's room for you and another guest.) ⏱ 1 hr. 15 Aviation Dr., Gilford. ☎ 603/250-6184. www. lakesbiplane.com. $225–$325 for 2 adults, depending on length of flight. Call to reserve.

Return to Rte. 11 and go 17 miles east; turn left onto Rte. 28 and go north 11 miles.

❹ ★ Wolfeboro. Colonial governor John Wentworth built Kingswood—the first summer country estate in northern New England—here in 1771, and the destination has remained a popular one ever since. Situated on the eastern shore of the lake, this picturesque village has both small-town charm and plenty to do and see. Stop by the information center at **Wolfeboro Station** for updates on current activities, check out the **New Hampshire Boat Museum,** and browse shops like **The Country Bookseller,** 23 N. Main St. (☎ 603/569-6030; www.thecountrybookseller.com). Be sure to get out on the lake; the paddle-wheel replica ***Winnipesaukee Belle*** leaves from the docks right in the middle of town for 90-minute narrated cruises. ⏱ 3 hr. See p. 434, ❶.

Take Rte. 109 18 miles north out of Wolfeboro and turn left onto Whittier Hwy. (Rte. 25). Go 5½ miles west to Center Harbor; turn right onto Rte. 25B and go east 3½ miles to Rte. 3. Take Rte. 3 north 6 miles to Holderness, where you will spend the night. On Day 3, follow signs to to I-93N. Go 30 miles to exit 34A.

❺ ★★ Franconia Notch. Yes, this is where the fabled Old Man of the Mountain used to live (see p. 417), but the 6,692-acre state park has plenty more up its sleeve. To get to the **Flume Gorge** (p. 440, ❺), a narrow crevasse with towering granite cliffs on both sides, start at the visitor center and walk uphill to the wooden walkway, from which you can view the spectacular cascading water of Flume Creek. A short drive down the street is the **Basin** (p. 440, ❺), a pool of the Pemigewasset River where thousands of years of falling water have carved a 20-foot-wide pothole in the solid granite base. And farther on up the road, the aerial tramway at **Cannon Mountain** (p. 440, ❻) brings you up the eastern face of Cannon for a panoramic view of the Presidential Range. ⏱ 3 hr.

Take I-93N 7 miles to exit 35. Merge onto Rte. 3 north, go 10 miles, and turn right onto Rte. 302 east. Go 4½ miles and turn left onto Base Station Rd.

❻ ★★ **Mount Washington Cog Railway.** The brainchild of one Sylvester Marsh, who, after nearly getting lost while hiking to the top of "the Rockpile" (Mount Washington), decided there must be a better way. His solution raised some eyebrows at first, but time has vindicated Sly, and this sturdy railroad has been delivering passengers safely to the summit since 1869. The train carries you nearly straight up the mountainside, for a trip of just over 3 miles, and the brakeman will make sure it stays fun and informative. You can reserve a ticket ahead of time, but trains board 15 minutes before departure. ⏱ 4 hr. Base Rd., Bretton Woods. ☎ 603/278-5404. www.thecog. com. $62 adults, $39 kids 4–12. Daily 8:30am–4:30pm (but check website for schedule, as times vary by season).

Drive back down Base Station Rd. and follow signs to:

❼ ★★★ **Omni Mount Washington.** We can't think of a better way to finish up a Granite State tour than with a visit to the glorious Omni. Established in 1902 by William Stickney, the hotel hums with history: Thomas Edison and Babe Ruth are among the long list of notable guests, and the World Bank and International Monetary Fund were born here at a 1944 conference. Once you've driven up onto the stunning setting, you probably won't want to leave. But whether or not you choose to stay the night, spend some time: Have dinner at either the **Dining Room** (jacket required) or **Stickney's Pub and Steakhouse,** enjoy a drink at one of the lounges, and soak up the ambience. See p. 443.

> *In 1852, the New Hampshire state legislature told Sylvester Marsh of his cog railway, he "might as well build a railway to the Moon."*

New Hampshire in 1 Week

The Granite State has long been renowned for its fiercely independent politics, perhaps most markedly in its steadfast resistance to an income or sales tax, and in its official motto: "Live Free or Die." This flintiness of spirit is equaled by the ruggedness of the glorious White Mountains, but you'll find evidence of that maverick attitude—and pleasant eccentricity—throughout New Hampshire, from the shops of Portsmouth to the farms of Walpole to the country inns and eateries. This full week gives you a chance to dig deeper into each region covered in our shorter itinerary (p. 416), and you'll also catch a couple of the best museums in the state.

> At 6,288 feet, Mount Washington is, according to the Mount Washington Observatory, home to the "world's worst weather."

START Portsmouth is 58 miles from Boston.
TRIP LENGTH 315 miles.

❶ ★★★ **Portsmouth.** For an introduction to the city's historic homes, take a look at the **John Paul Jones House** (p. 444, ❶). A short drive will bring you to two examples of Georgian architecture: the 1760 **Wentworth**

Gardner House. Climb onboard **Portsmouth Harbor Cruises** (p. 444, ❷) for the noon trip 6 miles out to the nine islands known as the Isles of Shoals. Then, enjoy a fun night on the town, following some of our suggestions for drinks and eats (p. 447).

On Day 2, see the harbor from a different perspective with **Portsmouth Kayak**

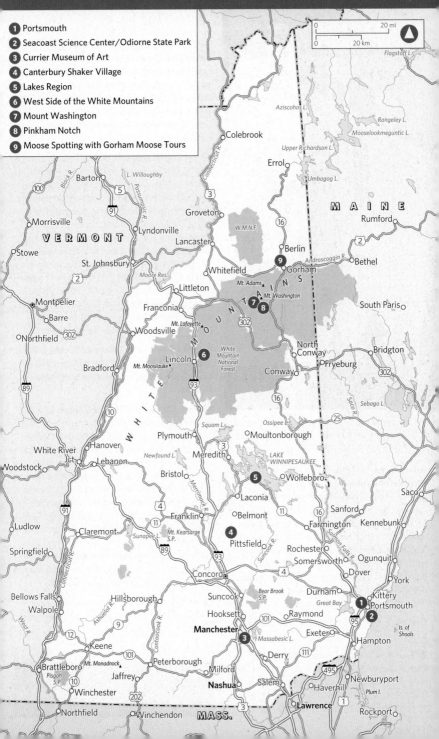

1 Portsmouth
2 Seacoast Science Center/Odiorne State Park
3 Currier Museum of Art
4 Canterbury Shaker Village
5 Lakes Region
6 West Side of the White Mountains
7 Mount Washington
8 Pinkham Notch
9 Moose Spotting with Gorham Moose Tours

> The paneled door with elaborate pediment at the Wentworth Gardner House is a classic element of late-Georgian architecture.

Adventures (p. 428). Then take your time at **Strawbery Banke** (p. 445, ④). Try to time your trip to make the **Smuttynose Brewery** (p. 446, ⑦) 3pm Friday or 11am Saturday tour, for an in-depth peek into the world of beer making. If this doesn't jibe with your visit, the **Red Hook Brewery,** 1 Redhook Way (☎ 603/430-8600; www.redhook.com), hosts tours daily. Spend the rest of your afternoon exploring the narrow streets and shops (p. 446) of this easy-to-love city. ⏱ 2 days.

On Day 3, take Rte. 1A south through a traffic circle, 3 miles to:

❷ **Seacoast Science Center/Odiorne State Park.** After breakfast, head here for a refreshing walk along the ocean, and make a quick stop in the Science Center—you've got a full day ahead, so don't linger! ⏱ 1 hr. See p. 446, ⑥.

Go back to the traffic circle and take the second exit onto Elwyn Rd. Go 1½ miles and turn onto Rte. 1 Bypass north. At the next circle, take the third exit onto I-95S. Go 8¼ miles to exit 2 and merge onto Rte. 101 west. Go 31 miles to I-93N, go less than a mile, and take exit 8, turning right onto Wellington Rd. Continue onto Bridge St. and in 1 mile turn right onto Ash St.

❸ ★★ **Currier Museum of Art.** Time for an art fix! This is one of the best art museums in northern New England, with a collection encompassing European and American painting, photography, sculpture, and decorative arts, including works by Monet, Picasso, Matisse, Hopper, and O'Keefe. What's more, you can take a by-reservation tour of the Frank Lloyd Wright–designed Zimmerman house, the only house by the groundbreaking architect open to the public in New England. ⏱ 2 hr. 150 Ash St., Manchester. ☎ 603/669-6144. www.currier.org. $10 adults, free for kids 17 & under. Sun–Mon & Wed–Fri 11am–5pm; Sat 10am–5pm.

Head back to I-93N. Take exit 15E onto I-393E, and take exit 3 onto Rte. 106 and go north 6¾ miles. Turn left onto Shaker Rd. and follow signs to:

❹ ★★★ **Canterbury Shaker Village.** Explore this well-preserved village, home to more than 300 Shakers during the Christian sect's mid-19th-century peak (see "The Shakers: Radical Chic"). The Ken Burns film screened in the visitors' center is a good primer, but we recommend the Shaker Story Tour (75 min.; hourly 11am–3pm) or the interactive (singing! dancing!) family tour (45 min.; summer daily 11am and 2pm) if you've got kids in tow. **Tip:** If you want to time your day to arrive here for (Shaker) family-style lunch at **Greenwoods**—last seatings are at 1:30 and 2:30pm—skip Odiorne State Park above. ⏱ 3 hr. See p. 436, ⑤.

❺ ★★ **Lakes Region.** Follow our Lakes Region itinerary stops ❶ through ❹. ⏱ 1½ days. See p. 434.

Travel Tip

Reserve a ticket for the **Mount Washington Cog Railway** (p. 419, ⑥) for Day 6.

> Keep an eye out for the mighty moose—you may spot one as you make your way through the state. If not, you can always take the Gorham Moose Tour.

On Day 5, take Rte. 113 27 miles to:

6 ★★ West Side of the White Mountains. Follow our White Mountains itinerary stops **4** through **7**. ⏱1 day. See p. 440.

On the afternoon of Day 6, take Rte. 116 south ½ mile and turn left onto Rte. 302 18 miles east to:

7 Mount Washington. You can't come to the White Mountains—really, you probably shouldn't come to New Hampshire—without making it up "the Rockpile," as the tallest peak in the northeast is known. There are all sorts of ways to come at it, but the **Mount Washington Cog Railway** (p. 419, **6**) is an experience in its own right. When you've finally chugged to a stop back at the bottom, have a drink and dinner and stay the night at the majestic **Omni Mount Washington** (p. 443). ⏱ Half day. See p. 441.

On Day 7, go 24 miles east on Rte. 302 and go left onto Rte. 16 north; it's 15 miles to:

8 ★★ Pinkham Notch. Start your last day hitting the bike trails bright and early with **Great Glen Trails** (p. 426); rent your wheels for 2 hours. Next: Mount Washington, redux. This time: Tackle the 8-mile **Mount Washington Auto Road** (p. 441). With no

guardrails and an average grade of 12%, you're going to need to be able to lock your car into first gear coming down. Back at the bottom, get one last rush of adrenaline whizzing down the cable of the **ZipRider** at Wildcat Mountain Ski Area. ⏱ Half day. See p. 438, **2**.

Check in to a hotel and grab an early dinner before heading nearly 8 miles north on Rte 16 to:

9 ★★★ Moose Spotting with Gorham Moose Tours. While road signs everywhere have been warning you to beware of these behemoths crossing the road, we hope you haven't had to slam on your brakes yet. A great way to see a moose in the wild: Grab a spot with **Gorham Moose Tours.** ⏱ 3 hr. See p. 424, **3**.

Into the Wild

For a true wilderness experience, head way up to the Great North Woods. Tranquil **Umbagog Lake,** on the New Hampshire–Maine border, is a wonderful place to paddle about, observe wildlife, and generally get away from it all. Forest, marshland, and other habitats provide sanctuary to the state's most abundant mix of birds, so bring your binocs—you may spot loons, osprey, chickadees, and even bald eagle. Angling for some action? The lake has plentiful bass, salmon, and trout pickerel. Rent a boat at **Umbagog Lake State Park** (☎ 603/482-7795; www.nhstateparks.org).

Plan Ahead

You'll want to call at least a few days in advance to reserve a spot on a **Moose Tour** (see **9**) for the evening of Day 7.

New Hampshire with Kids

While the motto "Live Free or Die" does sound a bit severe, the good folks of New Hampshire will neither eat your children nor enforce upon them the hard, cold realities of frontier living. Quite to the contrary: There is a surprising amount of kid-friendly and kid-centric activity throughout the state; the only challenge is covering so much ground. Base yourself in the White Mountains (see Spending the Night, below, for our suggestions) and plan on 3 days.

> 'Tis the season year-round at Santa's Village, a kid-friendly if slightly kitschy Christmas theme park in Jefferson.

START Lincoln is 110 miles from Portsmouth. **TRIP LENGTH** 119 miles.

❶ ★ Chutters. This shop has the longest candy counter in the world; exercise self-control! ⏲ 30 min. See p. 440, **❼**.

Take Rte. 116 20 miles east; turn left onto Rte. 2 west.

❷ ★ Santa's Village. You don't have to wait until December to sit on Santa's lap or visit his reindeer, though this *is* the farthest north you may get on this trip. Traditional rides include antique cars and a Christmas Ferris wheel, while newer additions like the Ho Ho H2O Water Park are decidedly summer oriented. Don't leave without decorating your own gingerbread cookie, and have the village smithy pound out a good-luck ring sized just for junior. ⏲ 4 hr. 528 Presidential Hwy. (US-2), Jefferson. ☎ 603/586-4445. www.santasvillage.com. $25. Call for hours & seasons.

Head east on Rte. 2 for 18 miles. Turn right onto Main St. and go 1 mile.

❸ ★★ Moose Spotting with Gorham Moose Tours. Maybe you'll get lucky and glimpse one of these gentle giants roadside, but if you go with the pros at Gorham Moose Tours, you'll have a 94% chance of seeing one, plus other wildlife. Their 21-passenger 3-hour guided bus tours leave at 6 or 6:30pm. ⏲ 3 hr. Rte. 16, Gorham. ☎ 877/986-6673. www.gorhamnh.org. $25 adults, $15 kids 5–12, $5 kids 4 & under. Late May to early Oct Mon & Wed–Sat; July & Aug Mon–Sat.

On Day 2, take Rte. 16 19 miles north to:

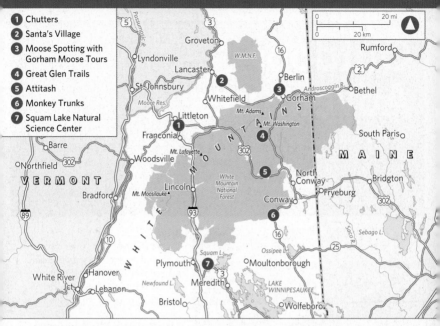

1. Chutters
2. Santa's Village
3. Moose Spotting with Gorham Moose Tours
4. Great Glen Trails
5. Attitash
6. Monkey Trunks
7. Squam Lake Natural Science Center

④ ★★ **Great Glen Trails.** Bring a picnic lunch, and spend the morning exploring the 25 miles of trails on mountain bikes. ⏱ 4 hr. See p. 426.

Take Rte. 16 south for 15 miles. Turn right onto Rte. 302 west and go 3½ miles.

⑤ ★★ **Attitash.** The Nor'easter Mountain Coaster—a downhill roller coaster—is the big draw at this ski resort, but your tickets allow unlimited use of the alpine slide, water slides, play pool, mountain bikes, bungee trampoline, climbing wall, and scenic chair ride. For this itinerary, you'll need an afternoon ticket only. ⏱ 3 hr. Rte. 302, Bartlett. ☎ 603/374-2368. www.attitash.com. Tickets by height (over/under 48 in.); adult afternoon ticket $25, child afternoon ticket $10. Mid-June to early Sept daily 10am–6pm.

On Day 3, take Rte. 16 south 15 miles.

⑥ ★★ **Monkey Trunks.** Lock into your harness and swing from one platform to the next at this high-rope and zipline park. Bigger kids (over 48 in. tall) can test their mettle on the 65-foot-high Discovery Course, while the 25-foot Mini-Monkey Course is suitable for ages 3 and up. ⏱ 2 hr. 1853 Chocorua Mountain Hwy., Chocorua. ☎ 603/367-4427. www.monkeytrunks.com. Jungle Course & Discovery Course $49; Mini-Monkey Course $39; Dropzone Course $10; all-course day

pass $79. Late May to late June Sat–Sun 10am–7pm; late June to early Sept daily 10am–7pm; early Sept to mid-Oct Sat–Sun 10am–4pm.

Take Rte. 16 south 3½ miles and turn right onto Rte. 113 west. Go 5 miles and turn right onto Rte. 25 going west 14 miles, then right onto Rte. 25B, going west 3¼ miles. Turn right onto Rte. 25/3 north and go 5 miles, and then right onto Rte. 113 east.

⑦ ★★ **Squam Lake Natural Science Center.** Kids are the obvious audience here, but adults too will enjoy the trails and checking out the interactive exhibits with animals native to the region, such as bobcats, otters, mountain lions, and bears. ⏱ 2 hr. 23 Science Center Rd., Holderness. ☎ 603/968-7194. www.nhnature.org. $13 adults, $9 kids 3–15. May–Oct daily 9:30am–4:30pm.

Spending the Night

There are lots of choices, but the best place for families to stay in the area is the super-kid-friendly **Adventure Suites,** 3440 White Mountain Hwy. (☎ 603/356-9744; www.adventuresuites.com), which features themed suites like Tree House and Jungle. Doubles are $109 to $489.

Outdoor Adventures

If it isn't already obvious, the Granite State is all about the outdoors—hiking and skiing in particular—and you'll find opportunities to enjoy all sorts of activities just about wherever you go. Below we list a small sample of options—from extreme to extremely laid-back—that only scratch the surface of what the state has to offer.

> Bemis Brook drops over a granite cliff at Arethusa Falls, named for a nymph of Greek myth who was turned into a fountain.

Biking

The White Mountains offer myriad scenic routes for road riding, while many downhill ski areas (Bretton Woods, Attitash, Waterville Valley) provide summer lift service for mountain bikers. Families should consider **Loon Mountain Adventure Center,** 60 Loon Mountain Rd., Lincoln (☎ 800-229-5666; www.loonmtn.com), for its self-guided Franconia Notch Bike Tour. Shuttles leave Loon at 10:30am and 1pm for Echo Lake, where you'll start your mostly downhill tour on a paved path through the Notch back to Loon. In Pinkham Notch, **Great Glen Trails** (☎ 603/466-3988; www.greatglen-trails.com) has gentle carriage roads for family biking, while hard-core mountain bikers speed down Whiplash, Plunge, and other single-track woodsy trails.

Fishing

Trout- and bass-rich **Lake Winnipe-saukee** is an angler's dream. Novices can venture out with **Meredith Bay Guide Service** (☎ 603/344-1314; www.cwkenney.com); for bait and tackle, try **Wolfeboro Bay Outfitters** (☎ 603/569-1114). There's fine trout fishing to be had on the **Pemigewasset River;** find access points in **Franconia Notch State Park** (p. 440, ❺). Crystal-clear **Profile Lake** (☎ 603/823-8800; www.nhstateparks.com), at the head of the Pemi, is a good bet for brook trout.

Biking

Great Glen Trails 14

Loon Mountain Adventure Center 9

Fishing

Franconia Notch State Park 11

Lake Winnipesaukee 4

Meredith Bay Guide Service 5

Pemigewasset River 11

Profile Lake 11

Wolfeboro Bay Outfitters 3

Hiking

Arethusa Falls 15

Lonesome Lake 10

Mount Monadnock 1

Mount Washington 13

Kayaking & Canoeing

Lake Winnipesaukee 4

Out Back Kayak 9

Portsmouth Kayak Adventures 2

Wild Meadow Canoes 6

Skiing & Snowboarding

Attitash 17

Bretton Woods 12

Bretton Woods Nordic Center 12

Cannon Mountain 11

Jackson Ski Touring Center 16

Loon Mountain 8

Waterville Valley 7

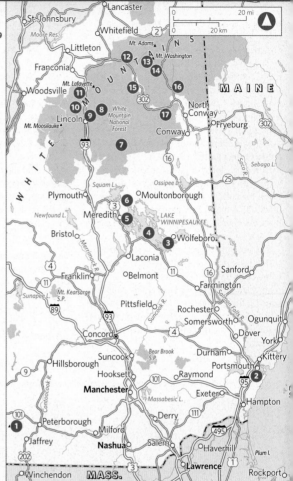

Hiking

New Hampshire is a nirvana for hikers of all experience levels. The best trails are within the White Mountains; the Appalachian Mountain Club's *White Mountain Guide* is a must if you want to do longer hikes.

The best trek in New England is the famous 23-mile journey over the **Presidential Range,** encompassing 8 peaks over 4,000 feet. It can be dangerous, with wildly unpredictable weather, steep climbs, and icy stream crossings. You'll need to be fit, and very well prepared. Intrepid souls complete this in 1 day, but most hikers take 2 or 3, overnighting in the wonderful AMC huts along the way (see p. 429). Another, albeit more minor, life lister

is tackling **Mount Washington.** See p. 441 for details.

There are loads of moderate and easy hikes, most of which showcase the singular beauty of New Hampshire. Check out www.nhstateparks. com and www.outdoors.org for more ideas.

Allegedly the most climbed peak in North

Don't Be a Law-Breaker

Don't forget your $15 New Hampshire **fishing license** (www.nhfishandgame. com), required for all freshwater fishing. You can get one on the spot at any local agent; see the website for a list of agents.

America, 3,165-foot **Mount Monadnock** (☎ 603/532-2416; www.nhstateparks.org) must be pretty special—or pretty easy. Though the climb to the summit along the rocky White Dot Trail is fairly tough, the 100-mile view—offering vistas of all six New England states—is worth the effort. And with 40 miles of trails, hikers of any level can find something to enjoy.

Other moderate hikes in the Whites include the **Arethusa Falls** (2.6-mile round-trip) trail in Crawford Notch. It is fairly steep but rewards you with views of the highest falls (200 ft.) in the Granite State. Take the access road off US-302, about half a mile south of Dry River Campground, and follow the path to the left of the (private) home.

A great option for families is Franconia Notch's popular 3.25-mile round-trip **Lonesome Lake** trail. A mere hour's hike from the road, AMC's Lonesome Lake Hut is beautifully sited on the crystal-clear lake, surrounded by spruce firs, with views of the Franconia Range. If you want to spend the night, reserve well in advance.

Kayaking & Canoeing

Out Back Kayak, in Lincoln (☎ 603/745-2224; www.outbackkayak.net), leads two fun 2-hour tours down the Pemigawasett River: One is more challenging; both require a change of clothing. Not into groups? Rent a kayak from Out Back and explore serene Mirror Lake on your own. Launch right onto **Lake Winnipesaukee** from the **Wild Meadow Canoes** shop, in Center Harbor (☎ 603/253-7536; www.wildmeadowcanoes.com). If you want to hit the open sea, try **Portsmouth Kayak Adventures** (☎ 603/559-1000; www.portsmouthkayak.com), which offers lessons on the basics before you head out on a guided tour. The full-moon tour in Little Harbor is magical.

Skiing & Snowboarding

It's New Hampshire's official state sport, so, yes, downhill skiers and snowboarders of all ages and expertise will have a lot to sink their teeth into here—all in the White Mountains. Expect to pay $60 to $70 for a lift ticket, with discounts for teens and children.

> *Whether you go on your own or with a guide, you'll find great freshwater fishing in New Hampshire.*

> Bretton Woods resort and ski area hired Olympic medalist Bode Miller as director of skiing; one run was partially designed by the athlete.

Attitash, in Bartlett (☎ 877/677-SNOW [677-7669]; www.attitash.com), encompasses 70 trails over two peaks, and has an excellent terrain park, wonderful scenery, great snow-making equipment, and good intermediate trails. With 464 acres of skiing, **Bretton Woods** (☎ 603/278-3320; www.brettonwoods.com) is New Hampshire's largest ski area; it also features gorgeous night skiing and excellent children's programs. State-run **Cannon Mountain,** in Franconia Notch State Park (☎ 603/823-8800; www.cannonmt.com), offers an old-school-style ski experience, with no base lodge, no condos, and a very cool tram. It's also a beautiful place to ski. Popular **Loon Mountain,** in Lincoln (☎ 800/229-LOON 5666; www.loonmtn.com), has lots of varied terrain, including some newish expert trails, while **Waterville Valley** (☎ 800/GO-VALLEY 468-2553; www.waterville.com) boasts well-regarded black diamond trails among its 52 runs, along with a terrific cross-country center.

For cross-country, head to the **Jackson Ski Touring Center** (☎ 603/383-9355; www.jacksonxc.org) for what is considered the best trail network in the east, covering 50 miles of varied terrain; or hit the 62 miles of beautiful trails at the **Bretton Woods Nordic Center**

AMC Huts & Lodges

The fabulous **Appalachian Mountain Club** is an invaluable source of information; the club also maintains eight **high mountain huts** (cabins with running water) that provide year-round relief for weary backpackers. Each (co-ed) bunkroom-style hut is about a day's hike from the next, and each includes breakfast and dinner. They book up fast, so reserve ahead.

The AMC also operates the **Joe Dodge Lodge** in Pinkham Notch, with private and family rooms in addition to bunkrooms. In Crawford Notch, guests can stay at the low-cost **Shapleigh Bunkhouse,** or go posh at the **Highland Lodge** with private guest rooms and bunkrooms. All three offer excellent trails, free guided hikes, and other activities. You can even borrow gear from the L.L.Bean center, for free. For more information on all of the AMC's offerings, call ☎ 603/466-2727 or visit www.outdoors.org.

(☎ 603/278-3322; www.brettonwoods.com). Expect to pay around $20 a day.

Monadnock & the Upper Valley

It's hard to beat the lure of the White Mountains, but the broad southwestern region of New Hampshire has a charm all its own. Largely bucolic, with rolling hills and long stretches of farmland, it bears little resemblance to the more severe terrain farther north, yet is also home to one of the most popular peaks in the country, Mount Monadnock. A big part of the appeal is getting outside for a walk or a hike, or letting the winding roads lead the way as you explore. When you occasionally need a destination, the trio of Peterborough, Walpole, and Hanover brings a healthy dose of good food or art into the mix. With some substantial driving involved, take 2 or 3 days to cover the area.

> *"Monadnock" is an originally Native American word that has come to mean an isolated or erosion-resistant mountain to geologists.*

START Peterborough is 82 miles from Portsmouth. **TRIP LENGTH** 117 miles.

1 ★★ **Peterborough.** Cited as the model for Thornton Wilder's *Our Town*—written in part while the playwright was here at the **McDowell Artists Colony**—little Peterborough has plenty to brag about, and is a cute place to while away an afternoon. Start your visit on a high point: A toll road brings you to the summit of Pack Monadnock Mountain (2,290 ft.) in **Miller State Park,** 4 miles east of town on 101 (☎ 603/924-3672; www.nhstateparks. org), where on a clear day you'll have a view of Boston, Mount Washington (p. 441), and the

Green Mountains. If you're visiting in the fall, don't miss the Pack Monadnock Raptor Migration Observatory, where New Hampshire Audubon Society staff do a daily count of the eagles, hawks, and other birds of prey that pass through (www.nhaudubon.org). In the easily walkable town center, known as Depot Square, you can find the **Sharon Arts Center ,** 457 Rte. 123 (☎ 603/924-2787; www.sharon arts.org) and the **Mariposa Museum & World Culture Center,** 26 Main St.(☎ 603 924-4555; www.mariposamuseum.org), offering a contrasting range of works from very local to decidedly exotic, along with the museum at the

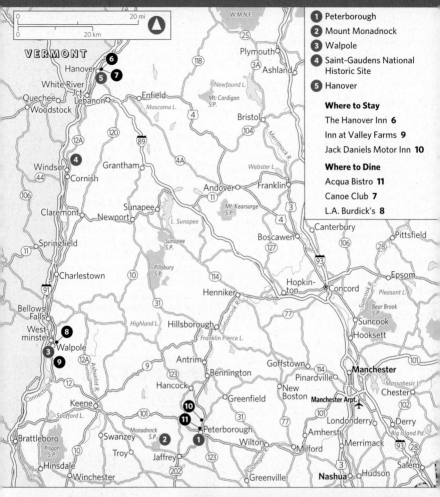

1 Peterborough
2 Mount Monadnock
3 Walpole
4 Saint-Gaudens National Historic Site
5 Hanover

Where to Stay

The Hanover Inn 6
Inn at Valley Farms 9
Jack Daniels Motor Inn 10

Where to Dine

Acqua Bistro 11
Canoe Club 7
L.A. Burdick's 8

Peterborough Historical Society, 19 Grove St. (☎ 603 /924-3235; www. peteroroughhistory.org). ⏲ Half day.

From Main St., head south on Grove St., which turns into Rte. 202. Follow it south 6 miles, and turn right onto Rte. 124 west. After 2 miles, turn right onto Dublin Rd., and after 1¼ miles, turn left onto Poole Rd.

2 ★★ kids **Mount Monadnock.** Hike up the most climbed peak in North America, not to be confused with Pack Monadnock. ⏲ Minimum 2 hr. See p. 428.

Who Was Daniel Webster?

This 19th-century statesman and native son was considered one of the finest orators of his time. A graduate of New Hampshire's own Philips Exeter Academy and Dartmouth College, he found success as a lawyer, state representative, senator, and secretary of state, though his nationalistic views were often polarizing. Arguing against the War of 1812—and in defense of the New England shipping industry—elevated him to the national stage. Today he may be best remembered from the Stephen Vincent Benet story "The Devil and Daniel Webster," in which a New Hampshire farmer who has sold his soul to the devil decides to sue over the terms of his deal, and is represented in court by the always eloquent Webster. Guess who wins?

Return to Rte. 124 west and go 10 miles; turn left onto Rte. 101 (Main St.); after 3¾ miles, go straight through the traffic circle onto Rte. 12/Rte. 10, staying on Rte. 12 for about 16 miles into:

❸ ★ Walpole. This rural town hidden away in the Connecticut River Valley has become a bit of a foodie mecca. It is home not only to **L. A. Burdick's Chocolates** (see p. 433)—famous for its bonbons, and with a wonderful restaurant—but also to a thriving little locavore scene. Some highlights include **Boggy Meadow,** 13 Boggy Meadow Lane (☎ 603/756-3300; www. boggymeadowfarm.com), for cheese; **Walpole Creamery,** 532 Main St. (☎ 603/445-5700; www.walpolecreamery.com), for farm-fresh ice cream; and **Alyson's Orchard,** 57 Alyson's Lane (☎ 800/856-0549; www.alysonsorchard. com), for pick-your-own fruit. Finally, there's the **Inn at Valley Farms** (see below), a magical little bed-and-breakfast where the owners offer by-appointment tours of their working farm. ⊕ 2 hr. www.walpolenh.gov.

Head back through town to Rte. 12 and go 19 miles north; turn left at Saint-Gaudens Rd.

❹ ★★ Saint-Gaudens National Historic Site. The first artist to design an American coin, Irish-born Augustus Saint-Gaudens made his summer home here in 1885, and later founded the Cornish Arts Colony. Walking the grounds, you'll find casts of his famous Shaw Memorial and Farragut Monument, while more than 100 works are on display in the galleries. The free tour of Aspet—his Federal-style house—usually runs five times daily; no reservations required. ⊕ 1½ hr. 139 Saint-Gaudens Rd., Cornish. ☎ 603/675-2175. www.nps.gov/saga. $5 adults, free for kids 15 & under. Memorial Day to Oct daily 9am–4:30pm; Nov–May limited hours.

Get back onto Rte. 12 and go north 13 miles; turn left onto S. Main St. and follow it 4½ miles into:

❺ ★★★ Hanover. First settled in 1765, this quintessential New England college town sits on the east bank of the Connecticut River, just across from Vermont. Established 4 years later, **Dartmouth College** has long been the center of cultural and social life here; its **Hood Museum of Art,** 4 E. Wheelock St. (☎ 603/

646-2808; www.hoodmuseum.dartmouth. edu), houses a collection ranging from Assyrian stone reliefs to Gilbert Stuart's portrait of New Hampshire hero Daniel Webster, while the **Hopkins Center for the Arts,** 2 E. Wheelock St. (☎ 603/646-2422; www.hop. dartmouth.edu), hosts performances and contemporary art. Browse the used selection at cozy **Left Bank Books,** 9 S. Main St. (☎ 603/ 643-4479); find cute pillows, colorful handbags, and other funky accessories at **Brambles,** 15 S. Main St. (☎ 603/643-1635); or check out the eclectic handmade pottery and furniture at **Shackleton Thomas,** 15 S. Main St. (☎ 603/676-7214). In nearby Enfield, the **Enfield Shaker Museum,** 447 Rte. 4A (☎ 603/ 632-4346; www.shakermuseum.org), is home to the Great Stone Dwelling—the largest building in northern New England when constructed in 1841. The museum comprises a collection of surviving Shaker structures, as well as the Mary Keane Chapel, built by the LaSalette seminary after acquiring the property in 1927. ⊕ 3 hr. www.hanoverchamber.org.

Cornish-Windsor Covered Bridge

One of 54 covered bridges in the state—and one of 4 in Cornish—this two-lane, 10-ton example is the fourth on this site; previous bridges washed away in floods. At 449 feet, 5 inches, it is the longest covered bridge in the country, and the longest two-span covered bridge in the world.

Where to Stay & Dine

> Get a taste of rural life at the Inn at Valley Farms.

★★ **Acqua Bistro** PETERBOROUGH *ECLECTIC/ NEW AMERICAN* The best restaurant in town, Acqua offers a stylish yet convivial atmosphere, good cocktails, and a tempting, grazing-friendly small-plates menu. 18 Depot Sq. ☎ 603/924-9905. www.aquabistro.com. Entrees $9–$18. DISC, MC, V. Dinner Tues–Sun, brunch Sun.

★★ **Canoe Club** HANOVER *NEW AMERICAN* The most happening spot in Hanover, with 24 beers on tap, live music regularly, and good, often locally sourced dishes like Malay curry shrimp, cappellini flan, and grilled lamb sirloin over seasonal ravioli. 27 S. Main St. ☎ 603/ 643-9660. www.canoeclub.com. Entrees $10– $25. AE, DISC, MC, V. Lunch & dinner daily.

★ **The Hanover Inn** HANOVER If you want to stay in downtown Hanover, this is your best bet, but remember, you're paying for location. It's more hotel than inn, with exactly the accommodations you'd expect to find on an Ivy League campus: Think white linens, Dartmouth green carpets, and dark furniture. 2 S. Main St. ☎ 800/443-7024. www. hanoverinn.com. 93 units. Doubles $269–$355. AE, DISC, MC, V.

★★★ **Inn at Valley Farms** WALPOLE We love this place—a friendly, welcoming B&B on a working farm. Inn rooms are country elegant, but we recommend a stay in a cottage, where you'll wake up to find that a basket of warm baked goods and farm-fresh eggs has magically appeared at your door. Don't forget to schedule a farm tour. 633 Wentworth Rd. ☎ 603/756-2855. www.innatvalleyfarms.com. 5 units. Doubles $175–$220 w/breakfast. MC, V.

★★ **Jack Daniels Motor Inn** PETERBOROUGH Lodging options are almost nonexistent in little Peterborough, but fortunately this well-run inn, just down the street from the town center, has you covered. The owners clearly take pride in their property: The rooms, while basic, are spotless, and the staff is friendly and knowledgeable. 80 Concord St. (Rte. 202). ☎ 603/924-7548. www.jackdanielsmotorinn. com. 17 units. Doubles $109–$139. AE, DISC, MC, V.

★★★ **L. A. Burdick Café** WALPOLE *BRASSERIE* They are renowned for their handmade chocolates, but this French-focused restaurant has a reputation all its own. The beef stew with roasted tomatoes and olives bursts with flavor, while roasted half-duckling was heavenly. 47 Main St. ☎ 603/756-9058. www.burdick chocolate.com. Entrees $10–$22. AE, DISC, MC, V. Dinner Tues–Sat, lunch Mon–Sat, brunch Sun.

The Lakes Region

Long inhabited by the Abenakis, the area around Lake Winnipesaukee (that's "Win-ah-pa-*sock*-ee")—a spring-fed body of water dotted with more than 250 islands—was "discovered" by Europeans in the 1650s. By 1771, governor John Wentworth had built not only an estate in what is now Wolfeboro, but also a road leading there from Portsmouth. The arrival of the railroad in the 1850s made the region even more accessible, and now it continues to draw folks in need of lakeside R & R. In summer, you could easily spend a week lingering on or by Lake Winnipesaukee and Squam Lake (of *On Golden Pond* fame), but our 2-day itinerary focuses on the highlights, with time built in to visit the blink-and-you'll-miss-'em farm stands and mom-and-pop shops scattered throughout.

> Take a ride on the Winnipesaukee Belle, *a 65-foot turn-of-the-century paddle boat operated by the Wolfeboro Inn.*

START Wolfeboro is 49 miles from Portsmouth. **TRIP LENGTH** 92 miles.

1 ★★ kids **Wolfeboro.** You've likely read about Wolfeboro's claim as the oldest summer resort in the country. True or not, this pleasant town on the banks of Winnipesaukee makes a good starting point for your tour. Hop on the 28-foot HackerCraft **Millie B,** Town Dock (☎ 603/569-1080; www.wolfeborotrolley. com), for a half-hour cruise costing about $20 for adults, $10 kids; or go for a 90-minute ride on the **Winnipesaukee Belle** (☎ 603/569-3016; www.wolfeboroinn.com). Then, shop: **Kalled Gallery,** 33 N. Main St. (☎ 603/569-

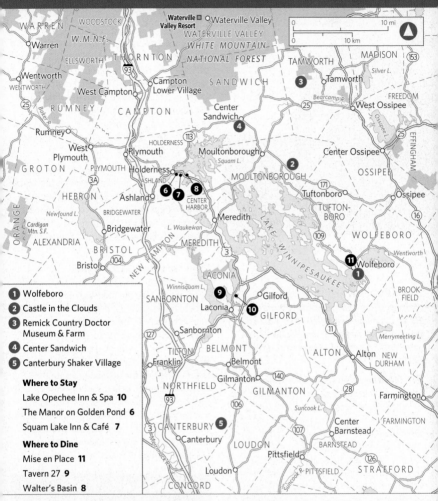

1 Wolfeboro
2 Castle in the Clouds
3 Remick Country Doctor
   Museum & Farm
4 Center Sandwich
5 Canterbury Shaker Village

Where to Stay

Lake Opechee Inn & Spa **10**

The Manor on Golden Pond **6**

Squam Lake Inn & Café **7**

Where to Dine

Mise en Place **11**

Tavern 27 **9**

Walter's Basin **8**

3994), for one-of-a-kind jewelry; **Yum Yum Shop,** 16 N. Main St. (☎ 603/569-1919), for whoopee pies. Hit the **New Hampshire Boat Museum,** 397 Center St. (☎ 603/569-4554; www.nhbm.org), to gawk at its fine collection of vintage vessels. ⏱ 3 hr. Wolfeboro Information Center: Wolfeboro Station, 32 Central Ave. ☎ 603/569-2200. www.wolfeboroonline.net.

Head 13 miles north on Main St. (Rte. 109) and turn right onto Severance St. At the end, turn right onto Old Mountain Rd. (Rte. 171) and go ½ mile.

2 ★★★ **Castle in the Clouds.** The setting of this 1914 Arts and Crafts home lives up to the promise of its name: Built by a millionaire

shoemaker named Thomas Plant, the mountaintop retreat commands spectacular views of the area's lake and hills. It's a fun, quirky place to explore (it's a self-guided tour). You'll find a secret reading room, needle showers, and a suit of armor the diminutive Plant used to wear to parties. ⏱ 2 hr. 455 Old Mountain Rd. (Rte. 171), Moultonborough. ☎ 603/476-5900. www.castleintheclouds.org. $15 adults, $5 kids 7-14. May to mid-June Fri–Sun 10am–4:30pm; mid-June to late Oct daily 10am–4:30pm.

Travel Tip

See p. 426 and p. 428 for tips on fishing and kayaking on Lake Winnipesaukee.

> *Thomas Plant's mountaintop Castle in the Clouds cost $7 million to build in 1914.*

Take Rte. 171 west until it becomes Rte. 109 north; go 2½ miles and turn right onto Rte. 25; go 8¾ miles east to Whittier Rd. (Rte. 113). Turn left and go 2½ miles; take a left onto Main St, and continue onto Cleveland Hill Rd.

3 ★ kids **Remick Country Doctor Museum & Farm.** Six generations of Remicks worked this farm before Dr. Edwin Remick, a country doctor like his father, created a foundation to preserve the property for the public. Now you can visit the working farm (with sheep and pigs), tour the senior doctor's original medical office, and check out changing exhibits on farm life. Best of all: Kids can partake in such programs as butter churning or ice harvesting. ⏱ 2 hr. 58 Cleveland Hill Rd., Tamworth. ☎ 800/686-6117. www.remickmuseum.org. $3 adults, $10 family. Mon–Fri 10am–4pm.

Take Cleveland Hill Rd. 2¾ miles west; go straight onto Brown Hill Rd. (which becomes Durgin) for 3½ miles. Cross the covered bridge, and take Fellows Hill Rd. to the end. Turn left onto Rte. 113A, continuing west onto Rte. 113. Go for 3½ miles to:

4 ★★ **Center Sandwich.** This tranquil, white-clapboard, artsy town is a lovely place to spend a bit of time. Stop by **Patricia Ladd Carega Gallery,** 69 Maple St. (☎ 603/284-7728), for a look at work by emerging contemporary artists, then move on to **Surroundings**

Gallery, 12 Main St. (☎ 603/284-6489), for art by local talent. The fantastic **League of NH Craftsmen craft shop,** 32 Main St. (☎ 603/284-6831; closed Nov–Apr), sells handmade jewelry, pottery, and metalware. And don't miss the **Sandwich Creamery** farm, 134 Hannah Rd., North Sandwich (www.sandwichcreamery.com), famous for homemade cheeses and ice cream sold by the honor system. ⏱ 2 hr.

Take Rte. 109 south out of town. Turn right onto Rte. 25 west, passing through Meredith, and continue onto Rte. 3 south. Go 5 miles and turn right onto Union Ave.; in 3 miles go left onto Rte. 106 (S. Main St.) and go 13 miles and follow signs to Canterbury Shaker Village.

5 ★★ **Canterbury Shaker Village.** Founded in 1792, Canterbury peaked in the 1850s, when 300 Shakers (see the box below) lived and worked here in 100 buildings. It's now an excellent, beautifully maintained museum that includes 25 historic structures—you could easily spend a few hours exploring the serene grounds on your own and taking a few tours (we recommend the house tour) with the knowledgeable guides. It's a fascinating place, and you'll come away with a renewed appreciation for this short-lived yet deep-rooted group. ⏱ 3 hr. 288 Shaker Rd., Canterbury. ☎ 603/783-9511. www.shakers.org. $17 adults, $8 kids 6–17. May 15 to Oct daily 10am–5pm.

The Shakers: Radical Chic

Formed in 1747 in England from a dissenting community of Quakers, this sect—named for their ecstatic form of worship, and noted for their celibacy—arrived in the New World in 1774, led by Ann Lee. The first small settlement sprung up just east of Albany, New York, but by the mid-19th century there were 18 communities stretching from Maine to Indiana. Leading a simple, self-sufficient agrarian lifestyle, they were as devoted to work as worship—their legacy of architecture, crafts, and furniture grew out of a dedication to efficiency, resulting in clean, elegant, and often innovative designs. In fact, their classic style is still considered quite fashionable.

Where to Stay & Dine

★★ **Lake Opechee Inn & Spa/O Steaks and Seafood** LAKEPORT Rooms here are spacious, impeccably kept, and—somewhat surprising given its hotel-like feel—charmingly appointed in a country or lodge style. All have gas fireplaces and are comfortable (feather beds, cozy armchairs, and ottomans). Upscale-casual **O,** the attached restaurant, is an area standout, with Kobe beef pops, short ribs with grits, and even fried Oreos. 62 Doris Ray Ct. ☎ 877/300-5253. www.opecheeinn.com. 34 units. Doubles $169–$339 w/breakfast.

★★ **The Manor on Golden Pond** HOLDERNESS Come to this dreamy English-style manor for sumptuous accommodations (we heart the Yorkshire suite), show-stopping lake views, and highly personalized service. (Make sure your Katherine Hepburn accent is up to snuff.) Not up for the splurge? Reserve a spot in the excellent **Van Horn Dining Room** or the casual **M** bistro, or at least hit the intimate **Three Cocks Pub** for a wee dram. 31 Manor Dr. ☎ 800/545-2141. www.manorongoldenpond.com. 25 units. Doubles $220–$540 w/breakfast. AE, DISC, MC, V.

★★ **Mise en Place** WOLFEBORO AMERICAN Chef-owned, romantic, and teeny—an excellent choice for date night. Start with an app like lobster wonton, or brie, duck confit, and tart cherry quesadilla; then go with the filet au poivre, or pork medallions with cranberry goat-cheese timbale. End with profiteroles. *Ahh.* 96 Lehner St. ☎ 603/569-5788. Entrees $15–$25. MC, V. Lunch Tues–Fri, dinner Tues–Sat.

★★ **Squam Lake Inn & Café** HOLDERNESS While the rooms at this welcoming inn are smallish, they are sparkling clean, are simply yet pleasingly furnished, and radiate charm. (We like Big Squam and Loon.) The cafe, which relies on locally grown produce, has a reputation all its own—try their peach curry chicken, or over-the-top lobster BLT. 28 Shepherd Hill Rd. ☎ 800/839-6205. www.squamlakeinn.com. 8 units. Doubles $160–$195 w/breakfast. AE, DISC, MC, V.

★★ **Tavern 27** LACONIA TAPAS Tapas? At a golf course? Yup. This little kitchen at the Mystic Meadows links turns out some inspired and well-executed small plates like

> *"Everything in its place"* at Mise en Place.

mustard-crusted pork bites and chickpea fries, along with creative pizzas. 2075 Parade Rd. ☎ 603/528-3057. www.tavern27.com. Small plates & pizzas $5–$15. AE, DISC, MC, V. Lunch & dinner Tues–Sun.

★★ **Walter's Basin** HOLDERNESS PUB FARE With huge windows overlooking Little Squam Lake, this casual standby is a sure thing for just about everyone. Watch the boats dock and dig into fish tacos at lunch, or hang with the locals in the pub over steak tips or a complete Shore Dinner. 859 Rte. 3. ☎ 603/968-4412. www.waltersbasin.com. Entrees $8–$29. AE, DISC, MC, V. Lunch & dinner daily.

The White Mountains

The rugged range that forms the centerpiece of the Granite State stands in stark contrast to the soft and rolling textures of Vermont's Green Mountains. You'll hear words like "tallest" and "coldest" thrown around, but don't let this put you off. The scenery is spectacular, whether from a vista on a hiking path, or while moving above it all in a gondola. Give yourself at least 4 days to explore and play.

> "The Kanc" Highway, along NH Route 112, is a prime route for fall leaf peepers.

START Pinkham Notch is 86 miles from Portsmouth. **TRIP LENGTH** 101 miles.

1 ★★★ kids **Mount Washington.** Start at the top! You can't visit the White Mountains without a trek up the tallboy of New England. See p. 441.

Take Route 16 south 1½ miles.

2 ★ kids **Pinkham Notch.** Stop in the Appalachian Mountain Club-run **Pinkham Notch Visitor Center** (☎ 603/466-2721) for hiking tips from the friendly staff, then hit the trails! The gorgeous **Tuckerman Ravine Trail** (see p. 441) takes hikers up to the summit of Mount Washington, but the lower portion of the trail, leading to the ravine itself, is a good, manageable hike (about 2 hr. one-way). Up the road, Wildcat Mountain's **ZipRider** is hard to resist, even if you're not the adventurous type. Strapped securely into a seat, you'll zoom above the trees for over half a mile at speeds up to 45mph. Sound scary? Opt for the gondola instead. ☺ Half day. Rte. 16. ☎ 603/466-3326. www.skiwildcat.com. $20. Memorial Day to mid-June Sat–Sun 10am–5pm; mid-June to mid-Oct daily 10am–5pm.

Take Rte. 16 south 6 miles.

3 ★ kids **Conway Scenic Railroad.** Catch your breath on this relaxing train ride. The Bartlett Excursion heads over the Saco River and through field and forest, with the mountains looming in the distance. Prices vary; get a first-class ticket for the extra space. ☺ 2 hr. Rte. 16 & Mountain Valley Blvd., N. Conway. ☎ 603/356-7606. www.conwayscenic.com. $23–$59 adults, $16–$44 kids 4–12, free–$17 kids 3 & under. Call for schedule; expect an 11:30am train.

Get back on Rte. 16 south to the Kancamagus Hwy. (Rte. 112) and turn right.

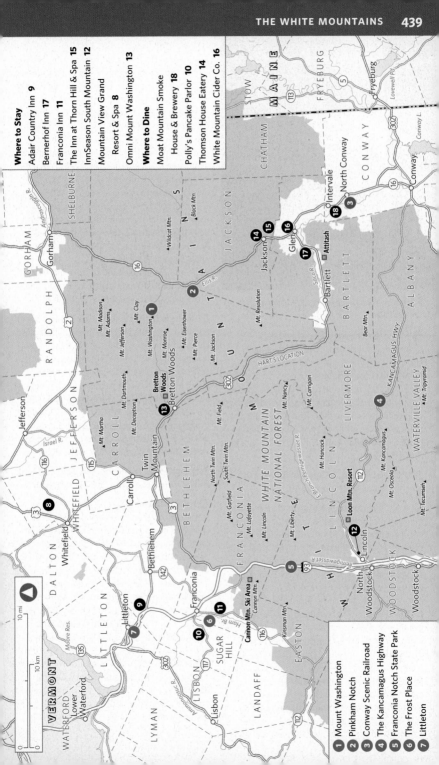

1 Mount Washington
2 Pinkham Notch
3 Conway Scenic Railroad
4 The Kancamagus Highway
5 Franconia Notch State Park
6 The Frost Place
7 Littleton

> *The renowned Flume Gorge at Franconia Notch State Park.*

❹ ★ The Kancamagus Highway. Mispronounced with impunity, the Kanc (keep it short; it's legit) has grown to be *the* scenic drive across the mountains since it first tied together two dead-end roads in 1959. The full ride from North Conway to Lincoln is less than an hour in a straight shot. Of course, there are plenty of hikes along the way; the 10-minute jaunt to **Sabbaday Falls** is easy, with a worthy reward. ⏱ 2 hr.

Take this scenic route west all the way to Lincoln, take I-93N to exit 34B.

❺ ★★★ 🄺 Franconia Notch State Park. This glorious mountain pass is rich with dramatic natural attractions. Start with the 800-foot chasm called the **Flume,** the park's most spectacular site. A shuttle bus or half-mile hike brings you to a path that leads to a wooden walkway along the inner wall of the gorge, through which the Flume Brook roars. The **Basin**—a beautiful glacial pothole carved in granite—is a brief ride away. This "remarkable curiosity," as Thoreau wrote, comes across best when the sun illuminates the crystalline blue water. Next, get away from the crowds on some of the many trails found throughout the park—we like the Lonesome Lake Trail (p. 428).

The 80-person **Cannon Tramway** (☎ 603/823-8800; www.cannontram.com) cable car climbs the eastern face of the 4,100-foot mountain, affording a broadside view of the White Mountains and beyond. If it's a nice day down at the base, take a dip at **Echo Lake,** clearly visible below from the Tram. Rainy? Stop in at the free **New England Ski Museum** (☎ 603/823-7177; www.skimuseum.org) for the story of skiing in the region, in gear and photos. In the winter, this is a prime spot for skiing and snowboarding (p. 429). ⏱ Half day. 9 Franconia Notch Parkway. ☎ 603/745-8391. www.nhstateparks.org. $13 adults, $9 kids 6–12; Discovery Pass provides a discount for the Flume & Aerial Tramway. Mid-May to late Oct daily 10am–5pm, weather permitting. Cannon Tramway, $14 adults, $10 kids 6–12. Mid-May to mid-Oct daily 9am–5pm.

Back on I-93N, take exit 38; turn left onto Rte. 116 and go 1 mile south; turn right onto Bickford Hill Rd. and left onto Ridge Rd.

❻ ★ The Frost Place. This little jewel is one of our favorite spots in the Whites. Robert and Elinor's home for 5 years, the humble 1860s house is now an understated museum, with some of his first editions on display. Plaques along a small nature trail dispense nuggets of verse at well-chosen intervals. ⏱ 1½ hr. 158 Ridge Rd., Franconia. ☎ 603/823-5510. www.frostplace.org. Suggested donation $5 adults, $3 kids 6–12. Memorial Day to June 30 Sat–Sun 1–5pm; July to Columbus Day Wed–Mon 1–5pm.

Turn right onto Ridge Rd., left onto Bickford Hill Rd., and follow Rte. 116 7½ miles north.

❼ ★ 🄺 Littleton. This charming mill town a stone's throw from the Vermont border is a welcome break from the more tourist-driven parts of the region. Head straight for the candy shop **Chutters,** 43 Main St. (☎ 603/444-5787), home of the longest candy counter in the world; drool over three gloriously long rows of jars packed with colorful sweet things from gummy fried eggs to malted milk balls. Stop to tour the free **Littleton Grist Mill,** 18 Mill St. (☎ 603/259-3205), then head next door to **Just L,** 16 Mill St. (☎ 603/238-7058), a cute mid-century-antiques store with some cool finds. Downstairs is **Miller's Café & Bakery,** 16 Mill St. (☎ 603/444-2146), where you can enjoy your latte on a porch right over rushing water.

Exploring Mount Washington

Mount Washington's resume is loaded with superlatives: "Highest Mountain in the Northeast" (6,288 ft.), "Fastest Wind Ever Recorded by Man" (231 mph in 1934), and "Worst Weather in the World" (what can we say?). Here's one more: The "First Mountain Railway of Its Kind," the **Mount Washington Cog** (pictured; p. 419, ⑥) is still one of the best ways to get to the top. Local Sylvester Marsh patented this design in 1861, and by 1868 tourists were riding up the mountain in a fire-powered steam train. So, what exactly is a "cog"? It's a toothed wheel, or *pinion,* which meshes with a special center "rack rail," to ensure the train grips the track as it heads almost straight up the mountain, at grades as steep as 37%. We recommend reserving, and note that trains run rain or shine. For the most authentic experience, a coal-fired steam locomotive runs at 9am on most days; prepare for lots of soot.

At 150 years old in 2011, the 8-mile **Mount Washington Auto Road** is $23 per car, plus $8 for passengers, and $6 for kids 5 to 12. Wait for a clear day to wind your way up the east side of the mountain from Pinkham Notch, and stop at the turnouts along the way for breathtaking scenery, for a short hike, or to just give your car a break. Note that there are vehicle restrictions, but unless you arrive in an RV, a limo, or a Hummer—and as long as you can put your car manually into first gear—you should be okay. Your ticket price includes a THIS CAR CLIMBED MOUNT WASHINGTON bumper sticker, along with an audio tour CD or cassette. If you'd rather enjoy the view, catch a ride on a **Van Tour** for $29, or $12 for kids 5 to 12. First offered via horse-drawn coaches in 1861, the "stage" rides run daily, weather permitting. A one-way ride is the same price, if you want to hike up. In the winter, the only vehicle that runs on the toll road is the **Snow Coach,** a nine-passenger, all-wheel-drive four-track van that costs $45 for adults and $30 for kids 5 to 12. Best of all: You can cross-country ski, telemark, or snowshoe down the road on this trip. Both the vans and the Snow Coach operate on a first-come, first-served basis. All of these can be found on Rte. 16, Pinkham Notch (☎ 603/466-3988; www. mountwashingtonautoroad.com).

If you're interested in ★★ **hiking** (www. mountwashington.org/about/visitor/ hiking.php) the old Rockpile, you'll be ascending roughly 4,000 feet in elevation, on rocky paths that are often steep; count on 4 to 5 miles each way, and at least a full day. Consider the Appalachian Mountain Club huts (p. 429) if you want to break it up over 2 days or more. Leaving from Pinkham Notch, the scenic **Tuckerman Ravine Trail** is the most popular route, heading right into the floor of the ravine. **Boott Spurr** is a bit longer, while the tougher **Lion's Head** has great views and less traffic.

Where to Stay

> *The Mountain View Grand prides itself on top-notch customer service, including an online concierge.*

★★ Adair Country Inn BETHLEHEM
Set on 200 acres and surrounded by gardens designed by the Olmsted brothers, Adair is elegant, welcoming, and unstuffy. Lounge in the downstairs granite room, walk the scenic trails through woods and meadow, and don't miss the popovers. 80 Guider Lane. ☎ 603/444-2600. www.adairinn.com. 9 units. Doubles $195–$375 w/breakfast. AE, DISC, MC, V.

★★ Bernerhof Inn GLEN
All 12 rooms were beautifully renovated in 2010, each with flat-panel TVs and fireplaces. There are no clunkers: Even the smallest room is appealing. Guests will appreciate touches like fresh cider donuts and complementary iPads. 342 Rte. 302. ☎ 877/389-4852. www.bernerhofinn.com. 12 units. Doubles $98–$264 w/breakfast. AE, DISC, MC, V.

★★ Franconia Inn FRANCONIA
We love this cozy, affordable, lodge-y inn. With gorgeous views—gliders take off from a field across the street—it offers all manner of outdoor recreation, including bicycling, tubing, horseback riding, and cross-country skiing. 1300 Easton Valley Rd. ☎ 800/473-5299. www.franconiainn.com. 34 units. Doubles $131–$191. AE, MC, V.

★★ The Inn at Thorn Hill & Spa JACKSON VILLAGE
As sophisticated an inn as you'll find in these parts, the immaculately kept burgundy-and-cream-accented rooms are matched by the lavish breakfast, full spa, four-diamond restaurant, and exceptional wine list. Thorn Hill Rd. ☎ 800/289-8990. www.innatthornhill.com. 25 units. Doubles $169–$440 w/breakfast. AE, DISC, MC, V.

★ InnSeason South Mountain LINCOLN
This well-maintained and friendly resort at the foot of Loon Mountain offers great value and convenience; spacious island-kitchen suites make the perfect home base for families. 23 InnSeason Dr. ☎ 800/456-2582. www.innseason.com. 70 units. Doubles $83–$239. AE, DISC, MC, V.

★★ **Mountain View Grand Resort & Spa** WHITE-FIELD The breathtaking view alone is worth the trip to Whitefield, but this hotel ups the ante with a top-tier spa, golf, tennis, farm activities for kids, two pools, and unique programs such as ax throwing. Book a treatment for the infinite tub in the tower, and feel like you're on top of the world. 101 Mountain View Rd. ☎ 603/837-2100. www.mountainviewgrand.com. 145 units. Doubles $139–$610. AE, DISC, MC, V.

★★★ **Omni Mount Washington** BRETTON WOODS Dramatically set at the foot of Mount Washington, this five-story Spanish Renais-sance–style grand old hotel—a majestic sight no matter how you approach it—is *the* place to stay. The recent $50-million renovation includes a new spa and considerable upgrades to guest rooms and public spaces, but the place still heaves with history. Rte. 302. ☎ 603/278-1000. www.omnihotels.com. 200 units. Doubles $189–$1,099. AE, DISC, MC, V.

Where to Dine

★ **Moat Mountain Smoke House & Brewing Company** NORTH CONWAY *BARBECUE* Featur-ing quality house-made brews on tap—and available to go by the growler. The down-home slant of the menu is offset by occasional unexpected Asian touches. 3378 White Moun-tain Hwy. (Rte. 16). ☎ 603/356-6381. www. moatmountain.com. Entrees $9–$22. AE, MC, V. Lunch & dinner daily.

★★★ **Polly's Pancake Parlor** SUGAR HILL *BREAKFAST* An essential part of your visit. Polly's does pancakes, and does them well. Choose from plain, buckwheat, whole wheat, oatmeal buttermilk—we like the cornmeal with chocolate chips. It gets packed, so call ahead to add your name to the list. 672 Rte. 117. ☎ 603/623-5575. www.pollyspancakeparlor. com. Entrees $4–$10. Cash only. Breakfast & lunch daily.

★ **Thomson House Eatery** JACKSON *AMERICAN* A sweet and much-loved country dining ex-perience, with such delectable mains as pork tenderloin with apple-cured bacon and roast-ed fig. Also open for lunch, serving hearty sandwiches and salads. 193 Main St. ☎ 603/ 383-9341. www.thomsonhouseeatery.com. En-trees $14–$32. AE, DISC, MC, V. Lunch & dinner, varies seasonally; call.

★★ **White Mountain Cider Co.** GLEN *NEW AMERICAN* Yes, the cider mill here churns out delicious donuts, but when the newish

> *Polly's Pancake Parlor specializes in...you guessed it, pancakes.*

restaurant—owned by Culinary Institute grads—opened, area foodies breathed a collective sigh of relief. We love the tempt-ing menu of updated classics (like a bacon-Gorgonzola-crusted pork chop) and the well-crafted cocktail list. Rte. 302. ☎ 603/383-9061. www.whitemountaincider.com. Entrees $18–$28. AE, DISC, MC, V. Dinner daily.

Portsmouth

Portsmouth is one of New England's most beautifully
preserved historic towns—its setting at the mouth of the Piscataqua River made
it an important port, once home to prosperous Colonial-era merchants, sea
captains, and revolutionaries. Today, it is home to more art galleries and crafts
shops than a town this size has any right to. Portsmouth is entirely walkable,
and abounds with great restaurants and well-curated boutiques. Plus, it has a
working waterfront, and is within spitting distance of beaches. You can make
this an excellent long-weekend visit, but it's a good overnight too.

> Portsmouth, with its still-active waterfront on the Piscataqua River, has been an important center of the coastal region's shipping trade for centuries.

START Portsmouth is 58 miles from Boston.

❶ ★ **John Paul Jones House.** Even those hard-pressed to recall JPJ's role in U.S. history will find something of interest in this lovingly restored 1758 house where he boarded. For the record, he was a Scottish sailor who emigrated to America and became the United States' greatest naval hero during the Revolution. Among its collections are china, portraits, and a very detailed exhibit on the 1905 Treaty of Portsmouth, also known as the Portsmouth Peace Treaty. It ended the Russo-Japanese War and marked the emergence of the U.S. as a diplomatic power. Then-president Teddy

Roosevelt won the 1906 Nobel Peace Prize for his efforts, and it's an obscure but fascinating part of our nation's past. ⏱ 1 hr. 43 Middle St. ☎ 603/436-8420. www.portsmouthhistory.org. $6 adults. May 22–Oct daily 11am–5pm.

❷ ★★ **Isles of Shoals.** For a different impression of the city, get out on the water. **Portsmouth Harbor Cruises** runs sunset cruises and river trips, but we suggest you instead take a tour to the rugged and mysterious Isles of Shoals. Reserve, bring binoculars for bird-watching, and get ready for intriguing tales of pirates (legend has it that Blackbeard stashed treasure here) and the infamous 1873

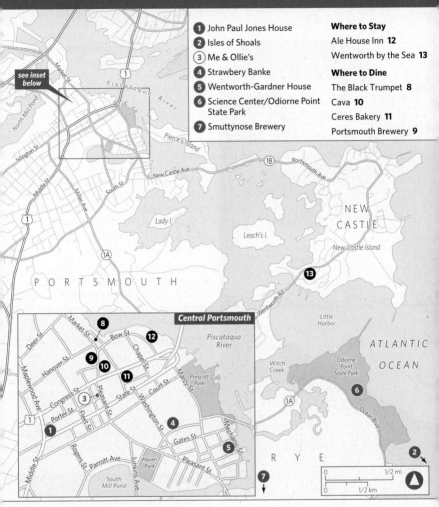

1 John Paul Jones House

2 Isles of Shoals

3 Me & Ollie's

4 Strawbery Banke

5 Wentworth-Gardner House

6 Science Center/Odiorne Point State Park

7 Smuttynose Brewery

Where to Stay

Ale House Inn **12**

Wentworth by the Sea **13**

Where to Dine

The Black Trumpet **8**

Cava **10**

Ceres Bakery **11**

Portsmouth Brewery **9**

Central Portsmouth

Smuttynose ax murder, novelized by Anita Shreve in *The Weight of Water*. ⏱ 2½ hr. 64 Ceres St. ☎ 800/776-0915. www.portsmouth harbor.com. $21 adults, $14 kids 3 & over. Mid-June to mid-Sept Tues–Fri at noon.

---

3 🍽 ★★ **Me & Ollie's.** There is truly pride of ownership at this minichain. We love the thoughtfully prepared sandwiches, the oatmeal–chocolate chip cookies, and the best granola (raisinless!) we've ever had. 10 Pleasant St. ☎ 603/436-7777. www. meandollies.com. $.

4 ★★★ **Strawbery Banke.** One of New England's best, this museum was established in 1958 when a group of locals banded together to rescue an old neighborhood from "urban renewal," aka demolition. It sprawls over 10 acres and comprises 42 historic buildings (the oldest from 1695); most stand on their original foundations. Some structures hold rotating exhibits, while others have been restored to particular periods—one even showcases two eras: life in the 1790s, and a 1950s household. There's also a sweet Victorian fairy garden, hearth-cooking demos, working coopers and masons, and costumed role-players. ⏱ 3 hr. 14

> *Portsmouth has had a long love-affair with the sea. 534J*

Hancock St. ☎ 603/433-1100. www.strawbery-banke.org. $15 adults, $10 kids 5–17. May–Oct daily 10am–5pm; Nov–Dec open only for guided walking tours & special events.

5 ★★ **Wentworth-Gardner House.** There are many attractive historic homes in Portsmouth, but we suggest this one because of its stunning Georgian architecture—perhaps the finest representation of the style in the country. ⏲ 15 min. 50 Mechanic St. ☎ 603/436-4406. www.wentworthgardnerandlear.org. $5 adults, $2 kids 4 & under. Mid-June to mid-Oct Wed–Sun noon–4pm.

Take Rte. 1A south to:

6 kids ★★ **Seacoast Science Center/Odiorne Point State Park.** Even if you don't have kids, this tranquil park and natural science center make for a nice visit. Take a walk along the gorgeous rocky shore, or through some of the six other environments inside the park. At the beautifully sited center you'll find seahorses, a blue lobster, and engaging interactive exhibits, including their newest: It's all about Tofu, the humpback whale, whose 800-pound skeleton hangs above the entrance. ⏲ 2 hr. 570 Ocean Blvd. (Rte. 1A), Rye. ☎ 603/436-8043. www.seacoastsciencecenter.org. $5 adults, $2 kids 3–12 (plus toll at Odiorne Point State Park toll booth in summer). Apr–Oct daily 10am–5pm; Nov–Mar Sat–Mon 10am–5pm.

Head north on Rte. 1A; at the traffic circle, take the second exit onto Elwyn Rd. After about 1½ miles, turn left onto Rte. 1 south, and in another 1½ miles, turn right onto Heritage Ave.

7 **Smuttynose Brewery.** What better way to end your visit? The folks at Smuttynose—whose hoppy Shoals Pale Ale we are big fans of—don't mess around. You'll get an in-depth behind-the-scenes look at how the magic happens (and of course, tastings!), though there are only two tours per week, so plan accordingly. ⏲ 1½ hr. 224 Heritage Ave. ☎ 603/436-4026. www.smuttynose.com. Free admission. Tours Fri 3pm, Sat 11am.

Downtown Shopping

We're not hard-core shoppers, but Portsmouth has such charming boutiques, even we can't resist their siren song. Check out the glassware at **NJM,** 8 Bow St. (☎ 603/433-4120; www.artglassusa.com); exquisite gifts and art at **Nahcotta,** 110 Congress St. (☎ 603/433-1705; www.nahcotta.com); and locally made wares at **Maine-ly New Hampshire,** 22 Deer St. (☎ 603/422-9500; www.maine-lynewhampshire.com). Don't miss the indy **RiverRun Bookstore,** 20 Congress St.; sublime small-batch chocolates at **Byrne & Carlson,** 121 State St. (☎ 603/559-9778; www.byrneandcarlson.com); and eclectic housewares at **City & Country,** 50 Daniel St. (☎ 603-433-5353).

Where to Stay & Dine

> The ever-changing menu at the family-owned Black Trumpet Bistro doesn't disappoint.

★★ Ale House Inn PORTSMOUTH
With brick walls, modernist furnishings, cool gray-and-blue details, flatscreen TVs, and complementary iPads in every room, the friendly owners at this former brewery warehouse in a prime downtown location clearly know their savvy audience. The boutique-style inn also offers guests use of its eco-friendly bikes, free of charge. 121 Bow St. ☎ 603/431-7760. www.alehouseinn.com. 10 units. Doubles $129–$299. AE, DISC, MC, V.

★★★ Black Trumpet Bistro PORTSMOUTH *NEW AMERICAN* The best meal in town. Dishes are always inspired, impeccably prepared, and locally sourced. Our pork shank with mashed yam, apple fritter, and bacon braised beans was pure bliss. 29 Ceres St. ☎ 603/431-0887. www.blacktrumpetbistro.com. Entrees $16–$28. AE, DISC, MC, V. Dinner daily.

★★ Cava PORTSMOUTH *TAPAS*
An atmospheric spot set down an alley. Watch chefs prepare tapas with modern twists—like chocolate, sea salt, and pistachio oil *bocadillos;* or ricotta gnocchi with Brussels sprouts and chanterelles. The sweets, too, are amazing. 10 Commercial Alley. ☎ 603/319-1575. Tapas $5–$19. AE, DISC, MC, V. Dinner daily.

★★ Ceres Bakery PORTSMOUTH *DELI*
Loved by the locals, the unassuming Ceres has freshly baked bread (try the anadama), plus terrific soups (African peanut!) and sandwiches. 51 Penhallow St. ☎ 603/436-6518. Entrees $3–$8. Cash only. Breakfast & lunch daily.

★ Portsmouth Brewery PORTSMOUTH *BREWPUB*
It's always happenin' (it can get loud), the pub-food-plus menu delivers, and—oh, yeah—the handcrafted draughts are just the ticket. Come for lunch if you have kids in tow; if not, come for beer flights and flavorsome chili. 56 Market St. ☎ 603/431-1115. Entrees $9–$17. AE, DISC, MC, V. Lunch & dinner daily.

★★★ Wentworth by the Sea NEW CASTLE
With a gorgeous setting on New Castle Island, top-notch dining, and great service, this Marriott-owned gem is a fabulous place to hang your hat. All rooms are done up in an attractive gold, cream, and brown decor, with exquisite furnishings, and most have good views of the harbor or ocean. We particularly love no. 501 and the Admiral's Suite above it: Both are located in the central turret, and both have spectacular views. 588 Wentworth Rd. ☎ 866/240-6313. www.wentworth.com. 161 units. Doubles $189–$899. AE, DISC, MC, V.

10
Maine

Our Favorite Maine Moments

Humorist Dave Barry once suggested that Maine's state motto should be changed to "Cold, but damp." That's cute, but it's also sort of true. Spring here tends to last just a few weeks and the long winters often bring a mix of blizzards and ice storms. Ah, but summer. Maine summers offer a serious dose of tranquillity; a few days in the right spot can rejuvenate even the most jangled city nerves. The trick is finding that right spot—if you were to iron out the kinks and peninsulas of the coastline, there's a *lot* of room to roam. Luckily, we've compiled a list of our favorites.

> PREVIOUS PAGE *Portland Head Light is said to be among the most photographed lighthouses in the world.* THIS PAGE *Nothing says "Maine" more than lobsters eaten right out on the rocks at Two Lights Lobster Shack.*

❶ Eating lobsters oceanside in Cape Elizabeth. There's no food truer to Maine than a steamed lobster with butter—preferably with a hunk of corn on the cob and a piece of blueberry cake on the side. And there's no more scenic place to eat this archetypal meal than right out on the windswept rocks behind **Two Lights Lobster Shack,** 225 Two Lights Rd. (off Rte. 77),

Cape Elizabeth (☎ 207/799-1677) . Walk off the calories at adjacent **Two Lights State Park** (☎ 207/799-5871).

❷ Camping at water's edge. What's better than unzipping your tent to make breakfast and walking out to a view of a shiny, empty bay? Nothing, in our book. Along the Maine

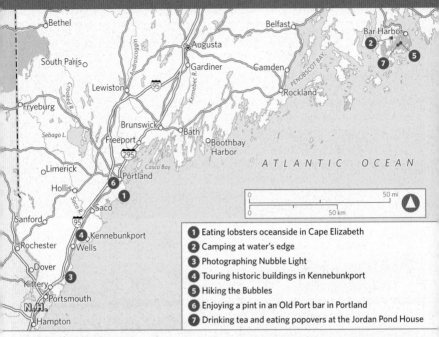

1 Eating lobsters oceanside in Cape Elizabeth
2 Camping at water's edge
3 Photographing Nubble Light
4 Touring historic buildings in Kennebunkport
5 Hiking the Bubbles
6 Enjoying a pint in an Old Port bar in Portland
7 Drinking tea and eating popovers at the Jordan Pond House

coast, you'll find campgrounds perched right beside the ocean, which is remarkable given how much of this coastline is privately owned. One of our favorites is **Mount Desert Campground,** 516 Sound Dr. (Rte. 198), Mount Desert (☎ 207/244-3710; www.mountdesert campground.com), just outside Acadia National Park on Mount Desert Isle.

3 **Photographing Nubble Light.** Maine's full of scenic lighthouses, but the one near York Beach is especially so. The tableau of a bright white lighthouse beside a cute red barn and the big blue ocean never fails to bring the summer crowds. Pack your best camera and lenses (including a polarizing lens), and come early or late in the day when the light is best for shooting. See p. 504, 7.

4 **Touring historic buildings in Kennebunkport.** The town of Kennebunkport is far better known for its wealth and First Family summer residents than its history or architecture. But if it's handsome old buildings you crave, this town holds as good a concentration of them as any place in Maine. Three historic districts all lie within easy walking distance of each other and the center of town. See p. 510.

5 **Hiking the Bubbles.** Sometimes you just want a quick walk to get the blood flowing. The Bubble Mountains are that sort of walk, if a bit too vertical to count as an "easy stroll." After a half-hour of hiking and clambering to the summit, you'll emerge with a view of Jordan Pond, the ocean, and Maine's coastal islands. See p. 485.

6 **Enjoying a pint in an Old Port bar in Portland.** If you're a beer drinker, the go-to Portland evening experience is a pint of locally brewed beer inside one of the city's pubs, followed by a responsible walk or taxi ride back to your hotel. See p. 499.

7 **Drinking tea and eating popovers at the Jordan Pond House.** The genteel days when Acadia was a Victorian-type resort, with horse-drawn carriages and steam trains bringing travelers from Boston, New York, and beyond, are gone. Well, nearly gone: You can still get a taste of that era at the Jordan Pond House, a sort of tearoom plunked down in the middle of the park beside a pond. Views are excellent, as are the popovers (the traditional snack). See p. 484, 6.

Maine in 3 Days

You could spend a month on the Maine coast and still not see it all—heck, that's why people buy summer homes here, so they *can* see it all. But Maine's remote position and size work to your advantage: The state has an amazing 5,500 miles of coastline, plus 3,000 or so coastal islands. With a little homework, you can book a room well in advance and enjoy the coast's lovely scenery without sweating any of the last-minute details. Basically, your main challenge when preplanning a vacation here boils down to simply this: Where to start? Luckily, this tour will take you through the best of Maine in just a few days.

> The crescent at Kennebunk Beach is perfect for both strolling and more serious athletic pursuits.

START Portland is 100 miles north of Boston. **TRIP LENGTH** 50 miles.

1 ★★★ **Portland.** Start your visit to this charming port city in **Eastern Promenade Park.** Take a walk along the shoreline path, sprawl out on the lawn to soak in the sea air, and take pictures of the islands, boats, and changing light. From there, head to **Commercial Street,** the heart of both Portland's working waterfront *and* its tourist trade. Move on to the **West End,** which offers more great architecture per square foot than almost anywhere in New England. The whole neighborhood could serve as a museum of 19th-century opulence. Must-sees include the John Calvin Stevens–designed homes on **Bowdoin Street** and the **Victoria Mansion** on Danforth Street. Nearby **Western Promenade Park** has splendid views of the western foothills.

Stop in at the **Portland Museum of Art** for a look at the Maine seascapes and the collection of European Impressionist works before paying a visit to the **Old Port,** a compact grid of streets in Portland's waterfront district where you can grab lunch or a pint.

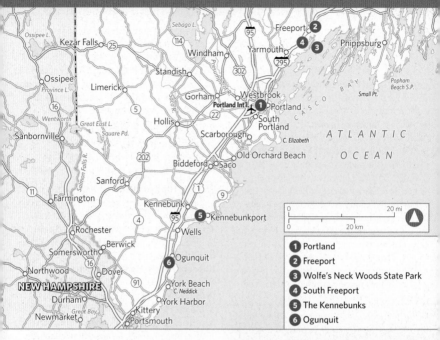

The following locations are marked on the map:

1 Portland
2 Freeport
3 Wolfe's Neck Woods State Park
4 South Freeport
5 The Kennebunks
6 Ogunquit

The shopping is great, too (shops are normally open 10am–6pm, sometimes later).

You'll need your car to make the trip to the **Portland Head Light** (p. 455). There are hiking, picnicking, and photo opportunities galore. From there, it's a quick drive to **Scarborough Beach Park** (p. 455). There are plenty of great beaches just south of the city—you can easily visit a half-dozen—but if you only have time for one, this is an excellent choice: clean facilities, good swimming, lifeguards, and a lunch place or two. ◷ 1 day. See p. 494.

Spend the night in Portland. On Day 2, drive 16 miles north on I-295 to exit 22. Turn left and continue ½ mile to Rte. 1 and turn left onto Main St. in:

2 ★ **Freeport.** History and shopping meet in this bustling little town. Your first stop should be the **L.L.Bean Flagship Store,** 95 Main St. (☎ 800/559-0747; www.llbean.com), before it gets shockingly crowded as the day goes on. This megastore is the patron saint of Freeport shopping, and has been since Leon Leonwood Bean invented a waterproof boot *and* was smart enough to market it to out-of-staters by mail. From there grew a business juggernaut, especially when L.L. decided to stay open

> *The 19th-century mansions lining Portland's West End, such as the George C. West House, are little-known architectural treasures.*

24 hours in 1951. You can find people nosing through camping, hiking, and other outdoor gear at 2 or 3am almost every night—there are no locks on the doors.

Once you're done shopping (and given how many outlet stores Freeport is home to, it may take you a while), head to the **Mast Landing Sanctuary,** Mast Landing Rd.

(☎ 207/ 781-2330), where a network of trails totaling 3½ miles crisscrosses through a landscape of eroded hills, mixed woodlands, and overgrown orchards. Streams trickle down to a marshland estuary. It's also a very peaceful winter hike if you've got snowshoes or cross-country skis.

Now that you've worked up an appetite, stop for lunch at **Jameson Tavern,** 115 Main St. (☎ 207/865-4196; www.jamesontavern.com). Built in 1779 as a combination eating/lodging place for stagecoaches heading up and down the coast, this little tavern has hosted poets (Longfellow) and presidents (Pierce) alike. For years, the Jameson was believed to be where Maine representatives negotiated and signed the papers separating the state from the Massachusetts Colony (which it had belonged to since the 1620s). That story was later proven unlikely, but a plaque remains in memory of the day Mainers rejoiced at their hard-won independence from the tax-happy Bostonians. ⏲ Half day.

Drive east on Bow St. (becomes Flying Point Rd.) to Wolfe's Neck Rd. Turn right and drive 2 miles into:

❸ ★ **Wolfe's Neck Woods State Park.** This attractive 233-acre park has quiet woodland trails that run through forests of white pine and hemlock, past estuaries, and along the rocky shoreline of the bay. **Googins Island,** just offshore and reached by following the park's **Casco Bay Trail,** has an osprey nest on it. This is a good destination for enjoying a picnic brought from town or for letting the kids burn off some pent-up energy—there are guided nature walks at 2pm daily during the summer. ⏲ 1½ hr. 426 Wolfe's Neck Rd. ☎ 207/ 865-4465. Day-use fee $4.50 per non–Maine resident adult, $1 kids 5–11.

Return to downtown Freeport. From Main St., turn left and follow South St. 3 miles into:

❹ **South Freeport.** Once the site of no fewer than four shipbuilding enterprises—huge trees were hauled here from the woods by teams of oxen—South Freeport has morphed from the town's main economic powerhouse into a sleeping boat landing where some fishing, marine repair, and charter-boating are still done. It's a good spot to get a quick look at the Maine coast and snap a photograph before settling down at a picnic table for a late-afternoon lunch or early dinner of the best lobsters in southern Maine at **Harraseeket Lunch & Lobster,** Main St. (☎ 207/865-4888). The **South Freeport Church,** 98 S. Freeport Rd. (☎ 207/865-4012), uphill from the harbor, was built by locals in 1884 and features a pleasing stained-glass rose window. ⏲ 2 hr.

Take Rte. 1 south 6 miles and merge onto I-295 S, then take exit 11 to I-95 S (a toll road). Follow I-95 26 miles to the Kennebunks, where you'll spend the night.

❺ ★★★ **The Kennebunks.** There's a ton to do in the twin towns known as the Kennebunks. Given a short schedule, you would do well to spend an hour strolling **Kennebunk Beach,** an hour shopping or dining in **Kennebunkport's Dock Square,** and a few hours in the lovely **Kennebunkport Historic District,** one of Maine's best. There are three distinct sections worth exploring in the District: the 3 blocks of Maine Street running from School Street to North Street, which contain numerous lovely 19th-century homes; an area concentrated around Pearl and Green streets, several blocks east of the square (plenty of inns and B&Bs here); and Church Street, only a block long but ending at the amazing, meetinghouse-style **South Congregational Church.** You can reach any of these areas easily on foot from Dock Square. Stop by the **Richard Nott House** at 8 Maine St. first to orient yourself, buy an inexpensive brochure describing local historic sights, or sign up for one of the historical society's excellent walking tours. ⏲ Half day. See p. 510.

From Dock Sq., Rte. 9 4 miles west and turn left onto Rte. 1, taking it 7 miles south to:

❻ ★★ **Ogunquit.** Once a summer art colony and now a beachy resort town, Ogunquit offers the traveler a little of everything—art, sand, shopping, fine dining, and a laid-back pace. Take your pick. The one don't-miss sight here is the wonderful **Ogunquit Museum of American Art,** while **Ogunquit Beach** is good for an hour's stroll or a lengthy suntan session. ⏲ Half day. See p. 506.

Either spend the night in Ogunquit, by the beach, or backtrack 10 miles north to the Kennebunks.

The Beaches of Lucky 77

One of the supreme pleasures of a Maine summer is discovering its beaches, many with island and/or lighthouse views as a free bonus—and lovely Rte. 77 will take you to them. Southern Maine, in particular, is blessed with an abundance of beaches and lighthouses—and greater Portland is the best place in the state to see a handful of each in one quick shot.

Even if you're pressed for time you can reach a beach in minutes: From downtown Portland, for instance, simply cross the Casco Bay Bridge to South Portland and follow Broadway to the end. This is **Willard Beach,** a small neighborhood strand with friendly locals, dogs, hiking trails, the ruins of an old fort, and tidal rocks to scramble over. There's plenty of free parking.

From there, drive south on Rte. 77 through **Cape Elizabeth,** past sweeping views of marsh, ocean, and cultivated field.

First you hit **Two Lights State Park** (☎ 207/799-5871), with two lighthouses (obviously) and **Two Lights Lobster Shack** (p. 450, ❶) besides. Ocean views are dramatic. Farther along, ★★★ **Crescent Beach State Park** (☎ 207/799-5871) is a gentle, mile-long curve of sand with ample parking, barbecue pits, picnic tables, and a snack bar.

★ **Fort Williams State Park,** a local park on Shore Road in Cape Elizabeth (just off Rte. 77), is a bit harder to find, but it's free and offers supreme vistas of both the sea and the much-photographed **Portland Head Light** landmark lighthouse. Three miles south, turn left onto Rte. 207 for two final options: **Scarborough Beach Park,** a longish strip of clean sand and dunes with changing facilities or—a little farther along, on the right—quieter **Ferry Beach,** with good views south to **Old Orchard Beach** (p. 512).

Maine in 1 Week

If 3 days in Maine are good, a week is even better. That's about enough time to take the two regions of the Maine coast: southern Maine ("down there," also sometimes referred to by locals as "Vacationland" or "not Maine") and Downeast ("up there" or "the real Maine"). The two regions are as different as night and day; the gourmet cuisine, fine cars, and luxury inns of the south coast gradually give way to cottages and fried fish. This tour will take you through both.

> Two generations of former Presidents summer at the Bush compound known as Walker's Point in Kennebunkport. 556A

START York is 66 miles north of Boston, 50 miles south of Portland, and 205 miles southwest of Bar Harbor. **TRIP LENGTH** 450 miles.

① ★ York Beach. The town of York is split into several neighborhoods, each with its own charms. On this tour, though, we'll just head straight for the beaches: Don't miss either **Long Sands** (p. 504, **⑥**) or **Short Sands** beaches. And a visit here isn't complete without a swing by **Nubble Light** (p. 504, **⑦**), a beacon to ships and a magnet to photographers. ⊕ 3 hr.

Continue north on Rte. 1 about 10 miles to:

② ★★ Ogunquit. Be sure to visit the **Ogunquit Museum of American Art,** and stretch your legs or catch some rays at **Ogunquit Beach.** ⊕ 3 hr. See p. 506.

Continue north on Rte. 1 about 10 more miles to:

③ ★★★ The Kennebunks. Spend some time on **Kennebunk Beach,** before checking out **Kennebunkport's Dock Square.** Cap the day with a 15-minute sunset drive out to scenic **Walker's Point.** ⊕ 3 hr. See p. 510.

Spend the night in the Kennebunks. On Day 2, follow Rte. 9 west to I-95N (a toll road); Go

> *Portland's Commercial Street is best known for shopping now—but you can still glimpse its maritime history in spots.*

about 40 miles to exit 44, where you'll pick up I-295N. Go 10 miles to Portland, where you'll spend the night.

4 ★★★ **Portland.** Maine's biggest city is an absolute must-see on almost any tour of the state, even if it's just for an afternoon or a day: There's more history, food, and architecture than first appears here. At an absolute minimum, check out the **Old Port** and **Commercial Street,** plus the restaurants in that neighborhood; the fine **Portland Museum of Art;** and the ocean view from **Eastern Promenade Park.** ⏱ 1 day. See p. 494.

On Day 3, take I-295N 15 miles to:

5 ★ **Freeport.** Maine's best single shopping destination, Freeport is also worth visiting for its history—best seen in places like **Jameson Tavern** and the village of **South Freeport** (p. ###, **4**). But let's be honest: You're here to dip into the wide sea of brand-name outlet stores inundating the town, and to check out fishing line/hunting vests/pocket knives/kayaks at all-hours retailer **L.L.Bean.** ⏱ Half day. See p. 453, **2**.

Continue north on Rte. 1 about 10 miles to Brunswick. Plan to spend the night either here or in neighboring Bath.

6 ★★ **Brunswick.** One of our favorite small towns in the southern half of Maine, Brunswick manages to be erudite—the beautiful quadrant-based campus of **Bowdoin College** (p. 514, **1**) and two great little **museums** (p. 515, **2** and **3**) are located here. But it's also fairly lovely, with a proud Maine Street, a big park, old churches, and a great collection of whitewashed 19th-century architecture—stroll down **Federal Street** (p. 516, **4**) to see some of the best of it. ⏱ 3 hr.

Continue north on Rte. 1 about 8 miles to:

Travel Tip

If you're flying into Portland rather than driving north from New York or Boston, you can also begin with stop **4** of this tour, do stops **1** to **3** the next day, and then pick up with stop **5** on Day 3. But either way, you'll need a car for this tour.

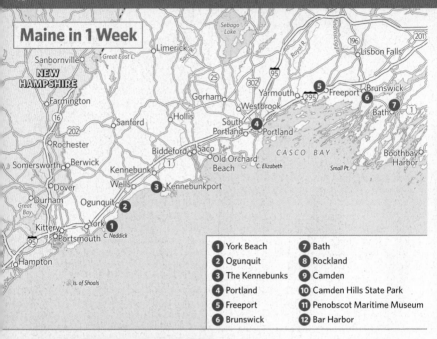

Maine in 1 Week

1 York Beach	**7** Bath
2 Ogunquit	**8** Rockland
3 The Kennebunks	**9** Camden
4 Portland	**10** Camden Hills State Park
5 Freeport	**11** Penobscot Maritime Museum
6 Brunswick	**12** Bar Harbor

> The Farnsworth Museum in Rockland features modern art in addition to impressive Wyeth holdings.

7 ★ **Bath.** The big claim to fame in Bath is shipbuilding (notice that huge crane looming over the town bridge as you approach or depart); whether you're intrigued by that sort of history or not, this little city is worth a few hours to a half day. The **Maine Maritime Museum** (p. 516, **7**) just south of the downtown district showcases the old art in all its glory, and runs actual boat trips from time to time to supplement the museum. Meanwhile, the handsome **Washington Street** (p. 516, **5**) and **Front Street** (p. 516, **6**) historic districts are easily worth a half-hour walk each for their architecture and the occasional shop and cafe. ⏱ 2 hr.

On Day 4, take I-95N (a toll road) 25 miles to exit 44 and pick up I-295N. Go 20 miles to exit 28, where you'll pick up Rte. 1 north. It's about 20 more miles to Wiscasset (p. 516, **9**), and make a mandatory stop at Red's Eats (p. 517). Continue on Rte. 1 about 35 miles to:

8 ★★ **Rockland.** The Midcoast's unofficial working-class capital is a good place to get a bite at a surprisingly upscale restaurant like **Primo** (p. 521); glimpse yachts, fishing boats, schooners, and tall ships all in one harbor, at **Harbor Park;** and stroll a **Main Street** that

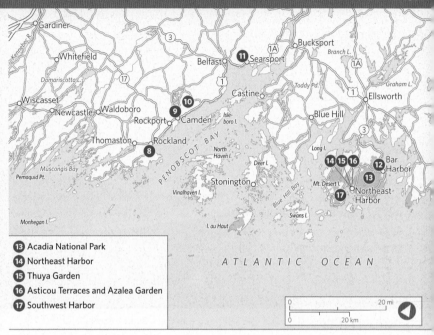

13 Acadia National Park
14 Northeast Harbor
15 Thuya Garden
16 Asticou Terraces and Azalea Garden
17 Southwest Harbor

actually still looks like, well, a main street. Art lovers, take special note—you will kick yourself eternally if you don't spend at least an hour at the **Farnsworth Museum,** one of Maine's finest thanks to its comprehensive collections of Maine art. ⏱ 2 hr. See p. 518, **1**.

Continue 8 miles on Rte. 1 to Camden, where you'll spend the night.

A Tent with a View

There are more inns and B&Bs on Maine's Midcoast (the area around Bath, Brunswick, Camden, and so on) than campgrounds—but you can find a few gems if you're really hankering to pitch a tent. One of the best is inside **Camden Hills State Park** (p. 520, **4**): For basically a dollar an hour, you get access to a sparkling bay, a tall mountain with foliage on its sides and a lake at its foot, open cliffs, an auto road to the summit. . . . It's hard to imagine a park offering families more than this one does. You can literally hike all day in the park, and tenters get their own quiet RV-free section. Expect to pay $25 a night from May to October, and a bit less the rest of the year.

9 ★★★ **Camden.** Put simply: the twee cousin to Rockland's denim jeans and dockline rope. The stretch of U.S. Rte. 1 running down Elm Street into the center of Camden, then back up out of town—now Main Street—tells you that you've switched gears. It's a mixture of old homes, B&B elegance, fishy chowder houses, tall ships, the sturdy **Camden Opera House,** and shops purveying anything from nautical souvenirs to T-shirts; it gets crowded, but never feels artificial. The lovely **Camden Public Library** and its adjacent natural amphitheater (known as **Harbor Park**) overlooking the harbor only add to the fun. ⏱ 3 hr. See p. 520, **3**.

From downtown Camden, drive north 2 miles on Rte. 1 to the entrance to:

10 ★ **Camden Hills State Park.** A good spot for sunset views of lovely Penobscot Bay, Camden's primo park lords over the water from some pretty impressive little twin peaks. You can picnic here, hike here, or just drive to good views; it all depends on how much time and energy you have. ⏱ 1 hr. See p. 520, **4**.

On Day 5, follow Rte. 1 north 25 miles to Searsport. Right on Main St. is the:

> *Schooners and tall ships regularly call at Camden's harbor—and many accept passengers.*

> *Bar Harbor's Shore Path takes a bit of looking to find, but yields tremendous sea views for the effort.*

11 kids **Penobscot Maritime Museum.** Though it's largely a working-class town today, Searsport was once one of the most important shipbuilding centers in the Midcoast. Sea captains built opulent mansions (many are B&Bs today), and coopers, brickyards, lumber mills, and factories followed. This museum/campus recounts the history of the shipyards and fisheries; holdings include a sardine boat, a sea captain's home, scrimshaw work, and huge photographic archives. ⏱ 1 hr. 40 E. Main St. (Rte. 1), Searsport. ☎ 207/548-2529 or 548-0334. www.penobscotmarinemuseum.org. May–Oct Mon–Sat 10am–5pm, Sun noon–5pm. $8 adults, $3 kids 7–15, $18 families.

Return to Rte. 1 and continue north 30 miles to Ellsworth. Bear right onto Rte. 3 east and go 15 miles into Bar Harbor, where you'll spend the night.

12 ★★ **Bar Harbor.** Begin your time here at **Agamont Park,** which looks out onto the islands of Frenchman Bay. Next, stretch your legs along the **Shore Path.** This little gem passes opulent "cottages" as it winds along a billion-dollar waterfront. It begins at the **Bar Harbor Inn** (p. 492), itself a fine example of the form with knockout views from its dining room and many guest rooms. But on the Shore Path, you get nearly the same view—for the price of your pair of sneakers. ⊙ Half day. See p. 486.

On Day 6, follow signs to:

⓭ ★★★ **Acadia National Park.** There's a lot to see and do here. Begin at **Sand Beach,** one of Maine's nicest beaches. It does actually have some sand—plus views of several mountains and the open ocean. If you have time, explore the Sand Beach and Great Head walking trails that both depart from the east end of the beach. The Sand Beach trail threads gently inland through the woods away from the water, while the latter trail climbs the adjacent cliffs; you'll see plenty of plant, bird, and flower life on either one. Wrap up your day with a stop at **Thunder Hole,** where crashing waves can send plumes 30 feet or more into the air—or can be an absolute dud if there's no wave action in the bay.

Get an early start on Day 6 and drive to the top of granite **Cadillac Mountain,** which reaches 1,528 feet from sea level to summit. *Trivia lovers note:* Until 1918, this hill was known as Green Mountain and a cog railway once ran to

the top from a hotel. The engines are now used to haul travelers up Mount Washington in New Hampshire (p. 419, ⑥) instead.

If you're serious about your outdoor time, you may want to skip the rest of the stops in this tour and spend your time exploring the park instead, and perhaps opting for a **whale-watch** (p. 463). ⊙ 2 days. See p. 482.

Spend the night in a park campground (p. 459) or in Bar Harbor again. In the morning, follow Rte. 3 to Rte. 233. Turn left and follow Rte. 233 west 5 miles inland to Rte. 198. Turn left and continue 5 miles south to:

⓮ ★★ **Northeast Harbor.** Northeast Harbor's main street is one of the cutest on Mount Desert Isle. It's worth a few hours to a half day of exploring. Sample the goods at the old-fashioned grocery **Pine Tree Market,** 121 Main St. (☎ 207/276-3335Ð), then browse through a surprisingly fine collection of shops and galleries such as the **Kimball Shop & Boutique,** 135 Main St. (☎ 800/673-3754 or 207/276-3300), full of classy bedroom, living room, and kitchen accents; sea-glass jeweler **Lisa Hall's studio** at 8 Summit Rd. (☎ 207/276-5900; call ahead); and Sam Shaw's **Shaw**

> Look sharp for the woodworking details on boats at the Penobscot Maritime Museum in Searsport.

> Sand Beach, the largest true beach in Acadia National Park, offers superb hiking and beachcombing.

Contemporary Jewelry at 126 Main St. (☎ 877/276-5001 or 207/276-5000). Later, turn left at the end of Main Street and head down Harbor Road to the **marina/ferry dock** for clear harbor views and photograph opportunities. Check **Redbird Provisions** (p. 493) if you want to make dinner reservations. ⏱ 3 hr.

Backtrack to Rte. 102. Turn right and drive 5½ miles north to Rte. 3. Turn right and continue 6 miles east and south (stay on Rte. 3) to:

⑮ Thuya Garden. A beautifully laid-out flower garden full of bright perennials, Thuya is a testament to Joseph Henry Curtis (1841–1928), the landscape architect who once resided here and was a staunch defender of the parkland. It's a wonderful spot for a picnic or for snapping photos, best in mid-summer when blossoms are at their height. ⏱ 1 hr. Peabody Rd. (Rte. 3), Northeast Harbor. ☎ 207/276-3727. www.gardenpreserve.org. Free; donations requested. May–Sept daily 7am–7pm.

Travel a half mile back along Rte. 3 to:

⑯ ★ Asticou Terraces and Azalea Garden. Uphill from the busy loop road traversing this section of the island, these gardens are a fine surprise—and nearby (at the junction with Rte. 198) is a wonderful Asian water world where you step from stone to stone in a pond, admiring the seasonal blooms. It's very Zen. ⏱ 1 hr. See p. 490, ⑦.

> Beal's, in Southwest Harbor: You know the lobsters are fresh when there's a dock attached to the restaurant.

Travel north 6½ miles on Rte. 198 to Rte. 102. Turn left and continue 6½ miles south to:

⑰ ★★ Southwest Harbor. Southwest Harbor stands just a mile across the fjord from Northeast Harbor, but it takes almost half an hour to get from one to the other by car. (By boat? It would be 2–5 minutes—if there were one.) Southwest has a different feel from Northeast: Highlights include the busy main street, the ferry dock, the town pier, a Coast Guard station (off-limits), and the you've-arrived-in-Maine lunch spot **Beal's Lobster Pound,** 182 Clark Point Rd. (☎ 207/244-7178). Shopping in town largely runs to T-shirts and ship models, but you can also find art and craft galleries like **Flying Mountain Artisans,** 28 Main St. (☎ 207/244-0404), and the quirky croquet supplier **Clarkpoint Croquet,** 8 Dirigo Rd. (☎ 207/244-9284). Rent a bike for exploring local fishing villages at **Southwest Cycle,** 370 Main St. (☎ 207/244-5856; www.southwestcycle.com)—a ride'll cost you $14 to $27 per day. ⏱ 3 hr.

Getting Out on the Water

Getting out onto the water is one of the primal joys of visiting Maine in summer, and thankfully there are plenty of opportunities to do so—whether you're an experienced boater or not.

Bar Harbor is one of the best places in New England for **whale-watching.** We haven't listed it as a specific stop in this tour, as it is dependent on both weather and time of year, but if you're even slightly interested, and you're in town between May and early September, our advice is to get on a boat posthaste. On any given cruise, you might see breaching humpbacks, finbacks, little minkes, or even the endangered right whale. **Bar Harbor Whale Watching** (☎ 888/942-5374 or 207/288-2386; www.barharbor whales.com) guarantees you'll see whales on its 2- to 3-hour tours late May through late October. (Cruises cost $27–$56 per adult, $16–$28 per child 6–14.)

Deep-sea fishing is another option. Maine's fishing grounds are some of the most fertile in the world. Want a piece of that? Pick an outfit with a track record, sturdy boat, and crew of guys tough enough to handle the perfect storm. South Portland's **Atlantic Adventures,** 231 Front St. (☎ 207/838-9902; www.atlanticadventures.biz), offers 2-hour, half-day, and full-day tours taking in fish, lobsters, and lighthouses. How tough are these guys? They've tussled with sharks—multiple times. Figure $400 to $1,000 per charter.

Maine abounds with great **kayaking** too. On Mount Desert Island, you can explore inland and coastal waters. In Bar Harbor visit **Coastal Kayaking,** 48 Cottage St. (☎ 800/526-8615 or 207/288-9605; www.acadiafun.com); **National Park Sea Kayak Tours,** 39 Cottage St. (☎ 800/347-0940; www.acadiakayak.com); or **Aquaterra,** 1 West St. (☎ 877/386-4124 or 207/288-0007; www.aquaterra-adventures.com). Expect to spend $50 per half day. You can also kayak Penobscot Bay; get gear or book a tour at **Maine Sport Outfitters** on Rte. 1 in Rockport (☎ 800/722-0826; www.mainesport.com) or **Old Quarry Charters** (☎ 207/367-8977; www.oldquarry.com) in Stonington. In the Portland area, with its plentiful bays, islands, and beaches, **Maine Island Kayak Co.** (☎ 207/766-2373; www.maineislandkayak.com) on Peaks Island is the best outfit.

If it's **seal- and puffin-watching** you seek, you're also in luck. Boats set out for rocky nubs like Machias Seal Island, which boasts thousands of puffins, razorbills, and seals. **Bold Coast Charter** (☎ 207/259-4484; www.boldcoast.com) operates out of Cutler May through August. Figure $80 per adult, $45 per child; Bar Harbor Whale Watching (see above) also offers puffin cruises out of Bar Harbor.

Finally, there's **windjamming.** (They don't call it "sailing" up here when you're on a schooner or tall ship.) Many captains will let you take a day sail or even charter you overnight on the water. Camden and Rockland are the acknowledged best harbors from which to do this; contact the **Maine Windjammer Association** (☎ 800/807-9463; www.sail mainecoast.com) for full info on outfits.

Undiscovered Maine: The Blue Hill Peninsula

The Blue Hill Peninsula is Maine: rural, remote, fog-swept, lovely—and somehow still largely undiscovered (or even unknown) by the majority of Maine's tourists, especially those hellbent for Bar Harbor. And that has made all the difference; it's beautiful, pastoral country but tough living for locals, something the essayist E. B. White recognized when he bought a farm here and memorialized the experience in such great little books as *One Man's Meat*. They take extra time to reach, but villages like Castine and Blue Hill are well worth building into any Maine-coast itinerary. They'll hold you captive with their simple water views, boatyards, tiny artists' communities, local fresh eats, and grass-roots radio.

> There's culture in Stonington, but at heart it's a fishing village that feels miles from nowhere.

START Blue Hill is 140 miles northeast of Portland. TRIP LENGTH 60 miles.

1 ★★ **Blue Hill.** Sitting on a pretty harbor at the junction of three roads, it's the preferred summer destination of many an out-of-stater precisely because it's so quiet and untouristed. The compact downtown features the general store **Merrill & Hinckley,** on the green at 11 Union St. (☎ 207/374-2821Ð); a natural foods store, **Blue Hill Food Co-op,** 4 Ellsworth Rd (☎ 207/374-2165); the great little **Jonathan Fisher House historical museum** at 44 Mines Rd. (☎ 207/374-2459); a changing roster of galleries; and a smattering of fine

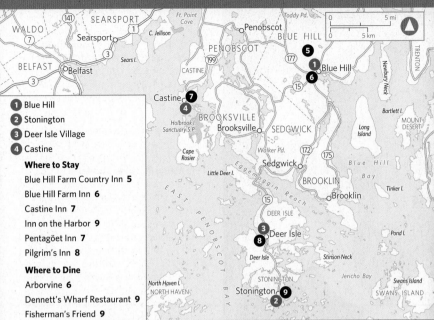

eateries, such as **Arborvine,** 33 Main St. (☎ 207/374-2119). ⏱ 3 hr.

From Blue Hill's village center, follow Main St. (Rte. 176/15) south 5 miles to the end. Turn left to keep on Rte. 15, continuing 12 miles to:

② ★★ **Stonington.** Stonington consists of one commercial street that wraps along a very scenic harbor's edge, plus a few side streets and fishing docks. It's still a somewhat rough-and-tumble fishing town, but gift, book, and craft shops have gradually taken over the main drag. Stop into **Bayside Antiques,** 131 W. Main St. (☎ 207/367-8714); **Dockside Books,** 62 W. Main St. (☎ 207/367-2652); or **Prints & Reprints,** 31 Main St. (☎ 207/367-5821), with its Wyeth focus, for example. The **town opera house,** 1 Opera House Lane, just off Main and School sts. (☎ 207/367-2788; www.opera housearts.org), is home to a summer-stock theater company. You can also eat well along the waterfront. *One more tip:* If you're here in July, do *not* miss the annual lobster-boat races (www.lobsterboatracing.com). ⏱ 2 hr.

Backtrack 5 miles north along Rte. 15 to:

③ ★★ **Deer Isle Village.** The town of Deer Isle (as opposed to the island) is tiny and noncommercial; you barely notice it unless you know to stop, yet it's chock-full of artists' studios and galleries. Some of the better choices include the **Red Dot Gallery,** 3 Main St. (☎ 207/348-2733), a local collective; **Conary Cove Glass Works,** 3 Black Point Rd. (☎ 207/ 348-9402); and **Deer Island Granite,** 70 Center District Crossroad (☎ 207/348-7714). Worth a look. ⏱ 30 min.

Fair Game

The ★★ **Blue Hill Fair** (☎ 207/374-3701; www.bluehillfair.com) is a traditional country fair with livestock competitions, vegetable displays, yummy fried dough, live music, and carnival rides—an end-of-summer rite on this peninsula. (It's also the fair from which Wilbur the pig escapes an unsavory fate in E. B. White's classic children's book *Charlotte's Web.*) The annual event takes place at fairgrounds northwest of the village on Rte. 172 on Labor Day weekend. Admission costs $5 to $8 per person (the price varies by day—weekends are more expensive), while rides are individually priced. Parking is free on the fairgrounds; when they fill up, locals nearby charge a reasonable $5 to $10 per car.

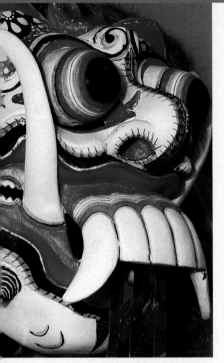

> You never know what's around the next corner at the Wilson Museum in Castine.

Continue north on Rte. 15 for 12 miles, staying straight through the junction with Rte. 176. Go north 2½ miles on Rte. 176, then turn right onto Rte. 175. Continue 7 miles west to Rte. 199; stay straight on Rte. 199 (which becomes Rte. 166) for 8 more miles to reach:

❹ ★★ **Castine.** Long considered one of Maine's most charming and attractive villages, Castine is best known to Mainers as the home of the **Maine Maritime Academy** (☎ 207/326-4311). In summer, the academy's training ship *State of Maine* can be toured for free whenever it's in port. Handsome mid-19th-century homes still fill the side streets, and towering elms overarch many of the avenues. The quirky **Wilson Museum,** at 120 Perkins St. (☎ 207/326-9247), is worth a stop, as is the adjacent **John Perkins House** (same phone and address)—it's Castine's oldest home. A quick walk through the woods at the edge of town leads to the 1829 Dyce Head (or Dice Head, depending on who you ask) lighthouse. You can't go inside, but if you're a lighthouse fanatic, you'll want to take a look. ⏱ 2 hr.

Where to Stay & Dine

★★ **Arborvine** BLUE HILL *SEAFOOD*
Arborvine is sleepy Blue Hill's best eatery, in a beautifully renovated Cape Cod–style house. Expect local crab, scallops, lobsters, oysters, haddock, and halibut, prepared with European twists, plus lamb and duck. Main St. ☎ 207/374-2119. www.arborvine.com. Entrees $27–$31. MC, V. Summer daily 5:30–8:30pm; winter Fri–Sun 5:30–8:30pm.

★ **Blue Hill Farm Country Inn** BLUE HILL
On 48 acres just north of the village center. Rooms in the former barn loft are more modern, while those in the main house share a bathroom. Rte. 15. ☎ 207/374-5126. www.blue hillfarminn.com. 14 units (7 w/shared bathroom). Doubles $85–$115 w/breakfast. AE, MC, V. "Limited accommodations" for kids 11 & under.

★★ **Blue Hill Farm Inn** BLUE HILL
Right in the center of town, this Federal-style inn is furnished in antiques. The breakfasts here are very good. 40 Union St. ☎ 800/826-7415 or 207/374-2844. www.bluehillinn.com. 12 units. Doubles $155–$205; suites $175–$275 w/breakfast. DISC, MC, V. Closed Dec to mid-May. Kids 13 & over welcome.

★ **Castine Inn** CASTINE
This handsome, cream-colored inn in Georgian Federal Revival style features a great wrap-around porch. The lobby is filled with wingback chairs, love seats, and a fireplace; there's a sauna too. 41 Main St. ☎ 207/326-4365. www.castineinn.com. 18 units. Peak season doubles & suites $90–$275 w/breakfast; off-season rates lower. MC, V. May weekends only; closed mid-Oct to Apr. Kids 8 & over welcome.

Dennett's Wharf Restaurant STONINGTON *PUB FARE* The upscale bar food served in a soaring waterfront sail loft includes everything from sandwiches, salads, fried clams, lobsters, and an oyster bar to pad Thai. Dine on the deck if you can. 15 Sea St. ☎ 207/326-9045. www. dennettswharf.net. Lunch entrees $5–$13; dinner entrees $9–$27. AE, DISC, MC, V. Daily 11am–midnight. Closed mid-Oct to Apr.

★ kids **Fisherman's Friend** STONINGTON *SEAFOOD* Right on the Stonington docks, the fresh fish and local lobsters here are cooked 30 different ways, but the specialty is the amazing lobster stew.. There's also a wine list and a choice of pastas. 5 Atlantic Ave. ☎ 207/367-2442. Lobsters market priced; dinner entrees $13–$20. DISC, MC, V. May–Oct daily 11am–10pm; Apr & Nov–Jan Thurs–Sun 11am–9pm. Closed Feb–Mar.

★ **Inn on the Harbor** STONINGTON Perched right over the harbor, and useful if you're catching an early boat to Isle au Haut (see right). The American Eagle suite features a glass-fronted woodstove, private kitchen, and private deck. 45 Main St. ☎ 800/942-2420 or 207/367-2420. www.innontheharbor.com. 14 units. Mid-May to mid-Oct doubles $149–$225 w/breakfast; mid-Oct to mid-May doubles $85–$135 (no breakfast). AE, DISC, MC, V. Kids 12 & over welcome.

★★ **Pentagöet Inn** CASTINE You can't miss the prominent turret. Most units sport king-size beds; some have clawfoot bathtubs and/or fireplaces. The pub and dining room are worth visits. 26 Main St. ☎ 800/845-1701 or 207/326-8616. www. pentagoet.com. 16 units. Peak season doubles $145–$280 w/breakfast; off-season rates lower. MC, V. Closed Nov–Apr.

★★ **Pilgrim's Inn** DEER ISLE This mid- to upscale inn features impressive diagonal beam work. Accents include private staircases, cherry beds, antique tubs, gasburning stoves, and fireplaces; breakfasts are big and fancy. 20 Main St. ☎ 888/778-7505 or 207/348-6615. www.pilgrimsinn.com. 15 units. Doubles $119–$219; cottage $189–$229 w/breakfast. MC, V. Closed mid-Oct to mid-May. Kids 10 & over welcome in inn, all kids welcome in cottages.

> Simple but comfortable: A room at the 1898-built Castine Inn on the village's Main Street.

High Times on Isle au Haut

★★ **Isle au Haut**—which is visible right from Stonington's town docks—might pique your appetite for a sudden offshore adventure. No museums, no hotels, no fancy restaurants? No problem. Famed for its lobstermen (and -women), the island is half-owned by the National Park Service and is a little-visited unit of Acadia National Park. There's not a whole to see here except nature—but *that* the Isle has in spades.

The ferry run by **Isle au Haut Boat Services** (☎ 207/367-5193; www.isleauhaut. com) lands at **Town Landing,** a small village of old homes, a handsome church, and a tiny schoolhouse, post office, and store. Get supplies here. During summer, a few boats also dock at **Duck Harbor,** a few minutes' walk from five **National Park lean-tos** (camping is $25 per site and must be reserved well in advance; book through www.nps.gov). Stroll the road circling the island or hike a rugged trail system stretching nearly 20 miles through foggy, towering groves of spruce. The **Western Head/Cliff Trail** circuit, at the island's southwestern tip, is the best walk; follow unpaved Western Head Road to the trail head. The 4-mile trail takes 3 to 4 hours of moderate to difficult walking but rewards one with ocean views. Be careful hiking over wet logs, stumps, and roots.

A Downeast Road Trip

Downeast Maine barely gets a thought from most coastal travelers, and there are reasons why: It takes time to get here, and sites are few and far between. Still, if you enjoy solitude, salty and foggy air, and empty roads lined with fir and spruce trees, this is the place for you. Bonus: You can dip into Canada. Bring your passport.

> Schoodic Point is the only portion of Acadia National Park on the mainland, and well worth the detour north.

START Schoodic Point is 50 miles east of Bar Harbor by car. TRIP LENGTH 155 miles.

1 ★★★ **Schoodic Point.** This remote, scenic unit of Acadia National Park is just 7 miles from Mount Desert Island and Bar Harbor, yet it's a 50-mile drive. It's worth it, though—and free. A one-way loop road hooks around the point, along the water, and through forests of spruce and fir. Good views of Acadia open up across the bay; park near the tip and explore the rocks—but stay a bit back from the edge, as waves can get big with little or no warning. ⏱ 1 hr.

From Schoodic Point, take Rte. 186 5 miles and turn right onto Rte. 1. Go just under 20 miles and turn right onto Rte. 187, going 12 miles to:

2 ★ **Jonesport.** This photogenic, lost-in-time fishing village at the end of a peninsula is still mostly the haven of lobstermen, fishermen, and boat builders and fixers. Besides the tableau, local color, and sea views, you'll also see lobster boat races (www.lobsterboatracing.com)—Maine's version of NASCAR, according to some—if you come on July 4th weekend. ⏱ 1 hr.

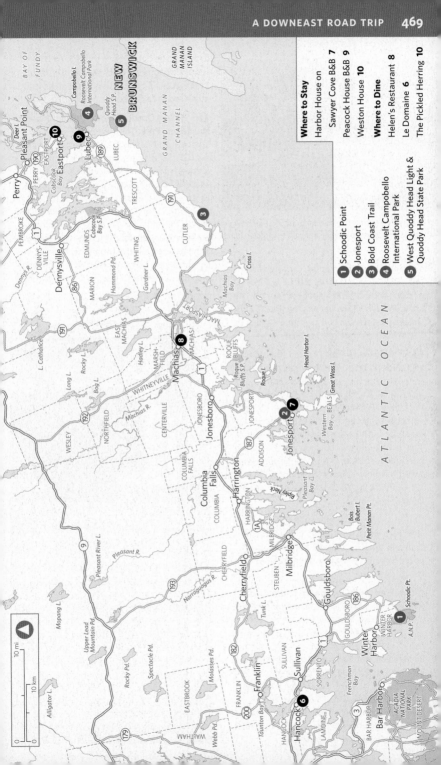

> *Tiny Jonesport is the launching-off point for racing lobster boats and whale- and puffin-watching tours.*

Continue around the point, turning north onto Rte. 187; go 11 miles to Rte. 1. Turn right and continue 24 miles north to Rte. 191. Turn right and drive 13 miles east on Rte. 191 into Cutler. Past the harbor, continue 4 miles to the turnoff on the right for the:

❸ ★★ **Bold Coast Trail.** Marked by a sign in a small parking lot, this dramatic trail loops through bogs, barrens, jumbled fields of stone, and forest. The highlight is a mile-long section along 150-foot cliffs rising high above the Atlantic—don't go if you fear heights, and step carefully, as there are no railings or fences. Just sample the trail if you're with the family, but budget at least 4 to 5 hours if you plan to walk the whole 10-mile (5-hr.) loop. ⏲ 1 hr. Rte. 191, Cutler. ☎ 207/827-1818. Free admission. Open year-round.

Continue 10 miles north on Rte. 191 to Rte. 189. Turn right. Continue 5 miles through Lubec to the U.S.-Canada border crossing. Enter Canada (passport required) and cross the bridge into:

❹ ★★ **Roosevelt Campobello International Park.** President Franklin Delano Roosevelt made an annual summer trek to this island; you can learn about Roosevelt at a visitor center or during a self-guided tour of the family mansion, but also take time to explore the grounds, which hold plenty of scenic walking trails. ⏲ 2 hr. 459 Rte. 774, Welshpool, New Brunswick. ☎ 506/752-2922. www.fdr.net. Free admission. Daily 10am–6pm; last tour at 5:45pm. Visitor center closed mid-Oct to mid-May; grounds open year-round.

Cross the bridge back to the U.S. (passport required) and Rte. 189. Head south; after 1 mile, turn left on S. Lubec Rd. and drive 3 miles south to the access road for:

❺ ★★ **West Quoddy Head Light and Quoddy Head State Park.** The candy-cane-colored Quoddy lighthouse is the easternmost point of the U.S. Visitors can photograph it from the park, and learn more in a visitor center inside the lightkeeper's house. The park's grounds include 500 acres of dramatic coast, with trails to the tops of the cliffs. ⏲ 1½ hr. West Quoddy Head Rd., Lubec. ☎ 207/733-0911 (park) or 733-2180 (lighthouse). www.westquoddy.com. Lighthouse free; state park $3 nonresident adults, $1 seniors & children 5-11. Lighthouse late May to mid-Oct daily 10am–4pm; grounds 9am–sunset. Closed mid-Oct to mid-May.

Eastport: The Big Fish

It's a 40-mile detour, but backtracking to Rte. 1 and visiting Eastport is a must-do when Downeast. In the 19th century, Eastport was a boomtown, home to 18 sardine plants. The plants are all gone, but the boomtown architecture remains. Walk the length of Water Street to see some prime examples, including the **Eastport Savings Bank** at no. 43, the **Shead Building** at no. 58, the **M. Bradish Bakery** at no. 68, the **Masonic Block** at no. 36, and the **Charles & M. A. Jackson Block** at no. 74. At a gap between Boynton Street and Furniture Avenue is an oddly Paul Bunyan–esque sculpture of a fisherman that inspires divided feelings among locals.

Where to Stay & Dine

> Helen's Restaurant in Machias has been a blueberry-pie mecca for foodies since 1950.

★ **Harbor House on Sawyer Cove B&B** JONE-SPORT Once the Jonesport telegraph office, this inn has just two suites, set above an antiques shop. Both feature truly impressive coastal scenery from their third-floor windows and private entrances. Breakfast is served on a great porch. 27 Sawyer Sq. ☎ 207/497-5417. www.harborhs.com. 2 units. Doubles $100–$125 w/breakfast. DISC, MC, V.

★ **Helen's Restaurant** MACHIAS *DINER*
This is the original Helen's, a cut-above-the-rest diner and one of the best places in Maine for pie. Specials run to pork chops, fried fish, burgers, and meatloaf—but save room for the strawberry rhubarb, blueberry, and cream pies. 28 E. Main St. ☎ 207/255-8423. Entrees $3–$16. DISC, MC, V. Breakfast, lunch & dinner daily.

★★ **Le Domaine** HANCOCK
Not far east of Ellsworth, this country inn serves some of the best French cooking on the coast. The original owner emigrated from Provence to the U.S. during World War II; now a young Maine chef has revitalized it. Rooms are comfortable and tastefully appointed without being pretentious. 1513 Rte. 1. ☎ 800/554-8498 or 207/422-3395. www.ledomaine.com.

5 units. Doubles $200–$370 w/breakfast & dinner. AE, MC, V. Closed Nov to mid-June.

★ **Peacock House Bed & Breakfast** LUBEC
Peacock House was built by an English sea captain in 1860. The suites are best, including one with an extra daybed and one with a fireplace, four-poster bed, and wet bar. 27 Summer St. ☎ 888/305-0036 or 207/733-2403. www.peacockhouse.com. 7 units. Doubles $90–$112 w/breakfast. MC, V.

★★ **The Pickled Herring** EASTPORT *NEW AMERICAN* Out of nowhere, the Herring has become the finest fine-dining experience in Eastport, or for miles beyond, with offerings like fire-grilled gourmet pizzas, salmon with dill butter, strip steak, and prime rib. 32 Water St. ☎ 207/853-2323. www.thepickledherring.com. Entrees $15–$29. AE, MC, V. May–Oct dinner Thurs–Sun.

★ **Weston House** EASTPORT
An 1810 Federal home looking out onto the water, this simple Eastport inn features rooms with antiques and Asian furnishings; classical music plays in the background. Breakfasts and brunches are elaborate. 26 Boynton St. ☎ 207/853-2907. 3 units (all with shared bathroom). Doubles $80–$90 w/breakfast. No credit cards.

LOBSTAH!

A Primer on Maine's Greatest Export BY KELLY REGAN

SO PLENTIFUL, AND SCORNED, WERE LOBSTERS IN THE 17TH CENTURY that Puritans and Native Americans alike ground them up for use as fertilizer, and they were a staple of the New England prison diet well into the 18th century. How did the homely *Homarus americanus* acquire its culinary cachet? One influential booster was John D. Rockefeller. At his Mount Desert Island compound one evening, at the turn of the 20th century, he was reportedly served a bowl of lobster stew meant for a servant. Wowed, he declared it a staple of his dinner menu. It was a lucky break for lobstermen, who, more recently, contributed $300 million to Maine's economy in 2010.

Lobster Lingo

BUG: What lobstermen call their catch. Lobsters are arthropods, in the same phylum classification as spiders and insects.

CHICK: A lobster weighing 1 to 1½ pounds.

CULL: A lobster with only one claw. Lobsters can spontaneously "amputate" one of their claws to escape perceived danger. Claws, legs, and antennae all grow back.

POT: A lobster trap, typically wire mesh over a wood or plastic frame. The basic design hasn't changed in 150 years; deliberate inefficiency allows small (and smart) lobsters to escape, and a "ghost panel" biodegrades to free a lobster if the trap is lost or forgotten.

SHORT: A lobster smaller than the legal limit for harvesting. It takes 5 to 7 years for a lobster's carapace to reach 3¼ inches, Maine's legal minimum size for harvesting.

TOMALLEY: The green organ inside the carapace is both liver and pancreas, filtering toxins from the ocean. Experts recommend limiting your intake of the tomalley, though it's often used to flavor sauces and stocks.

Myth vs. Fact

LOBSTERS ARE RED. MYTH. Cooking a lobster masks all pigments in the shell except the red (astaxanthin), which is why they turn a fiery shade after being boiled or grilled. Live lobsters are typically brownish-green. Thanks to rare genetic mutations, they may also be white (albino), yellow, symmetrically checkerboarded, and most surprisingly, an intense indigo blue.

LOBSTERS "SCREAM" WHEN YOU PUT THEM IN BOILING WATER. MYTH. Lobsters have no vocal cords. The sound—akin to a tea kettle whistling—is a buildup of steam releasing from underneath the lobster's carapace.

LOBSTERS ARE CANNIBALS. FACT. Lobsters are opportunistic, devouring whatever's nearby—fish, crabs, sea urchins, and even their discarded shells after molting. And when crammed into tanks, they become aggressive and will kill and eat each other if their claws are not banded or pegged beforehand.

LOBSTERS ARE LEFT- OR RIGHT- "HANDED." FACT. One claw is the "crusher" that kills prey; the longer, thinner "ripper" claw tears off meat for consumption. These claws are on different side's depending on the lobster—evidence that individuals exhibit a dominant-claw "preference."

Interior Maine: An Outdoor Adventure

Travelers intent on exploring Maine's coast often ignore northern and western Maine. But there's serious wilderness in places like Baxter State Park and Moosehead Lake, and some of the best hiking on the East Coast along Maine's portion of the Appalachian Trail. While the interior isn't totally wild—logging roads, paper-company plantations, and mill and farm towns see to that—this is the wildest place east of the Mississippi, a place that sometimes recalls the "mossy, moosey" wilds Henry Thoreau wrote about.

> If you time it right, you can see the fall foliage in full color at Baxter State Park.

START Baxter State Park is 200 miles north of Portland. **TRIP LENGTH** 350 miles.

1 ★★ **Baxter State Park.** Maine's premier state park was created in 1931 by Governor Percival Baxter, a heroic figure who set aside big chunks over the next 30 years for future generations to enjoy. The enormous park contains about 180 miles of backcountry hiking trails and incorporates more than 25 backcountry campsites—some accessible only by canoe. Most hikers come intent on seeing or climbing **Mount Katahdin,** but there are dozens of smaller mountains and shorter walks too; simply walking the woods here is a sublime, quiet experience. Consider a day hike up **South Turner Mountain,** with wonderful

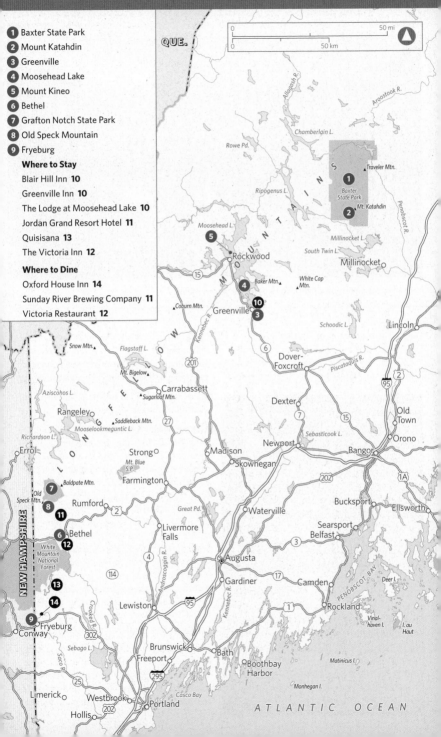

1 Baxter State Park
2 Mount Katahdin
3 Greenville
4 Moosehead Lake
5 Mount Kineo
6 Bethel
7 Grafton Notch State Park
8 Old Speck Mountain
9 Fryeburg

Where to Stay

Blair Hill Inn **10**
Greenville Inn **10**
The Lodge at Moosehead Lake **10**
Jordan Grand Resort Hotel **11**
Quisisana **13**
The Victoria Inn **12**

Where to Dine

Oxford House Inn **14**
Sunday River Brewing Company **11**
Victoria Restaurant **12**

> *You may see more moose than people in parts of interior Maine.*

views: The trail begins at Roaring Brook Campground and takes 3 to 4 hours round-trip. Other hikes begin at South Branch Pond Campground. ***Note:*** They don't accept credit cards within the park. ☉ 6 hr. 64 Balsam Dr., Millinocket. ☎ 207/723-5140. www.baxterstateparkauthority.com. Out-of-state cars $14 per day (Maine cars free) or $39 per calendar year.

Inside the park, bear left onto Main St. and continue 6 miles to the foot of:

❷ ★★★ Mount Katahdin. Maine's highest peak (5,270 ft.) is the northern terminus of the Appalachian Trail, and an ascent of this rugged, glacially scoured mountain is a trip you'll not soon forget. Formed a half-billion (yes, billion) years ago by a slow, grinding collision of ancient continental plates and islands, it's all that's left of a huge underground volcano. Today it's roamed by bears and moose, but plant life is mostly limited to hardy evergreens—the place is simply too cold, windy, and acidic for much else to grow. As for that name? Local native peoples made up a word for "the biggest mountain of them all," Henry David Thoreau wrote a book about it, and the name has stuck ever since. ☉ 2 hr.

Spend the night in the park. On Day 2, exit the park via the south entrance. Turn right onto Old State Rd. (becomes Golden Rd. and then Baxter Park Rd.) and continue 60 miles to Greenville, where you'll spend the night.

Spending the Night in Baxter State Park

The park maintains eight **campgrounds** accessible by car, plus two more that you can only walk into; most of the 10 are open from mid-May to mid-October. Don't count on finding a spot if you just show up without reservations; the park starts processing requests on a first-come, first-served basis in January, and some campers spend a cold night outside headquarters to secure the very best spots. You don't need to do that, though: Call in advance for forms that you can mail in. The cost of camping inside the park ranges from $7 to $30 per site, while a night in a bunkhouse is $11 per person per night; entire cabins can be rented for from $55 to $130 per night. Reservations can be made by mail, in person at the park headquarters, or by phone (but by phone only less than 14 days from arrival). Remember, reservations are required for backcountry camping.

> *Moosehead Lake is a summer tradition for many New Englanders.*

③ Greenville. Once a logging town, now a tourist base, the hamlet of Greenville doesn't offer much in the way of services—but up here, it's the only place you're going to find out-of-state newspapers, equipment rentals, and a decent selection of groceries. It's also blessed with one of the best collections of luxury-resort accommodations in all of New England. (Who knew?) Grab a bite at a local spot such as **Auntie M's,** 13 Lily Bay Rd. (☎ 207/695-2238), or pick up a fly-fishing guide at the **Maine Guide Fly Shop,** 34 Moosehead Lake Rd. (☎ 207/695-2266). Be sure to wander down to Thoreau Park and its info kiosk next to the boat docks, and check out the annual **Thoreau-Wabanaki Trail Festival** (www.nrecmoosehead.org) in mid- to late July, which offers lake cruises and other educational events. ⏱ 1 hr.

Greenville's dock is also the jumping-off point for:

④ ★★★ Moosehead Lake. Thirty-two miles long and 5 miles across at its widest, Moosehead is Maine's biggest lake by far. It's a great destination for hikers, boaters, and canoeists alike. This lake was historically a center of Maine's logging activity, which kept it unspoiled for years. Timber companies still own much of Moosehead's shores, but the state of Maine has also acquired a significant amount, and the 350-mile shoreline mostly consists of unbroken forest. The best thing you can do on

Tackling Katahdin

Hiking Katahdin is not to be taken likely: People have died up here. Allow at least 8 hours for the round-trip, and abandon your plans at once if the weather takes a turn for the worse while you're en route. (Helpfully, the home page of the park's website, www.baxterstateparkauthority.com, includes a direct link to daily weather forecasts.)

The most popular route departs from Roaring Brook Campground. You ascend first to Chimney Pond, set like a jewel in a glacial cirque, then continue to the summit along one of two trails. (The Saddle Trail is more forgiving, the Cathedral Trail more dramatic.) From here, if you have nerves of steel, you can descend via the Knife Edge, a narrow, rocky spine between Baxter Peak and Pamola Peak. (Do not take this trail if you are afraid of heights: The trail is just 2 or 3 feet wide, with a drop of hundreds of feet on either side!) Or simply retrace your steps back to the campground.

> *In addition to gorgeous scenery and great slopes, Sunday River offers early evening skiing on many of its trails.*

the lake is kayak it with a rental from **North-woods Outfiftters,** 5 Lily Bay Rd. (☎ 866/223-1380; www.maineoutfitter.com); rentals cost $25 to $35 per day. Failing that, take a cruise with **Katahdin Cruises** (mid-May to mid-Oct) at the docks in Greenville (☎ 207/695-2716; www.katahdincruises.com). ⏱ 3 hr.

From Greenville, take Rte. 6/15 20 miles west to Rockwood. Bear right on Village Rd., and park by the waterfront.

Roughing It on Moosehead

There are plenty of luxe resorts on and around Moosehead, but you can also camp right on this big, wild lake's shores. Greenville's **Lily Bay State Park,** 13 Myrle's Way (☎ 207/695-2700), is one of the primo places in Maine to pitch a tent. All tent sites in the park are quiet and woodsy-feeling, but if at all possible, try to reserve one of the cherished lakeside spots. You'll be able to fish, boat, or kayak the lake just steps from your sleeping bag. Sites cost $24 per night from mid-May to mid-October; $18 to $24 the rest of the year.

⑤ ★★ **Mount Kineo.** One of the best hikes in the Moosehead region is up the massive, broad cliff that rises from the lake's shores. Near the town of Rockwood, look for signs advertising shuttles across the lake to Kineo from the town landing. Prices vary, but it's usually quite inexpensive for a lift. Once across, explore the grounds of the former Kineo Mountain House (the huge 500-room hotel was demolished in 1938; the big building you see today was just the servants' quarters). Then cut across the golf course and follow the shoreline to a trail that leads to the 1,800-foot summit. Views from the cliffs are dazzling, but they might give you vertigo if you don't like heights. If you like steep vertical drop-offs, though, continue to the old fire tower, which you can climb for a hawk's-eye view that's even more spine-tingling—during peak foliage season, it's incredible. ⏱ 2 hr.

Return to Greenville. On Day 3, take Rte. 6/15 20 miles east to Rte. 16, and go 40 miles south. Pick up Rte. 23 west and go 11 miles to Rte. 27 south. Continue 12 miles to Rte. 2, which you'll take 50 miles west to:

6 ★ **Bethel.** The village of Bethel has a lot going for it: lovely whitewashed Colonial architecture, great natural surrounds (including mountains and river), and an agreeable pace of life. The **Sunday River ski resort** (www.sundayriver.com) is the prime draw in winter, but you can also mountain-bike the mountain, hike any of numerous hills in the area, or run rivers with the folks at **Bethel Outdoor Adventure** on Rte. 2 just outside the town center (☎ 207/824-4224 or 866/533-3607; www.betheloutdooradventure.com) in summer and fall. Stock up on snacks and craft beers at the great little **Good Food Store** (☎ 207/824-3754; www.goodfoodbethel.com) on Rte. 26, a combination natural foods store/gourmet grocer. ⏱ 2 hr.

From downtown Bethel take Rte. 2 north 6 miles to Rte. 26; take a left and go 9 miles north to:

7 ★★ **Grafton Notch State Park.** If Baxter is king of Maine's state parks, Grafton Notch is the successful little brother. We love this place: It's big, wild, inexpensive, and full of unexpected treats. If you've got your walking shoes on, head for **Old Speck Mountain;** if not, park and peer down at gorgelike **Screw Auger Falls.** ⏱ 1 hr. 1941 Bear River Rd., Newry. ☎ 207/824-2912. Mid-May to mid-Oct $3 adults, $1.50 kids 11 & under; rest of the year $1.50 adults, free for kids.

On the left side of Rte. 26, traveling north, is the parking area for:

8 ★★ **Old Speck Mountain.** At 4,170 feet, Old Speck is (surprisingly) Maine's third-highest peak. Even weekend walkers can tackle this hike. Look for the well-signed parking lot where Rte. 26 intersects the trail to the state park; park, pay, strap on boots (some parts are muddy), and join the trail. In just 500 feet, you'll intersect the **Eyebrow Trail**—a side trail ascending an 800-foot cliff called **The Eyebrow.** (Don't go this way it if you're afraid of heights.) Otherwise, stay on the main trail and climb past several great overlooks, over rushing streams and past mild cascades, into increasing views of the valley and its foliage. The summit is wooded, so there are no views from the top, but you can keep walking down into a bowl containing **Old Speck Lake.** There's also

another excellent hike directly across Rte. 26: up **Baldpate Mountain,** with its exposed cliffs and views all the way to Katahdin. (Though it looks smaller, Baldpate's summit is only 400 feet lower than Old Speck's.) The trail picks up right across the highway. ⏱ 2 hr.

From the park, backtrack to Bethel, then continue south on Rte. 5 for 35 miles to Fryeburg, where you'll spend the night.

9 ★ **Fryeburg.** Like Bethel, Fryeburg is also full of historic buildings and tales, and it also borders one of the most pristine, appealing smaller lakes in Maine, **Kezar Lake.** The 18th-century prep school **Fryeburg Academy** at 745 Main St. is worth a look for its made-from-local-brick architecture and its history—it was one of the first schools in New England to accept women. The **Oxford House Inn,** 538 Main St. (☎ 800/261-7206 or 207/935-3442; www.oxfordhouseinn.com) boasts the best kitchen in town, with a Culinary Institute–trained chef and eclectic New American menu items. ⏱ 1 hr.

Sampling the A.T.

En route to Mount Katahdin, the ★★★ **Appalachian Trail** passes through two amazing stretches you should sample if you can. Just prior to ascending Katahdin, the A.T. crosses the "100-Mile Wilderness," a remote stretch where the trail crosses few roads and no settlements. It's a place of loons and moose.

Then, at the Maine/New Hampshire state line, the trail crosses the Mahoosuc Range, just northwest of Bethel. (This is the stretch you can sample in Grafton Notch State Park, see left) Many who have hiked the entire 2,000-mile trail say this stretch is both the most demanding and the most strangely beautiful. Wear good boots: There are sheer, rocky ascents and rocky descents. And bring water: It's hard to find along this part of the trail in summer. Still, it's worth the effort for the views and the unrivaled sense of remoteness. Get lots more info on the A.T.'s Maine sections from the **Appalachian Trail Conference** (☎ 304/535-6331; www.appalachianantrail.org).

Where to Stay & Dine

> Take a break and try some local brews on the patio at Sunday River Brewing Company.

★★★ Blair Hill Inn GREENVILLE

A classy Queen Anne mansion on a hilltop with unbelievable views of Moosehead Lake. Inside, it's over the top: Oriental carpets, deer-antler lamps, fireplaces, and deep soaking tubs. The dining room serves five-course dinners, some of northern New England's best. 351 Lily Bay Rd. ☎ 207/695-0224. www.blairhill.com. 8 units. Doubles $300–$495 w/ breakfast. DISC, MC, V. Closed Nov & Apr. Kids 10 & over welcome.

★★★ Greenville Inn GREENVILLE

Everything's sumptuous at the Queen Anne–style lumber baron's home near Greenville's commercial district, with lots of cherry and mahogany woods and a lovely stained-glass window. Six simple cottages sleep four each, while three suites are the height of luxury. Don't miss the bar and dining room. Norris St. (2nd right off Lily Bay Rd.). ☎ 888/695-6000. www.greenvilleinn.com. 14 units. Doubles $185–$265, suites $215–$450, cottage $195–$265, all w/breakfast. DISC, MC, V. Kids 8 & over welcome.

★ kids Jordan Grand Resort Hotel BETHEL

Part of the Sunday River ski resort. Rooms are simply furnished in condo style, most with balconies and/or washers and dryers. Two hotel restaurants serve decent food, though parking is inconveniently distant—pay for valet. Sunday River Rd. ☎ 800/543-2754 or 207/824-5000. www.sundayriver.com. 195 units. Dec–Feb doubles $140–$210, suites $275–$460; Mar–Nov doubles $119, suites $235. AE, DC, DISC, MC, V.

Asia, and the American Southwest—from PEI mussels in wine to steak frites to decadent lobster mac-and-cheese to ale-braised bison ribs. 538 Main St. ☎ 800/261-7206 or 207/935-3442. www.oxfordhouseinn.com. Entrees $26–$32. AE, MC, V. Dinner Wed–Mon.

★★ Quisisana CENTER LOVELL

The views across Kezar Lake to the White Mountains are spectacular, but the real ear-opener is the music: Nearly the entire staff consists of students recruited from conservatories. The cabins are rugged and summer-campy; some have private bathrooms. Pleasant Point Rd. (off Rte. 5 just south of village market). ☎ 207/925-3500. www.quisisanaresort.com. 54 units, some w/shared bathroom. Mid-June to Aug doubles $320–$390 w/all meals; cottages $370–$470 w/all meals. 1-week stay required in most units. $600 prebooking deposit required. No credit cards. Closed Sept to mid-June.

★ Sunday River Brewing Company BETHEL

BREWPUB A good choice for quaffing locally brewed ales and porters. The motto? "Eat Food. Drink Beer. Have Fun." That about says it. Come early; it gets louder when bands take the stage. 29 Sunday River Rd. (at Rte. 2). ☎ 207/824-4253. www.sundayriverbrewpub.com. Entrees $8–$16. AE, MC, V. Lunch & dinner daily.

★★ The Victoria Inn BETHEL

This flowery inn with canopy beds and hand-made duvet covers sits on Bethel's main drag. The best rooms are four loft-style rooms in the attached carriage house, each with a gas fire-place, Jacuzzi, and soaring ceilings revealing original beams. 32 Main St.. ☎ 888/774-1235 or 207/824-8060. www.thevictoria-inn.com. 15 units. Doubles $109–$179 w/breakfast; suites $149–$309 w/breakfast. 2-night minimum stay Sat–Sun & holidays. AE, MC, V.

★ Victoria Restaurant BETHEL CONTINENTAL

Inside the inn of the same name, this place serves lobster in champagne butter sauce, grilled rib-eyes, filet mignon, grilled rack of lamb, and the like. Much better than you'd expect in a small town. 32 Main St.. ☎ 888/774-1235 or 207/824-8060. www.thevictoria-inn.com. Entrees $18–$28. MC, V. Dinner Mon–Sat.

★★ The Lodge at Moosehead Lake GREENVILLE

Luxury *and* woodsiness. Beds were carved by a local artist, and each room is themed to wildlife, and includes Adirondack-style stick furnishings, wingback chairs, antique English end tables, and Jacuzzis. Luxurious suites in the carriage house have swinging beds suspended from ceilings by logging chains, plus chandeliers, French doors, and whirlpools made of river stones. 368 Lily Bay Rd. ☎ 800/825-6977 or 207/695-4400. www.lodgeatmooseheadlake.com. 9 units. Doubles $250–$375 w/breakfast; suites $395–$680 w/breakfast. AE, MC, V. Kids 14 & over welcome.

★★ Oxford House Inn FRYEBURG NEW AMERICAN

High cuisine in western Maine? Yep. Meals here draw on influences from France,

Acadia National Park

Acadia, put simply, is one of America's most scenic national parks; it's a must-see on any extended trip to Maine. Carved by glaciers some 18,000 years ago, this craggy landscape promises one outstanding photo opportunity after another, from dramatic vistas (ocean cliffs falling away to the sea, columns of sea spray) to tranquil sights (horses in a stable). You can hit the highlights, which I've featured below, in just a day, but I strongly suggest you give this place a bit more time. There are plenty of great hikes, bike rides, and sites to keep your time well filled.

> When you get the timing right, Thunder Hole offers spectacular plumes of sea foam charging up the rocks at you.

START Bar Harbor is 175 miles northeast of Portland. **TRIP LENGTH** 50 miles.

Entering the Park. Acadia collects entry fees May through October (the rest of the year, entry is free) at a "tollgate" within the park boundaries. It's located on the Park Loop Road, just north of the parking lot for Sand Beach. You can save time waiting in line here by purchasing an entry badge on your way into town at park headquarters or on Bar Harbor's Village Green. At press time, park entry cost $5 per person, good for 7 consecutive days of park use, but families may find it more economical to purchase a weekly pass ($20; covers one vehicle and all occupants for 7 days) or an annual pass ($40; one vehicle for 1 year). Eagle Lake Rd. (Rte. 233). ☎ 207/288-3338. www.nps.gov/acad. Daily 8am–4:30pm.

1 Acadia Park Headquarters
2 Abbe Museum
3 Sand Beach
4 Thunder Hole
5 Jordan Pond
6 Jordan Pond House
7 Cadillac Mountain

1 Acadia Park Headquarters. Of the island's three visitor information centers, this one's the quietest and biggest. Set in a wooded, quiet clearing on a main road, the year-round center is full of information and helpful rangers. Eagle Lake Rd. (Rte. 233). ☎ 207/288-3338. www.nps. gov/acad. Daily 8am-4:30pm.

2 ★ Abbe Museum. This is the original Abbe Museum, before the directors decided to open a bigger, better version in downtown Bar Harbor (p. 487, 4). But it's worth a quick look if you don't mind paying the entry fee. The building—behind the nature center and up a hill—features a small but decent collection of Native American artifacts. A ticket here gets you a $3 discount at the downtown museum.

🕐 15 min. Park Loop Rd. ☎ 207/288-3519. www. abbemuseum.org. Late May to early Oct daily 9am-4pm. $3 adults, $1 kids 6-15.

3 ★★ Sand Beach. This small crescent beach is the only sand beach of substance on the island, and it's attractive, set between two rocky points. Views of the sea and the island's cliffs are stupendous, and there are clean bathrooms and changing facilities, plus a footpath to Thunder Hole and a hike rising above the shore. The strand and parking lot get packed on sunny summer weekends. The water's cold, though: Don't plan on swimming or wading for long unless you've got the constitution of a polar bear. Look for rafts of common eider (sometimes called eider ducks) in summer.

4 ★★★ **Thunder Hole.** This shallow, oceanside cavern draws hordes in summer. The pounding waves press into the cave, then shoot up in impressive geysers—*if* the ocean and tidal conditions are right. If the ocean is quiet, skip this stop or just snap a quick photo. When the seas are rough, though, this is a must-see; rangers say the best viewing time is 3 hours before high tide (check tide charts in town or at park headquarters). ⏱ 30 min.

5 ★ **Jordan Pond.** A small, lovely oval of water among forested hills, Jordan Pond is often photographed and easily hiked. A 3-mile loop follows the woods along the pond's shoreline, and a network of carriage roads converge at the pond. The view of the Bubble Mountains is superb.

6 🍽 ★★★ **Jordan Pond House.** There aren't any places to eat in the park, with the exception of Jordan Pond House at the tip of Jordan Pond, looking north toward the Bubbles. Afternoon tea with popovers and jam is a hallowed tradition here, but they also serve meaty dinners of prime rib, lobster, pasta, and stew. The restaurant is open from mid-May to late October for lunch and dinner daily. ☎ 207/276-3316. www.jordanpond.com. $$–$$$.

Two-Wheeling Acadia

Acadia's 57 miles of carriage roads are among its most extraordinary treasures. Originally built for horse-drawn carriages, they're also ideal for cruising on a mountain bike—which is both allowed and encouraged (except in a few spots where the roads cross private land). Park near Jordan Pond, then plumb the tree-shrouded lanes, admiring the stone work on the many bridges you pass over and under. The roads are superbly restored and maintained, with wide, hard-packed surfaces, gentle grades, and good signage. Rent wheels in Bar Harbor: **Acadia Bike,** 48 Cottage St. (☎ 207/288-9605 or 800/526-8615), offers the best choice, with bikes costing about $20 per day or $100 per week. Access points are at Rte. 3 (east of Seal Harbor), Jordan Pond, Bubble Pond, and Eagle Lake (www.nps.gov/acad/planyourvisit/maps.htm).

7 ★★★ **Cadillac Mountain.** Hordes converge atop this mountain at sunrise, the highest peak on the Atlantic coast between Canada and Brazil, because it's the first piece of U.S. soil touched by the sun's rays at daybreak. The parking lot fills early with tourists snapping shots on summer mornings. Views of Frenchman Bay and its islands are predictably spectacular in all directions. In September, rangers conduct a hawk watch here—if you're interested in catching a glimpse of raptors in flight, this is the place to do it.

Pitching a Tent in Paradise

There are no inns or hotels in the wild interior sections of this park. However, the National Parks Service does maintain two seasonal campgrounds, Blackwoods and Seawall. Both are simplistic and bucolic; don't expect lots of services, and don't expect your campsite to be tucked right at the base of Cadillac Mountain or on the ocean. Still, they're convenient, inexpensive, and family-friendly. **Blackwoods** is on Rte. 3, 5 miles south of Bar Harbor (☎ 877/444-6777 or 207/288-3274; www.recreation.gov); **Seawall** is on Rte. 102A, 4 miles south of Southwest Harbor (☎ 207/244-3600).

Hiking Acadia

Acadia is chock-full of great opportunities to commune with nature, from hikes along oceanside cliffs to meandering strolls through meadows and foothills. We've chosen a selection of our favorite hikes here; they range from easy walks almost anyone can manage to ladderlike climbs only experts should tackle.

★★ **Acadia Mountain** isn't a long walk, but it gets strenuous in spots, especially the final section. With time for lingering, this 2½-mile loop hike could be a half-day outing. From the trail head (3 miles south of Somesville on Rte. 102), you walk east through mixed forests, then begin a climb over ledges. The eastern peak has better views; look for clearings that open up unexpected vistas. Descend via the fire road.

★★ **The Bubbles,** at the northern end of Jordan Pond, are a pair of twin mounds. A trail heads up through mixed woods, then along ledges until you're presented with a choice: north Bubble or south. The southern Bubble has a better view. It's surprising how quickly you get to the top, with only a bit of huffing and puffing required. Views are amazing, not only of the pond but also of the ocean beyond. The whole thing takes about 1½ hours.

★★★ **Cadillac Mountain** (pictured) is the island's tallest. You can drive nearly to its 1,500-foot summit and walk a half-mile to the top, but serious hikers enjoy trying the trails along its flanks. The 4½-mile North Ridge trail (trail head on Cadillac Summit Rd.) is the shortest, easiest (but not easy), and most scenic of the options. The 7-mile South Ridge Trail (trail head on Rte. 3/Loop Rd., 300 ft. south of Blackwoods Campground) is best left to expert hikers. Can be done in a half day.

★ **Day Mountain,** a moderate 2½-mile hike, begins just west of Otter Creek (on the north side of Rte. 3, 1 mile east of Seal Harbor); the first stretches are fairly bland. But the trail soon does a dance with the island's carriage roads, where you'll see cyclists and even the occasional horse-drawn carriage or wedding party. The final climb takes you to an open, safe summit with views south of the Cranberry Islands. Can be done in 2 hours.

kids **Flying Mountain,** an easy-to-moderate hike, is great for birders. A half-hour walk (the trail head starts on Rte. 102) through dense fir trees and over boulders and twisted roots brings you up to a skinny ridge with views along Somes Sound to Northeast and Southwest harbors. Birds use the fjord as a flyway, so peregrine falcons are sometimes seen (which can cause the trail to be closed). Bring binoculars. Budget 1½ hours total.

Bar Harbor & Mount Desert Island

Bar Harbor is a summer-resort town, pure and simple; it has been that way almost since the moment city folks discovered the place in the 19th century. While it does get a bit crowded with buses and gawkers at times, it's a nice place to call home base—lots of gift shops, inns, views, and restaurants. Mount Desert Island is much more than Bar Harbor, though: As you circle the island, tick off quaint villages, hidden seaside mansions, hikes, lobster shacks, beaches, and gardens. Take 3 days for this tour.

> *Cottage Street in Bar Harbor is an amalgam of bars, tee-shirt shops, pizza parlors, hardware stores, and diners.*

START Bar Harbor is 155 miles northeast of Portland.

1 ★ Agamont Park. The best water views in town are from the foot of Main Street, at grassy Agamont Park. This popular green lawn with a gazebo overlooks not only the town pier, but also the Bar Harbor Inn (p. 492) and the panorama of Frenchman Bay. Best of all, the park is just steps from dozens of restaurants, bars, and gift shops. ⏱ 45 min. Main St. at West St. & Newport Dr.

2 ★★ Shore Path. It's only half a mile long, but Bar Harbor's winding walking trail follows the shoreline and passes in front of elegant summer homes (usually known around here as "cottages" despite their size, and some converted to inns). It's one of the best ways to get a quick insider's peek at the town's period

> *The bay views and lawns of Bar Harbor's Agamont Park are free for all to enjoy.*

architecture. ⏱ 30 min. Accessed from the lawn of Bar Harbor Inn, Newport Dr.

❸ ★★ **Main Street.** If Cottage Street is the commercial hub of this town, Main Street is its tourist hub. You can't throw a stone without hitting at least five restaurants, ice-cream shops like **Mount Desert Ice Cream,** 7 Firefly Lane (☎ 207/460-5515), or **Ben and Bill's,** 66 Main St. (☎ 207/288-3821); groceries like **Alternative—A Community Market,** 16 Mount Desert St. (☎ 207/288-8225); and souvenir shops. It's the one essential street to see when in town. ⏱ 30 min.

❹ ★ kids **Abbe Museum.** Since 2001, this has been the main site for the Abbe Museum, which also has a branch in Acadia National Park (p. 483, ❷). This is bigger and better than that one, showcasing a world-class collection of Native American crafts (check out the baskets) and artifacts. Highlights include a glass-walled section where visitors can watch archaeologists curating and preserving recently recovered items. Changing exhibits and videos mostly focus on the history and culture

> *The Abbe Museum in downtown Bar Harbor features the most extensive Native American holdings in New England.*

of tribes that lived in Maine and New England. ⏱ 45 min. 26 Mount Desert St. ☎ 207/288-3519. www.abbemuseum.org. $6 adults; $2 children 6–15. Late May to early Nov daily 10am–5pm; mid-Nov to Dec & Feb to mid-May Thurs–Sat 10am–4pm; closed Jan.

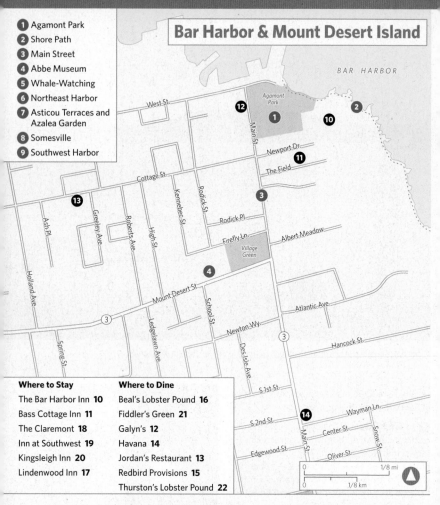

1 Agamont Park
2 Shore Path
3 Main Street
4 Abbe Museum
5 Whale-Watching
6 Northeast Harbor
7 Asticou Terraces and Azalea Garden
8 Somesville
9 Southwest Harbor

Bar Harbor & Mount Desert Island

BAR HARBOR

Agamont Park

West St.

Main St.

Newport Dr.

The Field

Cottage St.

Kennebec St.

Rodick St.

Rodick Pl.

Firefly Ln.

Albert Meadow

Village Green

Ash Pl.

Greeley Ave.

Roberts Ave.

High St.

Holland Ave.

Mount Desert St.

School St.

Atlantic Ave.

Spring St.

Ledgelawn Ave.

Newton Wy.

Hancock St.

Des Isle Ave.

S. 1st St.

Where to Stay

The Bar Harbor Inn **10**
Bass Cottage Inn **11**
The Claremont **18**
Inn at Southwest **19**
Kingsleigh Inn **20**
Lindenwood Inn **17**

Where to Dine

Beal's Lobster Pound **16**
Fiddler's Green **21**
Galyn's **12**
Havana **14**
Jordan's Restaurant **13**
Redbird Provisions **15**
Thurston's Lobster Pound **22**

S. 2nd St.

Wayman Ln.

Center St.

Snow St.

Main St.

Edgewood St.

Oliver St.

0   1/8 mi
0   1/8 km

> Bar Harbor's hidden Shore Path offers superlative views of the open sea, islands, and gorgeous summer homes.

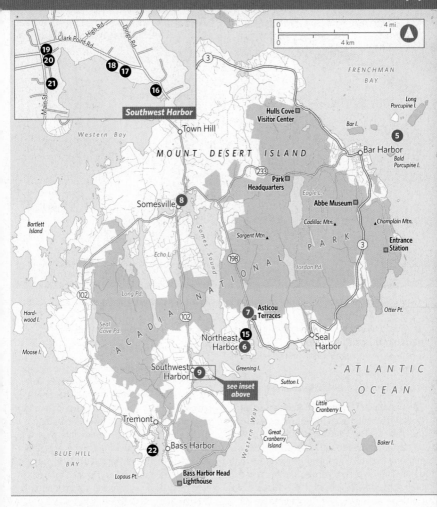

Southwest Harbor

5 ★★★ **Cruising with Bar Harbor Whale Watch Company.** Bar Harbor is an excellent base for whale-watching tours. Operators offer excursions in search of humpbacks, finbacks, minkes, and the infrequently seen endangered right whale. Along the way, you may see bottlenose dolphins, northern gannets, and other residents of Maine's summer waters. These days, the **Bar Harbor Whale Watch Company** seems to hold the monopoly on these excursions. No matter, as they run speedy excursion boats that can hold up to 200 passengers in their heated cabins. The proprietors guarantee sightings or a free ticket to try again. They also run tours to visit a puffin colony just off the coast. (Tours are

$27 to $56 for adults, $16 to $28 kids.) ⏲ Minimum 3 hr. 1 West St. ☎ 888/942-5374 or 207/288-2386; www.whalesrus.com.

Take Rte. 3 through Bar Harbor and continue 12 miles southwest (if you reach the Asticou Hotel, you've gone a half-mile too far) until you reach the sign on the right for:

6 ★★ **Northeast Harbor.** On the tip of the eastern lobe of Mount Desert Island is the staid, prosperous little village. It consists of elegant cottages plus one short main street and a marina. There's a bakery, an excellent small-town grocer, art and craft galleries, the great Redbird Provisions restaurant

> *Some of the back roads in Northeast Harbor get very up close and personal with the sea.*

(p. 493), a tourist information kiosk—even a laundromat for fishermen on shore leave. This is small-town coastal Maine at its best. ⏱ 2 hr. See p. 461, ⑭.

A few hundred yards farther along Rte. 3, is:

⑦ ★★ Asticou Terraces and Azalea Garden. One of the best places for enjoying views of the harbor is from these quiet terraces. Park on the left, cross the road (away from the water), and then hike the magnificent gravel path uphill. There's a third garden another few hundred yards down the road: The Asticou Azalea Garden—run by the same organization—is a groomed, Japanese-style wonder of water and plant life. ⏱ 45 min. Peabody Rd. (Rte. 3), Northeast Harbor. www.gardenpreserve.org. ☎ 207/276-3727. May–Oct daily dawn–dusk. Admission free; donations requested.

Backtrack to Rte. 198 and turn north, continuing 6 miles to Rte. 102; turn left. In ½ mile arrive in the town of:

⑧ Somesville. Believed to be the oldest settlement on Mount Desert Island, Somesville is genteel, lovely, and tiny. There's a bookstore, a town hall, a church, a dock with water views, a small repertory theater, and beautiful summer mansions. Yet the town is most famous for the whitewashed, curving **Somesville Bridge,** visible from the main road. ⏱ 15 min.

Continue south 6 miles on Rte. 102 to:

⑨ ★★ Southwest Harbor. Across the sound from Northeast Harbor, Southwest is a fishing town that went upscale, then became a culinary mecca. There are more good inns and restaurants here than anywhere else on the island save Bar Harbor, remarkable given the size of the town. Fishermen and boatbuilders still live here, too, giving the place an authentic feel. There's also a bakery, grocer, Internet cafe, ferry dock, and pocket waterfront park. ⏱ 1½ hr. See p. 462, ⑰.

A Rainy Day Alternative

When the weather's bad, the **Criterion Theatre,** 35 Cottage St. (☎ 207/288-3441; www.criteriontheater.com), becomes one of downtown Bar Harbor's best attractions. Built in the 1930s in classic Art Deco style, this 877-seat house shows mostly first-run movies in summer (but also classics like *It's a Wonderful Life*). The interiors alone are worth the price of a ticket, and while it costs extra, try to sit in the more plush seating upstairs in the balcony.

> Somesville's small, arched bridge is a must-stop for photography buffs no matter the season.

Where to Stay

> *The Lindenwood Inn's Australian owner has complemented his antique-filled inn with a wonderful little outdoor pool.*

★★ **The Bar Harbor Inn** BAR HARBOR
Right next to Agamont Park (p. 486, **1**), this inn mixes traditional styling with contemporary touches. Some units have spectacular bay views, and many have private balconies. There's also a newish spa with Vichy showers. Newport Dr. ☎ 800/248-3351 or 207/288-3351. www.barharborinn.com. 153 units. Doubles mid-Mar to Nov $79–$379 w/breakfast. AE, DISC, MC, V. Closed Dec to mid-Mar.

★★ **Bass Cottage Inn** BAR HARBOR
High marks for friendliness, service, luxe rooms, and proximity to the water. Units are decked out in cast-iron beds, woodstoves, silk canopies, love seats, armoires, and the like; some have Jacuzzis and/or views. 14 The Field. ☎ 866/782-9224 or 207/288-1234. www.basscottage.com. 10 units. Doubles $185–$370 w/breakfast. 2-night stay required on weekends. AE, MC, V. Closed late Oct to mid-May. No kids 11 & under.

★★ **The Claremont** SOUTHWEST HARBOR
An old New England sort of summer resort, the Claremont has retained its grace and quality level. Guest rooms are bright and airy, and there are 14 cottages on the property with fireplaces and kitchenettes. Clark Point Rd. ☎ 800/244-5036. www.theclaremonthotel.com. 44 units. Doubles May to mid-Oct $155–$335 w/breakfast. MC, V.

★ **Inn at Southwest** SOUTHWEST HARBOR
There's a late-19th-century feel to this mansard-roofed Victorian home, which is spare rather than frilly. All guest rooms are named for Maine lighthouses and outfitted simply—some with touches like sleigh beds and rosewood sofas. 371 Main St. ☎ 207/244-3835. www.innatsouthwest.com. 7 units. Doubles $105–$185 w/breakfast. DISC, MC, V. Closed Nov to late Apr.

★★ **Kingsleigh Inn** SOUTHWEST HARBOR
All rooms here are equipped with sound machines, wine glasses, and robes; the penthouse suite has great sea views and a telescope to see them with. 373 Main St. ☎ 207/244-5302. www.kingsleighinn.com. 8 units. Doubles $110–$195 w/breakfast. AE, MC, V. Closed Nov–Mar. Kids 13 & over welcome.

★★ **Lindenwood Inn** SOUTHWEST HARBOR
This inn features a striking interior decor in a captain's house near the harbor. Most units have balconies and plenty of windows; some have fireplaces, French doors, and/or private porches or decks. The heated in-ground pool is nice. 118 Clark Point Rd. ☎ 800/307-5335 or 207/244-5335. www.lindenwoodinn.com. 8 units. Doubles $95–$215 w/breakfast. MC, V.

Where to Dine

★★ kids Beal's Lobster Pound SOUTHWEST HARBOR LOBSTER

Some say Beal's is the best lobster shack in Maine. It's certainly got the right feel: creaky picnic tables on a plain concrete pier next to a Coast Guard base. Pick out a lobster from the tank. 182 Clark Point Rd. ☎ 207/244-7178 or 244-3202. www.bealslobster.com. Lobsters market priced. AE, DISC, MC, V. Mid-May to mid-Oct breakfast, lunch & dinner daily.

★★★ Fiddlers' Green SOUTHWEST HARBOR NEW AMERICAN

Island native chef Derek Wilbur's bistro is a big hit, from the creative lobster interpretations ("Ocean with Cow") to small plates of Thai-curried shrimp, fried catfish, grilled merguez, and baby back ribs. 411 Main St.. ☎ 207/244-9416. www.fiddlersgreen restaurant.com. Entrees $16–$32. AE, DISC, MC, V. Late May to late Oct dinner Tues–Sun.

★★ Galyn's BAR HARBOR SEAFOOD

Charming, unassuming Galyn's gets seafood right, from blackened and grilled Cajun shrimp to daily fish specials and seafood stews. Finish with real Indian pudding or the cappuccino sundae. A little streetside deck faces Agamont Park (p. 486, ❶) and the bay. 17 Main St. ☎ 207/288-9706. www.galynsbarharbor.com. Entrees $7–$31. AE, MC, V. Lunch & dinner daily.

★★ Havana BAR HARBOR LATIN

A menu inspired by Latino fare, with New American twists: crab cakes, duck empanadas, fig-and-blue-cheese tarts, beef and pork skewers dusted with cinnamon and vanilla. Desserts are creamy, sweet, and good. 318 Main St. ☎ 207/288-2822. www.havanamaine.com. Entrees $24–$32. AE, DC, DISC, MC, V. Dinner daily.

Jordan's Restaurant BAR HARBOR DINER

A slice of the "real" Bar Harbor, with grilled cheese sandwiches, omelets, and huge pancakes made with plenty of local blueberries. 80 Cottage St. ☎ 207/288-3586. Entrees $3–$13. MC, V. Mar–Feb breakfast & lunch daily.

★★ Redbird Provisions NORTHEAST HARBOR CONTINENTAL/SEAFOOD

You'll find local seafood with Asian, French, and Italian

> The fusion menu at Bar Harbor's Havana melds Latin American cuisine with New England-style New American fare.

accents, including trout salade niçoise or organic salmon with white bean ragout and figs, on Northeast Harbor's main street. The small, porchside outdoor dining space is nice in warm weather. 11 Sea St. ☎ 207/276-3006. www.redbirdprovisions.com. Entrees $9–$34. DISC, MC, V. Late Oct to late May Tues–Sat lunch & dinner, Sun dinner only.

★★ Thurston's Lobster Pound BERNARD LOBSTER

Great views of Bass Harbor plus lobster dinners, complete with corn on the cob? Sign us up. Eat either upstairs or down—both are convivial. Steamboat Wharf Rd. (on the waterfront). ☎ 207/244-7600. Lobsters market priced. MC, V. Late May to early Oct lunch & dinner daily.

Portland

Portland is often called one of the best small cities in America, and I can't disagree. The Old Port district burned flat twice but you'll still find fish markets, salty breezes, cobblestones, souvenir shops, ferries, gallons of coffee, a healthy vitality, and lots of brick architecture there. The West End, a mile west of the waterfront, offers graceful homes and parks; ascend gentle Munjoy Hill, just uphill from the Old Port, for the best sea views. You can walk the first three stops of this tour; you may need a car to see the rest. Plan on spending 1 to 2 days here.

> You'd have to be a bird to get a better view of Portland than from the top of Portland Observatory.

START Junction of Free, High, and Congress sts. Portland is 100 miles north of Boston.

❶ ★★★ **Portland Museum of Art.** This modern-looking, brick-faced museum contains one of New England's finest art collections. Holdings are particularly strong in American artists with Maine connections (Homer, Wyeth, Hopper), but there are also rooms of Early American furniture and crafts and a section on the likes of Renoir, Degas, and Picasso. Do not miss the adjacent McLellan House and its Sweat Galleries—they hold the best art.

🕐 2 hr. 7 Congress Sq. (Congress & High sts.). ☎ 207/775-6148. www.portlandmuseum.org. $10 adults, $8 students & seniors, $4 kids 6–17, free for kids 5 & under, free for everyone Fri 5–9pm. Tues–Sun 10am–5pm, Fri 10am–9pm; late May to mid-Oct also Mon 10am–5pm. Guided tours daily at 2pm.

❷ ★ **kids Children's Museum of Maine.** The centerpiece exhibit in Portland's excellent kids' museum is a camera obscura, a room-sized "camera" on the top floor. Children gather around a white table in a dark room,

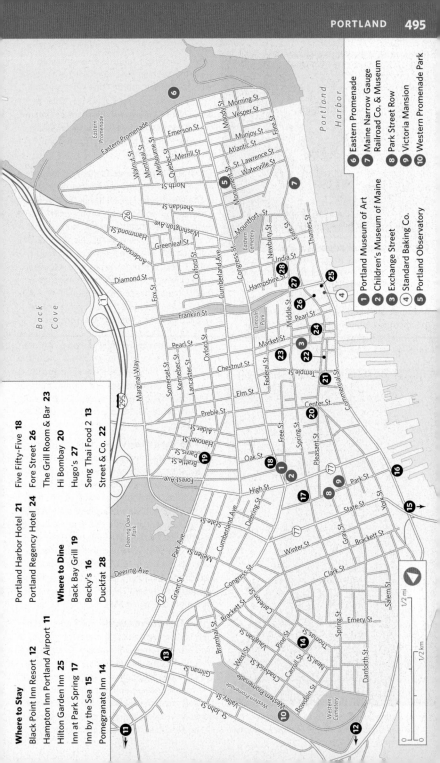

Where to Stay

Black Point Inn Resort **12**
Hampton Inn Portland Airport **11**
Hilton Garden Inn **25**
Inn at Park Spring **17**
Inn by the Sea **15**
Pomegranate Inn **14**
Portland Harbor Hotel **21**
Portland Regency Hotel **24**

Where to Dine

Back Bay Grill **19**
Becky's **16**
Duckfat **28**
Five Fifty-Five **18**
Fore Street **26**
The Grill Room & Bar **23**
Hi Bombay **20**
Hugo's **27**
Seng Thai Food 2 **13**
Street & Co. **22**

6 Eastern Promenade
7 Maine Narrow Gauge
Railroad Co. & Museum
8 Park Street Row
9 Victoria Mansion
10 Western Promenade Park

1 Portland Museum of Art
2 Children's Museum of Maine
3 Exchange Street
4 Standard Baking Co.
5 Portland Observatory

> *N.C. Wyeth's* Dark Harbor Fishermen *(1943) is but one of countless Maine-related treasures in the Portland Museum of Art.*

where they see magically projected images that include cars driving on city streets, boats plying the harbor, and seagulls flapping by. This never fails to enthrall, providing a memorable lesson in the workings of lenses. Other

attractions might range from a simulated supermarket checkout counter to a firehouse pole or a "space shuttle" that kids can pilot from a mocked-up cockpit. ⏱ 1 hr. 142 Free St. ☎ 207/828-1234. www.childrensmuseumofme. org. $8 per person, free for kids under 1. Apr–Nov Mon–Sat 10am–5pm, Sun noon–5pm. Closed Mon Nov–Apr.

❸ ★★ Exchange Street. Perhaps no street encapsulates modern-day Portland more than Exchange Street, even if it has become somewhat overrun with touristy shops, galleries, and restaurants. Running 4 short blocks downhill to bustling, beery Fore Street, this street physically and psychologically connects downtown to the Old Port. It's the go-to place for a souvenir, piece of jewelry, cup of gourmet coffee, or fancy meal. (You might see a few local skateboarders practicing moves, too; this isn't *only* a tourist district.) ⏱ 1¼ hr. Congress St. to Fore St.

④ 🍴 ★ Standard Baking Company. Across from the ferry terminal, this is one of the best little bakeries in New England. Order sticky buns (with or without pecans), focaccia, brioches, or a cookie and a cup of coffee. 75 Commercial St. ☎ 207/773-2112. $.

❺ ★ Portland Observatory. One of the best bird's-eye views on Casco Bay is from the top of this shaggy, shingled observatory, which was originally a ship-signaling tower—a sort of hilltop, landlocked lighthouse—when it was built in 1807. The exhibits within give a taste of local history, but everyone comes for the views from that tiny deck up top. ⏱ 45 min. 138 Congress St. ☎ 207/774-5561. www.portlandlandmarks.org. $7 adults, $4 kids 6–16. Guided tours daily late May to mid-Oct 10am–5pm, last tour at 4:30pm; late July to early Sept Thurs 5–8pm. Observatory closed late Oct to mid-May.

❻ ★★ Eastern Promenade. Portland's best bay view can be seen here from the sloping lawns of the Eastern Promenade, which is not so much a walkway as an experience. You can jog or dog-walk the mile-long pathway, but Portlanders also love to toss Frisbees and plunk down picnics on the soft grass; meanwhile, wonderful views of boats and islands occupy a panoramic sweep. ⏱ 1 hr. At northeast terminus of Congress St.

> *The distinctive hexagonal brick walls of the Portland Observatory, viewed from back down on the ground.*

7 kids **Maine Narrow Gauge Railroad Co. & Museum.** Maine was once home to several narrow-gauge railways, operating on rails just 2 feet apart. This small museum preserves their memory, as does a narrow-gauge train that chugs along the foot of the Promenade. Bay views are outstanding, though the 3-mile ride is molasses slow. ⏱ 1 hr. 58 Fore St. ☎ 207/828-0814. www.mngrr.org. Museum $2 adults, $1 seniors & kids 3–12; train $10 adults, $9 seniors, $6 kids 3–12; both free for kids 2 & under. Late May to early Oct daily 11am–4pm; late Oct to early May Sat–Sun 10am–4pm.

8 ★ **Park Street Row.** The outstanding row of Greek Revival brick town houses marching down little Park Street dates from 1835, and these buildings even survived the terrible July 4th fire that ravaged huge chunks of Portland in 1866. Today, it's Maine's longest connected section of homes surviving from the early 1800s. (Another half-block of these homes, south of Gray St., was razed in the 1960s.) The homes across the street (on the east side of Park) aren't too shabby, either. ⏱ 15 min. 88–114 Park St. (btw. Spring & Danforth sts.).

> The graceful State Street Church, redesigned by John Calvin Stevens in 1893, remarks the beginning of Portland's wonderful West End.

> Expansive bay and island views can be enjoyed by driving or walking to Portland's Eastern Promenade, a natural cliff.

> *Considered the finest surviving Victorian building in the U.S., the Victoria Mansion anchors Portland's West End.*

9 ★★ **Victoria Mansion.** Perhaps no building in Portland is more famous than this imposing High Victorian brownstone manse, built between 1858 and 1860 from plans by New

Fine Arts in Portland

When in Portland, you've got several excellent fine-arts options. The renowned **Portland Symphony Orchestra,** 477 Congress St. (☎ 207/842-0800 or 207/773-612; www.portlandsymphony.com), is a must-see if you're a classical music buff. They perform from September to May in a series of pops and classical concerts held at the city's Merrill Auditorium. Tickets cost $23 to $62 per person.

If you're a theater buff, you're also in luck. Portland theater companies come and go like the wind, but **Portland Stage Company,** 25A Forest Ave. (☎ 207/774-0465; www.portlandstage.com), endures. Its season runs October through May, with an eclectic schedule of shows including locally written works. Tickets cost $26 to $36, with discounts for seniors and children.

Haven architect Henry Austin (1804–91). It's the nation's premier showpiece of Victorian architecture. Details fill the interior, from wonderful and plentiful mural work to a grand staircase, gas-fueled chandeliers ("gasoliers"), Persian-style rugs hand-woven in Scotland, stained glass, and nearly all its original furniture. If you're serious about architectural history, you need to stop here. ⏱ 1¼ hr. 109 Danforth St. ☎ 207/772-4841. www.victoria mansion.org. $15 adults, $14 seniors, $5 kids 6–17, free for kids 5 & under, $35 families. May–Oct Mon–Sat 10am–4pm, Sun 1–5pm; Thanksgiving to Dec daily 11am–5pm. Closed first 3 weeks of Nov & Jan–Apr.

10 ★ **Western Promenade Park.** This park, a ¾-mile-long strip of greenery with a pathway, is a good spot to eat a picnic on a bench or sun on the lawn as majestic Victorian mansions overlook your indolence. If you lift your eyes above the sprawl on a clear day, you can see the outlines of the White Mountains on the horizon—some 90 miles away. The surrounding streets, especially Spring and Bowdoin streets, showcase some of Portland's very best residential architecture. ⏱ 45 min.

Portland's Best Beer

Portland can legitimately stake a claim to being the microbrew capital of New England—in fact, of the East Coast. It's astonishing how many good breweries are packed into this one small city. Here are a few of our favorites.

★★ **Shipyard Brewing.** Shipyard has risen from a pile of contenders to become the Big Daddy of Portland brewing. *86 Newbury St. (entrance on Hancock St.).* ☎ *800/789-0684 or 207/761-0807. www.shipyard.com.*

★★★ **Sebago Brewing Co.** This Old Port charmer is one of the city's finest—the Boathouse Brown Ale, Frye's Leap IPA, and Lake Trout Stout are popular, or try the Full Throttle Double IPA for a more hopped-up experience. *164 Middle St.* ☎ *207/775-2337.*

★★★ **Gritty McDuff's.** If you have time for just one beer in Portland before shipping out—this happens a lot—you should end up at Gritty's, the second-ever brewpub to

open in the city. Best beer in town? Maybe, maybe not. But the atmosphere is just right: a combination of geezers, ex-journalists, college kids, and tourists in an attractive space with big windows front and back. *396 Fore St.* ☎ *207/772-2739.*

★ **Three Dollar Deweys.** This Portland institution sports a row of perhaps three dozen taps dispensing wonderful microbrews, most of them from Maine, and still doles out free popcorn. The bar probably stocks another 50 beers in bottles, as well. This is local beer at its best. *241 Commercial St.* ☎ *207/772-3310. www. threedollardeweys.com.*

★ **The Great Lost Bear.** With more than 60 tap lines and extensive storage space, the Bear stocks an extremely broad and well-chosen selection of brews from Montreal, Belgium, Brooklyn, Vermont, Germany, and other places. *540 Forest Ave.* ☎ *207/772-0300. www.greatlostbear.com.*

Where to Stay

> Portland is surprisingly short on B&B's, but the Pomegranate Inn makes up for lack of quantity with its quality.

★★★ Black Point Inn Resort SCARBOROUGH
Just south of Portland, the Black Point is an elegant Maine classic with great coastal views and breezes near Winslow Homer's former studio. Rates are all-inclusive. 510 Black Point Rd. ☎ 207/883-2500. www.blackpointinn.com. 25 units. Doubles $380–$580 w/breakfast, tea & dinner. AE, DC, DISC, MC, V. Closed Nov–Apr.

★ kids Hampton Inn Portland Airport SOUTH PORTLAND
Of all the hotels clustered around Portland's airport and mall, this is our favorite. There's a pool, a free shuttle van, cookies, Internet, breakfast, good staff, and a quiet-ish location. 171 Philbrook Ave. ☎ 800/426-7866 or 207/773-4400. www.portlandhamptoninn.com. 117 units. Doubles $110–$170 w/breakfast. AE, DISC, MC, V.

Hilton Garden Inn OLD PORT
You can't stay closer to the Old Port than at this Hilton, across Commercial Street from the ferry and cruise ship docks and near plenty of restaurants, shopping, bars, and coffee-houses. But it's pricey for a chain hotel. 65 Commercial St. ☎ 207/780-0780. www.hilton.com. 120 units. Doubles $189–$369. AE, DISC, MC, V.

★ Inn at Park Spring WEST END
This small, friendly B&B in an 1835 brick home straddles downtown and the West End. All units are corner rooms, most with good light and some with views. 135 Spring St. ☎ 800/437-8511 or 207/774-1059. www.innatparkspring.com. 6 units. Doubles $99–$175 w/breakfast. AE, MC, V. No kids 9 & under.

★★★ Inn by the Sea CAPE ELIZABETH
This luxury inn gets it all right: seaside location, pool, bar, spa, gourmet food, eco-friendliness, and wonderful rooms and suites with double Jacuzzis. The walkway leads to one of Maine's best beaches. 40 Bowery Beach Rd. ☎ 800/888-4287 or 207/799-3134. www.innbythesea.com. 57 units. Doubles $189–$369; suites $259–$789. AE, DC, DISC, MC, V.

★★★ Pomegranate Inn WEST END
In a 19th-century Italianate home in the West End, this is the city's top B&B. Eight rooms feature distinct design touches, and gas fire-places. The carriage house room includes a private terrace; breakfasts are a highlight. 49 Neal St. ☎ 800/356-0408 or 207/772-1006. www.pomegranateinn.com. 8 units. Doubles $140–$295 w/breakfast. AE, DISC, MC, V. Kids 16 & over only.

★★ Portland Harbor Hotel OLD PORT
Adjacent to Portland's bar scene, this town house–like hotel offers good suites with deep tubs, plus a decent gourmet restaurant. 468 Fore St. ☎ 888/798-9090 or 207/775-9090. www.portlandharborhotel.com. 100 units. Doubles $159–$329. AE, DC, DISC, MC, V.

★★ Portland Regency Hotel OLD PORT
Centrally located in the Old Port, the brick Regency is both historic and thoroughly mod-ern. Corner rooms are best, with city views and Jacuzzis. The health club is among the best in town, and there's an excellent little bar. 20 Milk St. ☎ 800/727-3436 or 207/774-4200. www.theregency.com. 95 units. Doubles $159–$389. AE, DISC, MC, V.

Where to Dine

★★ **Back Bay Grill** DOWNTOWN *NEW AMERICAN*
The very skillful New American menu with continental accents includes plenty of local ingredients: Maine crab cakes, duck, and salmon. 65 Portland St. ☎ 207/772-8833. www.backbaygrill.com. Entrees $17–$33. AE, DC, DISC, MC, V. Dinner Mon–Sat.

Becky's OLD PORT *DINER*
A classic Maine diner, where fishermen hang out over mugs of coffee before or after a day's (or night's) work—the place opens at 4am. Nothing fancy here; stick with eggs, pancakes, fish, and fish chowder. 390 Commercial St. ☎ 207/773-7070. www.beckysdiner.com. Entrees $2–$8. AE, DISC, MC, V. Breakfast, lunch & dinner daily.

★ **Duckfat** OLD PORT *CAFE*
Belgian-style fries with curried mayo, or truffled ketchup, plus *poutine* (Canadian-style fries with cheese and gravy), beignets, even a meatloaf-filled panini—don't tell your doctor. 43 Middle St. ☎ 207/774-8080. Entrees $6–$10. AE, MC, V. Lunch & dinner Mon–Sat.

★★ **Five Fifty-Five** DOWNTOWN *NEW AMERICAN*
Steve and Michelle Corry's restaurant excels at small plates, plus a fuller menu of lobster mac-and-cheese, hand-rolled pastas, and the like. The wine list is tops. 555 Congress St. ☎ 207/761-0555. www.fivefifty-five.com. Small plates $6–$15, entrees $31–$35. AE, MC, V. Brunch Sun, dinner daily.

★★★ **Fore Street** OLD PORT *NEW AMERICAN*
Chef Sam Hayward uses his wood-fired brick oven and grill in an open kitchen to create memorable, widely acclaimed meals with an eye to local sourcing. This is some of the city's finest food, in warm and inviting space. 288

> *Sam Hayward's Fore Street leans heavily on local ingredients such as Maine-caught fish.*

Fore St. ☎ 207/775-2717. www.forestreet.biz. Entrees $13–$29. AE, MC, V. Dinner daily.

★ **The Grill Room & Bar** OLD PORT *AMERICAN*
Harding Lee Smith works the wood-fired grills in this great Old Port eatery. You can get steak, seafood, even thin-crust pizza; the house sauces are a highlight. 84 Exchange St. ☎ 207/774-2333. Entrees $13–$27. AE, DISC, MC, V. Lunch & dinner daily.

Hi Bombay OLD PORT *INDIAN*
The best Indian food in town, steps from the Old Port: fiery vindaloos, great mango *lassi* shakes, good *shami korma*, *masala*, and *biryani* dishes—and superb puffed-up *poori* fried breads. 1 Pleasant St. ☎ 207/772-8767. www.hibombay.com. Entrees $9–$14. AE, DISC, MC, V. Lunch & dinner daily.

★★★ **Hugo's** OLD PORT *NEW AMERICAN*
Chef Rob Evans runs one of Maine's most exciting kitchens, buying local ingredients and crafting unusual meals. The offerings run largely to substantial "small" plates: salads, steak tartare, Arctic char. 88 Middle St. ☎ 207/774-8538. www.hugos.net. Small plates $10–$21. AE, MC, V. Dinner Tues–Sat.

Seng Thai Food 2 EAST END *THAI*
For Thai food, this lowbrow corner eatery is the finest in town. The Thai iced tea is excellent, and the staff are unfailingly friendly. 921 Congress St. ☎ 207/879-2577. Entrees $6–$16. AE, MC, V. Lunch & dinner daily.

★★ **Street & Co.** OLD PORT *SEAFOOD*
This brick-walled bistro off an alleyway has cooked Portland's best seafood for decades, in an open kitchen looking out on a small, divided dining room with a pleasantly rustic decor. 33 Wharf St. ☎ 207/775-0887. Entrees $14–$24. AE, MC, V. Dinner Mon–Sat.

The Yorks

You won't find "The Yorks" on a map of Maine. That's because York is one town composed of several neighborhoods. Each part is distinct in character: York Harbor's where the old money is; York Village is where you go for Colonial history, gas, local eats, banks, bagels, and groceries; and then there's York Beach, whose Long Sands beach is long and overpoweringly scenic. You can finish this tour in about 1 to 2 days, depending on beach time.

> *Long Sands, long and pretty, is one of a handful of "must-see" beaches in mostly-rocky Maine.*

START York village is 45 miles south of Portland.

① ★★ Old Gaol. The big, reddish, vaguely barnlike structure with a cannon in front of it is neither a barn nor a fort, but rather Maine's original jail. Constructed in 1719, it was both the state's only prison *and* a tiny home for the jail keeper and his family (talk about close quarters) for years. Yes, prisoners were whipped on a post outside. ⏱ 30 min. East side of York St. at Lindsey No. 2 Rd. (across from town hall). ☎ 207/363-4974. $6 adults, $5 seniors, $3 kids 5–15, free for kids 5 & under, $15 families. June to mid-Oct Mon–Sat 10am–5pm.

② ★★ Jefferds' Tavern. This yellow tavern looks somewhat as it did when it was built in 1750, though it has since been moved (from Wells) and considerably added onto during restoration. The hive-shaped brick oven works, and is sometimes used to bake simple breads. ⏱ 30 min. East side of York St. btw. Lindsey Rd. & Lindsey No. 2 Rd. (across from town hall). ☎ 207/363-4974. $6 adults, $5 seniors, $3 kids 5–15, $15 families. June to mid-Oct Mon–Sat 10am–5pm.

③ First Parish Congregational Church. This meetinghouse-style church, built in 1747, features an attractively inlaid black clock face

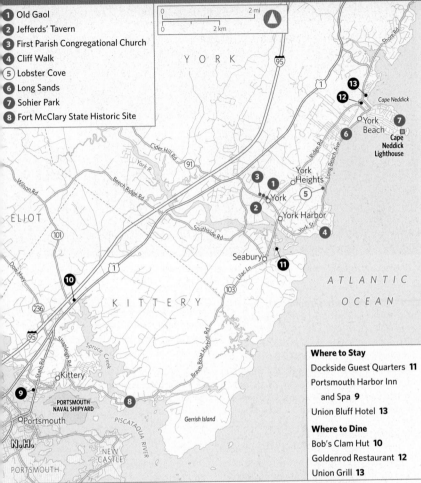

1. Old Gaol
2. Jefferds' Tavern
3. First Parish Congregational Church
4. Cliff Walk
5. Lobster Cove
6. Long Sands
7. Sohier Park
8. Fort McClary State Historic Site

Where to Stay

Dockside Guest Quarters **11**

Portsmouth Harbor Inn
and Spa **9**

Union Bluff Hotel **13**

Where to Dine

Bob's Clam Hut **10**

Goldenrod Restaurant **12**

Union Grill **13**

and graceful spire. Behind the church is an extensive parish cemetery dating from 1837; visitors are welcome to stroll through during daylight hours, though pets and bicycles are not welcome. ⏱ **15 min. 180 York St.**

The York Historical Pass

One of southern Maine's outstanding historical bargains is the York Historical Pass, sold at Old York's headquarters inside the Remick Barn on Main St. in York (☎ 207/363-4974; www.oldyork.org). The pass costs $12 per adult, $10 seniors, $5 kids 5 to 15, and $25 for a family. It gets you into eight properties, including the Old Gaol and Jefferds' Tavern.

> You don't want to end up in Maine's original jail, the Old Gaol, for the wrong reasons.

> *Fort McClary features a variety of catacomb-like spaces to explore, plus harbor views and a small museum.*

4 ★ **Cliff Walk.** From Harbor Beach, follow the sidewalk and dirt path as it ascends a set of stairs (handrails help guide you) along cliffs, and nearly right through the front yards of multimillion-dollar mansions. Beach roses lend their scent to the pathway, and views are breathtaking (but not too scary). Walk carefully and stay on the path—careless tourists have fallen from the 30-foot cliffs. ⏱ 45 min.

5 🍽 kids **Lobster Cove.** A spot for families to eat lobster dinners, broiled seafood, and fish platters right across the road from York Beach. Old-timey Maine dessert choices include blueberry pie in season. 756 York St. (south end of Long Sands). ☎ 207/351-1100. $–$$.

6 ★★ **Long Sands.** York's biggest and prettiest beach stretches 2 sandy miles alongside the Atlantic, is free to enter, and offers great surfing, beachcombing, and safe swimming. There's even a takeout seafood restaurant and changing facilities, as well as a bushel of cheap motels and cottages across from the water. Rte. 1A.

7 ★★★ **Sohier Park.** You don't come for the park: You come for the view of **Nubble Light**, probably one of the most photographed lighthouses in the world. The park is free; gawk at Nubble and its tiny island from the rocks across the inlet. Coin-operated looking glasses help you get a better view. Expect a parking lot crammed with RVs and vans: People come from around the nation to take this picture. ⏱ 1½ hr. Nubble Rd. (off Long Sands Dr.), Cape Neddick.

8 ★★ **Fort McClary State Historic Site.** This hidden historic park backs up against a lovely inlet and commemorates a spot used for coastal defense since at least the late 1600s. The fort was built in 1808 but was little used in wartime and eventually went to seed; in 1987, it was finally restored. The hexagonal blockhouse is now a small museum. ⏱ 30 min. Kittery Point Rd. (Rte. 103), Kittery. ☎ 207/384-5160. $3 adults, $1 seniors. Grounds & museum open year-round dawn–dusk; no staff Oct to mid-May.

The Kittery Outlets

Kittery's outlets (www.thekitteryoutlets.com), a few miles south of York, aren't a "sight" per se, but you'd be amazed at the numbers of visitors and the miles they travel here to snag a bargain. The mile-long strip coats both sides of Route 1; here, you score cut-rate deals on merch from name brands like Coach, Seiko, Crate & Barrel, Banana Republic, Nike, and the like.

Where to Stay & Dine

> *The Portsmouth Harbor Inn & Spa sits in Maine, but it's just a half-mile walk from New Hampshire.*

★ kids **Bob's Clam Hut** KITTERY *SEAFOOD*
This outlets-adjacent Rte. 1 staple fries clams like nobody else in Maine. You can also get fish and chips and local ice cream at the window. 315 Rte. 1. ☎ 207/439-4233. www. bobsclamhut.com. Entrees $8–$29. AE, MC, V. Lunch & dinner daily.

Dockside Guest Quarters YORK
Off the beaten track, this family-owned compound features a private dock and shared, town house–style cottages with private decks overlooking the harbor. 22 Harris Island Rd. ☎ 888/860-7428. www.docksidegq.com. 25 units. Doubles $117–$265 w/breakfast; suites $236–$312. DISC, MC, V. Closed Jan–Apr & Mon–Fri in May, Nov & Dec. 2-night minimum stay in summer.

★ kids **Goldenrod Restaurant** YORK BEACH
DINER Here since 1896, this combination malt shop/candy factory/diner anchors York's Short Sands neighborhood. Buy a box of taffy "kisses" or "birch bark" to take home. 2 Railroad Ave. (at Ocean Ave.). ☎ 207/363-2621. www.thegolden rod.com. Entrees $5–$8. MC, V. Late May to early Sept breakfast, lunch & dinner daily; early Sept to mid-Oct Wed–Sun breakfast & lunch.

Portsmouth Harbor Inn & Spa KITTERY
Across the drawbridge from Portsmouth, this inn features homey rooms with harbor views and a comfortable spa in an adjacent building. 6 Water St. ☎ 207/439-4040. www.innat portsmouth.com. 5 units. Doubles $120–$200 w/breakfast. MC, V. Not recommended for kids 11 & under.

★★ **Union Bluff Hotel** YORK BEACH
Old-looking but actually from the 1980s, this York Beach lodging is improving into a boutique-type hotel with the addition of the upscale Union Grill (see below). Off-season rooms are deeply discounted. 8 Beach St. ☎ 800/833-0721 or 207/363-1333. www.unionbluff.com. 61 units. Doubles & suites $59–$399. AE, DISC, MC, V.

★★ **Union Grill** YORK BEACH *AMERICAN/SEA-FOOD* Seafood predominates in the Union Bluff Hotel's dining room, but you can also eat duck, calamari, Kobe short ribs, lobster "mignon," and boar with béarnaise. 8 Beach St. ☎ 800/833-0721 or 207/363-1333. www.unionbluff.com. Entrees $11–$30. MC, V. May–Oct breakfast, lunch & dinner daily; Nov–Apr Sat–Sun dinner only. Pub open year-round lunch & dinner.

Ogunquit

Ogunquit is a bustling, genteel beachside town that has attracted summer tourists and artists for more than a century. Though certainly notable for its abundant and elegant summer-resort architecture, it's most famous for its 3½-mile white-sand beach backed by grassy dunes. The beach serves as the town's front porch, and most everyone drifts over there at least once a day when the sun is shining. Ogunquit's history as an art colony dates to around 1890, when Charles H. Woodbury arrived and declared the place an "artist's paradise." There's a great museum—but even if you're not an art lover, you'll adore the walking trail that climbs along the town's rocky cliffs for outstanding views, not to mention the abundance of inns, cafes, and restaurants. You'll need about 2 days to see it all.

> *Marginal Way is one of southern Maine's best easy coastal walks; views and coves abound.*

START Ogunquit is 40 miles south of Portland.

❶ ★★★ Ogunquit Museum of American Art. It's been called the "best small museum in America," and it's certainly way up there on the list. The legacy of Ogunquit's artist-colony days is recalled through this terrific collection, housed in a tranquil, waterside complex. You'll see Maine-associated artists like Neil Welliver, Charles Woodbury, Marsden Hartley, Robert Henri, and more, plus modern sculpture, graphical art, and photography from artists across the country. ⏱ 1½ hr. 543 Shore Rd. ☎ 207/646-4909. www.ogunquitmuseum.org. $7 adults, $5 seniors, $4 students, free for kids 11 & under. July–Oct Mon–Sat 10am–5pm, Sun 1–5pm.

❷ ★★ Perkins Cove. Marginal Way (see ❺) might be more picturesque, but Perkins Cove is the "scene" in Ogunquit, and it's a must-visit—if you can find parking. An attractive collage of yachts, fishing boats, rowboats, narrow alleys, shops, restaurants, and a small drawbridge keep visitors shopping and shutterbugging. Consider taking the town "trolley" (bus) instead of driving right to the cove—parking is expensive. ⏱ 1 hr. Oarweed Rd. (off Shore Rd.).

3 ★ kids Ogunquit Beach. The longest and most popular beach in town, Ogunquit Beach is *the* reason many families return to this town reliably summer after summer. Situated on a sandbar by the harbor, the beach offers access to gentle waves and several miles of soft white sand, plus views of the town's mansions and cliffs. It's got facilities—bathrooms, snacks—that the other local beaches don't have, making it the best choice for families. Lifeguards patrol in summer. **From main intersection, follow Beach St. to end.**

④ ☕ ★ kids Congdon's Doughnuts. Chocolate-chocolate is popular at this family style restaurant/doughnut shop, but you can't go wrong with almost any of the doughnuts—like filled blueberry, butter crunch, or one of the seasonal specials such as maple or apple. They also serve diner fare. 1090 Post Rd. ☎ 207/646-4219. $.

5 ★★★ Marginal Way. One of the best walking trails in coastal Maine is tucked into the cliffs rising above Ogunquit Beach (see above). It begins at the beach, then runs about 1¼ scenic miles up above sea level and out to a point of land, passing weird rock formations, little pocket coves, hotel balconies, and fancy summer cottages en route to Perkins Cove. About 30 benches are scattered along the path, all with great views. ⏱ 1 hr.

A Little Theater?

If you're spending a night in Ogunquit, consider checking out a show at the **Ogunquit Playhouse,** 10 Main St. (☎ 207/646-2402; www.ogunquitplayhouse.org), a 750-seat summer-stock theater slightly south of the town's main intersection. Founded in 1933, it has retained its elegance over the years, and in its heyday, it attracted stars like Bette Davis and Tallulah Bankhead. Performances run from mid-May to mid-October, and tickets range from $30 to $45.

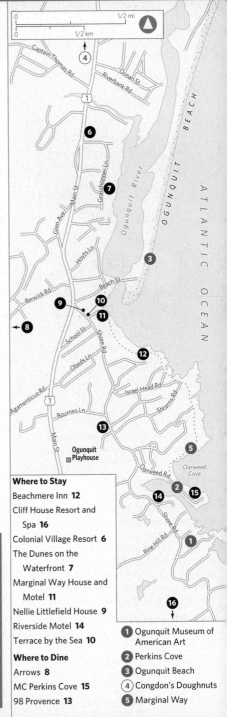

Where to Stay
Beachmere Inn **12**
Cliff House Resort and Spa **16**
Colonial Village Resort **6**
The Dunes on the Waterfront **7**
Marginal Way House and Motel **11**
Nellie Littlefield House **9**
Riverside Motel **14**
Terrace by the Sea **10**

Where to Dine
Arrows **8**
MC Perkins Cove **15**
98 Provence **13**

1 Ogunquit Museum of American Art
2 Perkins Cove
3 Ogunquit Beach
4 Congdon's Doughnuts
5 Marginal Way

Where to Stay & Dine

> Arrows, a few miles inland from Ogunquit's beaches, remains one of the top New American-cuisine restaurants in Maine.

★★★ Arrows NEW AMERICAN

Mark Gaier and Clark Frasier do some of the most innovative cooking in the region, using local products, home-grown greens, and house-cured prosciutto. Expect roast chicken, local fish, steaks, lobster, and a great wine list. 41 Berwick Rd. ☎ 207/361-1100. www.arrows restaurant.com. Entrees $42–$45. MC, V. June to mid-Oct dinner only Wed–Sun; mid-Oct to Dec & mid-Apr to May dinner only Thurs–Sun.

★★★ kids Beachmere Inn

A well-run cliff-top inn with a scenic lawn and access to Marginal Way (p. 507, ⑤). The original Victorian inn dates from the 1890s with turrets, porches, and angles, while the other building is more modern. Rooms are simple, pleasantly furnished, maritime in theme, and never overdone; the focus is on the sea views. Kids' programs abound, and there's a children's playroom on the ground floor. 62 Beachmere Place. ☎ 800/336-3983 or 207/646-2021. www.beachmereinn.com. 53 units. Doubles $95–$250 w/breakfast; suites & cottages $155–$460. 3-night minimum in summer. AE, DC, DISC, MC, V.

★★★ Cliff House Resort and Spa

This complex of modern buildings replaced a former grand hotel. Views are stunning, and the Cliffscape wing features new beds and furniture. A spa, vanishing-edge outdoor pool, and restaurant look out on the sea. Shore Rd. ☎ 207/361-1000. www.cliffhousemaine.com. 200 units. Doubles & suites $160–$385. AE, DISC, MC, V. Closed Dec to mid-Apr.

★ kids Colonial Village Resort

This certainly is *not* a resort—rather, it's a budget- and family-friendly motel with two pools, a Jacuzzi, a tennis court, free doughnuts, coin-op laundries, and weekly rates for its cottages and apartments. Most rooms have kitchenettes and full-size refrigerators. 548 Rte. 1. ☎ 800/422-3341. www.colonial villageresort.com. Doubles & suites $54–$262 w/breakfast. AE, MC, V. Closed Dec–Mar.

★★ The Dunes on the Waterfront

A fancy motor court? Indeed. These gabled cottages are decked in vintage maple furnishings, braided rugs, maple floors, louvered doors, full kitchens, and wood-burning fireplaces. 518 Rte. 1. ☎ 888/295-3863. www. dunesonthewaterfront.com. 36 units. Doubles $95–$345; cottages $160–$435. MC, V. Closed Nov to late Apr.

★ Marginal Way House and Motel

A quiet, old-fashioned compound centered around a four-story guesthouse, this is a spare but centrally located place with good customer service. Some rooms have little decks with views; all have refrigerators and televisions. 22–24 Wharf Lane. ☎ 207/646-8801. www. marginalwayhouse.com. 30 units. Doubles early June to Labor Day $82–$199; mid-Apr to early June & early Sept to Oct $49–$159 double. MC, V. Closed Nov to mid-Apr.

> *The Beachmere Inn is both exceptionally family-friendly and architecturally quirky.*

★★★ MC Perkins Cove NEW AMERICAN/SEA-FOOD

Mark Gaier and Clark Frasier of Arrows (see p. 508) run this bistro, featuring small plates, salads, mussels and oysters, and fish. Desserts are terrific. Perkins Cove Rd. ☎ 207/646-6263. www.mcperkinscove.com. Entrees $19–$31. DC, DISC, MC, V. Late May to mid-Oct lunch & dinner daily; mid-Oct to Dec & Feb to late May lunch & dinner Wed–Mon.

★★ Nellie Littlefield House

Of the many B&Bs in Ogunquit, this might be the friendliest. Rooms are carpeted and feature a mix of modern and antique reproduction furnishings; several have refrigerators. One third-floor suite features a Jacuzzi, another a turret. But those traveling with children should be forewarned: Only kids 13 and older are welcome. 27 Shore Rd. ☎ 207/646-1692. www.nellielittlefieldhouse.com. 8 units. June–Sept doubles $108–$230 w/breakfast; Mar–May & Oct–Dec doubles $85–$170 w/breakfast. 3-night minimum high season & holidays. DISC, MC, V. Closed Jan–Feb.

★ Riverside Motel

The Riverside offers wonderful marina and harbor views and free Wi-Fi, plus a convenient footbridge right over to Ogunquit's Perkins Cove—all at a fraction of the cost of downtown hotels. Rooms are spare and white-washed, but comfortable enough. 50 Riverside Lane. ☎ 207/646-2741. www.riversidemotel.com. Double $99–$209. MC, V. Closed mid-Oct to mid-Apr.

★★ Terrace by the Sea

The Terrace by the Sea is a fairly upscale choice, a nice surprise in a town where there's a lot of variability in the lodgings. Many rooms have great sea views, and there's also a heated outdoor pool, plus the innkeepers are friendly. Eight motel-style rooms have kitchenettes. One big caveat, though—kids 6 and under aren't accepted during high season (Memorial Day to Labor Day). 3 Wharf Lane. ☎ 207/646-3232. www.terracebythesea.com. Doubles $52–$242. MC, V. Closed mid-Dec to late Mar.

★★ 98 Provence FRENCH

A truly French menu that changes three times yearly to reflect the seasons. Lobster is cooked in puff pastry; a fish stew is Provençal; and there's rabbit, escargots, cassoulet of duck, and rack of lamb. A bistro menu offers lighter meals. 262 Shore Rd. ☎ 207/646-9898. www.98provence.com. Entrees $23–$28. AE, MC, V. Late Apr to mid-Dec dinner Wed–Mon.

The Kennebunks

"The Kennebunks" consist of the side-by-side villages of Kennebunk and Kennebunkport, both situated along the shores of small rivers and both claiming a portion of rocky coast. This region of southern Vermont was first colonized in the mid-1600s and flourished after the American Revolution, when ship captains, boat builders, and prosperous merchants constructed imposing, solid homes. The Kennebunks today are known for their striking historical architecture and expansive beaches; leave 1 to 2 days to explore both.

> The end of a day in Kennebunkport's Dock Square, the hub of this coastal town.

START Kennebunk is 30 miles south of Portland.

1 ★★ **St. Anthony's Franciscan Monastery.** This monastery is a peaceful spot for walks through quiet grounds, chapels, and sculptures. The estate and property were purchased by Lithuanian Franciscans in 1947, who then added the grotto, statuary, and worship spaces. There's a section of sculpture from the Vatican Pavilion at the 1964–65 World's Fair, a chapel, an outdoor shrine, English gardens, statues, and a walking trail with some of the best river views in town. Park in the visitor's lot and be respectful of the grounds. ⏲ 1 hr. North side of Beach Ave., less than ½ mile from Lower Village & the intersection of Rte. 9 & Rte. 35.

2 🍴 kids **Port Bakery and Café.** This unpretentious bakery/cafe sits in the heart of Lower Village and serves ever-changing soups, salads, breads, pastries, and homemade desserts. 181 Port Rd. ☎ 207/967-2263. $.

3 ★★★ kids **Kennebunk Beach.** Actually a string of several beaches broken up by a jetty or two—each section has its own name

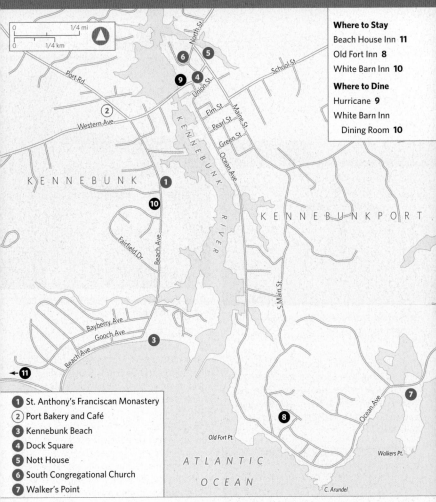

1 St. Anthony's Franciscan Monastery
2 Port Bakery and Café
3 Kennebunk Beach
4 Dock Square
5 Nott House
6 South Congregational Church
7 Walker's Point

and devotees—Kennebunk Beach is among Maine's finest. Sunrises, sunsets, swimming, beachcombing, and dog-walking are all superb here. There's even a section of rocky tide pools (keep an eye on the kids). A local parking permit is required (buy at town hall). ⏱ 2 hr. Beach Ave.

4 ★★ **Dock Square.** Kennebunkport life revolves around this square, which in summer slows to a crawl of bumper-to-bumper sports cars pausing while shoppers cross at the pedestrian walkway marked by a small-scale lighthouse. Among the highlights are several excellent restaurants (such as Hurricane,

p. 513) and upscale specialty stores, galleries, and studios purveying everything from fine tableware and candles to furniture, pottery, antiques, ice cream, and even maps. ⏱ 1½ hr. Ocean Ave. at Spring St. (Rte. 9).

5 ★★ **Nott House.** The stout, Doric-columned Nott House (built 1853) is a heavyweight, both literally and figuratively; it's not only a solidly footed example of Greek Revival design, but it also holds the town's historical society. Period rugs, furniture, wallpapers, and other items keep one in that 19th-century state of mind. The society also offers excellent local walking tours of the neighborhood (11am daily; $7

> Kennebunk Beach goes by several names, yet it's graceful any time of day.

> Look, but don't touch: The Bush family compound at Walker's Point.

adults) beginning here whenever it's open. ⏱ 1 hr. 8 Maine St. at Spring St. ☎ 207/967-2751. $7 adults, free for kids. House tours July–Aug Thurs–Fri 10am–4pm & 7–9pm, Sat 10am–1pm; Sept to early Oct Thurs–Fri 10am–4pm, Sat 10am–1pm.

Old Orchard Beach

Summer vacationers flock by the thousands to Old Orchard, which is a town, an impressive ocean pier, and a 5-mile motel- and condo-fronted beach. The beach is a good spot for a long, long walk; the pier, a place for cotton candy. A few peppy bars and restaurants sit directly on the sand, and there's an annual sandcastle-building contest over the July 4th holiday (☎ 207/934-9078). You can brush up on your French-Canadian simply by strolling around—the town attracts Quebecers like a magnet—and kids won't want to miss the adjacent **Palace Playland** amusement park, 1 Old Orchard St. (☎ 207/934-2001; www.paceplayland.com). ⏱ 2 hr. Foot of Old Orchard St., from East Grand Ave. to West Grand Ave. (Rte. 9).

6 ★★ **South Congregational Church.** Kennebunkport's most recognizable icon is the enormous clock of this whitewashed, meetinghouse-style church (built 1824), down a lane off Dock Square and close to the tidal river. The huge clock faces are the originals, and are made of wood (which is very unusual); they no longer keep the correct time, but this is still as lovely a church as you'll find in southern Maine. Inside, the simple, spare theme continues but for some stained-glass work and an outsized, impressively columnar pipe organ—though it's only from 2004. ⏱ 30 min. 2 North St. at Temple St., just off Spring St. ☎ 207/967-2793. Office Mon–Fri 9am–2pm; Sun services 10:30am.

7 ★ **Walker's Point.** When you drive to Walker's Point, you not only get a peek at the lives of presidents, but also get to sample free and breathtaking views of the sea that the families around here paid millions to enjoy every day. The Bush family has resided here since the late 19th century (the present-day compound was begun in 1903). You cannot enter the property, which is guarded by Secret Service agents at all times. But you can park on the road and snap long-lens photos of it. ⏱ 30 min. Ocean Ave.

Where to Stay & Dine

> *Seasonal displays complement the seasonally changing menus in the White Barn Inn's outstanding dining room.*

★★ **Beach House Inn** KENNEBUNK
Right across from one of Kennebunk's best stretches of beach. Rooms are comfy, and many come with panoramic views of the ocean; a front porch, bikes, and canoes are additional draws. 211 Beach Ave. ☎ 207/967-3850. www.beachhseinn.com. 35 units. Doubles late June to mid-Sept $255–$390, early June to late June & mid-Sept to Oct $185–$399, Nov–Dec $155–$300 w/breakfast & afternoon tea. AE, MC, V. Closed Jan–May.

★★ **Hurricane** KENNEBUNKPORT *AMERICAN/ ECLECTIC* This fusion restaurant is the best in Dock Square. Expect healthy sandwiches and salads, pan-roasted local fish, seared scallops, and lobster cioppino. 29 Dock Sq. ☎ 207/967-1111. www.hurricanerestaurant.com. Small plates $8–$22; entrees $15–$45. AE, DC, DISC, MC, V. Lunch & dinner daily.

★★ **Old Fort Inn** KENNEBUNKPORT
Units in this upscale inn retain yesteryear charm, yet have in-floor heated tiles, plush robes, and fridges. Breakfasts are very good. Old Fort Rd. ☎ 800/828-3678 or 207/967-5353.

www.oldfortinn.com. 16 units. Doubles & suites $125–$395 w/breakfast. AE, DC, DISC, MC, V.

★★★ **White Barn Inn** KENNEBUNK
The White Barn pampers guests like no other in Maine, with luxe rooms, a spa, a parlor, afternoon tea, and a prize-winning restaurant (see below); the adjacent May's Cottage suites are spectacular, as is the outdoor pool. 37 Beach Ave. ☎ 207/967-2321. www.whitebarn inn.com. 29 units. Doubles $310–$620; cottages & suites $540–$925 w/breakfast. AE, MC, V.

★★★ **White Barn Inn Dining Room** KEN-NEBUNK *NEW AMERICAN* The White Barn Inn's (see above) classy dining room, a former barn, is among Maine's best. Jonathan Cartwright cooks lobster spring rolls, seared diver scallops, grilled chicken, steamed lobster over fettuccine, and other seasonally changing treats. 37 Beach Ave. ☎ 207/967-2321. www. whitebarninn.com. Prix-fixe dinner $91–$125 per person. AE, MC, V. Dinner Mon–Fri. Closed early Jan.

Bath, Brunswick & Beyond

Bath/Brunswick is one of the best places to get a compact history lesson in Colonial Maine: Both towns prospered in the wooden-ship days of the late 18th and early 19th centuries, and each has taken a different path (Brunswick went for education, while Bath became the site of a massive ironworks) to survive in the modern era. You'll also want to make a brief detour to Popham Beach—a beach, not a town, with expansive sea views, long strands of sand, and plenty of bird life—and the village of Wiscasset, with its two quirky museums and blasts of quaintness.

> Bowdoin College (founded in 1794) is one of America's oldest colleges, and still maintains very high standards today.

START Bath is 35 miles northeast of Portland; Brunswick is 8 miles west of Bath.

❶ Bowdoin College. This "little Ivy" was Maine's first educational institution, and has one of the toughest admissions standards in the U.S. Among the highlights of its campus are squarish, Federal-style **Massachusetts Hall** (when Bowdoin opened, the entire school fit inside this one building); a stone chapel; Pickard Theatre, which comes alive with musical performances during summer; and Coles Tower, a bit of '70s Space Needle architecture that lords oddly above the otherwise pleasant architecture. ⏲ 30 min. 5000 College Station, Brunswick. No scheduled tours; campus open to visitors daily.

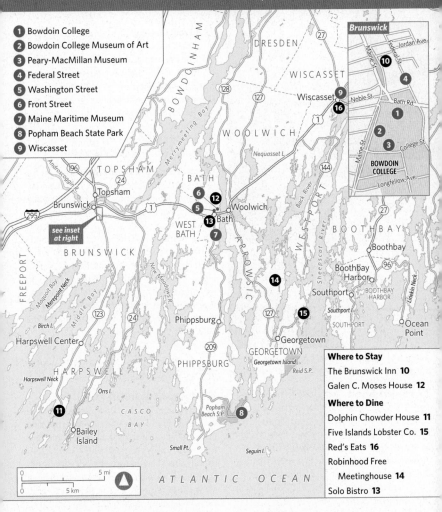

1. Bowdoin College
2. Bowdoin College Museum of Art
3. Peary-MacMillan Museum
4. Federal Street
5. Washington Street
6. Front Street
7. Maine Maritime Museum
8. Popham Beach State Park
9. Wiscasset

Where to Stay

The Brunswick Inn **10**
Galen C. Moses House **12**

Where to Dine

Dolphin Chowder House **11**
Five Islands Lobster Co. **15**
Red's Eats **16**
Robinhood Free
   Meetinghouse **14**
Solo Bistro **13**

2 ★★ **Bowdoin College Museum of Art.** This is one of the best small museums in New England. The holdings include a number of American artists—some with close ties to Maine, such as the Wyeths and Winslow Homer—but there's also a significant collection of work from classic European painters and plenty of modern art. The rotunda entrance is grand; the basement was redesigned in 2008 by an Argentine architect to bring in light, color, and style. ⏱ 1 hr. 9400 College Station, Brunswick. ☎ 207/725-3275. www.bowdoin.edu/art-museum. Free admission. Tues–Wed & Fri–Sat 10am–5pm; Thurs 10am–8:30pm; Sun 1–5pm.

3 ★★ **Peary-MacMillan Museum.** Just as good as the art museum, in its own way, is Bowdoin's song to the Arctic. Two of history's most famous Arctic explorers, Admiral Robert Peary and Donald MacMillan, graduated from Bowdoin in consecutive years late in the 19th century. When they returned from their polar travels, both men donated items to their alma mater. Among the museum's holdings are the obligatory stuffed polar bears, but also journal pages, native Canadian craft work, and thousands of photographs of the polar region. ⏱ 45 min. 9500 College Station, Brunswick. ☎ 207/725-3416. www.bowdoin.edu/arctic-museum. Free admission. Tues–Sat 10am–5pm; Sun 2–5pm.

> *Real wooden ships can still be found—and boarded—at the Maine Maritime Museum in bath.*

④ ★ Federal Street. This straight mile-long street is home to one of New England's best concentrations of whitewashed, Federal-style architecture. None of the homes here is open to the public, but the sidewalk is. The entire street is attractive and worth a walk (Maine Street's restaurants are just a block west); if you're pressed for time, the first ½ mile from the college to Center Street is prettiest. ⏱ 15 min. Bath Rd. to Mason St., Brunswick.

Take Rte. 1 north 8 miles. Bear right and exit for downtown Bath, then turn left beneath the underpass onto Middle St. Continue 3 blocks to Oak St. and turn right. In 1 block you'll reach:

⑤ ★ Washington Street. Bath's maple-framed Washington Street was the place the wealthy captains, shipbuilders, and merchants built their ostentatious (for the time) Victorian homes late in the 19th century. Along with Brunswick's Federal Street (see above), it's one of northern New England's best-preserved residential streets. Don't miss the big white Winter Street Church. ⏱ 30 min. Off Rte. 1, Bath.

⑥ ★ Front Street. Bath's compact downtown, on a small rise overlooking the river, is home to some remarkable brick and stone Victorian commercial architecture. Note especially the blond, stone Richardson-style **Patten Free Library** at Summer Street—its park features a gazebo, fountain, and view of the Winter Street Church—and the bell tower on the big **City Hall** at no. 55. Its bell, from 1802, was probably cast by Paul Revere. ⏱ 1 hr. Off Rte. 1, Bath.

⑦ ★★ kids Maine Maritime Museum. This historical museum, which backs up to the tidal Kennebec River, teaches you everything about wooden boat building you ever wanted to know, and more. The site's a former shipyard where more than 40 schooners were built in the late 19th and early 20th centuries. The main building features maritime art and artifacts; also don't miss the "display" ships (they sometimes sail) and boat-building shop. 243 Washington St., Bath. ☎ 207/443-1316. www. bathmaine.com. $10 adults, $9 seniors, $7 kids 6–17. Daily 9:30am–5pm.

Follow Washington St. south until it ends on High St. (Rte. 209). Continue south on Rte. 209 for 12 miles until you reach:

⑧ ★ Popham Beach State Park. This was the location of the first Colonial attempts at settling Maine. Those efforts failed, but shipping and fishing interests eventually did take hold here. Today the park is best known for its long sand beach with views of island and lighthouse. Rare birds nest in the sand dunes; please step carefully. ⏱ 2 hr. 10 Perkins Farm Lane, Phippsburg. ☎ 207/389-1335 or 389-9125. Summer $4 adults, $1 kids 5 to 11; rest of the year $1.50 adults, free for kids.

⑨ ★★★ Wiscasset. "The Prettiest Village in Maine"? So it claims. Dozens of structures have some form of historic designation. Look for the brick **Lincoln County Courthouse** (the longest continuously operating courthouse in the U.S., since 1824) at 32 High St. (☎ 207/ 882-6311); the gray, granite-slabbed stone **jail** (1811) at 133 Federal St. (☎ 207/882-6817), which operated until the 1950s; and the 1808 Federal-style **Nickels-Sortwell House** at 121 Main St. (☎ 207/882-7619) with its multiple chimneys. ⏱ 1 hr.

Where to Stay & Dine

★★★ The Brunswick Inn BRUNSWICK

Brunswick's best B&B is also its most central, on Park Row a block from Federal Street. Expect wingback chairs, homey quilts, and comfortable suites. 165 Park Row. ☎ 800/299-4914 or 207/729-4914. www.brunswickbnb.com. 15 units. Doubles $125–$190 w/breakfast. MC, V. Closed Jan. Kids 6 & over welcome.

★★ Dolphin Chowder House SOUTH HARP-

SWELL SEAFOOD Located next to a working-class marina just outside of Brunswick, this is the best chowder in the state of Maine. Table or booth, it doesn't matter: You're facing a full bay view and real fishermen. The muffins are great, too. 515 Basin Point. ☎ 207/833-6000. Entrees $4–$17. MC, V. May–Oct breakfast, lunch & dinner daily.

★★ Five Islands Lobster Co. GEORGETOWN

LOBSTER After a scenic drive to the end of Rte. 127, this unprepossessing "lobster pound" on the wharf is a welcome nosh. Zero atmosphere; excellent lobsters. 1447 Five Islands Rd. (from Bath, cross Rte. 1 bridge & turn right). ☎ 207/371-2990. Entrees priced according to market. MC, V. May–Oct lunch & dinner daily.

★★ Galen C. Moses House BATH

This Italianate 19th-century manse is full of Victorian clocks, antiques, and original stained glass. Unusually for a B&B, rooms have fun themes: Check out the stripy Safari Room. 1009 Washington St. ☎ 888/442-8771 or 207/442-8771. www.galenmoses.com. 7 units. Doubles $119–$259 w/breakfast. AE, DISC, MC, V.

★★★ Red's Eats WISCASSET LOBSTER

This little red shack at the bridge in Wiscasset is the best place to get a lobster roll for miles. Traffic stops here. Literally. Expect big chunks of lobster meat on toasted hot dog buns, picnic tables, and long waits. Rte. 1 at Water St. ☎ 207/882-6128. Entrees $6–$16. No credit cards. May–Sept lunch & dinner daily.

★★★ Robinhood Free Meetinghouse GEORGE-

TOWN SEAFOOD The world beats a path to chef Michael Gagné's fine-dining experience, inside an actual mid-19th-century meetinghouse. Asian influences are evident, and

> Inside, the Galen C. Moses House is one of the more offbeat 19th-century B&B's you'll ever find in Maine.

seafood is the strongest suit. 210 Robinhood Rd. ☎ 207/371-2188. www.robinhood-meeting house.com. Entrees $22–$28. AE, DISC, MC, V. June to mid-Oct dinner daily; rest of the year dinner Thurs–Sun.

★★ Solo Bistro BATH BISTRO

This bistro/jazz club serves hearty burgers, stews, seafood, and risotto among the possible offerings. The interior's Euro-cool, too— the owners run a design shop next door. 128 Front St. ☎ 207/443-3373. www.solobistro.com. Entrees $13–$24. AE, MC, V. Dinner Mon–Sat.

Rockland, Camden & Rockport

Camden and Rockland are polar opposites. Rockland's a blue-collar town, founded on fishing and fish processing; elegant Camden was where sea captains built mansions (now fine inns) with their booty. Yet Rockland is catching up—it has become a place to dine well, stay overnight, and visit art galleries, and is home to one of Maine's best museums. Meanwhile, Rockport, a cute fishing village nearby, is a detour that must be seen to be appreciated; no wonder a photography school was established here.

> Harbor Park overlooks Camden's gracious, boat-filled harbor with wide, sloping lawns perfect for picnicking.

START Rockland is 80 miles northeast of Portland. Camden is 8 miles north of Rockland.

❶ ★★ **Rockland.** Rockland's main square and long Main Street have plenty of brick buildings of architectural interest, but the waterfront and its small park are where you really feel the town's character. Watch real windjammers and schooners come, go, or just bob in the harbor; some of the ships and

shipbuilders here have acquired national historic designation.

When in Rockland, make sure to visit the ★★★ **Farnsworth Art Museum.** Philanthropist Lucy Farnsworth bequeathed the funds that established the museum in the 1930s; it has since become one of the most important collections of regional art in New England. The museum holds a superb collection of paintings

> The Farnsworth Museum features an outstanding variety of work by New England painters. Here: Will Barnet's *Way to the Sea*.

and sculptures by renowned American artists with connections to Maine—three generations of Wyeths, Rockwell Kent, and the like. The spaces here are big, well-lit, and stylish; the quality of the exhibits is tops. ☉ 1½ hr. Museum: 356 Main St. ☎ 207/596-6457. www.farnsworthmuseum.org. $10 adults, $8 seniors & students 18 & over, free for kids 17 & under. Late May to early Oct daily 10am–5pm; rest of the year Tues–Sun 10am–5pm.

From Rockland, drive north 6 miles on Rte. 1 to Pascal Ave. and bear right. In a half-mile arrive at:

② ★★ Rockport. Rockport is not just another of Maine's quaint fishing-harbor towns, though it *is* cute. This is also one of the hidden centers of Maine art, with a thriving visual-arts school (the **Maine Media College,** at 70

> *Camden Hills State Park may not offer lobster, but it offers everything else that's great about this state.*

Camden St.) and a scenic harborside footpath that winds past docks, a boat landing, a small park, and a cafe—it should win awards for the views and the way it introduces, rather than intrudes upon, the landscape. The collectively owned **Center for Maine Contemporary Art,** 162 Russell Ave. (☎ 207/236-2875), is one of the best small galleries in the Midcoast. This town is a great place to rest after a bike ride or a short stroll in the sea air; bring a camera. ⏱1 hr. Foot of Main St., off Central St.

From Rockport, drive north 2 miles on Russell Ave., which becomes Chestnut St. and brings you into Camden. The street comes to a T-junction with Elm St. Proceed into:

❸ ★★★ **Camden.** Rte. 1 suddenly becomes graceful as it approaches the center of downtown Camden; Elm Street is lined with Federal-style buildings, many converted into bed-and-breakfasts. Note the **Camden Opera House,** 29 Elm St. (☎ 207/236-7963), on the left. As you reach town, parking becomes tight and buildings become commercial; seafood restaurants and souvenir shops are ubiquitous. Stroll through it all, browsing and grazing, then take a break. **Harbor Park,** a natural amphitheater beside the **Camden Public Library,** 155 Main St. (☎ 207/236-3440), whose real estate must be worth about a zillion dollars, was donated by a generous local, Mary Louise Curtis Bok Zimbalist, in the 1920s. Today it's on the National Register of Historic Places. Bring a picnic and while away some time. ⏱1 hr.

❹ ★★★ **Camden Hills State Park.** This 6,500-acre park may not be as big as the White or Green mountains, but it's got the ocean views those mountains don't. There's a free ocean-side picnic area, more than 100 campsites, and a small toll road to the summit of the "mountain" with awesome Penobscot Bay views. You can take any number of hikes, too (p. 459). ⏱1¼ hr. Rte. 1 at Mount Battie Rd. ☎ 207/236-3109. $3 adults, $1 kids 5–11. Mid-May to mid-Oct sunrise–sunset.

Taking In Camden's Waterfront

In summer, the Camden docks are a virtual carnival as vendors hawk hot dogs and ice cream; whale-watch tours arrive and depart; and shutterbugs click cameras at the yachts and wooden ships tied up on the docks. This is the best spot to sample Camden if you're pressed for time. Also be sure to explore the various unnamed alleys leading down to the waterfront, where there are restaurants, a bakery, and curio shops.

Where to Stay & Dine

★★ Atlantica CAMDEN *SEAFOOD*
Seafood with flair on the Camden waterfront. Expect thick chowders, poached lobsters, seared scallops, and a fresh fish dish of the day. 1 Bayview Landing. ☎ 888/507-8514 or 207/236-6011. www.atlanticarestaurant.com. Entrees $26–$36. AE, MC, V. Apr–Oct dinner Wed–Mon.

kids Boynton-McKay CAMDEN *CAFE*
A former pharmacy (with bottles and pillboxes still on the wall), this funky downtown diner serves good sandwiches, coffee, and lunch specials like meatloaf to famished families. 30 Main St. ☎ 207/236-2465. Entrees $8–$14. MC, V. Lunch Tues–Sat, dinner Tues–Sun.

★★ Cafe Miranda ROCKLAND *INTERNATIONAL*
One of the craziest, most inventive menus in New England, with items like "Ducks of Spanish Pleasure" (a sort of duck curry). 15 Oak St. ☎ 207/594-2034. www.cafemiranda.com. Entrees $9–$22. DC, MC, V. Dinner daily; brunch Sun.

★★★ Camden Harbour Inn CAMDEN
This 1871 captain's house offers king beds, a spa, a gourmet restaurant, and wine refrigerators. Suites are designed with Thai, Mauritian, and other themes. 83 Bayview St. ☎ 800/236-4266 or 207/236-4200. www.camdenharbourinn.com. 22 units. Doubles $175–$450 w/breakfast. AE, DISC, MC, V. Closed Dec–Apr. No kids 11 & under.

★★★ Francine Bistro CAMDEN *FRENCH*
An elegant, urbane bistro manned by a talented chef, tucked away on a little street in little Camden. The food leans local and the tea-brined duck is amazing. 55 Chestnut St. ☎ 207/230-0083. www.francinebistro.com. Entrees $17–$25. MC, V. Dinner Tues–Sat.

★★ The Hartstone Inn CAMDEN
Great food in a comfortable inn near the water: This is Maine. Rooms are furnished with antiques. Do not miss dinner or a cooking class with the owners. 41 Elm St. ☎ 800/788-4823 or 207/236-4259. www.hartstoneinn.com. 21 units. Doubles $105–$190. MC, V. Closed late Nov to late Apr.

★★★ Inn at Ocean's Edge LINCOLNVILLE BEACH
The name says it all. You'll find spa services, a gourmet restaurant, and and many rooms

> *Water on water: The seaside pool at the Samoset Resort cozies right up to Penobscot Bay.*

have balconies. 2268 Atlantic Hwy. (Rte. 1). ☎ 207/236-0945. www.innatoceansedge.com. 33 units. Doubles $195–$425 w/breakfast. AE, DISC, MC, V.

★★★ Norumbega CAMDEN
You can't miss this stone castle–like mansion just north of downtown. Rooms are immaculate. The suites are worth a splurge for the views alone. 63 High St. ☎ 877/363-4646 or 207/236-4646. www.norumbegainn.com. 12 units. Doubles $125–$475 w/breakfast. AE, DISC, MC, V. Kids 7 & over welcome.

★★★ Primo ROCKLAND *NEW AMERICAN*
Change your plans: Chefs Melissa Kelly and Price Kushner run this incredible bistro in a century-old home, and you need to eat here now. The menu has French and Italian accents plus the best desserts in Maine. 2 S. Main St. ☎ 207/596-0770. www.primorestaurant.com. Entrees $23–$38. AE, DC, DISC, MC, V. May–Oct dinner daily.

★★ Samoset Resort ROCKPORT
This classic old-Maine resort has recent upgrades: a heated pool and hot tub with sweeping ocean views, plus a tiki bar. Most rooms have balconies or porches, flatscreen TVs, and marble vanities—and the golf course is Maine's best. 220 Warrenton St. ☎ 800/341-1650 or 207/594-2511. www.samoset.com. 178 units. Doubles $129–$369; cottages $539–$769. AE, DC, DISC, MC, V.

New England's History & Culture

A Timeline of New England History

EARLY HISTORY

CA. 9000-7000 B.C. Native American tribes first settle in what is now New England (a village map, left).

CA. 1000 A.D. Vikings travel south from Canada, possibly venturing as far south as the northern New England coast.

1524 Giovanni de Verrazano lands at Rhode Island's Narragansett Bay and explores the Maine coast.

1542 French explorer Jean Allefonsce sails south from what is now Canada, and claims he discovered a vibrant city, Norumbega, in what is now Maine. Later explorers searched for the city, but no such place was found.

1600

1604 French explorers establish a settlement in Maine.

1609 Samuel de Champlain claims Vermont for France.

1616 Outbreak of a major epidemic of smallpox, to which New England's native population has no immunity.

1620 The *Mayflower* (left) lands at what is now Provincetown, Massachusetts, and continues to Plymouth, Massachusetts, New England's first permanent English settlement.

1623 Fishermen from England settle Rye, New Hampshire.

1636 Roger Williams establishes Providence, Rhode Island. Connecticut Colony is founded. Harvard College opens.

1675-76 King Philip's War leads to the death of thousands of Native Americans and colonists.

1700

1770 With resistance to British government policies growing, royal soldiers kill five colonists in the Boston Massacre.

1773 The Boston Tea Party, a show of rebellion by colonists, occurs.

1775 The first battles of the American Revolution take place at Lexington and Concord in Massachusetts on April 19. On June 17, British troops win the Battle of Bunker Hill near Boston, but suffer significant losses.

1776 Signers of the Declaration of Independence (left) include representatives from Connecticut, Massachusetts, New Hampshire, and Rhode Island (which in 1790 becomes the last of the original 13 colonies to ratify the Constitution).

1777 Colonial militias prevail in New England's last major Revolutionary War battle, near Bennington, Vermont.

1791 Fourteen years after declaring itself an independent republic, Vermont becomes the 14th state.

1800

1815–65 New England rises to literary and intellectual prominence. The region's numerous rivers power the mills that drive the growth of industry after the War of 1812.

1820 After 168 years as a territory of Massachusetts, Maine becomes the 23rd state.

1850s Underground Railroad guides such as Harriet Tubman (left) lead fugitive slaves from the South to Canada via New England, a hotbed of abolitionist sentiment.

1861–65 Hundreds of thousands of New Englanders fight in the Civil War. A raid at St. Albans, Vermont, in 1864 is the war's northernmost engagement.

1897 The first Boston Marathon is run. The first subway in America opens in Boston.

1900

1918 Following World War I, New England industry falls into decline.

1930 America's Cup yacht races move from New York to Newport, Rhode Island.

1935 Mount Mansfield in Stowe gets a towrope, the start of the transformation of Vermont into a major skiing destination.

1938 Historic hurricane causes devastation across New England, killing hundreds of people.

1975 Connecticut elects Ella Grasso, the first female governor in the U.S. who is not the wife or widow of a previous governor.

1992 Nine years after receiving federal recognition as a tribe, the Mashantucket Pequot open Foxwoods Resort Casino in Connecticut (left).

2000s

2004 The Boston Red Sox win the World Series for the first time in 86 years (left). Massachusetts legalizes same-sex marriage, followed by Connecticut (2008), Vermont (2009), and New Hampshire (2010), continuing New England's tradition of progressive politics.

2007 After 15 years and $15 billion, the "Big Dig" highway project wraps up. Replacing an ugly interstate is the new jewel of downtown Boston, the Rose Kennedy Greenway.

2009 The death of Senator Ted Kennedy, and the decision of Congressman Patrick Kennedy not to run for reelection, ends the Kennedy family's 64-year stretch of representing New England in national politics.

A Brief History of New England

> PAGES 522–23: A painting, by Paul Revere, of the Boston Massacre. THIS PAGE: An illustration shows Roger Williams rejecting Pequot pleas for assistance during the Pequot War in Rhode Island Colony in the 1630s.

Viewed from a distance, New England's history mirrors that of its namesake, England. The region rose from nowhere (by European standards) to gain tremendous historical prominence, captured a good deal of overseas trade, and became an industrial power-house and center for creative thought. And then the party ended relatively abruptly, as commerce and culture sought more fertile grounds to the west and south.

To this day, New England remains linked to its past. Walking through Boston, lay-ers of history are evident at every turn, from the church steeples of Colonial times (dwarfed by glass-sided skyscrapers that bespeak the refined sensibility of the late Victo-rian era) to verdant park-lands that bespeak the refined sensibility of the late Victo-rian era.

History is even more in-escapable in off-the-beaten-track New England. Travelers in Down East Maine, northern New Hampshire, Connecti-cut's Litchfield Hills, the Berk-shires, and much of Vermont will find clues to what Henry Wadsworth Longfellow called "the irrevocable past" every way they turn, from stone walls running through woods to Federal-style homes.

Indigenous Culture

In the 16th century, some 10,000 years after humans first reached New England on foot, European explorers began arriving by sea. Algon-quian-speaking native people lived throughout the region, where they fished, hunted, trapped, and farmed, often moving their settlements according to the seasons. By 1600, the pace of exploration was picking up, with dire con-sequences for the indigenous peoples. They had no natural immunity to smallpox, syphi-lis, and the other scourges the Europeans brought with them, and within decades, disease wiped out a sub-stantial portion of the native population. French Catholic missionaries succeeded in converting many of those who survived, and most tribes sided with the French in the French and Indian Wars in the 18th century, which cost them dearly. Afterward, the Indians fared poorly at the hands of the British and were quickly pushed to the margins.

The legacy of the New England Natives displaced by the earliest European set-tlers endures mostly in place names: Abenaki, Aquinnah, Kennebunk, Massachuset, Mikmaq, Mohegan, Nar-ragansett, Passamaquoddy, Penobscot, Pequot, Quinni-piac, Wampanoag, and many, many more. There are still a handful of tribes. Today they are found in greatest concen-tration at several reservations in Maine, while the Wam-panoags have a reservation on Martha's Vineyard. The Mohegans and the Pequots, once thought to have been extinct, have established a thriving gaming industry in Connecticut (p. 272). Sadly, other than that, the few clues left behind by Indian cultures were more or less obliterated by later settlers.

The Colonial Era

Viking explorers from Newfoundland may or may not have sailed southward into New England—stories abound—but what's certain is that the European colonists arrived in the very early 17th century and eventually displaced entirely the Native American culture that existed in the region.

It began in 1604, when some 80 French colonists spent a winter on a small island on what today is the Maine–New Brunswick border. They did not care for the harsh weather of their new home and left in spring to resettle in present-day Nova Scotia. In 1607, 3 months after the celebrated Jamestown, Virginia, colony was founded, another group of 100 settlers (this time from England) established a community at Popham Beach, in present-day Phippsburg, Maine. The Maine winter demoralized these would-be colonists as well, and they returned to England the following year.

The colonization of the region began in earnest with the arrival of the Pilgrims at Plymouth Rock in 1620. The Pilgrims—a religious group that had split from the Church of England—established the first permanent colony, although it came at a hefty price: Half the group perished during the first winter. But the colony began to thrive over the years, in part thanks to helpful Native Americans. The success of the Pilgrims

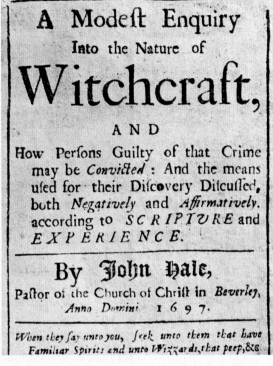

> The title page from a 1702 edition of A Modest Enquiry Into the Nature of Witchcraft, written by John Hale, a local minister who was instrumental in the Salem witch trials.

lured other settlers from England, and they established the Massachusetts Bay Colony, with Boston as its capital. Its leaders expelled Roger Williams in 1636 because of his liberal religious beliefs; he founded the city of Providence, Rhode Island. The great Puritan migration helped increase the population, and the settlers' religion exerted a strong influence on society. They associated belief in the supernatural (which was widespread in both Europe and the colonies) with rejection of God, a philosophy that helped lead to the mass hysteria we now know as the Salem witch trials in 1692.

Throughout the 17th century, colonists from Massachusetts pushed northward into what are now New Hampshire and Maine, and southward into Connecticut and Rhode Island. The first areas to be settled were lands near protected harbors along the coast or on navigable waterways. The more remote settlements came under attack in the 17th and early 18th centuries in a series of raids by Indians conducted both independently and in concert with the French. These proved temporary setbacks; colonization continued throughout New England into the 18th century.

The Revolutionary War

The colonists who settled New England were a contrarian bunch, and as early as 1687, Connecticut residents were flouting the Crown appointee who wanted to invalidate the colony's charter. Legend has it that they hid the document in the tree that became known as the Charter Oak, a symbol of the state. Relations between Great Britain and its American colonists continued to deteriorate in the 18th century. After the 1754–63 French and Indian War (known in Europe as the Seven Years' War), the situation grew openly hostile. Taxes the colonists considered unjustifiable fanned discontent, and "no taxation without representation" emerged as a rallying cry.

Starting around 1765, Great Britain launched a series of ham-handed economic policies to reign in the increasingly feisty colonies. These included a direct tax—the Stamp Act—to pay for a standing army. The crackdown provoked strong resistance. Under the banner of "no taxation without representation," disgruntled colonists engaged in a series of riots, resulting in the Boston Massacre of 1770, when five protesting colonists were fired upon and killed by British soldiers. In 1773, the most infamous protest took place in Boston. The British had imposed the Tea Act (the right to collect duties on tea imports), which prompted a group of colonists dressed as Indians to board three British ships and dump 342 chests of tea into the harbor. This

> Henry Hudson Kitson's Minuteman Statue on the Battle Green in downtown Lexington, where the American Revolution began.

incident was dubbed the Boston Tea Party.

The Revolutionary War eventually raged from Quebec to Georgia, but it started in New England, where the first shots fired in battle rang out in Lexington, Massachusetts, early on April 19, 1775. A contingent of British soldiers was sent to seize military supplies and arrest two high-profile rebels—John Hancock and Samuel Adams. The militia formed by the colonists exchanged gunfire with the British, thereby igniting the Revolution ("the shot heard round the world").

Two months later, the British prevailed at the Battle of

Bunker Hill but suffered such devastating losses that they abandoned Boston within a year. George Washington took control of the Continental Army on July 3 in Cambridge, where he made his home and headquarters for the next 10 months. The last major conflict in New England took place near Bennington, Vermont, on August 16, 1777, when forces from Vermont, New Hampshire, and Massachusetts defeated British troops and their allies. Hostilities formally ended 6 years later, in February 1783, and in September of that year, Britain recognized the United States as a sovereign nation.

Independence to Civil War

The United States established itself as an economic power in the years following independence, a trend that accelerated following the War of 1812. Across New England, trade and industry flourished. The region's large, fast-moving rivers powered textile and lumber mills and shoe and boot factories. Vermont diversified its agrarian economy with the opening of quarries that produced slate, granite, and the state's famed marble. Connecticut, home to inventors Eli Whitney and Samuel Colt, was a center of munitions and clock manufacturing. Whaling vessels and clipper ships constructed and based in New England ports like Nantucket, Massachusetts, and Mystic, Connecticut, circled the globe, returning laden with treasures. Many of the lighthouses that helped guide them back into port survive, a lasting symbol of the region's seagoing legacy.

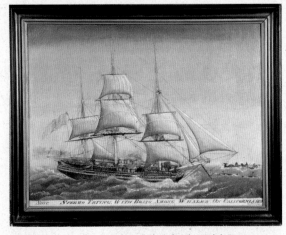

> Whaling ships sailing out of Nantucket often hunted their prey in the Pacific, as in this painting by John Fisher at the Nantucket Whaling Museum.

Meanwhile, in 1796, John Adams had been elected the second President of the United States, the first of seven native New Englanders to hold the office. Adams was a member of the Federalist Party, whose influence persisted in New England well after it declined elsewhere—an early indication of the region's tendency to go its own way politically. Another important regional export that emerged in this period was prominent authors and philosophers, notably Ralph Waldo Emerson, Henry David Thoreau, Nathaniel Hawthorne, Herman Melville, and Henry Wadsworth Longfellow. Three 19th-century New England writers whose work endures were women: Louisa May Alcott, Emily Dickinson, and Harriet Beecher Stowe, author of *Uncle Tom's Cabin.*

Stowe and her fellow abolitionists, including the fiery William Lloyd Garrison, were the heirs to long-standing beliefs about individual liberty. Slavery was widespread in Colonial New England and persisted after the Revolution, but resistance dated to early Colonial days. By the time of the Civil War, the courts and people of the region typically took an abolitionist stance.

New England fueled the Union war effort with the products of its thriving industries, including firearms, and hundreds of thousands of troops. They included the 54th Massachusetts Colored Regiment, the first army unit made up of free black soldiers (and the subject of the 1989 film *Glory*).

The Gilded Age

Profound changes swept across the United States in the decades following the Civil War, a period of unprecedented economic growth in most areas. Immigrants poured into Connecticut, Rhode Island, Maine, and Massachusetts, where mills drove demand for labor and the expanding railroad system aided the distribution of goods. Boston, a magnet for new arrivals from Ireland, was also an intellectual powerhouse proud to call itself the "Athens of America." The growth of the railroads was a mixed blessing for inland areas such as Vermont, which enjoyed expanded markets for exports but saw considerable emigration in pursuit of nonfarming jobs. Resourceful New Englanders took advantage of the transportation network to develop a new use for the region's natural resources: tourism.

Newly mobile Americans

> *Marble House, a Newport "cottage" designed by Richard Morris Hunt for a grandson of Commodore Cornelius Vanderbilt.*

made New England a desirable vacation destination. Mountain resorts and beach communities flourished. Magnificent residences sprang up in the Berkshires, the White Mountains, Bar Harbor, and especially Newport. Newport's cottages are one of the enduring legacies of this period, along with tension between some year-round New England residents and "summer people." The Panic of 1893 effectively ended the Gilded Age, but its legacy endures to this day.

The 20th Century

The first half of the 20th century found New England's one-time prominence on the national stage a fading memory. The slow decline of the region's agriculture continued in tandem with the relocation of many manufacturing jobs west and south, where labor

> *President John F. Kennedy stayed true to his New England roots, spending time on Cape Cod even after he took office in 1960.*

was cheaper and resources more plentiful. World War I saw an uptick in economic activity, but the ravages of the Great Depression soon took their toll. With the outbreak of World War II, the tide began to turn.

The wartime economy was strong, and defense contracting boosted factories in southern Connecticut and parts of the Maine coast, among other places, an influence that endured as the Cold War took hold. More important was the influx of veterans attending college on the GI Bill in the 1940s and 1950s, sowing the seeds of the tech revolution of the second half of the century. In 1946, Bostonians elected to Congress a young veteran who would help change New England's reputation for stuffiness to an image of innovation and youth: John F. Kennedy.

In the mid–20th century, it became clear that national trends would be dictating New England's future rather than the other way around. The postwar rise of the interstate highway system echoed the transformation the railroads had worked on New England's economy a century earlier, but this time the ascendant sector was services rather than goods. Higher education, long a privilege of the elite, became a given for the middle class, creating a boom for New England's many colleges and universities. Tourism became even more important, especially in northern New England. Vermont and New Hampshire expanded their ski areas, and Maine added the word "Vacationland" to its license plates. In the last quarter of the century, high-tech businesses brought great prosperity to Boston and its suburbs as far away as New Hampshire and Rhode Island. New York City's revival boosted southern Connecticut's fortunes, driving up real estate prices in commuter suburbs; it also raised the profile of vacation destinations such as the Litchfield Hills, in the northwest part of the state.

> *The Rose Kennedy Greenway, the mile-long, block-wide park that graces downtown Boston.*

The 21st Century

Even as the United States grows ever more homogeneous, New England's regional identity helps make it an irresistible draw for visitors. The phrase "New England" evokes many associations—skiing, sailing, college, the Red Sox, lobster, maple syrup, clam chowder, fall foliage—but almost never "just like everywhere else." Politically and socially, the region remains generally more liberal than much of the rest of the country. Even famously conservative New Hampshire has a Democratic governor and legal gay marriage, and Maine's Republican U.S. Senators are considered among the most moderate members of their party. The urban-rural divide persists, but today it's likely to signify the difference between a research scientist and a telecommuting Web designer rather than between a factory worker and a subsistence farmer. The northern New England states in particular cling to their distinct identities, remaining as different from their southern neighbors as they are from one another: Consider Vermont's independent-minded legislators, New Hampshire's starring role in presidential politics, and Maine's open-door policy for Somali refugees (and the resulting conflicts). The mall-ification that's sweeping so many other places has certainly affected Connecticut, Rhode Island, and Massachusetts, but they remain uniquely appealing destinations. Pay attention during your travels, and you can write your own ending to this story.

THE WITCHING HOUR

Salem's Dark Defining Moment

BY MARIE MORRIS

SALEM OWES ITS WORLDWIDE FAME NOT TO ITS RICH HISTORY as an early American settlement and a prominent 19th-century seaport, but to an incident that lasted less than a year—the witch trials of 1692. The story of the trials endures as an unforgettable lesson in the dangers of prejudice and groupthink.

Whispers of Witchcraft

THE SETTING

Salem Village (now the town of Danvers), was an insular community under the repressive control of the work-and-prayer-minded Puritan clergy. The white

settlement in Salem was fewer than 70 years old, and even well-educated colonists believed in witchcraft—the devil was as real as God to the pious Puritans.

THE CHARACTERS

The household of Salem Village's minister, the Rev.

THE ACCUSED

At first, only Tituba, and Sarah Good and Sarah Osborne (both social outcasts and neighbors) were accused of casting spells. Tituba was arrested and confessed, saying that she had seen the devil and that Good and Osborne were her conspirators. Before long, an accusation of witchcraft became a handy way to settle a score. Anyone who didn't quite fit in was a potential target, though some of the accused were prosperous, upstanding citizens caught up in the hysteria.

THE TRIALS

A special court convened in Salem, and although the girls recanted, trials ensued. Defendants had no counsel, and objecting or pleading not guilty was considered akin to confessing. Spectral evidence, such as accounts of dreams and visions, was considered legitimate testimony. From March 1 to September 17, the court convicted and

sentenced to death 25 of the 150-plus people accused. In the end, 14 women and five men went to the gallows, including Good. Eighty-year-old Giles Corey refused to plead and was pressed to death by stones piled on a board on his chest over an agonizing 2 days. The other convicted "witches" died in custody, including Osborne.

In October, with the jails overflowing, Governor William Phips dissolved the court, and eventually all those accused and convicted were freed.

What Really Happened?

In his play *The Crucible*, Arthur Miller blamed repression for the trials, but scientists offer other theories. Some scholars blame a bird-borne pathogen, while others posit that encephalitis explains the spasms and cries of some "bewitched" people and livestock. One intriguing theory points to ergot, an LSD-related fungus that affects rye and causes symptoms that would be familiar to any resident of Salem in mid–1692: convulsions, sensations of heat and pinpricks in the arms and legs, even hallucinations. The weather in 1691 had been rainy and damp, creating perfect conditions for ergot to thrive in rye, an important grain in the colonists' diet. In 1692, as the witchcraft accusations died down, the weather turned warm and dry.

Samuel Parris, included his 9-year-old daughter, Elizabeth (Betty); her 11-year-old cousin Abigail Williams; and Tituba, a slave who told stories of witchcraft and sorcery to amuse the girls during the long, harsh winter. Around January 1692, the children and their friends began acting out the stories, claiming to be under a spell, shouting, and wailing. They fell into delirious fits, reported pains in their limbs and bellies, and had what we now recognize as hallucinations. Physicians could find no medical explanation, and prayers provided no relief. The leap from the inexplicable to suspicions of witchcraft was a short one indeed.

The Lay of the Land

An Inside Look: State by State

New England is more diverse than one might think by looking at a map. Each of the six states this book covers has a distinct personality of its own. Here is a brief look at each.

MASSACHUSETTS

The Bay State has always been the place in New England with the most drama and intrigue. (Remember the Boston Tea Party and Paul Revere's Ride?) And it still is. The place that brought you the Kennedys hit the news wires hard again in early 2010 when the state's famously Democratic voters elected (the horror!) a Republican senator—the first time that had happened in ages. A few years previous, Bay Staters had elected their first black governor, former Attorney General Deval Patrick, to office. And Massachusetts political figures continue to make waves nationally, such as Senator John Kerry, who narrowly lost the nation's Presidential election to incumbent George W. Bush in 2004.

Still, through it all, there are always the Red Sox—the single-most-unifying force in the six New England states. Two recent World Series titles (in 2004 and 2007) brought unspeakable joy to the entire region—followed by a return to the usual grousing about the Yankees—while the New England Patriots and Boston Celtics won Super Bowls and an NBA Championship, cementing the city's claim as America's new "Titletown."

> *Connecticut's upscale shoreline is known as the Gold Coast.*

CONNECTICUT

The state of Connecticut, quite frankly, for many years, was basically one big plot of farmland with a strip of shipbuilders on its fringe of a coast. You can still find the odd tobacco barn, boatyard, naval base, or orchard here and there, but otherwise those days are long gone; today the state has found some interesting new niches in which to sustain itself. The Hartford suburb of Bristol has found a surprising second life as the world headquarters for ESPN, the planet's largest sports broadcasting network.

Meanwhile, the southwestern coast—such towns as Greenwich and Fairfield—has become one of the wealthiest places in the entire country, thanks to its location within commuting distance of New York City. Hedge funds are particularly fond of setting up shop in these parts. Yale University continues to breathe erudite life into New Haven; Stamford is experiencing a minirevival as an alternative business center to high-rent Manhattan; and the many quiet byways stretching into forested hills continue to attract leaf peepers, second-home buyers, and vacationers just as they have always done.

RHODE ISLAND

Pretty little Rhode Island just goes about its business, staying out of the news and seemingly immune to all the barbs about its size. Quick, what's the top industry in America's smallest state? Tourism? No. Manufacturing? Not. Try "health services" (chain pharmacy CVS is based here, among other companies). There's also a smattering of light industry and business and insurance services, plus tourism as visitors come to gawk at the lovely mansions of Newport or enjoy the capital city of Providence (home to Brown University).

> *The Flume Gorge draws visitors to Franconia Notch State Park, in New Hampshire's White Mountains.*

> *Cape Elizabeth Light is one of the two iconic Maine beacons that gave Two Lights State Park its name.*

VERMONT

Change is afoot in the Green Mountains. Of course, this has always been a place of gorgeous hiking and ski trails, Robert Frostian walks, scenic back-road drives, and wonderful inns. It's both the fall-foliage and the maple syrup capital of the Western world. Yet something else is up: Hotshot gourmet chefs are pouring into the place at what seems like a breakneck pace.

Even quite small towns—Manchester, Essex, Warren, Wilmington, and Vergennes, to name just a few—have Michelin-worthy restaurants. It's somehow all appropriate for the U.S. state with the smallest capital (Montpelier, pop. 8,000).

Meanwhile, Lake Champlain still beckons with its lovely sunsets; and Burlington is slowly changing from a hippie town (though it still has a progressive-party mayor) into a sophisticated little place of light industry, technology, and gourmet eats.

NEW HAMPSHIRE

Like Vermont, tough and historic New Hampshire is also changing. In a state where it was unthinkable to vote anything but Republican, the state has elected Democratic governors, senators, and representatives in recent years—though it still stubbornly resists a state sales tax.

Some things remain unchanged, thankfully: Portsmouth is still an odd amalgam of pierced baristas, antique homes and inns, fishermen, folk musicians, and good restaurants. Hanover still stars Dartmouth College. Lake Winnipesaukee is still a huge, lovely, placid body of water ringed with quiet towns (such as Wolfeboro) and honky-tonk attractions. Finally, the White Mountains will never change. New England's best backcountry hiking and camping are still found here, and always will be.

MAINE

Maine is holding its own. You can still see a loon here, or catch a glimpse of bestselling horror author Stephen King, who bases many of his books here. You can still eat lobsters and fresh-caught fish, and photograph some

> *The Appalachian Trail passes through five of the six New England states.*

of the world's most famous lighthouses. The economy isn't booming, but it's not at rock bottom, either. Portland remains one of New England's best places to visit and dine in, with architecture and restaurants that rival anywhere else, while the Kennebunks and the Yorks offer choice beaches for summer lazing and strolls plus plenty of souvenir shops. Maine's rocky coast is still the stuff of legend, art, and poetry—a list of quaint towns and drives would fill an entire book and then some.

An uncomfortable divide is starting to develop in places. As you get upcountry, for instance, you can feel a difference between affluence (huge summer mansions on Mount Desert Island or around Penobscot Bay) and the hard-working locals who fish, lobster, or wait tables in summer, then tow cars or shovel and plow snow the rest of the year to get by. Land values have shot up in these lovely

regions. Regardless, they're some of my favorite places to visit in New England: towns such as Freeport, Camden, and Blue Hill, plus the natural wonders of amazing Acadia National Park. Finally, the big Woods of Maine pose a future battleground—for now, timber and paper companies, forest activists, and developers maintain a standoff. But one day, when the economy kicks upward again, values may clash. Meanwhile, Mount Katahdin and Moosehead Lake will always be worth a visit, no matter what.

New England's Geography

New England began to take shape about a billion years ago. Magma rose through the planet's mantle and hardened, oceans rose and receded, continental masses collided. Sediment became sedimentary rock, which smashing landmasses converted into metamorphic rock. After hundreds of thousands of years of upheaval, the Appalachian Mountains arose, extending

from southern Canada to the southeastern U.S. If you think of the Appalachians as being farther south, remember that the Appalachian Trail cuts across New England. The region's highest peak is Mount Washington, in New Hampshire's White Mountains, which are part of the Appalachians. At 6,288 feet, Mount Washington is tiny compared to the behemoths of the American West, but scientists believe that the Appalachians were once comparable in size to the Himalayas. Their weather-worn contours indicate their immense age.

Ice Age glaciers also helped create the appearance of present-day New England. Glaciers as much as a mile deep repeatedly advanced and receded, carving grooves in the rocky surface of the earth and depositing huge boulders in random places. Melting glaciers helped determine the course and size of many New England rivers, including the Connecticut, Merrimack, and Housatonic. They gouged out Lake Champlain and Lake Winnipesaukee, and they created moraines—huge deposits of geologic debris—that became islands when thawing ice created oceans. Block Island, Martha's Vineyard, and Nantucket are all moraines; the most prominent moraine in New England is Cape Cod. The coast of the Cape is in constant flux, as you can see by visiting the Monomoy Islands, which are (for now) on the constantly shifting coast of Chatham.

The geologic transformations that created New England's mountains and

> *Moose are the largest members of the deer family, and male moose can weigh over 1,400 pounds.*

rivers also shaped the coast. New London, Newport, New Bedford, Boston, Gloucester, Portsmouth, and Portland grew up around deep, sheltered harbors that made them important commercial centers. Visitors today who aren't arriving by cruise ship probably associate the rocky, treacherous New England coast with a more eye-catching feature: lighthouses.

New England Flora

Diverse terrain makes New England an excellent place for wildflowers. They range from plants that thrive in low-lying coastal areas to alpine species around the peaks of Vermont, New Hampshire, and Maine. Evergreen trees and shrubs are a familiar sight throughout the region; they include fir, hemlock, juniper, pine, spruce, and yew.

The best-known plants in New England—even more famous than Maine blueberries and potatoes—are deciduous trees and shrubs that change color in the fall. A quick biology lesson: Chlorophyll makes most leaves appear green in the spring and summer. When cold weather hits, chlorophyll production slows, revealing hidden colors. The duration and intensity of foliage season depends on the weather. Ash trees, birches, chestnuts, elms, hickories, and lindens turn yellow; maples orange to vibrant red; dogwoods, magnolias, sumacs, and sycamores red; elms and oaks mostly brown; and American beeches gold. Most trees eventually fade to a muddy brown. Larch trees, which have leaves resembling evergreen needles that change color and drop in autumn, turn yellow.

New England Fauna

The mammal population of New England is roughly the same assortment you see elsewhere in the Northeast U.S. and eastern Canada. Deer are so plentiful that some frustrated gardeners compare them to squirrels. Dairy cows ply their trade across the region and are a symbol of Vermont (do hands-on research with a container of Ben & Jerry's).

Moose live largely in Vermont, New Hampshire, and Maine but are spotted in Connecticut and Massachusetts. Gray wolves, which were extinct in New England by the mid-19th century, began reestablishing themselves in far northern areas in the early 21st century.

The creatures that distinguish the region, for the most part, aren't land dwellers; they're migratory birds, fish, and shellfish, as well as some unforgettable marine mammals. The presence of the Atlantic flyway makes the New England coast a magnet for serious birders, who often spot rare species passing through in the spring and fall. Although the fishing stocks of the north Atlantic are depleted, fresh seafood remains an important element of life in New England. Species range from codfish, which were once so plentiful that a whole peninsula bears their name, to the tasty crustaceans that make Maine synonymous with lobster. The five states with ocean beaches produce clams as well as oysters and mussels (you need a license to harvest shellfish). The biggest attraction in the waters off the region are the migrating whales that pass through every summer. Humpback, finback, and minke whales—which eat fish, crustaceans, and plankton—sometimes share their habitat with sharks. Although *Jaws* was filmed partly on Martha's Vineyard, the appearance of a great white is rare enough that it can create a boom in tourism, as it did in Chatham, on Cape Cod, in the summer of 2010.

New England's Art & Architecture

> When Winslow Homer's Breezing Up *was first exhibited in 1876, it was hailed as a masterpiece, and a symbol of the U.S.'s adventurous spirit.*

Since Colonial times, New Englanders have embraced the visual arts, building temples to them in the cities and establishing artists' colonies in mountain and beach communities. Even in the 17th and early 18th centuries, when the demands and expenses of day-to-day life tended to outweigh aesthetic concerns, itinerant painters could make a living creating portraits. Gold- and silversmiths, cabinetmakers, quilters, and even headstone carvers demonstrated their artistic talents in practical ways.

The most prominent artist in Colonial America, **John Singleton Copley** (1738–1815), established himself as a portraitist in Boston. The Museum of Fine Arts in Boston (p. 70, ❺) owns an excellent collection of his work. Also at the MFA is an iconic portrait of George Washington by Rhode Island native **Gilbert Stuart** (1755–1828),

who painted the first six U.S. presidents. **Winslow Homer** (1836–1910) was born in Boston and became one of the most prominent American painters of the 19th century. **James Abbott McNeill Whistler** (1830–1903) made his reputation in London but was a Lowell, Massachusetts, native. **Fitz Henry Lane** (1804–65) painted iconic images of the New England coast, many of which are collected in his native Gloucester, Massachusetts, at the Cape Ann Museum (p. 130, ❹). **John Singer Sargent** (1856–1925), an American born and raised in Europe, left his mark on New England in his magnificent murals at the **Boston Public Library** and the **Museum of Fine Arts** (p. 70, ❺).

Two New Englanders loom large in the sculpture of this era. **Daniel Chester French** (1850–1931) created the *Minute Man* statue in Concord,

Massachusetts (p. 121, ❹), and the John Harvard statue in Harvard Yard (p. 59, ❸), Cambridge, as well as the figure of Lincoln that dominates the Lincoln Memorial in Washington, D.C. **Augustus Saint-Gaudens** (1848–1907) designed the Robert Gould Shaw Memorial on Boston Common (p. 50, ❷) and eventually moved to New Hampshire, where his home is a National Historic Site (p. 432, ❹).

A museum devoted to the work of beloved painter and illustrator **Norman Rockwell** (1894–1978), who lived in Vermont and western Massachusetts, is in Stockbridge, Massachusetts (p. 237, ❷). His contemporaries include **Andrew Wyeth** (1917–2009), who had a summer home in Maine. One of his best-known paintings, *Christina's World*, depicts a neighbor. The Farnsworth Art Museum in Rockland (p. 518, ❶) houses a notable collection of Wyeth's work. Other part-time New England residents include **Edward Hopper** (1882–1967), who sought inspiration on the coast of Maine and later spent summers on Cape Cod, and muralist **Thomas Hart Benton** (1889–1975), a sometime resident of Martha's Vineyard. Sculptor and painter **Louise Nevelson** (1899–1988) grew up in Maine.

The best way to get a sense of New England's artists, past and present, is to visit one of its dozens of museums. Beyond the big names in Boston and Hartford, you'll

> On the easel in Norman Rockwell's studio at the museum in Stock-bridge, MA, that bears his name is The Golden Rule (Do Unto Others), a Saturday Evening Post cover.

> A clapboard house on Cape Cod.

find worthwhile institutions on many college campuses, in vacation destinations, and even in unlikely places such as Manchester, New Hampshire, and St. Johnsbury, Vermont.

Architecture

New England's wide variety of architecture makes it a visual treat. From utilitarian 17th-century homes to eco-conscious 21st-century class-room buildings, the region has it all.

The oldest structures (found in every state but Vermont) date to the 17th century, when most buildings were made of wood and heated and lighted by fire—it's a miracle any survive. These **Colonial** structures are boxy, no-frills affairs, often covered in shingles or rough clapboards. They're typically Tudor, rather than stereotypically Colonial (which is actually Colonial revival) in style. Ipswich, Massachusetts, is a treasure-trove of "First Period" houses, such as the 1677 Whipple House. Other good examples are Boston's Paul Revere House (ca. 1680) and the Sherburne House (1695/1703) at the Strawbery Banke Museum (p. 445, ❸) in Portsmouth, New Hampshire.

Georgian style is fancier, reflecting the greater variety of building materials available in the 18th century. Brick and stone come into use, and windows are larger. These structures have Palladian windows, decorative moldings, and symmetrical features. Deerfield, Massachusetts, in

> *A stately Beacon Hill home.*

> *Betts House, originally a private home, is now a Yale University administration building.*

> *The stunning Institute of Contemporary Art, in Boston, was designed by noted architects Diller Scofidio + Renfro and completed in 2006.*

the Pioneer Valley, has many early Georgian homes. Good places to see examples of later Georgian style include Providence, Rhode Island, and Portsmouth, New Hampshire.

The iconic New England architectural style is **Federal** (1780–1820). Popularized by Boston architect Charles Bulfinch, it draws on the conventions of classical antiquity for its austere features: Ionic and Corinthian detailing, frequently in white against brick or clapboard; fanlights over doors; and an almost maniacal insistence on symmetry. **Kennebunkport, Maine** (p. 510), is a good place to see Federal-style buildings, as is the **Beacon Hill** neighborhood of Boston (p. 78).

Greek Revival (1820–60) buildings are easy to identify thanks to their massive columns supporting projecting porticos. More popular in the South than in New England,

where the most prominent example is **Quincy Market** (1826), home of the Faneuil Hall market in Boston (p. 52, ⑧), this style also left its mark in several Vermont towns. The Meeting House and General Store at the Shelburne Museum (p. 383) are two good illustrations.

The impressive scale and ornamentation of **Gothic Revival** and **Carpenter Gothic**

(1840–80) architecture made these styles popular for college buildings. The Boston College and Yale University campuses abound with examples, as does the town of Oak Bluffs, on Martha's Vineyard (p. 218).

Victorian (1860–1900) is an umbrella term for the elaborate styles that prevailed during most of Queen Victoria's reign. Newport,

Rhode Island, is a good place to get a sense of its wide variety. Betts House (1868) on the Yale campus is a typical mansard-roofed Victorian building. The South End of Boston is the largest Victorian neighborhood in the country.

On Cape Cod and all along the Maine coast, **Shingle** (1880–1900) architecture prevails. This style abounds with gables and porches; shingles typically cover the buildings from roofline to foundation.

Notable examples of **Modern** (1900–present) architecture in New England are mostly on college campuses, often in the Boston area. The angular, airy **International Style** is well represented at Harvard, where Bauhaus veterans Walter Gropius and Marcel Breuer were on the faculty. Yale abounds with outstanding designs (and superstar professors), as does the MIT campus, with its Saarinen chapel.

An eye-catching **Postmodern** (1975–present) design is Boston's Institute of Contemporary Art (2006; p. 85), which is dramatically cantilevered over the harbor. But New England's most significant recent structure isn't a building. Boston's Leonard P. Zakim Bunker Hill Memorial Bridge (2003) is a cable-stayed structure that echoes the rigging of the USS *Constitution,* the warship anchored nearby.

Portrait Sculptures

Gratifyingly often, as you're exploring a New England area associated with a person, you can satisfy your curiosity about his or her appearance almost immediately. The art of portrait sculpture dates to classical antiquity, so of course the Victorians embraced it; many of these pieces were commissioned in the second half of the 19th century. Look for politicians, war heroes, and other historical figures, authors, and more. Here are just a few to get you started.

State capitols and college campuses are good places to see portrait sculptures. You'll find **Franklin Pierce** and **Daniel Webster** at the New Hampshire State House in Concord, **John F. Kennedy** and **Anne Hutchinson** at the State House in Boston, and **Ethan Allen** at the Vermont State House in Montpelier. **Nathan Hale** is on the campus of his alma mater, Yale; **John Harvard** (pictured above) is on the grounds of the school that bears his name. And **Emily Dickinson** appears at her museum in Amherst, Massachusetts (p. 244, ⑤). Boston is great for this: **Benjamin Franklin** crops up downtown at two points on the Freedom Trail (p. 51, ⑤ and p. 74, ⑨), and equestrian renderings of **George Washington** (in the Public Garden; p. 47, ⑧) and **Paul Revere** (in the North End; p. 83, ⑤) are well worth a visit.

Some sculptures are less highfalutin but perhaps more relatable. In downtown Portland, Maine, movie director **John Ford** is captured sitting in a director's chair. Entertainment legend **George M. Cohan** is depicted in downtown Providence, Rhode Island, his birthplace. And outside Fenway Park (p. 66, ❶) in Boston, Red Sox great **Ted Williams** appears twice, placing his baseball cap on a young fan's head, and standing with teammates Bobby Doerr, Johnny Pesky, and Dom DiMaggio.

New England in High & Popular Culture

In addition to reading some of the books discussed below, visitors planning an extended trip to New England should check out the Frommer's guides to New England (all published by Wiley Publishing, Inc.), including the Complete and Day by Day guides to Boston; Cape Cod, Martha's Vineyard & Nantucket; Vermont, New Hampshire & Maine; and the Maine Coast.

Books

The first book printed in the English colonies was produced in Cambridge, Massachusetts, in 1640, and a list of books and authors connected to New England could fill a whole volume and still barely scratch the surface. To help set the scene before you leave home, seek out titles related to your destination and interests. Here are just a few suggestions to get you started—an online search or a stroll around a library or bookstore will surely generate more suggestions.

Religious tracts dominated early New England literature, and the region was soon known for poetry. In 1650, **Anne Bradstreet** (ca. 1612–72), a member of the band of Puritans who founded Boston, published a book of poems in London; she's considered the first American poet. Fellow Bostonian **Phillis Wheatley** (1753–84) was the first published African-American woman poet. **Henry Wadsworth Longfellow**

> Henry David Thoreau's Civil Disobedience, *in which he argues the need to take a moral stand against unjust laws, is still required reading among activists.*

(1807–72), a Maine native who settled in Cambridge, was one of the foremost American poets of the 19th century. He wrote "The Courtship of Miles Standish," set in Plymouth, and the stirring but historically inaccurate "Paul Revere's Ride." The genius of **Emily Dickinson** (1830–86) wasn't recognized until after her death; her home is now part of the Emily Dickinson Museum, in Amherst, Massachusetts (p. 244, **5**). **James Russell Lowell** (1819–91), of Cambridge, was an influential poet, critic, and editor. Later poets include imagist **Amy Lowell** (1874–1925), from Brookline, Massachusetts, and **Edna St. Vincent Millay** (1892–1950), from Camden, Maine. The iconic New

> Poet and essayist Ralph Waldo Emerson led the 19th century Transcendentalist movement.

England poet of the 20th century is **Robert Frost** (1874–1963), who lived in Massachusetts, New Hampshire, and Vermont and famously said, "Literature begins with geography." Today, New Hampshire alone is home to two former poets laureate of the U.S., **Maxine Kumin** and **Donald Hall.**

Any discussion of New England fiction must include **Nathaniel Hawthorne** (1804–64), author of *The Scarlet Letter* and *The House of the Seven Gables,* who was educated in Maine and spent much of his life in Massachusetts. His neighbor and sometime-student **Louisa May Alcott** (1832–88) based *Little Women* and her other children's books on her early life in Concord. *Moby-Dick,* by **Herman Melville** (1819–91), is the definitive introduction to the whaling trade that was vital to southern New England in the late 18th and 19th centuries. One of the most influential American writers of this period was the abolitionist **Harriet Beecher Stowe** (1811–86), author of *Uncle Tom's Cabin;* President Lincoln reputedly said she "wrote the book that made" the Civil War. She lived much of her life as a neighbor of **Mark Twain** (himself an adopted New Englander) in Hartford, Connecticut, and you can visit their respective homes (p. 298, ❺ and ❻).

John Updike and **John Cheever** both chronicled the malaise of the New England suburbs. Cheever's *Wapshot* books provide a particularly illuminating—and hilarious—view of New England sensibilities in the mid-20th century.

The uncontested big name (as in mega-bestselling) among contemporary fiction writers is **Stephen King,** a Maine resident with a soft spot for the Boston Red Sox. Give his *Salem's Lot* a read before you get to Maine and you may have trouble sleeping. **John Irving,** author of *The Cider House Rules,* lives in Vermont but is better known for his novels set in New Hampshire. Others whose fiction takes place largely in New England include **Jodi Picoult** of New Hampshire, **Chris Bohjalian** of Vermont, **Wally Lamb** of Connecticut, and **Alice Hoffman** and **Anita Shreve** of Massachusetts. **Dennis Lehane's** crime novels, including *Mystic River,* bring Boston to life.

New England continues to attract writers drawn to the noted educational institutions

> *Pulitzer Prize–winning novelist Philip Roth has set several of his books, including* The Ghost Writer *and* The Human Stain, *in the Berkshires.*

and the privacy of rural life. Prominent contemporary writers and poets who live in the region at least part of the year include **Nicholson Baker, Christopher Buckley, P. J. O'Rourke, Philip Roth,** and **Bill Bryson.**

Nonfiction writers whose work still resonates include Concord residents abolitionists, and champions of the individual **Ralph Waldo Emerson** (1803–82) and especially **Henry David Thoreau** (1817–62), whose back-to-nature outlook seems particularly prescient in the eco-conscious present. Be sure to read *Walden* before you pay a visit to the Boston area. Countless historians have made New England their home and subject; one of the most prominent in recent years was **David McCullough,** a Martha's Vineyard resident whose *1776* and *John Adams* helped bring the American Revolution and its aftermath to life. *The Perfect Storm,* by **Sebastian Junger,** tells the

story of a Massachusetts-based fishing boat caught in historically bad weather; it will change the way you look at seafood on a menu.

Children's books make a fantastic introduction to New England, even for adults. *One Morning in Maine, Blueberries for Sal,* and *Make Way for Ducklings* are classics by **Robert McCloskey,** a summer resident of Maine. His neighbor **E. B. White** set one of the best-loved books in children's literature, *Charlotte's Web,* in Maine, and made Boston an important part of *The Trumpet of the Swan. The Witch of Blackbird Pond,* by Massachusetts and Connecticut resident **Elizabeth George Speare,** takes place in the Connecticut Colony but sheds light on the Salem-witch-trial hysteria of 1692. Another excellent historical title is *Johnny Tremain,* by **Esther Forbes,** a fictional boy's-eye-view account of Boston during the Revolutionary War.

Movies & TV

New England has been a movie star since 1920, when Lillian Gish starred in the Maine-set *Way Down East*. Hollywood soundstages often stand in for city streets, but there's only one way to capture the beauty of New England's countryside and seacoast, and that's to make the trip. The backdrops shine in films ranging from soapy efforts such as *Peyton Place* (1957; Maine) and *The Four Seasons* (1981; Vermont) to dramas *Amistad* (1997) and *Revolutionary Road* (2008), which both shot in Connecticut. *Amistad* also used some Rhode Island locations, as did Connecticut-set *Mystic Pizza* (1988). Peter and Bobby Farrelly's *Dumb and Dumber* (1994) and *Me, Myself & Irene* (2000) feature scenes set in the filmmakers' native Rhode Island; at the other end of the classy scale is *High Society* (1956), which showcases Newport's mansions and Grace Kelly in her final film role.

Vermont shines in *Baby Boom* (1987) and *Funny Farm* (1988), both of which paint the state as the perfect antidote to high-powered city life, and Alfred Hitchcock's *The Trouble with Harry* (1955), a considerably less sunny effort. Stephen King wrote the source material for many films set in Maine, most of which were filmed elsewhere; an exception is *Thinner* (1996). Lillian Gish's final film, *The Whales of August* (1987), was shot in Maine. Other Maine productions include *Carousel* (1956), *Forrest Gump* (1994), and *Jumanji* (1995),

> *Matt Damon and Robin Williams in* Good Will Hunting. *Damon shared the Academy Award for Best Original Screenplay with Ben Affleck, and Williams captured Best Supporting Actor.*

which also used some New Hampshire locations. New Hampshire stars along with Henry Fonda and Katharine Hepburn in *On Golden Pond* (1981), which filmed on and around Squam Lake and Lake Winnipesaukee. The 1940 version of *Our Town*, the dramatic work perhaps most closely associated with New Hampshire, used some local background shots but filmed mostly in California.

Thanks to favorable tax laws, Massachusetts has soared in popularity with filmmakers in recent years. The movie that helped launch the trend was *Good Will Hunting* (1997), which was followed by some future classics and

> *Angela Lansbury in the hit tv series* Murder, She Wrote, *which was set in Maine.*

a whole lot of clunkers. Films worth boasting about include *Mystic River* (2003), *The Departed* (2006), *Gone Baby Gone* (2007), *The Great Debaters* (2007), *Shutter Island* (2010), *The Town* (2010), *The Fighter* (2010), and *The Social Network* (2010). If you have a high tolerance for sports and sentiment, rent *Fever Pitch* (2005), which filmed partly at Fenway Park and got a new ending after the Sox won the World Series for the first time in 86 years.

Television has done as much as any movie to familiarize international audiences with New England. *Cheers* (1982–93) was so popular that two Boston bars are named after it. *Empire Falls* (2005), an HBO miniseries based on the Richard Russo novel, shot in multiple locales in Maine, and *Brotherhood* (2006–08) made good use of its Rhode Island locations. *Newhart* (1982–90) was set in a Vermont B&B, and *Murder, She Wrote* (1984–96) took place in a crime-ridden Maine community, the fictional Cabot Cove. More recently, *Boston Public, The Practice,* and *Boston Legal* explored facets of public schools and legal practice in that city.

Music

New England musicians have contributed mightily to the American music scene. An exhaustive list of stars is impossible here, but following are a few of the notable highlights: Folk-pop singer **James Taylor** was born in Boston, long ensconced on Martha's Vineyard, and now resides in

> *Phish guitarist Trey Anastasio, who was a University of Vermont student when he co-founded the band in 1983.*

his beloved Berkshires. His former wife, **Carly Simon,** still calls Martha's Vineyard home.

Pop stars **Michael Bolton** and **John Mayer** were both born in Connecticut, while jam-band **Phish** was formed in Burlington, Vermont, in 1983 by college friends. Texas-based country-folk musician **Slaid Cleaves** was raised in western Maine. Nashville singer-songwriter **Patty Griffin** was also born and raised in Maine.

The still-going-strong band **Aerosmith** has roots in Boston (and first played together in a barn in New Hampshire), while '70s rock group **Boston** was fronted by residents of that city. Indeed, Boston has had a wildly diverse music scene over the years. The **J. Geils Band** and **The Cars** scored Top 40 hits, while seminal alternative bands like **The Pixies, Throwing Muses, Mission of Burma,** and **Galaxie 500** inspired legions of musicians. My suggestion? Download the **Standells'** "Dirty Water," their ode to '60s-era Boston (the title refers to the Charles River) before hitting the town.

Eating & Drinking in New England

> Homarus americanus, *known to its fans as "Yum, lobster!" See pp. 470-71 for the juicy details.*

> *A competitor in a chowder cook-off in Newport.*

Live lobsters, clam chowder, or cheddar cheese can be at your door less than a day after you develop a craving, but there's a lot to be said for going to the source for New England's famous foodstuffs.

From the Ocean
Seafood is a world-famous New England specialty, and you'll find it on the menu at many restaurants, no matter the cuisine or price point. Maine **lobsters** are the star of the show, and well worth a trip to the source. Order a boiled or steamed lobster and you'll usually get a plastic bib, broth and drawn butter (for dipping), a nutcracker (for the claws and tail), and a pick (for the legs). Restaurants price lobsters by the pound; expect to pay at least $15 for a "chicken" (1- to 1¼-lb.)

lobster and more for bigger specimens. Lobster out of the shell may be available in a "roll" (lobster-salad sandwich on a grilled roll), in a "pie" (casserole), stuffed and baked or broiled, in or over pasta, and in creamy bisque. The rough-hewn restaurants known as lobster pounds dot the Maine coast, and clam shacks crop up on the seashore everywhere else in New England, notably on Cape Cod and in Rhode Island and Connecticut.

Cod is sublime fresh out of the ocean. **Scrod** or schrod is a generic term for fresh white-fleshed fish, usually served in filets. The fish in fish and chips is often Atlantic **haddock.** Local **shellfish** includes clams, oysters, scallops, mussels, and shrimp; the restaurant staff can often

tell you exactly where they're from (tiny Maine shrimp, available only in winter, are especially delectable). Well-made **New England clam chowder** is studded with fresh clams and thickened with cream. Recipes vary, but they *never* include tomatoes. (Tomatoes go in Manhattan clam chowder.) **Fish chowder,** often prepared in a spicy style attributed to Portugal or Italy, is a worthy alternative. If you want clams but not soup, many places serve **steamers,** or soft-shell clams cooked in the shell. More common are hard-shell clams—**littlenecks** (small) or **cherrystones** (medium-size)—served raw, like oysters.

> *Maine is famous for its blueberries—and its blackberries are excellent, too.*

From the Land

Maine is the word here, too: **Blueberries** and **potatoes** are major crops, but the berries are the real find. If you see a farmers market or roadside stand selling fresh blueberries, clear your schedule, and leave time in case you run across someone hawking pie.

The region's only challenger to Maine's culinary domination is Vermont. **Vermont cheddar** is the headliner, with other cow and goat cheeses gaining in popularity. Some producers will let you tour their cheese-making operations, perhaps as you're checking out the state cheese council's "Cheese Trail." The

> *Vermont is the country's top producer of maple syrup. It takes approximately 43 gallons of sap to make 1 gallon of syrup.*

state is also home to Ben & Jerry's, maker of some of the finest ice cream you're likely to encounter—and given New Englanders' love of ice cream, that's saying something. Speaking of sweets, all of the New England states produce **maple syrup,** but Vermont's crop is tops in the nation. During sugaring season (the month of Mar, give or take a week or two), visitors are welcome at many sugarhouses—where the sap is collected

from maple trees and boiled down into syrup—in rural areas of all six states. Fall is harvest season for **cranberries,** a major Massachusetts export, and **apples,** which grow in orchards across New England.

Other culinary traditions relate to preparation rather than production. **Baked beans** date from Colonial days. They earned Boston the nickname "Beantown," and you'll see excellent beans on the menu at diners and church suppers in New Hampshire and Maine too. Boston baked beans often precede **Boston cream pie,** which is actually golden layer cake sandwiched around custard and topped with chocolate glaze—no cream, no pie.

In parts of Connecticut, notably the New Haven area, the signature dish is **apizza,** known elsewhere simply as pizza. And Rhode Island is about the only place to find **johnnycakes,** cornmeal cakes sometimes sweetened with molasses and fried on a griddle, pancake-style. It's also home to the **cabinet,** a drink known in old-time businesses in eastern Massachusetts as a **frappe** (pronounced *frap*). Blame the fast-food chains for the near-demise of these odd terms and just order a milkshake.

From the Tap

New England's breweries and microbreweries are numerous and excellent. Sam Adams, based in Boston, helped the New England beer scene get noticed, and today, every decent-size liquor or package store in the area offers a variety of products you can't get elsewhere, including the Olde Burnside Brewing Company in Connecticut, Sea Dog of Maine, Wachusett from Massachusetts, New Hampshire's celebrated Smuttynose, Rhode Island's Newport Storm, and Long Trail and Magic Hat from Vermont, which reputedly has more breweries per capita than any other state.

> *Johnnycakes, Rhode Island's answer to flapjacks.*

> *Boston cream pie, a delicious misnomer.*

> *The Magic Hat Brewery in South Burlington, VT, is open for visits and tours.*

Local Lingo

Thanks in large part to New England's enormous population of college students, many of whom arrive in the area in their late teens and never leave, regional quirks in language and pronunciation are less common than they once were. But you'll still hear **rotary** instead of traffic circle, **packie** (short for "package store") rather than liquor store, **statie** to mean a state trooper, and sometimes **tonic** as a generic term for a carbonated beverage. The oblong sandwich that's a hero, hoagie, or wedge elsewhere in the world is a **sub** (short for submarine) or **grinder** in New England. In parts of Maine, people speak of going "up to Boston," the reverse of the common term **"down East,"** which refers to the fact that a ship sailing from Boston to Maine is traveling downwind. In Maine you'll also hear **"a-yuh"** to mean yes, which brings us to the local accent.

In linguistics theory, the stereotypical New England accent is "nonrhotic," meaning speakers pronounce "r" only when it falls before a vowel. In practice, that means the wiseguy going on about "pahking the cah in Hahvahd Yahd" is closer to accurate than many people are willing to acknowledge. Although the accent is usually associated with Boston, you'll notice versions and variations wherever you go in eastern New England (Vermont and western Connecticut gravitate toward New York linguistically). To prepare your ears before you go, rent *Good Will Hunting;* ignore Robin Williams and pay close attention to Ben Affleck. Or just keep your ears open, and try not to smile when someone from eastern Massachusetts or Rhode Island refers to a statie as "lore enforcement." And remember that there's no public parking in Harvard Yard (pictured above).

12

The Best
Special
Interest Trips

> *PREVIOUS PAGE Kayakers take to the Concord River near the North Bridge in Concord, MA. THIS PAGE A mountain biker at Kingdom Trails in Vermont.*

Escorted General Interest Tours

Escorted tours of New England are most popular, and available in the most configurations, during foliage season. "Peak color" strikes between mid-September and early November, depending on the location and the weather; the leaves generally change from north to south, but trees on the coast tend to lag behind their inland counterparts. Tours typically begin in Boston or New York and last 7 to 11 days. Note that the stereotypical itinerary—10 towns in 8 days—means you'll spend a lot of time looking at the inside of a bus window. If possible, consider booking a trip that lets you linger for more than a few hours at major destinations on your route.

Tauck World Discovery in Norwalk, Connecticut (☎ 800/788-7885; www.tauck.com), is just one of the many outfits offering fall-fo-

liage tours of New England. They even have a resident "foliologist" (and no, that isn't really a word) on staff to monitor the peak leaf color in various spots. Tauck's "Grand Autumn in New England" tour covers four of the six states in this book, including overnight stays in hotels and inns in the region for most of its 11 nights.

Multi-activity Outfitters

A good introduction to New England's diverse terrain is an excursion with the **Appalachian Mountain Club** (☎ 617/523-0655; www.outdoors.org). The recreation and conservation organization is best known for its indispensable trail guides and maps. It also coordinates volunteer-led activities that range from walking dogs on a beach to multiple-day backpacking tours. Though closely associated with New Hampshire's White Mountains, where it operates a camp, the AMC has chapters all over the Northeast.

All six New England states are home to active chapters of the **Audubon Society,** which has expanded its original bird-centric mission to advocate for conservation and environmental awareness. Audubon operates wildlife sanctuaries and offers programs that help people of all ages connect with nature. Classes, workshops, and special events of all types, many for children and families, take place throughout the year. Visit www.audubon.org and click "Audubon Near You" for information about your destination.

L.L.Bean Outdoor Discovery programs (☎ 888/LLBEAN1 552-3261; www.llbean.com/ods) include low-risk introductions to skills such as kayaking, fly-fishing, snowshoeing, and archery. For as little as $15, Walk-On Adventure instructors help students gain some proficiency in just a few hours. More extensive day trips and weekend excursions let participants test out their new (or renewed) skills.

Road Scholar programs offered by **Elderhostel** (☎ 800/454-5768; www.roadscholar.org) include New England destinations. College instructors and local experts lead the trips, which might range from meeting winemakers and fishermen to learning about geology while snowshoeing. The nonprofit organization no longer specifically targets seniors, but it retains the focus on educational travel that has made it popular since 1975.

> *Get a close-up look at lobster boats by hitting the water in Maine.*

Outdoor Activities A to Z

Here's a brief rundown of the many outdoor activities available in New England. For our recommendations of the best places to go, the best shops for renting equipment, and the best outfitters to use, see the individual chapters earlier in this book.

Biking

Someone, somewhere offers a New England bicycle tour that's right for you. Bring a bike or rent one? Guided or self-guided journey, supported or not? Small or large group? Experienced or novice? Day trip or longer excursion? Strenuous or relaxing? Rustic cabin or plush B&B? It's all out there.

Bike the Whites, P.O. Box 1785, North Conway, NH 03865 (☎ 800/421-1785; www. bikethewhites.com), offers self-guided biking tours between three inns in the White Mountains. Each day requires about 20 miles of biking, and luggage is shuttled from inn to inn.

Other resources include **Bike Walk Connecticut** (www.wecyclect.org); the **Bicycle Coalition of Maine** (☎ 207/623-4511; www.bikemaine. org); the **Massachusetts Bicycle Coalition** (☎ 542-BIKE 2453; www.massbike.org); the **Granite State Wheelmen** of New Hampshire (☎ 603/989-5479; www.granitestatewheelmen.org); the **Narragansett Bay Wheelmen** of Rhode Island (www.nbwclub.org); and the **Green Mountain Bicycle Club** of Vermont (www.thegmbc.com). For info about mountain biking, contact the **New England Mountain Bike Association** (☎ 800/57-NEMBA 576-3622 or 978/635-1718; www.nemba.org).

Birding

New England falls within the Atlantic Flyway migration route, and the entire region offers excellent birding. Coastal areas are especially active during spring and fall. The Audubon Society (see "Multiactivity Outfitters," opposite) is an excellent resource for travelers interested in observing and learning about birds. State chapters post recent sightings on their websites and offer plenty of advice for interested visitors of all ages and levels of expertise. Budding and experienced naturalists can expand their understanding of marine wildlife while residing on 333-acre Hog Island in Maine's wild and scenic Muscongus Bay through the *Maine Audubon Society,* 20 Gilsland Farm Rd., Falmouth, ME (☎ 207/781-2330; www. maineaudubon.org). Famed birder Roger Tory Peterson once taught birding classes here, and I can personally vouch for Maine Audubon's educational programs. Call or visit their lovely headquarters just north of Portland.

Boating

New England offers an exhilarating variety of waterborne experiences, from cruising on windjammers off the coast of Maine (p. 463), to powerboating on Lake Winnipesaukee (p. ###), to poking around a pond in a borrowed Sunfish. Several lines offer cruises that take in much of the New England coast, calling at Newport, Boston, Gloucester, Portland, Bar Harbor, or some combination thereof. Embarkation points include Baltimore, New York/ New Jersey, Boston, Quebec City, and Montreal. **Holland America Line** (☎ 877/

> *A sea kayaker explores Barnstable Harbor, which opens onto Cape Cod Bay.*

932-4259; www.hollandamerica.com) offers the most numerous and varied cruises; **Royal Caribbean International** (☎ 866/562-7625; www.royalcaribbean.com), **Princess Cruises** (☎ 800/774-6237; www.princess.com), **Silversea Cruises** (☎ 877/276-6816; www.silversea.com), **Carnival Cruise Lines** (☎ 800/764-7419; www.carnival.com), and **Norwegian Cruise Line** (☎ 866/234-7350; www.ncl.com) are among the other operators that sail to and from New England ports. See individual chapters for information about sightseeing cruises and day trips.

Camping

Public and private campgrounds and campsites abound throughout New England. The White Mountains, Green Mountains, and Berkshires are popular destinations, as is virtually the entire coast, with especially busy areas in Maine and on Cape Cod. For most people, camping is a summer activity, but it's popular enough in cold weather that the Appalachian Mountain Club publishes a *Guide to Winter Camping*. The listings under "National & State Parks," on p. 564 in the "Savvy Traveler" chapter, can give you a sense of the options in your destination. Also see "Multiactivity Outfitters," p. 552, for information about the Appalachian Mountain Club, an excellent resource.

Canoeing & Kayaking

Sea kayaking in the Atlantic Ocean is a popular way to see the New England coast; paddling a canoe or kayak on river, lake, or pond is less taxing but no less enjoyable. In areas where these activities are popular, local visitor information centers can recommend rental outlets and tour operators.

For longer tours, try **Allagash Canoe Trips,** P.O. Box 932, Greenville, ME 04441 (☎ 207/237-3077; www.allagashcanoetrips.com), which leads 5- to 7-day canoe trips down Maine's noted and wild Allagash River and other local rivers. You provide a sleeping bag and clothing; they take care of everything else. In Vermont, **BattenKill Canoe Ltd.,** 6328 Historic Rte. 7A, Arlington, VT 05250 (☎ 800/421-5268 or 802/362-2800; www.battenkill.com), runs guided canoeing and walking excursions in Vermont (as well as abroad). Nights are spent at quiet inns. **Maine Island Kayak Co.,** 70 Luther St., Peaks Island, ME 04108 (☎ 207/766-2373; www.maineislandkayak.com), has a fleet of seaworthy kayaks for camping trips up and down the Maine coast, as well as to such places as Canada and Belize. The firm has a number of 2- and 3-night expeditions every summer and plenty of experience in training novices.

> *A hiking pole is a useful companion for negotiating rocky New England terrain.*

Finally, **New England Hiking Holidays,** P.O. Box 1648, North Conway, NH 03860 (☎ 800/869-0949 or 603/356-9696; www. nehikingholidays.com), has an extensive inventory of trips, including weekend trips in the White Mountains, as well as more extended excursions to the Maine coast, Vermont, and overseas. Trips typically involve moderate day hiking coupled with nights at comfortable lodges.

Fishing

Saltwater and freshwater fishing are wildly popular throughout New England. Deep-sea fishing charters are available in every port with a fleet of any size, and the region's rivers are famous for their great fly-fishing. The outdoor equipment giant Orvis operates an **Orvis Fly Fishing School** (☎ 802/362-4604; www. orvis.com) at its headquarters in Manchester, Vermont, and offers guided trips. **L.L.Bean** (see "Multiactivity Outfitters," p. 552) offers fishing and casting lessons as well as fishing trips from its headquarters in Freeport, Maine, and other locations.

Note that everyone other than children under a certain age (12, 15, or 16, depending on the state) must have a fishing permit; your guide or outfitter can help you buy one.

Hiking & Walking

The incredible diversity of the landscape makes New England an unforgettable hiking destination. Trails of every description crisscross the region, up mountains, through woodlands, and along the rocky coast. In cities and many towns and villages, walking tours are a top sightseeing option. National parks, historic properties, historical societies, and for-profit and nonprofit companies offer innumerable guided walking tours throughout the year. Pack your broken-in hiking boots or walking shoes, and check the chapters earlier in this book for suggestions.

The **Appalachian Trail** is one of the great long-distance hiking routes in the United States. En route from Maine's Mount Katahdin to Springer Mountain, Georgia, it passes through every New England state except Rhode Island. The **Appalachian Trail Conservancy** (☎ 304/535-6331; www.appalachian trail.org) is a good resource whether you're planning a day trip or a "through hike" of the whole 2,179 miles.

New England Hiking Holidays (☎ 800/ 869-0949; www.nehikingholidays.com) offers 3- to 5-day inn-to-inn trips to central and far-northern Vermont, the White Mountains

> *Bretton Woods is the largest ski area in New Hampshire.*

> *Migrating whales visit New England waters every summer, followed by human whale-watchers.*

of New Hampshire, Acadia National Park in Maine, and the Berkshires of western Massachusetts. Guides can adjust the pace, usually 5 to 9 miles per day, to accommodate slower and faster participants.

Country Walkers, P.O. Box 180, Waterbury, VT 05676 (☎ 800/464-9255 or 802/244-1387; www.countrywalkers.com), has a glorious color catalog (more like a wish book) outlining supported walking trips around the world. Among the offerings: walking tours in coastal Maine and north-central Vermont. Trips generally run 4 to 5 nights and include all meals and lodging at appealing inns.

Skiing

The primary reason for many people to visit the region, skiing is ingrained in the life of northern New England. Vermont has the most ski areas and the greatest range of accompanying accommodations and diversions. Popular destinations include Jay Peak, Killington, Okemo, Smuggler's Notch, Stowe, Stratton, and Sugarbush. See p. 370 for more information. High-profile ski areas in New Hampshire include Attitash, Bretton Woods, Cannon Mountain, Loon Mountain, Waterville Valley, and Wildcat. See p. 428 for the scoop on skiing the White Mountains. In Maine, Sugarloaf and Sunday River are the big names. See p. 479 for information. Ski areas

in Massachusetts, Connecticut, and Rhode Island (where the single ski area tops out at 310 ft.) cater almost exclusively to locals; state tourism bureaus can supply information. If you're interested in booking a package, the largest group-tour operator in New England is **Ski 93** (☎ 800/451-1830 or 603/665-9650; www.ski93trips.com).

Stargazing

Light pollution in New England's cities makes amateur astronomy frustrating, but in the region's less populated areas—wow. When the skies above the mountains and coasts, especially in northern New England, are clear, the spectacle is breathtaking. Summer is prime season for meteor showers, with the Perseid shower in mid-August the high point.

Museums and observatories throughout New England schedule public viewing sessions and other activities. The **New England Space Science Initiative in Education** lists events in all six states at www.mos.org/nessie.

Whale-Watching

The waters off New England are prime territory for whale-watching cruises. From April or May to October, boats and catamarans visit the migrating mammals' feeding grounds almost daily. Species spotted in the area are mainly humpback, finback, and minke whales, who dine on sand eels and other fish. The whales often perform for observers by jumping out of the water, and dolphins occasionally join the show. Naturalists onboard narrate the trips, pointing out the whales—many of which they recognize and call by name—and describing birds and fish that cross your path. See p. 463 for whale-watch tours in Maine; pp. 130 and 173 for those in Massachusetts; and p. 318 for those departing from Rhode Island. And to be sure you're picking an operator who respects the safety and well-being of the whales, see the "Sustainable Tourism" section on p. 568 in "The Savvy Traveler."

Learning Trips

See "Multi-activity Outfitters," p. 552, for information about **Road Scholar** programs. Also worth investigating are the offerings of **Smithsonian Journeys** (☎ 877/338-8687; www.smithsonianjourneys.org), which include bus tours and cruises.

Food & Wine Trips

See the destination chapters earlier in this book for information about city and neighborhood walking tours that concentrate on food. The state and local tourism authorities and trade associations in your destination can supply lists of food producers and wineries that welcome visitors. All six New England states have wineries, many but not all of them near the coast, with its relatively hospitable microclimates and moderating breezes.

The big cheese is the **Vermont Cheese Council** (☎ 866/261-8595; www.vtcheese.com), which offers abundant information, including a map of the Vermont Cheese Trail, links to cheese makers, and recipes, on its website. The **Coastal Wine Trail of Southern New England** (www.coastalwinetrail.com) links some of the region's highest-profile vineyards, in Massachusetts and Rhode Island; visiting all seven takes 2 to 3 days. The Southeastern New England appellation includes part of Connecticut; the **Connecticut Wine Trail** (☎ 860/677-5467; www.ctwine.com) adjoins the Coastal Wine Trail.

Two prominent universities offer continuing education classes that are open to the public: Johnson & Wales (☎ 401/598-2336; www.jwu.

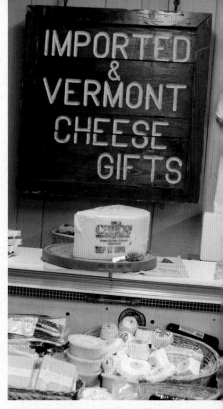

> *Cheddar cheese is one of Vermont's signature foods, along with maple syrup and Ben & Jerry's ice cream.*

edu), in Providence, Rhode Island, and Boston University (☎ 617/353-9852; www.bu.edu/foodandwine), which also offers 1-day gastronomic walking tours in the Boston area.

Volunteer & Working Trips

Habitat for Humanity (www.habitat.org) has multiple chapters in every New England state. Volunteers staff construction sites for at least 1 day; check with the local chapter near your destination for more information, including the schedule of orientation sessions. The **Appalachian Mountain Club** and the state chapters of the **Audubon Society** (see "Multiactivity Outfitters," p. 552) rely heavily on volunteers. Most opportunities require long-term commitments, but some take as little as half a day.

13
The Savvy Traveler

> A familiar sign on northern New England highways indicates a moose crossing; this one is in Maine.

Before You Go

Tourist Offices

All six New England states and most municipalities in the region offer abundant visitor information online, by mail, over the phone, and in person. These are the state tourism bureaus:

Connecticut Commission on Tourism & Culture, 1 Constitution Plaza, 2nd floor, Hartford, CT 06103; ☎ 888/CT-VISIT (288-4748) or 860/256-2800; www.ctvisit.com.

Maine Office of Tourism, 59 State House Station, Augusta, ME 04333; ☎ 888/624-6345 or 207/287-5711; www.visitmaine.com.

Massachusetts Office of Travel & Tourism, 10 Park Plaza, Suite 4510, Boston, MA 02116; ☎ 800/227-MASS (6277) or 617/973-8500; www.massvacation.com.

New Hampshire Division of Travel and Tourism Development, P.O. Box 1856, 172 Pembroke Rd., Concord, NH 03302; ☎ 800/FUN-IN-NH (386-4664) or 603/271-2665; www.visitnh.com.

Rhode Island Tourism Division, 315 Iron Horse Way, Suite 101, Providence, RI 02908; ☎ 800/250-7384; www.visitrhodeisland.com.

Vermont Department of Tourism and Marketing, One National Life Dr., 6th floor, Montpelier, VT 05620; ☎ 800/VERMONT (837-6668) or 802/828-3237; www.vermontvacation.com.

Best Times to Go

The well-worn joke about the climate in New England is that it has just two seasons—winter and August. Though this bromide might have originated as a ploy to keep outsiders from moving up here (and it worked, partly), there's also a kernel of truth to it. But don't worry. The ever-shifting seasons here are precisely what make New England so distinctive, and three of the four are genuinely enjoyable. The fourth (which is not the one you might have guessed) is, well, tolerable.

The peak **summer** season in New England runs from Fourth of July weekend until Labor Day weekend. That's a pretty slim sandwich, only about 8½ weeks. But summers here are exquisite, particularly since the daylight lasts so long—until 9 or 9:30pm in late June and early July. Forests are verdant and lush; the sky is a deep blue, the cumulus clouds puffy and almost painfully bright white. In the mountains, warm days are the rule, followed by cool nights. On the coast, ocean breezes keep temperatures down even when it's triple-digit steaming in the big cities. (Of course, these sea breezes sometimes also produce thick, soupy fogs that linger for days.) In general, expect moderation: In Portland, Maine, the thermometer tops 90°F (32°C) for only 4 or 5 days each year, at most.

Rain is rarely far away in summer—some days it's in the form of an afternoon thunderstorm, sometimes a steady drizzle that brings a 3- or 4-day soaking. On average, about 1 day in 3 here will bring some rain.

For most of this region (we'll get to Vermont in a moment), midsummer is prime time. Expect to pay premium prices at hotels and restaurants. (The exception is around the empty ski resorts, where you can often find bargains.) Also be aware that early summer brings out scads of biting black flies and mosquitoes, a state of affairs that has spoiled many north-country camping trips. Come prepared for these guys. They've been up here a lot longer than we have, and they seem to like it just fine.

Don't be surprised to smell the tang of **autumn** approaching even as early as mid-August, when you'll also begin to notice a few leaves turning blaze-orange on the maples at the edges of wetlands or highways. Fall comes early to New England, puts its feet up on the couch, and stays for some time. The foliage season begins in earnest in the northern part of the region by the third week in September; in the southern portions, it reaches its peak by mid-October. But it's beautiful everywhere.

Fall in New England is one of the great natural spectacles in the world. When its rolling hills tart up in brilliant reds and stunning oranges, grown men pull to the sides of roads and fall to their knees weeping (and snapping, and taking video); the scenery is garish in a way that seems deviously designed to tease and embarrass shy, understated New England. The best part? This spectacle is nearly as regular as clockwork, with only a few years truly "bad" for foliage (due to oddly warm or wet weather). Though you can never predict exactly when it will strike, you can more or less guess where.

Keep in mind, however, that this is the most popular time of year to travel—bus tours flock like migrating geese to New England in early October. As a result, hotels are invariably booked solid. (Local radio stations have been known to put out calls for residents to open up their doors to stranded travelers who otherwise might have to sleep in their cars.) Reservations are essential. Don't be surprised if you're assessed a foliage surcharge of $10 or $50 or more per room at your inn or hotel; deal with it. You can't buy scenery like this.

Some states maintain seasonal foliage hot lines and/or websites to let you know when the leaves are at their peak: Call **Maine** (☎ 888/624-6345; www.mainefoliage.com), **New Hampshire** (☎ 800/258-3608), or **Vermont** (☎ 800/VERMONT 837-6668; www.travel-vermont.com/seasons/report. asp). The **U.S. Forest Service** also maintains a foliage hotline at (☎ 800/354-4595), updating conditions within the White Mountain National Forest in New Hampshire.

New England **winters** are like wine—some years are good, some are lousy. During a good season, mounds of light, fluffy snow blanket the deep woods and fill the ski slopes. A "good" winter offers a profound peace and tranquillity as the fresh snow muffles all noise and brings such a thunderous silence to the entire region that the hiss and pop of a wood fire at a country inn can seem noisome. During these good winters, exploring the forest on snowshoes or cross-country skis is an experience bordering on the magical.

During the other winters, though—the yucky ones—the weather fairies instead bring a nasty mélange of rain, freezing rain, and sleet (um, frozen rain). The woods become filled with crusty snow, the cold is damp and bone-numbing, and it's bleak, bleak, bleak as gunpowder-gray clouds lower and linger for weeks. Keep in mind, the higher in elevation you go into the mountains of northern New England, or the farther north you head (to places like Jay Peak (p. 370), in Vermont), the better your odds of finding snow.

On the other hand, meteorologically speaking, the coast in winter is a crapshoot, at best, more likely to yield rain or sticky, heavy "snowball" snow. Yes, winter vacations on the ocean can be spectacular—think Winslow Homerian waves crashing savagely onto an empty beach—but after a day or two of trying to navigate your car around big gray slushy snowbanks, you, too, will soon be heading for Stowe.

Naturally, ski areas get crowded during the winter months. Some of them get very crowded. Expect maximum pricing. The resorts get especially packed during school vacations, which is just when many resorts choose to employ the rather mercenary tactic of jacking up rates at hotels and on the slopes. See "Outdoor Adventures" in Vermont on p. 366 and "Outdoor Adventures" in New Hampshire on p. 426.

By the way, if you visit a small town in this region during winter, there is another pleasure to enjoy: public ice skating and ice hockey. You'll find locals skating on town greens, lakes, ponds, rivers, and probably on top of swimming pools, for all we know—anywhere that will hold a little water. How do you find these spots? Easy. Look for a clump of cars beside an iconic little warming hut with a wood-burning or oil-burning stove inside, sending up smoke puffs like a signal to the masses.

After the long, long winters, **spring** in New England is a tease. It promises a lot and comes dressed in impressive finery (see: delicate purple lilacs, which blossom for just a week). But in many years, spring lasts only a week, sometimes less than that (we're not kidding), "occurring" around mid-May but sometimes as late as June. There's a reason New Englanders hardly ever use the word "spring" in conversation with peers. They just call this time of year "mud season."

It happens quickly. One morning the ground is muddier than muddy, the trees are barren, and gritty snow is still collected in shady hollows. The next day, it's in the 80s and humid, maple trees are blooming with little red cloverlike buds, kids are swimming in the lakes where the docks have just been put in, and somewhere in New Hampshire a blue cover is being ripped off an aboveground pool.

Travelers need to be awfully crafty to experience spring in New England—and once they get here, they often have trouble finding a room. That's because a good number of innkeepers and restaurateurs close up for a few weeks for repairs or to venture someplace warm. The upside? Rates are never cheaper than they are in spring. It's simply jaw-dropping how little you can pay in March for the same room that would cost 3 to 10 times more in the middle of summer or October.

Festivals & Special Events

Please note that, as with any schedule of this kind, the following information is subject to change. Always confirm details before you plan your trip around an event. For an exhaustive list of events beyond those listed here, visit events.frommers.com, where you'll find a searchable, up-to-the-minute roster of what's happening in cities all over the world.

JANUARY

Celebrations of **Martin Luther King Jr.'s Birthday** take place across New England on the third Monday in January, and are especially popular in Boston, Massachusetts, where Dr. King attended graduate school. Numerous other destinations schedule observations and activities, ranging from gospel music performances to children's events to panel discussions. At the other end of the spectrum, the 10-day **Stowe Winter Carnival** in Stowe, Vermont (www.stowewintercarnival.com), held at the end of the month, celebrates traditional pastimes such as ski racing and ice carving, as well as offbeat activities like "snowgolf" and "snowvolleyball."

FEBRUARY

The second weekend in February, Maine's Camden Snow Bowl ski and recreation area plays host to the **U.S. National Toboggan Championships** (☎ 207/236-3438; www. camdensnowbowl.com), a raucous event contested on wooden sleds hurtling down a 400-foot-long ice-coated wooden chute. Hundreds of teams vie for titles, and being overweight is actually an advantage. A tradition dating to 1911, the **Dartmouth Winter Carnival** (☎ 603/646-3399) held midmonth at Dartmouth College in Hanover, New Hampshire, features athletic events, a polar bear swim, and an immense snow sculpture on the village green. First contested in 1945, late February's **Stowe Derby** (☎ 802/253-7704;

www.stowederby.com) is a 12½-mile downhill/cross-country ski race that runs from Mount Mansfield to the picturesque village of Stowe, Vermont.

MARCH

On March 17, wear something green for **St. Patrick's Day,** celebrated with surprising zeal all over New England with parades and other events. Boston, Massachusetts, throws the biggest party. The spring thaw signals the beginning of **maple syrup season,** when farmers tap sugar maple trees and boil down the resulting sap to produce flavorful syrup. Vermont (www.vermontmaple.org) is the leading American producer of maple syrup and the best place to experience the harvesting tradition up close.

APRIL

Brush up on the story of Paul Revere's midnight ride if you plan to visit Massachusetts on **Patriots Day,** the third Monday in April. The state holiday (also observed in Maine) commemorates the events of April 18 and 19, 1775, when the Revolutionary War began. Ceremonies and reenactments take place in **Boston** at the **Old North Church** (p. 83, ⑥) and the **Paul Revere House** (p. 53, ⑩). Suburban **Lexington** stages a battle reenactment beginning at dawn; **Concord**'s reenactment starts later. Both towns stage parades and pancake breakfasts. Consult the **Battle Road Committee** (www.battleroad. org) or contact the **Lexington Chamber of Commerce** (☎ 781/862-1450; www.lexington chamber.org) or the **Concord Chamber of Commerce** (☎ 978/369-3120; www.concord chamberofcommerce.org) for information.

Patriots Day is also the day of the **Boston Marathon** (www.bostonmarathon.org), one of the oldest and most famous in the world. Cheering fans line most of the route, which begins in Hopkinton, Massachusetts, and ends on Boylston Street just outside Boston's Copley Square.

A sure sign of spring is the late-April **Boothbay Harbor Fishermen's Festival** (☎ 207/633-2353; www.boothbayharbor.com) in Boothbay Harbor, Maine. Competitions for children and adults, a crafts show, the Miss Shrimp Princess pageant, and a fish fry are among the event's highlights. At the same time, spring fever grips Nantucket, Massachusetts, during

NEW ENGLAND'S AVERAGE DAILY TEMPERATURES & MONTHLY RAINFALL

BOSTON, MA

MONTH	JAN	FEB	MAR	APR	MAY	JUNE	JULY	AUG	SEPT	OCT	NOV	DEC
TEMP °F	30	31	38	49	59	68	74	72	65	55	45	34
TEMP °C	-1	-1	3	9	15	20	23	22	18	13	7	1
RAINFALL (IN.)	3.8	3.5	4.0	3.7	3.4	3.0	2.8	3.6	3.3	3.3	4.4	4.2

BURLINGTON, VT

MONTH	JAN	FEB	MAR	APR	MAY	JUNE	JULY	AUG	SEPT	OCT	NOV	DEC
TEMP °F	18	20	30	44	56	66	70	68	60	48	37	24
TEMP °C	-8	-7	-1	7	13	19	21	20	16	9	3	-4
RAINFALL (IN.)	1.9	1.7	2.1	2.7	3.2	3.6	3.8	3.8	3.4	3.1	3.0	2.3

HARTFORD, CT

MONTH	JAN	FEB	MAR	APR	MAY	JUNE	JULY	AUG	SEPT	OCT	NOV	DEC
TEMP °F	26	29	38	49	60	69	74	72	63	52	42	31
TEMP °C	-3	-2	3	9	16	21	23	22	17	11	6	-1
RAINFALL (IN.)	3.8	3.0	3.9	3.9	4.4	3.9	3.7	4.0	4.1	3.9	4.1	3.6

PORTLAND, ME

MONTH	JAN	FEB	MAR	APR	MAY	JUNE	JULY	AUG	SEPT	OCT	NOV	DEC
TEMP °F	22	25	34	44	54	63	69	67	59	48	38	28
TEMP °C	-6	-4	1	7	12	17	21	19	15	9	3	-2
RAINFALL (IN.)	3.5	3.3	3.7	4.1	3.6	3.4	3.1	2.9	3.1	3.9	5.2	4.6

the **Nantucket Daffodil Festival** (☎ 508/228-1700; www.nantucketchamber.org). A flower show, multiple parades, and millions of blooming bulbs help the island shake off winter and welcome spring.

MAY

Festivals, tours, exhibits of art and artifacts, and other fun activities make up the month-long **Cape Cod Maritime Days** (www.ecape chamber.com/maritimedays). Communities across the Massachusetts peninsula celebrate the Cape's seagoing legacy in the weeks before the summer tourist crush begins. At the early-May **Spring Farm Festival** in Woodstock, Vermont, sheep shearing, plowing, and wagon rides help introduce visitors to the seasonal routine on a traditional farm. Activities and demonstrations take place at the **Billings Farm & Museum** (p. 396, ③). Three times a year (mid-May, mid-July, and early Sept), the **Brimfield Antique and Collectibles Show** (☎ 800/628-8379; www.brimfieldshow.com) draws thousands of dealers to fields lining a country road in Brimfield, Massachusetts. It's New England's largest outdoor antiques show. For many dealers, the May event is the first show of the season, and they're eager to hawk the treasures they've been stocking up over the winter. At Mystic Seaport's **Lobster Days** (☎ 888/973-2767; www.mysticseaport.org), in late May in Mystic, Connecticut, visitors can learn some lobster lore, participate in kids' activities, and crack open a tasty crustacean at a picnic.

JUNE

Early in the month, the historic waterfront district of Portland, Maine, plays host to the state's largest 1-day festival, the **Old Port Festival** (☎ 207/772-6828; www.portlandmaine.com). It includes a parade, family activities, crafts displays, and live music. A festival with an eco-conscious focus begins with the **Strolling of the Heifers Parade** (☎ 802/258-9177; www.strollingoftheheifers.com) through the streets of Brattleboro, Vermont. The placid counterparts to Pamplona's running bulls don flowers and traverse downtown to kick off the event in early June. Around the same time, the north bank of the Charles River plays host to the **Cambridge River Festival** (☎ 617/349-4380; www.cambridgeartscouncil.org) in Cambridge, Massachusetts. The celebration of the arts

---

National & State Parks

The saying "your tax dollars at work" will gain new meaning when you realize what a great resource the National Park Service and the New England state park systems are. The National Park Service website, **www.nps. gov**, is an essential tool if you're interested in outdoor activities in New England (or the rest of the U.S.). Search by park name, activity, or topic, or simply click a state on the interactive map and go from there.

State park websites and staffs can offer information about outdoor activities, licenses, camping, parking, fees, and much more. Another good resource is the **state tourism bureaus** (see above). The state parks systems are listed here:

Connecticut State Parks and Forests, Department of Environmental Protection, 79 Elm St., Hartford, CT 06106 (☎ 860/424-3000; www.ct.gov/dep/stateparks).

Maine Bureau of Parks and Lands, 2 State House Station, 18 Elkins Lane, Augusta, ME 04333 (☎ 207/287-3821; www.maine.gov/doc/parks).

Massachusetts State Parks, Department of Conservation and Recreation, 251 Causeway St., Boston, MA 02114 (☎ 617/626-1250; www.mass.gov/dcr).

New Hampshire Division of Parks and Recreation, 172 Pembroke Rd., P.O. Box 1856, Concord, NH 03302 (☎ 603/271-3556; www.nhstateparks.org).

Rhode Island State Parks, Department of Environmental Management, Division of Parks & Recreation, 2321 Hartford Ave., Johnston, RI 02919 (☎ 401/222-2632; riparks.com).

Vermont State Parks, 103 S. Main St., Waterbury, VT 05671 (☎ 802/241-3655; www.vtstateparks.com).

---

includes live music and family-friendly activities. The second week in June sees the **Boston Pride Parade and Festival** (☎ 617/262-9405; www.bostonpride.org), a weeklong celebration of diversity in Boston, Massachusetts. In late June, a sailboat parade is the centerpiece of the **Annual Windjammer Days** (☎ 207/633-2353; www.boothbayharbor.com) in Boothbay Harbor, Maine, a tradition since 1952. The waterfront festival also includes a parade on land, fireworks, live music, a craft show, pancake breakfasts, and tours of participating vessels. Also in late June, New England's gay mecca, Provincetown, Massachusetts, celebrates its ethnic heritage at the **Provincetown Portuguese Festival** (☎ 508/246-9080; www.provincetownportuguesefestival.com). P-town is also a fishing port; the festival features the blessing of the fleet in addition to food, music, and family activities. The blessing of the fleet is also an important part of **St. Peter's Fiesta** (www.stpetersfiesta.org) in Gloucester, Massachusetts. The Italian-American fishing community throws an open-air party, with carnival rides and lots of music and food. Highlights include a competition that involves racing across a greased pole suspended over the water.

JULY

Fourth of July revelry lasts nearly a week in Boston, Massachusetts, which calls its party **Boston Harborfest** (☎ 617/227-1528; www.bostonharborfest.com). Events include concerts, children's activities, cruises, fireworks, Chowderfest, guided tours, talks, and USS *Constitution*'s turnaround cruise. The big day concludes with a beloved tradition, the **Boston Pops Concert and Fireworks Display** (www.july4th.org), which ends with pyrotechnics over the Charles River. The program includes the *1812 Overture*, featuring real cannon fire and church bells.

Throughout July and into August, international attention focuses on tiny Becket, Massachusetts, during the annual **Jacob's Pillow Dance Festival** (☎ 413/243-0745; www.jacobspillow.org). The event draws dozens of companies, hundreds of artists, and thousands of enthusiasts with performances, workshops, tours, talks, and other events. Many offerings are free. At the same time, another internationally renowned event, the **Williamstown**

Theatre Festival (☎ 413/597-3400; www.wt festival.org) of Williamstown, Massachusetts, is famous for launching Broadway hits, but hard-core theater aficionados flock to check out rising stars, both actors and playwrights. Complementing the mainstream main-stage productions are new works, readings, workshops, and cabaret. The musical component of the Berkshires' summer arts explosion is the **Tanglewood Music Festival** (☎ 888/266-200; www.bso.org), which runs from late June to early September near Lenox, Massachusetts. The summer home of the Boston Symphony Orchestra is a magnet for jazz, opera, pop, world music, and, of course, classical performers. Arrive early, explore the lovely grounds, and picnic on the lawn.

Mid-July sees a host of events, including the **Wickford Art Festival** (www.wickfordart.org), one of the oldest art festivals on the East Coast, held in lovely Wickford, Rhode Island. It attracts hundreds of artists. New England's largest free jazz event is the **Greater Hartford Festival of Jazz** (☎ 860/727-0050; www.hartfordjazz. org) in Hartford, Connecticut. Live music is the soundtrack for the **Market Days & Summer Music Festival** (www.mainstreetconcord. com) in Concord, New Hampshire. The event features nonstop family activities, carnival rides, street performers, and abundant shopping. A parade through Yarmouth, Maine, kicks off the **Yarmouth Clam Festival** (☎ 207/846-3984; www.clamfestival.com). Live music, pancake breakfasts, a craft show and art sale, and races on water (in canoes and kayaks) and land highlight this event.

On weekends from mid-July to mid-August, chamber music aficionados pour into Marlboro, Vermont, for **Marlboro Music** (☎ 802/254-2394; www.marlboromusic.org). The Green Mountain town plays host to musicians and vocalists who explore the genre and mount dozens of performances. Finally, at the end of the month, the legendary **Newport Folk Festival** (www.newportfolkfest.net) books some of the biggest names in folk music.

AUGUST

Newport, Rhode Island, is also the home of the **Newport Jazz Festival** (www.newportjazzfest. net). The storied event, held early in the month, features legendary artists and established

musicians as well as promising students.

Mid-month sees a number of food and arts festivals. The **Machias Wild Blueberry Festival** (☎ 207/255-6665; www.machiasblue berry.com) in Downeast Maine celebrates with a parade, live music, kids' activities, a "blueberry musical" featuring local performers, a fun run, and a pie-eating contest. Another Maine product takes center stage at the **Maine Lobster Festival** (☎ 800/LOB-CLAW 562-2529; www.mainelobsterfestival.com) in Rockland. A classic small-town event, it includes a parade, carnival rides, and a great addition to the typical menu: fresh lobster. Live music, unusual food offerings, and a variety of local beers add to the fun at the **Southern Vermont Art and Craft Festival** (☎ 802/425-3399; www.craftproducers.com). Hundreds of artisans visit the grounds of Hildene, a historic home on a magnificent estate in Manchester, Vermont, to show and sell their creations. Newbury, New Hampshire, plays host to the **Annual Craftsmen's Fair** (☎ 603/224-3375; www.nhcrafts.org), the oldest craft fair in the country (since 1933). The League of New Hampshire Craftsmen stages the 9-day affair, which features top-notch crafts in every medium, on display and for sale. Music and theater performances, workshops, and demonstrations round out the schedule.

The third weekend in August, the **Martha's Vineyard Agricultural Society Fair** (www. mvas.vineyard.net) in West Tisbury, Massachusetts, features a carnival midway, live music, and family-friendly events. The horse pull, livestock and crafts competitions, and farm and garden exhibits help recall the posh island's agricultural legacy. On weekends from late July to August, **Italian-American Feasts** take over parts of the North End in Boston, Massachusetts. The street fairs feature live music, dancing, carnival food, tacky souvenirs, and lively crowds of locals and out-of-towners. The two biggest events are the **Fisherman's Feast** (www.fishermansfeast.com), in mid-August, and the **Feast of St. Anthony** (www. saintanthonysfeast.com), in late August.

SEPTEMBER

The **Blue Hill Fair** (☎ 207/374-3701; www. bluehillfair.com), held on Labor Day weekend, makes a good excuse to visit Blue Hill, one of

New England Insects

Mosquitoes, ticks, and flies are the same nuisance in New England that they are in other places, with some additional dangers to be aware of. Always take precautions in the summer, and be aware that a warm spring or late frost can extend the season.

Mosquitoes in the Eastern U.S. can spread Eastern equine encephalitis from birds to horses and humans. Most of those infected suffer few or no symptoms, but in rare cases, mostly involving those with weakened immune systems, a serious infection develops. The result can be brain damage or death. Mosquitoes are especially aggressive at dusk.

Across New England, deer **ticks** spread Lyme disease, named for the Connecticut town where it was identified. The infection can result in fever, aches, chronic fatigue and, in severe cases, heart damage. Tuck your pants into your socks if you're walking in woods or high grass, wear light colors to help spot the insects, and check yourself and your pets daily for signs of bites. If you develop a bull's-eye-shaped rash, even if you don't remember being bitten, see a doctor immediately.

Biting flies plague many parts of the Northeast in the summer, especially near the coast. Horseflies are enormous, and their bite is more painful than that of a mosquito. Deer flies also deliver a nasty nip. Black flies, also known as buffalo gnats, swarm unpredictably; cover your mouth and eyes if you find yourself under attack. Greenheads are especially plentiful near salt marshes and can ruin a trip to the beach.

To ward off insects, slather on insect repellent. Some people swear by natural deterrents such as citronella, and others won't go without their Avon Skin So Soft lotion. The most popular repellents contain **DEET.** Whatever you choose, apply it to all of your exposed skin, not forgetting your neck, ears, and feet. Unlike sunblock, insect repellent doesn't need to be reapplied until you sense its effects wearing off; if you're using a product that combines the two, it's a good idea to pack some straight sunblock to avoid overexposure to the chemicals in the bug stuff.

Maine's cutest villages. Livestock exhibits, blueberry pancake breakfasts, fireworks, live entertainment, a carnival midway, and lumberjack competitions are just some of the offerings. That same weekend, gorgeous sailboats parade into the Camden, Maine, harbor to kick off the **Camden Windjammer Festival** (☎ 207/236-4404; www.camdenwindjammer festival.com). The celebration includes musical performances, a heritage fair with maritime crafts demonstrations, kid-friendly activities, and a pancake breakfast.

From early to mid-September, the huge and hugely popular **Vermont State Fair** (☎ 802/775-5300; www.vermontstatefair.net) in Rutland features the can't-miss combination of agricultural exhibits and competitions, live music, a carnival midway, and fried food. Beginning in mid-September, **The Big E** (☎ 413/205-5115; www.thebige.com), at Eastern States Exposition in West Springfield, Massachusetts, is New England's largest agricultural fair. A supersize version of a state fair, the 2½-week event features a large variety of food, carnival rides, and other activities, as well as agricultural displays and big-name musical acts.

OCTOBER

Kicking off the month is Maine's largest agricultural fair, the **Fryeburg Fair** (☎ 207/935-3268; www.fryeburgfair.org) in Fryeburg, Maine, which dates to 1851. The 8-day event incorporates old-school activities—cooking contests, horse pulling, and kids' events that include a "pig scramble"—with a carnival midway and live music. Columbus Day weekend, New England's signature soup is the main course at the **Mystic Seaport Chowderfest** (☎ 888/973-2767; www.mysticseaport.org) in Mystic, Connecticut. The outdoor museum schedules live music and kids' activities to accompany its celebration of chowder. The third weekend in October brings the preppiest event in New England: the **Head of the Charles Regatta** (☎ 617/868-6200; www.hocr.org), in Boston and Cambridge, Massachusetts. Hundreds of thousands of spectators line both riverbanks and six large bridges for a tailgate-style event centered on rowing races from the Charles River basin to West Cambridge. The busiest day of the year in Salem, Massachusetts, is **Halloween,** the high point of **Haunted Happenings** (☎ 877/SALEM-MA

725-3662; www.hauntedhappenings.org), the city's month-long Halloween party. Events include parades, fortunetelling, cruises, and tours.

NOVEMBER

Giant helium balloons, marching bands, and floats roam the streets of downtown Stamford, Connecticut, during the **UBS Parade Spectacular** (☎ 203/348-5285; www.stamford-downtown.com), the third weekend in November. Like Salem with Halloween, Plymouth, Massachusetts, makes a big deal of its **Thanksgiving Celebration** the third Thursday in November. "America's Hometown" highlights 17th- and 19th-century Thanksgiving preparations in historic homes. Menus at Plimoth Plantation, which re-creates the colony's first years, include a buffet and a Victorian Thanksgiving feast. Reservations (☎ 800/262-9356 or 508/746-1622; www.plimoth.org) are accepted beginning in June.

DECEMBER

The seaside village of Kennebunkport, Maine, starts its holiday celebrations the first 2 weekends in December with the **Christmas Prelude** (☎ 207/967-0857; www.christmasprelude. com). The event includes trolley rides, an arts-and-crafts show, a bonfire, and appearances by Santa, who arrives by lobster boat and by fire engine. Nantucket, Massachusetts, celebrates Christmas all month, and the high point is the **Nantucket Christmas Stroll** (☎ 508/228-1700; www.nantucketnoel.com) the first weekend in December. The shopping extravaganza features costumed carolers, wandering musicians, and the arrival of Santa and Mrs. Claus on a Coast Guard vessel.

In mid-December, history comes to life at the **Boston Tea Party Reenactment** (☎ 617/482-6439; www.oldsouthmeetinghouse.org) in Boston, Massachusetts. The Old South Meeting House enlists audience members of all ages in the debate over taxation without representation. Throughout the month, Boston Ballet puts on one of the biggest and best American productions of *The Nutcracker* at the Boston Opera House in Boston, Massachusetts. The annual holiday extravaganza is popular with locals and visitors alike. Buy tickets (☎ 617/695-6955; www.bostonballet. org) as soon as you plan your trip. A highlight of the holiday season in Portsmouth, New Hampshire, is the **Candlelight Stroll,** held the first 3 weekends of the month. The Strawbery Banke Museum adorns its historic homes with period decorations and illuminates its 10-acre campus with hundreds of candles. The stroll is part of **Vintage Christmas** (☎ 603/433-1100; www.vintagechristmasnh.org), which features live music, crafts demonstrations, and horse-drawn carriage rides. December weekends also see high-energy performances at the **Black Nativity** (☎ 617/723-3486; www.blacknativity.org), a holiday tradition in Boston, Massachusetts. Poet Langston Hughes wrote the "gospel opera," which features a cast of more than 100.

Mystic Seaport in Mystic, Connecticut, celebrates **Christmas by the Sea** (☎ 888/973-2767; www.mysticseaport.org). The festively decorated museum village schedules storytelling, hands-on crafts, and a gingerbread lighthouse competition on weekends throughout the month. Another monthlong event, **Christmas in Newport** (☎ 401/849-6454; www.christmasinnewport.org), in Newport, Rhode Island, includes concerts, tours, open houses, train rides, and abundant shopping opportunities. To evoke candlelight, only clear bulbs are used in decorations, lending the gorgeous seaside city and its stately mansions a romantic glow.

Finally, New Year's Eve is also known as **First Night** in more than a dozen New England communities, which ring in the New Year with family-friendly celebrations of the arts, including live performances and elaborate ice sculptures. **Hartford,** Connecticut, **Portsmouth,** New Hampshire, and **Burlington,** Vermont, get in on the fun, as does **Providence,** Rhode Island, which calls its event Bright Night. Check with local tourism bureaus and chambers of commerce for details. **Boston**'s party (☎ 617/542-1399; www.firstnight.org) is the original no-alcohol, citywide festival. It includes a parade and a double hit of fireworks, over Boston Common just before 7pm and over Boston Harbor at midnight.

Weather

New England weather is famously changeable—variations from day to day and even hour to hour can be enormous. Swings as large as 30° in less than a day are not common but are certainly not unheard of. Always dress in layers, especially near the ocean, which tends to keep the shore cooler than inland locations in summer and (slightly) warmer in winter. Another way to keep cool is to seek altitude; the higher you go, the lower the mercury. The record high at the top of Mount Washington, New England's highest peak, is a balmy 72°F (22°C)—but the record low is -47 °F (-44 °C).

Spring and fall are the best bets for moderate temperatures. **Spring** (also known as mud season) can be brief and often doesn't settle in until early May, especially in northern New England, but is consistently changeable. You'll almost certainly need an umbrella. Layers will come in handy, too, if snow falls (which can happen as late as Apr) or a rogue heat wave sets in. **Summer** is hot, especially in July and August, and can be uncomfortably humid. Seek relief near the ocean, at a lake or pond, or in the mountains. A sure sign that the end of the season is near is an unexpectedly cool late-August night—grab a sweater, because you're going to need it. **Fall** is when you're most likely to catch a comfortable run of dry, sunny days and cool nights. In northern New England, the first snow often comes in October, but colorful foliage can linger into November along south-facing coasts. **Winter** is cold and usually snowy—bring a warm coat and sturdy boots.

Sustainable Tourism

Traveling the eco-friendly way in New England is not all that difficult. The six states we cover in this book are all fairly progressive when it comes to environmental issues, and you're likely to find lots of sustainable cuisine, energy-efficient lodgings, and spots you can explore by bike or on foot, rather than by car.

Local statewide chapters of the National Audubon Society and The Nature Conservancy turn out to be some of the very best resources. Each of these offices runs education programs and tours and maintains trail systems and nature preserves.

In Maine, the **Maine Audubon Society** (☎ 207/781-2330; www.maineaudubon. org) maintains an impressive nature center and extensive grounds just 10 miles north of Portland. It's a good spot to bird-watch. The Maine chapter of **The Nature Conservancy** (☎ 207/729-5181; www.nature.org) has a small office in a Brunswick mill complex but maintains a huge selection of parks, preserves, and other natural areas throughout the state—absolutely consult them on places to go.

In New Hampshire, contact the **Society for the Preservation of New Hampshire Forests** (☎ 603/224-9945; www.spnhf.org) and **New Hampshire Audubon** (☎ 603/224-9909; www.nhaudubon.org). In Massachusetts, the **Massachusetts Audubon Society** (☎ 781/259-9500; www.massaudubon. org) must be one of the nation's most active chapters, maintaining everything from island beaches holding rare birds to a farm converted into an education center.

In Connecticut, the **Connecticut Audubon Society** (☎ 203/259-6305; www.ctaudubon. org) maintains impressive bird-watching and hiking areas plus a kid-friendly headquarters and nature center. In Rhode Island, it's the **Audubon Society of Rhode Island** (☎ 401/949-5454; asri.org) you want to see.

If you really want to travel responsibly, consider a hiking or inn-to-inn bike tour. Boston cycling maps and tips are available from the **Massachusetts Bicycle Coalition** (☎ 617/542-2453; www.massbike.org). In New Hampshire, get in touch with the club known as the **Granite State Wheelmen** (www.granitestatewheelmen.org).

Also ask about "green" ecotour outfits that take care to leave only small footprints on the landscapes they're traveling through. These sorts of outfitters bring only small groups into the wilderness, and they usually use "light" transportation methods (kayaks, sailboats, snowshoes, bicycles, what-have-you) while traveling in them. They might also contribute a portion of their profits to wildlife organizations or land trusts, or pay for carbon "credits" to offset the fuel they use.

New England's six state tourism offices can point you to these sorts of outfitters and many additional resources. So can the various local tourism offices dotting the region's villages, towns, and cities. All you need to do is ask.

Getting There

By Plane

Most air travelers to New England, particularly those arriving from abroad, will book their flights into Boston's **Logan International Airport** (☎ 800/23-LOGAN (235-6426); www.massport.com/logan) or Hartford's Bradley International Airport. Airports serving other major New England cities handle fewer carriers and fewer flights. Deciding whether to connect at Logan and continue to a smaller regional airport means weighing multiple factors, including price, schedule, convenience, and your comfort with small commuter aircraft. During high season, flying to Logan or Bradley and renting a car or taking public transit to your destination is almost always cheaper than flying all the way. Be aware, however, that travelers to Logan are subject to Boston traffic, long security lines, and flight delays, especially in the winter.

If you're traveling to New Hampshire, you can fly into **Manchester,** and if you're going to explore Rhode Island, you may want to consider flying into **Providence.** If you're exploring the northern reaches of Vermont or New Hampshire, you can fly to Burlington, Vermont. The region's other midsize airports include Bangor, Maine (perfect if you're exploring interior Maine); Portland, Maine (a great start for visits to either southern New Hampshire or the Maine coast); and Hyannis, Massachusetts, which offers a quick way to avoid Cape Cod traffic.

By Car

Interstate highways crisscross New England, connecting the larger cities. But to investigate the small towns and winding back roads that help make this part of the country so popular with travelers, you'll need to leave the major roads and spend most of your time on the routes that wind their way through the region. Also, and I can't stress this enough: buy a good map (see "Getting Around" p. 571). New England's roads are notoriously confusing.

Most of the other major routes in New England (and all of the minor ones) are narrower and slower than the interstates. Mapping websites do a decent job of accounting for local quirks, but it's always a good idea to leave extra time when you're venturing into an unfamiliar area.

E-ZPass transponders work at the tolls in New Hampshire and Maine; the Massachusetts system, **Fast Lane,** is compatible. The devices can be invaluable at bottleneck-prone toll plazas, such as those on I-95 in New Hampshire and on the Mass. Pike at the I-84 interchange.

For information about renting a car, see "Getting Around," p. 571.

Travel Tip: Flying to New England

There are many airlines that fly into New England—if you're pricing tickets to Boston, it's always worth taking a look at fares to Hartford and other cities. Here are some things to keep in mind:

Southwest (☎ 800/435-9792; www.southwest.com) flies into Boston; Hartford; Manchester, New Hampshire; and Providence, Rhode Island.

JetBlue (☎ 800/538-2583; www.jetblue.com) offers direct service into Boston, Massachusetts, Burlington, Vermont, and Portland, Maine, from New York City's John F. Kennedy Airport.

Continental (☎ 800/523-3273; www.continental.com) flies into Manchester, Burlington, and Portland from Newark's Liberty International Airport.

Cape Air flies Cessnas from Boston to Rutland, Vermont.

Continental flies into Bangor, Portland, Manchester, and Providence, in addition to Boston and Hartford.

Delta flies into Providence from Atlanta, Detroit, and Minneapolis.

Northwest flies into Burlington and Portland, in addition to Boston and Hartford.

United flies into Burlington, Portland, and Manchester, in addition to Boston and Hartford.

US Airways and its commuter subsidiaries fly into Boston, Hartford, Burlington, Manchester, and Portland, as well as some smaller airports in Maine, such as Bar Harbor and Presque Isle.

By Train

Commuter trains connect New York City with southern Connecticut and link Boston to Rhode Island, but the major interstate routes are served exclusively by **Amtrak** (☎ 800/USA-RAIL 872-7245; www.amtrak.com). Fares fluctuate with season and demand; book at least 3 days ahead (with your AAA membership number, if you have one) for the best prices.

High-speed **Acela** and standard **Northeast Regional** trains serve Boston's South Station from Penn Station in New York and points south, stopping in Connecticut and Rhode Island; service to Springfield, Massachusetts, via New Haven, Connecticut, is available. The **Vermonter** connects Washington, D.C., and New York with St. Albans, Vermont, near the Canadian border, and the **Ethan Allen Express** runs between New York and Rutland, Vermont. North Station in Boston is the southern terminus of the **Downeaster,** which stops along the New Hampshire and Maine coasts en route to Portland.

If you're connecting in Boston, note that the South Station–North Station transfer isn't much fun with a lot of luggage: Pack light, and if the weather's fine, walk the mile or so on the Rose Kennedy Greenway. Otherwise, hail a cab or take the subway, which involves a transfer.

If you plan a lot of train travel, consider buying Amtrak's USA Rail Pass, which covers a limited number of tickets within 15, 30, or 45 days. It's available online and through many travel agents.

By Bus

The bus is the only way to reach (and leave) many small New England towns. The regional service hub is **Boston's South Station Transportation Center** (☎ **617/737-8040;** www.south-station.net), on Atlantic Avenue next to the train station.

The major bus company is **Greyhound** (☎ 800/231-2222 or 617/526-1816; www.greyhound.com); **Peter Pan** (☎ 800/343-9999; www.peterpanbus.com) coordinates service with Greyhound. Greyhound sells a Discovery Pass that covers unlimited travel for 7, 15, 30, or 60 days. Visit www.discoverypass.com to get more information and to buy passes online.

Regional operators include **C & J** (☎ 800/258-7111; www.ridecj.com), **Concord Coach Lines/Dartmouth Coach/Boston Express** (☎ 800/639-3317; www.concordcoachlines.com), and **Plymouth & Brockton** (☎ 508/746-0378; www.p-b.com).

Most Americans consider long-distance bus travel a last resort. Service between New York and Boston is an exception: It's frequent and relatively fast (4–4½ hr.), and the price is about half the regular train fare. If you can catch an express bus, which makes only one stop, it's worth the extra $5 or so.

If you book at exactly the right moment, the trip from Boston to Manhattan can cost as little as $1 on **BoltBus** (☎ 877/865-8287; www.boltbus.com) and **MegaBus** (☎ 877/462-6342; www.megabus.com). Both offer onboard Wi-Fi access, as does **World Wide Bus** (☎ 877/992-8797; www.worldwidebus.com), which serves New York from Cambridge and Newton, Massachusetts.

Another option is the so-called **Chinatown buses;** the highest-profile operator is **Fung Wah** (☎ 617/345-8000 or 212/925-8889; www.fungwahbus.com), which connects South Station to Canal Street in New York's Chinatown for about $15 each way. While they remain the cheapest option, the Chinatown bus lines made the news in early 2011 after two fatal crashes.

LimoLiner (☎ 888/546-5469; www.limoliner.com) is a business-oriented service between Boston's Back Bay Hilton, 40 Dalton St., and the Hilton New York, 1335 Ave. of the Americas (with an on-request stop in Framingham, Massachusetts). The luxury coach has Internet access and work tables. Fares are higher than Greyhound's but cheaper than most plane flights.

By Cruise Ship

Cruising is an increasingly popular way to see New England. Ships call at **Boston, Nantucket,** and **Martha's Vineyard,** Massachusetts; **Portland** and **Bar Harbor,** Maine; **Newport,** Rhode Island; and numerous smaller New England ports. If you choose not to participate in a shore excursion arranged by your cruise line, make sure you have the number of a reliable cab company programmed into your phone before you disembark, and leave plenty of time for the trip back to the dock.

Getting Around

By Car

Driving is the most flexible way to see New England. It allows you to set your own itinerary, covering more ground than you could if you relied on public transportation. If you have the option to put a passenger in charge of navigation, do so, because after you leave the interstates (and sometimes even while you're still on them), New England traffic patterns can be confusing.

When driving in or near cities, especially Boston, allow for rush-hour traffic. Even better, stay off the roads during the busiest times, from about 6 to 9am and 4 to 7pm on weekdays. Traffic around popular beach and ski destinations slows to a crawl on Friday afternoon and Sunday evening during their busy seasons, and areas near airports are subject to congestion year-round, especially before and after holidays during the school year and all long weekends. Out-of-towners often have no choice but to be in the car at what feels like exactly the wrong time and place; it's small consolation, but know that this is actually one of the most authentic New England travel experiences you can have.

The following travel times are approximate and subject to traffic conditions: From Boston, it's about 1 hour to Portsmouth or Manchester, New Hampshire; Sturbridge or Plymouth, Massachusetts; or Providence, Rhode Island. Allow about 2 hours to reach Portland, Maine; Springfield, Massachusetts; Hartford or Mystic, Connecticut; or the mid-Cape area of Cape Cod. In 3 hours, you can reach Boothbay Harbor, Maine; North Conway, New Hampshire; Bennington or St. Johnsbury, Vermont; or New Haven, Connecticut. Four hours away are Camden, Maine; Dixville Notch, New Hampshire; Burlington, Vermont; and New York City.

AAA, the American Automobile Association (☎ **800/AAA-HELP** 222-4357; www.aaa. com) provides members with maps, itineraries, other travel information, and emergency road service if you break down. Membership can be a worthwhile investment, especially if you're venturing into the countryside and not completely confident in your car.

Other sources of good maps and road atlases include Maine-based **DeLorme** (☎ **800/561-5105;** www.delorme.com),

which has a store at its headquarters in Yarmouth, and **Jimapco** (☎ **518/899-5091;** www.jimapco.com).

Car Rentals

For booking rental cars online, the best deals are usually on company websites. U.K. visitors should check **Holidayautos** (☎ 0871/472-5229; www.holidayautos.co.uk). Major companies with New England offices include **Alamo** (☎ 877/222-9075; www.alamo.com), **Avis** (☎ 800/331-1212; www.avis.com), **Budget** (☎ 800/527-0700; www.budget. com), **Dollar** (☎ 800/800-3665; www.dollar. com), **Enterprise** (☎ 800/261-7331; www. enterprise.com), **Hertz** (☎ 800/654-3131; www.hertz.com), **National** (☎ 877/222-9058; www.nationalcar.com), and **Thrifty** (☎ 800/847-4389; www.thrifty.com). Independent local operators can be cheaper, but if you're planning a long trip, bear in mind that a major chain is more likely to be able to help if you run into trouble far away from the office where you rented your vehicle.

If you are **under 25** or **over 70,** check before you leave home to make absolutely sure that your chosen operator will honor your reservation. Some firms won't rent to younger and older drivers; others impose a surcharge (calculated per day, not per rental) on drivers 21 to 24 years old, won't rent young drivers certain classes of vehicles, or require that the renter use a credit card rather than a debit card.

International travelers should note that quoted rates almost never include insurance and taxes. Some companies are becoming more transparent about this, but don't commit to a reservation until you fully understand what's covered and what isn't. Also note that although foreign driver's licenses are usually honored in the U.S., an **international driving permit** can be a good idea, especially if your home license is not written in English.

By Bus

The days when buses were cheap and went everywhere are long gone, but travelers to some locations, especially small towns in northern New England, must rely on them. You don't need reservations, but you may save some money if you buy your ticket online.

Greyhound (☎ 800/231-2222 or 617/526-1816; www.greyhound.com) is the major bus company serving New England, mostly from stations near the interstate highways.

The regional carrier **Peter Pan** (☎ 800/343-9999; www.peterpanbus.com) is a major presence in Connecticut, Rhode Island, and Massachusetts. **Concord Coach Lines** (☎ 800/639-3317 or 603/228-3300; www.concordcoachlines.com) is the dominant player in Maine and New Hampshire, with service to Boston; it has two affiliates: **Dartmouth Coach** (☎ 800/637-0123 or 603/448-3800; www.dartmouthcoach.com), which connects New Hampshire's Upper Valley (Hanover, Lebanon, and New London) with Boston and New York; and **Boston Express** (☎ 800/639-8080; www.bostonexpressbus.com), which operates between southern New Hampshire, Tyngsboro, Massachusetts, and Boston. **C & J** (☎ 800/258-7111; www.ridecj.com) serves southeastern New Hampshire from Boston and Newburyport, Massachusetts. **Cyr Bus Lines** (☎ 800/244-2335; www.cyrbustours.com) serves northern Maine from Bangor. **Plymouth & Brockton** (☎ 508/746-0378; www.p-b.com) connects southeastern Massachusetts, including Cape Cod, with Boston.

By Train
Amtrak (☎ 800/USA-RAIL 872-7245; www.amtrak.com) serves Portland, Maine; Boston and Springfield, Massachusetts; Providence, Rhode Island; New Haven, Connecticut; Rutland and St. Albans, Vermont; and numerous intermediate points, as well as New York City. It's an expensive way to get around, especially compared with fares on the commuter-rail systems that serve some of the same destinations.

In southern Connecticut, the **MTA Metro-North Railroad** (www.mta.info/mnr) provides service between New York and New Haven, with numerous stops en route and spur lines to Danbury and Waterbury. **Shore Line East** (☎ 800/255-7433 or 203/777-7433; www.shorelineeast.com) service connects New Haven and New London. In eastern Massachusetts, the **MBTA commuter rail** (☎ 800/392-6100 or 617/222-3200; www.mbta.com) operates a dozen routes out of Boston's two main train stations. Its service to Providence, Rhode Island, is both cheaper and more frequent than Amtrak's trains on the same route.

By Plane
The airport security process is so time-consuming and distances between most New England destinations are so (relatively) short that driving within the region is often faster than flying. Even when that's not true, your budget may preclude flying. Airfares within New England tend to be steep during high season, though they can be surprisingly reasonable at other times. Although small commuter aircraft aren't for everyone, the convenience is undeniable, especially if you're going to or around northern New England. The east-west roads through Vermont, New Hampshire, and Maine are mostly two-lane affairs, and the coastal roads are subject to unpredictable traffic snarls. Even with a connection in New York, flying from Portland, Maine, to Burlington, Vermont, isn't much slower than driving—and is probably less taxing than half a day on the road. And flying to Martha's Vineyard or Nantucket from Boston or Hyannis, Massachusetts, rather than driving and taking the ferry, can add precious hours to your vacation.

The busiest regional airline is **Cape Air** (☎ 866/CAPE-AIR 227-3247 or 508/771-6944; www.flycapeair.com), which serves every New England state other than Connecticut. The major carriers that fly within New England are Continental (☎ 800/525-0280; www.continental.com), Delta Air Lines (☎ 800/221-1212; www.delta.com), JetBlue Airways (☎ 800/538-2583; www.jetblue.com), Southwest Airlines (☎ 800/435-9792; www.southwest.com), and US Airways (☎ 800/428-4322; www.usairways.com).

By Ferry
Seasonal and year-round ferries connect various ports on the New England coast to offshore islands and other points. Destinations include New London, Connecticut (from Orient Point, New York); Block Island, Rhode Island (from Point Judith and Newport, Rhode Island, and New London, Connecticut); Martha's Vineyard and Nantucket, Massachusetts (from New Bedford, Woods Hole, and Hyannis, Massachusetts); Provincetown, Massachusetts (from Boston); and numerous Maine locations. In addition, Lake Champlain ferries connect Grand Isle, Burlington, and Charlotte, Vermont, with upstate New York.

Some ferry trips never require a reservation, even for vehicles. One example is the 12-minute route between Grand Isle and Plattsburgh, New York, which operates 24 hours a day, year-round. At the other extreme is the conventional ferry from Hyannis to Nantucket, which sells out of vehicle slots on its six daily 2-hour-15-minute trips months before the summer season. If your plans include a ferry, especially if you'll be driving aboard, do your homework to avoid an unpleasant surprise. Consult individual chapters for specific information about your destination.

Tips on Accommodations

New England offers a full range of accommodations, and it's always a good idea to make a reservation. And the earlier you book, the better your chances of landing a (relative) bargain. You probably won't wind up sleeping in the car if you spontaneously set off for the seashore on an August weekend or the mountains at the height of foliage season, but you'll almost certainly wind up paying through the nose for whatever guest room happens to be available. Book well in advance for travel between April and November, when conventions, college graduations, vacations, and foliage season drive demand. Your budget will thank you.

A note for smokers: If you must smoke in your room, make sure the property you're considering allows it—many don't. Most inns and B&Bs and an increasing number of hotels and motels forbid smoking anywhere on their premises, and they charge rule-breaking guests steep cleaning fees.

Hotels & Motels

Most of the major chains have locations in New England, with the amenities that make them both unexciting and comforting—you know what to expect, and you'll get it. Independent establishments can't guarantee the same consistency, but they do tend to offer more personal service. This category includes everything from posh international brands and luxury boutique hotels to cookie-cutter extended-stay lodgings and mom-and-pop motels.

Inns & B&Bs

These are the fuzziest categories of New England accommodations. Roughly speaking, inns are larger and more expensive. They charge for breakfast, if they serve it. Bed-and-breakfasts are homier and include the morning meal in their room rates. Exceptions abound, however. Some "innkeepers" are just renting out a couple of rooms the family wasn't using anyway, while some B&Bs are so elegant you'll think twice before speaking above a whisper. Rest assured that the inns and B&Bs we recommend in this guide are all warm and welcoming.

Campgrounds & RV Parks

New England's camping facilities are as diverse as its terrain. Whether you're looking to moor a giant RV near the ocean or spread out a sleeping bag deep in the forest, you'll find a place that suits your needs. Options include national and state parks and forests as well as private establishments. The state tourism authorities listed on p. 560 all list campgrounds on their websites. To reach the **National Recreation Reservation Service,** which books federal facilities, call ☎ 888/448-1474 (customer service) or 877/444-6777 (reservations), or visit www.recreation.gov.

Fast Facts

ATMs/Cashpoints

Most communities of any size have at least one ATM; if you don't see a bank branch, seek out a convenience store or gas (petrol) station. In addition, many stores and post offices offer cash back when you pay with a debit card. Before heading to rural areas, however, you should always have some cash on hand. Cirrus (☎ 800/424-7787; www.mastercard.com), PLUS (☎ 800/843-7587; www.visa.com), and NYCE (☎ 888/456-2844; www.nyce.net) cover most New England banks. Unless you can find an ATM operated by your home bank, expect to pay a $1.50 to $3 access fee. **Tip:** Before you leave home, find out your daily withdrawal limit.

Business Hours

Most banks are open weekdays from 8 or 9am to 4 or 5pm, and sometimes Saturday morning. All banks close on national holidays, but most locations allow ATM access 24/7. Most offices are open weekdays from 8 or 9am to 5 or 6pm. Shopping centers and malls typically close Sunday morning and keep long hours the rest of the week; smaller retail businesses tend to stay open late (8 or 9pm) on 1 night each week and may close altogether or keep limited hours during the off season.

Customs

International air travelers and virtually every international traveler arriving in the U.S. by land or sea—including citizens of the U.S. and Canada—must present a passport at the airport, border crossing, or ship terminal. Many international visitors must fulfill other requirements before leaving home; for example, citizens of countries that do not participate in the U.S. State Department's Visa Waiver Program must obtain a visa. For complete information about entry requirements, visit **travel.state. gov/visa**. For up-to-date information on U.S. Customs & Border Protection policies, including the rules for carrying food and currency across the border, consult your nearest U.S. consulate or embassy, or visit the Customs website, **www.cbp.gov**.

Electricity

Like Canada, the U.S. uses 110 to 120 volts AC (60 cycles), compared with 220 to 240 volts AC (50 cycles) in most of Europe, Australia, and New Zealand. Downward converters that change 220–240 volts to 110–120 volts are difficult to find in the U.S., so bring one with you.

Embassies & Consulates

All embassies are in the nation's capital, Washington, D.C. For addresses and phone numbers, visit www.embassy.org/embassies or call directory assistance in Washington, D.C. (☎ 202/555-1212). Countries with consulates in New England include **Canada,** 3 Copley Place, Suite 400, Boston, MA 02116 (☎ 617/247-5100; www.boston.gc.ca); **Ireland,** 535 Boylston St., 5th floor, Boston, MA 02116 (☎ 617/267-9330; www.consulate generalofirelandboston.org); **Japan,** Federal Reserve Plaza, 600 Atlantic Ave., 22nd floor, Boston, MA 02210 (☎ 617/973-9772; www. boston.us.emb-japan.go.jp); and the **United Kingdom,** 1 Broadway, Cambridge, MA 02142 (☎ 617/245-4500; ukinusa.fco.gov.uk).

Emergencies

Call ☎ **911** for the fire department, the police, and ambulance service. This is a free call from pay phones. From land lines, 911 connects to the local emergency dispatcher; from cellphones in New England, it reaches the state police.

Health

New Englanders, by and large, consider themselves a healthy bunch. Besides the common cold or flu, you shouldn't face any serious health risks when traveling in the region. See the "New England Insects" box, earlier in this chapter, for tips on dealing with insects.

Holidays

Banks, government offices, post offices, and some stores, restaurants, and museums close on the following legal national holidays: January 1 (New Year's Day), the third Monday in January (Martin Luther King Day), the third Monday in February (Presidents' Day, Washington's Birthday), the last Monday in May (Memorial Day), July 4th (Independence Day), the first Monday in September (Labor Day), the second Monday in October (Columbus Day), November 11 (Veterans' Day/Armistice Day), the fourth Thursday in November (Thanksgiving Day), and December 25 (Christmas Day). Also, the Tuesday following the first Monday in November is Election Day and is a federal government holiday in presidential-election years (held every 4 years, next in 2012). State offices in Massachusetts and Maine close for Patriots Day on the third Monday in April, and Vermont government offices close on Bennington Battle Day, August 16.

Internet Access

Nearly all large hotels, and most smaller accomodations, now offer Internet access. If not, your best bet in many New England destinations, including smaller towns, is the free terminals at the **public library.** Use may be subject to a time limit, and the staff will probably ask for a picture ID, which you surrender when you start surfing and get back when you're done. For a partial list of cybercafes, visit www.cybercafe.com. Listings of businesses that offer Wi-Fi are available at www. wififreespot.com and www.jiwire.com.

Legal Aid

If you are "pulled over" for a minor infraction (such as speeding), never attempt to pay the fine directly to a police officer; this could be construed as attempted bribery, a much more serious crime. Pay fines by mail or directly into the hands of the clerk of the court. If accused of a more serious offense, say and do nothing before consulting a lawyer. Once arrested, a person can make one telephone call to a party of his or her choice. International visitors should call their embassy or consulate.

LGBT Travelers

New England is among the most gay-friendly destinations in North America. At press time, four of the five states where same-sex marriage is legal are in New England—Connecticut, Massachusetts, New Hampshire, and Vermont—and Rhode Island recognizes marriages performed elsewhere. As is true elsewhere, larger communities tend to be more accommodating to gay travelers than smaller towns, with some high-profile exceptions. Provincetown, Massachusetts, at the tip of Cape Cod, has a year-round population of just over 3,000 and a well-deserved international reputation for open-mindedness. There are large, lively gay communities elsewhere throughout the region, notably in and around Boston and Cambridge, Massachusetts; Burlington, Vermont; Ogunquit, Maine; and the lesbian mecca of Northampton, Massachusetts. A good guide to gay- and lesbian-owned and -friendly businesses in New England is the **Pink Pages** (www.pinkweb.com).

Liquor Laws

The legal age for buying and drinking alcohol in the U.S. is 21. Proof of age is required; be ready to show government-issued identification. Many bars, nightclubs, and restaurants, particularly those near college campuses, check the ID of everyone who enters. Do not carry open containers of alcohol in your car or any public area that isn't zoned for alcohol consumption. The police can fine you on the spot. Don't even think about driving while intoxicated.

Some restaurants have "full" liquor licenses, while others serve only beer, wine, and sometimes cordials. If you must have hard liquor, make sure you're in a place that serves spirits. Following are specific state rules for retail sales: In **Connecticut,** wine and spirits are available only at liquor stores, but grocery stores and convenience stores may sell beer. **Maine**'s liquor stores sell spirits and fortified wine; beer and table wine are available at retail stores. In **Massachusetts,** most chain convenience and grocery stores do not sell any alcohol. In **New Hampshire,** state-run liquor stores handle all alcohol sales. In **Rhode Island,** only liquor stores may sell alcohol. Rather than operating state stores, **Vermont** licenses private retailers ("agency stores") to sell spirits and high-alcohol beer and wine; grocery and convenience stores may sell table wine and beer whose alcohol by volume is less than 16%.

Mail & Postage

To find the nearest post office, call ☎ 800/ASK-USPS (275-8777); www.usps.com. At press time, domestic postage rates are 28¢ for a postcard and 44¢ for a letter. For international mail, a first-class letter of up to 1 ounce or a postcard costs 98¢ (75¢ to Canada and 79¢ to Mexico). If you aren't sure what your address will be in the U.S., mail can be sent to you, in your name, c/o General Delivery at the main post office of the city or region where you expect to be. The addressee must pick up mail in person and must produce proof of identity, such as a passport. Most post offices will hold mail for up to 1 month.

Money

Don't carry a lot of cash in your wallet, but be prepared to deal with businesses, such as small restaurants, that don't accept credit cards. Ask first, and be ready to run to the ATM. See "ATMs/Cashpoints," p. 573, for more information. Traveler's checks are something of an anachronism from the days before ATMs; American Express (☎ 800/221-7282) and Visa (☎ 800/227-6811) sell them.

For help with currency conversions, tip calculations, and more, download the convenient Frommer's Travel Tools app for your mobile device. Go to www.frommers.com/go/mobile/ and click on the Travel Tools icon.

Passports

Keep your passport and other valuables in the hotel or room safe. Always keep a photocopy of your passport with you when you're traveling. If your passport is lost or stolen, having a copy facilitates the reissuing process at your consulate (or embassy). See "Embassies & Consulates" and "Customs," p. 574, for more information. Allow plenty of time before your trip to apply for a passport; processing can be slow at busy times.

For Residents of Australia
Contact the **Australian Passport Information Service** (☎ 131-232; www.passports.gov.au).

For Residents of Canada
Contact the central **Passport Office** (☎ 800/567-6868 or 819/997-8338; www.ppt.gc.ca).

For Residents of Ireland
Contact the **Passport Office** (☎ 01/671-1633; www.foreignaffairs.gov.ie).

For Residents of New Zealand
Contact the **Passport Office** (☎ 0800/225-050 in New Zealand or 04/474-8100; www.passports.govt.nz).

For Residents of the United Kingdom
Visit your nearest passport office, major post office, or travel agency, or contact the **Identity and Passport Service** (☎ 0300/222-0000; www.ips.gov.uk).

Pharmacies
Rhode Island–based **CVS** (☎ 800/SHOP-CVS 746-7287; www.cvs.com) is the largest pharmacy chain in New England. Major competitors include **Walgreens** (☎ 800/WALGREENS 925-4733; www.walgreens.com) and **Rite Aid** (☎ 800/RITE-AID 748-3243; www.riteaid.com). Most **Walmart** locations (☎ 800/WAL-MART 925-6278; www.walmart.com) have on-premises pharmacies. Finding a 24-hour pharmacy can be tough, especially in northern New England and outside metropolitan areas, so plan ahead.

Safety
New England is generally a safe destination, but you should still take all of the same precautions you would in any unfamiliar area. Stash wallets in your least accessible pocket, don't wave your big map or expensive-looking camera around, and always be aware of your surroundings. Try to stay in well-lit areas when walking around after dark; if that's not possible, travel in a group. All of this is especially true in cities, but also be careful in outdoor destinations, such as parks and beaches. Never swim alone. Don't leave valuables in an unattended car, even in the trunk, and if you're going to be on rural roads at night, fill the gas tank beforehand.

Senior Travelers
Most attractions and some hotels, restaurants, and performing arts organizations offer discounts to people over a certain age (usually 62, 65, or 70) with identification. Members of **AARP** (☎ 888/OUR-AARP 687-2277 or 202/243-3525; www.aarp.org) are usually eligible for these discounts. One tour organizer affiliated with AARP is **Elderhostel** (☎ 800/454-5768; www.roadscholar.org), which offers excursions to New England destinations. The nonprofit educational-travel organization's **Road Scholar** programs no longer specifically target seniors, but their focus on travel and learning make them popular with many older travelers.

Smoking
New England is a bastion of antitobacco sentiment. All six states have strict laws that ban smoking in bars and restaurants, and every state other than New Hampshire forbids smoking in most other workplaces. Most B&Bs and inns and many hotels, motels, resorts, and vacation rentals are entirely smoke free or restrict smoking to small (often outdoor) areas. Vermont and the city of Boston have laws banning smoking in all hotels and motels, and the Marriott, Sheraton, and Westin chains forbid smoking in their U.S. properties.

Taxes
The U.S. has no value-added tax (VAT) or other indirect tax at the national level. Every state, county, and city has the option to charge its own local tax on all purchases, including lodging, eat-in and takeout food, alcohol, car rentals, and airline tickets. These taxes do not appear on price tags. Posted prices at gas stations do include tax, which every state imposes. The state sales taxes in New England, as of 2011, are as listed here: Connecticut, 6%; Maine, 5%; Massachusetts, 6.25%; Rhode Island, 7%; Vermont, 6%. New Hampshire has no sales tax.

Telephones
For directory assistance ("information"), dial ☎ 411; for long-distance information, dial 1, then the appropriate area code and 555-1212. Pay phones, when you can find them, usually charge 35¢ or 50¢ for a local call. In most of New England, **local calls** are 7-digit numbers; some areas, mostly in Connecticut

and Massachusetts, have 10-digit dialing, and you'll hear an error message if you forget to use the area code. To call **long-distance** within the U.S. and Canada, dial 1, the area code, and the 7-digit number.

To place an **international call,** dial 011, then the country code, city code, and number. The country code for Australia is 61; for Ireland, 353; for New Zealand, 64; and for the U.K., 44. **To call the U.S.** from a country other than Canada, dial your country's international code, the country code (1), the area code, and the number.

As for mobile phones, which most Americans call "cellphones," the major North American service providers cover New England, but outside urban areas, you can expect to encounter dead spots. Don't count on reliable service in rural areas, especially if your phone is on the GSM network, which most of the world uses. Among major U.S. carriers, AT&T and T-Mobile are compatible with GSM, and Sprint and Verizon use CDMA. To see where GSM phones work in the U.S., check out www.t-mobile.com/coverage.

Time Zone

The continental U.S. is divided into four time zones. New England is on Eastern Time, like New York, Washington, D.C., and Miami. When it's noon in Boston, it's 11am in Chicago (Central Time), 10am in Denver (Mountain Time), 9am in Los Angeles (Pacific Time), 5pm in London (GMT), and 2am the next day in Sydney. The U.S. observes daylight saving time from 1am on the second Sunday in March to 1am on the first Sunday in November (except in Arizona, Hawaii, the U.S. Virgin Islands, and Puerto Rico). DST moves the clock 1 hour ahead of standard time.

For help with time translations and more, download our convenient Travel Tools app for your mobile device. Go to www.frommers.com/go/mobile/ and click on the Travel Tools icon.

Tipping

Tipping is ingrained in the American way of life, and many service providers rely on gratuities for a substantial portion of their earnings. Some guidelines: In hotels, tip bellhops at least $1 per bag ($2–$3 if you have a lot of luggage) and tip the chamber staff at least $2 per day (more if you've left a mess). Tip the doorman or concierge only if he or she has provided you with a service (for example, calling a cab for you or obtaining difficult-to-get theater tickets). Tip the valet-parking attendant $1 every time you get your car. In restaurants, bars, and nightclubs, tip service staff and bartenders 15% to 20% of the check, tip checkroom attendants $1 per garment, and tip valet-parking attendants $1 per vehicle. As for other service personnel, tip cab drivers 15% of the fare; tip skycaps at airports at least $1 per bag (more if you have a lot of luggage); and tip hairdressers and barbers 15% to 20%. For help with tip calculations and more, download our convenient Travel Tools app for your mobile device. Go to www.frommers.com/go/mobile/ and click on the Travel Tools icon.

Toilets

Public toilets are available in many hotel lobbies, bars, restaurants, coffee shops, museums and other attractions, shopping centers, department stores, train and bus stations, highway rest areas, state and national parks, and gas stations. Some businesses post signs saying restrooms (as they're known) are for the use of customers only; buying a soft drink or pack of gum qualifies you as a customer. Your best bet in many New England destinations will likely be a fast-food restaurant or a branch of Starbucks or Dunkin' Donuts.

Travelers with Disabilities

Most public establishments in New England, including chain hotels and larger attractions, meet federal requirements for accommodating people with disabilities. Public transit in the major cities is accessible, as are most state and national parks, at least to some degree. Most sources of online visitor information include tips about access, and many allow users to search for accessible businesses. But in some parts of the region's centuries-old communities, with their antique buildings, narrow streets, cobbled thoroughfares, and brick sidewalks, getting around and getting comfortable can be a challenge. Check ahead, being as specific as possible about your concerns and asking follow-up questions. For example, the accessible rooms at many lodgings are on the first floor only; that lovely suite you saw on an inn's website may be at the top of a staircase you can't use.

Index

Photo Credits

Note: l= left; r= right; t= top; b= bottom; c= center